TH[illegible]
BART[illegible]
COMPANION

THE BARTÓK COMPANION

edited by

MALCOLM GILLIES

faber and faber

First published in 1993
by Faber and Faber Limited
3 Queen Square London WC1N 3AU

Typography by Humphrey Stone
Typeset by Anna Pinter Design & Editorial
Music examples typeset by Linda Lancaster
Printed in England by
Clays Ltd, St Ives plc

A CIP record for this book is available
from the British Library.

ISBN 0-571-15330-5
0-571-15331-3 (Pbk)

2 4 6 8 10 9 7 5 3 1

Contents

PIANO MUSIC

CHAMBER MUSIC

Illustrations

Editorial Preface

Companionship is not a characteristic readily associated with Bartók or Bartók studies. The man himself was a loner most at home within the walls of his own mind; his legacy has often proven divisive and engendered many a hostility between family members, associates, competing archives and scholars alike. During the 1950s to 1980s his musical, intellectual and even physical residue were the subject of some intense wrangling between his homeland, Hungary, and the land of his death, America. Although most of these issues have now been resolved or simply become irrelevant with the passing of time, the consideration of his life and music in the 1990s is still very much stamped with the intellectual camp allegiances of this prolonged 'cold war'.

The Bartók Companion brings together a selection of scholars from these disparate traditions. Several, indeed, meet together for the first time within these covers. The *Companion*'s purpose is in no way to provide a homogeneous guide to the composer and his output – that can be found in the half dozen life-and-works studies already available to readers – but rather to show the range of approaches in circulation at the time the wall between East and West came down, and so to encourage a more liberal scholarship. As the reader will see, the Hungarian scholars have tended to be more concerned with placing works in their cultural and historical context, with authentic interpretation according to Bartók's own word, with elucidating the ethnic roots of so much of his thinking, and with describing the 'dramaturgical' qualities of the works. The Western scholars have tended to pay most attention to 'internal' musical concerns, in particular to providing rationalist interpretations of forms, pitches and rhythms, and to relating identified characteristics to documented folk sources or, alternatively, to issues of performance. The latters' contributions, therefore, generally call for more study with score in hand and sometimes a greater awareness of music theory, while the Hungarians often assume a not inconsiderable knowledge of east European history and culture over the last century. Both traditions, however, do come together in highlighting those essential qualities in so much of Bartók's music: his debt to a huge range of folk styles, his attraction to symmetries of all types and his incurable love of variation at all structural levels.

After the introductory 'Perspectives' chapters, the chief divisions of the volume are drawn according to musical genre – piano, chamber, stage, vocal and orchestral – and internally organized according to chronology of creation. Most of Bartók's works receive some commentary, although there is no equality of coverage. To some of the major works entire chapters have been devoted, while the juvenilia and many folksong arrangements have tended to be treated more cursorily. Placement of a few works was problematic. The Divertimento and Music for Strings, Percussion and Celesta, both written for chamber orchestra, are here found in the 'chamber' category, within which the development of their characteristics appears to be more conveniently explained than in the 'orchestral'. A number of other works, such as the violin rhapsodies, are found in more than one arrangement, in which case the first composed form has generally been taken as primary, even if now sometimes less performed. Titles of works mostly follow traditional practice, although with the violin concertos we have used the titles now generally found on score covers and in publishers' catalogues, that is, First and Second, rather than the more historically accurate Violin Concerto Op.posth., and Violin Concerto (1937–8). In specific musical references bar numbers or rehearsal cues (e.g., fig.5.2–3, meaning second and third bar after rehearsal cue 5) have been given according to what is found in today's scores. With much of the solo piano music, however, neither form of reference is found in current scores, and readers, like the authors before them, have no option other than to start counting the bars.

This *Companion* is designed as much for the reader wanting a compact account of a particular work as for the one interested in the full gamut of Bartók's life and works. The chapters can, therefore, be read in isolation. In consequence, where authors have set out to examine different works from similar historical or analytical viewpoints there is occasional repetition of introductory data or of key quotations. Concerning terminology, however, it has sometimes proven just too cumbersome to redefine all terms fully in each chapter. When the meaning of a term is not immediately apparent, then, readers are advised to seek help through the cross-references of the notes or through the terminological entries in the General Index.

Acknowledgements

To Boosey & Hawkes Music Publishers Ltd acknowledgement is due for musical examples from the following of Béla Bartók's works: Three Piano Pieces (1894), Three Piano Pieces (1898), Improvisations Op.20, *Mikrokosmos*, Sixth String Quartet, Sonata for Two Pianos and Percussion, Sonata for solo violin, Eight Hungarian Folksongs, Twenty Hungarian Folksongs (1929), Second Suite Op.4, First Violin Concerto, Second Violin Concerto, Concerto for Orchestra, Third Violin Concerto, Viola Concerto. Acknowledgement is made to Boosey & Hawkes Inc., New York, for musical examples from the following works: Romanian Christmas Carols, Suite for piano Op.14, Sonata for piano (1926), *Out of Doors*, Nine Little Piano Pieces, Second String Quartet Op.17, Second Violin Sonata, Third String Quartet, Fourth String Quartet, Forty-four Duos for violins, Fifth String Quartet, Music for Strings, Percussion and Celesta, *Duke Bluebeard's Castle*, *The Wooden Prince*, *The Miraculous Mandarin*, *Village Scenes*, Five 'Ady' Songs Op.16, *Cantata profana*, Dance Suite, First Piano Concerto, Second Piano Concerto.

To Universal Edition (London) Ltd, for musical examples from the following works: Romanian Christmas Carols, Suite for piano Op.14, Sonata for piano (1926), *Out of Doors*, Nine Little Piano Pieces, Second String Quartet Op.17, Second Violin Sonata, Third String Quartet, Fourth String Quartet, Forty-four Duos for violins, Fifth String Quartet, Music for Strings, Percussion and Celesta, *Duke Bluebeard's Castle*, *The Wooden Prince*, *The Miraculous Mandarin*, *Village Scenes*, Five 'Ady' Songs Op.16, *Cantata profana*, Dance Suite, First Piano Concerto, Second Piano Concerto, Five Songs Op.15.

To Editio Musica (Budapest), for musical examples from the following works: Four Pieces for piano (1903), Rhapsody Op.1, Bagatelles Op.6, *Two Elegies* Op.8b, Two Romanian Dances Op.8a, Sonatina for piano (1915), First String Quartet Op.7, *Kossuth*, Scherzo Op.2, First Suite Op.3, Two Pictures Op.10.

Acknowledgement is due to the following publishers from whose books quotations are made: Faber and Faber Ltd., London (*Béla Bartók Letters*, *Béla Bartók Essays*, *Bartók Remembered*), Zeneműkiadó, Budapest (*Bartók Béla levelei*, *Bartók Béla családi levelei*, *Bartók Béla írásai I*), Corvina, Budapest (Tibor Tallián's *Béla Bartók* and József Ujfalussy's *Béla Bartók*), Magvető, Budapest (Tibor Tallián's *Cantata profana*), Hungaroton, Budapest (record booklet notes), the State University of New York Press, Albany (Bartók's *The Hungarian Folk Song*), Occidental Press, Washington DC (Vilmos Juhász's *Bartók's Years in America*). Péter Bartók has granted permission for inclusion of passages from Bartók's unpublished correspondence; the editors of *The New Hungarian Quarterly* and *Studia musicologica* have granted permission for inclusion of quotations from articles appearing in these journals.

Illustrations nos 1, 7, 9, 12, 15, 21, 24–6, 28, 30–32 are reproduced by courtesy of Péter Bartók (Homosassa, Florida); illustrations nos 2–6, 8, 10, 11, 13, 14, 16, 17, 19 by courtesy of Béla Bartók Jun. (Budapest) and the Budapest Bartók Archive; 18, by courtesy of Guy Whitaker (Folkestone); 20, by courtesy of Ernest Nash (New York) and Harriett Stevens (Los Angeles); 22, by courtesy of Malcolm Gillies (Brisbane); 23, by courtesy of Paul Sacher (Basle); 27, by courtesy of Wide World Photo and Harriett Stevens (Los Angeles); 29, by courtesy of Yehudi Menuhin.

Katalin Komlós is acknowledged as the translator of the chapter by Miklós Szabó, Judit Rácz as translator of the chapter by Béla Bartók Jun., Malcolm Gillies as translator of the chapter by János Demény, and Stewart Spencer and Malcolm Gillies as translators of the four chapters by Günter Weiss-Aigner.

The assistance and advice in preparation of this volume of David Pear, Simon Perry, Adrienne Gombocz, László Somfai, András Wilheim, Kathleen Nelson, Simon Perry and Christine Buckley is gratefully acknowledged. Finally, the editor and authors express gratitude to Faber and Faber music book editors Patrick Carnegy, Helen Sprott and Andrew Clements, and their staff, under whose various directions this ambitious volume was commissioned, supported and published.

Key to Abbreviations

BBcl	*Bartók Béla családi levelei* [Béla Bartók Family Letters], ed. Béla Bartók Jun., Budapest (Zeneműkiadó), 1981
BBE	*Béla Bartók Essays*, ed. Benjamin Suchoff, London (Faber and Faber), 1976
BBí.i	*Bartók Béla írásai I* [Béla Bartók's Writings I], ed. Tibor Tallián, Budapest (Zeneműkiadó), 1989
BBL	*Béla Bartók Letters*, ed. János Demény, London (Faber and Faber), 1971
BBlev.i–v	*Bartók Béla levelei* [Béla Bartók Letters], ed. János Demény, Budapest (Magyar Művészeti Tanács), 1948, (Művelt Nép Könyvkiadó), 1951, (Zeneműkiadó), 1955, 1971, 1976
BR	Malcolm Gillies: *Bartók Remembered*, London (Faber and Faber), 1990
DB.i–vi	*Documenta Bartókiana* (Budapest), 1964, 1965, 1968, 1970, 1977, 1981
DD	Numbering of Bartók's youthful works found in Denis Dille: *Thematisches Verzeichnis der Jugendwerke Béla Bartóks, 1890–1904*, Budapest (Akadémiai Kiadó), 1974
HFS	Béla Bartók: *The Hungarian Folk Song*, ed. Benjamin Suchoff, Albany (State University of New York Press), 1981; originally issued in English as *Hungarian Folk Music*, London (Oxford University Press), 1931
Kroó	György Kroó: *A Guide to Bartók*, Budapest (Corvina), 1974

MTA BA-B	Hungarian Academy of Sciences, Institute of Musicology, Budapest Bartók Archive collection
MTA BH	Bartók Estate collection of Béla Bartók Jun., housed in the Budapest Bartók Archive
NHQ	*New Hungarian Quarterly* (Budapest)
NYBA	Private collection of Péter Bartók (Homosassa, Florida), previously the New York Bartók Archives
RFM.i–v	Béla Bartók: *Rumanian Folk Music*, ed. Benjamin Suchoff, The Hague (Martinus Nijhoff), 1967–75 (5 vols)
SM	*Studia Musicologica* (Budapest)
Stevens	Halsey Stevens: *The Life and Music of Béla Bartók*, third edition, ed. Malcolm Gillies, Oxford (Clarendon Press), 1993
SV.i–ii	Béla Bartók: *Slovenské l'udové piesne / Slowakische Volkslieder*, ed. Alica Elscheková, Oskár Elschek, Jozef Kresánek, Bratislava (Academia Scientiarum Slovaca), 1959, 1970 (2 vols)
TFM	Béla Bartók: *Turkish Folk Music from Asia Minor*, ed. Benjamin Suchoff, Princeton (Princeton University Press), 1976
YFM.i–iv	Béla Bartók: *Yugoslav Folk Music*, ed. Benjamin Suchoff, Albany (State University of New York Press), 1978 (4 vols)
ZD	*Zenetudományi dolgozatok* [Musicological Papers] (Budapest)
ZT.i–x	*Zenetudományi tanulmányok* [Studies in Musicology] (Budapest), 1953–62

PERSPECTIVES

I

Bartók and his Music in the 1990s

MALCOLM GILLIES

As century's end draws near, the Hungarian composer Béla Bartók remains firmly placed in the first tier of twentieth-century 'classical' musicians. Although only so recognized by a narrow circle during his lifetime, he was more widely accorded this high regard during the upsurge of interest in his music which occurred in the late 1940s and 1950s. The authors of books on twentieth-century music have since generally placed him about fourth in their line-up of leading innovators – if number of pages be the guide – after Debussy (as father of impressionism in music), Schoenberg (pioneer of atonality and serialism) and Stravinsky (rhythmic innovator and neo-classicist). Bartók is, almost invariably, given as the chief representative of folk influence in art music. Normally following the lead of Bartók's many essays on this topic,[1] the historian traces the progression from unadorned transcriptions of folksongs through song settings of growing complexity to examples where Bartók's folk-music experiences infuse his composition but are not actually quoted. He, above all musicians of the century, is credited with bringing the sounds of the swineherd and peasant girl into the concert hall and with putting the urban middle class in touch with a variety of ethnic roots. There is, of course, much more to Bartók for those who wish to stray beyond this simple characterization with its regulation examples and prescribed movements for study.

Béla Viktor János Bartók was born on 25 March 1881 in Nagyszentmiklós (now Sînnicolau Mare, Romania), a medium-sized town in the southern Hungarian section of the Austro-Hungarian Empire.[2] The county of Torontál into which Bartók was born was ethnically mixed, with significant populations of Romanians, Germans, Hungarians and Serbs. It was a time of peace and economic buoyancy in provincial Hungary as the new railways opened up increasingly remote regions to easier trade. Bartók's father, also Béla, was in 1881 aged twenty-five and had already for four years been director of the local agricultural school; his mother, Paula Voit, was one year younger than her husband and had been a schoolteacher in the town before marrying. Until his teenage years Bartók's life was unsettled. He suffered from several contagious illnesses which kept him at home and prevented him from forging normal childhood friendships. The death of his father in 1888 caused financial problems for the family, which was forced to move from town to town as Bartók's mother sought a suitable place for her children's education and her own employment. Only in 1894 did they settle finally in Pozsony (now Bratislava in Slovakia), where Bartók completed the last five years of his secondary schooling. Despite chronic lung problems which emerged in his final year at school Bartók commenced studies at the Budapest Academy of Music in 1899, where he specialized in piano and composition. He graduated with high recommendations in 1903.

The years between 1903 and 1907–8 were transitional years, as he experimented, to limited success, with a career as composer–pianist, wrote his first large-scale orchestral and chamber works and increasingly came to dedicate himself to the collection of genuine folk music. Initially his interest was in Hungarian folk music, which he saw as a suitable material from which to build a new national music, but he soon expanded his horizons to the ethnic musics of the many minorities within the Empire, in particular the Slovaks and, a little later, the Romanians. By 1907 he had been appointed a professor of piano at the Budapest Academy of Music, and had also started to include folk-music characteristics in his compositions, beginning with the last movement of the orchestral Second Suite Op.4 (1905–7). In the following years, from the Bagatelles Op.6 (1908), onwards, he tended to more free-wheeling experimentation with these rural experiences. His new compositions found little favour at home or abroad, however, except among small bands of progressive, younger musicians, such as the Waldbauer–Kerpely Quartet and his colleagues in the short-lived New Hungarian Musical Society. By 1912 he was thoroughly disillusioned and withdrew from public musical life, although he continued with those teaching duties which brought in his Academy salary. During these 'hermit' years, in which he withdrew increasingly even from his own young family, he poured most of his energies into folk-music collection and analysis – even visiting French north Africa in 1913 – and occasional composition. Some real recognition as a composer did unexpectedly come in 1917, during the height of the war, when the Budapest Opera mounted his ballet *The Wooden Prince* Op.13, which he had started to write in 1914. Pleased with its reception, the Opera agreed to stage his earlier stage work, the opera *Duke Bluebeard's Castle* Op.11, in the following year. These successes led to something Bartók had longed for: a comprehensive agreement to publish his compositions, both past and future, with one of the leading promoters of contemporary music, Universal Edition of Vienna. The end of the war did not immediately improve his lot, however. Hungary was thrown into chaos, from which it started to steady only in 1920. During that chaotic period Bartók had briefly been involved as a musical adviser to the short-lived Communist government of Béla Kun, and although he had become disillusioned with the Communists, his collaboration did not endear him to the right-wing governments which then ruled Hungary during the 1920s and 1930s. Bartók, therefore, moved determinedly to cultivate a more international career, and even thought for some time of emigrating.

From 1920 onwards, as normal musical life was resumed in Europe, he was more seen and heard both in Hungary and abroad. His many concert tours, usually as a pianist playing his own works, led him to most countries of Western Europe, in 1927–8 to the United States and in 1929 to the Soviet Union. These tours spurred him on to write and perform new works, such as the violin sonatas, violin rhapsodies, the first two piano concertos and the various solo piano pieces of 1926. His compositions became increasingly available throughout Europe and several – the *Allegro barbaro* (1911) for piano, Romanian Folk

Dances (1915) in various settings, and the orchestral Dance Suite (1923) – scored particularly well in the mid–late 1920s. From chamber-music connoisseurs his body of string quartets, to which a Third was added in 1927 and a Fourth in 1928, was gaining respect for its tight construction and Beethovenian profundity.

During the inter-war years Bartók became more occupied as an ethnomusicologist in the transcription and analysis of his own and others' collections, rather than the further gathering of new material on expeditions. (He did, however, travel to Turkey in 1936 to collect folksongs in Anatolia.) Although he prepared volumes of Hungarian, Romanian and Slovak folk music during these decades only his Hungarian volume of 1924 gained wide dissemination. Finally in 1934, after years of petitioning, he was relieved of his responsibilities as a piano professor at the Academy of Music and appointed to the folk-music section in the Hungarian Academy of Sciences. There he happily worked for six years, with occasional interruptions for concert tours, and wrote one or two works each summer, normally in response to international commissions. These years produced Bartók's most consistently mature body of works, including his final two string quartets, the Music for Strings, Percussion and Celesta, the Sonata for Two Pianos and Percussion, the Second Violin Concerto and a stunning collection of Twenty-seven Choruses, which is still little known outside Hungary.

The growing tensions in Europe during the later 1930s caused Bartók to think again of emigrating. In 1938 he sent his most valuable manuscripts out of the country, but was only prepared to make definite plans to leave after the death of his mother in December 1939. A trip to America in April–May 1940 convinced him of the good sense of settling in New York, which he and his wife did later that year. Initially performing opportunities were forthcoming, and he was offered a research fellowship at Columbia University working on Serbo-Croatian folk materials. As the United States itself moved to a war footing, however, these opportunities became more limited. 1942 was a low point for Bartók. He felt unable to compose and was showing the first signs of leukaemia. Once placed under appropriate medical treatment, however, he did manage to work productively again. He completed studies of Turkish and Serbo-Croatian folk music and revised his Romanian collections. The Concerto for Orchestra and Sonata for solo violin were written during these final years, while his Third Piano Concerto and Viola Concerto were sufficiently advanced for his friend Tibor Serly to complete them after his death on 26 September 1945. Whether or when he intended to return to Hungary, itself by this time under Russian occupation, remains a matter of debate.

In the near half-century since Bartók's death the events of his life have been thoroughly investigated and are now well documented.[3] His character, too, has been relatively consistently depicted by those who knew him.[4] In 1918 his visage and attitude were finely painted in these words by the Hungarian writer Viktor Papp:

> Bartók is not tall, rather thin, clean-shaven, prematurely greying, unassuming but still self-conscious in appearance, reserved by nature, laconic, sullen. He is like a Cuman warrior. His sharp-featured Hungarian head is dominated by exceptionally shrewd eyes, whose fire almost burns through his glasses.[5]

This portrait, dating from when Bartók was aged thirty-seven, could have been written at almost any time between 1915 and 1940, so ageless did he appear to his contemporaries. Those bright eyes as well as his generally taciturn behaviour certainly made many feel awkward in his presence. The qualities which emerge from the accounts of those who did penetrate the cool, sharp exterior are still hardly warm, but point to a highly moral being. Although some of his actions in personal, particularly sexual, relations could be construed as immature, even irresponsible, and his political behaviour tended to naivety, Bartók is usually credited with a high degree of professional and personal integrity. He could not be corrupted by promises of power, social status or money, and clung steadfastly to his self-appointed mission as an ethnomusicologist, despite its scant material rewards. The rewards were, for him, to be found in pushing back the frontiers of knowledge and becoming familiar with many concepts which would later inform his compositions. Despite occasional pupils of composition early and late in his life, he rejected several lucrative offers of chairs in composition in the belief that such work, if systematically undertaken, would undermine his own integrity as a composer. As for many years he had to teach, his chosen subject was the piano, although he preferred his students not to learn his own works. This firm sense of professional integrity could, however, make life difficult for those around him and make his own progress through life less than easy. He was simply unable to participate in those polite banalities and mutual statements of half-truths which so often grease human interactions. Despite a fine sense of educational method in his pedagogic compositions he would often drive his piano students to distraction through an unbending insistence on the exact turn of phrase, tone or rhythmic pattern that he had determined was needed.[6] His wives – Márta Ziegler, from 1909, and Ditta Pásztory, from 1923, both originally his piano students – early had to learn a role of service, not so much to the man as to his musical endeavours and career. His activities modulated between composition, pianism, ethnomusicology and pedagogy, with one or other coming to the fore depending on the demands of his employment, the need to promote his works, his concert career, or just artistic or scholarly inspiration. Rarely, even during family holidays, would Bartók bend from the ordered succession of his musical tasks.

This uncompromised dedication over forty years to his art leads to a bland image of the personality, which is only reinforced by the writings of his that have survived. His letters, apart from those written during a passing romantic phase in the century's first decade,[7] were chiefly a medium for disseminating details about his day-to-day activities or conducting his musical affairs. Their humour was only occasional, and personal interest in or compassion for the affairs of others was, at best, spasmodic. His essays and treatises are likewise dry, meticulous tracts of musical description or argument. They are matter-of-fact and well show his aversion to theorizing.[8]

Notwithstanding the settled interpretation of many aspects of his life, personality and music inherited by us in the 1990s, the Bartók debate is by no means over. On some points, both major and minor, the selection and weighting of evidence remains problematic and needful of review; on others, some fundamental assumptions may need to be reappraised. Bartók's character, it must be admitted, appears somewhat *too* neatly presented. In the inherited image, for instance, he comes across as a model, almost saintly musician of multiple talents, but are his contributions as performer, composer, teacher and ethnomusicologist being rated candidly, in his contemporary Hungarian context and more broadly within the history of twentieth-century music? Our own ears can tell us, through listening to his recordings,[9] that Bartók was not one of the best pianists of his day, despite some occasional, magnificent performances of certain repertories. Contemporary evidence suggests that Ernő Dohnányi was much the better and more resourceful pianist. The accounts of Bartók's piano students and his lack of creation of a personal school of talented performers – despite holding a teaching position at the Budapest Academy of Music for twenty-seven years – suggest that he was an insensitive teacher, both to individual student needs and to more enlightened educational methods. Others, such as the violinist Jenő Hubay and even the pianist Árpád Szendy, were more effective and probably more respected as teachers at that Academy. Bartók considered himself, particularly in later years, as primarily an ethnomusicologist; from 1934 onwards he certainly devoted more of his time to this than to any other musical pursuit. His work was immense: over a dozen volumes of his folk-music treatises have now been published,[10] and several others from his Slovak and Hungarian collections still remain unpublished. In the international history of that discipline, none the less, his significance is still disputed. He had a magnificent ear but may be considered to have failed to see 'the wood for the trees' in important aspects both of the notational representation of melodies and their analysis.[11] On the home scene, too, Zoltán Kodály can be seen to rival his scholarship and to have better achieved the aims they jointly set in making such collections. These candid estimates of his significance should not diminish Bartók's overall standing but rather help us to appreciate better what posterity has, for good reason, decided: that in the remaining field of his musical endeavour, composition, Bartók far eclipsed all his national contemporaries and was of a truly international significance. But let us not stop there, with this note of eulogy. His compositions were not all great works. I personally do not hear in his output a truly great work – at least, not one that brings him close to Schoenberg's or Stravinsky's achievement – until his pantomime, *The Miraculous Mandarin*, written in 1918–19 when he was in his late thirties. By then he had finally found some novel solutions to many of the constructive problems and unevennesses of style which had bedevilled his earlier compositions. Then over the following quarter-century there are many great works, of which the Fourth String Quartet, the Music for Strings, Percussion and Celesta, and Sonata for Two Pianos and Percussion rank especially highly in my mind. Different scholars would undoubtedly come up with different favourites, but would find it difficult to deny that the years from 1926 to 1939 were Bartók's *floruit*.

Another area where Bartók still suffers from stereotyping is his supposed role as a left-wing artist–intellectual and conscience of society. He is seen as steadfast, true to his convictions, 'a beacon of humanity' in a dark age, an 'ideal East European', an internationalist preaching 'the brotherhood of peoples'.[12] But was he so steadfast in the name of humanity? Did not that character trait sometimes lead to inflexibility, intolerance and expressions of arrogance? Was he not sometimes human enough to be inconsistent in his attitudes? His views on ethnic questions provide a good example of how the current image of Bartók has tidied up a less than tidy body of evidence. From a distance it is now possible to see Bartók as just another confused player in the fiery ethnic cauldron which was – and is – Eastern Europe. In 1903 we find him espousing the downfall of the Habsburgs and evidencing an intense Hungarian patriotism:

> Everyone, on reaching maturity, has to set himself a goal and must direct all his work and actions towards this. For my own part, all my life, in every sphere, always and in every way, I shall have one objective: the good of Hungary and the Hungarian nation.[13]

Or was this simply ethnic chauvinism? In 1905 he would write to a Hungarian friend: 'The place [Budapest] has attracted a haphazardly heterogeneous, rootless group of Germans and Jews; they make up the majority of Budapest's population. It's a waste of time trying to educate them in a national spirit.'[14] By the following year, as he went on more expeditions collecting folk music, he came to realize the crassness of the provincial Hungarian gentry, too, and was starting to idealize the peasantry.[15] He was developing a sympathy for various ethnic minorities within Hungary's borders. That sympathy was not one based on equality of all men or an internationalist ideal, however, but arose from his self-confessed desire to side with the underdog: the Hungarian against the ethnic Germanic, the Finn against the Russian, the Romanian or Slovak against the Hungarian.[16] In his various public clashes over his Romanian collections between 1914 and 1936, with both Romanian and Hungarian critics, he does not acquit himself particularly well and argues on grounds that are less than consistent. In 1920, as Hungary formally lost over half its land area through the Treaty of Trianon, he incoherently and bitterly lashed out at Hungarian allegations of his lack of patriotism because of his study of the music of Hunedoara Romanians:

> Its publication now is downright desirable, because it makes evident the cultural superiority of the Hungarians. I cite the following from my article: 'From among the peoples of our country (that is, Hungary) the Romanians are the ones who have conserved in a relatively intact form the ancient condition of their folk music.' Anyone who is not completely illiterate in the science of ethnography knows that the survival of such 'ancient conditions' is possible only on a low cultural level. The article also makes it quite plain that not a single Romanian has appeared who is suitable for the systematic study of the Romanian folk music: a Hungarian had to undertake this scientific research which is extremely important from the Hungarian viewpoint. – Is this not proof of our cultural superiority?
>
> The publication of my article was also desirable in order to show those abroad in what high esteem we held our nationalities, the extent of our concern for their cultural questions, how little we oppressed them. Or does Hungary's interest possibly not require that we refute our enemies' charge that we oppress our nationalities?[17]

In following decades these ethnic issues continued to simmer, and Bartók's responses were similarly confusing and liable to misinterpretation; the poor man was, after all, being attacked from a number of ethnic quarters. He could see these issues only through musical glasses. Even the enunciation of his 'brotherhood of peoples' ideal of 1931 was not a political or social statement but an ideal he had conceived as a composer, and which he sought to serve in his music. Its little-quoted continuation is important, too. Bartók had described to his Romanian correspondent Octavian Beu how he tried to draw his musical ideas from any ethnic source that was 'clean, fresh and healthy!', but then continued:

> Owing to my – let us say geographical – position it is the Hungarian source that is nearest to me, and therefore the Hungarian influence is the strongest. Whether my style – notwithstanding its various sources – has a Hungarian character or not (and that is the point) – is for others to judge, not for me. For my own part, I certainly feel that it has. For character and milieu must somehow harmonize with each other.[18]

Bartók's musical ideal, then, was not one so much of internationalism as of integration of foreign ethnic elements within a Hungarian-dominated style. Whether this reflected his wider ideal for humanity is hard to determine, but if it did it places him in the middleground of tempered nationalism between the ultranationalism of the emerging forces of fascism and Marxist internationalism. But so to rationalize his views at all involves too close a cropping of the evidence from a man politically and ideologically naive. His response to the heightened tensions from 1938, such as the Vienna Awards, which partially restored Hungary's pre-1920 suzerainty, or the succession of Hungary's Jewish Laws, was similarly less than definitive. Characteristically, he was most concerned with his own security and that of his music. On 13 April 1938, for instance, he wrote: 'As far back as Nov. I noticed that Hungarian policy was being diverted from the right track: I then conceived the idea of putting at least the original manuscripts of my musical compositions in some safe place.'[19] So begins the progression of events which would end with his emigration – itself a popular Cold War battlefield for stereotypic interpretations now often more soberly depicted.[20]

In what matters most, the understanding and appreciation of his music, the debate has been more intense than that concerning his life, as so many different, sometimes conflicting, theories have been proposed. Although Bartók's mature works have an almost lapidary quality, appearing so firm and purposeful in their construction, the paradox for analysts has lain in their defiance of exact conformity to any one model. The root cause of this defiance is Bartók's ever-present tendency to variation, which can best be attributed to his decades of studying the intricacies of folk music. Any phenomenon is likely to return defective or skewed, extrapolated or mirrored; the proportion apparently so perfect at first occurrence is unexpectedly shortened or lengthened at subsequent hearings. Even where he has provided his own detailed analyses, as with the Fifth String Quartet or Music for Strings, Percussion and Celesta,[21] the stark, logical structures described are sometimes obscured on the surface of the music and occasionally directly flouted. The task for the analyst of Bartók's music is a daunting one. It is easy enough to pick out characteristics in most of his pieces to illustrate a variety of theories, but such activity can become a travesty of analytical process. The real challenge lies in providing a comprehensive illumination of the music, not mounting a 'fishing expedition' to justify a theory; it lies in explaining clearly the dynamic of formal and stylistic phenomena of a piece while neither erring on the side of undue normalization of features, thereby denying deviations and variations their potency, nor losing sight of that underlying dynamic through too exclusive a focus on aspects of deviation. Bartók studies suffered their greatest normalizing threat in the theories of the Hungarian Ernő Lendvai. Lendvai in the late 1940s made a most important discovery: that Bartók's music sometimes exhibits a natural, almost magical, sense of internal proportion. From that undeniable truth, which less justifiably equated to the Golden Section or Fibonacci series, he spun a dialectical Bartókian theory, encompassing features of form, pitch, rhythm and even tempo and dynamics.[22] Although many of the terms in Lendvai's inventory are useful in describing particular musical phenomena, the on-off twinned nature of his approach limited its usefulness and, more seriously, encouraged a crass normalization which distorted the interpretation of a work's more intricate – but sometimes crucial – features, so as to fit the limited range of sanctioned models. The essence of the piece so frequently slipped between those standard prototypes by which it was meant to be illuminated. The opposite tendency, of restricted focus, emerges in those studies of Bartók's techniques of melodic or rhythmic variation, which, often taking their models in folk-music studies or semiotics, analyse the detail and difference of each variation (even transposing materials to make clearer the deviations), but do not provide any substantial understanding of the formal, tonal or thematic context in which these variations occur.

Another broad matter for debate concerns that by which Bartók is best known, as the folk-influenced composer. Folk-music influence is almost universally viewed as something wholesome and a worthy undergirding to a style. In the Bartók literature an important task has been to identify, classify and even glory in the web of these influences. But specific influences from Western art music in his style are treated more reticently. It is, for instance, one matter to point out the precise sources of a passage's Romanian rhythmic or Hungarian melodic features, but quite another to set about identifying the sources of Stravinskyan rhythmic or Szymanowskian pitch features in his music. Traditional musicology frowns on the latter as unfortunate if they can too easily be identified in the composer's mature works. Such influences smack of contamination and, if emphasized by a scholar, could raise serious questions about the composer's stylistic integrity. Writing in 1921 Bartók stated: 'Peasant music itself plays the part in composition that natural objects play in painting. Real folk music can be regarded as a natural phenomenon from the point of view of higher art music.'[23] In Jakob Grimm's expression, 'folksongs emanate in silence from the tranquil strength of the whole'.[24] There is no question of specific ownership of the song; it is a 'common material' for all to use. The Western Romantic notion of genius has, on the other hand, encouraged most scholars to treat art music as an artificial, individual product. In this perspective, the adoption of specific features by others would constitute a violation of the original composer's intellectual property, and suggest the borrower's second-rate status and questionable morality. But Bartók himself was of much more liberal outlook. He decried the obsession of his critics with the invention of themes, condemning it as 'a Romantic conception which values originality above all'.[25] In his essays of later years he three times referred approvingly to Molière's dictum 'je prends mon bien où je le trouve',[26] and in 1943 praised Stravinsky's neo-classicism as a fine application of purely evolutionary principles, which in no way lessened his standing as a composer.[27] A continuing challenge in Bartók studies remains for these borrowings and influences from other composers or schools to be probed just as intensively as those materials of folk music once were and to become the subject of more candid discussion. For too long has the concern with folk influence deflected attention from this other, equal partner in the formation and continuing renewal of his style. The determination of such art-music influences is more prone to conjecture, with the evidence needing to be drawn very widely, from his memorabilia, the contents of his bookshelf, his concert and repertory lists, but, above all, from the detailed comparison of scores.[28] A more balanced representation of the folk- and art-music influences upon Bartók's output will lead to a richer, more varied portrayal of the musician: a less consistent character, less sure of himself, who remained concerned into his sixties with what his contemporaries – Schoenberg, Stravinsky, Debussy, Szymanowski, Kodály, to name just some – were composing, and drew great inspiration from them, as well as from the great composers of previous generations; a composer who did sometimes err on the side of importation, rather than inspiration or influence, but generally realized where he had overstepped the mark and took appropriate steps to withdraw, suppress or discourage performances of such compositions; a more human, more fallible Bartók, but in his finest hours just as great.

NOTES

1 See *BBE*, pp. 301–96.
2 For a year-by-year account of Bartók's life see the Chronology at the back of this volume.
3 The most methodical summary of his life is found in the chronology compiled by his son Béla Bartók Jun., *Apám életének krónikája*, Budapest (Zeneműkiadó), 1981. The detail of his professional career was first charted in 1954–62 by János Demény in four issues of *ZT*.
4 See *BR*, in particular pp. 58–89.
5 *Arcképek a zenevilágból*, Budapest (Franklin-Társulat), 1918, p. 54.
6 See *BR*, pp. 133–49, for a series of recollections of his piano students.
7 See, for instance, two letters of 1907 to Stefi Geyer in *BBL*, pp. 75–87.
8 See *BBE*, p. 376, where in 1943 Bartók stated his personal 'hatred' of creating theories of composition in advance and 'preference' not to deduce such theories in retrospect.
9 See the two-volume *Centenary Edition of Bartók's Records*, Budapest (Hungaroton), 1981, LPX 12326–33 and 12334–8.
10 See Select Bibliography.
11 See, for instance, Bruno Nettl, *Theory and Method in Musicology*, London (Collier-Macmillan), 1964, pp. 105–6.
12 See *BBL*, p. 201.
13 *BBL*, p. 29.
14 *BBL*, p. 50.
15 See his letter of 25 November 1906 in *BBlev*.v, p. 115.
16 See his letter of 25 December 1916 in *BBcl*, p. 248.
17 *BBE*, pp. 201–2.
18 *BBE*, p. 201.
19 *BBL*, p. 268.
20 Tibor Tallián, to my mind worryingly, rolls many issues from the 1930s into an idealized, heroic vision of Bartók: 'The questions of Eastern European history he saw in terms of music, and gave his answer in that homogeneous medium. A result of his guileless and whole-hearted devotion to his profession was that he experienced problems of society as the problems of art, thereby coming closer than any of his fellows to their artistic and human solution. In his complete professionalism Bartók became the ideal East European . . . as a least gesture, by no means easy to make, he carried out the duty of a humanist citizen by his action in breaking away from a Europe turning fascist. With this he acknowledged that a completely new phase had arrived for the European artist with the war, a phase in which artistic decisions proved to be insufficient and had to be substituted by political ones. In preserving his own integrity, Bartók preserved that of Eastern Europe . . . Both his own times and those that followed did not find it easy to acknowledge the consistency and greatness of his conduct.' (*Béla Bartók: the Man and his Music*, Budapest (Corvina), 1988, p. 216.)
21 See *BBE*, pp. 414–16.

22 See his *The Workshop of Bartók and Kodály*, Budapest (Editio Musica), 1983.
23 *BBE*, p. 324.
24 See Constantin Brăiloiu, *Problems of Ethnomusicology*, ed. and tr. A. L. Lloyd, Cambridge (Cambridge University Press), 1984, p. 6. Bartók doubted if any one peasant was able to invent a 'quite new tune'; he only recognized an ability to make substantial alterations to an already existing tune (*HFS*, p. 2).
25 See *BBE*, pp. 346–7.
26 *BBE*, pp. 343, 346, 360.
27 *BBE*, p. 360.
28 See my exploratory study 'Stylistic integrity and influence in Bartók's works: the case of Szymanowski', *International Journal of Musicology*, vol. 1 (1992), pp. 139–60.

2

The Private Man

BÉLA BARTÓK JUN.

More than four decades have elapsed since Béla Bartók died.[1] He is becoming an ever more distant figure, even from those who do personally remember him. Most of his contemporaries have also passed on, and so today it is virtually only those who saw or met him in their youth who have recollections of him – and their memories are, as a result, often rather vague. Over the years a good many descriptions of my father have appeared. A large number of them have contained errors of fact, inaccurate characterizations or just plain misunderstandings. The main reason for this state of affairs is that Bartók was rather reserved when in the company of strangers, and so it was difficult for them to form a full and accurate picture of him.

Within the family, of course, the situation was different. As well as offering my own personal recollections I want to characterize the human qualities of Bartók by drawing on various written materials, some of which have not yet been published. My first memories are naturally associated with Bartók as a father figure. Even from my earliest years I was brought up to believe that I was living with an exceptional human being. As my father was more than usually sensitive to noise I had to learn to keep completely quiet when near him. But this was not a burden for me as we had a garden in which I could make noise to my heart's content. It was a double pleasure, then, when my father could spare the time to be with me. His parents had been outstanding teachers, and the pedagogic sense which he had inherited from them showed itself in the way he sought to educate children.

Although taking their ages into account, he looked on children as full human beings. He sought to give them every possible help in improving their level of education. As far as music went, he tried to establish a basic musicianship in the malleable core of a child's character, which would enable the child to develop into a more worthwhile member of the human race. Very early on he wrote the *Piano School* with Sándor Reschofsky, but the series *For Children*, the Violin Duos, the systematic series of *Mikrokosmos* pieces and the Two- and Three-part Choruses all served this same goal. With his own children he did not pay undue attention to musical development (and he would not have achieved much with me, anyway), but did take every opportunity to teach us about a broad range of phenomena. He was a real nature-lover and studied all its forms. Animals interested him, above all. When he was a child he bred silkworms, and once even took them from Pozsony to Nagyszentmiklós. Later on, he systematically collected insects and put together a lovely collection of them. Even when I was very young I helped him with it, and made up my own little collection, too, from left-over specimens. The most important instruction he gave in doing this was that no pain whatsoever was to be inflicted on the animals. And so he always took the appropriate drug with him on his insect-collecting expeditions. The insects, therefore, died and came into his collection without any suffering.

His refusal to go to the circus was another indication of his love of animals. He did regularly visit the zoo, however, both in Budapest and on his journeys abroad. He considered bullfights absolutely ignominious. When we were living in Rákoshegy we kept some chickens. During the difficult years of the war we fed the orphaned little chickens by hand, and so they became personal friends. My father would not consent to their being killed, even during the most severe shortages of food.

The presents he gave were also primarily didactic in nature, mainly being concerned with nature or the arts. I used to receive some beautiful papier-mâché animals, and over time amassed a veritable army of them. I also received a big, colourful picture book of animals, in which the pictures were accompanied by explanatory texts in German and Latin. My father carefully added in the relevant Hungarian names. When I was ten I received the ten-volume Brehm.[2] From his journeys abroad he brought back presents which were, as far as possible, long-lasting. He brought home my first pocket watch from Holland, and my first fountain pen, likewise, from one of his concert tours. At home, I usually received books. Even before I was of school age I received art reproductions whose originals I would only manage to see decades later. From the well-known children's literature I received mainly the works of Verne and Cooper, and we always discussed together their geographical descriptions, thereby increasing my desire to travel. He also tried to acquire for me as much Hungarian literature as he could: the complete Hungarian Classics series; from among his contemporaries, the works of Zsigmond Móricz and Endre Ady, principally, although there were some others. Of course, I received foreign works as well.

My father liked to draw, and when I was small he kept a special booklet just for that purpose. There, as a reward for something, he would sketch various real events – a walk in the zoo, collecting folksongs, an outing – mostly in a humorous way. He was interested in my studies at school, but only from a distance. He never went to the teachers to ask about me, and only twice did he ever come to one of my exams. He expected me to see my studies through dutifully, but with a sense of interest and enjoyment rather than of pressure. The idea of giving a special financial reward or present for a good school report was foreign to him; we both looked on a good report as something perfectly natural. When I acquired my engineering diploma he asked my mother (who had, by then, separated from him) in a letter: 'Are you glad that our son has gained his diploma?'

In my eighth year of secondary school I received a scholarship. At that time he was on his first concert tour of America. I wrote to him and he immediately replied, congratulating me and asking that I hold off spending the money until he had returned home, as he wanted to suggest something to me. The suggestion was that after my matriculation exams I go to see the world and engage in language study. I accepted this idea willingly, and spent five weeks in Austria at my own expense.

When my father came to Budapest as a student of the Academy

of Music he regularly went to concerts, and went to the Opera three or four times a week. As time went by he attended less frequently, only going now and then to some exceptional concert or performance. He did try to stimulate my interest, however, and took me to concerts or opera performances which he deemed suitable. I even went to the rehearsals of his first two stage works, and enthusiastically listened to their first and subsequent performances. He took me, also, to performances of Miklós Radnai's ballet *The Infanta's Birthday*.[3] His own concerts remain forever in my memory. I would listen delightedly to performances of works which I had heard him practise many times. Afterwards, when we were back home, my father would be in high spirits and would recall each episode of the concert with a sense of relief. He would ask us about the comments we had heard from the audience.

He often accepted the help of members of his family in his musical work. When he was still single his mother and sometimes his sister helped him by copying out scores. Later on, my mother copied out the manuscripts of his compositions and made fair copies of his folksong transcriptions. Even at the age of eight or ten I would frequently help him with the mechanical classification of folksongs, for a modest remuneration. In later years he liked to show me the texts of his lectures or the translation of his *Cantata profana*. When he gave his lectures over the radio I would help him operate the phonograph.

He held that the study of languages was an important way of gaining a broad education, and showed exemplary application to such study. When he set out to learn a language he bought the best available textbook and dictionary, and some kind of fairly simple reader. He always studied alone – or, perhaps, together with his wife – but never with a teacher or with any other assistance. He prepared a precise and detailed word-list, effecting at the same time a study of comparative linguistics. Frequently he compiled a vocabulary of two foreign languages. While still at secondary school he became acquainted with Latin and Ancient Greek, and then studied German, French, Romanian and Slovakian. (Regarding his Slovakian, there is no question – as some would like us to believe – that he took to studying it because of his mother's coming from Túrócszentmárton (Slovakia). His mother did not even speak the language.) Later, he learnt Italian and English. He took up Spanish, Arabic, Ruthenian, Serbian and Finnish – and Turkish in greater detail – although he could not speak in these languages.

Naturally, he loved the Hungarian language best of all. He subscribed to the journal *Magyarosan* and bought the successive volumes of the Gombocz–Melich etymological dictionary at their regrettably slow appearance. He was interested to learn the origin of the word 'Bartók' from this dictionary, acknowledging with satisfaction that it was Hungarian. He was occupied with the origin of his family in other ways, too, and during his early youth he had even used the title 'of Szuhafő', for which there is no documentary substantiation. Our family's origins in Borsod county had long been well known, but he would have liked to have gained more information about this. When I was unemployed for quite some time after gaining my engineering diploma, he suggested that I do some research to throw light on the earlier history of the family.

He loved the members of his family more than anyone else. He remembered birthdays and never failed to commemorate them – even if sometimes after the event. Some of his works also have family associations. He often went to visit his sister in Békés county and collected folksongs there. I personally knew Péter Garzó and Julcsa Varga, who feature in the folksongs from the neighbourhood of Vésztő. His sister later moved to Szöllőspuszta, near Pusztaföldvár, where my father created 'The Night's Music', in which he immortalized the frogs' chorus and the other mysterious sounds of the night which can be heard in the quiet regions of the Plain.

My father considered physical exercise was important as well as intellectual exertion. He enthusiastically championed every new achievement in health matters. It was partly through the influence of Kodály that he became such a meticulous follower of the sun-and-air health movement which was popular in the early years of the century. In those homes of ours which had a garden he always worked outdoors, weather permitting. As far as the situation allowed, he would undress, but used a handkerchief tied with four knots to protect his head against the sun.

He acquired the series of books of Müller's *Mein System*, and regularly went through the exercises (not unlike the television gymnastics of today) with members of the family. On one of his trips abroad he got hold of a peculiar ball game that consisted of two half drums with which the two players used to hit a tennis ball. He really liked to play this game. He loved walking and going off into the mountains. Even in this he proceeded methodically. In 1915 he made a folksong collecting tour of Zólyom county (in Slovakia). My mother and I joined him there for a while. As I was only five, he wrote beforehand to my mother that she was to prepare me for the mountainous terrain by letting me practise climbing up and down on the slope of a former gravel pit near our house in Rákoshegy. Later, when I had grown up and we were going on expeditions together, he came upon the idea of our taking half-hour turns in carrying a rather heavy knapsack. By doing this, one of us could always be relaxed as we went along.

Another contact with sport was his invitation in 1924 to join the jury for the intellectual competition of the Olympic Games, being held in Paris then for the second time. There was a musical contest, too, and he was supposed to help in assessing the works submitted. Because of lack of time he turned the offer down, but he paid great attention to this linking of intellectual and physical contest. Incidentally, prizes were not awarded for the musical contest because of a paucity of suitable works.

During his lifetime Bartók suffered many disappointments. This made him rather pessimistic – almost a family tradition! The difficulties he encountered in propagating his works often discouraged him, and this sense of depression, in turn, hindered his further work. He wrote to my mother in 1916 that he knew for sure that he would never live to see the performance of *Bluebeard*. He was sorely tried by both world wars. In the first, the danger of being drafted hung over him. When the Russians invaded Máramaros – his brother-in-law Lieutenant Károly Ziegler died there at that time – Bartók feared that nothing would stop them reaching Budapest, and packed up all his folksong materials to put them in a safe place. He started a strong garlic treatment against the threat of cholera, although it was still only a distant threat. Faced with the Second World War, he worked hard to gain a secure place for the manuscripts of his works. On the basis of his earlier bad experiences he accumulated supplies of paper, candles and the like so that he could continue with his work even if the worst came to the worst. The change in boundaries which followed the Trianon peace treaty cut him off from his mother and rendered impossible the further realization of his plans for collecting folksongs.

No compromise or 'golden mean' ever existed for him. In his eyes people and circumstances were either outstanding or contemptible. Because of this view many people thought he was rigid and humourless, although the contrary was, in fact, true. Amid family and friends he could be very cheerful, and he liked to play jokes. He bought some amusing bits and pieces in a 'magic shop', and enjoyed fooling his friends and our domestics with them. His private correspondence is full of humorous descriptions and strange addresses. He was delighted by inaccurate or incorrect addresses on letters arriving from abroad. Our homes were in streets which had names containing composite sounds; foreigners would amusingly mangle these names. He kept a special collection of such envelopes, which he liked to show to people. His humour is found in his compositions, too, as in 'A bit drunk', 'Bear Dance' and a few of the choral works. As a rule he threw nothing away, keeping every document, letter, bill, receipt, and even train and boat tickets. Most of these are still extant, and by using them it is possible to trace the course of his life reliably.

The early death of his father placed the family in a difficult financial position, and it was necessary for them all – his mother, his sister, and his aunt, who ran the household – to live very carefully. This thriftiness remained a feature of his character throughout his life. When he was a child he diligently conserved his writing materials, not wasting any bit of his paper in doing his schoolwork. To the end of his life he would never throw away any letter or sheet of paper which had a blank side to it: he used them for his drafts. When he was a student in Pozsony the previous day's newspapers were available at half price in a in a nearby café. Perhaps this was the origin of his practice, later in life, of not subscribing to a newspaper but only buying them copy by copy. He hardly spent anything on clothes, but somehow he always looked neat and tidy, although he would wear the same suit for many years. When travelling he was particularly thrifty. He always travelled second or third class, rarely used a sleeping car, and if he was not to be put up in a private home, he expressly asked the concert agent to book him in at a cheap hotel.

In just one regard he was not thrifty: medical care. Having often been ill since his childhood, he had great faith in the work of doctors and tried to follow their instructions with an exactitude which bordered on the pedantic. He did everything he could to maintain the good health of his family and himself. When he was twenty he spent considerable time undergoing treatment to cure his tuberculosis in Meran (now Merano, in northern Italy). In 1917, despite the difficult circumstances of the war, he took my mother to be treated in the Tátra, and in 1926 took his second wife to the Swiss resort of Davos. His fear of tuberculosis was so strong that when I was seventeen he took me for a chest X-ray, although I was suffering from no complaint, and was relieved to learn that I was perfectly healthy. He made a gift of the manuscript of *Allegro barbaro* to one of the doctors attending my younger brother, in lieu of payment, as the doctor would not accept a fee. His trust in doctors did, however, lead to some unfortunate errors of judgement. Before his final journey to America he entrusted the charge of my younger brother – then still under age but remaining for the time being in Hungary – to another doctor, who did not prove fit to act in such an executive capacity. In America, too, it was one of his émigré doctors from Budapest who advised him to get in touch with Victor Bator. Through his use of American laws quite incomprehensible to Europeans, Bator persuaded my father to make a will, the adverse consequences of which affected both his family and Hungary for several decades.

My father was interested in so many things besides music. His love of nature was religious in its devotion. I have already mentioned his collection of insects. He collected minerals and plants as well, and studied the specialist botanical literature; he loved the stars of the sky, and sought to impart his knowledge of them to others. He closely followed our century's rapid advances in technology although, while appreciating these achievements, he was also worried by the increasing mechanization, foreseeing with startling precision its dehumanizing consequences. Photography interested him – he used an 8 × 14 Kodak camera for a long time – and he would finish off collecting folksongs by photographing the singers. Members of the family would help to develop and make prints of the pictures back home. The spread of machine-made music did worry him, although he accepted that this was the only way for music to reach the masses, and for that reason (at least in part) he often played over the radio in Budapest and abroad. He did not have a radio of his own, however, and had no experience of television.

It is common knowledge that studying folksongs was his favourite activity. Everything he did served that end, and he spared no trouble or expense. His journeys were primarily through the length and breadth of pre-Trianon Hungary, although he also visited Algeria and Turkey. The First World War seriously constrained him in his work, but even then he found a way to continue with his collecting. He gained permission from the military authorities to go to certain barracks and to collect songs from the new recruits. He managed to carry out this plan in different regions of the country: Besztercebánya, Pozsony, Arad and Marosvásárhely. In 1919, too, he recorded a few songs from the Moldavian Csángó soldiers of the occupying Romanian army who were billeted in our home. He mostly went on his collecting tours during the Academy's non-teaching periods, after making careful advance preparations by correspondence. We loved to hear the vivid accounts of his experiences which he always gave when he came home. He was interested in other fields of ethnology, too. He carefully studied Kriza's *Vadrózsák* ('Wild Roses'),[4] as well as other collections of folk poetry. He collected various items of folk art, including embroidery, instruments and furniture; indeed, he furnished his home with carved pieces most of which he had had made in Körösfő.

An important part of his life was taken up with concerts and other public appearances. In his younger years he liked giving concerts; later, the activity took its toll upon him. During forty-six years, that is from when he was eighteen until his death, he appeared in public 630 times, in twenty-two countries on four continents. That means that he performed once a month on average for nearly half a century. He prepared meticulously for both his concerts and his lectures, practising for five or six hours each day and taking part in rehearsals. He would keep the windows closed while practising – even in the hottest weather – since he was mindful of just how much he was himself disturbed by extraneous noises, and did not want, in turn, to disturb others. The travelling associated with these appearances, which was nearly always undertaken by train or boat, took up a good deal of his time, but he could stand this strenuous lifestyle quite well and was rarely afflicted with illnesses at such times. On his trips he took every opportunity to savour the particular attractions of a city or country, and then to share that experience with others. When on his trips, he always sent delightful letters or picture postcards to members of the family and to certain close friends. He was constantly short of time, but organized what time he did have very well.

The poor, slapdash arrangements made by his concert managers forced him forever to oversee their work – it once happened that they proposed a concert for him on 31 November. He himself handled such travel matters as his passport, visas, tickets and exchange. Whenever these trips took him in a westerly direction he tried to go via Pozsony, so that he could call on his mother, who lived there. Although he loved travelling, he made only one trip abroad unconnected with his musical work. This journey, to Norway, was undertaken with my mother in 1912. They travelled by boat from Bergen to Hammerfest simply for a holiday. From the 1920s he tried to take summer holidays regularly, if possible in the mountain regions of Italy, Austria or, above all, Switzerland. On these holidays he would renew his strength, but also work at composing, giving lessons or appearing in the occasional smallish concert. The compositions written during these periods usually took their final form at the end of the summer, when he was generally back in Budapest.

While he composed he would withdraw into himself. By the time he put his works on to paper they were already so well developed in his mind that his manuscripts are usually very neat, and show few signs of correction. Occasionally he would show works in progress to a limited circle of family or friends. For instance, once, when the Kodálys were visiting us, he played the second movement (but the last finished) of the Second String Quartet. When giving the work its final form he took account of Kodály's remarks. He was always careful about the practical performing issues raised by his pieces. He would measure the tempo of each piece with a metronome and its duration with a stopwatch. When planning a concert he would always note performing durations, sometimes even to an accuracy of half a minute. When scoring a work he would experiment with various sound effects (particularly those involving percussion). He was fond of percussion instruments and liked to use them in his works.

He greatly loved Hungary and the Hungarian people, and repeatedly gave expression to this sentiment. In a small composition, *The Course of the Danube*, written when he was ten or eleven years old, the personified Danube greets Hungary cheerfully, but becomes sad when it has to leave the country at the Iron Gate. Forty-five years later, in his inaugural address before the Hungarian Academy of Sciences, he devoted a special section to the Hungarianness of Ferenc Liszt, saying: 'Ferenc Liszt declared himself a Hungarian. Everyone, whether Hungarian or not, is obliged to acknowledge this statement and become reconciled to it.'[5]

One of his last letters, written in America shortly before his death, ends in this way: 'And yet I, too, would like to return [home], for good . . .'[6] This is further proof of the falsity of the popular myth that my father *emigrated* to the United States in 1940. At the time, he intended to stay for only one year. He left everything at home, and in his increasingly infrequent letters from America he always mentioned the difficulties which prevented him from carrying out this plan of returning home.

NOTES

1 The author has drawn the material for most of this chapter from his contribution to *Így láttuk Bartókot*, ed. Ferenc Bónis, Budapest (Zeneműkiadó), 1981, pp. 58–71.
2 *Állatok világa* [The world of animals] by the German zoologist Alfred Brehm (1829–84) [ed.].
3 Miklós Radnai (1892–1935) was one of Bartók's colleagues at the Budapest Academy of Music, and from 1925 director of the Budapest Opera [ed.].
4 This early collection of Transylvanian (Székely) folk poetry, compiled by János Kriza (1811–75), dates from 1863 [ed.].
5 For the fuller context of this opinion see *BBE*, pp. 508–10 [ed.].
6 *BBL*, p. 347.

3

In his 'Compositional Workshop'

LÁSZLÓ SOMFAI

Bartók was generally less communicative in explaining his compositions and his 'compositional workshop' than many of his famous contemporaries. It was rare for even his close acquaintances to gain insights into a work while it was in progress, or to become familiar with his sketches or drafts. Consequently, an idealized conception emerged, even among his followers, that 'Bartók produced his compositions in a similar fashion to Mozart: he worked them out to a finished state in his head and then noted them down with passionate speed.'[1] His family, too, was kept at a distance from the process, as his son Béla has recalled: 'he always sought to use the most isolated room as his study and isolated it further from outside noises by fitting a double door or in some other way.'[2] If even more isolation was needed Bartók had recourse to ivory ear-plugs. His first wife, Márta, has stated that 'when he composed he did not speak about it; neither did he allow questions nor, by and large, did he volunteer information as to whether he was working on something or what it was. Only when a work was completely finished would he play it.'[3]

Bartók did not work regularly on his compositions, but rather, in intensive, short bursts. From the 1920s his habit was to begin his major compositions in the seclusion of late summer. When asked in 1925 about his compositional practice he stated:

Q. How do you work? Regularly?
A. I would say that I don't like mixing my work. When I undertake something, then, I only live for it, until it is finished.
Q. [Do you compose] At a desk? At the piano?
A. Between the desk and the piano.[4]

Indeed, as a true pianist, he developed many of his new ideas at the instrument, up to the point where a continuity draft could be put down on manuscript paper. That paperwork often kept him up well into the night. During a typically intensive summer, in 1926, he wrote to Ditta, his second wife:

> I am now really engrossed in my work . . . Ordinary bedtimes, e.g., are out of the question. The other day it happened that I had prepared for bed, around midnight, when all at once an idea came to me, which I just had to write down right away . . . Another time I was already in bed, and then jumped up to note something down. Afterwards, on these occasions, my sleep is restless. I am generally tired at breakfast-time and in the morning, and so prefer to use the time for copying or letter-writing.[5]

Such revelations of his working method are, however, rare.

Bartók's natural sense of modesty prevented him from speaking about the actual composition of a work. As several of his statements indicate, he himself looked upon the 'creation' of a piece of music as some kind of unfathomable wonder. He did not want to understand or analyse his 'creations'. This was the main reason why Bartók stubbornly refused to teach composition (apart from occasional consultations, normally motivated by the prospect of some extra income). His statement to Denijs Dille in 1937 is entirely convincing:

> I must state that all my music . . . is determined by instinct and sensibility; no one need ask me why I wrote this or that, or did something in this rather than in that way. I could not give any explanation, other than that I felt this way, or I wrote it down this way.[6]

In his Harvard Lectures of 1943 Bartók also stated:

> I never created new theories in advance . . . This attitude does not mean that I composed without . . . set plans and without sufficient control. The plans were concerned with the spirit of the new work and with technical problems (for instance, formal structure involved by the spirit of the work), all more or less instinctively felt.'[7]

In the midst of public discussions about contemporary musical systems and methods Bartók strongly maintained that intuition played a central role, and wrote in 1938 that 'the spontaneous expression of Genius is sometimes more complicated than a mechanical creation'.[8]

A deep understanding of Bartók's 'compositional workshop' can only be based on a deductive method: on the comparative study of all existing sources; on the understanding of his typical working procedures; on discoveries of the genesis of individual compositions. Such a study needs no less elaborate research of sources or detailed musical analysis than that brought to bear on Bach chronology or Beethoven's sketches. Unfortunately, during the first four decades after the composer's death, while style analyses and work descriptions based on the printed music were produced in great quantities, genuine source study of Bartók's manuscripts was paid little attention. As a result of the geographic and legal separation of the sources – above all, the holdings of the American and Hungarian Bartók Estates – only a handful of pilot studies could be published up until the late 1980s. The following is something of a preliminary survey, based on this author's singular acquaintance with all American, Hungarian and other, complementary sources.

The existing sources

Bartók was a very thorough man who kept practically everything: drafts of his compositions, folk-music transcriptions, essays, letters, bills, overseas transport tickets, and much more. This thoroughness helps us greatly, since he frequently 'recycled' these papers. Empty pages of phonograph transcriptions were used for sketches; the discarded page of a fair copy could be used for the next draft.

How complete is the existing material? Bartók seldom let 'workshop'-stage manuscripts out of his hands. There were some exceptions, however. Between about 1903 and 1920 Emma Kodály frequently took for herself isolated sketches and drafts from Bartók's desk. Occasionally, also, Bartók presented sketches or drafts to friends, former pupils or musical associates,[9] and he was sometimes willing to write down short *Albumblatt*-type incipits of works or themes after a concert. On the basis of Kodály's recollections and recent surveys of all existing sources, however, it appears that until the mid-1910s Bartók destroyed many of his sketches. He was surely just continuing the old tradition among composers that embryonic ideas and imperfect first forms do not belong to posterity. But, probably after becoming acquainted with some Beethoven facsimile editions, he changed his mind and recognized the right of succeeding generations to study the germination of ideas in a composer's hands. Immediately after the German annexation of Austria, in March 1938, Bartók sorted his manuscripts, having decided temporarily to secure them in Switzerland. At this time he also listed the lost or missing autographs, and put to one side his juvenile works as well as a series of pages of diverse fragments and jottings. These two collections were left behind by him in Budapest. The manuscripts of his mature, published works – from the Study for Left Hand (from Four Pieces for piano DD71) to the Sonata for Two Pianos and Percussion – were numbered from 1 to 51 and forwarded to Switzerland. With the addition of his latest European works Bartók then had the whole collection sent via London to New York, where after his death it formed the basis of the New York Bartók Estate and Archives (supplemented, by this time, with the manuscripts of his American-period compositions). In subsequent years the Trustee of this New York estate succeeded in acquiring the primary sources from Bartók's two main publishers, Universal Edition and Boosey & Hawkes,[10] as well as quite a number of less substantial materials. The Bartók Archive in Budapest obtained the extant material from Bartók's Hungarian publishers, such as Rozsnyai and Rózsavölgyi, and various other manuscripts from those who held them. As a rough estimate, then, more than ninety-five per cent of the known sources can be studied either in the collections of the Budapest Bartók Archive, Béla Bartók Jun., or Péter Bartók, who assumed control of all the New York material in the mid-1980s.[11]

Owing to the two world wars, the dismemberment of Old Hungary after Trianon and large-scale emigrations, quite a number of manuscripts are either lost or missing. Curiously, not one of the publishers' archives was intact. From the Hungarian publishers about a dozen autograph, or revised, manuscripts appear to be missing; in the collection of Universal Edition some six works cannot be found; in the Boosey & Hawkes material two or three engraver's copies are missing. Of the publisher's proofs, so carefully corrected by Bartók, a majority cannot be traced. Of the more than eighty Bartók works published during his lifetime (more than one hundred if variant forms are admitted, and yet more when revised or rearranged editions are included), proofs to barely thirty-five have survived. Each of these works went through two or three proof stages. All in all, however, the ratio of presently available sources to all sources that probably once existed is still very high. The sources of many compositions seem to be fully represented; for most of the rest, only one or two stages are missing.

Source types and source chains

For a clear understanding of Bartók's compositional process and working psychology it is necessary to classify existing sources and to analyse the chain of sources of each composition. Six or more stages can be distinguished in the course of Bartók's composition, from the first sketch to the final form: (1) thematic memos, sketches; (2) draft(s); (3) fair copy, written by Bartók; or (4) by a member of the family, or a professional copyist, with Bartók's corrections; (5) proof(s) with corrections and changes; (6) authorized edition(s). To this chain could be added two further stages: (7) corrected printed copies, alternative corrections; (8) recording(s) by Bartók as pianist. For some works links in this chain either never existed or have now been lost; in other cases a particular source type may exist in more than one, successive form. At times Bartók wrote quickly and found it easy to make compositional decisions, but he also had 'graphomaniac' periods when, although making few essential changes, he would write out, in turn, three full autograph copies before considering the piece ready for publication. The average number of working stages also changed during the course of his life, and certain genres became associated with particular working procedures.

His earliest compositions are exclusively preserved in the copy of his mother, who was his first piano teacher. The first existing autograph draft dates from 1893, when he was twelve years old, and the earliest extant examples of pieces in two forms – as the young Bartók sketched them in pencil and his mother copied them in ink – date from 1894–5. Starting in the spring of 1898 Bartók himself wrote out the final copy in ink, producing at this time a set of dedication copies for the inauguration of his third series of opus numberings.[12] While studying composition at the Academy under Koessler (1899–1903) he carried out his exercises and free compositions in two steps: a draft in pencil, a final copy in ink. The output of the following years, however, suffered substantially from the destruction of his sketches and drafts. Some large-scale works written between 1903 and 1907 exist virtually only in the form of autograph full score. Incidentally, after graduating Bartók rarely used pencil. His handwriting in sketch, draft and copy alike was a fast but clear notation in ink. In later years he used a fountain pen. Crossings out, interpolations, abbreviations, and immediate or subsequent corrections all occur in his fair copies, too.

1908 marked not only the beginning of a new style of composition, but also of a new, regular publishing arrangement in Budapest. The last series of opus numbers given to his mature works was introduced in the summer of 1908, with its numbering being assigned, in part, retrospectively. From this time he gave his autograph manuscript, often a draft, or a revised copy made by a professional copyist, to the engraver. Fortunately, from 1909–10 Bartók had a dedicated helper in his first wife, Márta, who made copies under Bartók's own supervision. The musical text of the original editions of these years needed revision later on (although these revisions do not always coincide with his playing of his piano works on gramophone recordings in later life), and so the chain of sources is quite long.

This working procedure did not change much in the first years of his relationship with Universal Edition in Vienna (from 1918). In 1923, however, Bartók remarried, thereby losing a family copyist who could perfectly read his abbreviations and intentions. For a time his second wife, Ditta, was asked to undertake copying, but this arrangement was less successful. Finally (and reluctantly), Bartók decided that he would himself produce an extra copy for his publisher, and this partly motivated the almost 'graphomaniac' routine of the very productive year 1926. To save at least this extra copying, or having to pay for a copyist and check that work, Bartók made an attempt in 1928–9 to use photoprints of his original manuscripts of the Third and Fourth String Quartets as well as of both violin rhapsodies, although this 'solution' proved inconvenient. But then, when he observed that Universal Edition were trying to save costs by lithographing rather than engraving some of his full scores, he began making *Lichtpaus* (transparent tissue, onion-skin) fair copies of his works. In this way he could make copies quickly for his own working purposes, as well as for sending to performers, to his publisher, or simply for keeping as his own concert copies. A few scores were even printed directly by Universal Edition from Bartók's tissue masters.[13]

The indian ink fair copy on transparent tissue was also used in the Boosey & Hawkes period from 1939, sometimes involving several, differently corrected copies of the tissue master (as, for instance, with the Sonata for Two Pianos and Percussion). A significant exception, however, was the autograph score of the Concerto for Orchestra, which is on ordinary manuscript paper. It is also worth noting that the degree of 'authenticity' of the Boosey & Hawkes editions varies considerably. Some were proofread and authorized by Bartók (the full score of the Second Violin Concerto and Concerto for Orchestra, even though they were printed after his death); some were edited from a reliable source by others after the death of the composer (Sonata for solo violin and the Second Suite for orchestra, for instance, in which Erwin Stein played a key editorial role); some had to be completed by others (Third Piano Concerto, Viola Concerto, both completed by Tibor Serly).

Apart from these chronological changes, as outlined above, certain genres were associated with particular working procedures. The continuity draft, that is, the first fully notated rough form, was immediately written as a score, with one stave for each instrument, up to the level of the quartet. Even the Divertimento for string orchestra and Sonata for Two Pianos and Percussion were drafted in this way. With symphonic compositions Bartók used to write a draft in the *particella* form of (mostly) two staves, as in *The Wooden Prince* and the Dance Suite, whereas a concerto was drafted as a quasi piano reduction (Scherzo Op.2, the violin concertos, First and Third Piano Concertos, Viola Concerto). Similarly, vocal works, such as *Duke Bluebeard's Castle* and *Cantata profana*, were drafted as quasi-piano reductions. Occasionally, probably because of a particularly dense or unusual texture, Bartók drafted in a two-piano or four-hand format (Four Orchestral Pieces, *The Miraculous Mandarin*). Two major compositions would appear to have been drafted immediately in full score: the Second Piano Concerto[14] and Music for Strings, Percussion and Celesta. These are exceptions, however, and the procedure, at least in the case of Music for Strings, Percussion and Celesta, must have been connected with lack of time. To show how different the number of autograph sources can be, I present two extremes. For the First Piano Concerto, in addition to his short sketches, Bartók wrote four full autograph manuscripts: the continuity draft in two-piano form; the rough full score (which he kept for himself); a copy of the full score (which he sent to Universal Edition as the printer's copy); the engraver's copy of the two-piano reduction. By way of contrast, for Music for Strings, Percussion and Celesta he made only the one single draft which, although full of corrections, crossed-out and discarded pages, was directly copied in Vienna for Paul Sacher (who conducted its first performance in Basle) and also for the first printed edition.

Sketches – the plan of a new work

On the basis of a thorough analysis of the complete extant material I am inclined to believe that Bartók wrote down sketches only in connection with actual, planned compositions. In other words, he was not the type of composer who entered musical thoughts into his notebook instantly and later, when inspiration was needed, searched for useful themes among his old sketches. On the contrary, in his obsessive compositional mood he was able to comprehend long progressions in his mind, even though he often 'matured' them by improvising at the piano. Therefore, he put sketches on paper simply as a practical aid and did not have any mystifying purpose. Nor did he date his sketches.[15]

Sketches can emerge at two points in Bartók's compositional process. They can be either preliminary 'memo' notes or 'partial sketches', the latter being made during the writing of a draft or the working out of instrumentation, with the purpose of resolving contrapuntal, harmonic, textural or scoring problems. Naturally, each 'memo' sketch contains wonderful information which must be evaluated with great care and empathy. When considered in their full context many of these sketches prove extremely interesting from the viewpoint of creative psychology. Bartók sketched the opening and some other themes of his Sixth String Quartet, for instance, immediately after he had finished the second movement of Divertimento. Likewise, the trio theme of the finale of *Contrasts* came to his mind while working on the very last bars of the second movement of the Second Violin Concerto.

As to terminology, it is true that in several instances 'sketch' and 'continuity draft' can only be differentiated arbitrarily, or are subsequent steps of the same process on the same page. The unfinished draft of 'With Drums and Pipes', from *Out of Doors*, which Bartók sent to his wife in a letter during the summer of 1926, can be called a sketch (as Bartók indeed referred to it in his letter), since it is not complete. Alternatively, it can be called an unfinished draft. The real mystery is this: was it left incomplete because, at that time, the end had not yet been decided, or because it was self-evident to Bartók? Instances of two subsequent steps as part of the same compositional process can be seen in the sketches of Concerto for Orchestra or the Sonata for solo violin, where short thematic sketches (in ink) were followed by a full-length draft (in pencil) on the same page.

Bartók did not keep ordinary 'sketch books' for regular use, as did Beethoven or Webern. For sketching he would use any paper to hand. The extant sketches from his grammar-school years have mostly survived in the margins of his school books. Later, he would sketch on such materials as empty manuscript sheets, left-over pages, or in the empty staves of another manuscript on which he happened to be working at the time. There are, however, three pocket-sized books (with ten-stave manuscript paper, of the type he regularly used on folk-music collecting expeditions) which can rightly be called Bartók's sketch books. He took these with him when he was far from his home and his piano. The first, the so-called *Black Pocket-book*, was used repeatedly between 1907 and 1922 and includes themes and short continuity drafts for fourteen compositions and six unrealized pieces.[16] The second, originally a notation book for Bartók's folk-music tour of Anatolia in 1936, was also used by him during his 1943 stay at Saranac Lake for a major part of the sketches for Concerto for Orchestra.[17] The third, another field notation book used on Bartók's tour to north Africa in 1913, contains his drafting of the Sonata for solo violin undertaken in Asheville (North Carolina) during early 1944, and also other late sketches.[18] These pocket-books might be the most valuable sources for further studies. No other type of sketches displays so directly the 'plan' of the composition, or the course of events in the building up of a piece. Countless questions are raised: what was written first? how did Bartók continue? what did he not sketch (either because it was just routine for him, or because he could not yet make up his mind)? Short pieces were conceived as a unity (the first and third of *Four Dirges*, for instance), but complex forms or multi-movement structures were often sketched in parallel channels. As can clearly be seen in the *Black Pocket-book* Bartók sketched the opening themes of the movements of the First and Second Violin Sonatas on subsequent pages first, and then enlarged the memos into more coherent drafts. With these already worked out, he could easily make the continuity draft proper when he had returned home and had access to his study and piano.

There are several important common features of memo and other preliminary sketches which seem characteristic of Bartók. The key of the music in the sketch is practically always identical with that of the final form. (As is well known, Bartók had very secure absolute pitch.) Metre and rhythm are seldom changed, and it was not Bartók's habit to change to augmented or diminished values. He also did not devise preliminary, strategic 'plans' which employed letter symbols or words as formal or other structural designations.

In his own terminology Bartók did not differentiate between sketches and drafts. When he packed up and sent off his manuscripts in 1938 the terms he used alternately were the German *Skizzen* or *Konzept*, and the French *brouillon*, meaning basically the same thing.

The draft – the key manuscript

The draft represents the most valuable link and informative source in Bartók's source chain, from the viewpoint of the genesis of a work, and contains the greatest amount of information relevant to the study of his compositional method. Although his notation leaves the general impression that a determined and composed act of writing has taken place, it is far from a simple matter to read and interpret his drafts. Even though his use of abbreviations was accurate, a good many problems remain. These include the separation of the compositional layers (were changes made immediately? were revisions later made with the same pen, or ink?) and the reconstruction of sections which have been deleted, erased or stuck over.[19]

The study of the micro-chronology of a composition in its drafting period often depends on the results of paper studies. Bartók was economical in using manuscript paper and had certain habits. For a start, he liked to write on good-quality manuscript paper, of various numbers of staves, which included the trademark of a major printer of music. More than sixty sorts of manuscript paper are found among his manuscripts, but prior to his American period he mostly used an assortment delivered by Eberle of Vienna, marked 'J.E. & Co.', or just 'J.E.'. Some paper types are a direct help in dating manuscripts, similarly to the watermark in seventeenth- and eighteenth-century manuscripts. The starting point of paper studies, in Bartók's case, is the bifolio (one folded sheet: that is, four pages). When he drafted a new work he habitually took one bifolio and filled it, before moving on to the next. When he copied the work out, or undertook the instrumentation, he was already able, then, to calculate the amount of paper needed, and so assembled a neat gathering of bifolios in advance. After all, it was easier to handle one or two fascicles than a bunch of loose bifolios or pages. Although there are exceptions to this procedure, the reconstruction of the original paper arrangement still provides a good start in the detailed study of a composition.[20]

Even without these paper studies the order of compositional events is often evident. Both *Contrasts* and the Divertimento, for instance, were clearly drafted in the sequence of movements, first, third, and, last of all, second. But authoritative paper studies can reveal many more important facts about the microchronology of the composition. And this information can be 'negative' as well as 'positive' in nature. The four, published movements and the unpublished Andante of the Suite for piano, Op.14, for example, were all drafted on individual sheets of paper, and the final succession of movements appears to have been determined subsequently. The Third String Quartet, however, provides 'positive' evidence that when the composer drafted the opening themes of what would become his 'Prima parte' and his 'Seconda parte', the sequence of a slower and then a faster movement might not yet have been determined; furthermore, he stopped before the 'Ricapitulazione', made further sketches and clearly needed time to make up his mind about the rest of the attacca structure. In the Hungarian Peasant Songs (1933) we can determine, on the basis of paper study, that the instrumentation of the fourth movement was a later addition. In the Third Piano Concerto there is clear evidence that Bartók worked in parallel on the first and second movements, shifting from one to the other bifolio. The most exciting 'secret' to emerge from these paper studies, however, is that Bartók originally meant the Fourth String Quartet to be in four movements rather than in its eventual, symmetrically arranged five movements. The idea of the published fourth movement – and with it, the realization of his first multi-movement arch form – was an 'afterthought', which only emerged after he had already finished the fair copy of the four-movement version.

Deletion, insertion, and substitution during the drafting period are other crucial aspects of the genesis of Bartók's compositions. One particular problem concerns the composite form of his loose series of pieces, most of which are folksong arrangements. Quite a number of finished, but discarded short pieces can be found among his drafts. Bartók clearly did not find them good enough for publication. Here are some examples: two additional arrangements are found among the draft for the Bartók–Kodály Hungarian Folksongs (1906); four additional pieces were written for the Hungarian half of *For Children* (1908–9); one extra dance was drafted for his Romanian Folk Dances (1915); from twenty-four pieces written between 1914 and 1918 Bartók selected the Fifteen Hungarian Peasant Songs (published in 1920 by Universal Edition), and much later picked out three further ones for the memorial Paderewski Album (published by Boosey & Hawkes in 1942), leaving six which still remain unpublished. At least one violin duo and half a dozen *Mikrokosmos* pieces also remain stuck in the 'workshop'. Important cuts and insertions were also made in a fair number of his large-scale works. The most famous case is that of the Sixth String Quartet, which was originally planned with a fast finale. A whole movement was also dropped from the Dance Suite at some stage before the work's orchestration. This movement was placed between the published second and third movements, and represented the (now missing) Slovak character in Bartók's multi-national concept for the work. The movement now known, in an extended form, as 'Musettes' (from *Out of Doors*) was originally the middle episode in the finale of his Piano Sonata. From the 'Friss', second movement of his First Violin Rhapsody (in both its violin–piano and violin–orchestra forms) a whole dance episode was deleted, and this deletion was made even after parts had been copied for its première. It is true to say that each of these stated cuts improved the overall form of the work considerably, but each to some extent also distorted the 'spirit of the work' (that is, its 'secret programme', or its special message relating structure and content).

Sometimes months or years elapsed between the composition and substantial revision of a work. To take the Sonata for Two Pianos and Percussion as an example, Bartók and his wife Ditta gave numerous première performances, over a period of eighteen months, in which they played another version, fifty bars in length, of the published bars 229–73 (forty-five bars) leading to the recapitulation of the first movement.[21] I suggest that this rewriting was solely motivated by Bartók's own empirical criticism of his work rather than by any consideration of overall numbers of bars, Fibonacci numbers or the like.[22] Incidentally, hundreds of numbers and little 'sums' can be found in Bartók's drafts and scores. These are primarily connected with the planned page and stave arrangement of the full score, or with the way in which the tissue mastersheets were to be arranged, or even with the honorarium to be given to the copyist. But calculations of actual proportions of a composition, using Fibonacci or other number systems, have not been found anywhere in the source materials of Bartók's music. In composition Bartók followed an extremely sensitive natural instinct for balance and proportion, seeking to achieve a perfect balance, not in terms of ratios, but in terms of the natural growth of a performance.

The Bartók literature has already made the point that the satisfactory ending of several major works (above all, the stage works) was born with difficulty. Bartók was satisfied only with his third ending to *Duke Bluebeard's Castle*. So, too, was he only happy with the third ending, dating from 1931, to *The Miraculous Mandarin*, even though the work had already been published by that time with its second ending. The 'alternative endings', as printed in original editions of the First Violin Rhapsody, Second Violin Concerto and Concerto for Orchestra, were mostly 'second thoughts', motivated by practical considerations or written in response to an external request.

Any change in basic aspects of a work during its primary compositional process, because of external criticism, was out of the question, however – with one exception. For more than a decade, from about 1908 to 1920, Bartók frequently asked Zoltán Kodály for his advice. In an article about Kodály, written in 1921, he mentioned these cases where his friend's criticism had led to revisions: 'Bear Dance' (from Ten Easy Pieces), First String Quartet (second movement), Second String Quartet (second movement).[23] These revisions are confirmed by manuscript markings, and we can even add to the list the third movement of the Second String Quartet and the last of the Five 'Ady' Songs. In details of musical grammar such as pitch notations, too, Bartók sometimes accepted Kodály's advice. Kodály's enharmonic suggestions for a certain passage in the orchestral *Two Pictures* Op.10 are found as *marginalia* on the work's proof sheets.

After a first survey of Bartók's drafts several puzzles still remain to be solved: Why did Bartók switch from the original Romanian words to Hungarian after two-thirds of the draft of *Cantata profana* had been completed? Why did he interrupt the composition of the Second Piano Concerto (probably at the point of recapitulation in the first movement) for a year? Were only personal circumstances the cause of the delay in his completion of *The Wooden Prince* and the Second String Quartet, or were problems with form or lack of inspiration contributory factors? These and similar questions require further detailed study.

Orchestration, reduction, arrangement, fair copy

In Bartók's working process the orchestration was a more or less mechanical task. As his first wife recalled: 'It was often not in his study that he completed . . . the scoring of orchestral works, but at the big dining-room table amid the family . . . and while sunbathing.'[24] Original ideas and notes about the later orchestration, or desired timbres, can seldom be found in his drafts. If he had a draft in *particella* form – as in most cases – he took the draft once again and prepared it for the orchestration, marking how many bars would make a system and how many staves and which instruments he would need in a system. In a section with intricate texture (such as one involving counterpoint or string harmonics) he would make partial sketches on extra pages. The autograph full score was so clearly written by Bartók that the engraver or conductor could use it without further ado. In the exceptional cases when he made a second autograph score it was not because one was merely conceptual and the other a fair copy, but rather because he needed two scores, one to remain with him and one to go to the publisher. Carelessness only crept into an autograph score when he had to work in haste, as on *Duke Bluebeard's Castle*, and knew that his wife would be copying out the work immediately. From 1930 onwards, with the

Lichtpaus at his disposal, the issue of scoring becomes more complex. If Bartók knew that a score would go to the engraver almost immediately, then the scoring was quickly done on normal manuscript paper (as with the Transylvanian Dances and *Hungarian Sketches*). If several copies were soon needed, however, or the printing was to be made directly from Bartók's indian ink copy, then a *Lichtpaus* copy became essential. So, either he copied the already existing full score on to the tissue mastersheets (*Cantata profana*), or else he drafted the work in advance in full-score format and, after a revision, put it on to the tissues (Second Piano Concerto), or from the *particella* directly he scored on to the tissues (Hungarian Peasant Songs, Second Violin Concerto, Third Piano Concerto).

Piano reductions of orchestral and stage works were not 'reduced' from the finished orchestration but rather adapted from Bartók's original draft, which was normally already in something like a piano texture. Alternatively, if he really had to make a reduction, as was the case with the 1944 piano version of Concerto for Orchestra, he produced it directly in the form of a fair copy on the tissue mastersheets.

The source chain of a Bartók arrangement of his own work for another ensemble tends to be quite simple. With the concerto version of his Sonata for Two Pianos and Percussion, for instance, he did not even produce a full score. He considered it enough merely to write down the orchestral contribution, which could then be cut, pasted and rearranged together with the old form of the work. When in 1941 he worked on the Suite for two pianos, a transcribed and revised version of his Second Suite for orchestra, Op.4, only the first and second movements and revised sections of the work were drafted. Bartók put the third and fourth movements directly on to his tissue mastersheets.[25]

The documentation is less reliable for works of the composer which were transcribed by others (such as Szigeti, Székely, Weiner, Serly) but published with Bartók's authorization. The manuscript of the transcription inspected by Bartók is usually missing, although two valuable such sources are extant: Gertler's transcription of the Sonatina for violin and piano, made in 1930, which Bartók not only revised thoroughly but also used as his *Vorlage*, when he orchestrated the work as Transylvanian Dances in the following year; Országh's transcription of Hungarian folksongs from *For Children*, made in 1934, which Bartók carefully rewrote and rearranged.

A 'final copy' or 'fair copy' of a composition, that is, a form of the work ready for performance and publication, was not always in the style of a fair-copy manuscript. As already mentioned, during the early period, when he was dealing with Rozsnyai and Rózsavölgyi, even a revised draft with added performing instructions could serve this purpose. Bartók, of course, was a skilful copyist who produced first-class, easy-to-read copies in a large size of notation, and sometimes copied instrumental parts as well. He preferred, however, to have the 'family copy workshop' produce a basic copy, which he then revised and furnished with performing instructions. Sometimes Emma Kodály also helped the ladies of the family. Bartók occasionally employed 'anonymous' professional copyists (although the names of a few are now known), mainly during the period 1908–9 and during the late 1920s. From the mid–1930s Jenő Deutsch, his former pupil, was his chief copyist. Deutsch worked primarily on Bartók's folk-music projects, but also assisted in making fair copies of some of his compositions. His handwriting has often been mistaken for Bartók's.

Concerning the final or 'authentic' musical text of a composition by Bartók, a warning is needed: whether the last manuscript be Bartók's autograph or an authorized copy, if the work was prepared for publication during his lifetime he practically always changed details for the edition. And he did this on the proof sheets at the time. These final changes were, of course, not re-entered into the 'last' manuscript!

Edition, revision, author's performance

A brief essay such as this is not the place for a detailed exposition of the evolution of Bartók's notation, his running controversies with editors, engravers and house rules, or the various misprints in authorized and even revised editions of his music. Work on these issues has already been undertaken in the

Budapest Bartók Archive as part of the preparations for the Béla Bartók Complete Critical Edition. A few essential points can none the less be made in laying the basis for a general understanding of the role of the printed score in the 'compositional workshop': (1) some Bartók scores were prematurely published and so contained many errors (Second Suite, lithographed first edition; First Piano Concerto, first edition of 1927); (2) some full scores can be regarded as intermediary, rather than final forms, as they were lithographed directly from Bartók's manuscript, before the definitive form of the work had crystallized (as with the Second Piano Concerto), or, with the stage works, reflected a certain point in the continuing revision of his ideas; (3) revised reprints made during his lifetime overrule first editions (look for the frequently changing metronome numbers!), but in many cases, of course, there was neither time nor occasion for a revised printing; (4) because of the evolution of Bartók's notation and the different notational house rules of his various publishers, a comparison of editions (for instance, a study of the same phenomena in the First, Second and Sixth String Quartets published by Rózsavölgyi, Universal Edition and Boosey & Hawkes, respectively) rarely solves performing problems, as these editions are fundamentally incompatible; (5) published 'revised editions' may represent a truly authentic and improved form (as with the 1943 revision of *For Children*), but may also represent authorized forms which can probably best be considered, from an historical perspective, only as 'alternative' versions (as with the two versions of the 'Friss' movement of the Second Violin Rhapsody, or the three forms of the Second Suite); (6) printed copies corrected or changed by Bartók in the personal copies of pupils or performers – now scattered all around the world – do not necessarily relate to the formation and revision of a work, but might represent ossia versions (technically simpler versions, occasional concert-style changes etc.); (7) at the same time, Bartók's own concert copies present a great many little changes which add to the final shape and performing style considerably. As an extreme case, in actual performances Bartók even added unpublished movements to those presented in the published edition. He recorded *Petite Suite* in America in a six-movement form, with 'Wallachian Dance' as the second movement. That movement was only posthumously inserted into the printed score.

Bartók's gramophone recordings of his own music definitely belong to his 'compositional workshop', whether they were made in the studio (and even referred to, by Bartók himself, in contemporary published editions), or played in live concerts and recorded by amateurs.[26] Of course, it is necessary to learn how to handle and make the best use of these sound documents. But it has been proven that the written form of a Bartók piano piece, with its customary revisions, and the step-by-step crystallization of the 'acoustic form', as represented in Bartók's own performance, often developed along somewhat different lines.

Fragments, unrealized compositions

Given Bartók's working process, it is not at all surprising that very little manuscript evidence exists of planned, but unrealized, compositions. There are fragments from his youth and, quite naturally, fragmentary pieces and exercises from the time of his compositional studies under Koessler.[27] Two other fields were also investigated many years ago: the unrealized stage works, plans, and librettos held in Bartók's estate;[28] the compositional plans outlined in his correspondence with his publishers, and his publishers' suggestions.[29] The plan for a series of 'three (or four) cantatas', which included the *Cantata profana*, is already well-known to the reader of Bartók's letters.

Based on a survey of the manuscripts, the following emerge as the most significant fragments:[30] (1) a slow piece for cello and strings, about fifty bars in length, written around 1907–08; (2) a fugue based on the Stefi Geyer theme (found in the second movement of the posthumous First Violin Concerto), seventeen bars in length, dating from 1908, and six unidentified sketches, among them two piano pieces in the style of the Fourteen Bagatelles and the *Seven Sketches* (respectively), probably from 1908–9; (3) a fragment of thirty-one bars for piano, dating from 1918, probably intended for the planned longer series of Three Studies Op.18; (4) two Hungarian folksong arrangements for piano, of thirty-three and twenty-one bars, from 1926–7; (5) an orchestration of thirty-one bars of 'With Drums and Pipes' from *Out of Doors*, dating from around 1932, written for an orchestral composition based on his piano pieces which had been discussed with Universal Edition; (6) a 103-bar fragment for orchestra, found among the sketches of Concerto for Orchestra, but actually planned as an episode for the orchestral version of the chorus 'Hussar'; (7) some twenty-two to twenty-four bars of sketches, found in the same field book as those to the Sonata for solo violin, which may belong to the Seventh String Quartet that Ralph Hawkes was encouraging Bartók to write in 1945.

In summary, excepting the Viola Concerto's draft, no Bartók sketch or fragment seems to remain which could be reconstructed as a complete work. Bartók's supposed comment shortly before his death that 'I am only sorry that I have to leave with my baggage full' probably concerned plans and compositional ideas still only in his imagination.

NOTES

1 Antal Molnár, *Bartók művészete, emlékezéssel a művész életére*, Budapest (Rózsavölgyi), n.d., p. 73.

2 *ZT*.iii, p. 284.

3 *DB*.iv, p. 175.

4 Dezső Kosztolányi, 'Bartók, Béla', *Pesti Hirlap*, 31 May 1925, reprinted in *Bartók breviárium*, ed. József Ujfalussy and Vera Lampert, third edition, Budapest (Zeneműkiadó), 1974, p. 590.

5 21 June 1926, *BBcl*, p. 381.

6 Reproduced in József Ujfalussy and Vera Lampert ed., op. cit., p. 478.

7 *BBE*, p. 376.

8 *BBE*, p. 516.

9 For instance, two songs written in 1916 to the critic M.-D. Calvocoressi, a draft of *Allegro barbaro* to Ignác Péteri (his children's doctor), sketches for the Second Violin Concerto to the violinist Tossy Spivakovsky, the draft of Fifteen Hungarian Peasant Songs to his friend Agatha Fassett, and of the second and third of Three Rondos on Folktunes to his former pupil Wilhelmine Creel.

10 Details of these publishing relationships are provided in Adrienne Gombocz's chapter 'With his Publishers' in this *Companion*.

11 Other important manuscripts are held in Washington DC (Library of Congress), Philadelphia (University of Pennsylvania), New York (Pierpont

Morgan Library), London (British Library), Basle (Paul Sacher Stiftung), Vienna (Stadtbibliothek, Österreichische Nationalbibliothek), Budapest (Országos Széchényi Könyvtár, Történeti Múzeum), as well as in further public and private collections.

12 This copy of his 'Op.1' Piano Sonata in A♭, of 1898, is now held in the Pierpont Morgan Library, New York.

13 Second Piano Concerto, full score; Hungarian Peasant Songs for orchestra; *Cantata profana*, full and vocal scores.

14 See Illustration no. 21.

15 His diary-like memo sketches from 1908, with their accompanying dates, refer to sad events in his relationship with Stefi Geyer, and are exceptions resulting from this romantic crisis.

16 Facsimile edition, ed. László Somfai, Budapest (Editio Musica), 1987.

17 See Illustration no. 28.

18 These second and third sketch books are held in the collection of Péter Bartók.

19 Among the drafts held in the Budapest Bartók Archive the affixed revisions and their covered counterparts have mostly been checked. The drafts held in America remain untouched, however.

20 The study of the American manuscripts is problematic because, when the New York Bartók Archives were being established, the original bifolios and fascicles were cut into separate folios. The researcher needs to match up the halves of the former bifolios on the basis of any irregularities evident along the cut edges.

21 See Illustration no. 25.

22 cf. Roy Howat's chapter, 'Masterworks (II): Sonata for Two Pianos and Percussion', in this *Companion*.

23 See *DB*.v, pp. 63, 65.

24 *DB*.iv, pp. 174-5.

25 When in the mid–late 1920s Bartók transcribed a number of Italian keyboard pieces and an organ sonata by J. S. Bach for piano, he did produce regular autograph manuscripts. The process was simpler for his numerous performing editions of 'Classical' masterworks, however. With these, he took an existing printed edition, or a copy of it, and added the performing instructions in red ink or pencil.

26 See *Centenary Edition of Bartók's Records (Complete)*, ed. László Somfai, János Sebestyén and Zoltán Kocsis, 2 vols., LPX 12326–33, 12334–8, Budapest (Hungaroton), 1981.

27 These early fragments are described in Denis Dille, *Thematisches Verzeichnis der Jugendwerke Béla Bartóks, 1890–1904*, Budapest (Akadémiai Kiadó), 1974.

28 László Somfai, 'Nichtvertonte Libretti im Nachlass und andere Bühnenpläne Bartóks', *DB*.ii, pp. 28–52.

29 György Kroó, 'Unrealized Plans and Ideas for Projects by Bartók', *SM*, vol. 12 (1970), pp. 11–28.

30 Juvenile sketches and discarded pieces obviously belonging to completed compositions have been omitted from this listing.

4

The Ethnomusicologist

SÁNDOR KOVÁCS

'Now I have a new plan: to collect the finest Hungarian folksongs and to raise them, adding the best possible piano accompaniments, to the level of art song.' In this way Béla Bartók wrote to his sister Elza in December 1904.[1] He had heard genuine peasant songs for the first time only a few months before in the northern Hungarian resort town of Gerlicepuszta, where he had gone to rest, practise and engage in creative work. The experience had led to a fundamental change in his earlier ideas about Hungarian folksong. Moreover, it led to a change in his entire artistic outlook. Until then he had considered music 'Hungarian' and 'folk' in the same way as Brahms or Liszt would have done, thinking primarily of the folk-like popular songs which were composed by various, frequently amateur 'song writers' from the turn of the nineteenth century onwards and generally gained currency through gypsy musicians in inns. Bartók may have known such songs as a child – according to his mother he knew about forty at the age of four – but certainly became keenly interested in them at the beginning of 1903. At this time Bartók was under the spell of the nationalist movement which was then reaching its height of influence in Hungary. This great nationalist ardour, however, soon led to a kind of schizophrenia.The composer Bartók found the melodies less than inspiring while the patriot Bartók found himself obliged to cherish them and use them in his compositions. This contradiction was resolved by the singing of Lidi Dósa, a maid of some acquaintances of his at Gerlicepuszta. Bartók realized that another world of music existed beyond that sphere which he already knew, a world which might provide that new impetus which had until then eluded him.

Of course, his first thoughts were not about the scholarly potential of these songs. It was the artist, rather than the scientist, who sought to collect the finest of Hungarian folksongs. Although by his mid-twenties Bartók may already have displayed a systematizing inclination, his knowledge of ethnomusicology was practically nil. All he knew was that from then on he would no longer approach his urbanized relatives and friends for 'interesting' melodies but, rather, turn to the peasants. Above all he would have liked to go to Transylvania, to the land of the Székely people, from where Lidi Dósa had originated. During the spring of 1905 he appealed to the Ministry for Religion and Public Education for a grant. Although his request was favourably received he decided to postpone any journey so that he would be free to prepare for the Paris Rubinstein competition of August that year. He only noted down a few songs from servants and labourers at Sziladpuszta, where he was holidaying with his sister's family. While he collected only a few melodies in 1905, that year was of decisive importance to the development of Bartók's career as an ethnomusicologist: he became acquainted with Zoltán Kodály. Despite having studied at the Budapest Academy of Music at the same time, they had not been in the same class and so had not come to know each other. They first met in the salon of Emma Gruber (later Kodály's wife) on 18 March 1905, and soon became friends, not least because of their mutual interest in folk music. Kodály had much more experience in the field, and was soon to graduate from the University in Budapest with a doctoral treatise on the stanzaic structure of Hungarian folksongs. In this treatise he had presented a literature survey as well as material which he had collected himself. He was able, therefore, to act as a guide for Bartók – at least in the initial stages of their joint work – advising him and drawing his attention to important publications. It is probable, although not definite, that Kodály introduced Bartók to Béla Vikár, the first person in Europe to use a phonograph when collecting folksongs. Vikár was primarily interested in the texts rather than the music. Indeed, his inability to read music led him to decide to use Edison's invention, for he realized that the precise analysis of the melodies was likely to be just as important as the analysis of the song texts. Between 1896 and 1910 he recorded about 1500 melodies on phonograph cylinders. Kodály became familiar with Vikár's collection in the autumn of 1903, and by 1906 Bartók had determined to use the phonograph on his first properly organized expedition to collect folksongs.

In that year Bartók and Kodály issued an 'Appeal to the Hungarian People' in which they asked for support in accomplishing a 'scientifically precise and complete collection of folksongs', as well as for subscribers to their jointly edited publication 'Hungarian folksongs for voice with piano accompaniment'(which was then forthcoming).[2] This volume was intended as the first of a series which would popularize *genuine* folksongs among those of the middle classes interested in domestic music-making. They had hoped that these songs would sell well and the resultant income cover the expenses of their scientific collecting, at least partially. But these hopes were not realized. The volume of twenty songs, with piano accompaniments written ten each by Bartók and Kodály, went on sale at the end of 1906 but elicited few buyers. This lack of support did not upset the young composer–researchers too much. In the summer of 1907 Bartók still managed to realize his original dream of visiting the villages of Transylvania. The result was remarkable, as Kodály recalled: 'He came back with such a pile of pentatonic melodies that . . . the fundamental importance of this hitherto unnoticed scale suddenly became obvious.'[3] It was also found that this anhemitonic pentatony (lacking any intervals of a semitone) did not play a fundamental role in the folk music of any of the neighbouring peoples. Bartók and Kodály had realized from the start that an analysis of the music of these neighbouring peoples was indispensable to a scholarly examination of Hungarian peasant music. At the turn of the century, however, the research into the folk music of these nationalities – with the exception of the Germans – had reached approximately the same rudimentary state as in Hungary, or, in some cases, even lagged behind it. This comparative work particularly attracted Bartók. He regularly collected Slovak folksongs from 1906, and Romanian tunes from 1909. In 1912 he collected some eighty-one Ruthenian melodies, and while touring the southern region of the Bánát collected twenty-one Serbian and seven Bulgarian melodies. He also planned a further expedition to the Volga region, to the Chuwash and Tartar peoples, from where the Magyars were believed at that time to have originated. This plan was not realized, but Bartók did manage to organize another trip, to the north African oasis of Biskra in 1913. There he took down about two hundred Arabic melodies on his phonograph.

Bartók continued his collecting work energetically even during the years of the First World War. Although the war did frustrate some of his ideas – he would have liked, for instance, to have returned to north Africa or to have visited the villages of Moldavia inhabited by ethnic Hungarians – he could continue relatively freely with much of his work. Indeed, in some regards, the war made his work easier: in the army barracks a large number of melodies could be collected in a short time from soldiers drawn from a variety of regions. At the end of 1918, however, fundamental political changes took place. The disintegration of the Austro-Hungarian Empire and consequent redistribution of its territory (later ratified by the Trianon treaty) resulted in the loss to Hungary of those very areas which had hitherto provided Bartók with the most valuable and interesting folk materials: Transylvania (to Romania), the 'Felvidék' (to Czechoslovakia), the Bánát (to Yugoslavia and Romania). Given these new circumstances Bartók decided to call a halt to his field work. After 1918 he only went on one formal collecting tour, to Turkey in 1936, although he did occasionally note down melodies sung by maid servants or by peasant singers who were – mostly on his initiative – brought to record their songs at the Hungarian Radio towards the end of the 1930s.

Although Bartók's time of intensive field work lasted barely a dozen years, he collected and noted down during that time almost ten thousand melodies and gained unique experience as a researcher. Equally importantly, his thinking and outlook on the world underwent a major transformation. His initial extreme, Romantic nationalism soon vanished as his perception of social problems deepened. He was shocked by the backwardness of much of the country, particularly among its ethnic minorities. His original image of an ideal Hungarian nation came to be replaced by that of an ideal village. At one time, around 1906, he expressed hatred of urban 'frivolity', and although this anti-urban, essentially anti-capitalistic attitude was less prominent in his later years it never fully disappeared.

From 1908 Bartók's articles about folk music began to be published. The Budapest journal *Ethnographia* published two early articles about Székely and Transdanubian ballads and, in 1911–12, a study of Hungarian folk instruments.[4] His views on comparative music folklore were also published in 1912. Meanwhile, in 1910, he had initiated enquiries about publishing his collections of Slovak and Romanian melodies, leading to the publication in 1913 of his collection of Romanian melodies from the (Hungarian) county of Bihar through the Romanian Academy in Bucharest. This was Bartók's first major, self-standing scholarly treatise. It contained 371 melodies, along with notes, song texts and an introduction, in which Bartók described the main types of dances, instruments, and metric schemes of the texts, as well as providing broad characterizations of the most important genres. The melodies were not presented in genre groupings, however, but according to the 'amended Krohn system', which Kodály had taken over from the work of the Finnish collector Ilmari Krohn when preparing his doctoral dissertation, and had early recommended to Bartók.[5] The principle was simple. All vocal tunes were transposed to a common final note of G. Assuming the basic four-section form common to so much East European folk music, the ordering of the melodies was then determined according to the end-notes of the second, first and, last of all, the third section. The undoubted advantage of the system was its transparency and lexical simplicity. The disadvantage, which Bartók started to ponder when this first volume went to press, was that certain other important connections in the material could not adequately be expressed, or were even concealed. But Bartók kept on trying to refine his systems, so as to separate the most important stylistic layers not just lexically, but also 'grammatically'.

The principles of 'grammatical' classification of the Hungarian melodies were formalized only some years later, because of a lack of outside support for Bartók's and Kodály's research. In 1913 they sought sponsorship from the Kisfaludy Society, then well known for its sponsorship of literary and humanistic endeavours, to publish their collected materials using an amended Krohn system of categorization. Their application, formulated by Kodály, was never answered. In the absence of such support Bartók and Kodály carried out only preparatory and archival work, in addition to their collecting activity. They wrote out clean copies (*támlaps*) of the melodies which they had taken down in small notebooks during their trips, including also such information as place of collection, name and age of singer. Bartók, in particular, also started to note down the folk material recorded by the phonograph, and not just his own recordings, but most of those of Vikár as well. It was only towards the end of the war that a new commission provided the impetus for renewed attention to theoretical classifications. The imperial War Ministry asked Bartók (and Kodály) to collect and analyse soldiers' songs. On 12 January 1918 an 'historic concert' was held in Vienna, at which the finest of these songs were presented. Bartók also summarized his research findings in the concert's programme booklet. In this essay he outlined, for the first time, the 'old' and 'new' styles of Hungarian folk music. Into the first category he put pentatonic melodies displaying a descending design and containing four lines with an equal number of syllables; into the second he placed melodies of architectonic construction, which exhibited a 'dome-like' melodic design and repetition. He hypothesized that these 'new' songs were mainly created in the second half of the nineteenth century. (Modern research has, indeed, confirmed that the 'new' style was primarily a product of the 1870s and 1880s.) With this distinction of 'old' and 'new' styles the basis of Bartók's ordering of Hungarian folk music was laid. During the next few years he elaborated the system into one of minute detail.

In the chaotic time which followed the collapse of the Austro-Hungarian monarchy Bartók retreated into the world of folk music analysis. He attempted to give up his burdensome piano teaching at the Budapest Academy of Music, and concluded a contract in the autumn of 1918 to work at the Ethnographic Department of the National Museum (although this contract was revoked in 1920). For a short time he even thought of earning his living abroad as an ethnomusicologist, and with this in mind visited the renowned phonogram archives of Erich Hornbostel in Germany during early 1920. But with no concrete offers of employment, he settled down in Hungary to the writing of various studies of his collected material. By 1921 these writings had taken the form of a book, *The Hungarian Folk Song*, which was published in Hungarian in 1924, followed by a German translation in the following year and an English version in 1931.

In this book Bartók divided the stock, strophic material of Hungarian peasant music into three classes: A. 'old'; B. 'new'; C. 'miscellaneous'. Within Class A further ordering seems primarily to have been intended to illustrate the 'history of origin' of the material. First came the isometric melodies of twelve or eight syllables (Subclass AI), which possessed the 'most ancient' stanzaic structure. Then followed the melodies of six syllables (Subclass AII), and finally the 'derived' structures (with seven syllables (AIII), with eleven (AIV), with ten (AV), with nine (AVI)). In fact Bartók was here furthering and summarizing into a system theories first expounded by Kodály in his early dissertation. The basic idea was evolutional: more complicated (asymmetrical) formations were deemed 'of later origin'. Bartók also regarded one particular rhythmic phenomenon as being 'of later origin': the dotted rhythm – quaver + dotted crotchet; dotted crotchet + quaver – with its accommodation of Hungarian speech patterns. He believed that Class A melodies which showed such a rhythmic characteristic were transitional towards the 'new' style of Class B, where the dotted rhythm is generally found. At the time, however, he did not consider it necessary to illustrate this historical line of development in the system itself, only hinting at it in his detailed descriptions. Although Bartók did not divide the stylistically highly unified Class B into subclasses, he did so with his Class C, distinguishing seven subclasses based on a variety of criteria. In this book he published 349 melodies in illustration of his system. In fact, by this time the number of Hungarian songs collected totalled around 7800, of which 2721 (according to the book's statistics) had been collected by Bartók himself.

When writing *The Hungarian Folk Song* and various articles at this time Bartók repeatedly had to confront several basic theoretical issues, not least of which concerned the accurate definition of the subject of his research. For him 'folk music' meant peasant music, as he elaborated in his Introduction to the book:

> The term 'Peasant music' connotes, broadly speaking, all the tunes which endure among the peasant class of any nation, in a more or less wide area and for a more or less long period, and constitute a spontaneous expression of the musical feeling of that class ... Taken in a narrower sense, the term peasant music connotes the totality of the peasant tunes exemplifying one or several more or less homogeneous styles.[6]

Bartók also considered the origins of such music:

> Whether peasants are individually capable of inventing quite new tunes is open to doubt. We have no data to go by. And the way in which the peasant's musical instinct asserts itself encourages no such view. Yet peasants – even individually – are not only capable of altering, but strongly inclined to alter, all the musical elements of which they get hold ... And there can be no doubt that with peasants who people one geographical unit, living close to one another and speaking the same language, this tendency to alter, in consequence of the affinities between the mental disposition of individuals, works in one way, in the same general direction. It is thus that the birth of a homogeneous musical style becomes possible.[7]

Peasant music born in this way was, for Bartók, the outcome of a natural, unconsciously operating force: 'it is impulsively created by a community of men who have had no schooling; it is as much a natural product as are the various forms of animal and vegetable life.'[8]

After *The Hungarian Folk Song* Bartók's scholarly activity was less intensive, although it did not stop completely. By 1926 he had completed another Romanian volume, and between 1922 and 1928 he worked continuously on the classification and preparation for publication of a large study of Slovak folk music containing 3409 melodies. He did not succeed in having either collection published in its original form. The Romanian study, containing 484 Christmas carols (*colinde*), was only published in 1935 in an incomplete form and at Bartók's own expense. Only some preliminary pilot proofs of the Slovak collection were completed during Bartók's lifetime.

During the later years of the 1920s and early 1930s Bartók's ethnomusicological work virtually stagnated, and it was only in 1934 that this situation changed. The Hungarian Academy of Sciences decided to include the publication of a 'universal' collection of Hungarian folksong in its approved programme of works. At last Bartók was able to accomplish his plan of old: to stop teaching completely and work on his folksong materials at the Academy of Sciences. First of all, he looked through the new collections of folk music. Since Kodály – in contrast to Bartók – had continued collecting during the 1920s and a number of young researchers had joined in this work, the collection of 7800 melodies in the early 1920s had increased to about ten thousand melodies in 1934 (and would reach about 13,500 by 1938). But only a select few of these collectors had been able to undertake the meticulous transcription of phonographed melodies, so most of this work awaited Bartók. In addition, Bartók listened to and revised his earlier notations of phonographed recordings. He strove not only for a more detailed transcription, but as the years went by came to the conclusion that the transcriber had to notate in the most accurate way possible the *actual* performance of the melody, including all its chance peculiarities, and without making any kind of biased or analytical interpretation. This 'positivist' approach differed starkly from that of Kodály, who always kept in mind the 'typical' form of a given melody characteristic of a larger social unit, and sought in his notations to distinguish this form from any chance elements of the actual performance. In his later years, however, Bartók noted the obvious 'mistakes' of the performance so closely that he often found it necessary to put down the melodic skeleton on a separate line lest it be lost amid the microscopic detail. Even this level of detail did not satisfy him, and he looked to a future in which the latest recording techniques would be used to produce gramophone records of folk music to which precise notations of the pieces would be added. During a visit to Bucharest in 1934 he found that, in this respect, Romanian folk music research was ahead of the Hungarian – the Romanian Academy had already funded the production of almost one hundred gramophone records of peasant music – and, on returning to Budapest, initiated a similar programme. In 1936, therefore, a limited commercial edition of four gramophone records of peasant music was prepared under his guidance and placed on sale. During the immediately following years, financial support from the Hungarian Radio led to the commencement of a much more extensive recording project, for which Bartók prepared an unbelievably detailed supplement of song notations.

These detailed notations, along with those of his close colleagues Jenő Deutsch and Sándor Veress, were the last which he included in the Academy's large Hungarian folk music collection. At around the end of 1938 he closed that collection, believing that new collecting work could not be expected to turn up any hitherto unknown types of tunes and that the most important task was the final reclassification of the collected material. To begin with, he did not plan any essential changes in the system which he had described in *The Hungarian Folk Song*. But then, probably during the spring of 1940, he changed his mind and decided that a large-scale revision was warranted. He now included part of his original Class C material in his new Class A, thereby undermining the practicality of the existing subclass system in Class A. Bartók now only distinguished two subclasses: AI, those melodies without dotted rhythms; AII, those with dotted rhythms. Within his new Class C he made changes of order also according to this dotted/non-dotted criterion, as well as earlier line and syllable characteristics, rhythmic features and the patterns of final notes of sections. To illustrate his revised system Bartók prepared a detailed table of rhythmic forms which his colleagues could use in arranging the complete melodic material and undertaking the references. The preparation of the references may have been carried out under his personal supervision, but it is more probable that it was only completed after he left for the United States in October 1940 and control of the project had passed into the hands of Kodály.

In addition to the compilation and classification of this mass of Hungarian folk material, Bartók dealt untiringly with the peasant music of other peoples during the 1930s. Indeed, he became thoroughly acquainted with the folksong treasures of several nations at this time. He originally wanted to publish the Hungarian collection in such a way that it would also prove informative about the international affinities of a particular song or song type. On the basis of his experiences he had formed some rather definite views about the 'interrelationship' of Slovak, Ruthenian, Romanian and German folksong with Hungarian peasant music, which he summarized and exemplified in his essay of 1934 entitled 'Hungarian Folk Music and the Folk Music of Neighbouring Peoples'. He claimed, for instance, that there was no essential relationship between German and Hungarian peasant music; Slovak music had, however, exerted a major effect on that of the Hungarian villages, although recently the direction of influence had switched around, with the Slovaks starting to take up the new-style Hungarian songs. After 1934 he extended his comparative research to Polish, Ukrainian, Yugoslav and Bulgarian folk musics, obtaining the most important publications in these fields and seeking contact with renowned fellow researchers such as the Croatian Vinko Žganec and the Bulgarian Raina Katzarova. In agreeing to collect folk melodies in Turkey during 1936 he hoped to find a melodic kinship with Hungarian music, but his expectations were only partly fulfilled in that he did find and record some melodies which were reminiscent of Hungarian 'old'-style peasant songs.

During the final, American years Bartók was engaged on three important ethnomusicological works. As well as finalizing his large Romanian and more modest Turkish collections, from the spring of 1941 he spent two years transcribing the recordings of the Parry collection, held at Columbia University. During the mid-1930s Professor Milman Parry had started to record folk epics in Yugoslav villages, and, based on their examination, to draw conclusions about the origins of Homeric epic and its performance in ancient times. After Parry's unexpected death his collaborator Albert B. Lord continued to work on the material.

Bartók was very pleased to join in this work, being not only fascinated by the richness of the epic material but also attracted by the lyric songs which Parry had only incidentally recorded. As he could now thoroughly examine this type of lyric song from recordings, and not just from transcriptions, he felt the time ripe for the publication of a book on the subject. Hence emerged *Serbo-Croatian Folk Songs*, in which he clearly summarized his general views about the classification and systematization of these lyric songs. His study was accompanied by seventy-five transcriptions in fifty-four groups of variants. Bartók had firm hopes that this volume would soon be published, but these hopes proved vain. The volume only appeared six years after his death.[9] The fate of the Romanian and Turkish collections was even sadder. Bartók had originally intended to complete his vast Romanian collection by the end of the 1930s, and did indeed accomplish most of the work then. He set up a very complicated system of classification, which took into account genre, line structures, rhythms and other factors, and completed making fair copies of 1115 instrumental and 1440 vocal tunes in a form ready for duplication. (In this number he included revised notations of the tunes of his early Bihar study.) In fact, only the introduction needed to be written and a few minor gaps filled. By December 1942 these deficiencies had been remedied, but no publishing house would agree to take on such an expensive publication. Bartók's Turkish study also failed to find a publisher during these war years. He accordingly deposited the manuscripts in the library of Columbia University, doing so 'for those few (really very few) people who are interested in them'. During 1944, with no prospect of publication whatsoever, he none the less completed a third Romanian volume, a classification involving 1752 folksong text types. The Romanian material was only published in 1967 and the Turkish material in 1976.[10] But these collections, even if long delayed, have finally been published. This is not the case with the Slovak thesaurus of melodies, which he had left behind in Europe. Even today only about two-thirds of this collection is accessible in published form.[11] Nor is Bartók's main research work on the vast Hungarian collection yet substantially available. Until 1991 none of it had been published in Bartók's final form,[12] although a considerable proportion of its melodies has been published in the *Treasury of Hungarian Folk Music* series of publications launched in 1951.[13] But this series has not used Bartók's classificatory system and includes many melodies collected since Bartók left Hungary in 1940.

NOTES

1 *BBcl*, p. 125.
2 See Béla Bartók and Zoltán Kodály, *Hungarian Folksongs*, reprint of the original manuscript, ed. Denijs Dille, London (Boosey & Hawkes), 1970. The appeal is published on p. 50.
3 'Bartók, the Folklorist', in *The Selected Writings of Zoltán Kodály*, ed. Ferenc Bonis, Budapest (Corvina), 1974, p. 102.
4 See relevant portions of *BBE*, pp. 239–84.
5 The same system was followed in his volume of 339 melodies from the Máramaros county, prepared with the hope of immediate publication in 1913 but only published in a revised form in 1923 (*Volksmusik der Rumänen von Maramureş*, Munich, Drei Masken).
6 *HFS*, pp. 1–3.
7 *HFS*, pp. 2–3.
8 *HFS*, p. 3.
9 New York (Columbia University Press), 1951, jointly authored with Albert B. Lord. This volume appears as *YFM*.i.
10 See *RFM* and *TFM*, respectively.
11 *SV*.i–ii; iii, in preparation.
12 A first volume, containing 416 songs and their variants, has recently appeared: *Magyar népdalok: Egyetemes gyűjtemény I*, ed. Sándor Kovács and Ferenc Sebő, Budapest (Akadémiai Kiadó), 1991.
13 *A magyar népzene tára*, Budapest (Akadémiai Kiadó).

5
The Pianist

JÁNOS DEMÉNY

The piano was Bartók's companion from the very beginning. It was in his birthplace, Nagyszentmiklós, that he took his first piano lessons, from his mother in 1886–8. Later, in Pozsony (Bratislava), he learnt from László Erkel, son of the famous nationalist composer, and, after his death in 1896, from Anton Hyrtl. Between 1899 and 1903 he studied piano at the Budapest Academy of Music with István Thomán, a pupil of Ferenc Liszt, who played a major role in Bartók's development as a pianist. It had actually been because of the growing international success of Bartók's older colleague from Pozsony and fellow Thomán pupil, Ernő Dohnányi, that Bartók had been inspired to go to Budapest instead of the nearby Vienna, and there to cap his training amid the Hungarian traditions of the Liszt school. On graduating from the Academy in 1903 Bartók took some masterclasses from Dohnányi at the Austrian resort town of Gmunden. He did not attain Dohnányi's level of international success, however. In 1905 he was unsuccessful, both as composer and as pianist, in the Rubinstein Competition in Paris, and this led to a break in his pianistic career. Fortunately, this break had its compensations in his greater commitment to composition and the development of his interests in folk-music research.

Bartók's musical personality, however, remained piano-centred, as can be seen particularly in two formative periods of his life: 1908–11, when the development of his 'radical' compositional style was largely worked out in many piano pieces, ranging from his Valse (the last of the Op.6 Bagatelles) to *Allegro barbaro*; 1926–31, when he poured out many piano works, including his first two piano concertos. In these two periods he was also involved in educational piano writing with *For Children* (1908–9) and the first of the pieces in 1926 of what would become *Mikrokosmos*. In looking at his output for piano it is surprising that he held back so long from writing a concerto for the instrument. For over twenty years his early Rhapsody for piano and orchestra, Op.1 – written under the inspiration of the Romantic Hungarian style of Liszt – was his only 'fundamental' work as a pianist–composer, and despite his many shorter piano pieces in more modern idioms he did not forsake this work. Even in the 1920s and 1930s he continued to play his Rhapsody, either because he did not wish to alienate an untrained audience with his more radical, recent concertos, or because particular conductors would not take on his new works or would prepare them so poorly that Bartók had to substitute this earlier work.[1]

What were the hallmarks of the pianist Bartók, from his student days until his last public performance, in New York, in January 1943? To answer this question we shall look firstly at two illuminating reports of his playing, and then consider in greater detail the nature of his concert programmes and where he performed them.

Bartók's characteristics as a performer reflect those very traits found in his personality and his compositions. They are most graphically and concisely expressed in relation to two concerts he gave in Budapest, on 27 February 1921 and 22 April 1936. The first of these concerts involved Bartók in a matinée performance of his own works. The noted Hungarian critic, Aladár Tóth, wrote in a review of this concert that while Bartók's pianistic predecessors, such as Paderewski, Sauer, Lhévinne, excelled through their brilliant passagework, hidden wonders of pedalling and sensuous glitter of touch, and at best, with such as d'Albert, Busoni and Dohnányi, discovered and stretched the potentialities of the piano, Bartók broke through that pianistic refinement and beauty of melody to summon up a monumental strength and demonic vision, perhaps in the finest tradition of Liszt, and to cultivate this decisive character in the rationale behind the performance of his own music.[2] Tóth claimed that Bartók's style of playing could most aptly be characterized by the word 'intensivity', if it were possible to call such a personal style of playing, so bound up with someone's life work, a school. In saying this Tóth had in mind, first of all, that concentrated monumental quality which was present in small surface features and pervaded Bartók's miniature pieces. Bartók's graceful 'schizothyme' physique[3] made this magic aura of fear-inspiring veracity felt in the concert hall. None the less, Tóth continued, this mode of performance would remain puritanically silver-grey if there were not present at every moment a brilliantly fine and balanced sense of proportion to the compositional whole. You could call this a kind of Japanese watchfulness: sharply intellectual, with a miraculous form of communicativeness and kaleidoscopically colourful subtlety of rhythm. And it was perfectly natural that this style and approach to performance was especially effective in his renditions of Bach's compositions, quite apart from his explosive interpretations of his own works.

The concert on 22 April 1936 featured the two most illustrious, but diametrically opposed, Hungarian pianists of the day: Dohnányi and Bartók. Together they performed a concert of two-piano music: Bach's C major Concerto, Mozart's D major and Brahms's F minor sonatas, and, finally, Liszt's *Concerto pathétique*. Bartók and Dohnányi provided a cross-section of almost the whole of Classical and romantic music, attempting to bridge those opposite tendencies evident in their characters, both as men and artists (Dohnányi, contrary to Bartók, being a jovially open, 'cyclothyme', romantic being). In the limelight of the stage these differences were only demonstrably magnified. Because of this incompatibility of character the works performed on this occasion perhaps inevitably lost something, but they gained much more through the impromptu dialogue which took shape between these two artistic personalities, 'great spirits, when they meet'. With the interpretation of Bach, Bartók's constructivist–structuralist stance was dominant. Mozart's painfully doleful music, thanks to Dohnányi, came through with the most staggeringly consolatory clarity. The 'depressing' atmosphere of the Brahms – well known through its many performances – was clarified through the good co-ordination of the two musicians' masterly chamber playing. But the real co-ordination came with Liszt's pathetic and demonic concerto, which started off with minutes of unforgettable real unity of performance. With its huge contrasts, however, the whole evening provided an exceptional opportunity for exposing to the audience, with strength and certainty, those qualities of Bartók's playing already outlined. Against the backdrop of Dohnányi's greatness as a performer, romantic build and human character, it also provided an opportunity on this unforgettable evening for illuminating dazzlingly Bartók's genius, regarding which attempts to separate the performing artist from the tone poet and man are futile.[4]

We must now consider in detail the concert programmes of the pianist Bartók, to see which composers he considered closest to his inner impulses at various times in his life, which were performed most frequently, and where these works were played. Of the many Baroque, Classical and Romantic composers whose works featured on his programmes, it was Beethoven and Bach who appear to have been closest, at different times in his life, to those inner artistic impulses. The beginnings of the Beethoven ideal, which he acknowledged as dominating the first half of his life's work, stretch back far into the years of his childhood. It was under the direction of the local choirmaster in Nagyvárad (Oradea), Ferenc Kersch, that Bartók in 1891–2 learned Beethoven's 'Waldstein' Sonata. He performed its first movement at a charity concert in Nagyszöllős (Vinogradov) on 1 May 1892. His first important rendition of a work by Beethoven, however, was of the 'Emperor' Piano Concerto. This he played in Vienna on 4 November 1903, in the season immediately following his Academy graduation. We can consider this as Bartók's first, truly substantial, even 'heroic' début. In the course of his solo and chamber music concerts in Hungary during 1904–5 he included the A♭ major Sonata Op.26 and the A major Sonata Op.101 in his programmes, and in the 1905–6 season took part in a performance of Beethoven's 'Archduke' Trio in Budapest. In the early 1910s he participated in a performance in Szeged of the Piano Trio in D major Op.70 no.1, and on 27 November 1911 concluded the first concert of the New Hungarian Musical Society with Beethoven's early Twenty-four Variations on Righini's arietta 'Venni amore'. During the early 1920s as his concert tours abroad multiplied he took part in performances of the C minor Violin Sonata, of the 'Archduke' and E♭ major (Op.70 no.2) trios when in England, and of the C major Cello Sonata while touring in Transylvania. From the mid-1920s his broadcasts over Budapest Radio afforded him the opportunity of playing a good number of the piano sonatas. Most performed was perhaps the F major Sonata Op.10 no.2; this appears more than a dozen times in his programmes between 1922 and 1928. Mention must also be made of the A♭ major Sonata Op.26 and the G major Op.31 no.1, the E♭ major Op.31 no.3 and 'Les Adieux'. Of Beethoven's violin sonatas he performed the 'Kreutzer' most frequently, with such artists as Zoltán Székely, Jelly Arányi, Henry Marteau, Imre Waldbauer, Endre Gertler and Ede Zathureczky. His performance of this sonata can be relived through the recording he made with József Szigeti in Washington on 13 April 1940.[5] In Bartók's playing of Beethoven's music his spontaneous and explosive nature is coupled with a sense of rigorously disciplined inner tension to produce an interpretation of elemental strength.

Although Bartók stressed at the verge of the 1930s that his new 'ideal of beauty' was Bach and pre-Bachian music, hints of this direction can actually be seen developing some twenty years before, near the beginning of his 'modern' phase. At the 1911 concert of the New Hungarian Musical Society already mentioned, for instance, he played a selection of works by Scarlatti, Couperin and Rameau. Of these composers, it was Scarlatti who would interest him in the most sustained way; in later life Bartók played works drawn from his *Opere Complete* as introductory items to some fifty of his piano recitals. These series of pieces placed at the start of his programmes were so characteristic of him that we could consider them as a veritable 'intonational colour' of his own conscious creativity. So important did he consider this pre-Classical atmosphere that he later undertook to prepare transcriptions of selected pieces of cembalo and organ music dating from the seventeenth and eighteenth centuries.[6] He first played from these transcriptions over Budapest Radio on 15 October 1926. He later further enriched his range of pre-Classical styles by introducing transcriptions of the

English composers Henry Purcell and Giles Farnaby into his programmes.[7] The way led naturally for Bartók from these pre-Classical composers to a compositional renewal in the spirit of Bach and also to a renewed interest in interpretation of Bach's music. Bach's art came in his later times to be a focal point in Bartók's concerts, even if in the first period of his life Bach's name hardly features at all. It is only after the big season of Liszt performances in 1904–5 that the Chromatic Fantasy and Fugue appears, and then many times, in concerts in such varied places as Sopron, Temesvár, Graz, Pozsony, Anklam, Manchester and Porto. Later on, in the 1920s and 1930s, he took part in performances of each of Bach's violin sonatas, with a succession of famous violinists, often including these works as companions to one or other of his own violin sonatas. The Hungarian poet Attila József even commented in 1936 that Bach had to be understood from Bartók's music, and not vice-versa. Bartók's playing of Bach invariably involved an intense, hugely strong tenderness arising from his icy calm. With his subdued, restrained, artistic mode of playing, which kept its power in reserve for the appropriate moments, he succeeded in outlining the structure of Bach's music. Among the many works of Bach in his repertory the C minor French Suite, G minor English Suite, Italian Concerto, B♭ major Partita and A minor Fantasy and Fugue were performed at the peak of his performing career. His transcription of the G major organ sonata, BWV530, published in 1930, could be considered to establish this profound connection with the spiritual works of the keyboard player Bach. During the 1930s Bartók also played several Bach concertos: that in C major for two pianos, on 22 April 1936, with Ernő Dohnányi (see above); those for three pianos in D minor and C major on 4 May 1937, with Edwin Fischer and Dohnányi.

Among modern composers it was Debussy who stood out above all for Bartók, representing for him the ever-present mood, timbre and good taste of French impressionism.[8] It is little wonder that among Bartók's orchestral compositions, too, works such as the first of the *Two Pictures* Op.10 and *Duke Bluebeard's Castle* Op.11, were initially – erroneously –

perceived as impressionistic music. In his recital and chamber music programmes the following works of Debussy are represented: *Pour le piano*, the *Images*, *Children's Corner*, the *Préludes*, *En blanc et noir* (performed with his wife Ditta Pásztory in 1938 and 1939), the Cello Sonata (performed with Jenő Kerpely in 1917 and Emanuel Feuermann in 1935 and Gregor Piatigorsky in 1937) and the Violin Sonata (with Székely, Waldbauer, Zathureczky and Szigeti).[9] It was typical of Bartók's devotion to Debussy's music that at a Budapest concert of the Collegium Musicum on 12 February 1934, built around the theme 'Debussy and French folksong', he accompanied all items on the programme: sixteenth-century Jesus songs, eighteenth-century shepherd songs, a troubadour song, Debussy's *Aquarelles* and selections from Debussy's opera *Pelléas et Mélisande*. Besides Debussy, the other composer whose works Bartók continually included on his programmes was Zoltán Kodály. He frequently undertook the piano accompaniment of Kodály's early songs from Opp.1, 5, 6 and 9, and other collections of Hungarian songs, in association with such Hungarian singers as Oszkár Kálmán, Vilma Medgyaszay, Dezső Róna and Ferenc Székelyhidy, and especially with Mária Basilides. In over seventy of his concert programmes Bartók included solo piano pieces from Kodály's Op.3 and Op.11 collections or othewise represented his works. With the works of his composer-friend, Bartók was, in fact, demonstrating the continuing presence of the new Hungarian musical movement. We could say that Kodály's works in Bartók's repertory had a function of dissolving his sense of artistic loneliness. These works were mainly from Kodály's more youthful years; he was involved with vocal rather than piano composition in more mature times. However, Kodály did make a piano transcription of his Dances of Marosszék, written for orchestra in 1930, which Bartók performed both at home and abroad in 1930–2. In chamber recitals Bartók played Kodály's youthful Cello Sonata Op.4 with many different cellists between 1910 and 1935.

Works by modern composers other than Debussy or Kodály are also represented in his repertory but rather more sporadically, as demanded by particular occasions. These performances were often of symbolic significance, although Bartók rarely explained their external circumstances. On 13 September 1927, for instance, he entered two Hungarian peasant dances by Zoltán Kodály's first wife, Emma, into the programme of a Budapest Radio concert. He played Ernest Bloch's Suite for viola and piano on 18 January 1922 in Budapest with Zoltán Székely, his First Violin Sonata on 24 October 1923 in Vienna with Imre Waldbauer, and his Improvisation for violin and piano, again with Székely, on a tour of Holland in October 1925. Bartók put this last piece on the programme out of consideration for Székely, for whom it was a show piece. This was clearly the case, too, with Ravel's *Berceuse sur le nom de Gabriel Fauré*, which he included on a London programme of 30 November 1923 for the sake of the violinist Jelly Arányi. It was not a difficult step to take for the artist for whom he had composed both his violin sonatas in 1921–2, nor for Ravel, Debussy's most important successor. Bartók's repertory did, therefore, contain further works by Ravel: 'Scarbo', from *Gaspard de la nuit*, and 'Oiseaux tristes' from *Miroirs*, both of which he performed at the New Hungarian Musical Society concert on 12 December 1911 and the latter also on 13 September 1929; the Violin Sonata, which he performed several times between 1929 and 1936 with Székely and Szigeti; the 'Laideronnette, impératrice des pagodes' from the *Ma mére l'oye* Suite, which he played in a Budapest Radio concert of 11 November 1930, with fellow pianist Lajos Hernádi (Heimlich); and the Piano Trio, in which he twice participated, in 1920–21.

Among other modern composers whose works Bartók publicly performed were Manuel de Falla, whom Bartók especially esteemed because of his music's relation to folk music; Bartók performed his 'piano concerto' *Nights in the Gardens of Spain* in Budapest on 26/27 October 1924 with the orchestra of the Philharmonic Society. He also performed works by the Polish composer Karol Szymanowski – the *Mythes* and *Notturno e tarantella* – with violinists Adila Fachiri, Jelly Arányi and Székely between 1921 and 1923, and took part in a performance of Albert Roussel's *Divertissement* for wind instruments and piano in Budapest during March 1923. Works which he practised or only performed in private include Alfredo Casella's Piano Trio and Darius Milhaud's *Le boeuf sur le toit*.

In his appearances as pianist Bartók placed special emphasis on the works of Arnold Schoenberg and Igor Stravinsky, establishing thereby a continuity with our century's most decisive musical geniuses. And Bartók attempted his interpretations of their music amid Hungary's regressive musical milieu. On 23 April 1921 he played the first two of Schoenberg's Three Piano Pieces Op.11 at an evening of Debussy's and Stravinsky's music in Budapest.[10] The Hungarian press responded with: 'Even Bartók's performance could not persuade us to accept this nervous-shock music.' (He also played these Schoenberg pieces in Paris during April of the following year.) On this same programme three of Stravinsky's works were included: the *Piano-Rag-Music*, the second of *Three Tales for Children* and Four Russian Songs. Bartók accompanied the singer Erzsi Gervay in these latter two items. In an article for the Italian periodical *Il Pianoforte* he said of the last of the Russian songs: 'This song is a veritable gem among small, modern lyrics; it is full of moving intimacy . . .'.[11] With Lajos Hernádi at their radio concert on 11 November 1930 Bartók performed Stravinsky's Five Easy Pieces, and he combined with his wife Ditta Pásztory in four performances of the Concerto for two solo pianos: on 24 March 1939 and 29 January 1940 in Budapest, on 9 December 1939 in Florence and 12 December 1939 in Rome.

With such an important representation of Stravinsky in his repertoire, this survey of the performing interests of the mature Bartók in the music of his contemporaries concludes. The question remains, however, of what was 'modern' during Bartók's youthful period. Bartók, aged twenty-two in 1903, was surrounded by a different 'contemporary music' from that of twenty years later. The music of Ernő Dohnányi is represented in the early repertoire: the Passacaglia Op.6, which he performed at a recital in Berlin on 14 December 1903; the Cello Sonata Op.8, performed with Jenő Kerpely in Pozsony on 10 January 1906; the Piano Quintet Op.1, in which he performed on 21 March 1903, and also at the other end of his career, on 23 January 1938, in Hilversum. On the occasion of his memorable début in Paris, 12 March 1910, Bartók played from the *Aphorismes* of his piano colleague at the Budapest Academy, Árpád Szendy, and at the concert of the New Hungarian Musical Society on 12 December 1911 he performed the Preludium, Nocturne and Scherzo Op.7 of the young Hungarian composer Leó Weiner. Apart from Hungarian contemporaries, the German Richard Strauss was in the years 1902–4 still a world-class contemporary model for the young Bartók. At a performance in Vienna on 16 December 1904 Bartók took part in Strauss's Violin Sonata Op.18, with the violinist Rudolf Fitzner. The previous month he performed his own solo piano transcription of Strauss's song *Sehnsucht* during a recital in Pozsony, following up his playing of his own transcription of Strauss's *Ein Heldenleben* in Vienna on 26 January 1903. During the years 1907–10 Max Reger's music was also highly valued by Bartók, who mounted several Reger premières in Budapest: on 10 December 1907 playing from Reger's *Aus meinem Tagebuch*, on 8 March 1908 performing the Violin Sonata Op.72 with Vilmos Grünfeld, and on 28 February 1910, the Cello Sonata Op.78 with Kerpely. Through his role in the New Hungarian Musical Society Bartók also encouraged performances of others' works, including songs by Egon Wellesz, Mussorgsky and Reger at the Society's concert on 12 December 1911, so keeping abreast of more recent compositional developments.

A prominent feature of Bartók's several hundred concerts was his interpretation of his own works, particularly if the première of a new work was involved. Bartók's piano music consists of just on five hundred pieces or separate movements, nearly all of which he performed, some many times and a few on only one occasion. His Three Studies Op.18 were played as the closing item of his recital in Budapest on 21 April 1919. According to the programme he intended to play the work twice, with one performance immediately after the other. Much later, in 1934, when the progressive 'Aurora' society of Békéscsaba requested that he include this work on his programme, Bartók refused, saying that he had not programmed these studies anywhere since that première, and so was unable to play them any more.[12]

He is currently believed only once to have performed the two-piano arrangement of *The Miraculous Mandarin*, on 8 April 1926 over Budapest Radio, with György Kósa. At the other extreme are those works which he frequently performed. The *Allegro barbaro* often turns up on Bartók's programmes as a final item and antithesis to his opening Scarlatti sonatas, but pride of place for frequency of performance goes to the fifth of the Ten Easy Pieces, 'Evening with the Szeklers', dating from 1908.[13] In his performances of this early piece in later periods of his life Bartók started to make spontaneous, arbitrary little changes in the rhythm, distinguishing his performance from what is in the printed score. When he arranged the piece for orchestra in 1931, as the first of the *Hungarian Sketches*, he took the opportunity to incorporate these smallish alterations, which he then also played in the work's solo form. This piece was recorded in two variants,[14] which well show the 'improvisatory conversational' nature of Bartók's performing art. Characteristic, too, of 'Evening with the Szeklers' is the alternation between 'tempo rubato' and 'tempo giusto', two fundamental style elements in Hungarian and neighbouring folk music. The 'rubato' playing is actually founded upon conversational features; a correct perception of both the music and mode of playing lies in an understanding of the articulation of the Hungarian language. The 'giusto' playing is tightly rhythmic but is not interpreted in a machine-like way. Of Bartók's pianism László Somfai has observed: '[He] did not at all play in some exotic, East European 'dialect' of musical language. His manner of playing was fortified with his rich experiences of Classical interpretation and adopted very carefully the truly personal "accentuations" of his own music.'[15]

During his career as a pianist Bartók gave concerts in over twenty countries. The study of those concerts well depicts the different types of musical life in these countries. Bartók also visited several other countries – French north Africa in 1913, Egypt in 1932 – for strictly ethnomusicological or folkloristic reasons. His performing connection with his homeland, or more specifically, Budapest, was an uneven one. The First World War caused the progressive movement in Hungary, of which Bartók was a member, to retreat. Although Bartók's first 'composer's evening' took place on 19 March 1910, it would be over nine years before the second such concert, on 21 April 1919.[16] A true momentum was only established in 1921, reaching a high point in 1926 and 1928 with the premières in the city of many of his new compositions and his collaborations with many world-famous Hungarian violinists. But after his concert of 30 January 1930, with the singer Mária Basilides, he withdrew for years as composer and pianist from before the city's audiences. Only on 12 January 1934 did he again appear as a chamber-music player, and then playing works by Brahms, Mozart, Debussy and Beethoven. It was not until 7 May 1937, after a break of more than seven years, that he again appeared as composer playing his own works, at this time sixteen of the *Mikrokosmos* pieces. From then on, until 1940 when he left Hungary, he found his way back to the city's audiences. His final, farewell concert there on 8 October 1940, given in conjunction with his wife, featured works by Bach and Mozart, and a further selection from *Mikrokosmos*. In contrast with this fluctuating attitude to performing in Budapest, Bartók's connection with the musical centres of provincial Hungary remained unbroken. He frequently performed in the largest cities on the Plain, such as Szeged and Békéscsaba. He visited all thirteen of the Hungarian counties that remained after 1920, in the course of his concert tours. In the inter-war years he also gave a good number of performances in many of those parts of Czechoslovakia and Romania which had formerly been part of Hungary.

Looking further afield, we find Bartók frequently performing in Austria and Germany, with Vienna and Berlin featuring most prominently. By 1905 he had performed half a dozen times in Vienna and collaborated in a number of première performances of his own compositions; in 1918 he took part in a concert there of folksongs of the Austro-Hungarian Empire, organized by the Ministry of War; between 1923 and 1936 he performed at least eight times in the city, and was often there to see his publisher, Universal Edition. Berlin was significant as the location for his first piano recital on foreign soil, in December 1903, and as the destination of his first post-war concert tour, in February–

March 1920. Three concerts of his music were also arranged there in February 1923. Bartók did, however, perform in over a dozen other German cities, of which Frankfurt was most important. He premièred his first two piano concertos there in 1927 and 1933, the latter being his last appearance in Germany. Still within German-speaking areas, he performed many times in Switzerland, between 1910 and 1939, with a famous performance on 16 January 1938 in Basle, when he premièred the Sonata for Two Pianos and Percussion with his wife and two local percussionists.

France, for Bartók, effectively meant Paris,[17] where he had early performed in the Rubinstein Competition (1905) and Festival Hongrois (1910). Between the wars he returned at fairly frequent intervals, with perhaps his most memorable day in the city being on 8 April 1922, when he played firstly in a concert of his own works and then after dinner again played his First Violin Sonata (with Jelly Arányi) to a private gathering including Stravinsky, Ravel, Szymanowski, Roussel and several members of the French 'Six'. With Italy, the first concert connections came only in 1925–7, when he undertook four short tours. His only later tours were in 1929, with Szigeti, and two in 1939, in association with the violinist Ede Zathureczky and Bartók's wife. The performances in Spain, too, were only occasional: an early tour, in 1906, with violinist Ferenc Vecsey, a performance in Barcelona in 1927 and concerts in four cities (including Lisbon in Portugal) during 1931. His one visit to Turkey, in 1936, although mainly for ethnomusicological purposes, did give him the opportunity also to perform.

In northern Europe Bartók appeared a limited number of times in Sweden, Denmark, Poland, Belgium, Luxembourg and, it appears, in Latvia, all during the late 1920s or 1930s. Holland, however, was a frequent port of call, and the country played an important role in the recognition of Bartók's genius. He toured its musical centres nine times, appearing in some two dozen concerts between 1923 and 1939 and visiting every year between 1935 and 1939. His only visit to the Soviet Union occurred at the beginning of 1929, when he gave recitals in Khar'kov, Odessa, Leningrad and Moscow, and performed his First Piano Concerto in Leningrad under the conductor Alekszandr Gauk.

In the English-speaking world Bartók was a regular visitor, gaining there, as indeed throughout Western Europe, a continually growing significance, not just as a composer but also as a pianist. In the years after the First World War he performed a dozen times in London and added into his tours many provincial English towns and cities; in 1932–3 he also twice visited Glasgow, in Scotland. Of his many concerts, two of especial significance were a BBC broadcast on 6 January 1930 which also involved his Hungarian colleagues Basilides and Szigeti, and his last performance in Britain, on 20 June 1938, when he took part in the performance of his Sonata for Two Pianos and Percussion at the London festival of the International Society for Contemporary Music.

Finally, there are his three tours of the United States, the last constituting also his so-called emigration. The coast-to-coast tour which lasted from December 1927 to February 1928 took in some fifteen cities, with the most significant concerts being recitals with Szigeti and two performances of his First Piano Concerto, in New York and Cincinnati, under the direction of Fritz Reiner. On his second tour, during the spring of 1940, his most important engagement was the Washington recital with Szigeti which was one of the rare occasions when a full Bartók performance was professionally recorded. In October 1940 Bartók left Hungary with his wife to seek refuge in America. During the first two concert seasons he appeared in thirty towns. These were, by and large, recitals of his own compositions, but he did also participate in occasional orchestral and chamber concerts, including a number of two-piano concerts with his wife and two performances of his *Contrasts*, one involving its dedicatee Benny Goodman. His final public appearance was on 21 January 1943, when he performed under the direction of Fritz Reiner in the orchestrated version of his Sonata for Two Pianos and Percussion. His partner was again his wife. With this concert Bartók bowed out of concert life, although not composition. After the Concerto for Orchestra (1943) and Sonata for solo violin (1944), the piano-centred nature of his personality re-emerged, again with amazing strength. In the autumn of 1945, then, Bartók's fading life was poetically closed with his Third Piano Concerto.

NOTES

1 The latter eventuated at Bartók's first appearance in America, in New York on 22/23 December 1927, when the American première of his First Piano Concerto had, at the last minute, to be postponed and the Rhapsody substituted for it.
2 *Nyugat*, 16 March 1921, reproduced in *ZT*.vii, pp. 152–3.
3 The terms 'schizothyme' and 'cyclothyme' refer to the character typologies of Ernst Kretschmer.
4 Several reviews of this concert are found in *ZT*.vii, pp. 537–9.
5 Reissued in the Hungaroton collection *Bartók at the Piano*, LPX 12331.
6 His published transcriptions of 1926–30 include works by Benedetto Marcello, Michelangelo Rossi, Azzolino Bernardino Della Ciaia, Girolamo Frescobaldi and Domenico Zipoli. Further transcriptions of works by Pasquini, Pescetti and Paradisi were performed but not published.
7 Bartók's transcriptions from 1929–30 of two preludes by Purcell were published, but not his Farnaby transcription.
8 For a listing of contemporary works performed by Bartók, and dates of these performances, see my article 'Zeitgenössische Musik in Bartóks Konzertrepertoire', *DB*.v, pp. 169–76.
9 Bartók's performance with Szigeti, dating from 1940 in Washington, is issued on Hungaroton LPX 12331 (see above).
10 See *BR*, p. 112, for facsimile.
11 *BBE*, p. 480.
12 *BBL*, p. 227.
13 Also known as 'Evening in the Country' and 'Evening in Transylvania'.
14 Found in Hungaroton's *Bartók at the Piano* set, LPX 12326 (from 1929) and LPX 12329 (from *c.*1920).
15 For Somfai's study of the published and recorded variants of 'Evening with the Szeklers', see *DB*.v, pp. 193–201.
16 Bartók did, however, participate in Kodály's second 'composer's evening', on 7 May 1918, and there was a series of other sporadic performances between 1911 and 1913.
17 He did once perform the Second Piano Concerto in Strasbourg (9 August 1933).

6

The Teacher

MALCOLM GILLIES

Bartók did not like teaching. His correspondence, his conversations and his essays leave no doubt that he found the task irksome; his students picked up that same impression strongly from their lessons. Teaching was the lowest priority in Bartók's hierarchy of professional activities. As his friend and associate Antal Molnár has stated: 'When he was tired of composing, he played the piano; when he was exhausted by playing, he turned to his work with folklore; when the incessant transcribing led to cramp in his fingers, he would go to teach.'[1] But this constant turning from one activity to another still allowed Bartók to achieve a great deal as an educator. He taught piano for almost half a century, and – very occasionally – composition; he composed numerous works with pedagogic aims, and not just for piano but also for strings and voices; he edited a vast amount of Baroque, Classical and Romantic piano literature for use by piano students at all levels from the beginner to the graduating professional. Reluctant though he may have been as a studio teacher, Bartók took all his educational responsibilities seriously and never allowed the 'meal ticket' nature of his employment as a professor to influence the quality of his pedagogic work.

Although Bartók's main teaching position was as professor of piano at the Academy of Music in Budapest, he started teaching informally while still a schoolboy in the provincial Hungarian city of Pozsony (now Bratislava, Slovakia) during the 1890s. One of his first pupils there was Sándor Albrecht, who later became cathedral organist and a leading conductor in the city. On matriculating from the grammar school in Pozsony in 1899 Bartók decided to study music in Budapest, rather than in

Vienna (where he had already been offered a scholarship). Despite some help from his mother his financial position in Budapest was very tight, and he soon turned to teaching a small number of pupils, firstly only piano, but later, also theory. Emma Gruber, later Kodály's wife, was one early student of his in Budapest.

In 1903 Bartók graduated from the Academy with fine results both as pianist and composer, and commenced a period when he was frequently absent from Budapest on concert or ethnographic tours. His pedagogic activities were, accordingly, spasmodic. Towards the end of 1906, however, he was appointed on a temporary basis to teach the students of his own piano teacher, István Thomán, at the Budapest Academy of Music, a position which was confirmed as permanent early in the following year when Thomán formally retired. There, apart from a short break in 1919–20, Bartók remained as a piano professor until 1934, when he transferred to the Academy of Sciences to head its newly established folk music section. His colleagues in the piano department over these years included Kálmán Chován, Árpád Szendy, and later, Ernő Dohnányi. The list of his Academy pupils – nearly 120 in total – reveals surprisingly few really illustrious names, although the following did study with him: Ernő Balogh (1909–13), Lajos Hernádi (Heimlich) (1924–7), László Lajtha (1910–11), Fritz Reiner (1907–8) and Georg Solti (briefly in the mid-1920s). His second wife, Ditta Pásztory, also studied with him for one year before they married in 1923.

Already in his earliest years as a professor Bartók had established his fundamental approach to teaching the piano. He took over the practice of demonstrational teaching which Thomán, a late pupil of Liszt, had employed so extensively in teaching him. Thomán, like Bartók, believed that set pedagogic formulas led only to artificial musicianship, and that ideas could never be imposed on a pupil. Through personal demonstration, however, a teacher could hope for an awakening of correct ideas and interpretations, and the development of a natural musician.[2] But Bartók differed from Thomán in being less interested in issues of keyboard technique. One of Bartók's earlier pupils at the Academy, Ernő Balogh, has written:

> The essence of his approach as a teacher was that he taught music first and piano second. Immaculate musicianship was the most important part of his guidance and influence. He clarified the structure of the compositions we played, the intentions of the composer, the basic elements of music and the fundamental knowledge of phrasing. He had unlimited patience to explain details of phrasing, rhythm, touch, pedalling. He was unforgiving for the tiniest deviation or sloppiness in rhythm. He was most meticulous about rhythmical proportion, accent and the variety of touch. Bartók insisted on first solving the musical problems and then the pianistic ones. In fact, he was not deeply interested in pianistic problems. He had a natural technique and although he was recognized in time as a virtuoso, virtuoso problems did not interest him.[3]

Bartók's teaching by demonstration often, however, encouraged imitation of his own mannerisms rather than the natural self-driven interpretation of the student. His pedagogic persona, too, was unbending. About questions of rhythm, tempo and accentuation he was particularly strict, bringing a rigour and logic to issues which were assigned by so many teachers of the day to 'taste' or 'sentiment'. In choice of repertory he was domineering, but relatively broad and up-to-date, including recent French, Hungarian and German works among his teaching pieces. But few students ever managed to study a concerto with him – Bartók himself was not a natural concerto player.

During his earliest years on the Academy's staff Bartók continued to teach a number of students privately, including Márta Ziegler (who became his wife in November 1909) and Gisella Selden-Goth, whom he taught composition between 1906 and 1908. Given Bartók's stated belief that composition teaching posed a threat to his own work as a composer and his reticence in saying anything about how others should compose, the following testimony of Selden-Goth about their lessons together is particularly valuable:

> His teaching was not orthodox, nor was it easy at first to follow his system, although in the long run it proved to be exciting and challenging. From the first, he insisted on my harmonizing the simplest four-part chorales in a 'progressive' way and not ending them on the usual cadences; he had me work out contrapuntally themes

> of Debussy, himself a vaguely frightening figure at that time; and he believed strongly that the music written for each instrument should be thematically independent – for example, in a duo-sonata the violin and piano should work out completely different thematic material, thus violating the constructive principles of traditional composition. Some lessons were devoted entirely to hearing him play by memory from Richard Strauss's *Salome* and *Zarathustra* – music forbidden at that time at the Academy as devilish and corrupting! – while I followed it closely with a pocket-score which he always carried around in his portfolio. Other lessons were spent in explanations of his own works, works that are today considered 'tame' but which at that time scared his colleagues as if they had been inspired by Satan himself.[4]

Although between the wars he became increasingly well known throughout Europe, both as composer and pianist, Bartók continued to teach at the Academy, probably because of a feeling of insecurity about his long-term financial position. During these years his 'nurturing' demonstrational method hardened further into an automatic, and sometimes counterproductive, classroom procedure. Lajos Hernádi (Heimlich), his student during the mid–1920s, generously explained the problem in this way:

> No one who heard him play could escape his magnetic influence. Well, this influence was, if possible, even greater when one heard him speak; when one saw the firm, blazing light in his eyes at arm's length. Bartók himself never wanted to impose his personality on his students, but close proximity to him made it impossible to avoid it . . . His wrists and arms were all fixed. That is why he sounded, as I said, as if he had carved each piece in stone. It was combined with an unmatched clearness and plasticity of sound, a sound that was convincing from him alone. No one with a personality different from Bartók could make use of this sound convincingly.[5]

For Hernádi, this explained why Bartók never established a 'school' of playing, as did Thomán and Szendy. These teachers lacked Bartók's extremely individual approach to piano-playing, but their more neutral approach was more productive in honing a greater diversity of talents. With more talented students Bartók's teaching attitude became increasingly laconic: a few words of instruction or criticism; his own playing of the piece in question; little, if any, praise. With those of lesser talent he insisted upon endless repetition of 'faulty' sections and undisguised modelling upon his own performances. Júlia Székely, in her book *Bartók tanár úr* (Professor Bartók), explained:

> Sooner or later it was impossible to stop turning into a slavish imitator . . . Once, when he had already played a section of a piano piece with me more than ten times (because it was still not precisely as he conceived it), I ventured the question:
>
> ——Well, am I playing this badly?
>
> ——I should like it otherwise.
>
> This, of course, sounded like an order.[6]

Székely recorded Bartók's distinctive ideas about piano repertory.[7] He reacted strongly against the dynamic waves of much nineteenth-century Bach performance, and sought exact, fixed angles, in a fabric of registers. Each voice had, ideally, to be presented in a different tone colour and live its own 'register life'. In playing Mozart, too, he approved of no emotionalism or sentimentality, but wanted hard *forte*s, and uniform *piano*s. Beethoven he demanded to be rendered 'cleanly', seeing this composer not as a precursor of the Romantics, but as a thoroughly Classical master. With Chopin's works, however, Bartók's demands for precise rhythm and unmuddied tone found him seriously out of step with prevailing opinions. Although he therefore rarely included Chopin's works on his own concert programmes, he did insist that his students studied a good selection of the *Etudes* and *Préludes*. Bartók was always a staunch supporter of Liszt's works, which were not central to the Academy's piano curriculum even in the 1920s (despite the adoption of the name Ferenc Liszt Academy of Music in 1925). He was also in advance of popular taste in his appreciation of Schubert's works.[8] Of the works of his contemporaries he prescribed firstly Debussy's works, especially the twenty-four *Préludes*, followed by Kodály's and Ravel's compositions, and showed some enthusiasm in teaching these recent works to his students. But he was reticent about recommending his own works for study, commenting on several occasions that 'they are strong enough to fend for themselves'.

After moving over to the Academy of Sciences in 1934, and later also in America, Bartók continued to teach a few piano students privately, but looked to ethnomusicology for his basic salary. Among his private students during these years were Dorothy Parrish, Wilhelmine Creel, Storm Bull, Ann Chenée and Agnes Butcher, and occasional composition students, Violet Archer and Jack Beeson. True to his principles, however, Bartók turned down a number of offers of faculty positions to teach composition, including one from the Curtis Institute in Philadelphia.

Despite the large amount of time he devoted to studio teaching, Bartók has had a much wider educational influence through his compositions. There, he stands along with Bach and Schumann in the first league of composers who could write truly great music for developing musicians. His first specific offering for young musicians, the *For Children* collection (1908–9), was written 'in order to acquaint the piano-studying children with the simple and non-Romantic beauties of folk music.'[9] Many of his other short pieces from these years around 1908 were also written with the post-Romantic repertory of the young piano student in mind, in particular the Ten Easy Pieces (1908) and several of the *Seven Sketches* Op.9b (1908–10).

In contrast with these earliest works for piano students, Bartók's earliest vocal arrangements of folksongs professed a much broader pedagogic aim: the education of the Hungarian population in the musical riches of its own folk tradition. As Bartók and Kodály stated in the Preface to their joint publication of twenty Hungarian Folksongs (1906): 'the choice pieces should be presented in a musical arrangement in order to make them more palatable to the taste of the public. If brought in from the fields into the towns, folksongs have to be dressed up.'[10] Although Bartók's views about the appropriate 'dressing up' of these tunes would change over the succeeding decades, he never withdrew from this aim of community education in his transcriptions and arrangements of folksong.

Bartók's next educational compositions involved the writing

of easy pieces for the *Piano Method* (1913) of Sándor Reschofsky, which were also published separately as *The First Term at the Piano*. His pedagogic works for more advanced pianists continued during the war years with various transcriptions of folk music, such as the Sonatina (1915), Romanian Folk Dances (1915), Romanian Christmas Carols (1915) and Fifteen Hungarian Peasant Songs (1914–18). During the mid–1920s he also composed the Nine Little Piano Pieces (1926) and Three Rondos on Folk Tunes (1916/27), most of which were highly suitable for amateur players.

It was during the 1930s, however, when Bartók was himself becoming less personally involved in teaching, that the greatest of his pedagogic works were produced: the Forty-four Duos (1931), which arranged tunes of seven different ethnic origins for violin students; Twenty-seven Two- and Three-part Choruses (1935), twenty-one of which were intended for children's voices (the remaining six being for women's voices); and his best known educational work, *Mikrokosmos* (1926–39), consisting of 153 'progressive piano pieces' and associated exercises.

Through editing the keyboard music of other composers, too, Bartók contributed significantly to the teaching of Hungarian piano students. From 1907 to 1926 he edited a vast amount of standard repertory from the Baroque, Classical and Romantic eras. Starting with his four-volume edition of the entirety of Bach's *Das wohltemperierte Klavier* in 1907–8, he had by 1914 fathered editions of twenty-five of Beethoven's sonatas, twenty sonatas and two fantasias of Mozart, seventeen sonatas of Haydn, and other piano pieces by Beethoven, Schumann and Schubert. Over the following twelve years he edited two further sonatas by Haydn, ten sonatas by Scarlatti, eighteen pieces by Couperin, volumes of studies by Köhler, Heller and Duvernoy, a selection of pieces from the *Notebook for Anna Magdalena Bach*, and editions of fourteen Chopin waltzes and Beethoven's *Ecossaises*.[11]

These editions were 'instructive' – something akin to the editions of standard classics prepared under Donald Tovey's supervision for Britain's Associated Board of the Royal Schools of Music during the 1920s and 1930s. Most were intended as texts to be used for the performance of pieces prescribed for the various grade examinations leading to entry into courses at the Academy of Music in Budapest, and also for the internal grades of the Academy itself. Because of the disparate nature of the students studying at the many grade levels – spread through the cities, towns and villages of the empire, and subject to varying standards of teaching – the editions were highly detailed. They purported to provide practical 'solutions' to all conceivable questions of technique and musicianship so that the diligent student might render a piece to a passable standard regardless of pedagogic circumstance. At the Academy these instructive editions were the 'set texts' from which examination pieces had to be learned.

The educational aims of Bartók's edition of Bach's '48', for instance, were reflected in numerous ways: the pieces were arranged in the volumes according to his assessment of their level of difficulty; formal analyses were frequently presented in the footnotes, and also, using abbreviations, on the score itself; in some passages an alternative metre was suggested to the regular one which Bach had employed, as a more 'helpful' interpretation of the contours of the music; colourful performing instructions were occasionally added (*quieto*, *allegro con fuoco*); fingerings, phrasings, dynamics and articulation marks were liberally proffered, especially in the revised, 1913 edition of the first two books. The training function of all this detail was evident when the student arrived at the last two preludes and fugues of each set of twelve. There, Bartók presented only quasi-*Urtext* editions and explained that performing decisions were left up to the 'taste' of the student.[12]

Bartók's instructive editions, especially those from before the First World War, appear strange to musicians today, and probably appeared so to many of his contemporaries as well. They present such a forest of signs that they probably intimidated all but the most determined of students. In his desire to provide the most detailed of scripts for lessons Bartók managed to produce editions that were probably counter-productive educationally, but, for our benefit today, provide an extremely accurate impression of how he taught the 'classics'. By and large, these editions were not carefully researched, integrated interpretations. Where Bartók had himself publicly performed the work the interpretative quality and consistency were noticeably higher than in the editions of works which he did not play. In certain musical parameters, such as articulation, Bartók took pains to follow the *Urtext* editions available to him. In parameters where the *Urtext* often had little to say – dynamics and accentuation, in particular – his individual interpretation was, obviously, more to the fore. Yet further, in many aspects of fingering, formal analysis and ornamentation he is found to be highly dependent on earlier secondary sources, and sometimes even careless.

Looking broadly at his editorial work, it is evident that Bartók's ideas about performance were rarely 'style specific' to the composer, or even period. Bartók was using the same basic technical and interpretative criteria whether editing Bach, Mozart, Beethoven or Chopin. This impression is reinforced by the recordings of his playing as well as the recollections of his students; the same approach, seeking an incisive clarity, informed his performing and teaching. As Júlia Székely has reported: 'Bartók interpreted and played Chopin as if it were Mozart. And he taught it like that, too. To him a melody of Chopin had to be unaffected, strict, like a chorale, never sentimental, not something to start sobbing about.'[13] His editions, then, reflect the popular view of the time that there was a broad style suitable for rendering most of the 'classics'. One played with a due sense of style rather than in distinctive 'styles'. Although Bartók's awareness of stylistic differentiation clearly increased during the 1920s and 1930s, as he expanded beyond the bounds of his previous *Schönheitsideal* of Beethoven, these new concepts were not reflected in further instructive editions or revisions of the existing editions. In contrast to Bartók's pioneering work as a composer, his pedagogical activity, particularly as evidenced in his editions, reflects more of late-Romantic values.

NOTES

1 *BR*, p. 35.
2 See *BBE*, pp. 489–91.
3 *BR*, p. 45.
4 *BR*, p. 49.
5 'Bartók – Pianist and Teacher', *New Hungarian Quarterly*, no.30 (Summer 1968), pp. 198–9.
6 *BR*, pp. 135.
7 *BR*, pp. 136–41.
8 See *BR*, p. 181.
9 *BBE*, p. 427. For detailed accounts of the pedagogic works of Bartók listed here see the relevant chapters in this *Companion*.
10 In facsimile edition, ed. Denijs Dille (London: Boosey & Hawkes, 1970), p. 43.
11 Bartók's concert arrangements of Baroque music and work for the Liszt critical edition are not considered here, as they were undertaken primarily for performing and scholarly purposes, respectively.
12 For a detailed study of Bartók's edition of Mozart's Sonata in D major, K311 (284*c*) see my 'Bartók as Pedagogue', *Studies in Music*, vol.24 (1990), pp. 64–86.
13 *Így láttuk Bartókot*, ed. Ferenc Bónis, Budapest (Zeneműkiadó), 1981, p. 132.

7
With his Publishers

ADRIENNE GOMBOCZ

Bartók spent much of his life producing musical scores, ethnomusicological treatises and journal articles – works which he then sent to be published or, at least, tried to have published. As a result, his most consistent correspondents were frequently his publishers – especially during the final quarter century of his life – and these gentlemen came to know the man and his mind better than most.

Was Bartók aware that his relations with his publishers could generally be characterized as positive? He probably was not, for owing to his sensitive and somewhat distrustful character and his uncompromising, constant striving for perfection he would hardly have perceived just how much respect his publishers accorded him, how much they recognized his genius, and how they venerated him, even to the point of helping him generously in financial matters. Many of his publishers over the years became his friends or tried to foster close relationships with him: Emil Hertzka, the director of Universal Edition in Vienna; M.-D. Calvocoressi, who worked for Oxford University Press; Ralph Hawkes at Boosey & Hawkes; Hans W. Heinsheimer, Erwin Stein and Ernst Roth, who all dealt with Bartók both through his Viennese and his London publishers. The voluminous correspondence of these individuals with Bartók reveals a concern for correctness of procedure, a comprehension of his difficult personality and, just occasionally, glimpses of personal feelings. Bartók's replies tended to concentrate on concrete matters and never showed any sign of personal affection. Heinsheimer recalls that Bartók, the correspondent, never wasted a word on polite questions about state of health or personal matters. Indeed, when Bartók died and Heinsheimer and his staff tried to trace some 'human interest' passages in his hundreds of letters, they found practically nothing which illuminated his character or his private life. His publishers, on the other hand, tried time and time again to impress upon him their appreciation of his work: 'Proud of our longlasting connections, we send you our hearty congratulations on this special day, and hope to continue contributing to the success of your monumental works', Emil Hertzka wrote to Bartók on his fiftieth birthday in March 1931.[1] The following day Bartók did manage a laconic 'thank you' but then immediately raised the contentious issue of the lack of performance of his pantomime *The Miraculous Mandarin.* In his book *The Business of Music* Ernst Roth provides a fascinating and candid portrait of Bartók, touching upon that inaccessibility of his character which Roth believed was an indication of his extreme impatience in musical as well as personal matters.[2] To Roth – in contrast to many others – this bluff behaviour did not represent Bartók's shield against an uncomprehending world, but was, rather, integral to his character, his only shield being, in fact, his music. Printers and proof-readers, in particular, held the uncompromising Bartók in awe, as he expected from them his own level of conscientiousness and would not tolerate even the slightest carelessness. His requests had to be fulfilled; mistakes were unpardonable. Once, in the midst of the Second World War, Heinsheimer took the liberty of protesting to Bartók about his unappreciative behaviour:

> I see from your last letter and from previous letters in the past that you seem to be under the impression that Boosey & Hawkes are trying to annoy you, that we do not have enough respect for your work, etc. Never in the long years of co-operation have I heard a single word of appreciation from you but even the smallest mistake is severely criticized and you profess indignation and annoyance at everything we are trying to do. I beg you to realize that we wish only to satisfy you and to make the best out of the great many important works which we have acquired and which we are proud and happy to have in our catalogue . . . If I could only find a little bit more confidence and co-operation we would certainly undertake this difficult task with even more enthusiasm. You must realize that all these things are being done under difficult conditions.[3]

There were three main publication periods in Bartók's professional life. First of all, there are the Hungarian publications, dating from 1904 onwards, issued variously by the publishers Bárd, Rozsnyai, and Rózsavölgyi, or privately by Bartók himself. Next is the major period of publication of his compositions with Universal Edition, which lasted from 1918 to 1938. Finally, from 1939 until his death his works were published by the British firm Boosey & Hawkes.

During the earliest years of his career Bartók's works were, naturally, published by local publishers. At the turn of the century Budapest publishers agreed to publish the works of young composers on the 'eternal price' basis of a non-recurrent honorarium. As time went by and works gained popularity this arrangement proved most disadvantageous, and Bartók and Kodály came to regret having yielded their early compositions to publishers on such a basis. The publishing house Ferencz Bárd and Brother issued Bartók's Four Songs for voice and piano (texts by Lajos Pósa) in 1904. Bárd was keen that the edition have a worthy cover and so they commissioned Bartók's cousin Ervin Voit, a designer and teacher, to produce one. This was the first of several imaginative score covers for Bartók's compositions.[4] In the same year Bárd also published as separate items the Four Pieces for piano DD71.

Editio Musica, the legal successor of the Budapest publisher Károly Rozsnyai, still holds contracts made by Bartók with Rozsnyai between 1908 and 1926.[5] Bartók's contracts with Rozsnyai were of two types: those for his own compositions; those for instructive editions of the music of famous Baroque, Classical and Romantic composers. As far as Bartók's own compositions were concerned Rozsnyai was hoping for something conservative and saleable. In December 1909 he expressed his willingness to publish Bartók's *For Children* piano pieces, but asked Bartók to opt wherever possible for the easiest level of technical difficulty and to use traditional harmonies. The 'old habitual path' could not be abandoned, he warned Bartók, who he feared would alienate his customers with a 'new style'. From this publishing relationship, however, the following piano compositions emerged between 1908 and 1911: Three Hungarian

Folksongs from the Csík District, Fourteen Bagatelles Op.6, Ten Easy Pieces, *Two Elegies* Op.8b, *For Children*, *Seven Sketches* Op.9b. *Two Portraits* for orchestra, Op.5, was also published in 1911, and Rozsnyai had earlier, in 1906, published the Bartók–Kodály twenty Hungarian Folksongs for voice and piano. Bartók's Rozsnyai editions of 'classics' involved the composers Bach, Beethoven, Mozart, Schubert, Schumann, Haydn, Couperin and Scarlatti. These many editions, dating variously from 1907 to 1926, resulted directly from the publisher's decision to issue Hungarian editions of piano and chamber music instead of continuing to import standard German editions.[6] Most prominent among Bartók's editions are Bach's Forty-eight Preludes and Fugues, twenty Mozart piano sonatas and nineteen Haydn piano sonatas.

The Budapest firm of Rózsavölgyi was also keen to contract with Bartók. In a letter of March 1908 the publishing house stated that it had recently been taken over by a younger staff, desirous of establishing an international reputation, and invited Bartók to submit works for publication. As a result, the first contract between Rózsavölgyi and Bartók was signed on 19 June 1908, for his Rhapsody for piano, Op.1.[7] Perhaps the most important Bartók composition published by Rózsavölgyi in the pre-war years was the First String Quartet Op.7, the contract for which is dated 31 July 1909, although the work did not become available until early the following year. According to a letter which Bartók wrote during July 1909 to his friend Etelka Freund, the firm had been very impressed that Bartók's Op.1 Rhapsody had sold forty copies abroad (although only four or five in Hungary). Other works published by Rózsavölgyi in the pre-war years were his piano works Two Romanian Dances Op.8a, *Three Burlesques* Op.8c, and *Four Dirges* Op.9a. In the early 1930s the firm also published Bartók's orchestral transcriptions *Hungarian Sketches* and Transylvanian Dances, which had both been completed in 1931.

Besides publishing Bartók's works Rózsavölgyi dealt with the composer in a number of other capacities. Between 1909 and 1912 the firm published Bartók's instructive editions of twenty-five of Beethoven's piano sonatas, and in later years issued his editions of piano pieces or studies by Bach, Köhler, Heller and Duvernoy. As with most publishing houses of the time, Rózsavölgyi acted as a concert bureau. One of the most outstanding of their organized concerts was that of the Waldbauer–Kerpely Quartet on 19 March 1910, when both Kodály's and Bartók's First String Quartets were premièred. In 1912 the firm (which had been in existence since the middle of the nineteenth century) moved into a new, stately shop, furnished in art nouveau style, and this shop quickly became a cultural focus for Budapest artists. At the back of the building there was a large oval table around which composers, performers and regular customers would gather in the afternoons and conduct lively debates. Bartók and Kodály were both among those who frequented the shop. Indeed, Bartók maintained a business relationship of one sort or another with Rózsavölgyi right up until 1940, when he left Hungary for America.[8]

In a letter of 6 June 1918 Bartók informed his Romanian friend Ion Buşiţia:

> The greatest success of the year, however, . . . is that I have succeeded in gaining a long-term agreement with a first-rate publisher. 'Universal Edition' (Vienna) had already in January made me a reasonable offer. At last, after protracted negotiations, we have agreed on everything, and just in these last days I have signed the contract, according to which all of my so far unpublished works, as well as those yet to be written, will appear in the next few years. That's a great thing because for about six years – thanks to our Hungarian publishers – nothing of mine has been published, and because this is perhaps the very first time that a foreign publisher has approached a Hungarian musician with such an offer.[9]

The contract with Universal Edition, dated 4 June 1918, was generous to Bartók. It covered all original compositions which he might compose until 1 July 1926, as well as existing unpublished works. Universal Edition became copyright owner of Bartók's works and committed itself to publishing four works each year. The contract was renewed several times, lasting until just before the start of the Second World War, when, owing to the Nazi influence over the firm, Bartók felt the relationship was no longer tenable.

Bartók was immensely happy about his contract with Universal Edition. Although only established in 1901, the firm could by 1918 be proud of its relationships with such important composers as Gustav Mahler, Arnold Schoenberg, Alfredo Casella, Karol Szymanowski, Frederick Delius, Leoš Janáček and Egon Wellesz. In the following year Universal Edition launched the review *Musikblätter des Anbruch*, in which it offered composers the opportunity to publicize their works either in the form of composition supplements or of articles. Thus, Bartók's *Allegro barbaro* appeared as a supplement to the journal in 1919, and the second of Five 'Ady' Songs Op.16 in a 1921 issue. *Musikblätter des Anbruch* also published many of Bartók's articles on such varied topics as Hungarian peasant music, Schoenberg's music in Hungary, and the 'piano' problem.[10]

The close relations between Universal Edition and Bartók can be witnessed in their exchange of hundreds of letters. Especially during the earlier years, when Emil Hertzka was director, the connection can be characterized as friendly, and Bartók often visited his publisher when passing through Vienna, or contacted the firm's Budapest representative, Hertzka's brother Julius. For about fifteen years he had the chance to see into print any composition he desired, and Universal Edition became the publisher of his œuvre from *Allegro barbaro* (1911) through to Music for Strings, Percussion and Celesta (1936), with the exception of the Sonatina for piano (1915), which was published by Rózsavölgyi. This situation started to become less favourable in the early 1930s with the onset of the Depression and the death of Emil Hertzka. The firm could no longer publish Bartók's compositions at the rate he desired, nor could it afford to have some of his full scores engraved. Those for which the demand was expected to be limited were only lithographed. When Bartók became aware of this change he quickly learned the technique of lithography himself and began making *Lichtpaus* fair copies of his works, writing his final copy directly on to transparent tissue master sheets for such works as the Second Piano Concerto, Hungarian Peasant Songs, and *Cantata profana*.[11]

The detailed correspondence between Bartók and Universal Edition shows that, however favourable his contract, the composer was not backward in complaining. One question exercised him above all: the correct translation of the words of his texted works. He hoped that his songs and choruses were to be performed all over the world and so wanted the texts to be printed not only in Hungarian but also good German verse translations. Frequently he entered into protracted debate with Universal Edition because he found translations unidiomatic, inaccurate, unmusical, inept or otherwise unsuitable. He experienced particular problems with his Five Songs Op.16, *Duke Bluebeard's Castle* Op.11 and Twenty Hungarian Folksongs (1929), and took to sending a rough German translation to Universal Edition in the hope of avoiding some of the more basic problems.

The annexation of Austria by Hitler's Germany in 1938 deeply affected Bartók. He forwarded his more valuable manuscripts firstly to Switzerland, and later via England to America; he set about extricating himself from his contract with Universal Edition, and started to plan to leave Europe altogether. During March 1938 he discussed the possibility of a contract for his new compositions with Ralph Hawkes of the London firm Boosey & Hawkes, and in mid-1939 – just before the outbreak of war – his links with Universal Edition were formally severed. Informal relations were not cut as abruptly, however, and even in March 1941, on the occasion of Bartók's sixtieth birthday, Universal Edition tried to send a congratulatory telegram to him in New York.

One reason for Bartók's change of publisher in 1939 was that several of his original editors at Universal Edition had, for political reasons, accepted appointments with Boosey & Hawkes in London. Among these editors were Alfred Kalmus, Ernst Roth and Erwin Stein. The contract with Boosey & Hawkes of 20 May 1939 referred both to new works, and to existing, published scores whose control Universal Edition had in many instances been persuaded to relinquish. The first work published under this contract was Bartók's *Mikrokosmos* collection of 153 piano pieces, on which his old Viennese editors lavished much care. Bartók's idea of illustrations to accompany the pieces was seriously investigated, although eventually had to be abandoned. A great deal of thought went into the translation of the titles, preface and notes into English and French (although not German at this stage), and the preface, in particular, was only written by Bartók after he had received much advice from Boosey & Hawkes's staff about the nature of the English market. The subtitle 'progressive piano pieces' was added because of a fear that the English, with little experience of abstract musical titles, might not know what to make of the term 'Mikrokosmos'. Ernst Roth personally supervised the production of the six books and, despite growing difficulties of communication between Bartók and his publisher during the early months of war, the volumes were released in 1940, to Bartók's apparent satisfaction.

Parallel with working on *Mikrokosmos* Boosey & Hawkes started work on Bartók's newly completed Second Violin Concerto and Divertimento for string orchestra, as well as making plans for reprinting some of his earlier works under its own imprint. When publishing nine of the Twenty-seven Two- and Three-part Choruses, Boosey & Hawkes came to appreciate Bartók's real concern with accuracy and style of translation, although the composer did, in the end, accept the English translations of the songs made by Nancy Bush. Of the reissues of earlier works, the Second Suite for orchestra, Op.4, is perhaps the most complex. This work was originally published by Bartók himself in 1907. Universal Edition published a revised version in 1921, which was reprinted by Boosey & Hawkes in 1939. Another orchestral version of 1943, based on the two-piano transcription made by Bartók in 1941, was published by Boosey & Hawkes in 1948, preceding the appearance of the two-piano version, Op.4b, by a decade.

During most of the time of his association with Boosey & Hawkes Bartók lived in New York. Although dealing with Ralph Hawkes during his occasional visits to the city and sometimes communicating directly with the London office, Bartók addressed most of his business to the local office of the firm. There, his most frequent contact was Hans W. Heinsheimer, who later recalled:

> I knew Béla Bartók well. I worked for him in a double capacity. Our little concert bureau tried to help him and his wife, the pianist Ditta Pásztory, in their attempts to fit themselves into the complicated machine of American concert business. And during the same

> period the house I was connected with published his music. No association in my life has been more inspiring; none, if I pause to look, more densely filled with an almost mystic atmosphere: the aura of a truly great man.[12]

Fortunate though he was in seeing most of his compositions into print during his lifetime, Bartók had no such luck with his folk-music studies. Only one of these studies, that of Hungarian folk music, gained significant international exposure, being published in Hungarian by Rózsavölgyi in 1924, and in German by the Berlin firm Walter de Gruyter in the following year. Oxford University Press also issued the book in English translation in 1931. Even this Hungarian study had its initial disappointments, however. Bartók had started work on the book in 1920 under a contract with the small Hungarian publisher Táltos. But this firm soon went bankrupt, and Bartók had to look elsewhere for publication. Although portions of his studies of Romanian folk music did gain publication during his lifetime, the bulk of this material – along with his Slovak, Turkish and Serbo-Croatian collections – was not published until well after his death.[13]

A further little-known publishing connection of Bartók was with the Leipzig firm Breitkopf & Härtel. In 1908, armed with a recommendation from Busoni, he had approached the firm with a proposal that it publish his Fourteen Bagatelles. Despite a negative response – the pieces were found to be 'extraordinarily difficult and modern' – Bartók was soon asked to assist with the firm's complete edition of Liszt's compositions by revising the works of an overtly Hungarian character or intention. Bartók, then recently appointed as professor of piano at the Budapest Music Academy, did accept the invitation and worked intensively on the project, especially in 1911–12. But the project was much delayed for organizational reasons, as well as by the First World War.[14] Furthermore, Bartók was not happy with the way in which his work had been supervised and evaluated, and eventually felt obliged to withdraw from the edition's team. Consequently, only the commentaries on the *Ungarischer Sturmmarsch* and *Ungarischer Königsmarsch* are signed by Bartók (dated January 1916), and only 'preparatory work' by him is acknowledged in the commentary accompanying the edition of the Hungarian Rhapsodies which appeared in 1926.

With the growth in popularity of Bartók's music since his death, publishers – both in Hungary and abroad – have keenly sought to hold his works in their lists. Editio Musica became the legal successor of his former Hungarian publishers. Through various agreements after the Second World War, Universal Edition and Boosey & Hawkes have remained the chief publishers of his compositions. Facsimile and reprint editions have also emerged of several of his compositions.[15] The most appropriate tribute to Bartók's genius, a complete critical edition of his works, is, nevertheless, still awaited.

NOTES

1 Unpublished letter (NYBA).
2 London (Cassell), 1969, pp. 164–6.
3 Reproduced in John Vinton, 'Hints to the Printers from Bartók', *Music and Letters*, vol.49 (1968), p. 230.
4 Voit's best was, perhaps, that of 1912 for *Three Burlesques* Op.8c.
5 Publisher no. 767–8.
6 See László Somfai, 'Nineteenth-Century Ideas developed in Bartók's Piano Notation in the Years 1907–14', *Nineteenth-century Music*, vol.11 (1987), p. 77.
7 Only the *Adagio mesto*, the first part of this work, was published in 1908; the full score and the two-piano version both appeared in 1910.
8 In addition to the above-mentioned Hungarian editions of Bartók's works, Magyar Kórus of Budapest published several of his choruses, including the Twenty-seven Two- and Three-part Choruses (1935) and *From Olden Times* (1935). Both of these works appeared in 1937.
9 *BBlev*.v, p. 247.
10 See *BBE*, pp. 304–15, 467–8, 288, respectively.
11 For further information about these *Lichtpaus* copies see László Somfai's chapter 'In his "Compositional Workshop"' in this *Companion*.
12 Reproduced in *Bartók's Years in America*, ed. Vilmos Juhász, Washington DC (Occidental), 1981, pp. 78–9.
13 For greater detail about Bartók's ethnomusicological publications see Sándor Kovács's chapter 'The Ethnomusicologist' in this *Companion*.
14 See László Somfai, 'Liszt's Influence on Bartók Reconsidered', *NHQ*, no.102 (Summer 1986), pp. 210–19.
15 See, in particular, the Editio Musica facsimile editions of his *Andante* for violin and piano (1902), the Sonata for piano (1926), and the Bartók–Kodály Hungarian Folksongs (1906).

PIANO MUSIC

8

Youthful Piano Works

GÜNTER WEISS-AIGNER

It was on 25 March 1886, on his fifth birthday, that Bartók first began to study the piano under his mother's watchful eye. Four years later he attempted his first piano compositions. According to Bartók's own listings he composed some twenty-nine short pieces between 1890 and 1894.[1] Most of these works were written down by his mother, and all have remained unpublished. They reflect the kind of music that Bartók must often have heard as the family moved from one provincial town to another during these years. Around half of them are dance numbers, including nine polkas and three mazurkas. There is also a march. Specifically Western influences can be felt in two ländlers and also in two waltzes, the first of which – his first Op.1 – is an unmistakable adaptation of melodies from Johann Strauss's *The Blue Danube*. Also imbued with dance rhythms are a number of pieces, such as *Sounds of Spring*, which were obviously influenced by the *Albumblatt* music fashionable at this time. *Echo of Radegund*, written when Bartók was ten, is noteworthy as the composer's earliest attempt at simple embellishing variations. (Its title refers to the spa which he had visited with his father, shortly before the latter's death.) This work was also the point of departure for Bartók's *The Course of the Danube*, a series of nine loosely related programme pieces, which included an Hungarian *csárdás* to represent the river's entry into Budapest. This was one of the pieces that he played at his first public concert, held on 1 May 1892 in Nagyszöllős. A second attempt to write a set of variations reveals Bartók's appropriation of a model from the middle movement of Beethoven's 'Kreutzer' Violin Sonata. The dedication of this work to an amateur violinist who had partnered Bartók in performing that Beethoven sonata throws further light on the background against which these early pieces were written.

Beethoven's influence is even more clearly discernible in a three-movement Sonata in G minor, dating from 1894, the opening of which bears highly recognizable traces not only of the 'Pathétique' Sonata (see Ex. 1a) and Fifth Symphony (see the 'Fate' motifs in Ex. 1b) but also, in its *presto* finale, of Beethoven's Sonata in D minor, Op.31 no.2, for piano.

EX. 1

With this G minor Sonata Bartók launched into a new creative period, which lasted until 1898. By 1894 Bartók was enrolled at the Catholic grammar school in Pozsony (now Bratislava, Slovakia). There he took piano lessons from László Erkel (son of the well-known opera composer Ferenc Erkel) and, after his death, piano and theory lessons from Anton Hyrtl. The orthographical errors which marred his earlier manuscripts now began to disappear, as he learned to notate music in a theoretical rather than purely empirical way.

After completing two further sonatas for piano Bartók temporarily turned his back on this genre and concentrated more on chamber music, for the most part cyclically conceived. This development was probably the result of his attendance at numerous local concerts – Pozsony was noted as a musical centre – and of his own involvement in amateur music-making. A marked stylistic change in his writing is also evident. Romantic elements increasingly find their way into Bartók's previously Classical vocabulary, being detected as early as 1895 in his piano Fantasie in A minor. This sonata-form work takes up elements from the development of the first movement of the G minor sonata of the previous year, but Bartók prefaces his main theme with an introductory melody reminiscent of Brahms.

With the three piano pieces of 1897 (Op.13 in Bartók's numbering system of the time) we find him unexpectedly moving away from the Classical world of Beethoven to the lighter, more melodically flowing style of Mendelssohn – specifically of his *Songs without Words* – as can be seen in the *presto* theme (Ex. 2) of the first of these pieces.[2]

EX. 2

Several echoes of Brahms can be heard in the Scherzo (Fantasie) for piano, Op.18, which also dates from 1897. Right from its first eight-bar phrase there is a kind of Romantic oscillation which clearly draws its inspiration from Brahms's Ballade in B major, Op.10 no.4. The opening motif is compressed to form that hemiolic 'waltz syncopation' which attests to the influence of Viennese dance rhythm, as mediated by Brahms.

By 1898 – a particularly productive year for the composer – Bartók was receiving an increasing number of invitations to appear in public as a pianist, and was inspired again to write a considerable number of works for the piano. Although several of these works are only known from the listings he kept, others, such as the three Op.21 fantasies (also known as Three Piano Pieces), have survived and are worthy of attention. They provide a stylistic and thematic link between Bartók's Piano Quartet in C minor, Op.20, and his unnumbered String Quartet in F major. The first two of these fantasies, an Intermezzo in C minor and an Adagio in G minor, show how in Bartók's hands a soaring melodic gesture becomes an emotional cardinal point, while the descending chromatic line that follows it is subjected to variation and extension. Ex. 3 shows this process in the Intermezzo.

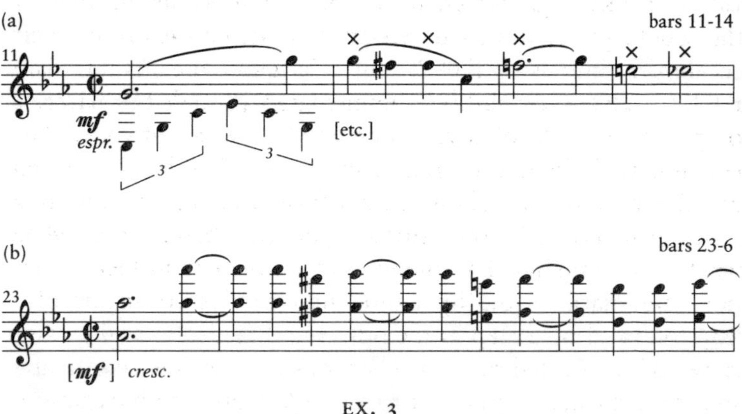

EX. 3

The result of this shared procedure is a remarkable sense of kinship between the two pieces. The Brahmsian thematic colourings are reinforced by the triplet crotchet accompanying figure in the Intermezzo and the rich, chordal texture of the following Adagio.

Well before taking his matriculation examinations in Pozsony Bartók had decided that he wanted to study music in Budapest, notwithstanding the greater geographical convenience of Vienna. In coming to this decision he was influenced by Ernő Dohnányi, his friend in Pozsony and by now already well known as a pianist and composer. In January 1899 Bartók underwent a private audition before István Thomán, Dohnányi's teacher at the Budapest Academy of Music, which opened the way for his enrolment at the Academy in the following September. He was admitted to the second year of piano studies and to the second/third year in composition, which he studied under Hans (János) Koessler, a man imbued with that spirit of Classical Romanticism associated with Brahms. If Bartók felt that his creative imagination was inhibited by Koessler's strictly conservative teaching, with its insistence on many formal exercises, his friendship with his gifted fellow student the pianist Felicie Fábián did inspire him to compose one of his more significant early piano works, a Scherzo in B♭ minor (DD63), written during the autumn of 1900. The very opening of the piece heralded the use of the variation technique which would be so important throughout the whole piece; it was based on a motif consisting of their combined initials F F B♭ B♭ (in German and Hungarian: F F B B). This work had been immediately preceded in Bartók's output by a cycle of love songs (DD62), which invoked far-reaching variational procedures, some involving themes written by Fábián, and was followed by a formal twenty-minute-long series of piano variations (DD64, 1900–01), based on a theme written by Fábián.[3] The theme and following thirteen variations are characterized by a three-note motive consisting of a leap followed by a step in the opposite direction, usually associated with a dotted rhythm. The work bears evidence of many stylistic influences: Liszt in the *marcia funèbre*, ninth variation; Schumann in the third variation, in which the original figures of the theme are now melodically overlapped; Beethoven in the fifth variation, the beginning of which is clearly inspired by the Scherzo from the Piano Sonata in E♭ major, Op.31 no.3; national Hungarian style, as seen in various neighbouring-note formulas and dotted or syncopated rhythmic patterns. In the use of some of these Hungarian features Bartók was already anticipating aspects of the writing in his symphonic poem *Kossuth* of 1903. The high point of Bartók's constructive thinking occurs in the sixth variation, the final phrases of which (bars 175–80) incorporate retrograde inverted forms of bars 13–14 of the original theme. Tonally, the piece is relatively unadventurous, however; with the exception of the seventh, G major variation, it is solidly based in E major–minor. In technical musical terms, these Variations are a good reflection of Bartók's level of pianistic skills at this time; they also indirectly reflect the kinds of piano music that he was then playing.

The straitjacket of composition instruction at the Academy soon caused Bartók's creativity to dry up, and it required the rousing experience of hearing Richard Strauss's *Also sprach Zarathustra* during February 1902 to spur him on to new compositional activity, including his first attempts at writing a symphony and – as a result of a series of public successes as a pianist – further piano pieces. The Four Pieces for piano (DD71) all date from 1903, another productive year for Bartók the composer. These pieces are contemporaries of the symphonic poem *Kossuth* and Violin Sonata in E minor (DD72), and share a common national Hungarian style with those works. Indeed, the thematic material of them all fits into a single broad framework of variation, which is overlaid with common elements of Strauss's style. The first of these piano pieces, a B♭ major Study for left hand which was destined to become one of Bartók's more popular early pieces, consists of two contrasting themes: the first, an instrumental version of a Straussian fanfare similar to the opening of his Symphony (1902) although more overtly Hungarian in style because of its syncopations; the second, a gentle, step-wise descending melody having its roots in popular song. It reappears in a stylistically neutral form as an apparently new theme at bar 33, and in two different variants in the opening movement of the Violin Sonata. Among the various processes used to develop the material the one which stands out is the mirror-like treatment of the principal theme (from bar 80). This treatment is tonally significant as well, being in F♯ major yet having a traditional dominant preparation of G. It is clear here that F♯ substitutes for its tritonal pole, C – an early sign of the procedures of axial substitution which become common in Bartók's later works. The intense alternation of F♯ (G♭) and G is also strikingly presented at bars 56–63 of the first Fantasy, the second of these 1903 piano pieces. This Fantasy is motivically based upon a dotted upbeat figure borrowed from the bright world of the 'Tanzlied' of Strauss's *Also sprach Zarathustra*. Other Straussian reminiscences are found at bars 21 and 26 (the parallel third movement), although these are not as blatant as the references to *Till Eulenspiegel* which occur in the Study at bars 90 and 132 (the descending dotted triplet pattern).

While Bartók's friends may not have known what to make of the first two piano pieces from 1903, the third piece, another Fantasy, in A minor, presented no such problem. It is simpler in structure and clearer in allegiance to a Hungarian national style, as witnessed in a detail from the first section of the piece (Ex. 4).

EX. 4

The starting-point for this purely monothematic piece is a theme whose dotted rhythmic structure demonstrates the influence of popular, perhaps peasant song, and whose characteristic sharpened fourth degree (D♯) and consequent melodic augmented second interval are further evidence of national colouring. (These rhythmic and melodic elements were also being explored more thoroughly in *Kossuth* at this time.)

The virtuosic Scherzo, the last of these Four Pieces, is dedicated to Bartók's pianistic idol of the time Ernő Dohnányi, and attempts to effect a synthesis between Western and Hungarian styles, that is, between the main section's ebullient waltz and the Trio's duple, *csárdás* rhythms. This synthesizing attempt is most energetically pursued at the point where the Trio returns to the Scherzo da capo. Bartók's upper and lower staves pursue different metres: triple ($\frac{3}{8}$) in the upper; duple ($\frac{2}{4}$) in the lower. For some thirty (triple) bars the upper part anticipates the returning waltz while the lower resolutely sticks with the duple *csárdás* rhythms of the Trio. Particularly interesting also at this point is the unfolding of an octatonic (alternating tone and semitone) line in the lower, duple part – G A B♭ C(B♯) D♭(C♯) D♯ E – which was probably inspired by Liszt. The interest in tonal polarization already seen in the earlier pieces of the set is also maintained in this final piece.

Bartók's next work for piano was his Rhapsody Op.1, the first work in his definitive, mature system of opus numbering. It was written during the autumn of 1904, with Bartók's own promotion as a pianist in mind, and harks back to Liszt's famous Hungarian Rhapsodies in a consciously national and Romantic sense, although it surpasses those works in textural density and concentration of structure. The two traditional parts of the rhapsody are the 'Lassú', a slow introduction with *verbunkos* (recruiting-dance) characteristics, and the 'Friss', a fast, *csárdás*-like section. Through skilful reworking of thematic material the two parts are held together.

Many of the ideas which Bartók expressed in his Rhapsody Op.1 had already been tried out in immediately preceding works: his initial descending motif A G♯ F D had been shaped in the Piano Quintet (1903–4), again following Liszt's example; the embellishing figures of the first theme (bars 1–4) had already been well tested in the Second Fantasy (see Ex. 4, above); the sharply dotted bass figures, as at bar 9, point back to *Kossuth*, the Piano Quintet, and further to the E♭ major Symphony (1902), and even to the ninth of the piano Variations of 1900–01. The secondary theme (from bar 22) also has its stylistic predecessors in a pool of variants shared by such earlier compositions as the Symphony (fourth movement), String Quartet in F (first movement) and Piano Quintet (third movement). The rhythmic similarity between the embellishing figurations of both themes allows them to be interwoven as the 'Lassú' (slow section) develops, producing a forceful but lively texture that goes beyond cimbalom stylization or mere Lisztian virtuosity. The fugato which Bartók initiates at bar 42 (*a tempo*) also is the result of imitative experiments in many of Bartók's earlier works. Here, however, Bartók is more liberal in his treatment of thematic material.

Already from bar 79 Bartók is anticipating the theme of the second, faster section of his Rhapsody, but the move to that new section is delayed by two transitional passages in traditional Hungarian *verbunkos* (recruiting-dance) style: from bar 85, and from 104. The movement to the 'Friss' (fast) section starts from bar 115, where the triadic material from bar 79 is restated *adagio molto* (Ex. 5a) and then stated *tranquillo* in an intervallically compressed, diminished seventh form (Ex. 5b). From this point the tempo and dynamics gradually increase, in a prevailing *molto capriccioso* mood, until the *vivacissimo* of bar 151 is reached. Bartók's new section develops in an irregular way, frequently recalling its opening theme, but also spasmodically developing other motifs including, at bar 170, a motif of a fourth (G♯–D♯) which had already been the focus of considerable

EX. 5

attention in the seventh section of *Kossuth*. At bar 423 an *allegro vivace* version of the work's opening *adagio* theme is introduced, and the second 'slow' theme (from bar 22) is, likewise, given a *presto* rendition from bar 471. In the *adagio* coda to the work, however, both these themes are again recapitulated in their original tempo and style. But between these various thematic blocks, Bartók's writing is highly improvisatory and cadenzas frequently occur at the section joins.

In 1905 Bartók arranged this Rhapsody for piano and orchestra, as part of his entry as a composer in the Paris Rubinstein competition, where it was performed with Bartók as soloist. The solo piano version was premièred on 25 May 1905 by Bartók in Újpest, Hungary, and repeated on 4 November 1906 in Pozsony, at a concert which Bartók had arranged to benefit the patriotic 'Tulip' movement.

NOTES

1 See Denis Dille, *Thematisches Verzeichnis der Jugendwerke Béla Bartóks*, Budapest (Akadémiai Kiadó), 1974, pp. 11–13.

2 This work and a selection of other adolescent piano works are published in *The Young Bartók*, vol.2, Piano Pieces, ed. D. Dille, London (Boosey & Hawkes), 1965.

3 See *The Young Bartók*, vol.2, pp. 18–42.

9

'At last something truly new': Bagatelles

ELLIOTT ANTOKOLETZ

On 28 June 1908 Bartók sent a note to Etelka Freund regarding his Fourteen Bagatelles Op.6, which he had completed only a month earlier, stating that

> Busoni was very pleased with the piano pieces. '*Endlich etwas wirklich neues*', he said. Tomorrow I'm going to play all fourteen of them at his piano-class. He has given me a very nice letter of recommendation for Messrs. Breitkopf & Härtel. We shall see how much it's really worth.[1]

Despite Busoni's enthusiasm the Bagatelles were rejected for publication on the grounds that they were 'too difficult and too modern for the public'.[2] They were published instead by Károly Rozsnyai in Budapest, about a year later. Breitkopf & Härtel's attitude toward these pieces as 'too modern' was largely due to the conservative tastes of the public. However, consideration of certain details of the new musical language in the context of Bartók's broader influences is intended to provide a more meaningful definition of their 'modernism'.

Bartók composed the Bagatelles shortly after his initial contact with both Eastern European folk music and the compositions of Debussy, and so they represent his first major attempt to absorb and transform these sources into a systematic network of divergent chords and scales. The result was one of the earliest sets of pieces to discard the triad as the exclusive harmonic premise. The so-called 'modernism' of this work seems, therefore, to lie largely in the tendency toward the dissolution of traditional harmonic construction and tonal functions, a tendency which gave rise to a new kind of tonal system based on the free and equal treatment of the twelve semitones. Although the Bagatelles remain rooted in a sense of tonal centricity, they also foreshadowed new aspects of pitch organization that were to appear more pervasively a year later in the more radical context of Schoenberg's first consistently atonal pieces. The intention in this study is to identify the means by which Bartók transformed certain folk-music and art-music sources into the new musical idiom of the Bagatelles.[3]

Each piece contains special features that had laid the groundwork for the development of Bartók's musical language. He asserted that in the Bagatelles,

> a new piano style appears as a reaction to the exuberance of the Romantic piano music of the nineteenth century; a style stripped of all unessential decorative elements, deliberately using only the most restricted technical means.[4]

His motivation to turn away from traditional Western influences led him to Eastern sources in his search to derive new pitch structures as the basis for harmonizing both the authentic folk melodies as well as his own original inventions. The potential for his new harmonizations was found in the folk tunes themselves. Among the characteristics of what Bartók referred to as the 'old Hungarian folksong style' is a pentatonic scalar basis for the melodies, with occasional transformations of the latter into the Dorian, Aeolian or Phrygian mode. Among the characteristics of what he referred to as the 'new Hungarian folksong style' is a heptatonic modal basis for the melodies, including Dorian, Aeolian and Phrygian scales with strong pentatonic inflections, as well as an occasional prominence of Mixolydian and even major scales.

From the pentatonic scale, which always occurs in its minor permutation (G B♭ C D F) in the Hungarian peasant tunes,[5] Bartók derived special limited possibilities for harmonization. These include two triads – one minor (G B♭ D), the other major (B♭ D F) – the minor-seventh chord (G B♭ D F) and the traditional harmonic inversions of these chords. He traced the consonant use of the minor-seventh chord to the old pentatonic melodies, where the seventh appears as an interval of equal importance with the third and fifth, so these three intervals could also have equal weight when used harmonically. The strong pentatonic outline in the new Hungarian folk tunes led Bartók to derive pentatonic harmonies here also. Such heptatonic modal melodies did, however, expand the number of harmonic possibilities, permitting the free use of chords to harmonize melody notes that are foreign to them.[6] This led to the use of traditionally dissonant intervals as consonances even within cadential chords. Since Bartók's point of departure for the development of his own musical language stemmed primarily from the folk sources, we may order our study of the Bagatelles by moving from these folk sources through increasingly abstract compositional procedures.

Harmonic and linear derivations from authentic folksongs and original modal constructions: Bagatelles nos I, IV, V, VII *and* XII

The pentatonic-modal features are essential to harmonic construction and progression in Bagatelle no.IV, based on an old Hungarian folk tune collected by Bartók in 1907 in Felsőiregh, Tolna, a district west of the Danube.[7] Its non-rounded quatrain structure (*A A B C*, with repeat of *B C*) and the isometric, eight-syllable lines are also characteristic of the 'old' Hungarian style. The principal melodic notes of the folk melody, D F A C, outline a minor-seventh chord, which is expanded into the D Aeolian mode by two passing notes, G and B♭. Both the symmetrical construction and modal-seventh degree (C) of the minor-seventh chord prevent any sense of traditional leading-note motion. The accompanying harmonic root progression of the first two phrases is exclusively based on the symmetrical pentatonic substructure, D F G A C, of the D Aeolian melody, the lack of semitones of which also contributes to the static harmony. Furthermore, both the vertical projection and parallel motion of the minor-seventh chord (or its modal triadic segments) preclude traditional voice-leading and directed harmonic motion. The tonality of D is, therefore, simply asserted by its prominent rhythmic and registral position in both melody and bass.

Following Bartók's initial investigations of Hungarian folk music in the summer of 1906, his increasing international interests also led him to collect the melodies of the Slovaks in the same year. This provided source material for several solo-voice, choral and piano arrangements, including the second volume of *For Children* (1908–9) and Bagatelle no.V, which is based on a Slovakian folksong from the province of Gömör.[8] This bagatelle is among Bartók's earliest experiments with the irregular 'tempo giusto' rhythm of the Slovaks. Guided by the syllabic structure of the original text, we can analyse the ambiguous quatrain structure of the melodic variant used in this arrangement into unequal lines of 13, 6, 13 and 6 syllables. As in the Hungarian sources, the G Dorian mode of the tune also strongly outlines the G pentatonic substructure, which is harmonically represented by its minor-seventh tetrachord, G B♭ D F. While the symmetrical structure of this chord contributes to the equally consonant status of its four notes, Bartók's choice of the first inversion (B♭ D F G) corresponds with the position of these notes in the descending contour of the melody. Such registral considerations in the harmonic projections tend to replace traditional voice-leading functions as the basis of cohesion between the linear and vertical levels.

The prominent linear occurrence of fourths in old pentatonic folk melodies also led to Bartók's use of fourth chords.[9] Since the pentatonic scale G B♭ C D F can be reordered as a five-note segment of the cycle of fourths, D G C F B♭, a pentatonic melody can be harmonized by the various fourth chords derived from it. Bartók had noted in Debussy's work 'pentatonic phrases' similar to those in Hungarian peasant music, and so we may assume that his studies of Debussy's music since 1907 would have also provided some impetus for his use of quartal harmony. The local harmonic occurrence of fourths in Bagatelle no.XII (bars 39–40) reveals Bartók's early concern for vertical symmetrical construction. Fourth chords are more extensively projected into the harmonic structure of Bagatelle no.XI.

Bagatelle no.I represents a more sophisticated example of folk-music absorption into an abstract idiom, where modal elements are gradually transformed into symmetrical formations.

The lower staff remains expressly modal while the upper staff moves from the modal form of C♯ Aeolian to a cyclic reordering of its intervals. Bartók stated that the bitonal key signature of C♯ minor and F minor was intended as a 'half-serious, half-jesting procedure'.[10] Although it does accord with his new concerns for employing the folk modes in a more distinctive contrapuntal context, his assertion that the combined modal lines produce a single 'Phrygian-coloured C major' is more relevant.[11] While the tonic C major triad serves as the convergent point of the two lines at prominent focal points, modal and cyclic pitch formations gradually diverge in the separate staves.

The development is induced by the combination of several pitch and rhythmic factors within a non-rounded quatrain structure reminiscent of the old Hungarian folksong style. The local cadences of phrase *a* are articulated by two descending C Phrygian segments, both of which begin on a weak part of the bar. Near the beginning of phrase b, a third descending segment from the same mode produces a sense of local closure by its metric shift to the strong beat. Within the first phrase of this section, the potential for symmetrical transformation of the C♯ Aeolian mode is suggested by the first foreground occurrence of a perfect fifth, C♯–G♯, which forms the boundary of the linearly stated C♯ tonic triad (bar 3). This interval-class increases in prominence at the end of phrase *b* (bars 7–8) as a cyclic reordering of the modal material begins in the amphibrachic (short–long–short) figures. Segments B F♯ E, F♯ C♯ G♯ and A B E all contain the same intervallic content (intervals 2, 5 and 7), but F♯ C♯ G♯ explicitly occurs in its perfect-fourth/fifth (5/7) cyclic ordering, as shown in Ex. 1a.

The pattern of closure is repeated in phrases *c* and *d*, the first two C Phrygian segments beginning on a weak part of the bar (bars 9 and 11), the third on the strong beat (bar 15). The pattern is intensified as the first two weak C Phrygian segments now overlap two statements of a new C Phrygian segment, D♭ C B♭ A♭ G, on the strong beat. The third statement of the basic C Phrygian segment then reverses its metrical position with the new segment to round out the passage (bar 15). Correspondingly, modal and cyclic interval collections reach their most extreme polarity in phrases *c* and *d* (bars 9–15). Phrase *c* opens (bars 9–11) with the main pentatonic substructure of the C♯ Aeolian mode, C♯ E F♯ G♯ B, against overlapping C Phrygian scalar segments. Phrase *d* (bar 12) is initiated by another, now explicitly symmetrical but not yet cyclically ordered, pentatonic segment from the same mode, E A B C♯ F♯. This foreshadows the final transformation of the C♯ Aeolian mode (at bar 13), in which six of its seven diatonic notes now unfold in cyclic ordering: E B F♯ C♯ G♯ D♯/A (Ex. 1b).

EX. 1

In the coda (bars 16–18), the three basic C Phrygian segments, the first statement of which is elided with the D♭ C B♭ A♭ G segment, appear in quicker succession, so the second and third statements overlap each other for the first time at the final cadence firmly to establish the complete C major triadic frame. Bagatelle no.VII is also based on linear cyclic-interval reorderings, but the modal source is less distinct.

Fusion of traditional and symmetrical concepts of tonal centricity: Bagatelles nos II *and* III

Bartók assigned a specific tonality to each of the Bagatelles. He addressed this information 'especially to those who like to pigeonhole all music they do not understand into the category of "atonal" music'.[12] However, in many of Bartók's works we often find an interaction of two different tonal concepts, one established by some allusion to traditional modal–tonal concepts, the other by the encirclement of a given space around an axis of symmetry. In Bagatelle no.II tonality is established primarily by linear motions to D♭ (first cadence, bar 5, and final one) and by the prevalence of the 'dominant' degree, A♭, throughout the opening section and last part of the recapitulation. At the same time, these sections are organized around a conflicting, non-traditional 'tonal' centre represented by a single axis of symmetry, A–A.[13] The latter is implied by the opening A♭–B♭ ostinato, which is expanded in the left hand by a series of symmetrically related dyads, B–G, C–G♭, D♭–F, D–F♭, and E♭–[E♭]. This movement is shown in Ex. 2. The A–A axis is locally disrupted by the first occurrence of the D♭ chromatic figure (bar 5). However, the latter is extended to the first main cadence (bar 7), where dyad G–B re-establishes the A–A axis.

The recapitulation is introduced (at bar 17) by the return of the repeated major second at the tritonal transposition, D–E. The implied axis is E♭–E♭, the dual intersection of the original A–A axis. At bars 20–23 the original D♭ figure is transposed to B♭ B𝄫 A♭, so its earlier disruptive function is dissolved as it is absorbed into the basic symmetry around the A–A axis (that is, B𝄫–B𝄫). The final phrase returns to the original axial whole step, A♭–B♭.

In Bagatelle no.III the concept of a modal–tonal centre is primary but the relationship between the exotic modal melody and ostinato is also based on symmetry. Bartók referred to the key of the modal tune as C major, undoubtedly because of the leading-note motions to C at the main cadences as well as the harmonic convergences between the fifth degree, G, in the

EX. 2

ostinato and the tonic and third degrees, C and E, in the theme. The mode is characterized by the augmented second and tritonal boundary, the latter, C–F♯ being symmetrically filled in by the rotating figure G A♭ A B♭ B.

Diatonic, octatonic and whole-tone interactions: Bagatelles nos VI, IX, XI, XIII, XIV

In his investigations of Hungarian folk music Bartók also came upon certain modes that were unknown in modal art music.[14] One of these non-diatonic scalar formations, G A B♭ C D♭ E♭ F, which contains seven different modal permutations analogous to the diatonic modes, has the potential for transformation into diatonic, octatonic and whole-tone collections. While segment G A B♭ C D♭ E♭ can be extended by the addition of F♭ and G♭ to a complete octatonic scale – a symmetrical eight-note scale of alternating whole and half steps, or alternatively, half and whole steps – and segment D♭ E♭ F G A to a complete whole-tone scale, segment B♭ C D♭ E♭ F can be diatonically extended to either the B♭ Aeolian or B♭ Dorian modes. Such pitch-set interactions are basic to Bagatelles nos VI, IX, XI, XIII and XIV.

In Bagatelle no.IX, a set of unison variations in three sections, ambiguous melodic segments serve as links among diatonic, whole-tone and octatonic collections. The descending pentatonic fourth at the first main (*molto sostenuto*) cadence is expanded to a tritone at the second (*molto sostenuto*) cadence and final (*largo*) cadence. Similarly, on the local level, the second phrase cadences with a gapped whole-tone segment, E♭ [] G A (bar 4), the tritonal boundary of which expands the descending perfect-fourth boundary of the preceding cadential E♭ minor triad. The content of segment E♭ G A is extended by the addition of C♯–E♯ to five of the six notes of a whole-tone scale, A [] C♯ E♭ E♯ G, as shown in Ex. 3a. At the end of this section (Ex. 3b) we find the complete whole-tone scale (A B D♭ E♭ F G), the surface details of which articulate transpositions of the originally gapped segment, D♭ [] F G and A [] D♭ E♭. A cadential segment, A B C♯, from this whole-tone scale is transformed into a diatonic segment, A B C♯ D.

At *Tempo I* the second phrase (bars 17–18) cadences on a transposition, D [] F♯ G♯, of the original whole-tone segment, which represents the other whole-tone scale. This time, however, the segment is expanded into a complete octatonic scale, D [] [] F♯ G♯ A B C D E♭ F (Ex. 3c). The next four dyads outline a second octatonic scale, G A B♭ C D♭ E♭ E F♯ (bars 20–21, beat 1), both octatonic collections of which are elided at the whole-tone tetrachord, E♭ F G A, based on the main gapped segment, E♭ [] G A (bar 4 and final cadence). The intersection between these two octatonic scales, A B C D E♭ F G A (bars 19–20, beat 1) outlines the special non-diatonic mode that Bartók found in certain Hungarian peasant tunes.

Interactions among diatonic, octatonic and whole-tone constructions are associated with leitmotivic transformations in Bagatelle no.XIII, a dirge entitled 'Elle est morte . . .', and no.XIV, a satire entitled 'Valse (Ma mie qui danse)'. The First Violin Concerto (Op.posth.) and *Two Portraits* Op.5 are based on the same leitmotif, D F♯ A C♯, which is also recognizable in its major and minor forms in the First String Quartet Op.7, as well as in these two bagatelles. While the leitmotif symbolizes the violinist Stefi Geyer, with whom Bartók was in love, these

gapped
W.T. segment
IX, 17-19
(c)
W.T.
octatonic (F♯ G♯ A B C D E♭ F)

EX. 3

works are also structurally related. Bartók had incorporated the first movement of the then unpublished Violin Concerto into the *Two Portraits*, with some alteration, and combined it with an orchestral version of Bagatelle no.XIV.[15] The two bagatelles were composed after Bartók had received a letter from Stefi Geyer saying that their relationship was at an end.

No.XIII opens with a descending inverted linear statement of the major-seventh leitmotif, A G♭ D D♭ (in enharmonically spelled root position, D F♯ A C♯), which reappears in the codetta (bars 22–3) in root position a half step lower. This expressive melody is accompanied exclusively by minor triads on E♭ and A. Although each triad suggests a segment of the major-seventh tetrachord, together they form an octatonic segment, E♭ E G♭ [] A B♭ C []. Two new notes, D♭ and G, are added to the E♭ and A triads in the last four bars, expanding both triads to minor-seventh variants of the leitmotif, E♭ G♭ B♭ D♭ and A C E G, to form the complete octatonic collection E♭ E G♭ G A B♭ C D♭.

In Bagatelle no.XIV the leitmotif D F♯ A C♯ serves as a pivotal construction between diatonic and whole-tone formations. The accompanying D major (tonic) triad alternates with a whole-tone trichord F♯ G♯ B♭. The addition of the held C♯ of the leitmotif expands the D major triad to a larger diatonic, major seventh construction and provides a diatonic meaning for the ambiguous whole-tone segment as well, expanding the latter to a larger pentatonic collection, [] F♯ G♯ B♭ C♯. This initial statement of the leitmotif initiates a series of motivic transformations (bars 9–43), the succession of cadential held notes outlining the perfect-fifth ordering, C♯ F♯ B E A, or an F♯ pentatonic scale, F♯ A B C♯ E. The chordal accompaniment below the held axis-note B of this pentatonic outline forms, through to bar 26, a five-note segment, G A B C♯ E♭, of a whole-tone collection around the same axis. Furthermore, the symmetrical relationship of both five-note collections is supported by the common axial placement of the larger whole-tone trichord A B C♯. Thus, whole-tone trichords are given both diatonic and whole-tone significance in the harmonizations of the leitmotif and its transformations.

Generation of the interval cycles from intervallic cells: Bagatelles nos VIII *and* X

An interval cycle is a series based on a single recurrent interval, the sequence of which is completed by the return of the initial pitch class. From the total complex of interval cycles,[16] Bartók derived symmetrical segments (or cells) as the basis for the generation of the cycles. He derived perfect-fourth cyclic segments from the diatonic folk sources, but his prominent use of the tritone for the first time in the Fourteen Bagatelles also stems from his folk-music studies. The Lydian mode, which is not found in the Hungarian tunes, is strongly characteristic of certain Slovak melodies. According to Bartók's own statement, 'Romanian and Slovak songs show a highly interesting treatment of the tritone . . . in a Lydian mode . . . These forms brought about the free use of the augmented fourth.'[17] Although Bartók considered five of the Bagatelles (nos I, VIII, IX, XI and XIII) as experiments, the entire set reveals his earliest attempt 'to use the supradiatonic tones with the greatest possible freedom'.[18]

In no.VIII cells prominently replace the traditional triad as the basis for generating the cyclic texture. The closing *ritenuto* unfolds all six tritones in chromatically descending pairs, so two cyclic intervals (tritone and semitone) are interlocked above a G pedal (Ex. 4).

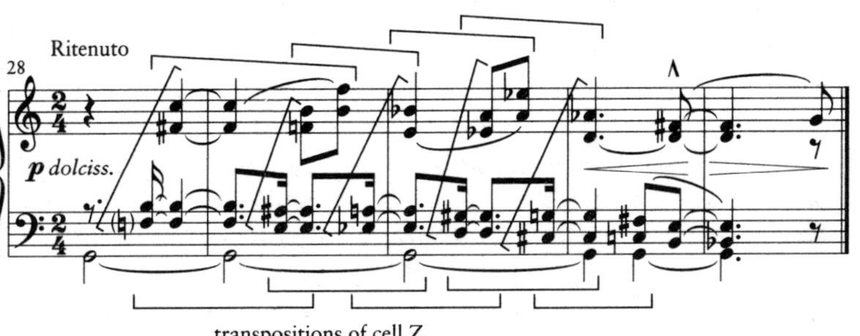

EX. 4

Furthermore, the specific linear and vertical joining of these tritones a half step apart produces all six transpositions of a special symmetrical, double-tritone, tetrachord: F F♯ B C, etc.[19] At the cadence, right hand, the double-tritone pairing of cell Z is contracted into a non-symmetrical three-note cell, D F♯ G. The latter is the tritonal transposition of that which opens the piece (G♯ B♯ C♯), and like cell Z, it generates a series of transpositions that linearly outline parallel segments of the semitonal cycle.

In Bagatelle no.X the interval cycles are generated from any one of the three interval couples – a pair of perfect fourths, tritones or minor seconds – of cell Z (G C D♭ G♭). At its first thematic statement (bars 17–18) this symmetrical tetrachord is harmonically partitioned into its two perfect fourths/fifths, G–C and D♭–G♭, while above the reiterated C–G tonic fifth the complete cell linearly unfolds in both its perfect-fourth D♭–G♭/G–C and tritonal D♭–G/C–F♯ pairings. At bars 19–20 the 'black-key' fourth G♭–D♭ is cyclically extended to F♯ C♯ G♯ A♭ E♭ A♯ (that is, G♭ D♭ A♭ E♭ B♭), while the 'white-key' fourth C–G is cyclically extended to C G D. At bars 37–9, right hand, the black-key and white-key arpeggiations extend both fourths of cell Z (G♭–D♭ and C–G) to the entire cycle in two partitions: G♭ D♭ A♭ E♭ B♭ and F C G D A E B. The slight reorderings of these two cyclic segments place the cell-Z fourths at the cadential points of the two arpeggiations, respectively. At the final, modified return of the theme (and especially from bar 82), the tonic thematic fourth C–G is more directly extended through the white-key cyclic partition in the rolled fourth chords, while the complete black-key segment is less noticeably dispersed throughout the passage.

The tritones of cell Z also serve as the basis of cyclic expansion to larger segments of the two whole-tone cycles. At the second appearance of the theme (bars 54–5) cell Z is reinterpreted as a pair of semitones, C–D♭ and F♯–G, against an incomplete linear statement, D♭ G C [], suggesting the principal notes of the modal (Lydian) source of cell Z. In the following bar the left hand joins one of the Z tritones, F♯–C, with a new one, E–B♭, so the semitones are expanded to two whole tones: E–F♯/B♭–C. The new tritone E–B♭ is then filled in by whole tones (at the end of bar 56) to extend the left hand tritones to five notes of the whole-tone cycle E G♭ A♭ B♭ C. At bar 61 the right hand extends D♭ of cell Z by whole tones to a segment of the other whole-tone cycle, D♭ E♭ F G.

In conclusion: virtually all the elements of Bartók's musical language that he was to absorb and transform throughout his career were already contained in microcosm in the Fourteen Bagatelles. The increasing tendency toward complexity and synthesis of these principles in his post-First World War compositions was largely due to his expanded folk-music investigations after 1908 and to his greater focus on composition after the outbreak of the war. Nevertheless, his post-war compositional and pianistic techniques, which were more radically developed in the Three Studies Op.18 (1918) and eventually codified in the *Mikrokosmos* (1926–39), ultimately have their roots in this early set of fourteen masterpieces.

NOTES

1 *BBL*, p. 89.
2 *BBL*, p. 90.
3 See further my 'The Musical Language of Bartók's 14 Bagatelles for Piano', *Tempo*, no.137 (June 1981), pp. 8–16, and *The Music of Béla Bartók*, Berkeley (University of California Press), 1984.
4 *BBE*, pp. 432–3.
5 Bartók transposed the *tonus finalis* of all his folksong transcriptions to G, following the system of the Finnish ethnologist Ilmari Krohn.
6 *BBE*, pp. 342–3.
7 See *HFS*, melody no.7a.
8 *SV*.ii, melody no.692a.
9 See *BBE*, pp. 331–9.
10 *BBE*, pp. 432–3.
11 *BBE*, p. 433.
12 *BBE*, p. 433.
13 An axis of symmetry is always represented by two notes (either unison or half-step), since the axis forms the intersection of two inversionally related interval cycles, as shown, for instance, in the lower diagram of Ex. 2. Such an inversional alignment of cycles is the source for all symmetrical formations.
14 *BBE*, p. 363.
15 See Malcolm Gillies's chapter 'Portraits, Pictures and Pieces' in this *Companion*.
16 The total complex of interval cycles consists of one cycle of minor seconds, two of whole tones, three of minor thirds, four of major thirds, one of perfect fourths and six of tritones.
17 *BBE*, pp. 336–8.
18 *BBlev*.i, p. 117.
19 Referred to as 'cell Z' by Leo Treitler, in 'Harmonic Procedure in the *Fourth Quartet* of Béla Bartók', *Journal of Music Theory*, vol.3 (1959), pp. 292–8, and first shown to be part of a larger system in Elliott Antokoletz, 'Principles of Pitch Organization in Bartók's Fourth String Quartet' (Ph.D. dissertation, City University of New York, 1975).

10

Fusion of National Styles: Piano Literature, 1908–11

BENJAMIN SUCHOFF

The second stage in Bartók's stylistic development, which I refer to as fusion of national styles, was primarily the outcome of his methodical articulation of the true folk music of Hungary and of the national minority peoples, and the resultant applications in his composed works.[1] This period began in late 1905 with studies of Zoltán Kodály's first publication of autochthonous Hungarian folksongs. Continuing his investigations in 1906, Bartók made his own field recordings of folk music in Hungarian villages and, moreover, in linguistically Slovak territory. He found an incredible variety of old ecclesiastical or old Greek modes in both materials and, during the summer of 1907, the ancient pentatonic scale in the melodies of the Transylvanian Hungarians.[2] Later on he collected Transylvanian Romanian folksongs 'with various, sometimes rather strange scales'.[3]

> The outcome of these studies was of decisive influence in my work . . . It became clear to me that the old modes, which had been forgotten in our music, had lost none of their vigour. Their new employment made new rhythmic combinations possible. This new way of using the diatonic scale brought freedom from the rigid use of the major and minor keys, and eventually led to a new concept of the chromatic scale, every tone of which came to be considered of equal value and could be used freely and independently.[4]

Bartók's new concept of the chromatic scale, which he designated 'polymodal chromaticism',[5] appears for the first time – in February 1908! – as the basic tonal language of his first *Elegy* Op.8b, and thereafter in the works he composed for piano solo until 1911:

> Just as the two types of the minor scale can be used simultaneously [ascending and descending melodic forms], two different modes can be used at the same time as well . . . As the result of superposing a Lydian and Phrygian pentachord with a common fundamental tone, we get a diatonic pentachord filled out with all the possible sharp and flat degrees.[6]

In addition to the folk modes Bartók found three kinds of prevailing rhythmic formations in Eastern European rural music: 'parlando rubato', a free, declamatory or recitative type (found in the second *Elegy*); 'tempo giusto', a more or less rigid type, in which change of barring may occur ('Bear Dance' from Ten Easy Pieces); and the so-called 'dotted' rhythm, where accentuated short values are followed by non-accentuated long values ('Evening with the Szeklers' from Ten Easy Pieces).

Another structural feature of Eastern European folk music is the preponderance of four-section melodies, except for those three-section, Transylvanian Romanian specimens which are 'absolutely independent, even very characteristic formations'.[7] 'Old'-style Hungarian quaternaries show a remarkable type of transposition in which the second half of the melody is a fifth lower than the first half.[8]

Tone colour is an important stylistic element in Bartók's piano writing. He considered the piano to be essentially a percussion instrument – somewhat similar to the hammered output of the Hungarian cimbalom – rather than a stringed one, and devised a special notation to indicate which way the piano was to be played.[9]

Above all, however, was Bartók's supernal talent that enabled him to homogenize polyglot musical folklore and develop five innovative levels of complexity for its use in composition: (1) Genuine folk tunes are featured, and the invented additions are of secondary importance. In other words, the folk tune is the 'jewel' and the added parts function as its 'mounting' (an example is the fifth *Sketch* Op.9b); (2) the folk tune and the invented material are treated equally (*For Children*, vol.2, 'Rhapsody'); (3) the folk tune is presented as a kind of musical 'motto', and the invented material is of greater significance (second Romanian Dance Op.8a); (4) the composition is based on themes which imitate genuine folk tunes (first Romanian Dance); (5) the highest level is abstract composition in which neither folk tune nor its imitation is used, but the work is nevertheless pervaded by the 'spirit' of folk music. Thus, for example, it might have Hungarian pentatonic turns (second *Dirge*), the Slovak Lydian tritone (third *Burlesque* Op.8c), or other characteristics of Eastern European rural music.[10]

In September 1907, following his return from collecting folk music in Transylvania, Bartók began the composition of his First Violin Concerto (Op. posth.), and his career as professor of piano at the Academy of Music in Budapest. Dedicated to his first love, the Hungarian violinist, Stefi Geyer, the main theme of its first movement is based on Bartók's 'declaration of love' leitmotif, D F♯ A C♯. No sooner had Bartók completed the work on 5 February 1908, than the beautiful young virtuoso terminated his courtship. Later that month the anguished suitor vented his innermost feelings in the first *Elegy*, during May in the last two of his Fourteen Bagatelles Op.6,[11] and on 13 July in the 'Dedication' of Ten Easy Pieces – all created from transformations of this leitmotif.

Ten Easy Pieces

The original title of the collection was Eleven Piano Recital Pieces, since it included what later became the sixth Bagatelle. Thus compiled, Bartók completed the work in June 1908, and a contract for its publication by Károly Rozsnyai of Budapest was signed later that month. During the summer Bartók changed the original title to Ten Easy Piano Pieces, in order to shift the sixth Bagatelle to its eventual place, and added his 'Dedication' as the eleventh piece, perhaps to satisfy his contractual obligation.[12] In 1945 Bartók described the composition as follows:

> The Ten Easy Pieces – with a 'Dedication' as an eleventh – are a complement to the Bagatelles. The former were written with pedagogical purposes, that is, to supply piano students with easy contemporary pieces. This accounts for the still more simplified means used in them.[13]

'Dedication': Analysis of this abstract composition reveals an ingenious blending of motifs from the First Violin Concerto and structural characteristics of 'mixed'-style Hungarian folksong. The melody is isometric quaternary with *A B C D* form. Each of the four melody-sections consists of thirteen syllabic notes, that is, as if underlaid with folk text.[14] There is no time signature.[15] The first four bars – the prelude – contain the famous leitmotif degrees, in augmented values. The first melody-section is an augmentation of the pentatonic rhythmic schema of the consequent phrase of the First Violin Concerto's main theme. All melody-sections, interludes and the postlude are polymodal collections, based on G, E and D as fundamental notes, which combine Phrygian and Lydian pentachords for the most part.[16]

'Peasant Song' (no.1): The unisonal texture of this Level 4 folksong imitation in Slovak style may well have been intended to underscore the monophonic character of Eastern European rural music. The four-section, heterometric melody is in the C♯ Dorian mode. Interest and variety are achieved by rhythmic means: equal and unequal phrase lengths, and different combinations of minim and crotchet values in duple metre.[17]

'Painful Struggle' (no.2): This is an abstract composition, based on Slovak folksong characteristics, particularly the four-section, heterometric melody. Note the unusual pitch content of the first melody-section: its incipit (bars 3–5) is the Lydian octave segment of the Dorian mode. The ostinato accompaniment, however, illustrates the first systematic use of a unique tetrachordal motif that pervades Bartók's oeuvre. Designated the 'Z-cell' by American theorists, the cell consists of the first (fundamental note or 'tonic'), minor second, augmented fourth, and fifth degrees of the Phrygian/Lydian polymodal pentachord.[18] If we tag such tetrachords with whatever designation will identify the fundamental note, the ostinato in bars 1–6, 15–18, 21 (second half) is a D Z-cell, in bars 7–9 (first half) an F Z-cell, in bars 10–11 a G Z-cell, in bar 19 a C-Z-cell, and in bar 21 (first half) an E Z-cell. The D and F Z-cells accompanying the first half of the Dorian melody (bars 3–9) also interlock to form an octachordal pitch collection of alternating half and whole steps – the well-known octatonic scale, which Bartók would later find among the Transylvanian Romanians and North African Arabs.[19] The resultant twelve-note tonality of the combined melody and accompaniment is the product of a D Phrygian/Lydian polymode.

'Finger Study' (no.9): An abstract composition, with Slovak structural characteristics, that explores another tetrachordal motive – the so-called 'Y-cell'.[20] The cell consists of four whole steps or, in other orientations, the first four degrees of the Lydian mode, an octave segment of the Dorian mode, or a partition of the whole-tone scale. The first and third melody-sections (bars 5–8, 13–16) of the four-section heterometric melody have a repeated dotted crotchet plus quaver rhythmic schema. Such repetitions, unknown in Eastern European folk music, stem from art music sources, and they seem to be deliberately stressed in the repetition of the melody (bars 29–40). The Y-cell ostinatos are arranged in alternation of the two cycles of whole-tone pentachords and complete scales, and, moreover, are concatenated to form chromatic octachords (as at bar 10) and octachordal polymodes (bars 43–8). In the case of the alternating pentachords, the ascending Y-cells in related bars outline an underlying Z-cell framework, C D E F♯ + D♭ E♭ F G = C Z-cell (bars 1–2).

For Children

Bartók's next contract with Rozsnyai, dated 23 March 1909, was for '21 juvenile music pieces' to be titled *For Children*. The manuscript apparently was delivered to the publisher on or about that date. Based on Hungarian musical folklore, the collection was followed by a second set of twenty-one Hungarian pieces, in accordance with a contract dated 23 June. On 6 December Rozsnyai shipped the newly published copies of Ten Easy Pieces, Fourteen Bagatelles, and *For Children* to Bartók, together with the following enclosure:

> Dear Professor Bartók,
> I was very glad to receive your cordial letter. I duly enclose the required pieces. I wish to emphasize that it would be better if the

> rules of classical harmony would be even more strictly observed than in the ones already published, without any modernization. I should not like to see a new trend in this undertaking but rather the beaten track on which you can continue working from time to time.[21]

When Bartók received this letter he had probably completed the forty-two pieces based on Slovak musical folklore for the last two volumes of *For Children*, yet publication was not achieved till 1911. Whether the postponement was related to Rozsnyai's criticism or the takeover of that company by another Budapest publisher (Rózsavölgyi) is uncertain. In 1931 Bartók transcribed no.42 (no.40, 'Swineherd's Dance', in the revised edition) as the last piece in *Hungarian Sketches*. And in November 1944 Bartók responded to the request of his then publisher, Boosey & Hawkes, to 'make some slight alterations' for copyright purposes. The next month he provided the music engraver with a 'revised (improved)' copy of the original Hungarian publication.[22]

At lecture–recitals given by Bartók during the 1940–41 concert season, his performance of pieces from *For Children* was prefaced by the statement that they were written 'in order to acquaint the piano-studying children with the simple and non-Romantic beauties of folk music. Excepting this purpose, there is no special plan in the work'.[23] The following pieces selected for analysis, however, should make it quite apparent that he had another, unmentioned reason: to provide piano students with a melodious and uncomplicated introduction to the sound of his newly invented musical language.

'Moderato' (vol.1 no.26): The original form of this isorhythmic Transylvanian melody is limited to the first four degrees of the Hungarian pentatonic scale: G B♭ C D. A number of variant or closely related melodies from that area have altered or expanded pitch collections, such as major or minor pentachords, a Mixolydian mode with lowered sixth degree, and one specimen where Mixolydian and Phrygian modes alternate to produce a peculiar 'neutral' tonality (that is, with superposed major and minor thirds).[24] The accompaniment begins in the G Aeolian mode, with the raised seventh degree (the 'colour' note of the modern harmonic minor) being added in bar 11. The repetition of the accompaniment has the lowered second degree (the Phrygian 'colour' note, bars 22–3) and the raised sixth degree (the Dorian 'colour' note, bar 27). In other words, this piece reflects the interaction of a simple pentatonic melody with a chromatic accompaniment, thus forming a ten-note minor polymode.

Among the other polymodal pieces in the first volume are no.9 (D Lydian/Aeolian eleven-note polymode) and no.18 (D Lydian/Phrygian twelve-note polymode). The latter piece is especially interesting with regard to its 'international' melodic structure: G pentatonic scale (the major or so-called Chinese form), with C as passing note; uniquely characteristic Hungarian 'dotted'-rhythm schemata; Ukrainian *kolomyjka* (round dance) syllabic structure (fourteen syllables in duple or quadruple metre, where the last two syllables are doubled values); Slovak heterometric four-section structure, in which the third melody-section (bars 11–12) is a 6 + 6-syllable double section; and Western European architectonic (*A A B A*) form.

'Mourning Song' (vol.2, no.39): Bartók's treatment of the Slovak folk tunes comprising the second volume of *For Children* indicates his indifference to the conservative attitude of his publisher, for it shows an increasing use of parallel fifths, unresolved dissonant chords and polymodal chromaticism. Whereas the first volume ends with a brilliant dance piece in *kolomyjka* rhythm (no.40), the second concludes with this 'Mourning Song', a dirge whose text reflects utmost despair:

> Down there, deep in the valley,
> A frightened black raven flies;
> Down there, deep in his grave,
> In blackness my father lies.

There may be extra-musical significance in the punctuation of the accompaniment by the 'declaration of love' leitmotif in bars 2, 17, 22 (altered pentachord), 30–35, 45 (fifth degree omitted) and 51. The E Phrygian/Lydian polymode provides a twelve-note tonality, but the last melody-section and the postlude (bars

43–53) are in the pure Phrygian mode. The piece ends *calando*, with the unaccompanied, almost indiscernible subtonic (D) as the final note.

Two Elegies Op.8b

Bartók points to this opus as 'a certain return to the old-style piano technique', indicating the tonality of no.1 as D minor and of no.2, C♯ minor: 'This information is addressed especially to those who like to pigeonhole all music they do not understand into the category of "atonal" music.'[25]

'Grave' (no.1): As already mentioned, this first piece was composed in February 1908, soon after Bartók received Stefi Geyer's letter announcing the end of their relationship, and several months prior to the composition of the experimental Fourteen Bagatelles Op.6. It is quite important for the reader to note that the only stylistic reversion in the first *Elegy* is in terms of the bombastic piano writing typical of Franz Liszt and other nineteenth-century virtuosos, and Bartók himself before 1908 (as in the Rhapsody Op.1). In point of fact, this musical memento of 'Stefi Lost' inaugurates Bartók's new style of composition.

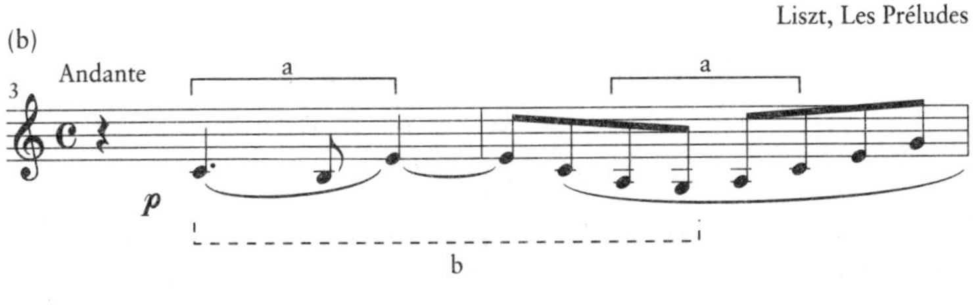

EX. 1

Ex. 1 illustrates the motivic relationship to the opening theme of Liszt's *Les Preludes*. This elegy's opening theme (that is, the first melody-section) combines two motifs: the trichord D♯ C♯ F♯ and the tetrachord E B G C. The former, indicated by 'a', is a transformation of Liszt's germinal trichord C B E; the latter, indicated by 'b', is a reordering of Bartók's 'declaration of love' leitmotif – itself a transformation of the second motif in Liszt's theme, E C A G. Ex. 2, based on C as the end note of the first melody-section (bar 3), reveals the underlying structure of Bartók's theme: an octatonic hexachord within the frame of a Z-cell, C C♯ F♯ G. Including B (the major seventh degree), the pitch collection represents a C Lydian/Phrygian polymode: the superposed Lydian pentachord, C E F♯ G B, and Phrygian tetrachord, C C♯ D♯ G.

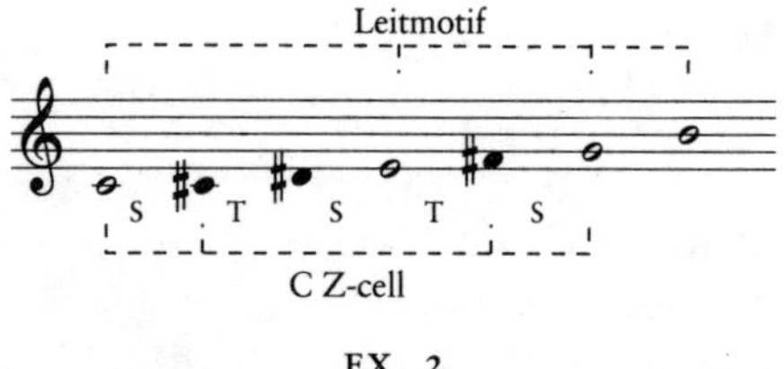

EX. 2

The second melody-section, transposed to F as end-note (bar 7), contains the F Z-cell, now within the frame of the octatonic hexachord E♭ F F♯ [] A B C []. Here, too, the leitmotif is provided by the addition of E, a non-octatonic degree. The third melody-section (bars 8–9) is the A octave-segment of the symmetrical Dorian mode. The placement of D as axis of symmetry underscores its main function as the fundamental note, notwithstanding the position of A as end-note of the section.

The intervallic structure is of 'old'-style Hungarian pentatonic orientation in terms of major seconds and minor thirds. The fourth melody-section (bars 10–14) is similar to the kind of double-section found in Eastern European folksongs. The quaternary structure of this first part of the piece, the syllabic structure of the individual melody-sections, and the 'parlando rubato' rhythm – delineated by irregular alternation of duple and triple metres – are other characteristics that point to the first *Elegy* as an abstract composition pervaded by the spirit of folk music.

Mention should be made that emphatic rendition of the C Z-cell, G♭ G C♯ C, occurs in bars 39–52 and in the closing section (bars 85–95). A unique cadence is found in the last two bars, where the altered leitmotif serves as a dissonant chord, D F A C♯, resolving to a D minor-seventh chord as a 'consonant' ending.[26] The two-part fugato that opens the fourth section (bars 53–71), perhaps an adaptation of the fugato form in Liszt's Piano Sonata in B minor,[27] is the first example of free, chromatic counterpoint as an outcome of polymodal structure. Another innovation by Bartók is the quartal harmony in bar 14, where the closing chord of the first section, B♭ E♭ A D, is the vertical projection of the main degrees of the D Phrygian mode. This bar, together with the preceding one, represents the ultimate in Bartókian polymodal chromaticism: twelve-tone tonality resulting from superposed Phrygian and Lydian modes.

'Molto adagio, quasi rubato (quasi improvisando)' (no.2): Almost two years elapsed until Bartók composed the second *Elegy* in December 1909. An agreement was signed with Rozsnyai for the complete work on 4 July 1910, and the publication appeared in 1911. Bartók alternately performed the two pieces well into the 1920s, when they were replaced in his repertory by the newer works of his 'Synthesis of East and West' period (1926–45).[28] The entire composition consists of an introductory 'motto' theme (bars 1–3) and its transformations or rhythmic permutations, all based on the A Lydian/Phrygian polymode. In other words this variation-like form is somewhat similar to a Level 3 transcription, where the invented material is of greater significance. The pentachordal theme, however, is a transformation of the 'declaration of love' leitmotif, in which a C♯ minor triad is encapsulated by the interval of a major seventh: A G♯ E C♯ A♯. If there is an extra-musical connotation in the descending structure of the leitmotif, then it may reflect a subliminal 'renunciation of Stefi': on 16 November 1909, some weeks prior to the composition of this second *Elegy*, Bartók married his sixteen-year-old pupil Márta Ziegler. In view of this possible ambivalence it seems appropriate to rename the leitmotif as a 'motif-chord' in the remainder of this essay.

Two Romanian Dances Op.8a

Bartók's vast collection of Romanian folk music material begins with four melodies he notated during November 1908, while on holiday in eastern Transylvania.[29] Their three-section structure and certain characteristics related to 'old'-style Transylvanian Hungarian melodies impelled him to investigate this music further. During the summer of 1909 he collected hundreds of vocal and instrumental melodies from Romanian villagers in Bihar county (now Bihor, Romania) and composed the first of his Two Romanian Dances soon afterwards.

'Allegro vivace' (no.1): The first dance is 'based on original thematic material and not on folk tunes'.[30] The piece, however, is a Level 4 transcription in which the thematic imitation is close enough to be considered a variant of an original folk tune. The rhythmic schema is a clone of a Romanian Drâmbå (jew's-harp) dance-melody motif,[31] including its drone-like accompaniment, and the downward tritone swoop on the last beat of the bar and the following bars is a borrowing from a Romanian jeering song.[32] There is also a simulation of the irregular repetition of bagpipe-type motifs (at bars 45–50, for instance) that characterize the indeterminate melodic structure of such dance music. The innovative aspect of this extraordinary composition is the fusion of Bartók's newly won tonal language with rural folk-music section-structure. Ex. 3 illustrates the harmonic application of the same Z-cell used in the melodic construction of the first *Elegy* (see Ex. 2, above), as a way of avoiding the commonplace I–V progressions characteristic of the gypsy-styled, urban folk music disseminated in Eastern Europe at that time. In terms of functional harmony the C Z-cell serves here – and more emphatically in the last five bars of the piece – as a surrogate dominant seventh chord in the C Phrygian/Lydian polymode, C D♭ D E♭ F F♯ G B. Certain motifs are cast in an impressionist mould; the two contrasting cycles of the whole-tone scale are represented by their segments in bars 47, 48 and 50. Indeed, a whole-tone scale is divided between the hands in bars 113–14, where an unusual cluster-chord, E F♯ G♯ A♯ B♯, serves as the accompaniment.

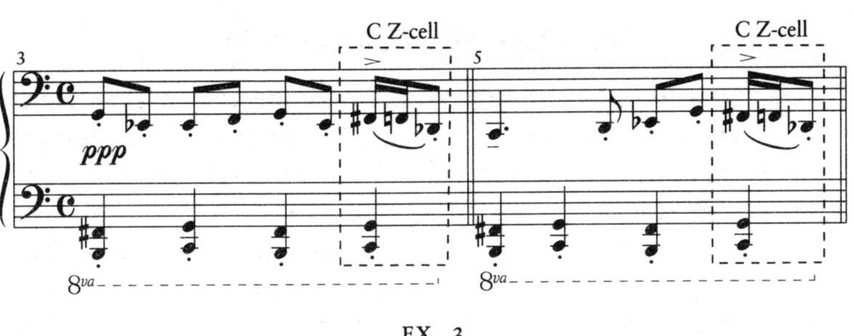

EX. 3

'Poco allegro' (no.2): In 1910, when Bartók sought a companion piece to round out the opus, he turned to the vocal source-melody of the first dance and borrowed its first melody-section as a motto theme, in order to create a Level 3 composition. The motto theme, however, appears as the second subject (L.H.: bars 17–20), alternating with related thematic material (L.H.: from bar 5) of Bartók's own invention. The quaver–crotchet –quaver rhythmic schema (bar 11) serves as a pentatonic or modal interjection (for instance, at bars 69–72 and 110–13, respectively), in what is otherwise a G Lydian/Phrygian poly-mode. Again drawing a parallel to functional harmony, the first half of the motto theme (bars 17–18) is harmonized by the same C Z-cell found in the first dance (see Ex. 3, above), in which the D♭ is a preceding grace note instead of an end-note. In the second half, the harmonic progression continues with the D Z-cell, D G A♭ D♭ (bar 19), and the G Y-cell, G A B C♯ (bar 20). Thus, in Bartók's system of modal chromaticism, traditional IV–V–I progressions can be replaced in whole or in part by cellular equivalents.

Three Burlesques Op.8c

Bartók's growing reputation as pianist and composer – the outcome of successful concert tours in imperial Hungary and abroad – gave him the incentive to expand his repertory with accessible recital pieces befitting his stature as a virtuoso, such as the *Three Burlesques*. Although the first piece of this opus was composed in 1908, the complete work remained unfinished until 1911. In 1931 the second *Burlesque* was transcribed for orchestra as the fourth piece of the *Hungarian Sketches*.

'Quarrel' (no.1): This first *Burlesque*, composed on 27 November 1908, is dedicated to Márta Ziegler, Bartók's first wife – then in her second year as his piano student at the Royal Academy of Music in Budapest. One of the drafts of this impressionist composition has an amusing entry that reads: 'Please choose one of the titles: "Anger because of an interrupted visit" or "*Rondoletto à capriccio*" or "Vengeance is sweet" or "Play it if you can" or "November 27".' The sketch version has other entries, such as 'angrily' (bar 1), 'with a weeping voice' (bar 60), and 'sorrowfully' (bar 88).

The eight-bar introductory section, in unison, partially establishes C as the fundamental note, by repetition of the cellular tritone G–D♭ as the last beat of each bar. The first section begins with the same melodic configuration but alternates with a different one (bars 9–14) whose first beat contains C–G♭, the fundamental tritone of the C Z-cell. Thus, by means of an innovative monophonic texture, the underlying harmonic foundation of the C Phrygian/Lydian polymode is laid.

The C whole-tone scale introduces the second inversion Z-cell 'dominant', D A♭ G D♭ (bars 22–25), the first inversion Y-cell 'tonic', D C B♭ A♭ (bar 28) and the second inversion Z-cell 'subdominant', C G♭ F C♭ (bars 26–9). The same scale and its other Y-cell segments are featured in the second section, in contrasting homophonic texture (bars 39–87). The reprise (bars 88–161) alternates homophonic with monophonic treatment of the thematic material, and the postlude (bars 162–76) iterates the introductory bars, ending with octave repetitions of the fundamental note, C.

Four Dirges Op.9a

Since the first draft of these pieces also includes the third *Sketch*, on the verso page of the third *Dirge*, its date of composition therefore is August 1910.[33] In 1931 Bartók transcribed the second

Dirge for orchestra as the third piece of his *Hungarian Sketches*.

The fateful year of 1909 also brought Bartók in contact with Romanian mourning songs whose 'strange scales . . . absolutely unknown from modal music [cannot be] expressed as octave segments of the diatonic scale'.[34] One of these non-diatonic formations – nowadays referred to as the octatonic scale – is represented by the heptachordal melody of Ex. 4, a Romanian mourning song recorded by Bartók in July of that year.[35]

EX. 4

It would be difficult to overestimate the impact of this finding on Bartók's evolving tonal language. The melody verified for him the existence of octatonicism in folksong, a scalar peculiarity he had previously discovered in Liszt's music and subsequently emulated in his own works (see Ex. 2, above), and he apparently memorialized the finding with the composition of the first *Dirge*.

'Adagio' (no.1): The binary *A B* form has a quaternary *a a b c* substructure. The first two melody-sections consist of gapped, octatonic pentachords: G [] A♯ B C♯ D, and the same configuration transposed a whole tone upward (bars 2–8). The other two, non-octatonic melody-sections have C as their end-note (bars 12 and 14, respectively).

The accompaniment, opening the piece with the suggestion of B major (bars 1–2), is for the most part a succession of consonant intervals and triads. The overall effect is a dialogue between the accompaniment and the melody-sections, resulting in an ambiguous (i.e., without a fixed fundamental note) twelve-note Lydian/Phrygian polymode. Part *B* continues the dialogue in an unstructured, improvisatory manner, and the piece ends as it began – but now with the fundamental note in place – in B major.

'Andante' (no.2): Although this piece has the same binary form as the first *Dirge*, its thematic properties are closely related to the Transylvanian Hungarian folksongs that Bartók collected in 1907.[36] Part *A* is an isometric (thirteen-syllable section-structure) quaternary (a a_v b b_v) involving mild variation of both *a* and *b* material. Both parts feature the flattened form of Hungarian 'dotted' rhythm.

The first two melody-sections (bars 1–21) emphasize the characteristic Hungarian 'old'-style pentatonic intervals: perfect fourths, minor thirds and major seconds. These intervals, moreover, are organized as pentatonic segments of the C♯ Dorian mode. The last half of the melody and its accompaniment, on the other hand, consist of Romanian-style, essentially octatonic scale segments (bars 22–9), with B♭ as the fundamental note. The outcome of the interaction between Hungarian mode and Romanian scale is a Bartókian polymode!

Part *B* is a heterometric a_v b_v a a quaternary. The first two melody-sections and its accompanying, arpeggiated motif-chord, F♯ A♯ C♯ E, are based on A♯ as the fundamental note of an incomplete Phrygian/Lydian polymode (bars 30–40). The missing twelfth note, B, is provided in the last half of the melody, where the reprise of the quasi-pentatonic opening theme is supported by inversions of the arpeggiated motif-chord, now expanded to an impressionist ninth chord.[37]

'Assai andante' (no.4): The last composition is a sectional arrangement in ternary form (bars 1–29, 30–53, 54–70), based on transformations of the octatonic motif in bars 2–3. The substructure in part *A* has some resemblance to a heterometric quaternary, in which the first melody-section and its chordal accompaniment are fashioned from an octatonic scale G A♭ B♭ B C♯ D E F (bars 1–5). The addition of E♭ in the second section (bar 9) and A, C, G♭ in the third (bars 10, 13) transforms the octatonic scale into a twelve-note, G Phrygian/Lydian polymode. The reprise of the motif in the postlude (bars 66–70) ends the piece as it began – with the G octatonic scale.

Seven Sketches Op.9b

In a statement written shortly before his death in 1945 Bartók refers to the *Seven Sketches*, composed between 1908 and August 1910, as representative of the new piano style that first appeared in his Fourteen Bagatelles Op.6. The one exception is the fourth *Sketch,* which is similar to *Two Elegies* with respect to 'the "decorative" broken chords . . . of the "old"-style piano technique'.[38] The varied styles of the present collection include the same mixed types previously met in Fourteen Bagatelles and Ten Easy Pieces, but the *Sketches* are closer to the Bagatelles as regards difficulty of piano technique.

'Portrait of a Girl' (no.1): In view of its modest technical demands the first *Sketch*, composed in 1908, may have been Bartók's first musical impression of its dedicatee, Márta Ziegler, rather than the first *Burlesque* Op.8c. Each of the four parts of the *A B C D* form has a song-like quaternary structure, developed from one or the other rhythmic schema of the theme (bars 1–2, 2–4, respectively).

The accompaniment features the motif-chord (bars 1, 3, 10, 13, etc.) and the whole-tone scale as a chain of inverted minor and major triads (bars 27–30). It is interesting from an extra-musical aspect that the tonality is the twelve-note G Lydian/Phrygian polymode, yet the piece ends unambiguously with the motif-chord, D F♯ A C♯ (the original leitmotif degrees), transformed into a functional V^7 chord for resolution to its tonic triad, G B D.

'Seesaw' (no.2): One of Bartók's drafts of the second *Sketch* has the complete piece in the form of a spiral, in which the piano score is notated so that it undulates outward from the centre of a sheet of ordinary paper. Instead of the title, a Latin caption appears in his handwriting, which can be translated as: 'In everlasting memory of the hours 6, 7, 8, 9, 10, 11 p.m. 16 February 1909'.

The descriptive title of this binary piece depicts neither a minor (R.H.) / major (L.H.) bitonal struggle nor the alternate motion of a child's seesaw, but rather the dual nature of minor and major chords in a Lydian/Phrygian polymodal environment. Thus, the E minor trichord (R.H.: bars 1–4) represents an octave segment of the C Lydian mode (a major scale with raised fourth degree), and the A♭ major tetrachord (L.H.: bars 1–4), an octave segment of the C Phrygian mode (a minor scale with lowered second, sixth and seventh degrees). The emphatic VII–I modal cadence and the abrupt change to unison texture in the last five bars also mark a change in tonality – to a C Aeolian/ Lydian polymode.

'Lento' (no.3): The third *Sketch*, dedicated to Zoltán Kodály and his wife Emma and dated August 1910, treats the whole-tone scale in a somewhat experimental manner – along the lines of the Fourteen Bagatelles. It was Kodály, Bartók's closest friend, who introduced Bartók to the music of Debussy in 1907. The A A_v form has a one-bar interlude (bar 10) and a four-bar postlude (bars 22–6), with C as fundamental note of a Lydian/ Phrygian polymode. The first part has the song-like character of a heterometric quaternary, and the thematic emphasis on the C whole-tone pentachord (bars 1–2, 4–5) and hexachord (bars 3–4) – each within the context of Lydian and Phrygian pitch content – underscores the close connection between Debussyan whole-tone collections and Bartókian modal chromaticism.

'Non troppo lento' (no.4): As mentioned in my introductory remarks to *Two Elegies* and *Seven Sketches*, Bartók intended this piece and *Two Elegies* to mark a certain return to the 'old'-style piano technique. Indeed, the fourth *Sketch* is also elegaic in terms of rubato performance and stress on the motif-chord, F A C E (bars 1–3).

The *A B C D* form is unusual with regard to the variegated substructure of the individual parts: *a b* | *a b c d* | *a b c* | *a b*. The connection with Hungarian folk music is evident in the 'dotted'-rhythm schemata that pervade the composition, particularly the 'softer variety' in the theme (bars 1–3),[39] as well as the octave segment of the pentatonic scale in the accompaniment of bar 13.[40]

The tonality is the C♯ Phrygian/Lydian polymode. It is interesting that the last bar ends with the 'dotted'-rhythm schema, A–E, accompanied by the fundamental chord, C♯ E G♯. These degrees are, of course, those of the motif-chord and, with the addition of A♯, constitute the pentachordal motif-chord that concludes the second *Elegy*.

'In Walachian style' (no.6): Walachia was the name given to Old Romania – the pre-First World War territory south of Transylvania – by its Slavic neighbours. The proper title of the sixth *Sketch* – a Level 4 composition based on imitation of genuine folk melody – should perhaps be 'In Transylvanian Romanian Style', since the piece is fashioned from the same Romanian folk music material Bartók collected in 1909.[41]

As in the case of the first Romanian Dance Op.8a, the melody is based on a specifically Romanian rhythmic schema, glissando and bagpipe drone. Except for the held notes, however, the entire two-part composition is in unison. Variety is achieved by changes in melodic contour, modal chromaticism and register.[42] The ten-note polymode results from superposition of C Lydian and C Dorian modes.

'Poco lento' (no.7): To the casual observer the last piece might appear to be an exercise in impressionist whole-tone polytonality. It is, however, a highly concentrated study of the two whole-tone scales within the context of polymodal chromaticism, particularly with regard to their chord forms.[43]

Part *A* of this binary composition begins with the first half of the theme as an introduction (L.H., bars 1–2), in the guise of a B Mixolydian pentachord, B C♯ D♯ F♯ A, whose main degrees are sustained to form the B major triad. In the next bar the repetition of the motif and its accompaniment (a stretto imitation of its altered self) reveals the possible polymodal content of the pitch collection, A B C C♯ D♯ F♯ G, to be superposed A Lydian and A Dorian modes, with emphasis on the Lydian whole-tone tetrachord, A B C♯ D♯.

The second half of the theme (bars 4–5) partially verifies the presumed tonality, since it commences with a whole-tone tetrachord, A G F D♯ (the mirror inversion of the preceding Lydian structure) and is accompanied by the harmonic interval, F–C. But the resultant F major triad – a tritone removed from the preceding B major chord – adds Aeolian colour to the pitch collection. Thus, with the fundamental note A as axis of symmetry, a complete whole-tone scale is formed from two seemingly discrete tetrachords, D♯ F G A and A B C♯ D♯. The two entities are, in fact, organically related Y-cell octave segments of the A Lydian/Aeolian polymode.

Part *B* highlights the two whole-tone scales as sustained pentachords, in parallel motion at the interval of a major sixth (bars 17–22), alternating with unisonal transformations of a tetrachord derived from the theme, C A B F♯ (bars 1–2). The climax is reached in bar 20, where the A and F♯ whole-tone pentachords are indirectly extended to complete whole-tone scales, thus expanding the tonality to the twelve-note A Lydian/Phrygian polymode. The piece ends with the mentioned pentachords as simultaneities, perhaps the first example of so-called cluster chords.

Allegro barbaro

Allegro barbaro – often cited as Bartók's most famous and frequently performed work – was composed in 1911, but not printed until 1918 (by his new publisher, Universal Edition of Vienna). Although the piece is a Level 4 composition, similar in concept to the first Romanian Dance, it epitomizes the fusion of Hungarian, Romanian and Slovak folk-music styles. The arrangement of sections is quite unusual: *A B C* A_V *D E* B_V, with a prelude, a postlude and several interludes. The quaternary substructure of Part *A* (bars 5–30) is that of a Slovak folksong: heterometric double-sections (alternating 5 + 5 and 7 + 7 syllabic-structure), in which portions of the larger double-sections (bars 13–15, 27–9) are expansions of the smaller ones by means of 'Slovak rhythm-contraction'.[44]

The first half of the melody, E G A B♯, is the tetrachordal form of the pentatonic scale used by various peoples of central Asia; the second half, in so-called Hungarian fifth transposition, is the 'old'-Hungarian anhemitone–pentatonic scale, A B♯ D E G.[45]

Pentatonicism notwithstanding, the tonal language is Romanian in orientation: the emphatic notes of the first melody-section and its accompaniment, indicated by *marcatissimo* accents, form the F♯ Z-cell, F♯ G C C♯ (bars 7 and 11);[46] and those of the second melody-section and its accompaniment, the C♯ Z-cell, C♯ D F𝄪 G♯ (bars 21 and 25).

Part *B* has three important differences: there are two single-sections, repeated to form a quaternary; the nine-syllable rhythmic schema is an artificial one, created from different halves of Slovak schemata that are occasionally met with in Hungarian folksong; and both melody-sections are created from the F Lydian pentachord. Parts *A* and *B*, however, are based on the F♯ Phrygian/Lydian polymode.

A final characteristic worth noting is that the postlude of *Allegro barbaro* (from bar 200), which immediately follows the reprise of Part *B*, features a return to the pure F Lydian mode, in the form of unisonal octaves, leading to the same F♯ minor ostinato chords with which the piece began.

NOTES

1 See my 'Notes on the Music' in *Béla Bartók: A Celebration*, New York (Book-of-the-Month Club), 1981, p. 5.

2 Transylvania was Hungarian territory until its cession to Romania in 1920.

3 See *RFM*.ii, p. 26.

4 *BBE*, p. 410.

5 *BBE*, p. 367.

6 *BBE*, p. 367.

7 *RFM*.ii, p. 13.

8 *HFS*, p. 22. It is interesting to note that *Allegro barbaro* has the order of fifth transposition reversed.

9 See *BBE*, pp. 288, 490, also my *Guide to Bartók's 'Mikrokosmos'*, New York (Da Capo), 1983, pp. 13–14.

10 The five levels, an extrapolation of Bartók's remarks in *BBE*, pp. 341–4, 350–52, are the subject of my essay, 'Folk Music Sources in Bartók's Works', in *Gedenkschrift Kurt Reinhard*, ed. C. Ahrens, R.M. Brandl and F. Hoerburger, Laaber (Laaber-Verlag), 1984, pp. 197–218.

11 See the chapter ' "At last something truly new": Bagatelles' in this *Companion*.

12 This 'Dedication', composed on 13 July, was intended to be the first in a series of 'Little Piano Pieces'.
13 *BBE*, p. 432.
14 An exception is the one-syllable extension introduced into the second melody-section to resolve the suspension on the third beat of bar 15.
15 cf. *RFM*.ii, p. 43: 'When no time signatures are used, the performance is parlando rubato'.
16 The chromaticized degrees of polymodal chromaticism have 'absolutely no chordal function; on the contrary, they have a diatonic–melodic function. This circumstance is clearly shown if the degrees are picked out and grouped into the modes to which they belong' (*BBE*, p. 376).
17 *BBE*, pp. 128–33.
18 See Elliott Antokoletz, *The Music of Béla Bartók*, Berkeley (University of California Press), 1984, p. 71, n.10.
19 In Bartók's modal chromaticism it therefore appears that Z-cells represent a quartal harmonic system, which has evolved from and has characteristics of the tertian system of functional harmony.
20 See Antokoletz, op. cit., p.70, n.9.
21 Quoted in the booklet to *Béla Bartók Complete Edition*, Budapest (Hungaroton), LPX 11394–5, p. 8.
22 Issued as forty Hungarian pieces in the first volume and thirty-nine Slovak pieces in the second. A comprehensive discussion of the first edition, including Bartók's comments and the facsimile reproduction of the available source melodies, can be found in my notes to *Piano Music of Béla Bartók*, Archive Edition Series II, New York (Dover), 1981, pp. vii–xxi.
23 *BBE*, p. 427.
24 *BBE*, pp. 368–9.
25 *BBE*, pp. 432–3.
26 See *BBE*, pp. 334–45, 371–3, for Bartók's comments on the consonant character of the modal seventh degree.
27 On *BBE*, p. 452, Bartók refers to this section of Liszt's masterpiece as expressing Mephisto's devilish irony.
28 See my chapter 'Synthesis of East and West: *Mikrokosmos*' in this *Companion*.
29 *RFM*.ii, melody nos 67d, 117, 353, 411.
30 *BBE*, p. 432.
31 *RFM*.i, no.648.
32 *RFM*.i, no.456b.
33 See my related comment under discussion of Op.9b, further below.
34 *RFM*.ii, p. 26; *BBE*, p. 363.
35 See source melody in *RFM*.ii, melody no.628L. The reader should note that a Z-cell, G♯ A D E♭, is the structural skeleton of the first and last bars.
36 See Béla Bartók and Zoltán Kodály, *Erdélyi magyar népdalok*, Budapest (A Népies Irodalmi Társaság), 1923, melody nos 53, 95. See also *HFS*, melody nos 26, 244.
37 The relationship of the second *Dirge* with *Duke Bluebeard's Castle*

and the Concerto for Orchestra is discussed in my *Béla Bartók: A Celebration*, p. 7, illustrated by facsimiles of Bartók's holograph.

38 *BBE*, p. 432.

39 A comprehensive explanation of such schemata will be found in *BBE*, pp. 76–7, 389.

40 *BBE*, p. 364, scale segment 4.

41 See my remarks about Op.8a, above.

42 This rhythmic schema is derived from *RFM*.ii, melody no.607; the glissando is a feature of melody nos.58a–k.

43 See discussion of the sixth Bagatelle in the chapter by Elliott Antokoletz, '"At last something truly new": Bagatelles'. The seventh *Sketch* is discussed as a model of 'whole-tone polytonality' in H. A. Miller, *New Harmonic Devices*, Philadelphia (Oliver Ditson/Theodore Presser), 1930, pp. 124–6.

44 The diminution of values, such as replacement of certain crotchets by quavers. See *HFS*, pp. 57–62.

45 See *BBE*, p. 364, scale segments 2 and 5, respectively. See also note 8 and its related comment, above.

46 cf. Ex. 2 and Ex. 3.

11

Piano Works of the War Years

JÁNOS KÁRPÁTI

Even in the years before the First World War broke out Bartók had been suffering a creative crisis leading to silence. His opera *Duke Bluebeard's Castle* (1911), written for a competition of the Lipótváros Casino, had been rejected as unperformable and the New Hungarian Musical Society, which he had founded along with Kodály and Sándor Kovács, had failed because of lack of interest from the general public. By August 1913 Bartók would write: '. . . a year ago sentence of death was officially pronounced on me as a composer'.[1] He ceased to act as a public figure any more, moved to Rákoskeresztúr on the outskirts of Budapest, and commuted to the city only to give his classes at the Music Academy.

He found solace in his scientific work and started to collect folk music more enthusiastically than ever, this time concentrating on the Romanian population of Transylvania. Between 1909 and 1914 he made several collecting tours to this region each year, and in 1915–16 visited the northern part of Hungary in order to enrich his collection of Slovak folksongs. He seems to have anticipated that the war, in addition to its general devastation, would unfavourably influence the collection of folk music. Writing on 20 May 1915 to his Romanian friend from Belényes, Ion Buşiţia, Bartók expressed his thoughts and problems of the moment:

> Dear Professor,
> I am really ashamed of having delayed for so long replying to your charming letter of January . . . My long silence has been due to the fact that every now and then I am thrown into a state of depression by the war – a condition which, in my case, alternates with a

> kind of devil-may-care attitude. In all my thinking there is a *ceterum censeo*; nothing matters, but to remain good friends with Romania; it would be a grievous thing to me to see my beloved Transylvania devastated, besides greatly hindering my prospect of finishing, or rather continuing, my work . . . You wouldn't imagine that in times like this I would find it possible to go on collecting folksongs, would you? Well, I do! Communications have been too disrupted for me to venture into Romanian regions; but I have been collecting among the Slovaks, first in my own locality (Rákoskeresztúr), and then in Zólyom county, for a week around Easter! . . . I have even found the time – and ability – to do some composing: it seems that the Muses are not silent in modern war.[2]

It is surprising, but none the less perfectly logical, that in this year of 1915, when Bartók started to do some composing again after more than two years' silence, he would chose to work on arrangements of his recent collection of folksongs. 1915 could well be called his year of Romanian folksong arrangements, for although he did compose pieces of Romanian provenance before and after, it was in this year that he wrote such works as the Sonatina, Romanian Folk Dances, Romanian Christmas Carols, and two unpublished series of works for women's choir as well as songs accompanied by piano.

Compared with the Two Romanian Dances Op.8a (1909–10), his new series of 1915 entitled Romanian Folk Dances is definitely a simpler and more meagre collection. The main difference between the two is that the former is a monumental, unbounded dance fantasy based on Bartók's own themes of Romanian character, whereas the latter is a folk-music arrangement in the narrow sense. Its material had been collected by the composer during his tours to the counties of Maros-Torda (Mureş), Bihar (Bihor), Torda-Aranyos (Turda) and Torontál in 1910 and 1912. Romanian folk music offered Bartók a number of elements that were attractive, not found in Hungarian folk music and, moreover, stimulating to his further renewal of twentieth-century art music. Above all, the Romanian instrumental folk music was much richer than that of Hungary, and involved such instruments or combinations as one or two violins, violin and guitar, peasant flute or bagpipes. When Bartók arranged the folksongs he had collected (and their origins are precisely identified by him in the scores), he naturally had to give up the original timbre, but chose the register and keyboard touch that would invoke it best. The rich decoration of the original tunes and sometimes the complex rhythms were also lost in the process of arrangement; however, through the left hand he provided an accompaniment of far greater harmonic richness than found in the original, and one which, by its moving rhythm, emphasized the dance-like character of the pieces. The choice of tempo was a similar device on the part of the composer. Bartók hardly ever preserved the tempos of the original tunes, but made fast dances even faster and the slow ones even slower, thereby giving an individual character to each of them.

Another interesting question concerns the compilation of the dances into a series. Besides the alterations referred to above, Bartók took advantage of the variety of tempos in arranging the pieces into a series of six movements, representing a kind of suite. The initial movement, a 'stick dance', is relatively quick (*allegro moderato*), and is followed by the *allegro* 'sash dance', the *andante* movement entitled 'In one spot', a *moderato* 'horn dance' and, finally, two closely connected *allegro* movements, a Romanian 'polka' and a 'fast dance', both composed in the typical style of Bartók's folk-dance finales.

It is a little surprising that the parallel composition of this year, Sonatina, uses a compilation of folk-dance movements in a Classical three-movement form. The original types of dances used in the Sonatina are not indicated, however, and the titles refer to the characters of the individual movements: 'Bagpipers', 'Bear Dance' and 'Finale'. The first movement contains several characteristic features of Romanian instrumental folk music, as if in a systematic paradigm. The moving bagpipe part is a dominant feature of the style, and the peculiar modal character of the work is closely connected with it. The combination of a Lydian-coloured fourth degree (here G♯) and Mixolydian seventh degree (C) plays a particularly important role in Bartók's music of Romanian character. The music literature often refers to this type of scale as 'acoustic' or even 'Bartókian' because of

EX. 1

its 'natural' and unique character (see Ex. 1). Another characteristic feature that is easily recognizable is the faltering quality of certain degrees of the scale. Bartók, when analysing Romanian folk music, always pointed out this phenomenon, most probably since he considered it also to be an important element of his own compositional technique.

The largest composition of 1915 is the two series of Romanian Christmas Carols, or *colinde*, each of which consists of ten pieces. The technique of the arrangement and the conspicuously easy piano texture (lacking any octave stretches, as is pointed out on the title page) both imply that the series were written for didactic purposes. In some ways these pieces are a continuation of the *For Children* collection of 1908–9. As its volumes had included Hungarian and Slovak folksongs, respectively, it was only to be expected that Bartók would write a similar collection for the third ethnic group of Hungary, the Romanians. Through his life, art and research work Bartók reflected a view of the brotherhood of the peoples of the Danube valley. The *Cantata profana* (1930) was originally intended as a Danube valley trilogy, but was unfortunately never completed.

As against the instrumental arrangements mentioned above, the series of Romanian Christmas Carols are based on original vocal material. This is an important point, as the musical elements of this material are entirely different from the Romanian dance tunes. The difference is clearly recognizable, even if the arrangement for piano of these carols is not able to reproduce all of the specifically vocal features explicated below. As well as being vocal, Bartók stresses genre in these carols. The work is based on a very old, special form of Romanian folksong: the *colindă*. Bartók even lists the original tunes and extracts from the original texts at the beginning of his score, and he not only uses the tunes as his 'raw material' but also extends his attention to the whole of the folk custom involved with these tunes. In 1933 he described this genre in a study of Romanian folk-music classifications:

> the song texts in this category include some which are invaluable to the historian of Romanian folklore, even the historian of local culture. We must not think of the *colinde*, however, in terms of the religious Christmas carols of the West. First of all, the most important part of these texts – perhaps one-third of them – have no connection with Christmas. Instead of the Bethlehem legend we hear about a wonderful battle between the victorious hero and the – until then – unvanquished lion (or stag), we are told the tale of the nine sons who – after hunting for so many years in the old forest – have been changed into stags, or we listen to a marvellous story about the sun who has asked in marriage the hand of his sister, the moon, and so on. Thus here are texts truly preserved from ancient, pagan times! . . . Carolling usually takes place in the following custom: after several weeks of 'study' (choral singing in unison) of the *colinde*, on Christmas Eve a group of eight to ten boys, under the leadership of a chief, set out for the performance itself. They stop in front of each house and ask whether the hosts will receive them. Once inside the house, the group sings four or five *colindă* songs in antiphonal fashion . . . At the end of the performance, the hosts present a gift to the carollers who go on to the neighbour's house.[3]

It seems that when choosing these twenty pieces from his immensely large collection of the various genres of Romanian folk music Bartók already had in mind his subsequent scholarly study. In the mid–1920s he prepared a critical edition of a collection of about 450 Romanian *colindă* tunes, including the words as well, as he considered them 'of special interest to researchers in music folklore, to ethnologists and to linguists'.[4] It is surely not by chance that the texts to the twenty pieces included in Romanian Christmas Carols encompass all the most important kinds of *colindă* texts identified by Bartók in his later study: religious (4 tunes); connected with the custom of carolling (4 tunes); pastoral (3 tunes); legendary (3 tunes); family-life (3 tunes); biblical (2 tunes); hunting (1 tune).

The texts of the *colinde* must have been of great interest to Bartók, as well as the distinctive rhythmic and melodic characteristics of these songs, which presented many novelties when compared with Hungarian folksongs. The structure of the stanzas distinctly differs from that of Hungarian songs, since here the dominant form is two- and three-line musical stanzas, and the four-lines stanzas so typical of Hungary are relatively rare. 'Stanzas' here definitely refers to musical stanzas, as Bartók himself pointed out the lack of formal stanzas in the text and the interchangeability of the tune and words connected with it. The refrains inserted between the lines, however, have a clear influence on the structure of the musical stanzas.

In the process of the arrangement for piano the composer certainly relied on the musical stanzas, thus preserving the original structure. We take the second piece of the first series as an example; the stanzas of this piece were considered to be of three lines by Bartók. The lower levels of form here are created by the repetition of the stanza shown in Ex. 2.

EX. 2

The asymmetric quality of the metre of the *colindă* tunes and their resultant uneven pulsation was a novelty for Bartók and proved a treasury of compositional ideas. Ex. 2 shows a circulation of $\frac{5}{8}$, $\frac{2}{4}$ and $\frac{3}{8}$ metres. By 'uneven pulsation' we do not mean just asymmetric, odd metres (as a musical piece in $\frac{5}{8}$ or $\frac{7}{8}$ metre can still have an even pulsation, as also can an asymmetrically-divided $\frac{8}{8}$ metre, such as the $\frac{2+3+3}{8}$ found in the seventh piece of the first series), but rather, refer to an unsystematic shortening or lengthening of rhythmic units, even though these *colinde* are not *rubato* pieces.

This rhythmic concept must have been a major discovery for

Bartók since it was obviously at variance with the metric structure of most European music, where the structuring of time is predominantly 'divisive', with larger temporal units being divided into smaller, equal ones. With this kind of Eastern European folk music, as with the music of other Eastern nations, the typical rhythmic arrangement is 'additive', and involves sequences of temporal units of different duration. From this point of view, the unsystematic alternation of odd and even metric units, as with the alternation of $\frac{2}{4}$, $\frac{3}{8}$ and $\frac{5}{8}$ in Ex. 2, is obviously the lengthening and shortening of the 'middle' pattern, in this case the $\frac{2}{4}$. This recognition led Bartók to the phenomenon of 'Bulgarian' rhythm, as he called it in deference to the work of Vasil Stoin on Bulgarian folk music published in 1927.[5] On becoming aware of Stoin's work, Bartók corrected the simple metres of certain of his transcriptions to take account of these 'unsystematic alternations'.[6]

Bartók was also excited by the melodies of these *colinde*. He already knew that their scale patterns differed from the traditional major or minor, but these pieces presented still other possibilities. A typical example of this is the sixth piece of the second series, with its augmented-second colourings (Ex. 3).

EX. 3

In his study of 450 *colindă* tunes Bartók identified thirty-five scales. This does not mean thirty-five different patterns of notes, but rather that Bartók was distinguishing between the position and significance of notes, within scales, relative to their final tonic. Hungarian folksongs have their final note at the bottom of the scalar range, and the 'descending' tune in many ways rests upon it. The final notes of *colinde*, however, are relatively high and consequently often lack a sense of cadence. This explains why Western listeners often find *colinde* unfinished, as if they had been left open.[7]

Bartók considered the tonal interpretation of monophonic tunes an exciting challenge, and took great care not to harmonize tunes according to any set pattern. As a result of this conscious compositional purpose, the relatively open *colindă* tunes gain their own sense of closure within the well-balanced series, without being forced into the clichés of the major–minor system.

Among the many folksong arrangements of Bartók the Fifteen Hungarian Peasant Songs (1914–18) occupy a central place for more than one reason. Although, as mentioned, Bartók considered the three major ethnic musics of the Carpathian Basin, Hungarian, Romanian and Slovak, equally important to his compositional work, he still preserved special, national ties with his native Hungarian folk music. These short pieces are also central in the sense that they are half-way between the simple and the complex (as, for instance, between the Romanian Christmas Carols and the Improvisations Op.20). In his simple arrangements the folksong is unmistakably in the foreground and is only supplemented with chords or polyphonic counter-voices. In his complex arrangements, however, the folksong is hardly recognizable amid the elaborate texture of an independent composition. The Fifteen Hungarian Peasant Songs are a borderline case in that the songs are unmistakably in the foreground of the composition but the additional musical material is an excellent, elaborate supplementation.

In the second piece of the series the folksong is preceded by swaying and mysterious (*senza colore*) chords, the higher notes of which form a folksong-like tune that was actually invented by Bartók. This combination of an original tune and a folksong imitation inaugurates Bartók's new compositional practice of not distinguishing between the two kinds. The various harmonizations of the original folksong are most characteristic: when first heard, the actual melody of the folksong is virtually merged in with the accompanying chords. When played for the second time it goes still further in terms of both dynamics and expressivity; the tune, played in octaves, is in the left hand and the chords above it include dissonant notes. It is noteworthy that these dissonant notes are a G♯ and an A♭, which can be considered as mistuned forms of A, the fifth degree of the scale.

The deepest level of interference on the part of the composer, or, alternatively, the highest kind of arrangement, is seen in the sixth piece, entitled 'Ballade (tema con variazioni)'. Its original is a folk ballad that Bartók had collected during the summer of 1918, not long before writing excitedly about it to Márta, his wife:

> I have harmonized seven of the Hung. songs collected in the summer, including the famous 'Angoli Borbála' of Róza Ökrös. I recommend that you listen to it, as it is quite sensational to hear such a song in Hungarian, right in the middle of the Plains, and what's more, in $\frac{7}{8}$ metre.[8]

The term 'harmonization' is an understatement in this case, as the composer has turned the identical stanzas of the original ballad into a sequence of fanciful variations. Variation in its traditional, classic usage involves a gradual broadening in the processes of transformation, with the subject becoming increasingly distant from its original form as the piece progresses. Bartók's great idea was to use this entirely musical structure as a dramatic device: through the gradual transformation of this short four-bar stanza he manages to translate the narrative of this folk drama into the language of music, right up to its tragic conclusion. The drama is thus 'miniaturized' into the proposition and eight variations of the tune.

Through the first four variations the dynamic level as well as the density of the musical supplementation constantly increases. In the fifth and sixth variations this increase suddenly stops and the melody moves to the high register of the piano, now displaying a *dolcissimo* character with *pianissimo* dynamics. New key dimensions appear; first comes E, which is closely related to the G keynote, but then the distant C♯ occurs, substituting for the dominant. (It is, in fact, a mistuned dominant.) Eventually, the cathartic conclusion of this dramatic variation process comes about: the eighth variation thunders through the original tune twice, firstly *f*, then *ff*, with frequent interruptions from screaming, accented chords.

Variation plays an important structural role more widely in the Fifteen Hungarian Peasant Songs. The final part, entitled

'Old Dance Tunes' (nos 7–15), is compiled in such a way that the individual songs are actually variations of each other. The variations are connected by their common fourth interval, and the connection between them is obvious in spite of the fact that the direction of the leap alternates in the tunes. Ex. 4 groups the variations according to affinity of contour, rather than chronological order.

EX. 4

This large-scale finale, consisting of these nine short movements, shows how Bartók preferred to have a superstructure of larger units rather than a series of minute units of equal importance. Indeed, he never concealed these groupings. In the published Universal Edition score of 1920 the first four pieces were published as 'Four Old Laments', the fifth as 'Scherzo', the sixth as 'Ballade (tema con variazioni)', and remaining nine under the title 'Old Dance Tunes'. Thus, the entire series outlines the structure of the Classical four-movement sonata, in which the *moderato* first movement (1–4) is followed by Scherzo (5), slow movement (6), and concluding, quick finale (7–15). These arrangements written through the war years, then, are an early attempt of Bartók to provide the original musical material of folksongs within the more 'elevated' structure of composed, art music.[9]

While the majority of Bartók's piano works of the war years were folksong arrangements, he did compose one work not rooted in folk music, the Suite Op.14 (1916), written at about the time he was composing his ballet, *The Wooden Prince*, and the Second String Quartet. This work is one of the most significant in Bartók's piano œuvre and a companion to his Piano Sonata of 1926. Both refer to a Classical structural pattern in their titles.

The Suite was originally intended to have five movements, as is evidenced by the unpublished 'Andante' preserved by Bartók's pupil Irén Egri. She learnt this 47-bar piece with Bartók in 1918, when it still formed the second movement of the Suite.[10] Perhaps this pedagogic 'experiment' persuaded Bartók to leave this movement out of the Suite, and to have it published in its current four-movement form. He was certainly paying particular attention in this work to the order of the movements and to questions of larger-scale structure in general. Even the progression of the tempos from movement to movement reveals a definite artistic intention. The first movement is a moderately quick, dance-like Allegretto; it is followed by a quick Scherzo and an even quicker, impetuous Allegro molto. This gradual acceleration is suddenly broken by the astonishingly slow, fourth movement (*sostenuto*), the character of which is painful and dejected. It is not accidental that Bartók used a similar structural scheme in the contemporaneous Second String Quartet as well as in his pantomime, *The Miraculous Mandarin* (1918–19).

Although so far we have emphasized the Classical pattern of the Suite, the influence of folk music is also important. The first movement, for instance, starts as if it were a Romanian folk dance, at least as regards the stress of the tune on the Lydian fourth degree and the flexible dactylic–anapaestic rhythm. A thorough analysis, however, shows that this is a typical example of Bartók's highly individual compositional technique, despite the undeniable inspiration of Romanian folk music. The scale here (Ex. 5) is a transformation of the 'Bartókian' scale mentioned earlier, or, to put it another way, it is a differently cut version of that scale, in which the fifth scale degree has now also been sharpened, leaving now no perfect fifth above the tonic B♭. To carry this idea to its logical conclusion, the chords accompanying the tune have no perfect fifth intervals either, so instead of the traditional alternation of tonic and dominant we have

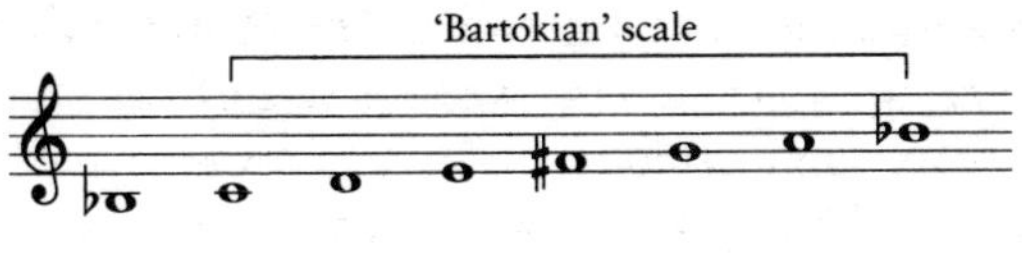

EX. 5

alternating B♭ major and E major (instead of F major). E major is a mistuned or substitute dominant, or, as Bartók says about the same relationship in his Fifth String Quartet, E has 'the role of a dominant' relative to the B♭ tonic.[11] It is the sign of mastery and firm control on Bartók's part that, after this rather unorthodox initial harmonization, he has the tune played a second time and now presents the traditional harmonization with its alternations of B♭ major and F major chords.

This duality of the unorthodox and the traditional is revealed in another aspect, as well. In the structure of the melody there are certain terraces, arranged in such a way that they deliberately overlap with the alternating modes of harmonization; when we have a perfect fifth interval in the melody there is a mistuned fifth in the chords, and vice versa. Fig.1, below, illustrates this ingenious arrangement.

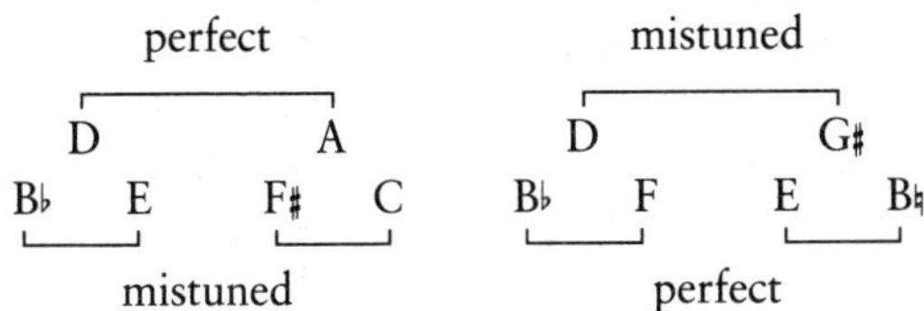

FIG. 1

This figure suggests the following unstated, but consistently observed principle of Bartók: to preserve the acoustically perfect intervals (octave, fifth, fourth) and, at the same time, to mistune them by one semitone in order to create tension and bring about an entirely new type of sound. In this way he created a dual system in which the perfect and mistuned functions are in a logical and complementary relationship. There is an infinite number of possibilities consequent upon breaking out of the traditional intervallic system through this technique of mistuning or sliding by a semitone: the temporary decomposition of tonality, new shadings of traditional triads, combinations of major and minor characteristics, earlier deemed incompatible.[12]

The second movement of the Suite contains the best instances of the application of mistuning by a semitone, this time far more explicitly than in the first movement. In this Scherzo movement the main role is played by a grotesque subject which is played with a *marcatissimo* touch in several variations. The first version consists of major thirds that, when stacked one upon the other, produce tonally faltering augmented triads (Ex. 6a). These augmented triads are put together with a semitone slide which, in principle, brings about the same 'pre-dodecaphonic' set as the one that starts Liszt's 'Faust' Symphony (Ex. 6b).

(a)

(b)

EX. 6

The stages of the metamorphosis of the Scherzo subject, in every case with a slide of a semitone are as follows: major thirds downwards (starting form); major thirds upwards; perfect octaves downwards; augmented fourths upwards; major sevenths downwards; major thirds downwards; perfect octaves upwards; augmented fourths downwards; major sevenths downwards; major sevenths upwards. As can be seen, besides the slide of a semitone which itself causes tension, many of these duplicated intervals are of a dissonant character and add to the pungency of the transformation of the subject through the movement.

As József Ujfalussy has pointed out, the Suite has the same structural scheme as *The Miraculous Mandarin*. In the centre of each work are two different but complementary scherzos.[13] In *Mandarin*, the 'Girl's dance', an ecstatically grotesque waltz, and the 'Mandarin's dance', an ecstatically wild chase, relate one to the other in precisely the same fashion as do the Suite's grotesque Scherzo in $\frac{3}{4}$ metre and even faster and more extreme *allegro molto* 'Scherzo' (literally, 'a chase'). It is also typically Bartókian that these two movements complement each other from a technical viewpoint. Analysis of the second movement shows that the pitch system underlying the intervallic transformation of the subject is the whole-tone scale, which contains major thirds, augmented fourths and octaves. These intervals, as with the whole-tone scale, create a 'spacious' atmosphere. On the other hand, the scalar alternation of whole tones and semitones in the third movement gives the impression of a 'compressed' musical space. But neither of these scales, as presented, contains a perfect fifth, being augmented in the whole-tone case and diminished in the octatonic scale of the third movement. Ex. 7 shows these two, complementary scales, expressed with C tonics to aid comparison.

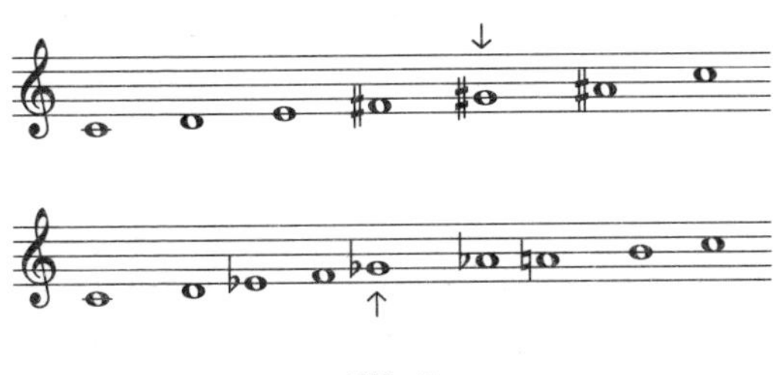

EX. 7

Bartók had come to know scales giving such a 'compressed' impression through the Arabic folk music of north Africa, from which he must also have adopted the wild, highly rhythmic character of this third movement. The composer referred to this influence in a letter of 1931, and later, in a lecture at Harvard University in 1943 identified north African Arabic music as one of the sources of his chromatic style.[14]

The tension of semitones provides the dynamism of harmony and melody in the final movement of the Suite. Faltering tonality is a well-known feature of Bartók's expressive movements, but even so, a tonal rudiment is given by the beginning and the cadence of the movement. Here the B♭ tonality can only be recognized in the second part of the movement and only because it is the logical entailment of the first and second movements, which are both in B♭. Once we accept this B♭ tonality as a foundation element we can account for several harmonic features of the movement. The melody, concealed in chords, extends semitone by semitone, and, after arriving at its first peak, rests on a note of B♭. Nevertheless, this B♭ is constantly contrasted with B♮, as shown in Ex. 8.

EX. 8

The middle part of the movement refers back to the first two movements, and to the second in particular, through the frequent moving major thirds which are combined here with the familiar slide of a semitone found in every part of this composition.

The tragic ending of the movement can only be explained by the phenomenon of mistuning or semitone slide. The unfolding melody seen at the beginning of the movement appears once again, while the bass part is slowly descending, as if following the scale, to the B♭ of the final chord. That chord, however, is not a traditional B♭ major or minor, but is 'shaded' by many of its semitonal neighbours. In particular, this final B♭ major is supplemented, or perhaps counterbalanced, by a G♭. However, as many of Bartók's own remarks confirm, when creating a dual tonality he always made one of the two keys more important.

Semitonal tension and friction is present throughout the final movement of the Suite, underscoring the expressive and grievous intentions of this music. But Bartók adds *dolce* and *dolcissimo* instructions, clearly considering that carefully measured portions of dissonance do match with a *dolce* character. This provides an important message for interpreters of Bartók's music: do not be deceived by the surface of the score, but go in search of the innermost logic of the music.

NOTES

1 *BBL*, p. 123.

2 *BBL*, pp. 131–2.

3 *BBE*, pp. 120–21.

4 See *RFM*.iv, p. xxxviii. Bartók's *Cantata profana* was also based on a *colindă* text, which he had translated himself.

5 See *BBE*, p. 43.

6 An example of such correction is the fourth movement, 'horn dance', of the Romanian Folk Dances, discussed above. In the piano version of 1915 it is in simple $\frac{3}{4}$ metre, but Bartók later re-transcribed the original tune into $\frac{10}{16}$ time. Such $\frac{10}{16}$ or $\frac{11}{16}$ metres are frequently found among his final *colindă* transcriptions, although not yet among the 1915 arrangements.

7 See, for instance, the fourth piece of the first series of the Romanian Christmas Carols for an 'open' ending and the seventh piece for a 'closed' one.

8 *BBcl*, p. 282.

9 The Three Hungarian Folk Tunes, published in 1942, also probably date from the years of the First World War, and may be 'left-overs' from Fifteen Hungarian Peasant Songs. They comprise a *parlando* and two *giusto* tunes, and, apart from the final piece, are relatively unadventurous.

10 See János Demény, 'Unpublished Bartók Documents', in Todd Crow ed., *Bartók Studies*, Detroit (Information Co-ordinators), 1976, pp. 137–8.

11 *BBE*, p. 414. Bartók's original French was: 'le rôle de la dominante'.

12 For further discussion see János Kárpáti, *Bartók's String Quartets*, Budapest (Corvina Press), 1975, pp. 137–58.

13 See József Ujfalussy, *Béla Bartók*, Budapest (Corvina), 1971, p. 142.

14 See, respectively, *BBL*, pp. 199–205, and *BBE*, p. 379.

12

Approaching Atonality: Studies and Improvisations

PAUL WILSON

The five major works that Bartók completed between 1918 and 1922 seem in some important ways to be separate from the main line of his compositional development. The musical centre of gravity in the period is clearly *The Miraculous Mandarin* Op.19, which is one of Bartók's most significant compositions. But the four pieces which, in a sense, accompany the *Mandarin* are not so widely admired. The Three Studies (*Etudes)* Op.18, the Eight Improvisations on Hungarian Peasant Songs Op.20, and the First and Second Violin Sonatas (1921 and 1922) are frequently characterized as products of 'crisis', 'struggle', 'experiment', even of 'creative confusion' and 'lack of direction'.

There are several interconnected causes involved in this perception of separateness and possible crisis. All four pieces participate to some extent in the expressive power and energy which explode with full force in the *Mandarin*, without of course sharing the scenario which called forth and supported that energy. All four pieces are, likewise, stylistically more distant from folk-music sources than the works composed before and after them. This is true even of the Improvisations, in ways that we shall soon explore. But the most obvious and most important cause is that all four pieces employ a harmonic language which greatly modifies and often abandons the modal and polymodal basis of Bartók's previous and subsequent work.

In this chapter we shall look at the two sets of pieces for piano, the Three Studies, and Improvisations. In doing so we shall come to grips with some aspects of what 'approaching atonality' (without fully arriving there) meant for Bartók compositionally. These two sets of pieces, whatever their other *raisons d'être*, gave him opportunities to compose small forms in the new style and also to try out two different ways of organizing and ordering a group of pieces in that style. In doing both, he came face to face with the perennial problem of atonal composition: that is, discovering within his musical ideas alone the whole basis for their expansion and realization within works of art.

Bartók wrote the Three Studies in the summer of 1918, while he and his family were living in Rákoskeresztúr. He apparently planned them as part of his concert repertoire and first performed them at a recital on 21 April 1919. Universal Edition published the set in 1920, but two letters tell us that they had a short and unsuccessful career as concert pieces. In his letter of 20 January 1934 to Ernő Südy, Bartók stated: 'By the way: I cannot play the 3 Etudes (!). I haven't played them – ever or anywhere – since 1918 [*sic*]'.[1] And in an earlier letter of 1925 to Jenő Takács he explicitly refused to programme the Studies, Improvisations or violin sonatas in places (specifically, 'Hungarian country towns') where the audience 'has not been trained to listen'.[2] It is not entirely clear from the first letter whether Bartók's inability to play the Studies was now permanent or simply due to a lack of recent practice on them. Either alternative is a testament to their extreme difficulty.

As in other celebrated sets of concert studies, notably Chopin's and Debussy's, each of these pieces makes its first distinct impression as a single-minded exploration of a particular texture and a particular pianistic technique. The first piece is a precipitous *moto perpetuo* featuring chromatic linear motifs which continually force both hands to stretch over ninths or tenths at top speed. The second combines two- and three-octave arpeggiated chords in one hand with a slow-moving and rhythmically irregular melodic line in the other. The third involves a quick tempo and smaller arpeggiations, but high-speed shifts of metre and accent are its true problem, especially during its first half.

Oddly enough in view of the presumed strangeness of these pieces, we have heard similar textures in other Bartók works. To pick some convenient examples, the third movement of the Suite Op.14 can show some family connection with the first study, as can the *Allegro barbaro*, at a slightly greater distance. The second study has the *Two Elegies* Op.8b as textural and expressive forebears. Only for the third study can we claim a more thoroughgoing originality within Bartók's output thus far. In contrast to their separate and distinctive textures, all three studies employ some version of the same basic solution to the problem of musical form, and in particular to the problem of ending the piece well. Each relies on the return of previous music – something in the nature of a recapitulation – as an element of design. And each reinterprets that music in its restatement, changing what had been an important beginning into something like a final event.

To stop its furious rush forward, the first study relies on the two carefully prepared arrivals (bars 38 and 119) of the primary motif which is also its basic harmonic event. Every section of the piece serves as either preparation, variation, or aftermath of one of these two arrivals. As a melodic motif, the events of bars 38 and 119 are a simplification of the work's opening bar, in which the G♭ and F of bar 1 become the F♯ and E♯ of bar 38, played in essentially the same rhythm. As a harmonic construction, the chord in bars 38 and 119 is ambiguous in ways which are quintessentially Bartókian. The complex six-note chord, as it appears in its final voicing from the last bar of the piece, is clearly a combination of two far more familiar triads, G major and F♯ major. But the chord's voicing denies both its dual triadic source and its possible atonal implications, emphasizing the perfect fifth between B and F♯ in the outer voices and thereby singling out B as a local tonal centre at both arrival points.

That sense of B as local tonic will, of course, give added weight to the forces for closure when the motif returns in bar 119. Bartók prepares its second arrival as carefully as before and with even greater rhythmic and dynamic impetus. But the motif, instead of generating more music in transformed versions of itself, as it did after bar 38, this time absorbs all the energy and uses it to punch out a final shattering cadence.

The second study uses the relative rhythmic, harmonic and

formal simplicity of the first as a foil against which to display its own complexities. The piece is shaped in two unequal parts, dominated overall by the imposing melodic line and by the insistent cadenza which ends the first part. Each part embodies one statement of a long harmonic progression, and the two progressions contain identical chords at crucial moments, as shown, somewhat simplified, in Ex. 1.

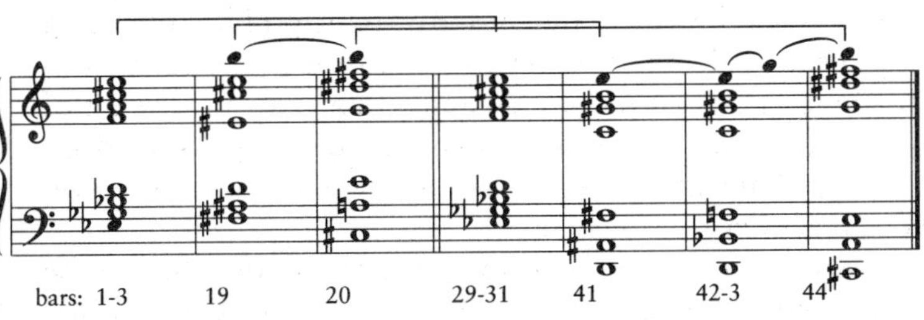

EX. 1

(The square brackets in Ex. 1 point out the paired chords in the two passages. Filled-in noteheads represent notes from the melody line.) Each progression begins from the same sonority, in bars 1–3 and 29–31, and each arrives at the same new chord by a similar path, in bars 19–20 and 41–4. But the chord in bar 20 serves as the beginning of a new section of the piece which gathers momentum and then sweeps on into the cadenza. This same chord is given an antithetical function in bars 44–6, serving there as final cadence for the entire study. As he goes about the business of reinterpreting the chord, Bartók is indescribably crafty in his artistry and musical tact. In particular, he uses bars 30–39 to alter the texture of the opening, breaking up its arpeggiations and its imperious melodic line, interrupting its flow until we hear it as only a shadow of itself. Then the subsequent resurgence of power (bar 40) and its quick dissolution (bar 44) almost compel acceptance of the final chord. Unlike the chord in the first study, this sonority lacks any tonal implications and cannot make that kind of contribution to its own meaning. To compensate, Bartók uses texture, tempo, rhythm and dynamics as even more vital participants in the task of shaping the cadence and of making the conclusion of the piece a convincing one.

Thematically and harmonically the third study is a standard three-part *A B A'* form with a brief introduction. After one hears the piece for the first time, this introduction takes on a certain air of the magician showing his audience that there really is no rabbit in the top hat. From this straightforward pair of arpeggiated chords (bars 1–4) comes the most dazzling music of the entire set. The first half is a mosaic of short phrases, repeated and transformed in a profusion of different metres and at breakneck speed.

The central section, bars 39–57, introduces new harmonic events and an almost lyrical melodic line, as well as a new regularity of metre. At bar 58 the chord of the introduction returns, but not within the same whirl of rhythmic complexity. Rather, in this recapitulation Bartók uses repetition of his central sonority to establish its centrality and to bind the two ends of the piece together in a relatively obvious way. Thus, although the piece is a clear three-part form, in another sense it follows a line of decreasing complexity of harmony and rhythm from the first to the last section.

This perhaps has something to do with the design of the Three Studies as a complete work. That design is most obviously a fast–slow–fast arrangement that echoes, with respect to tempo alone, a kind of three-movement keyboard sonata structure. More importantly, and in counterpoint to that three-movement structure, one can hear through the course of the work a rising level of musical complexity which reaches its climax in the first half of the third study. At that point, near bar 38, although Bartók allows no slackening of energy or pace, he does change the music to make it significantly easier to grasp by ear. The second half of the piece – the last thirty-nine bars – restores enough stability of metre and harmony to bring the whole set to a convincing close. Nevertheless, Bartók has not retreated to the level of simplicity of the first study, and the composition ends in a musical place which is quite different from where it began.

Bartók completed the Improvisations in 1920, and, as with the Three Studies, they were intended as repertoire for his recital tours. The seventh piece was dedicated separately 'to the memory of Claude Debussy', and appeared along with pieces by many other composers in a 'Tombeau de Claude Debussy' memorial review published in Paris in 1920. Universal Edition published the entire Op.20 in 1922. Bartók first performed the memorial piece to Debussy by itself in Budapest on 27 February 1921; he then played the entire set on 18 January 1922 in Budapest. He gave performances of the set in London and Paris later in the same year (on 24 March and 3 April, respectively), as well as in several other places. But after 1922 they appear to have suffered a public obscurity rivalling that of the Three Studies.

Nevertheless, the Improvisations were crucial to Bartók as compositional achievements, if not ultimately as concert pieces. As he said at Harvard University in 1943: 'In my Eight Improvisations for piano I reached, I believe, the extreme limit in adding most daring accompaniments to simple folk tunes.'[3] They are the primary examples of Bartók's folksong settings in which 'the added composition treatment attains the importance of an original work, and the used folk melody is only to be regarded as a kind of motto'.[4] Bartók's description here is perhaps overstated, since in each movement of the Improvisations the folk melody being set appears several times, usually in its entirety. Except in the sixth piece, the form of each thus appears as some type of strophic alternation between statements of the tune and interludes which vary widely in their length and complexity. Despite this kind of emphasis on the folk melody, one can hear a huge difference in approach between these pieces and, say, the settings of the Three Hungarian Folksongs from the Csík District (1907).

Of course, the main task for Bartók, which led him to such 'daring', was the combining of his old source material with his newly emergent style.[5] The result was a cycle of pieces which, as János Demény superbly remarks, 'rests on such an integral, coherent, deliberately planned design that its title (Improvisations!) might almost seem ironical'.[6] In the cycle Bartók apparently relies upon the modality of each melody to provide harmonic stability in the midst of his accompanimental extravagances. This seems to place melody and setting in opposition to one another, and some commentators, most notably Paul Griffiths, have made much of this opposition.[7] Nevertheless, Bartók himself was insistent that a folk melody and its setting should always be integrated, that – in his words – 'the musical qualities of the setting should be derived from the musical qualities of the melody, from such characteristics as are contained in it openly or covertly'.[8] It is perhaps more fruitful and more accurate, therefore, to hear the relationship between melody and setting in the various pieces as moving back and forth along a continuum between tension and mutual reinforcement. If we look for explicit derivations of the kind Bartók mentions, we also provide ourselves with the means for understanding some of the work's more hidden intricacies.

Perhaps the easiest way to make such connections is on the neutral ground of interval, in hearing the motivic intervals of the tunes as sources for harmonic structures. The simplest example of this in the Improvisations is the very opening, where the F–E♭ major second of the first bar's melody becomes the accompanimental sound in bar 2. That interval is then transposed throughout the phrase at the perfect fourth or fifth, which mimics the melody's overall descent from F to C. Another, more complicated instance appears in the fourth piece, where the semitone and major third of the melody engender in the right hand a pair of major thirds a semitone apart (A–C♯, C–A♭), as shown in Ex. 2.

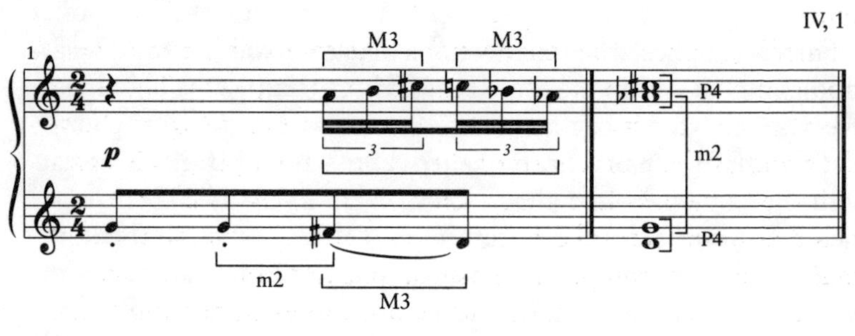

EX. 2

The complete interval in each hand is a perfect fourth, and the two fourths (D–G and A♭–C♯) are positioned vertically a semitone apart. The *pièce de résistance* of the technique is the seventh piece, where the opening minor third of the melody (F–A♭) is transposed, compounded, and deployed in myriad ways through the setting.

Not all the pieces contain this kind of explicit derivation of setting from melody. Identifying those which lack such a connection reveals another major facet in the design of the work. Bartók has used *attacca* markings to signal a gathering of the eight pieces into four larger 'movements'. The groups appear as follows: 1–2; 3–5; 6; 7–8. Within these, nos 2, 5, 6 and 8 lack a clear-cut intervallic connection between melody and setting. Each of these is, obviously, the culminating piece in its small group, except for the sixth piece, which has its own unique form. Each 'movement' thus begins with a setting, at a relatively slow tempo, which is carefully derived from its melody. As Bartók moves to the end of the group, the tempo becomes much faster and the internal intervallic connection is abandoned.

In its place, and to provide coherence on a larger scale, Bartók works out fairly explicit restatements of events or structures from the slow sections, sometimes in a form which seems like parody. The calmly meditative major second from the opening of the first piece, for example, becomes a harshly energetic minor second on the downbeat of the second piece. That event propels the new piece forward at the beginning, and indeed continues in the same role for every subsequent statement of the tune.

Bartók supplies other connections of greater subtlety and harmonic importance in moving from slow to fast pieces. The same five-note chord acts as a cadential event in bar 12 of the first piece and as the final chord of the second. Both pieces also end with the same bass-line progression, G♭ E♭ D D♭. The three folk melodies of the second group (nos 3–5) share a common modal final, G, and a common emphasis on paired phrases that span a perfect fourth. The seventh and eighth pieces both exploit the tension between their common modal final, C, and the bass note of their respective cadential chords, F♯, in a whole series of different situations.

The sixth piece deserves some separate comment because of

its unique form and its pivotal position in the whole work. It is the scherzo of the set, the only movement to avoid inclusion in the slow–fast pattern of a rhapsody. The introduction (bars 1–5) begins by sounding like the primary melody, but soon stutters its way into a kind of dead-end half cadence. The scherzo then proceeds as a tiny set of variations, in which accompaniment provides far more change than do embellishments of the theme. The movement, again uniquely, has no interludes between thematic statements. Its melody is pentatonic – the only one in the set – and placed entirely on the instrument's black keys. (How many very young pianists have delighted in discovering the pentatonic sound of the black keys alone!) Bartók emphasizes that fact at each end of the piece, surrounding the pentatonic melody line with white-key triads from the diatonic modes. The modal final of the introduction, B♭, is the 'dominant' of the E♭ final of the true melody, but the setting insists throughout on a permanent tritone, either A along with E♭ or (at bars 12–14) G along with D♭. The tritone, with its echoes of half- and fully-diminished seventh chords, undercuts the tonal stability of the tune. The close (at bars 27–32) repeats the music of the introduction but finally breaks through to a true cadence on E♭.

At the most extended level of his design, Bartók takes pains to create resonances between the two pairs of movements that begin and end the composition. These echoes have to do both with the melodies and with their respective settings. The corresponding melodies in each pair share some detailed similarities with regard to mode and to internal structure. The first melodies of these pairs (nos 1 and 7) both begin on F and end on C, a fourth below; likewise, each emphasizes E♭ as an important subsidiary note within that span and uses B♭ as a lower neighbour at the cadence. The concluding melodies (nos 2 and 8) both begin and end on C in their final appearances, and emphasize G, F and E♭ as internal accent points. The settings for all four of these melodies rely on the unresolved tension between the modal final C and the reiterated F♯ (or G♭) which serves as bass note at each final cadence, as shown in Ex. 3. That kind of tension seems to be the most lasting impression left to many people in hearing the Improvisations. But in the long run, far

EX. 3

more than tension alone is present in both these sets of pieces. Finding so many solutions for his compositional dilemmas here must have sustained and enriched Bartók's compositional imagination as he worked on new projects. The next stage would be large instrumental works, firstly the two violin sonatas and then the Dance Suite (1923), followed by the long series of celebrated pieces from 1926 onwards. Both the Three Studies and the Improvisations are essential parts of that development and essential parts of Bartók's musical legacy.

NOTES

1 *BBL*, p. 227.
2 *BBL*, p. 168.
3 *BBE*, p. 375.
4 *BBE*, p. 352.
5 The source material is old on its own terms, and old in Bartók's experience of it. Five of the tunes, those used in nos 1, 3, 4, 6 and 8, are from his own collection (*HFS*, melody nos 37, 40, 244, 64 and 46, respectively). The other three melodies are also authentic tunes but taken from other collections.

6 *BBL*, p. 149.

7 See his *Bartók*, London (J. M. Dent), 1984, pp. 98–100. Griffiths suggests that the Improvisations are designed, at least in part, as a mockery or 'quizzing' of their folk melodies, and therefore express Bartók's own self-doubt at this period in his career.

8 *BBE*, p. 342.

13

The 'Piano Year' of 1926

LÁSZLÓ SOMFAI

In June 1926, after finishing his piano classes at the Music Academy in Budapest, Bartók sent his family to vacation with his sister, who lived in Szöllős puszta, Békés county. He stayed on in their Budapest flat in Szilágyi Dezső Square in order to devote himself with full concentration to composition, as he had last succeeded in doing three years previously. His main aim was to compose a piano concerto, but he did not manage to begin work upon that concerto until the end of the summer.[1] Prior to its composition he made a whole range of sketches of large movements for solo piano, which were to lay the foundations for the new style of his 'piano music year'.

The sketches show that the movements of both Bartók's Piano Sonata and *Out of Doors* were composed during June, but not in the order in which they were published. It is probable that the first movement of the Sonata was the first to take a definite form. The initial drafts of 'With Drums and Pipes' and 'Barcarolla' (*Out of Doors*, nos 1 and 2) were made at the same time; their completed drafts were followed immediately by the drafts of the third, then the second, movement of the Sonata. 'The Night's Music' and 'The Chase' (*Out of Doors*, nos 4 and 5) also form a pair of movements and were, perhaps, the last of all to be sketched. The remaining *Out of Doors* piece, 'Musettes' (no.3), had not yet achieved its independence as it existed as an episode of the Sonata's finale.[2]

After having toiled throughout June the composer took time off for a summer vacation with his family. On 1 July he arrived at his sister's and subsequently travelled with his wife, visiting towns of artistic interest in Italy and relaxing in the Alps.

Returning to Budapest, he worked alone again between 9 and 25 August on his draft of the First Piano Concerto. It was presumably at this time in August that he also worked further on the third movement of the Piano Sonata, creating the final, shorter version and giving birth to the piece 'Musettes' from the excised episode.

In a letter written on 25 September to his publisher, Universal Edition Vienna, Bartók announced that he had completed a piano sonata in three movements, 'lasting about 13 minutes', five fairly difficult piano pieces and a volume of easier piano pieces. The last collection was the Nine Little Piano Pieces, which he had found most difficult to compose. Among their drafts can be found rejected pieces or rough sketches to three pieces that later appeared in the *Mikrokosmos* collection. The premières of these works soon followed. Using the manuscript Bartók gave the world première of the Piano Sonata over Hungarian Radio on 3 December 1926 and a second performance at a special Bartók concert in the Great Hall of the Music Academy on 8 December. Apart from the Sonata he also played on these occasions the first, fourth and fifth *Out of Doors* pieces and eight of the Nine Little Piano Pieces.[3]

In view of the enormous number of piano works that Bartók composed it is surprising that he gave the title of sonata to only one of these works from his maturity. It is no accident that his only sonata, just as his first piano concerto, was a product of the classicizing and distilling year of 1926. In its outer movements Bartók shows how he has embraced Viennese Classical formal principles of sonata and rondo construction. Yet despite this completely 'European' use of these models, his thematic material itself was fundamentally different from that of his Western contemporaries. The first movement – an Allegro moderato initially in a Lydian-flavoured E major tonality – has a long exposition – indeed, 134 of the movement's 268 bars – which unfolds a surprising number of themes representative of different pianistic styles.[4] External and internal organization provide cohesion to the form. The external cohesion is of rhythmic origin: tremendous momentum is created by the practically unbroken quaver hammering of the thematic or contrapuntal movement in the uniform, almost mechanical tempo. The force of the internal structure – the cohesion of the successive thematic and motivic profiles – operates more in the background. Each new theme makes a show of dissimilarity, but within seconds one senses that, in fact, it continues, varies or quotes from what precedes it.

The germ from which the thematic development of this first movement stems is the short head-motif, which Bartók early exposes within the first thematic area in two archetypes (Ex. 1).

EX. 1

These differ decisively in their rhythmic and metric position within the prevailing duple time. The first archetype and its rhythmic variants function in the exposition as an articulatory 'signal', heralding the onset of new themes – bars 38–43 herald the arrival of the second theme (bar 44); bars 69–72, the fourth theme (bar 76); bars 110–111, the fifth theme (bar 116) – or being inserted at a major point within a theme – as bars 87–8 divide the fourth theme. This is the element also which, when inverted at bar 135, initiates the movement's development. The second archetype (Ex. 1b), on the other hand, inspires motivic elaboration within the first theme and its following transition, and also plays a key role in the motivic connection of all the exposition's themes. To its three-note basic form – found both ascending and descending – can be joined a two-note conjunct motif – again either ascending or descending, as Bartók does at bars 33–4 (Ex. 2). There is a perfectly organic train of thought behind the way in which the semiquaver motif, C–D, inspires

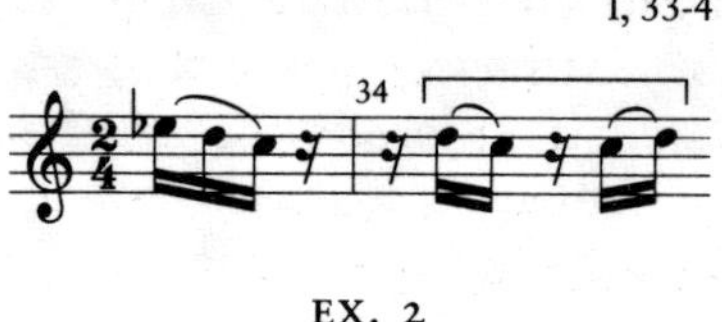

EX. 2

the opening C–D step of the second theme, at bar 44, and gains an independent existence in the third theme, at bar 57, now transposed to C♯–D♯. In the fourth theme this two-note motif is expanded and an organic variation of this quasi-*circulatio* motif commences in two-bar units, fairly obviously following folk-music practices (Ex. 3).

EX. 3

The two-bar units reappear in the fifth theme in exact or approximate inversion.[5] At around this point the listener begins to sense that he is not just listening to a colourful chain of independent pianistic themes, but to variations upon a central idea. Naturally, Bartók was familiar with nineteenth-century techniques of combining sonata form, with its thematic contrasts, and variation form; he knew Liszt's Piano Sonata in B minor intimately. Nevertheless, the procedure he applied here – the organic, step-by-step modification of motifs of two, three or four notes – is entirely his own, and based upon his study of variant forms and melodic types of folk music. Further variants of this second archetype appear in the second half of the movement. In the development the motivic elaboration of the second theme imperceptibly slips over into the motivic 'stock' of the fourth theme; in the carefully rewritten and shortened recapitulation (which begins, effectively, only with the statement of the second archetype at bar 187), motifs of the fourth and fifth themes unite in the tempestuous *più mosso* dance theme (bar 236). More broadly, the 'irregular' handling of themes in the recapitulation might throw into doubt the identification of five themes in the exposition. Only the first, fourth and ending of the fifth theme actually return in the recapitulation in any recognizable form. Yet, despite this technical formal consideration, the exposition does present five independent thematic formations, each with its own distinctive pianistic character. At a more basic interpretative level, however, all formal considerations become secondary in face of the motoric '*Allegro barbaro*' character of the movement, with its inexhaustible rhythmic invention and peerless combination of accent and metre.

In Bartók's second movement, a C-based Sostenuto e pesante, issues of rhythm and motion are consciously of secondary importance. It is a form of lament; the melody stirs only at bar 7 after a seemingly endless series of repetitions of the note E. It expands with large gestures, and shrinks again before becoming more restless. Perfect and imperfect fifth chords, from bar 24 onwards, provide the harmony with its hollow echoing quality.

The virtuoso *allegro molto* finale is a rondo form on the variation principle. Its growth and metamorphosis can be reconstructed through the study of the various manuscript stages, which reveal considerable differences with regard both to content and length. The first version consisted of 371 bars, the second 416 and the third, final version only 281 bars. In the first and second versions the same formal concept undergoes an extensive development, while in the third version Bartók's shortening is radical. The longest and most complete version, the second, is a monothematic rondo with five ritornellos and four episodes which themselves contain variations of the ritornello theme. The essential feature of the form of the movement, however, is that the theme, consciously evoking reminiscences of a folk tune (yet sufficiently abstract with its characteristically Bartókian features, such as the changes of metre) gives rise to episodes which recall the tone of genuine folk-music genres.

Moreover, the episodes, consisting of a simple rhythmic scheme over an ostinato accompaniment, seem to have been written consciously and systematically in Bartók's favourite types of peasant music. The first episode (from bar 53 in the published score) is an imitation of two verses of a strident vocal performance without ornaments; the second (from bar 143) constitutes a richly ornamented peasant flute setting; the third episode is a bagpipe scene which assumes immense proportions; the fourth (from bar 205) reflects the style of village fiddlers in Transylvania. A victory for Bartók's self-criticism over his latent preference for construction and conceptualization – and, at the same time, a great aesthetic advantage for the Sonata's finale – lies in his courage to cut out the bagpipe episode, which was slower in tempo and would have loosened the form because of its disproportionate size. Although it is true that the 'catalogue' is thus no longer complete, the rate at which the events occur experiences a favourable acceleration. The rewritten third block of ritornello, in its present form, is more hurried; the redrafted Transylvanian 'fiddler' episode does not even contain the entire melody, but accumulates and varies motifs found in a specific dance style of the Romanian peasant fiddlers. The bagpipe episode, of course, became the separate *Out of Doors* movement, 'Musettes', of 129 bars, where it stands as Bartók's most diabolical, self-composed bagpipe music.[6]

Although Bartók did not as a rule play all five pieces of his *Out of Doors* together in concert he does appear to have had a definite purpose in putting the five pieces in their particular order. *Out of Doors* is, in fact, a preliminary study of his five-part 'arch form'. Bartók had not worked out the symmetrical thematic structures later associated with that form (in such works as the Fourth and Fifth String Quartets) but he had considered the various functions of the pieces within the work and established an arched system of tonal relations: E G A G E (considering central, not closing, tonal centres). Bartók made no comment on the title of the work or individual pieces. It is not programmatic music, although the motivation for writing the fourth movement, 'The Night's Music', might well have been the chorus of frogs and other evocative sounds heard when visiting his sister's. Bartók has, more probably, recalled character and genre pieces such as Couperin's *Ordres* and Debussy's *Préludes*, which frequently featured in his concert programmes.[7]

Of the five pieces the final three are the more significant from the viewpoint of the composer's compositional development. 'Musettes' (no.3) reflects Bartók's fundamental attraction to the bagpipe, as one of the few polyphonic peasant instruments capable of playing tunes and dances in a harmonic setting and also producing with its middle pipe, stopped by the little finger of the right hand, a complementary middle-part rhythm. Among his great ethnomusicological experiences he listed hearing the bagpipers in Bihar county in February 1910, attending a swineherd's horn and bagpipe competition in the Ipolyság region in November 1910, and hearing an illiterate Romanian eighteen-year-old piper from Hunedoara in 1913–14. His subsequent composition included many references to the instrument, from the bagpipe finale (1914) of his Fifteen Hungarian Peasant Songs through to the brilliant bagpipe scene in the final movement of the Concerto for Orchestra (1943).[8] 'Musettes' is a remarkable poetic paraphrase. Its first fourteen bars press the listener's ear to the skin bag to hear, fearfully amplified, the air filling the instrument and bringing it creaking, whining and trembling to life in preparation for making music. The music starts with direct references to the bagpipe – the deep opening fifths, the puffing diminuendo motif (from bar 4), and the grace-note tremolos (from bar 8) – to which he adds characteristic references to the instrument's legendary poor tuning: the sharpened fourth within his perfect fifth (from bar 1) and later simultaneous major and minor thirds between the two hands. Of Bartók's three themes, the first (from bar 15) involves a narrow range and typical swineherd's rhythm, the second (from bar 39) a bagpipe-polka rhythm and the third (from bar 60, Ex. 4a) introduces a third tempo level, with leaps of a tenth above an E/C ostinato pendulum. It is the least related to bagpipe motifs although Bartók – after further development of his first theme (bars 67–80) and a condensed recapitulation – returns to it again to create an idyllic, realistic bagpipe coda reminiscent of genuine folk music (Ex. 4b).

EX. 4

The end of the piece brings still another splendid idea: the bag-piper puffs his last and the air starts to run out.

Nature, Ego and People – the musical symbols of the objective world, of individual poetry and of the powerful art of a folk community – provide the tripolar tension within the next piece, 'The night's music' (no.4). The first three sections of the piece provide an exposition of these three phenomena: Nature (bars 1–17), with its 'sounds of the night'; the Ego wandering in Nature (bars 17–34), with its two strophes of a Bartókian lament resembling a chorale melody; the People (bars 38–57), with its background music symbolically resembling that of the peasant flute. Bartók then opposes the materials of the Ego and the People (bars 58–66), with his playing together of the chorale and imitation flute-music, before returning in the piece's final bars (67–71) to the music of Nature, interspersed with ever more distant snatches of the flute. In this piece the 'Nature' music sounds more realistic than in any other related movement of Bartók. What he sought to do was to collect and stylize musical *gefundene Objekte*, sound 'godsends' of Nature, and to apply them in a particular musical genre-painting re-creating an experience of Nature. This stylization of the sounds of Nature in Bartók's works – reduction to frequencies, intervals, rhythms, tempos and forms of movements, and then their recomposition – simplifies them into musical motifs that assume their appointed places in a structure that is highly consciously designed.

The primary plan in the noises of the music of the night is the tonal system. Bartók's 'Nature scale' (Ex. 5) provides the key to understanding the way in which the various motifs share in the overall tonal scheme.

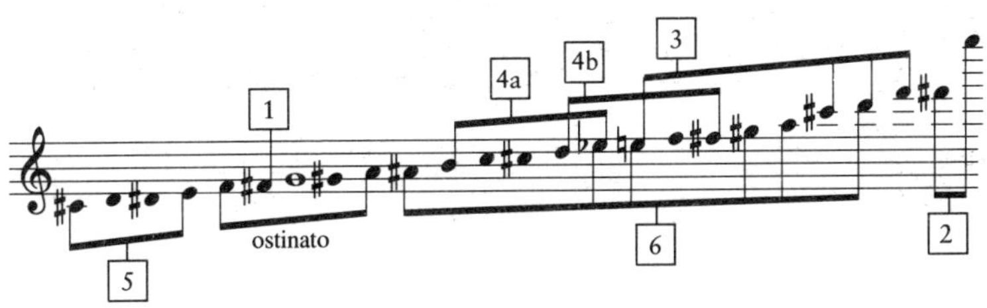

EX. 5

It is significant in three respects:

1) The scale, strongly restricted by comparison with the compass of the piano, contains, apart from the 1½-octave chromatic segment from initial C♯ to F♯, a few important complementary notes, mainly in the higher octaves. This stock of pitches remains unchanged both in the introductory section and the later recurrences of the 'Nature' background.

2) The motifs (Ex. 6) are built upon segments of this scale and never change in pitch during the piece.[9] The majority of the scale's notes result from one particular motif. It is rare for a pitch to appear in two or more motifs.[10]

3) For a piece in G the occurrence of G is surprisingly rare. Apart from the G in the ostinato there is only the very high final G of the scale. Bartók seems otherwise purposely to avoid G in any register. More generally, the omissions in Bartók's 'Nature scale' are part of another plan. His following chorale for the Ego moves precisely into these missing segments and uses all the Gs which were previously omitted in the various possible registers.

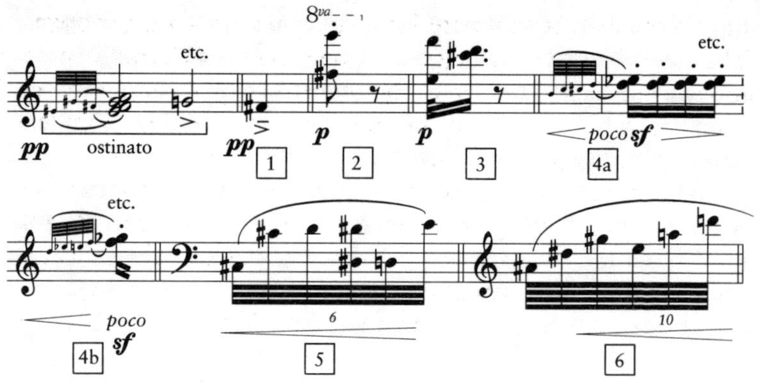

EX. 6

The frequency and ordering of Bartók's 'Nature' motifs can be translated into a hypothetical pictorial sequence of events. Bars 1–6 may represent the 'silence' of the night, with only the chirruping of the crickets audible. Then comes a stronger sound, perhaps from the signal for the 'croaking of a frog' (bar 7) and then the noise becomes denser with the awakening of other creatures (bar 11). Thereafter the other sounds are overwhelmed by the 'concert of the frogs' (bars 13–15), which then dies away; the noises become rarefied and stiffen again into the opening scenario. Bartók achieves this sequence so realistically by the precise rhythmic placement of his motifs within the prevailing $\frac{3}{2}$ metre, and by strategic placing of accents so as to inject tension.[11]

Bartók's final piece in *Out of Doors* is 'The Chase', a virtuoso counterpart to the 'chase' scene in his pantomime *The Miraculous Mandarin*. 'The Chase' is, however, more abstract than its predecessor, as the chase here has no goal that might be regarded as a programme. It is more a case of hunting. Bartók has deliberately set out to create an inarticulate music, in both physical and aesthetic terms. The ceaseless hammering, lashing chords, the passages of scarcely playable parallel ninths, the rude accents and the snarling crescendos become the more inarticulate the better the pianist overcomes the difficulties of the intentionally tough texture. The orgiastic, ostentatiously barbaric movements of Stravinsky's *The Rite of Spring* well show

how difficult it is to create inarticulateness in an artistic way. The credibility of the exaggerated vehemence in Bartók's chase, too, is only achieved by a comprehensive plan and through resort to a rich arsenal of techniques of motivic development and rhythmic manipulation.

The tension is primarily created by the ostinato conception. After the first four bars' hammering out of the beat, Bartók introduces the ostinato (Ex. 7) that, in increasingly widening range, will remain present throughout the rest of the work and offer a basic yardstick for the tonal and rhythmic events of its course.

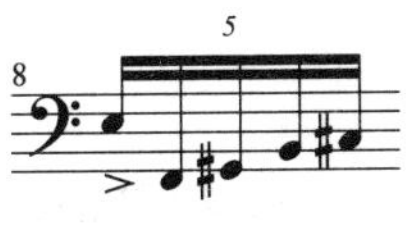

EX. 7

Against this left-hand ostinato pattern and its outgrowths Bartók presents themes in 'alien' keys. The tonal structure of his right-hand themes itself is frequently dissonant. The beginning and end of his first thematic stanza (bars 14–39), for instance, are in F, yet the theme soon runs through a scale which excludes octave equivalents, as it has F♯ and G♯ in its higher octave – see bar 17 – compared with F and G in its lower. Further tension stems from the choice of *repercussio* notes in the right-hand theme: G, D♯ and C in the first stanza. Yet the most important source of the inarticulate passion in 'The Chase' is not its tonal circumstance but the motivic–rhythmic composition in the right hand. This unfolds through the piece's five stanzas: the first, in which, after establishing a two-bar pulse, this feeling is undermined, leading to final eccentric rhythmic extensions and diminutions (bars 20–26); the second (bars 45–67), its varied reprise, which attempts its rhythmic disintegration, leading to a virtual $\frac{5}{8}$ pulse in bars 55–6; the third (bars 71–88), a fragmentary, brief development of anacrusis motifs, in which Bartók plays first with inverted forms and then with an 'endless screw' of contrary motion; the fourth (bars 96–129), which extensively develops the *repercussio* motifs in a texture dominated by major ninth chords; the fifth (bars 135–52), a coda, which acts also as a recapitulation but creates a series of rhythmic collisions, through its nervous right-hand leaps from register to register, which not even the *marcato* accents supporting the $\frac{6}{8}$ metre can smooth over. Bartók only heightens the sense of 'chase' by his highly effective use of tempos, which virtually forces the performer to give of the maximum and to create the very impression of being a chased man.

Bartók's Nine Little Piano Pieces is a looser cycle as far as both tonality and dramaturgy are concerned. Bartók's publisher grouped the works into three volumes: 1–4, 5–8, 9. The opening 'Four Dialogues' are two-part pieces in contrapuntal style, although no.2 does occasionally swell into three or four parts through the addition of pedal points. No.5, 'Menuetto', is historically important in Bartók's compositional output for being probably the earliest instance of his development of the content of a whole movement exclusively through manipulation of compressed and extended versions of the same subject (Ex. 8).[12]

EX. 8

It is of special interest that here the two forms remain in a state of irreconcilable dramatic 'dissonance', whereas in other works of Bartók they appear in an obligatory dramatic order, with the primarily chromatic form finally extending into the diatonic, as if gaining its 'natural' form. Within the work's ternary framework (bars 1–27, 28–41, 42–62) Bartók treats the compressed and extended forms as layers to be developed either individually or together. When played together (as from bar 9 and bar 28, for instance) they move in a rhythmic canon at one bar's distance. The meaning of the two kinds of dialectically contrasting material and their interrelationship is not predetermined or rigid; they exist in a vital, changing relationship. The compressed form, for instance, is even more distorted in the reprise than at the beginning of the piece. The extended form becomes even more *cantabile* in the coda (from bar 52) than in any previous section and now has a purely pentatonic content, exaggerating the contrast between the pitch content of the two versions of the subject even more. At the same time, however, there are signs of the two layers converging through the piece: the second canon more harmoniously presents the two versions than the first. But the momentum towards a 'synthesis' is absent: the 'ideal' does not conquer the 'distorted'; the diatonic does not triumph over the chromatic.

The sixth little piano piece is 'Air', in which a four-line isometric 'folksong' of Bartók's invention is found in the framework of a study in staccato and production of tone colour. No.7, 'Marcia delle bestie', belongs to the family of 'Bear Dance'[13] movements, although it is one of the less barbaric relations with its attention to imitative procedures and general compositional economy. No.8, 'Tambourine', was originally composed under the Hungarian title 'Csörgő-tánc', or 'rattle dance', but Bartók then introduced 'Tamburin' when giving the work its final German title, in clear reference to this drum instrument, and probably inspired by this common title in eighteenth-century French clavecin music. The piece is a study in dialectics – rhythm versus melody, right versus left hand, pairings of harmonic and rhythmic functions – although the expected formal synthesis is largely undermined by processes of decomposition. The form of the piece can be interpreted as consisting of four 'drumming' passages with interspersed thematic 'stanzas', the first (bars 17–51) devoted to the right hand, the second (bars 63–89) to the left hand, and a third (bars 99–107) involving both hands. The third 'stanza' is not, however, an independent section any more, for the third and fourth 'drummings' which precede and follow it are all part of a single process. They mark the breaking up of the symmetry and regular beat of the original drumming motion, which is followed by the 'explosion' of the piece rhythmically and, with it, the closing of the movement. Bartók's own gramophone recording of the piece[14] bears witness to his intention in this closing section to disintegrate the music. His performance is even more eccentric than the notation suggests, with an exaggerated *inégal* rhythm on the *marcatissimo* chords. Indeed, it suggests not destruction as much as a triumphant arrival. He really devastates his rhythmic fabric and beats the keyboard like a drum, almost with the flats of his hands, heedless of the actual pitches. Yet out of this brutal crescendo of noise he finally emerges triumphantly at the closing chord, in which the key of G is reinforced by the perfect fifth in the bass.

Bartók's final piano piece, the 'Preludio – All'Ungherese', has a slow–fast rhapsodic form. The beginning of an abstract, but unmistakably Hungarian, unison melody is heard in the 'Preludio', which becomes enlivened in the 'All'Ungherese' as one of Bartók's loveliest folksong imitations. The quasi 'new'-style folksong has a four-line *A B* |:*B A*:| structure and is repeated twice in variation, increasing in tempo and dynamics as it leads into a superb coda.

It is customary to view Bartók's 'piano year' of 1926 as the overture to a new period in Bartók's stylistic development. Although the piano accompaniment to the *Village Scenes* (1924) and even the piano texture of his 1925 transcription of the Dance Suite helped to prepare the way, the stylistic 'turn' of this year is still quite striking. Bartók's music became more polyphonic and linear – in the late 1920s he wrote to Edwin von der Nüll, the first essayist of his piano works: 'in recent years I have considerably occupied myself with music before Bach, and I believe that traces of this are to be noticed in the Piano Concerto and the Nine Little Piano Pieces.'[15] He also showed a greater fondness for using the percussive, colouristic and even noise potentialities of the piano, with the purpose of creating form. From the beginning of the 1920s Bartók had regularly played sonatas by Domenico Scarlatti and was studying the works of Couperin. In the summer of 1926, probably while preparing for his coming winter tour of Italy, he also learnt several pieces of

Italian pre-Classical keyboard music – a fresh experience for him. On 15 October and 10 November 1926 he performed sonatas, toccatas and polyphonic pieces by Michelangelo Rossi, Bernardo Pasquini, Azzolino Bernardino della Ciaia, Benedetto Marcello and Domenico Zipoli over Budapest Radio.[16] Meanwhile, he was also becoming acquainted with Stravinsky's neo-Classical endeavours. (On 15 March 1926, for instance, he had heard Stravinsky play the piano solo of his Concerto for Piano and Wind Instruments (1924) in Budapest.) Undeniably, Bartók's piano compositions of 1926 were to a certain extent also related to the general neo-Classical trend in European music at the time, and drew upon the style of the Classical masters, at least in many questions of technique and form. But what distinguished him from the Stravinsky trend was his flat rejection of any unilateral acceptance of 'old' music. He did not use the technique of quotation, nor did he resort to the artistic game of distorting Classical chordal passages with dissonances or fitting Baroque melodic models to modern settings. More profoundly than ever, the roots of his *melos* lay in folk music, despite the fact that no direct quotations from folk music can be found in his three piano cycles of 1926.

NOTES

1 See János Kárpáti's chapter 'The First Two Piano Concertos' in this *Companion.*

2 See from page 12 of the facsimile edition of the Sonata's manuscript held in Budapest's National Széchényi Library, ed. László Somfai, Budapest (Editio Musica), 1980.

3 Bartók appears to have only added a fourth Dialogue to this collection in late 1927, and previously to have divided the final piece, the Preludio – All'Ungherese.

4 Ernő Lendvai did not share my sonata-form interpretation of this movement, but saw it as a typical Bartókian bridge form. A study of recently discovered sketches for the movement, which Bartók sent to his wife in a letter at the time, supports the view of a 134-bar-long exposition. See *ZD* 1984, pp. 71–81.

5 cf. fourth theme bars 81–2 with fifth theme bars 117–18; similarly, 85–6 with 124–5.

6 A more extensive discussion of the Sonata's final movement appears in my chapter 'The Influence of Peasant Music on the Finale of Bartók's Piano Sonata', in *Studies in Musical Sources and Style: Essays in Honor of Jan LaRue*, ed. Eugene K. Wolf and Edward H. Roesner, Madison (A–R Editions), 1990, pp. 535–55.

7 Bartók had edited eighteen Couperin pieces for a Rozsnyai edition published in 1924 and had in the following year added to his repertory Couperin's suite 'Les Fastes de la grande et ancienne Ménestrandise'.

8 See from bar 188; Bartók was not directly quoting any folk-music source in this passage.

9 Note that motifs 4a and 4b are not transpositions since 4b only appears together with 4a.

10 See, for instance, the lowest F♯ in the ostinato and motif 1, and upper E♮ in motifs 3, 4b and 6.

11 For a more detailed statement of this and other qualities of the piece's opening section see my 'Analytical Notes on Bartók's Piano Year of 1926', *SM*, vol.26 (1984), pp. 5–10.

12 For Bartók's discussion in 1943 of this technique of compression and extension of themes see *BBE*, p. 383.

13 The last of Bartók's Ten Easy Pieces (1908).

14 Released on Patria MR 64 in about 1936, reissued in Hungaroton's *Centenary Edition of Bartók's Records (Complete)*, LPX 12326, also HCD 12326.

15 *BBlev*.v, p. 359.

16 See, further, my Introduction to *Béla Bartók XVII and XVIII Century Italian Cembalo and Organ Music Transcribed for Piano*, New York (Carl Fischer), 1990, pp. iv–vii.

14

Synthesis of East and West: Mikrokosmos

BENJAMIN SUCHOFF

> If there were such a man, I'd like to meet him,
> As Herrn Mikrokosmus I would greet him.[1]
>
> *Mephistopheles (to Faust)*

In the summer of 1939, at an interview in Paris, Bartók declared that he wanted to make a synthesis of Eastern European folk music and Western European art music, where the latter, in turn, would combine J. S. Bach's counterpoint, Beethoven's progressive form and Debussy's harmony.[2] It is curious that he omitted mention of Bach's Italian predecessors and contemporaries – Girolamo Frescobaldi (1583–1643) and Azzolino della Ciaia (1671–1755), among others – as having decisive influence on his stylistic development during the third, 'Synthesis of East and West' period of his career (1926–45). Indeed, just as Liszt had discovered and received creative inspiration from various works of earlier Italian composers during his stay in Italy in the 1830s, so did Bartók from his investigation of their seventeenth- and eighteenth-century keyboard pieces, in 1925.[3] In these compositions he found a contrapuntal style closer to his Hungarian temperament than the more or less rigid practice of the German composers of that period. Their imprint on his First Piano Concerto (1926) and, particularly, *Mikrokosmos* (1926–39) is so apparent. Before turning to examination of the textural and other stylistic aspects of selected pieces from the six volumes comprising *Mikrokosmos*, it seems appropriate to begin with an update of the historical background which led to its publication.[4]

In 1912 Rózsavölgyi, a Budapest music publisher, asked Bartók, then professor of piano at the Royal Academy of Music in Budapest, to write a number of volumes for teaching the piano from the beginning to the highest degree. In collaboration with a younger colleague, Sándor Reschofsky, who was assigned the task of preparing the technical exercises from which Bartók would write illustrative pieces, the first volume, *Piano Method*, was completed in May 1913 and published during that year. In 1929 Bartók selected eighteen of his pieces for reprinting as *First Term at the Piano*.[5]

On or about 1 May 1932 Bartók changed his Budapest residence from Kavics utca to Csalán út (now preserved as the national Bartók shrine). In view of the change in schools for his younger son Péter, then eight years old, and his dissatisfaction with the instruction previously given in the mandatory singing classes, Bartók arranged with the school authorities to have Péter excused from such classes: the father would personally attend to the son's musical education.[6] Then, on 12 October 1932, in response to the request of his Viennese publisher, Universal Edition, that he write some very easy piano pieces, Bartók replied:

> It coincides very well with my own plans that you are just now asking for some very easy piano pieces from me: during this past summer I wrote several – about 35 – beginning with the easiest (like the pieces that Rózsavölgyi published in the 'First Term') and progressing in difficulty. But because I have a many-sided project in mind, it will be a long time before I can complete it.[7]

During the following years Bartók added the remaining *Mikrokosmos* pieces and exercises, including three compositions he had previously intended, but not published, as part of Nine Little Piano Pieces (completed on 31 October 1926).[8] The last pieces to be undertaken apparently were those comprising the first volume and the related exercises (completed in June 1939). Later, beginning in 1939 or 1940, Bartók transcribed seven of the pieces (nos 69, 113, 123, 127, 135, 145, 146) for two pianos, for performance by his wife, Ditta Pásztory, and himself.

A substantial number of essays has been devoted to *Mikrokosmos* in whole or in part, including those written by the composer.[9] Bartók's interpretation of the work as 'a many-sided project' is only partially given in his Preface and Notes to the *Mikrokosmos* publication, where most emphasis is given to general directions for the teaching of the first four volumes. In a 1944 interview broadcast by WNYC (New York City radio), Bartók also referred to *Mikrokosmos* as 'a series of pieces in all (of) different styles to represent a small world.'[10] And in his last comment about the work, he states that it 'appears as a *synthesis* of all the musical and technical problems which were treated and in some cases only partially solved in the previous piano works', particularly with regard to his new trend of piano writing in which 'the percussive character of the piano' is accentuated.[11] Since Bartók's synthesis of musical and technical problems in piano playing is adequately covered elsewhere, the following *Mikrokosmos* pieces have been selected as exemplars of the composer's stated objective for his lifework: the synthesis of Eastern folk music and Western art music.[12]

Volumes One and Two (nos 1–66)

Bartók's original plan to publish the first sixty-six pieces in one volume was discarded by Boosey & Hawkes, who thought it would be more practical, in terms of a lower selling price, if the pieces were assembled in two books. 'It is a pity', Bartók wrote to the company on 3 February 1940, 'that this division has been made; now, the first book gives a very poor impression; besides, the contents of these sixty pages are a real unity; they are meant for the first year of piano-studying'.[13] The first two volumes are dedicated to Péter Bartók.

'Six Unison Melodies' (nos 1–6): Disguised as simple five-finger exercises, the purpose of these melodies is to introduce the novice to modal octave segments in the form of pentachords extracted from the C major scale. Nos 1 and 2a consist of the first five degrees; no.2b is the Aeolian octave segment; no.3, Dorian; no.4, Lydian (note the characteristic tritone, B–F); no.5, Aeolian, extended to a hexachord (note the VII–I modal cadence); and no.6, Mixolydian.

'Dotted Notes' (no.7), 'Repetition' (no.8): No.7 introduces the Phrygian pentachord as another octave segment of the C major scale. In tonal contrast is no.8, an undefined minor hexachord (Aeolian or Dorian: C or C♯ missing) transposed to E as fundamental note.

'With Alternate Hands' (no.10): The A♭ – a most unusual key signature! – highlights the equally unusual pentachord, D E F G A♭. This sequence can be interpreted as an octave segment of a non-diatonic folk mode, or, in more recent terminology, the first five degrees of the D octatonic (alternating tones and semitones) scale: D E F G A♭ B♭ B C♯.[14] The same type of pentachord, transposed to B as fundamental note, accounts for the C♯ key signature in no.25, 'Imitation and Inversion'.

'Village Song' (no.15): This piece is a structural variant of a Slovak folksong collected by Bartók in 1916.[15] The source melody consists of four isometric melody-sections (that is, four six-syllable lines) in the Phrygian mode, the third melody-section has a different rhythmic schema, and the form is *A B C D*. 'Village Song' has the same syllabic structure and rhythmic schemata, but with seemingly characteristic Slovak Lydian pentachords, C D E F♯ G and G A B C♯ D. These pentachords, however, are octave segments of the D Mixolydian and A Mixolydian modes, respectively, where the latter pentachord results from the fifth transposition in the second melody-section. By using real instead of tonal transposition (C♯ in place of C), Bartók converts a diatonic folk mode into a chromatic polymode,[16] which is based on the C Z-cell, C C♯ F♯ G, organized as juxtaposed Y-cells, C D E F♯/ G A B C♯.[17] The form is A A^5 B^5 A (a Western architectonic form with fifth transposition), a unique characteristic of the 'new' Hungarian folksong style as defined by Bartók. The piece ends with an unambiguous D Mixolydian, VII–I modal cadence.

'Slow Dance' (no.33): This is a 'textbook' example of Bartókian East–West synthesis. The Western architectonic form, A B C A_v, is in the rhythmic style of a Slavic *kolo* (round-) dance song.[18] The first three parts have a heterometric, quaternary substructure (bars 1–4, 5–8, 9–12), and the reprise is a half-section, somewhat like a short postlude (bars 13–15). There are cross-rhythms in sections *B* and *C*, moreover, which feature uniquely Hungarian dotted-rhythmic schemata (bars 5–6, 9–10). The last bar ends with the so-called Yugoslav cadence. Bartók commented: 'Has the character of D major, ending on the fifth degree in the L.H. and the second degree in the R.H. This is called a half-cadence, frequently used in Yugoslav music.'[19] The substructure of section *A* is also rounded, as a a_V b a melody-sections. The characteristic Slovak Lydian mode (represented by the pentachord G A B C♯ D in the L.H.) and the major pentachord of the melody, form together a G Lydian/major polymodal hexachord. The polyphonic treatment, in free counterpoint, includes a short ostinato (L.H., bars 1–3).

Exercises: Already mentioned above is the 1944 radio interview in which Bartók discussed his objectives in composing *Mikrokosmos*. Another purpose, he said, 'is to give pieces, piano pieces, which can be used from the very beginning and then going on.' And he stated that the title of the work also indicates 'a world, a musical world for the little ones, for the children'.[20] It therefore seems obvious that the chromaticism in the appended exercises is not intended to promote technical dexterity but to attune untutored ears to Bartókian twelve-note tonality.

Exercise 1*d* contains the ascending Lydian pentachord and the descending Phrygian pentachord, with A as fundamental note. The combined degrees form the A Lydian/Phrygian octachordal polymode or, in traditional terminology, an octave segment of the chromatic scale, bounded by a perfect fifth. Exercise 1*e* is in fifth transposition – the D Lydian/Phrygian octachordal polymode – where the octave segments are bounded by an augmented fourth. Exercise 1*f*, similar to 1*d*, is transposed to G as fundamental note.[21]

Ex. 1 shows the pitch contents of Exercises 1*d* and 1*e*, graphically delineated to indicate their Y-cell (whole-tone tetrachord) and Z-cell (dual-tritone tetrachord) components. These cellular partitions have important melodic, harmonic, and – especially in *Mikrokosmos* – textural (that is, polymodal contrapuntal) functions in Bartók's tonal language.

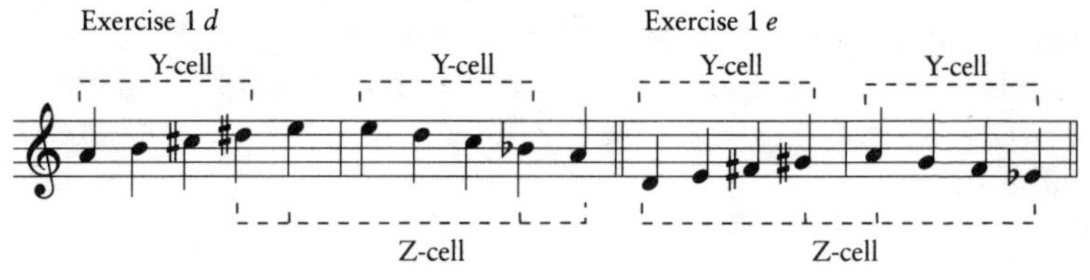

EX. 1

Exercises 2–4 are miniature studies in polymodal counterpoint, in which R.H. pentachords and tetrachords are combined with L.H. inverted forms. Exercise 2*a* has a C Lydian pentachord and C octatonic tetrachord, with C as non-symmetrical axis, resulting in a C Lydian/major polymodal octachord. Exercise 2*b* has the same polymodal pitch content, except that C is no longer axial in function: the R.H. consists of a D major pentachord, beginning on E, that provides the exercise with a minor atmosphere. The first two bars in Exercise 3 show that the mirror (that is, real) inversion of the C major tetrachord results in an octatonic tetrachord. Both tetrachords, however, are octave segments of the modern A harmonic minor scale. Bars 4–5 contain the D minor tetrachord and its mirror inversion, resulting in the symmetrical Dorian mode with the fundamental note as axis of symmetry. Exercise 4 demonstrates that the E major pentachord in the R.H. and its mirror inversion represent octave segments of the A melodic minor scale, with E as axis of symmetry.

'In Lydian Mode' (no.37): This piece is in Romanian *colinde* (Christmas songs) style, but ending with a Yugoslav semicadence on the fifth degree. The imitative free counterpoint, which begins in the R.H. (bar 5), is in emulation of the so-called change song. This song is performed by two alternating choruses of village boys, each group singing the various text stanzas in unison, in such a way that the entry of one group occurs just before the other finishes and thus momentarily creates a contrapuntal effect.[22]

'Melody with Accompaniment' (no.41): As the small-head notation indicates, the tonality is ambiguous: (a) the melody is an octatonic pentachord, the accompaniment is a Lydian pentachord, both pitch collections are octave segments of the D melodic minor (ascending form), and the piece ends on a V–IV plagal semi-cadence; or (b) the two pentachords are partitions of a G Lydian/Mixolydian polymode, ending with a modified V–I authentic cadence.

'In Hungarian Style' (no.43): The style is 'new' Hungarian, having an *A* A^5 *B A* architectonic form, in which *A* consists of thirteen-syllable melody-sections in dotted rhythm.[23] The third melody-section (*B*), however, has a 'mixed'-style 7 + 7-syllable double line, a heterometric structure of Slovak provenance. In version a) the unison melody is Dorian, with D Mixolydian colour (major third, minor seventh degrees) in the third melody-section, and the accompaniment is a D Phrygian/Lydian eleven-note polymode. The contrapuntal version b) is transposed to the G Dorian mode, with the exception that the same F♯ previously met in version a) now transforms the Dorian mode into an octachordal polymode with minor and major thirds.

'Waves' (no.51): The *A B A B* form features octave segments of the D♭ major scale, as pentatonic tetrachords (bars 1–8, 17–25) and major pentachords (bars 9–16, 26–32). The pentatonic scale is of the asymmetrical eastern Russian – central Asian type, consisting of a major second, a minor third and two major seconds.[24] The piece ends on the fifth degree, in the style of a Yugoslav half-cadence.

'Chromatic' (no.54): Ex. 2 shows the skeletal form (principal notes) of the melody, enharmonically extracted to highlight the melodic contour.[25] The basic structure is a Hungarian 'mixed'-style (Slovak, popular art-song provenance) heterometric quaternary,[26] in which the principal notes of the five-syllable melody-sections can be grouped into an octatonic hexachord: E F♯ G A B♭ (A♯) C♯. The octachordal pitch content of the third melody-section (*B*) includes a chromatic hexachord. The twelve-note Phrygian/ Lydian polymode is partitioned into seven semi-

EX. 2

tone tetrachords (beginning with E F F♯ G in bar 1, ending with C♯ D D♯ E in the L.H. of bars 10–11). These chromatic motifs – so-called X-cells – are one of the characteristic cellular structures in Bartók's unique tonal language.

'Line and Point' (no.64): Version a) consists of E minor and G minor octave segments of the G Dorian/major polymode. The juxtaposition of B and B♭ provides a neutral octachord, that is, the tonality wavers between minor and major. The tonal ambiguity is further stressed at the cadence (the last three bars), where the final sonority can be interpreted as an added-note G major chord or, preferably, as a 'consonant' E minor seventh chord.[27] Version b) illustrates an innovative Bartókian device, chromatic compression of diatonic octave segments, which he was later to find during his study of chromatic style in Dalmatian folk music.[28] The compression is in terms of interval size: version a) is based on diatonic pentachords bounded by a perfect fifth; version b), on chromatic tetrachords, bounded by a major third. What appears to be a chromatic octachord, with C as the fundamental note, is a C Phrygian/Lydian octachord. This pitch collection, segmented by means of Bartók's characteristic polymodal counterpoint and liberally sprinkled with X-cells, yields two related Z-cells: the cellular dominant, G D C♯ A♭ (for instance, bars 2–3) and the cellular tonic, C F♯ G C♯ (bars 5–6). The two cells appear together as chromatic trichords in contrary motion (bars 21–2), leading to the augmented triad in the last two bars. The compression also works in the vertical direction for harmonic intervals.

Bartók compares chromatic compression and its converse –

diatonic extension of chromatic octave segments – to the Baroque contrapuntal devices of diminution and augmentation of note values. And he explains that thematic 'extension in range'

> will considerably change the character of a melody, sometimes to such a degree that its relation to the original, non-extended form will be scarcely recognizable. We will have mostly the impression that we are dealing with an entirely new melody. And this circumstance is very good indeed, because we will get variety on the one hand, but the unity will remain undestroyed because of the hidden relation between the two forms.[29]

Volumes Three and Four (nos 67–121)

In these two volumes, beginning with 'Variations' (no.87), Bartók introduces the concept of 'poetically colouring the piano tone', an aspect of technique imparted to him by his Academy teacher, István Thomán. Thomán, a former pupil of Liszt, had acquired the means by direct observation of Liszt's instinctively applied piano touch. Bartók's first use of special tone-colour symbols began in 1907, while he was preparing an edition of Bach's *Das wohltemperierte Klavier*. The following year he applied them to his own works (as in the first Bagatelle Op.6). In 1916 Bartók edited another Bach collection, Twelve Little Piano Pieces, as a supplement to the Bartók–Reschofsky *Piano Method* (1913). Although his Preface to that Bach edition includes an explanatory list of special tone-colour symbols, a similar tabulation was not prepared for *Mikrokosmos*.[30]

'Hommage à J.S.B.' (no.79): This study in polymodal counterpoint is based on the E Lydian/Phrygian octachordal polymode, E F F♯ G G♯ A A♯ B. The figurations begin with E major, minor and pentatonic octave segments as triads and tetrachords, in canonic imitation at the fifth (bars 1–8). The midpoint bar consists of the pentachordal octatonic segment E F♯ G A B♭, followed by chromatic compression to an X-cell, G G♯ A A♯ (bars 10–12).

The last five bars consist of the E Lydian and Phrygian pentachords, also in canonic imitation but at the octave. The clever use of stretto, in which E major and minor triads are superposed as harmonic intervals – major thirds and a perfect fourth (bar 15) – provides a momentary, neutral tonality till the final E major triad is sounded in the last bar.

'Wandering' (no.81):[31] This exemplar of twelve-note linear counterpoint is based on the C Phrygian/Lydian polymode, in which the tonal 'wandering' is the outcome of cellular construction. The first two parts of the architectonic *A B* A_v form have quaternary substructure, but the reprise has only three melody-sections. The upper voice of Part *A* contains the octatonic cell A G F♯ E, extended to D as the boundary fifth (bars 1–2, 8–9), and F E♭ D C, similarly extended to G (bars 4–5, 11–12). The lower voice begins with diatonic octave segments, which are followed by an octatonic pentachord, G F E D C♯, and a Y-cell, D E F♯ G♯ (bars 4–7, 11–14). The interactions of the two voices return the tonic Z-cell, C F F♯ B (bars 1–4, 8–11), and the dominant Z-cell, G C C♯ F♯ (bars 4–6, 11–13). The first half of Part *B* features D, A, C and G Y-cells, each extended to its boundary fifth (that is, Lydian pentachords, bars 14–18), followed by F♯ and E octatonic cells (bars 19–20). The second half (bars 21–7) superposes diatonic and chromatic strands that are based on the rhythmic schemata in *A* (bars 4–6). The attenuated reprise has the tonic Z-cell as its tonal framework, and the last two bars end in Yugoslav style, with a half-cadence on the dominant triad.

'Duet for Pipes' (no.88): In this composition, whose original title was 'Triplets', the D Phrygian/Lydian ten-note polymode is partitioned into the interlocked Z-cell tetrachords that form the D octatonic scale. Rhythmic variety is obtained by grouping quaver triplets with beamed pairs as basic patterns in duple metre, then concatenating them to produce twin-bar rhythmic schemata (e.g. 3, 2 / 2, 3 in bars 1–2 and 2, 3 / 3, 2 in bars 7–8). These divisive subdivisions in $\frac{2}{4}$ also serve as a visual introduction to the contrasting additive ones in $\frac{5}{8}$ time – that is, 3 + 2 and 2 + 3 – that are later met in 'Bulgarian Rhythm' (no.113). The first melody-section contains the Z-cell, C F G♭ B, and its related X-cell, G A♭ A B♭, and ends with the fundamental note D (bar 4). The last melody-section, exclusively octatonic in construction, begins with emphatic rendition of the fundamental Z-cell, D A♭ A E♭ (bars 23–5), which interlocks with the preceding Z-cell to form the complete octatonic scale (bars 29–30), and ends with the tonic minor-seventh chord as a consonant sonority.

'Chromatic Invention' 1, 2 (nos 91, 92): Since the two pieces have more than the shared title in common, they may be considered as a contrasting pair – *Lassú–Friss* (slow–fast) – of Hungarian folk dances, a genre that Liszt emulated in his innovative Hungarian Rhapsodies.[32]

The form of no.91 is *A B* A_v, each part having a ternary sub-structure of *a a b* (bars 1–6) or *a a a* (bars 7–11, 12–17). The twelve-note A Phrygian/Lydian polymode features the octatonic scale, A B C D E♭ F F♯ G♯, as its basic framework.

The theme consists of two tetrachordal partitions of the polymode: the Z-cell, A G♯ E♭ D, followed by its related X-cell, G F♯ F E. The introduction of the Z-cell, F G♭ B C (L.H., bar 3), provides the other, interlocking nodes of the fundamental octatonic scale. The third Z-cell, A B♭ D♯ E (R.H., bar 5) is the inverted form of the first Z-cell; it, too, is followed by a related X-cell, B C C♯ D. The fourth Z-cell, G A♭ C♯ D, and its related X-cell, A B♭ B C (L.H., bars 5–6), also interact with the overlying cellular tetrachords but with a different structural outcome: a ten-note chromatic scale of three interlocking X-cells. Part *B*, from the end of bar 6, consists of descending Z-cells in a whole-tone scale sequence, thus partitioning the twelve-note polymode into its constituent whole-tone scales, B♭ A♭ F♯ E D C and E♭ C♯ B A G F (bars 6–11). In the reprise (bars 12–17) a fifth Z-cell appears in the lower voice, E F A♯ B, with its related but altered X-cell, F♯ G G♯ A♯. The substitution of A♯ for the X-cell fundamental A creates a deceptive cadence on the tritone A♯–E, thus implying *attacca* treatment of the two inventions.

The form of no.92 is *A B C*, each part with varying sub-structures based on the E Phrygian/Lydian octachordal polymode, that is, a chromatic scale bounded by a perfect fifth.The monophonic theme consists of two tetrachordal partitions of the polymode: the Z-cell, E F A♯ B, followed by its related X-cell, A G♯ G F♯ (bars 1–8). It should be noted that the Z-cell is the same tetrachord that made its first appearance in the last three bars of no.91.

Part *B* features contrapuntal variations of the X-cell (bars 9–19). Part *C* juxtaposes the Z-cell and an ostinato of minor seconds (from bar 20). The latter is taken up in unison, five octaves apart, until the Z-cell makes its final appearance to close the piece.

'Harmonics' (no.102): Although Bartók's analysis of this piece includes a reference to Arnold Schoenberg as 'the first to use harmonics in three atonal pieces, Op.11',[33] neither this piece nor any other Bartók work should be construed as atonal. His music 'is always based on a single fundamental tone, in its sections as well as in its whole'.[34] The *A B C* form and its interlude (bars 29–30) coincide with each change of harmonics. Part *A* is in the B Mixolydian mode; Part *B* begins with the Locrian mode, but is chromatically expanded to the twelve-note B Phrygian/Lydian polymode by the addition of 'black-key' pentatonicism (bars 22–7). The interlude features a 'white-key' pentatonic submediant ninth chord, followed by a return to the polymode in the third part. The piece ends with superposition of seemingly unrelated chords: B major against D minor seventh. This combination, however, provides seven nodes of the fundamental octatonic skeleton of the B Phrygian/Lydian polymode (B C D D♯ F F♯ [] A).

As far as the harmonics are concerned, their rendition represents purity in tonal colour, that is, they are devoid of the principal noise elements peculiar to the piano tone. These elements, which are emphasized when the piano is played with the various percussive (that is, key-striking) touch-forms, include the impact of finger against key, key against key bed, hammer against string, and rattling of parts during key descent and ascent.[35]

When *portamento* (*portato*) touch is used – as indicated by slurred staccato marks for the last two D minor seventh chords in no.102 – what would otherwise sound as unresolved dissonances are thereby 'coloured' consonantly.

'Minor and Major' (no.103): A study in rhythm, in binary form, with A as fundamental note of a Dorian/Lydian octachordal polymode. Part *A* begins with four bars of $\frac{9}{8}$ time in additive rhythm as 4 + 5 quavers. The remainder, similar to Bulgarian-influenced, Romanian *colinde* in its change of time, shows the manifold ways that groups of two and three quaver units can be permuted rhythmically. The polymode is partitioned into minor (L.H.) and major (R.H.) pentachordal octave segments. The first half of Part *B* has $\frac{9}{8}$ and $\frac{6}{8}$ in their traditional compound rhythm. The octave segments, too, are reorganized, as irregular pentatonic entities of a major second, minor third and perfect fifth. The double-bar (bar 29) marks the introduction of $\frac{5}{8}$ time as a Bulgarian *pajdushko* dance rhythm. The minor and major octave segments are ingeniously reconfigured, as regularly alternating broken triads and dyads, to produce a cross-rhythm between the upper and lower voices. The piece ends in Yugoslav style, with a semi-cadence on the dominant.

'Wrestling' (no.108): Bartók's impression of 'A picturesque struggle between tones of a minor second'.[36] The formal structure is *A B A* and the tonality is the D Lydian/Phrygian octachordal polymode. In Part *A* the 'struggle' is between the major third drone and the minor third of its encapsulating tetrachord, D E F A, which is resolved by the cadence on the tonic major third (bar 11). The first half of Part *B*, consisting of the Phrygian and Lydian tetrachordal octave segments of the polymode, superposes the minor-second drone and its neighbouring major second, within the boundary of the tritone, E♭–A. The section ends on the drone and its major third (the Neapolitan form of the supertonic, bar 15). In the second half of Part *B* the Lydian augmented-fourth drone is superposed with its neighbouring perfect fourth, within the boundary of the fundamental tritone, D–G♯ (bars 15–19). The two tritones are the Phrygian and Lydian components of the tonic Z-cell, D E♭ G♯ A. The reprise of Part *A* alternates F and F♯ as drones, bounded by the fundamental perfect fifth, D–A. Their emphatic rendition delineates the polymodal octatonic skeleton, D E♭ F F♯ G♯ A (bars 20–29). The appearance of E and G forms the related chromatic tetrachord,

E F F♯ G, that is, the dominant X-cell (bar 30). The struggle ends in a deadlock between the major and minor colour notes, since they are superposed as a 'neutral' chord, D E F♯ A, in the last bar. And this remarkable cadence illustrates the essence of Bartók's system of modal chromaticism, where the individual polymodal degrees 'have absolutely no chordal function; on the contrary, they have a diatonic–melodic function'.[37] In other words they are independent notes which have no interrelation except their relation to the fundamental note. One of the sources from which Bartók drew inspiration for this new tonal language is the instrumental folk music performed on the eastern central-European bagpipe, which he collected in Transylvanian Romanian villages from 1910 to 1914. This bagpipe has three pipes: the tonic drone, the tonic and dominant middle-pipe, and the chanter whose peculiar scale shows alternation of diatonic and chromatic third and fourth degrees, thus forming the polymodal octachord, G A B♭ B♮ C C♯ D E.[38]

'From the Island of Bali' (no.109): This piece joins nos 107 and 108 in a trio of impressionist compositions. It is 'possibly describing a tropical scene. Then, some action or dance takes place in the *risoluto* section, finally returning to the original tempo and mood'.[39] The Bach–Beethoven–Debussy aspect of Bartók's 'East–West Synthesis' concept is exceptionally well illustrated, since the construction also includes invertible counterpoint and other polyphonic devices, and palindromic ('bridge' form) structure, *A B* A_V *B A*, all within the context of modal chromaticism. Part *A*, in free counterpoint, superposes the two interlocking Z-cells, D E♭ G♯ A and C F G♭ B, that constitute the fundamental D octatonic scale (bars 1–11). Part *B* is fashioned from the C Z-cell, with A𝄫 added (bars 12–16); A_V returns to polyphonic texture, in canonic imitation (bars 16–23); and the unisonal reprise of *B* is a non-cellular permutation of the tonic D Z-cell, in which B♭ replaces G♯.

The reprise of Part *A* introduces another, related form of the C Z-cell, C F♯ G D♭ (the two cells share a tritone in common), which expands the tonality to the D Phrygian/Lydian eleven-note polymode. The last four bars contain an unusual, innovative cadence and consist only of the D octatonic scale degrees. Instead of cellular tetrachords these degrees are structured as two minor seventh chords – played with non-percussive, dotted-*tenuto* touch! – and enharmonically labelled to highlight the contrary motion resolution, by half-step, to the tonic. The addition of the staccato F♯ and A♭ in the penultimate bar serves as a sonic memorandum that the piece is, after all, not in the tertian system of functional harmony but in Bartók's system of modal chromaticism.

'Bulgarian Rhythm' 1 (no.113): The so-called Bulgarian rhythm – usually designated by additive time signatures – can be defined as regularly recurring bars which contain asymmetrical groups of very short, basic values.[40] The $\frac{7}{8}$ time signature actually represents the 2+2+3 Bulgarian *ruchenitza* dance rhythm. The melody, according to Bartók, is Hungarian in origin (a variant is published in his *The Hungarian Folk Song*).[41] The source melody and closer variants, however, can be found in Bartók's Bulgarian and Romanian folksong materials.[42] The *A B A* form is established by repetition of the introduction (bars 1–3) as a postlude (bars 24–9). The isorhythmic melody is syncopated by the placement of slurs and staccato marks, which shifts the accent from the first to the third quaver in each bar. Although the first and fourth melody-sections end on D, the emphatic rendition of A and G♯ (the leading note) in the ostinato accompaniment together with B♭ (the Phrygian second degree) in the introduction and postlude indicate that the tonality is an A Phrygian/Lydian polymode.

Volumes Five and Six (nos 122–53)

The last two volumes introduce pieces which are technically and musically quite difficult and were intended to serve as material for professional pianists; in fact, Bartók included most of them in his concert programmes and recordings. Polymodal counterpoint is mostly in four parts, and complex rhythmic structures are encountered by way of diverse Bulgarian rhythms, syncopation, and change of time.

'Village Joke' (no.130): Two-part in form (*A* A_v), with a characteristic Hungarian fifth-transposition substructure (*a* a^5 *b b*). This piece is based on the C Lydian/Phrygian twelve-note polymode. The subtlety of Bartók's humour becomes evident when the first part is played without accidentals: the music sounds traditional and follows the rules of functional harmony. The chromaticism, however, transforms the piece into programme music, as if it were a transcription notated with certain characteristics of 'off-pitch' or 'wrong-note' peasant performance. But these peculiarities are not in the least musical errors; they are essential, polymodal ingredients of rural tonal language! The skeletal structure of the theme and its accompaniment consists of the two, interlocked tritones comprising a diminished seventh chord. Its body is a Y-cell, extended to a Lydian hexachord and followed by a minor tetrachord. In the last half of the first melody-section the inversion and alteration of the skeletal structure encapsulates another Y-cell, D C A♭ B♭, which is extended to a whole-tone pentachord and followed by a major tetrachord (bars 7–12). Meanwhile, the accompaniment unfolds a descending X-cell, C C♭ B♭ A (bars 10–12), followed by – surprise! – a functional IV–I^6_4–V–I cadence. The first melody-section of the second part has its chordal accompaniment fashioned from one octatonic-scale partition of the polymode, C B♭ A G F♯ E E♭ []; the second melody-section, from the other partition, G F E D C♯ B B♭ [] (bars 15–20). The last half of the melody and its repetition are accompanied by interacting semitone and whole-tone dyads, resulting in sequences of the two whole-tone scale partitions of the polymode.

'Fourths' (no.131): The binary melody, in Arab narrow-range chromatic style and Ruthenian *kolomyjka* dance rhythm, appears to be an inverted, repeated-note transformation of the first theme from Bartók's Dance Suite.[43] Although the tune and its five variations are based on the E♭ Phrygian/Lydian twelve-note polymode, the first and last thematic statements have the 'pentatonic feeling' that results from emphatic rendition of black-key (E♭ anhemitone-pentatonic) fourths and tetrachords.[44] In variation 1 the polymodal counterpoint contrasts

R.H. pentatonic and L.H. diatonic fourths, then juxtaposes them as integrative Z-cells, G C D♭ G♭ and A D E♭ A♭ (bar 15). The beamed quavers delineate the hemiolic cross-rhythms in variation 2, which could also be indicated by a $\frac{3}{8}$ time signature for bars 16–18 and 20–22. The section ends with F as final note, that is, in Romanian style on the major second degree. The fourths in variation 3 are constructed from a chromatic octachord: two parallel X-cells, E♭ E F G♭ and B♭ B C D♭. The last four bars have a different pentatonic structure, E♭ F A♭ B♭ D♭, the scale used by various peoples in eastern Russia and central Asia. The *ossia*, however, offers Dorian fourth chords as an alternative ending.

'Major Seconds Broken and Together' (no.132): the form is three-part ($A\ A^4\ A_V$), with quaternary substructure. The piece is based on the G Lydian/Phrygian twelve-note polymode. The chromatic motif in the first melody-section of Part *A* (L.H., bars 1–2) is a closely related transformation of the second phrase of Bartók's fugue subject in Music for Strings, Percussion and Celesta. The accompaniment is derived from pentachordal octave segments of the two whole-tone scales that divide the polymode,[45] in the form of alternating dyads and trichords. The sixth whole-tone is placed among the chromatic degrees of the melody-sections. The piece ends on a 'consonant' tonic seventh chord.

'Bagpipe' (no.138): Bartók commented, 'Use of all three pipes: chanter, tonic and dominant [that is, middle-pipe], and drone. Interesting division of the pipes. Squeaky effects are typical'.[46] A certain class of Romanian bagpipe melodies – and their imitations on the violin and peasant flute – has an indeterminate structure in which a number of two- or four-bar motifs are repeated without fixed form or cadences. Another class includes dance melodies with sections of four $\frac{2}{4}$ bars.[47] The $A\ A_{V1}\ B\ C\ A_{V2}$ rounded form of no.138 is based on the G Dorian/Lydian ten-note polymode. The substructures, on the other hand, are either non-architectonic or indeterminate, as in the case of the above-mentioned melody classes. Part *A* has a four-section (*a a b b*)substructure, whose ostinato accompaniment represents an innovative hemiolic schema in Romanian 'shifted' rhythm. The $\frac{3}{8}$ hemiola in $\frac{2}{4}$ time results from the syncopated, upward-stemmed quaver and crotchet grouping of G and D (the tonic–dominant 'middle-pipe'), which is juxtaposed with the downward-stemmed dotted crotchet or its tied-note equivalent, G (the tonic 'drone' pipe). The hemiola shifts the rhythm so that G and D fall on different $\frac{2}{4}$ subdivisions of each three-bar phrase (L.H., bars 1–27). Part *B* is in the major mode and part *C* adds the Mixolydian seventh degree, F, as a colour note. Both parts are indeterminate in structure, consisting of repeated motifs which are accompanied by different ostinatos (bars 28–51). The extended reprise of part *A* is in the G Lydian/Dorian ten–note polymode, and the principal notes in the last two cadential bars, G A C D F, represent the eastern Russian – central Asian type of anhemitone-pentatonic scale.

'Free Variations' (no.140): Excepting the third variation, which is in quaternary form, the theme and variations are binary sub-structures. The theme and first three variations are separated by an interlude, and an unusually long postlude follows the fourth variation. The D Lydian/Phrygian twelve-note polymode emphasizes repeated-note ostinatos on the first and fifth degrees, in emulation of the tonic drone and tonic–dominant 'middle-pipe' of the Eastern European bagpipe.[48] The change of time throughout the composition is another manifestation of its Romanian folk-music style. The theme consists of a descending, octatonic tetrachord, G♯ F♯ F E♭, with a superposed ostinato, A (the dominant), extending the scale to a tonic Z-cell, D E♭ G♯ A (L.H., bars 1–7). The dotted-rhythm schema that closes the theme is accompanied in the upper part by a descending, related X-cell, B♭ B C C♯. This tetrachord, however, is appended to the superposed ostinato, D (the tonic), thus forming a tonic X-cell, D C♯ C B. Then follows the transitional interlude, further extending the modal chromaticism to twelve notes (bars 10–12).

In the first variation a dominant Z-cell, A B♭ D♯ E, results from inversion of the preceding tonic Z-cell, in which the ostinato common note, A, serves as axis of symmetry. The cellular continuity is maintained by the following, related X-cell, F F♯ G G♯

(bars 13–20). An expanded ten-bar interlude (bars 24–33) leads to the second variation, in which the theme and its inversion are in canonic imitation and *kolomyjka* dance rhythm (bars 34–41). Another ten-bar interlude, also based on the dominant Z-cell (bars 34–51), is followed by the octatonic third variation in quaternary form and slow tempo. The last variation is a reprise of the opening section (bars 65–72); the ten-bar postlude is based on X-cell partitions of the chromatic scale; and the last two bars juxtapose an octatonic tetrachord and an X-cell in contrary motion so that both tetrachords end on the dominant – as a semi-cadence in Yugoslav style.

'From the Diary of a Fly' (no.142): About this 'diary' Bartók commented,

> I wanted to depict the desperate sound of a fly's buzz, when getting into a cobweb. He was buzzing about and didn't see the spider web. Then he is caught in the web (*Agitato*: 'woe, a cobweb'!), but manages to get himself free before he is eaten, and he escapes. A happy (*con gioia*) ending.[49]

The piece is a programmatic study in cellular formations, with F as fundamental note of a Phrygian/Lydian twelve-note polymode, and its five-section form follows the action described by the composer. Section 1 begins on the second degree of the F major trichord, as the R.H. enters with the G♭ major tetrachord, together forming a Phrygian X-cell, G♭ G A♭ A. Although the parts have C and C♭ as common tones, they are discrete segments of the polymode and in pentatonic organization – their superposition at a minor second creates a chromatic 'buzzing'.[50] The second half of the section is transposed a whole-tone higher, so that the lower part forms a G major tetrachord in augmented values, and the upper part, a G♭ Y-cell. These superposed tetrachords expand the fundamental polymode to a chromatic octachord (bars 13–25).

The first two bars of section 2 repeat those of section 1 but a whole-tone lower, resulting in a different X-cell, F♭ F G♭ G, with B♭ and A as common tones. The parts expand in contrary motion till a ten-note fundamental polymode is formed (bars 26–34). The linear counterpoint in the second half of this section masks the ingenious cellular structure, in which the twelve-note polymode is partitioned into a two-bar series of three ascending X-cells in the lower part, from F♯ to F, and three ascending octatonic tetrachords in the upper part, from F to F♯ (bars 35–40). The contrapuntal treatment can also be construed as a series of six ascending X-cells, formed by the interaction between upper and lower parts of each bar. Simultaneously, moreover, the sustained notes of the individual parts divide the chromatic scale into its F♯ (upper part) and F (lower part) whole-tone octave segments.

Whichever interpretation is taken, the progression is interrupted by a Y-cell, D E G♭ A♭ (bars 41–2). Then follows a non-serial X-cell, D E♭ E F – the buzzing fly? – which is repeated as an encapsulated nucleus of the subdominant Z-cell, B♭ E♭ E A – the cobweb? – to end the section and the flight (bars 43–8). The *agitato* section, depicting the fly's struggle to free itself, extends this cellular complex to a symmetrical hexachord by the addition of C♭ and G♯ (bars 49–51). In the next three bars the Z-cell outer degrees, A and B♭, are discarded – shredding of the cobweb? – and thus transform the pitch collection into contiguous octatonic tetrachords, with the same nuclear X-cell and dual axis, B C D E♭/E F G A♭ (note the enharmonic equivalents). At the crescendo the outer degrees are again discarded, but D♭ and F♯ are added to transform the collection into two discrete X-cells. The transformation, moreover, creates a dominant Z-cell – escape from the cobweb? – with the same dual axis at its core, C D♭ D E♭/E F F♯ G (bars 55–9).

The more intricate construction of the first half of the *con gioia, leggero* section is similar to the second half of section 2, with regard to whole-tone octave segments. In the present case, however, there is a succession of descending Y-cells a tritone apart, on A♭ and D in the upper part, G and C♯ or D♭ in the lower part (bars 59–68). These four degrees constitute the supertonic Z-cell framework which interrelates the two otherwise discrete whole-tone octave segments. There is, moreover, another relational tetrachord in the guise of a diminished seventh chord, whose tritones serve as emphatic 'foreign' notes which are interposed between each Y-cell: A or E♭ in the upper part, F♯ or C in the lower part. Here, too, the linear counterpoint can be analysed on the vertical plane as a series of X-cells – beginning with A♭ G F♯ F, ending with E E♭ D D♭ – whose descent from bar to bar also maps whole-tone octave segments. Now the above-mentioned 'foreign' notes intersect with X-cell degrees as gapped (trichordal) Z-cells on A, F♯, E♭, and C (bars 61–2, 63–5). In the last half of the *con gioia, leggero* section the upper and lower parts are also superposed as a series of ascending X-cells and chromatic pentachord, all within the framework of the inverted tonic Z-cell, C F F♯ B.

The first half of the last section has superposition of diatonic and chromatic pentatonic scales on D (lower part) and E♭ (upper part) in their symmetrical, Hungarian form, as indicated by the sustained axial notes G and A♭, respectively (bars 76–87). The remaining bars consist of superposed F Lydian and F Phrygian tetrachords, ending in Romanian style on G, the major second degree of the polymode. Is this the diary of a Transylvanian fly?

NOTES

1 *Goethe's Faust*, tr. Walter Kauffmann, New York (Doubleday), 1961, pp. 190–91, lines 1801–2. Bartók underscored lines 1806–9 in his personal copy of *Faust* (MTA BH).

2 See Serge Moreux, *Béla Bartók*, London (Harvill), 1953, pp. 91–2.

3 See my essay, 'The Impact of Italian Baroque Music on Bartók's Music', in *Bartók and Kodály Revisited*, ed. György Ránki, Budapest (Akadémiai Kiadó), 1987, pp. 183–97.

4 See my essay, 'History of Bartók's *Mikrokosmos*', *Journal of Research in Music Education*, vol.7, no.2 (Fall 1959), pp. 185–96.

5 In 1954 I corresponded with Reschofsky about his work with Bartók. He informed me that Bartók asked Zoltán Kodály to contribute music theory materials, but these were not provided in time for the publication.

6 I am indebted to Péter Bartók for this information (personal interview, December 1988).

7 John Vinton, 'Toward a Chronology of the *Mikrokosmos*', *SM*, vol.8 (1966), pp. 41–69.

8 Nos 81, 137, 146.

9 See the selected listing in Elliott Antokoletz, *Béla Bartók: A Guide to Research*, New York (Garland), 1988, p. 338.

10 See Benjamin Suchoff, *Béla Bartók and a Guide to the 'Mikrokosmos'*,

Ann Arbor (UMI), 1957, p. 107.

11 See *BBE*, p. 432 (emphasis added). Bartók listed Fourteen Bagatelles Op.6, Suite for piano Op.14, and the Sonata for piano.

12 See further my book, *Guide to Bartók's 'Mikrokosmos'*, New York (Da Capo), 1983, and the chapter 'Fusion of National Styles: Piano Literature, 1908–11' in this *Companion*. A comprehensive analysis of *Mikrokosmos* and other Bartók works will be found in Benjamin Suchoff and Elliott Antokoletz, *Sources of Bartók's System of Composition*, currently in preparation.

13 Suchoff, 'History of Bartók's *Mikrokosmos*', p. 192.

14 See, respectively, *BBE*, p. 363, and my essay, 'Ethnomusicological Roots of Bartók's Musical Language,' *The World of Music*, vol.29, no.1 (1987), pp. 53–4, 59–60.

15 *SV*.i, melody no.128.

16 See *BBE*, p. 376.

17 For descriptions of these cells see the earlier chapters in this *Companion* by Antokoletz and by Suchoff.

18 North Slav (Slovak) sources can be found in Bartók, *SV*.ii, Type 21, melodies nos 700 and 701. The South Slav (Yugoslav) source, a Slovak variant, is found in *YFM*.iv, melody no.1365.

19 Suchoff, *Guide to Bartók's 'Mikrokosmos'*, p. 29.

20 Suchoff, *Béla Bartók and a Guide to the 'Mikrokosmos'*, p. 107.

21 See *BBE*, p. 367.

22 *RFM*.iv, p. 25.

23 cf. nos 15 and 17.

24 *BBE*, p. 364.

25 cf. no.55.

26 cf. *HFS*, p. 284, melody no.246.

27 cf. the cadence to no.66.

28 See *BBE*, pp. 382–3.

29 *BBE*, pp. 381–2; cf. no.112, bars 32–44. See also Bartók's Music for Strings, Percussion and Celesta (1936), where the opening chromatic theme is extended to diatonic 'scarcely recognizable' form in the second movement (bars 1–7), and to close variant relationship in the fourth movement (bars 203–9).

30 See my chapter 'Fusion of National Styles: Piano Literature, 1908–11' in this *Companion* for related discussion.

31 The $\frac{2}{2}$ time signature, reinstated in *The New Definitive Edition* (1987) of *Mikrokosmos*, made its first appearance as a typographical error in the original 1940 publication. Following my comparative study of the *Mikrokosmos* manuscripts, the obviously correct $\frac{2}{4}$ signature was substituted in reprinted editions. See my essay, 'Errata in the *Mikrokosmos* Publication', *Piano Quarterly Newsletter*, no.16 (Summer 1956), p. 11.

32 See *BBE*, p. 503.

33 Suchoff, *Guide to Bartók's 'Mikrokosmos'*, p. 89.

34 *BBE*, p. 371.

35 See Otto Ortmann, *The Physiological Mechanics of Pianoforte Technique*,

New York (Dutton), 1925, pp. 178–82, 231–4. My application of Ortmann's findings to Bartók's principles of piano playing and pedagogy can be found in Suchoff, *Béla Bartók and a Guide to the 'Mikrokosmos'*, pp. 56–68.

36 Suchoff, *Guide to Bartók's 'Mikrokosmos'*, p. 95.

37 *BBE*, p. 376.

38 See *RFM*.i, pp. 19–23, and melodies nos 558–60.

39 Suchoff, *Guide to Bartók's 'Mikrokosmos'*, p. 95

40 See *BBE*, pp. 46–7, where Bartók writes: 'For the present all we know is that it is best known and most widespread on Bulgarian soil. For this reason, even if it should someday be discovered that its origin is not Bulgarian, we may rightly call it Bulgarian rhythm.'

41 Suchoff, *Guide to Bartók's 'Mikrokosmos'*, p. 95; *HFS*, melody no.119.

42 See Suchoff, 'Ethnomusicological Roots of Bartók's Musical Language', p. 58, and *RFM*.ii, melodies nos 178d, 178e.

43 cf. no.62; see also *BBE*, p. 377, and *HFS*, p. 73.

44 Suchoff, *Guide to Bartók's 'Mikrokosmos'*, p. 114.

45 cf. no.136.

46 Ibid., p. 120; cf. *Mikrokosmos*, no.108.

47 *RFM*.i, pp. 50–2 and 659–69. The apparent source melody of the present composition is no.278a (p. 261), a four-section (*aabb*) dance tune played on the peasant flute.

48 cf. nos 108 and 138.

49 Suchoff, *Guide to Bartók's 'Mikrokosmos'*, p. 125.

50 cf. no.63, 'Buzzing'.

CHAMBER MUSIC

15

Youthful Chamber Works

GÜNTER WEISS-AIGNER

Bartók was fourteen years old when he first ventured, with a violin sonata, into the realm of chamber music. By that time he had already written more than thirty piano works, an experience which stood him in good stead for his writing in this new genre. This early violin sonata is the fifth in a second series of works associated with Pozsony (now Bratislava in Slovakia), and although it showed the influence of that town's stimulating musical climate – one predominating with German influence – the instrumental concept also contained living resonances of those Beethoven sonatas which Bartók, as a twelve-year-old, had come to know in the cultural backwater of Beszterce (now Bistriţa in Romania). There he had frequently accompanied the young amateur violinist Sándor Schönherr. Bartók's Violin Sonata (DD37, 1895)[1] was written in the 'Beethovenian' key of C minor and extended the line of development initiated in his Piano Sonata in G minor (DD32) during the preceding year. However, it approached its Classical model with a more succinct handling of richly gestural motivic forms and forged new ways of generating tension – in contrast to the merely formulaic use of rhythms and stereotypical periodic structures of so much of his childhood composition. In the first movement, as a result of its soaring melodic gestures the *cantabile* secondary theme (drawn from an old and widespread recitative formula) comes close – as though by chance – to the movement's principal theme (Ex. 1). The starting point for the other movements is a supranational type of 'descending' melody, which moves from the tonic triad's degrees of the third or fifth downwards through the root to the lower fifth. Bartók was thoroughly

EX. 1

familiar with this strategy, having only recently employed it on two occasions in his piano Fantasie (DD34). In his Violin Sonata's second, slow movement his employment of it is reminiscent of the *adagio* theme in Beethoven's 'Spring' Sonata. (Even as late as 1937 Bartók would give the soloist in his Second Violin Concerto a similar melody to play). In the final movement, too, a similar 'descending' melody appears both in the *moderato* introduction and in the following *allegro vivace* theme.

The only proof of the existence of Bartók's next chamber works is a list of compositions he drew up while living in Pozsony.[2] Several individual pieces for violin were listed – including two fantasies (DD40, 41) of 1896 – as well as two string quartets (DD42, 43, both 1896) and a Piano Quintet (DD46, 1897). His following chamber work, the Violin Sonata in A major (DD49) has, however, survived. It was written during November–December 1897 and is notable for the way in which Bartók has developed thematic relationships between the individual three movements to create a coherent gestural and emotional atmosphere in the work. The change in Bartók's compositional technique over the two years since his C minor sonata is unmistakable. In place of motifs tentatively forcing their way upwards, but held back by rests (see Ex. 1), we now hear in the main theme of the opening Allegro an arching *cantabile* melody, which is immediately intensified by a sequential shift upwards (Ex. 2).

EX. 2

The chromatically rich piano accompaniment also heralds Bartók's decisive move towards Romanticism, in particular towards the spirit of Schumann.

Bartók's Violin Sonata in A major offers remarkable insights into the growing boldness of the composer's compositional thinking at the age of nearly seventeen. The work presents rhythmic contrasts between the violin and piano parts, as at the end of the first movement's exposition where he establishes a syncopated type of motif in the piano part, foreshadowing his motivic practice during his following period of confrontation with the style of Hungarian national Romanticism. So, too, in the third movement his main theme presents a contrast between the more Mendelssohnian, gently rippling figurations of the piano and the Schumannesque $\frac{3}{4}$-metre hemiolas of the violin's part. Tonally, a new boldness is seen in the first movement's development, which begins with a forthright shift of key from C♯ to C major. Formally, the work is interesting for its combination of elements of sonata and rondo forms in the finale.

During the following year, 1898, Bartók's compositional lines of development culminated in two remarkable chamber works: the Piano Quartet in C minor (DD52) and the String Quartet in F major (DD56). The Piano Quartet was written during March–July, although it was based in part on earlier sketches. It reveals the increasing influence of Brahms, especially upon Bartók's piano writing (Ex. 3). The musical argument, from the outset, is tighter than in his previous writing. The opening eight-bar statement for the piano shows this new, more condensed Brahmsian attitude. The work is rooted, none the less, in a basic material comparable to that of his A major Violin Sonata of 1897. The scalar melodic model of the later work's initial motif (as marked in Ex. 3) and its sequential repetition is from bar 3 sharpened in its rhythm and articulation through the ascending forays,

EX. 3

producing a level of intensity only matched during the development of the corresponding movement of the Violin Sonata. The subsequent pendulum-like, imitative oscillations provide an even clearer reference to a type of melodic movement already familiar from his Violin Sonata, and also from the Trio section of his Scherzo (Fantasie) for piano (DD50, 1897). Much of the remainder of the movement is dominated by bar 1's dotted rhythmic pattern, with a recollection of Beethoven's 'fate' motif overtaking him as the movement draws to a close. The second movement, a scherzo, is entirely in the spirit of Brahms, with the initial rhythmic impulse being drawn from the finale's theme in Brahms's Piano Sonata in C major Op.1. Other Brahms works recalled are the Horn Trio Op.40, Piano Trio in C major Op.87, and even the Piano Concerto no. 2 in B♭ major Op.83 (although the transmission here may be via Dohnányi's Op.1, his Piano Quintet). The third movement (Adagio) also shows the clear influence of Brahms, in particular his Piano Quartet in C minor Op.60. The theme of Bartók's finale (Ex. 4) mirrors the outline of a popular Hungarian melody before culminating in a formula which anticipates the stylistic world created five years hence in his symphonic poem *Kossuth*.

EX. 4

Hungarian and Western elements come together in this movement. Again the main influence is that of Brahms, who not only provides the model for the trio-like central section but also for

Bartók's principal theme, where the melodic outline and dotted rhythmic figure point to the opening theme of Brahms's Violin Sonata in D minor Op.108. Formally, the movement combines sonata form with a series of variations, which are already hinted at by the subsidiary theme's *cantabile* reconstruction of the opening's melodic outline.

As with the Piano Quartet in C minor, the String Quartet in F major (DD56) was based on earlier sketches. Its predominating influence was more that of Schumann, however. This is seen in the opening theme (Ex. 5), which follows an impulse similar to that of the concluding theme of Schumann's First Symphony, the 'Spring'.

I, 1-8 (violin I)

EX. 5

The Piano Quartet's gestural urge here seeks new forms of expression in the syncopated leaps of bars 4–8, which later, at bar 27, take on a dotted character, and at bars 37–41, at the height of the thematic restatement, start to assume a lively triplet figuration. The subsidiary theme, starting at bar 63, introduces a new formulation of melodically widening intervals, the chromatic descent of which is clearly an extension of techniques seen in the Adagio of Bartók's Three Piano Pieces (DD53), composed some months earlier. The Schumannesque background to Bartók's quartet is reinforced later in the subsidiary thematic section (from bar 77), where resonances of the Fourth Symphony in D minor are clearly to be heard. The proportions of the opening sonata movements in Bartók's three extant chamber works of 1897–8 are very similar. In each instance the main theme's exposition follows the principle of repeated entry and continuing development by splitting up the theme's various motifs and using sequences frequently. Among Bartók's personal compositional advances, however, is the introduction of polyphony into the interplay of an increasing number of instrumental voices (more so in the piano, rather than the string, quartet).

The second movement of the String Quartet in F major, an Adagio, throws remarkable light on the associative nature of Bartók's thinking. The main melody harks back to the sequential opening motif of the Violin Sonata in A major (see Ex. 2), while the secondary theme, starting at bar 31 and then from bar 42 developing to its climax (Ex. 6), is influenced by the theme in the corresponding position in the Piano Quartet.

EX. 6

Its oscillating rhythm is soon (bar 46) caught up in congested syncopations and soaring melodic gestures, which then (bar 48) lead back to motivic material derived from the first movement. In Bartók's third movement only the trio shows signs of the inspiration of Schumann; the opening octave leaps in dotted rhythm appear to echo the Scherzo from Beethoven's Ninth Symphony, while the syncopated waltz-like model creates the impression of a Czech *furiant*. The finale, too, shows further reworking of ideas of syncopation under the influence of Beethoven, in particular his Allegretto from the second 'Razumovsky' Quartet Op.59 no. 2.

As well as these fully extant compositions, a number of isolated movements or fragments of chamber music have survived from Bartók's later school years, although their dating and context remain uncertain. They, too, intrude upon that area of contact between Eastern and Western styles which was taking an increasingly prominent position in Bartók's overall output.

In the autumn of 1899 Bartók commenced his studies at the Academy of Music in Budapest. There the overtly academic and conservative teaching of composition inhibited his creative urge, and it was only in 1902, with the stirring experience of hearing Richard Strauss's symphonic poem *Also sprach Zarathustra*, that any serious dedication to composition returned. He wrote a number of shorter violin pieces in 1902, such as the Duo (DD69) and Andante (DD70), but it was his Violin Sonata in E minor (DD72) of 1903[3] that first showed, in the medium of chamber music, the depth of Bartók's new commitment to the stylistic renewal of Hungarian national music. As with the piano pieces written at this time, this sonata reflects the critical confrontation which he was bringing about between Straussian 'Western' and traditional 'Eastern' styles. While presenting these elements in opposition to each other he also tried, repeatedly, to incorporate them into a specifically Hungarian synthesis, of which his symphonic poem *Kossuth* (1903) is perhaps the most compelling example. The very indication 'molto rubato' at the beginning of the opening Allegro serves notice of Bartók's overtly Hungarian aspirations. Both his initial themes, in their different ways, also serve that purpose: the first (Ex. 7), from bar 3, is inspired by the declamatory style of the national *verbunkos*, or 'recruitment dance'; the second (Ex. 8), which varies material found in the first of Bartók's Four Piano Pieces of 1903, is somewhat more regular in its movement, although, like the opening theme, ends with the characteristic 'Hungarian' fermata involving a rising fourth interval.

EX. 7

The first theme (Ex. 7) is already on its way to becoming a theme from *Kossuth*. It is based on the 'gypsy scale' (with a sharpened

EX. 8

fourth degree, D♯), the descending line of which produces numerous variants, not only in this movement but also in *Kossuth* and the piano Rhapsody Op.1. Characteristic, too, of Bartók's striving for a Hungarian stylistic synthesis is his contrapuntal handling of his themes. With the return of his first theme at bar 32, now performed full of emotion, he launches into the exposition, following in the footsteps of Liszt, in particular the Piano Sonata in B minor which Bartók knew so well as a pianist. By bar 120 he has turned this first theme into the starting-point of a chromatically condensed, five-part fugato. The stream of polyphonic motifs drives the music increasingly upwards to bar 150, and then initiates its descent towards the reprise (bar 157). In a dynamically analogous process, the first section of the development (bars 81–119) moves from the first to the second of the opening themes, with a related modulation from A minor to its tonal 'opposite' E♭ major.[4] Bartók ends the movement with the 'Hungarian fourth' formula first seen at the fermata points of both opening themes.

The Violin Sonata's second movement, in A minor, is constructed of six variations on a two-part *andante* theme, the last of which produces a cyclic conclusion. The first pair of variations adopts the traditional rhapsody sequence of *lassú* (flexible, 'gypsy' soloist figures interacting with 'cimbalom' passages on the piano, as from bar 34) and *friss,* or *csárdás* (more rhythmically strict and faster writing, as from bar 65). The second pair of variations is characterized by chromatically rich stylistic experiments influenced by the later writing of Wagner and Liszt. In Bartók's fifth variation he explores the depressive mood associated with the sense of national tragedy in *Kossuth* (which he had written by this stage in the year).[5] He takes Lisztian models but far exceeds them in the resultant depth of despair.

The energetic, *csárdás*-like final Rondo (completed some months before the second movement) follows a similar tendency towards syncopation, adapting itself gradually to the dotted rhythm of the *verbunkos*. Bartók further experiments with the melodic and harmonic manifestations of the 'gypsy scale', whose raised fourth, A♯, featured prominently in the very first bar of the movement. Through numerous processes of thematic variation and Lisztian chordal sequences Bartók produces a most extensive movement, of 625 bars, again ending with the 'Hungarian', rising fourth figure.

After completing the Violin Sonata Bartók resumed his concert activities, travelling to Berlin in October 1903 to develop his then promising career as a pianist. There, in Berlin, he began to compose his Piano Quintet (DD77), although he did not complete the work until July of the following year, when he was staying at Gerlicepuszta, in Slovakia. With this piece Bartók again projected his ideal of national Romanticism and sought an even closer integration of 'Western' and 'Eastern' influences. The stylistic centre of the work, as far as Hungarian influence is concerned, is the third movement, an Adagio which – in tight connection with the following finale – emphasizes the rhapsodic progression of *lassú–friss* already seen in the first pair of variations in his most recent Violin Sonata's slow movement. Both sections of Bartók's Adagio are linked, monothematically, with the first movement, and are manifestations of his broader principle of recharacterization of the same thematic material, which can be traced back to connections within his Symphony of 1902. The main thematic framework for the work is formed by changing formulations of a supranational melodic core, which also adopt the Hungarian version based on the (gypsy) minor scale. With this Bartók associates various tonal aims. The lively C-based *csárdás* theme of the finale (from bar 1084) and its 'augmented' version in the first movement (bar 3), immediately following the opening in F♯ minor, forge connections with the 'distorted' *adagio* version, based on the whole-tone scale, found at bars 963–5. The tonal importance of F♯ (usually, minor), seen here, is embedded in the work's overall plan. It is also seen in the thematically identical secondary themes of the outer movements[6] and the main theme of the second, Scherzo movement, from bar 262. But these various interrelated themes are held together by a further connection which extends to the Adagio as well. All of them oscillate around F♯'s fifth degree, C♯. The same is even true of the jaunty melody which forms the central axis of the Scherzo's Trio (from bar 545), and which is itself a varied form of outer-movement themes.

The outer movements function, then, at the broadest level of musical architecture, as a form of exposition and reprise to the composition. In this perspective, the fugato of the final movement (from bar 1337) – locally evolved from the initial expression of that movement's secondary theme – can be seen also to correspond with the similar passage in the opening movement, although that passage has been derived from one of its movement's side themes. While the Scherzo, with its multipartite, mirror-like structure, heralds the 'bridge form' seen in several of Bartók's mature works, the Adagio develops the works crucial 'Hungarianness' in two ways: declamatory pathos, developed in several waves of intensity from bar 961, and 'gypsy' improvisation, which rises up painfully from mysterious depths (from bar 1047), anticipating Bartók's further exploitation of the technique in his following piano Rhapsody. That Rhapsody is also foreshadowed, in its motivic procedures, by this Adagio's particular use of the syncopated dotted figure, which involves a typically Straussian emphasis on the upbeat followed by a dying away into a new 'Hungarian' formulation.[7] The influence of Strauss is even clearer at bar 1008, where the music soars upwards from an originally 'Hungarian' ground.

Bartók himself played the piano part at the Piano Quintet's première in Vienna on 21 November 1904 with the Prill–Jeral Quartet. Although he suppressed nearly all of his pre-opus compositions he did continue to play this work in later life, in 1910 and in 1921, but he was truly shocked at the latter performance by how well this youthful work was received in comparison with his more mature compositions. At the time it was believed that he had destroyed the score. It was, however, preserved in his Hungarian estate and published by Zeneműkiadó of Budapest in 1970.

NOTES

1 This work, as with most of Bartók's juvenile compositions, remains unpublished.
2 See Denis Dille, *Thematisches Verzeichnis der Jugendwerke Béla Bartóks, 1890–1904*, Budapest (Akadémiai Kiadó), 1974.
3 Published in *DB*.i, pp. [144]–[179] and *DB*.ii, pp. 175–200.
4 Note a similar tonal process in nos 1, 2 and 4 of the Four Piano Pieces.
5 cf. the passage from bar 177 with that from bar 418 in *Kossuth*.
6 See I, bar 17, and IV, bar 1230.
7 See, for instance, bars 1037–8.

16

Early String Quartets

JÁNOS KÁRPÁTI

Bartók's First String Quartet Op.7 is closely related to the posthumous First Violin Concerto. He composed that concerto for the young violinist Stefi Geyer between 1 July 1907 and 5 February 1908. Its very first sketches already contain germs of the quartet, even though the quartet was not completed until January 1909, many months after the concerto had been finished. The connection is evident, however, not only from the chronology but also from the musical material of the two pieces. The double leap of a sixth outlined by the two violins in the first bar of the quartet has a close kinship with the theme of the Violin Concerto's second movement. Bartók himself made this connection explicit in his last, unpublished letter to Stefi Geyer: 'I have begun a quartet; the first theme is the theme of the [Violin Concerto's] 2nd movement: this is my funeral dirge'.[1]

The quartet's first movement was, then, born as a dirge, expressing Bartók's grief at the recent rejection of his overtures of love towards Stefi Geyer. It is the concentrate of the Violin Concerto in a dual sense. While the outline of its opening theme is clearly related to the theme of the concerto's second movement, the slow tempo, polyphonic texture and sensitively Romantic harmonic construction link it to the first, 'Ideal' movement of the concerto. These are the two slow movements in which the young Bartók came closest to a yearning and resigned musical tone, which was inspired by his reading of Nietzsche and Schopenhauer and aptly expressed in the sensitive harmony and meandering melodic writing. Under such influences it was natural that the composer should express his passionate affection with the same musical character as his torment, resignation and longing for death. Musically, his direct model was Wagner; in fact, the beginning of the quartet's first movement can be taken as a kind of counterpart to the *Tristan* Prelude (with an upward sixth in the latter and a downward sixth in the former). Bartók's youthful enthusiasm for Wagner had found its way by this time into his compositions.

The first movement also shows signs of other influences. Its imitative counterpoint echoes Beethoven, especially the fugue-like opening of his String Quartet in C♯ minor Op.131. At first the slowly unfolding imitative structure suggests a fugue in Bartók's piece, too, but it later becomes clear that a wholly individual solution has been found: the parts entwine in closely knit pairs. In this counterpoint both the Bachian archetype and the direct example of Beethoven fade into the background; the parts interlace like the winding ornaments best resembling the trailing plants typical of the new style in fine art. If anything exists that can be labelled musical art nouveau, then Bartók's First Quartet is surely one of the best examples. In it ornamentation becomes content.

This music is fairly eclectic in character. In the middle section of the first movement, for instance, some typically French chordal sequences appear, strongly reminding one of Ravel's *Ma mère l'oye*, yet this possible model was only being composed at this time and Bartók could not have known it. Another surprising aspect is that these Ravelian chords are played above a typical cello melody *à la Kodály*. Bartók anticipates here the specific sound quality, based on the melodic lines of Hungarian folksongs, that would later become associated with Kodály, but which Bartók himself would never use again. It is not surprising, however, that the French sound and Kodály's intonation are so strongly intertwined: Kodály's individual melodic construction was a result precisely of his conscious, deliberate orientation towards French music.

In the middle section of the first movement a fundamental change in character takes place, which also entails a change in construction: strict polyphony gives way to homophony and a melodic–chordal relationship. At the end of the movement, however, the fugue-like polyphony of the opening returns, now transposed an octave higher into an 'ethereal sphere'. This high, floating music also appears in the concerto's 'Ideal' movement and in other movements of the quartet, and represents a tone of 'transfiguration', excellent examples of which are found in Richard Strauss's and Schoenberg's music. The young Bartók also was trying to find solace in such music.

After the condensed, 'transfigured' repeat the movement remains open both tonally and thematically, and progresses into the next, faster movement without interruption. The gradual transition is carefully planned. The melodic lines, moving in parallel thirds, keep rising and falling as the tempo accelerates step by step to the *allegretto*, reached at bar 21 of the new movement. This second movement unfolds a sonata construction permeated by the monothematic tendencies of the late Beethoven quartets. The central idea of not just this movement, but also the entire quartet, is a four-note motif. It first appears in complete form in the framing theme of the second movement (Ex. 1a).

EX. 1

Immediately afterwards, the first subject's ostinato accompaniment is formed from its mirror inversion (Ex. 1b). Related to

Ex. 1b is the emphatic main theme of the finale (Ex. 1c) and its scherzando-like and transitional fugato theme (Ex. 1d).

The melodic root common to all these themes is a four-note motif in which a 'clinging' melodic step is followed by a larger interval and another close step in the opposite direction. It is not difficult to recognize in this pattern a monothematic idea sometimes found in the late Beethoven quartets, such as the introduction to the String Quartet in A minor Op.132 (Ex. 2a), or the theme of the *Grosse Fugue* Op.133 (Ex. 2b).

EX. 2

When viewed from this angle, we realize that the melodic construction of the first movement of Bartók's quartet is also determined by this pattern, although more secretly, being hidden in the long, seemingly endless part-writing, as demonstrated in Ex. 3. In the second movement the solemnity of the previous 'funeral dirge' begins to dissolve; some chilling, weirdly objective moments appear (as from bar 105, with the drumming of the cello against a superimposed whole-tone scale), and some grotesque patterns constructed of two-note figures. The mood is still passionate, however, and sometimes heated or sensitive. The movement ends in a high register, with the same 'transfigured' tone as found in the opening movement.

The third, final movement of the quartet (Allegro vivace) is preceded by an 'Introduzione', which forms a bridge in both tonal and character terms. The main source of its material is a solitary *recitativo* melody, again reminiscent of Beethoven's Op.132 Quartet with the short recitative introduction to its final

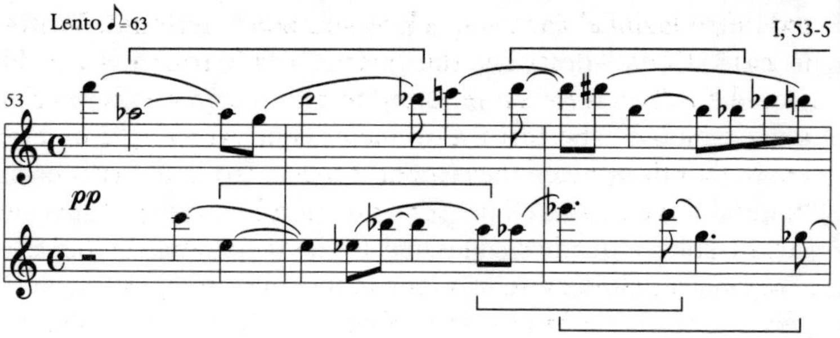

EX. 3

movement. Bartók's cello recitative melody (Ex. 4a), however, is of a typically Hungarian character, recalling the well-known nineteenth-century art song 'Just a fair girl' by Elemér Szentirmai (Ex. 4b).

EX. 4

It might seem odd that Bartók here practically quotes a popular art song, especially as by this time he had embarked upon his folksong collecting tours in Transylvania. One possible explanation is a bent for programme-like references and travesty, techniques which were not alien to Bartók's compositional method.[2]

If this quartet is the musical outcome of Bartók's 'recovery' from the crisis of his love for Stefi Geyer, then it can be assumed that the reference to 'Just a fair girl' in the strange 'dialogue' of the 'Introduzione' carries mocking, parodic overtones. Writing in 1918, Kodály described this quartet as a 'retour à la vie'. He would hardly have been referring just to the gradually accelerating tempo of the three movements, but rather felt, or even knew, that they traced the road of recovery from the crisis of the 'funeral dirge'. Bartók's parodic intention in quoting this popular art song is further suggested by his emphatic reference to true, ancient Hungarian folksong in the following movement. In July 1907, after a brief visit to Stefi Geyer's family in the town of Jászberény, Bartók set out on his first important trip collecting folksongs in Transylvania, which lasted for nearly two months. At Csíkrákos he found the pentatonic tune that he was to employ, though stripped of its vocal ornamentation, for the closing movement of his quartet.[3] But the gesture of its use there (bars 94–105) still seems more significant than its actual compositional value. The first line of the folksong sits isolated within the musical process, leaving the impression that the composer was still uncertain about how to use this otherwise impressively prepared melody. In fact, he only managed to spin out its iambic cadence.

The second movement, as mentioned, begins to introduce a lighter tone after the 'funeral dirge' of the first movement. This relaxation culminates in the third movement although the overall tone is still not carefree or serene. It seems that the 'retour à la vie' for the young Bartók led past witty, grotesque or sarcastic characters. It is noteworthy, for example, that the sharply engraved main theme (Ex. 1c) runs into a light, playful section. Its rhythmic pattern, which plays a major role throughout the movement, emphasizes the popular folk character via a Hungarian choriambic extension (as can be seen from bar 106). Another rhythmic pattern of great importance in the movement is a similarly popular formula. One of its variants is that wittily grotesque, somersaulting theme (Ex. 1d) which the composer uses in the centre of the movement to develop his fugato. The direction *grazioso* at the beginning of the fugato (bar 158) suggests a subtle humour, but with the growing number of parts and the increasing complexity of the contrapuntal texture the music becomes ever more cruel and sarcastic, reminding one of

Liszt's Mephistophelean fugue in his B minor Sonata. We know that Bartók held Liszt's music in high esteem, being especially attracted to that sonata, which he often played.

Viewing the three movements of the First String Quartet as a whole, we may contend that the work testifies to a substantial transformation in Bartók's tonal and harmonic thinking. The first movement is constructed of tense seventh chords enriched by chromatic passing notes in the manner of late Romanticism. The tonality of the movement is ambivalent, as the starting key, which is closest to F minor, shifts to A♭ minor by the end of the movement. Instead of a precise definition of the key it is better to approach the tonality of the movement through the ambiguous augmented triad, E A♭ C, and to compare the tonal uncertainties of the beginning with the last emphatic outburst of the movement, at bar 67 (Ex. 5).

EX. 5

The end of the second movement is tonally firmer, clearly being in B major. The tonal scheme of the third movement is even more unequivocal: the A key of the final cadence sheds light on several, hitherto tonally ambiguous moments. Nevertheless, the chord without thirds that is sounded at the end of the movement reinforces a neutral (neither major nor minor) A tonality. Compared to the first movement the chordal structure of the last is also different: chromatically built seventh chords are fewer, the chords are emptier, and they link up in a simpler way. Accumulations of fourths also appear. These are not yet vertical structures of fourths, as the fourths are not piled up in chords but are spread out in melodies, but the resultant sound already anticipates them. In the coda of this third movement, for instance, we first hear the cadential A E B fifths inverted as fourths, B E A. A new system of relations belongs with Bartók's new chordal structure: we arrive at the closing A fifth chord not through functional progression but through a double melodic leading-note step, progressing upwards and downwards simultaneously from either end of a scale of six whole tones, as shown in Ex. 6.

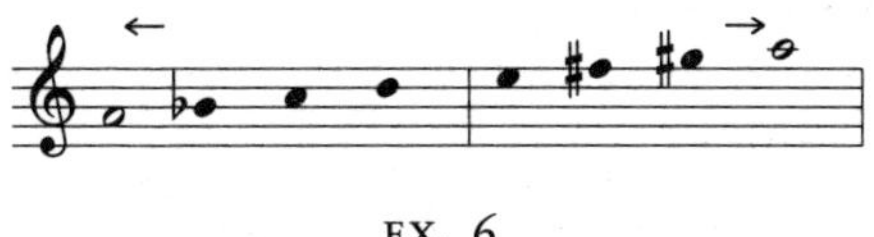

EX. 6

This reveals that the 'retour à la vie' symbolizes not only a personal recovery but also a compositional transformation: the post-Wagnerian Bartók of the first movement gives way to a colder, harder, 'twentieth-century' Bartók by the end of the composition, a Bartók who has the courage to face up to life.

Over a year passed after the completion of the First String Quartet before it was premièred. This première occurred at Bartók's first 'composer's night', on 19 March 1910, in the company of a series of his piano pieces and his Piano Quintet of 1904. It is a memorable date in the history of modern Hungarian music: Bartók's début was preceded by Kodály's similar concert by a mere two days. These two closely connected concerts were like an unfurling of the banner of new Hungarian music. The sweeping success of the First Quartet's performance was due to the highly talented young ensemble led by Imre Waldbauer which, from that time onwards, became a faithful and reliable interpreter of the chamber music of both Bartók and Kodály.

*

Nearly a decade separates Bartók's Second String Quartet Op.17 from his First. No exact date is available for this work beyond the broad period of 1915–17 noted at the end of the score. At this time Bartók was living in great seclusion at Rákoskeresztúr, on the outskirts of Budapest, and was anxious about the course of the war. Even so, he managed to compose a good many works, including the Sonatina, Romanian Folk Dances, Romanian Christmas Carols, Op.15 and Op.16 songs, the Suite Op.14, and his ballet, *The Wooden Prince*. The Second String Quartet was first performed by the Waldbauer–Kerpely Quartet on 3 March 1918; it had been composed expressly for them and was dedicated to them.

If the structure of the First Quartet, gradually accelerating from its opening slow movement, marked a break with traditional structure, then the break is far more radical in the case of the Second Quartet. There are, again, three movements, but the Moderato–Allegro–Lento structure suggests quite a different model. We could go as far as George Perle, who sees in this quartet a simpler variant of the later symmetrical 'bridge' form.[4] I am inclined, however, to interpret it rather as the 'dramaturgy' of oscillation, in two directions from the initial moderate tempo, showing kindred traits with the process of tempo polarization in Alban Berg's *Lyric Suite* (1926): Allegretto–Andante–Allegro–Adagio–Presto–Largo. Of course, in a set of six movements a tendency to polarize towards very fast and very slow is more marked than in a three-movement piece.

A similar structure, ending with a slow movement, can be found in the piano Suite Op.14, composed at almost the same time as this quartet. It seems that compositions ending on a note of resignation, suffering or pessimism best suited Bartók's compositional ideal at this time. Although in the case of great artists it may be misleading to look for direct links between the external world and a work of art, it cannot be overlooked that these compositions were born in the troubled years of the First World War. Their tone of crisis and their dark and sombre mood are due not only to their tempos but also to the painful and resigned gestures and disturbing harmonies.

During the relatively long period separating the composition of Bartók's first two quartets, a substantial change had occurred in his composing. The works from this period show a deepening awareness of how to use folk music yet also brought Bartók closer to his European contemporaries. (He first learnt of the works of Schoenberg and Stravinsky, for instance, shortly before the war.)[5] The great test of the integration of folk music into his serious composition was *Duke Bluebeard's Castle* (1911), in which the composer's experiments included how to develop continuous, highly organized, dramatic declamation from the tonal system and melodic idiom of 'old'-Hungarian folksongs. As well, Bartók was detaching himself more fundamentally from the chromaticism of late Romanticism, with its structures of thirds, and turning more firmly towards the idea of disrupting the traditional tonal and chordal systems.

Bartók's dissolution of tonal relations has already been discussed in connection with the First Quartet. There, the technique leads to tonal uncertainty or ambivalence in the first movement, while in the Second Quartet the disruption of the tonality is far more consistent. This is not a twelve-note, serial work, but is part of a preparatory phase leading towards such composition. In it the composer came to realize that the only way to make the twelve notes of the scale equal was to assign them equal roles in the musical texture. Without attempting to impose a serial analysis on to Bartók's quartet, it is still possible to demonstrate the systematic extension of the note range as far as the eleventh scalar degree within the first three bars of the first movement (Ex. 7).

Of course, there is much more to the 'atonal' method of Bartók, and it cannot be systematically analysed in these simplistic terms. It is far more important to note that in the first and third movements of the Second Quartet Bartók approached atonality by giving an equal weight and frequency to sets of fourths and seconds beside his third-based chords. Another special feature is that the thematic–motivic organization of these outer movements is determined by an intervallic model of fourth plus minor second, applicable in both melodic and chordal orientations. The model first appears concealed in the melody of

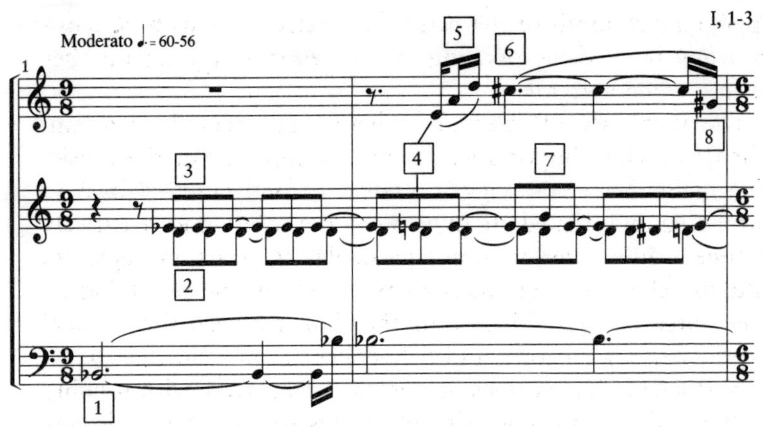

EX. 7

the main theme, as can be seen in bars 2–3 of Ex. 7, and is duplicated many times in the extension of this theme in the recapitulation (see two bars before fig. 17, in particular). The superior unity of the musical material is also evidenced by the fact that the model of fourth plus minor second appears in a chordal form, too, demonstrating that the model can be constructed either by placing perfect fourths one upon the other or by interlocking augmented fourths. The augmentation of the fourth interval and the interchangeability of elements are fundamental principles in the movement's variations of motifs. An appropriate example is the characteristic double fourth appoggiatura motif of the main theme (Ex. 7), which is, within a few bars of the opening, being heard in a great number of intervallic variants.

The flexibility of intervals, whether augmented or diminished, is a chief importance to the development of the music. The main theme's appoggiatura motif, for example, displays surprising and immediate dynamism: the subtly and sensitively outlined tune soon becomes gesticulating, even swaggering, and stretches its range to span two and, at one point (fig.2), even three octaves. This is another link between the musical expressivity of Bartók's and Schoenberg's music in the 1910s. Nevertheless, Bartók does not break conclusively with tonality as the main organizing principle of his musical form, despite the spreading of his chords of new structure and the expansion of his atonal 'patches'. Although he resigns from the functional resolutions of traditional chordal progression, he is still striving to create some sort of tonal centre at certain points in the musical process. The effect of such tonal centres is similar to that of the final note in Hungarian or other modal folk cultures. In the Second Quartet's first movement this tonally distinct point is associated with the third theme. It complies with Classical sonata principles in that it is in C♯ in the exposition but in A in the recapitulation.

At the same time, it is very hard to determine the tonality of the first movement as a whole because the tonal principle Bartók was later to adopt – the identity of the starting and finishing pitches – is not yet found here. The final chord, for example, appears to be tonally ambiguous, through its augmented quality (F A C♯) and apparently unrelated melodic note of resolution (E). The return of the closing (third) theme in A gives a valuable clue for the solution of the tonal problem here, suggesting that the cello melody of the coda is also in the tonality of A. Thus, when in the last bar the cello finishes with E, below the augmented triad, this can be interpreted as the plagal final note of the tune in A, and that, in turn, reinforces the claim of A in the augmented triad to be the root and assigns a colouring role to the uppermost *pp* note, F. In short, the movement ends in A major.

Bartók applied the technique of complementing chordal notes with colouring notes in other works of this period, such as the Suite Op.14. At the end of that composition, all the notes of the B♭ major triad, which determines the basic key of the piece, are flanked on one or other side by neighbouring chromatic notes with a colouring function. This practice also highlights Bartók's widespread exploitation of the tension inherent in semitonal relations, including their inversion or octave transposition.

By virtue of its robust folk-dance character, the second movement of the Second String Quartet (Allegro molto capriccioso) shows a kinship with his *Allegro barbaro* (1911). The musical material used is not Hungarian but comes from the Arabic folk music which the composer collected near Biskra in north Africa during 1913. Although Bartók himself only explicitly identified elements of Arabic folk music in his Suite Op.14 and Dance Suite (1923), it is beyond doubt that its influence is felt in other works, notably the Second and the Fourth String Quartets.[6] Although in the second movement of this Second Quartet the steady, tapping beat of the quavers in the accompaniment and the narrow-range tune above it (Ex. 8a) cannot be seen as direct Arabic quotations, the general effect is clearly reminiscent of the vocal or instrumental tunes, with their drum accompaniment, collected by Bartók around Biskra. Ex. 8b gives a few bars from one such folk example.[7] The ostinato, minor third (augmented second) motif introduced here occurs in other Bartók works, too, nearly always conveying a similarly barbaric or peasant impression.

In keeping with the verse-line structure of the theme, the movement is a combination of rondo and variation. Whenever the Arabic-inspired rondo theme appears it presents a new variation. The process of variation has a definite tendency: the theme of narrow range at its first appearance gradually spreads over a wider range, and, after a relatively large middle section, the duple-metre theme turns into triple metre – an increase resembling the *proportio* of Renaissance dances. The variational process is finally activated in the coda, where it includes both the narrowest and the widest of motions and synthesizes the duple and triple divisions.

EX. 8

In the middle section of the second movement two typical motifs of Bartók's instrumental dramaturgy can be discerned. One is the crude clashing of materials of different, even opposed, characters. Between fig.25 and fig.27 the sharply rhythmicized minor third motif is pitted against the solo violin's *dolce* tune. It is noteworthy that at this point of the form the weaker of the two is victorious: the power of the minor-third motif gradually weakens, its dimensions decrease, while the *dolce* melody is maintained, allowing it to take over the leading role from fig.27. The second dramaturgical effect is the switching of the *grazioso* tone into sarcasm, a change which was earlier seen in the fugato of the First String Quartet. Here, the *dolce* melody turns into one of mocking, ironic character (see figs 31–2). A strikingly similar example can also be cited in the third movement of the First Violin Sonata (1921), at fig.26.

These three instances well demonstrate that in Bartók's mind a sustained serene or *grazioso* character is all but inconceivable. His humour is mostly one of cruel irony and sarcasm.

The second movement ends with a coda in *prestissimo* tempo, comprising quite a wide range of the melodic and rhythmic variants of the rondo theme. This acceleration and condensation of the musical progression assumes quite a new musical quality. The muted timbre, *pianissimo* dynamics, extremely fast tempo and dense motion produce a mysterious, fleeting, almost transcendental musical vision. Reminiscent of Berg's Allegro misterioso of the Lyric Suite, although preceding it by a decade, this passage represents the appearance of Bartók's 'Prestissimo misterioso', the prototype of the fugato of the Third String Quartet, the second movement (Prestissimo, con sordino) of the Fourth String Quartet and the middle section of the second movement of the Second Piano Concerto.

The last movement (Lento) refers back to the first in several ways, but is consistently more extreme: the tempo is slower, there are still fewer firm indicators of the tonality, sadness turns into anguish and despair, the tension becomes oppressive. There are also thematic–motivic connections between these outer movements. It is not hard to recognize the slow variant of the main theme of the first movement (Ex. 9a) in the first violin's melody heard at fig.2 (Ex. 9b). This variant incorporates that model of fourth plus minor second which was so important in the first movement.[8]

EX. 9

This *dolce* melody with its painful resignation – almost lament – tells us much about how Bartók integrated the material of folklore into his own music at a higher, more original level than mere quotation or adaptation. In this melody can be discerned the descending melody of gesticular rhythm which is so characteristic of 'old'-style Hungarian folksong: the octave range may be filled in by a single line descending through the degrees of a pentatonic scale. Many such examples are found in Bartók's published collection of folksongs,[9] and in other Hungarian collections, as with Ex. 10, the opening of a lament collected by Kodály in 1922.[10]

EX. 10

Bartók's melody also appears to be built to this pattern, but he has added to its character by mistuning its perfect octave–fifth frame, bursting it, so to speak, from the inside. Instances of this process can be seen in other of his works, as well, and in two different forms. In some instances the 'perfect' form is only an imagined archetype behind the actual mistuned form; at other times the 'perfect' form is itself heard and the mistuning takes place as part of the musical process 'before our very ears'.[11] There can be no doubt in this instance from the Second String Quartet that Bartók considered this expansion of his melody the propelling force of his wider musical process, as is demonstrated by subsequent further expansions of its intervals. The crux of this mistuning technique is that the composer inserts the folk-music pattern with its perfect octave–fifth frame into his atonal or ultra-tonal system, in which the twelve chromatic degrees are to be used equally. This leads to the augmentation or diminution of intervals by semitonal intervals.[12]

Bartók's frequent use of chords built of other than third intervals is found in this final movement, too; for several bars at fig.4, in particular, he provides a breathtaking example of contrary-motion movement of paired fourth intervals. But Bartók claimed that the inspiration for this apparently Schoenbergian technique had come from folksong, observing in 1931 that 'the frequent use of fourth-intervals in our old melodies suggested to us the use of fourth chords.'[13] The fact remains, however, that in the 1910s Bartók was paying serious attention to contemporary art music. The right approach, therefore, is not to set the folk inspiration against that from contemporary music, but to try to show how these two sources mutually buttressed, justified and complemented each other. With that approach, then, the Second String Quartet can be seen to constitute a paradigm of the Bartókian synthesis: not only Hungarian and Arabic folk music, but also the peasant tradition and European art music are blended to produce a unified composition of the highest order.

NOTES

1 *DB*.ii, p. 92.

2 Similar references to art song are found in the First Violin Concerto ('Der Esel ist ein dummes Tier') and Concerto for Orchestra ('You are beautiful, you are wonderful, Hungary').

3 *HFS*, melody no.21, p. 224.

4 'The String Quartets of Béla Bartók', in *A Musical Offering. Essays in Honor of Martin Bernstein*, ed. Claire Brook and E. H. Clinkscale, New York (Pendragon Press), 1977, p. 198.

5 *BBE*, pp. 467–8.

6 See János Kárpáti, 'Béla Bartók and the East', *SM*, vol.6 (1964), pp. 179–94.

7 Ex. 8b is taken from melody no.15 in Béla Bartók, 'Die Volksmusik der Araber von Biskra und Umgebung', *Zeitschrift für Musikwissenschaft* (Leipzig), vol.2 (1920), pp. 489–522 (pp. 506–7). In Ex. 8b the sign '+' indicates a slight sharpening of the scalar degree, and 'o' a slight flattening.

8 Bartók was apparently unaware of this relationship between the themes. See John Vinton, 'New Light on Bartók's Sixth Quartet', *Music Review*, vol.25 (1964), p. 233.

9 See, for instance, *HFS*, melody nos 7b, 7c, 8, p. 221.

10 *A magyar népzene tára*, ed. Béla Bartók and Zoltán Kodály, vol.5, Budapest (Akadémiai Kiadó), 1966, melody no.56, p. 307.

11 See examples of these two types, respectively: Fifth String Quartet, I, bars 5–9; Sixth String Quartet, I, bars 24–5 (cf. I, bars 26–7).

12 For further discussion see János Kárpáti, *Bartók's String Quartets*, Budapest (Corvina), 1975, pp. 137–57.

13 *BBE*, p. 343.

17
Violin Sonatas

PAUL WILSON

By 1921 Bartók had completed the main compositional work on *The Miraculous Mandarin* Op.19, and had composed two of the four pieces which serve as companions to it. These two collections of short pieces for piano, the Three Studies Op.18, and Improvisations Op.20, provided him with repertory for his recitals and with further opportunities to work out the quasi-expressionist style and harmonic language so important in the *Mandarin*.

His next two works, the First and Second Violin Sonatas, were also intended as concert repertory, this time for his appearances in Western Europe with the violinist Jelly Arányi, to whom he dedicated both works. He composed the First Sonata in the last three months of 1921. The première took place in Vienna on 8 February 1922; Mary Dickenson-Auner was the violinist and Eduard Steuermann – now renowned for his long association with Arnold Schoenberg – was the pianist. Bartók and Arányi first performed the sonata on 15 March 1922 at a private recital organized by the chargé d'affaires at the Hungarian legation in London. A public performance in London followed on 24 March. Returning to Budapest after his concert tour, Bartók began work on the Second Violin Sonata in July, finishing it in November. Imre Waldbauer and he gave this Second Sonata its première in Berlin on 7 February 1923.[1] Bartók later took the work to London, where he played both sonatas with Arányi on 7 May.

The violin sonatas, like the Studies and Improvisations, have long been considered 'problem' works, their problems stemming, in part, from Bartók's supposedly increasing distance from his wonted sources in Hungarian folk music. A closer look at all four pieces shows not so much a complete departure from those sources as an attempt to include them within a wider frame of reference. The Improvisations are, after all, settings of authentic folk melodies, albeit settings of a particularly complex and elaborate kind. Movements from the other three pieces, especially the first study and the finales of the violin sonatas, have clear precursors among Bartók's earlier works, and the finales draw their melodic and rhythmic character quite directly from a folk idiom. But the new style of the *Mandarin* does dominate the music and, in turn, creates new, truly compositional problems for Bartók to solve. Such problems have mostly to do with the coherence and intelligibility of the musical process in each piece.

In the two groups of piano pieces, each separate movement is small enough for Bartók to rely on relatively straightforward tactics of repetition (in the Studies), or on the continual presence of a folk melody (in the Improvisations), to help give each piece internal coherence and expressive clarity.[2] The violin sonatas represent a more challenging undertaking: the extension of an essentially non-tonal idiom to large instrumental works.

Despite a general recognition that these sonatas are difficult works, not everyone agrees that Bartók employed a 'non-tonal idiom' in these compositions. Hungarian scholars, in particular, deny the atonality or non-tonality of Bartók's music from this period, or any other, and have worked out different points of departure for understanding the pieces. Mounting a direct argument for the position adopted here is beyond the scope of this essay. Instead, I have simply assumed Bartók's (temporary and incomplete) atonality as a kind of axiom (although it is grounded in my experience of listening to all the works of the period), and drawn out some of its implications. Readers will and should, of course, develop their own views of the pieces, but they should be aware that more than one general approach is possible.[3]

Part of the coherence of *The Miraculous Mandarin* depends on its scenario, with its brutality, its mystery, and especially it narrative symmetries; Bartók's score possesses a style and form which musically reflect all of those characteristics. But with the sonatas his problem was to write a lengthy work, in a comparable style, lacking a scenario to suggest for it a convincing overall shape. In response, he explored two quite different solutions to the problem, the success of which ultimately provided him with foundations for his more celebrated successes in the future.

In a sense the First Sonata is an adaptation of the Classical European model: a work which, externally at least, looks back and mimics the three-movement structure of violin sonatas by Mozart and Beethoven. That model, of course, includes a relatively long and complex first movement in some type of sonata form, balanced by a slow, lyrical middle movement and a rapid finale, often a rondo. In Mozart or Beethoven all three of these movements would rest solidly on a clear foundation in tonal harmony and key relationships, and they would deploy a series of separate but perhaps related themes, motivically pregnant and lyrically entrancing by turns. For the First Violin Sonata Bartók retains the general length and shape of each movement in the model, but the details of theme, harmony, progression and expressive design undergo huge changes. A look at each movement will show some of the most far-reaching of them.

Older sonata forms depend harmonically on a clear perception of a single tonal centre and on clear movement away from and back to this centre. In the First Sonata's first movement we are given no such tonic. In its place, and serving some of the same functions, Bartók provides a complex chord which appears at three crucial junctures in the movement: at the opening, at bar 187 (at what we will provisionally call the recapitulation), and at the end. Ex. 1 shows a simplified version of the chord's texture and voicing in each of these locations; open noteheads in the example show the notes common to all three appearances of the chord.

The return to this chord during the piece clearly signifies and sounds like the return to a home base, in some sense. Bartók himself suggested that the chord was an expression of C♯ minor, and that the piece itself was in C♯ minor.[4] The chord seems too complex for such a simple designation, and the way in which Bartók revoiced it at the movement's end makes C♯ much more

EX. 1

unlikely as a root for the chord, or as tonic for the piece. The chord is, however, sufficiently stable and complex to act also as a source for the other harmonies in the movement. Most of these sonorities are transposed groups of notes selected from within the primary chord. That chord itself thus provides at least two types of musical coherence for the movement: a moment-by-moment similarity of harmonic sound and the widely separated recurrence of a single event which marks important moments in the form.

However, Bartók must still create analogues or alternatives for the large sections and processes of a sonata form. In doing so, he adapts procedures from the altered sonata form of the nineteenth century; he radically changes the character and function of the development section (bars 103–86, that is: fig.10.8 to fig.20). Instead of a Beethovenian 'working out' of motifs, he makes the development a kind of meditative variation on the themes, with some new material also being added. For example, the themes which begin in bars 3, 16 and 82 reappear, transformed but complete, at bars 123, 134 and 159, respectively. One can cite two likely reasons for this change of character in the development. The first we have already touched on – that is, the impossibility in this idiom of heightening harmonic tension by transposing motifs or themes to an ever greater distance from the tonic. But the second has to do with Bartók's own lifelong habits of melodic writing: his incorrigibly variational approach to the treatment of themes. In this movement, for instance, every 'theme' presented by the violin takes the form of a single note, sustained and then increasingly embellished as the particular section of the exposition proceeds. The embellishments, in their variety and increasing complexity, are already developmental to the point where a Beethovenian development section would have nothing new of this sort to add. Instead, therefore, the themes are transformed in tempo, register, texture, dynamics and expressive character, but presented in relatively complete form. A list of composers who followed this kind of procedure would probably begin with Schubert and Schumann, but Bartók's most important model here is likely to be Liszt, especially his Sonata in B minor. The central section of the first movement of Schumann's Piano Concerto is also particularly apropos.[5]

The recapitulation, which begins at bar 187 (fig.20), thus loses a good deal of its dramatic force as a return and a release of large-scale tension. Instead, though clearly meant as a return of sorts – as witnessed by the revoiced presence of the movement's primary chord – it becomes a third statement of the exposition material in yet another version. Bartók greatly alters the internal proportions of each section from the exposition, but only one such section is missing entirely, that is, the piano theme from bar 35 (fig.3), which was already used in an untransposed form in the development at bar 146 (fig.15.5). The movement ends, as we have seen, with the last return of the primary chord and an embellished sustained C–A minor third in the violin.

In sum, then, Bartók's reworking of sonata form here has resulted in a large three-section piece, which one might symbolize as *A A' A''*. This is a perfectly worthwhile and viable design, with its own expressive meaning and impact, but it is certainly different from older and more forcefully directional kinds of sonata form. Its unfamiliarity may account for some of the puzzlement and the suggestions of obscurity with which the piece has been burdened. In its broad outlines, however, this piece is anything but obscure, and Bartók's simplicity of large design here actually allows him a wider scope for variational richness and complexity.

The second movement adheres more closely in form to its traditional model. It is a three-part design, *A B A'*, on the largest scale, with large paired subsections within each of the three main parts. Fig. 1 shows the plan of the movement in three levels of subdivision. Bartók once again treats the simplicity of his large design as a licence for rich embellishments of material already heard. The most important changes are from *A* to *A*', and especially in the way the piano participates in what had previously been solo violin material. *A*' thus shows both a compression of the material and an expressively meaningful increase of collaboration between the two instruments. The individual parts are also greatly changed in detail, although not in basic line, not only from *A* to *A*' but within smaller subdivisions, as well.

Section:	*A*			
Pair division:	1		2	
Subsection:	*a*	*b*	*a*'	*b*'
Bar numbers:	1–15	16–28	29–38	39–52
Rehearsal cues:			2	2.10
Section:	*B*			
Pair division:	1		2	
Subsection:	*c*	*d*	*c*'	*d*'
Bar numbers:	53–62	63–8	69–73	74–80
Rehearsal cues:	4	5	7	8
Section:	A'			
Pair division:	1		2	
Subsection:	*a*	*b*	*a*'	*b*'
Bar numbers:	81–9	90–3	93–102	103–11
Rehearsal cues:	10	11.4	12	13.5

FIG. 1

Harmonically, too, the movement is more traditional, deploying triads and seventh chords in ways that catch the ear without giving any single triad a central significance. Most frequently, Bartók – in a manner reminiscent of Debussy – places root-position triads in a whole-tone line spanning a tritone. In the *B* section (from bar 53, fig.4) he jettisons triads for a direct use of the tritone, in one of those inexorably building crescendos which are important for slow movements later in his career (as seen in the piano Sonata, the First Piano Concerto and the Sonata for

Two Pianos and Percussion). The harmonic flavour of this section is partially retained in the final third of the piece, where major and minor triads give way to diminished or augmented, and then finally to a five-note chord at the close, a kind of super-triad in which all four types overlap.

The finale to the First Violin Sonata is an unabashed folk dance, in which Bartók seems to have suddenly abandoned the Classical model for something even more traditional. But lurking beneath the surface of this celebration of energy are the familiar lineaments of the seven-part rondo, altered in certain respects, but discernible none the less. The piece is thus a synthesis – one of many in Bartók's output – of the two foundations of his musical thought. Fig. 2 shows how the movement uses, without completely adopting, the form of the rondo. The important innovations are two: the radical change of tempo and character in the section marked *C*, and, as usual, the progressively varied restatements of *A*, including its reharmonization at each new appearance.

Section:	*A*	*B*(1)	*B*(2)	*B*(3)
Bar numbers:	1–90	91–126	127–82	183–214
Rehearsal cues:		8	12	18.5
Section:	*A*'	*C*	*A*''	
Bar numbers:	215–58	259–371	372–422	
Rehearsal cues:	21.12	25.14	33	
Section:	*B*(1)	*B*(2)	*B*(3)	*A*''' (coda)
Bar numbers:	423–44	445–56	457–89	490–571
Rehearsal cues:	37.6	40	41	43.13

FIG. 2

One reason for the change in *A* is the character of the main theme. Because of both its rhythmic drive and its contour, it cannot achieve an effect of true closure on its own, unlike most rondo themes, which are self-contained sections. Both the huge size of the first *A* section and the greatly altered statement of *A* in the coda are consequences of this. In the first *A* section the theme's natural momentum seems to carry it through a whole series of restatements and variations, until it runs headlong into

EX. 2

the sustained B♮ in the transition, bars 76–89 (fig.6.10 – fig.7.9), which serves as 'dominant' and upbeat to the violin's E♮ of section *B*(1). At the movement's close Bartók gives us only a fragment of section *A* (beginning with bar 546), locking it into a circumscribed pattern that supplies energy without forward motion, and then reducing it finally to an embellished B♮ over the C♯ in the bass.

Bartók also returns part of the way toward tonality in this movement, actually to a modality that has far more to do with the folk-like character of the piece than with rondo form. The perfect fifth C♯–G♯ controls the left hand of the piano at each end of the movement, supplying at last sufficient stability for a true tonic focus on C♯. But the same types of harmonic complexity still govern the interior of the movement, giving it, along with the rest of this sonata, continued harmonic and expressive kinship with *The Miraculous Mandarin*.

Having appropriated the Classical model for the First Violin Sonata, Bartók turned in another direction for the Second. Its two-movement design is clearly an expansion of the pattern of the rhapsody, a slow and relatively lyrical opening section followed by a much quicker dance-like finale. Bartók carried out his expansion at two levels. He gave each movement a clear internal structure of its own, using techniques similar to those we have seen in the First Sonata. He also worked the two movements into a single large design, in which the full significance of the beginning is revealed only at the end.

The most memorable theme in the work is also Bartók's cornerstone for the structure. Ex. 2 shows the theme's first appearance, in bars 1–6 of the first movement. Both of its parts are crucial: the widely separated sustained notes in violin and piano, which act as a call for attention, and then the graceful and melancholy violin line which follows. The sonata returns to this theme five times, each occasion marking the initiation or closing of a major part of the work. The theme also carries out another kind of large design that we will touch on later.

The first movement uses Ex. 2 as its own first theme and thereby sets in motion a kind of sonatina form (a sonata without a development section), which takes the shape mapped out in Fig. 3. (The notation 'P' in this figure marks the presence of the theme shown in Ex. 2.) Although there is no separate development, Bartók as usual varies his themes extensively from exposition to recapitulation. Because of their similarity in texture and dynamics he can combine *b*' and *c*' into a single, longer section, mingling elements from *b* and *c* (which is certainly a developmental technique). The coda contains two statements of P, the first beginning a perfect fourth lower than usual and the second returning to E, but an octave higher than at the opening. The piano part for the entire coda rests upon a beautifully extended stepwise line in the bass, a gesture which will return.

Section:	Exposition			
Subsection:	*a* (P)	*b*	*c*	*d*
Bar numbers:	1–20	21–33	34–50	51–60
Rehearsal cues:		2.7	5	7

Section:	Recapitulation			Coda	
Subsection:	*a*' (P)	*b*' + *c*'	*d*'	*a*'' (P)	*a*''' (P)
Bar numbers:	61–72	73–99	100–105	105–19	119–25
Rehearsal cues:	8.5	11	15	15.5	18

FIG. 3

Harmonically, Bartók is using what seem to be his favourite small chords in this part of his career. Ex. 3 is a partial listing of them.

(a) Three-note chords

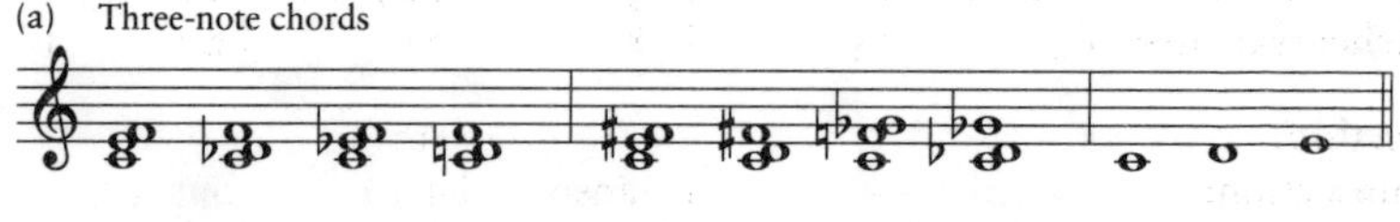

(b) Four-note chords

EX. 3

His practice for three-note chords seems to be to take a single interval and to use it as a 'frame' within which to place one other note. The most frequent 'frame' intervals are the perfect fourth and the tritone, although the three-note whole-tone scale segment is also very important. Bartók seems to prefer two types of four-note chord, either a pair of fourths or tritones a semitone apart or a triad with an added chromatic note. Ex. 3 shows one type of each of these in the order just mentioned.

The second movement is a large rondo-like form with some family resemblance to the last movement of the First Sonata. It is, however, more lavishly provided with themes and more elaborately organized than its precursor. Fig. 4 shows the layout of the movement. The overall design is still ternary, in that Bartók uses two themes in the outer, *A* sections, and constructs a central section around a third idea. (In the figure, 'P' is again used to show the primary theme from the first movement. The asterisks by bars 254 and 274 in the figure represent a restatement of material from bars 85–90 of the first movement.)

Section:	*A*					
Subsection:	*a*		*b*			
Theme:	1	2	1	1	1	1
Bar numbers:	1–32	33–60	61–74	75–86	87–105	106–23
Rehearsal cues:		3	6.4	8	9	11

Section:				*B*	
Subsection:					
Theme:	1	2	2	3	3
Bar numbers:	124–36	137–57	158–82	183–227	228–53
Rehearsal cues:	13	15	18	21	27

Section:				*A'*	
Subsection:			trans.	*a*	
Theme:	* + 3	* + 3	P + 1	1	1
Bar numbers:	254–73	274–98	298–307	308–41	342–64
Rehearsal cues:	29	31	34	35	38

Section:					
Subsection:		*b*			*c*
Theme:	1	2	2	2	1
Bar numbers:	365–90	391–418	419–27	428–47	448–62
Rehearsal cues:	40.4	43	46.5	48	49.9

Section:				Coda	
Subsection:					
Theme:	1	1	1	P	P
Bar numbers:	463–75	476–82	483–516	517–24	525–35
Rehearsal cues:	51	52	53	56	57

FIG. 4

The first *A* section thus presents two themes in fairly short order and in undecorated form. The remainder of the section presents a series of variations on the first theme, followed by a shorter reworking of the second. The central section exploits only its own theme and initially at a much slower tempo. The section marked *A'* has its own three-part plan, using the first and second themes, and the coda returns to the primary theme of the work.

The first theme of the second movement has a close kinship with the primary theme. The relationship is a sharing of the central six notes, which are arranged in each case as a stepwise line, with, of course, the reversal of direction and a considerable difference in tempo. Bartók has made this clear (not necessarily on purpose) by placing the two themes side by side not only at the join between the movements but also at the transition back to *A'*, in bars 298–307 of the second movement.

The most striking and beautiful aspect of the work, however, is the plan that links the beginning with the end, in a fashion strongly recalling T. S. Eliot's often-quoted lines from 'Little Gidding':

> We shall not cease from exploration
> And the end of all exploring
> Will be to arrive where we started
> And know the place for the first time.[6]

Here the beginning is in the two parts of the primary theme, the high violin E against the low piano F♯ and then the violin line (see Ex. 2). These two events are fused into one at the expressive climax of the entire work, starting at bar 517 (fig. 56) of the second movement. As the violin and piano hammer out their E and F♯, sounding the head motive of the theme over and over until finally it sinks exhausted, we understand that this is the moment toward which the very opening of the piece had pointed. But the piece still has not reached its end. It does so with the final return of the violin to an extremely high E and the piano's move to C and G, to complete the C major triad. As with the First Sonata, Bartók offered an identification of key for this work: C major.[7] One hardly knows how seriously Bartók meant this, although it is characteristic of a certain kind of statement to which he was prone later in his life. The problem with this key, and even with this triad, in context is that they seem unearned in the harmonic language of the piece. And yet the triad, though not the key, is in fact justified within the work-spanning harmonic structure that again depends upon the primary theme. That structure is depicted in Ex. 4.

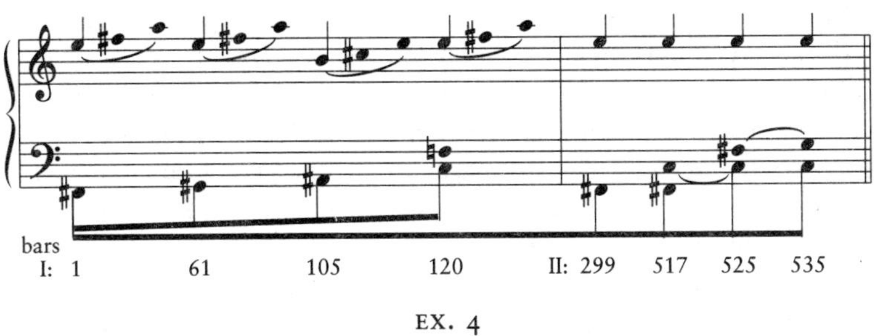

EX. 4

This example shows that the violin E is a stable element in widely spaced statements of the primary theme but that the piano bass notes are working out a long connection between F♯ and C. The connection appears in the first movement as a whole-tone stepwise line, arriving on C in bar 120. In the second movement F♯ reappears twice, at bar 299 and again at the climax at bar 517. C then replaces it at bar 525 and is affirmed at the close after another long bass-line descent.

In this long two-phase drive toward C it is hard not to regard as crucial the note that is joined with C in each appearance. The F♮ in bar 120 thus arrives as a beautiful sound for accompanying the theme, but it nevertheless lacks the stability to unite with C in bringing the work to a successful conclusion. The F♯ in bar 525 of the second movement is better, because at that point F♯ is in the final stages of relinquishing its prior status in the piece. The G at the close is at last the required element, taking over from the F♯ and stabilizing C and E in a triad which is the true culmination of this long process.

The long-range connection between F♯ and C is, of course, reminiscent of structures in the axis system of Bartókian tonality devised by Ernő Lendvai.[8] In my view the connection between tritone-related pitches is real and important in Bartók's music, but it is difficult to regard such pitches as functionally equivalent. If one defines a tonic function in part as a point of repose, then C is that kind of final tonic in this piece, and F♯ has a different function, as the primary harmonic point of departure. In tonal music these points are the same, but where they are not, as here, it seems correct to reserve 'tonic' as a name for the primary goal note, and to devise another way of speaking about notes which are basically points of departure.

In any case, the whole design is one of Bartók's most successful and beautifully realized plans. It makes of the Second Violin Sonata a fitting conclusion to a series of works which enriched both his technical craft and his expressive powers, leaving him poised to embark upon the great works of his final twenty years of life.

NOTES

1 For facsimiles of the programmes to the sonatas' première performances see Heinrich Lindlar, *Lübbes Bartók Lexikon*, Bergisch Gladbach (Gustav Lübbe), 1984, pp. 134–5.

2 See my chapter 'Approaching Atonality: Studies and Improvisations' in this *Companion* for a more detailed discussion of these works.

3 For a brief but representative example of 'tonal' commentary about the First Violin Sonata, see László Somfai, 'Bartók, Béla', in *The New Grove Dictionary of Music and Musicians*, ed. Stanley Sadie, London (Macmillan), 1980, vol.2, pp. 211–12.

4 Bartók's comment is quoted in Stevens, p. 63, but without a specific source or occasion. Similar statements appear in László Somfai, 'Bartók, Béla', p. 211, and Paul Griffiths, *Bartók*, London (J.M. Dent), 1984, pp. 100–102.

5 See Bartók's account from 1911 of the 'absolutely perfect' form of Liszt's Sonata in *BBE*, p. 452. He considered this form a 'revolutionary innovation'.

6 *The Oxford Book of Twentieth-century English Verse*, Oxford (Oxford University Press), 1973, p. 257.

7 See Stevens, pp. 63, 205.

8 See his *Béla Bartók: An Analysis of his Music*, London (Kahn & Averill), 1971, especially pp. 1–16.

18

Middle-period String Quartets

ELLIOTT ANTOKOLETZ

The evolution of Bartók's musical language toward increasing synthesis of divergent folk-music and art-music sources is most comprehensively reflected in his set of six string quartets. Composed over a period of thirty-one years, 1908–39, the quartets reached the most intensive stage of this evolution in the late 1920s. Bartók systematically transformed the earlier influences of German late-Romanticism, impressionism and Eastern European folk music that were juxtaposed in the First String Quartet into the highly original and unified musical language of the Third and Fourth String Quartets, composed in September 1927 and July–September 1928, respectively.

External political and social circumstances, as well as Bartók's own activities in the 1920s, were decisive in contributing to the expansion of the basic principles of pitch organization, texture and instrumental writing in these two middle-period quartets. Prevented from any further folk-music investigations after the signing of the Treaty of Trianon in 1920, Bartók was forced to shift his activities more toward composition and an intensive concert career. This change of activities can in part be observed in the increasing transformation of the folk-music materials. In those works of the early 1920s that still incorporated authentic folk tunes, Bartók shifted musical interest from the tune to the accompaniment. This led toward ever greater abstraction, complexity and concentration in both the pitch and rhythmic construction of his third and fourth quartets.

At the same time, new art-music influences had become manifest in Bartók's works immediately preceding these two middle-period quartets. In 1925, when Bartók toured Italy with performances of Baroque Italian music, he was inspired to investigate contrapuntal techniques in the keyboard works of Marcello, M. Rossi, della Ciaia, Frescobaldi and Zipoli, transcribing some of their works for piano.[1] Bartók's studies of Bach were also to be more intensely felt in his works of this period. His piano works of the mid-1920s foreshadowed the move toward the more densely chromatic and highly contrapuntal fabric of the two quartets, which include narrow-ranged motifs that often unfold in contexts based on systematic and pervasive use of canons, fugatos and strettos.

Bartók's approach to instrumental technique as well as to pitch organization may also have been given some direction by his contact with the music of his contemporaries during this period. It was shortly after 26 July 1927, when Bartók heard Berg's Lyric Suite for string quartet at an ISCM concert in Baden-Baden, that he composed his third and fourth quartets. Although the two Bartók quartets show little stylistic resemblance to the lush Romantic textures of the Lyric Suite, we may observe a superficial yet striking similarity in their common use of exotic instrumental colours. A comparison of the Allegro misterioso movement of the Lyric Suite with the coda of the Third Quartet and second movement of the Fourth reveals similarly light rapid textures that include such devices as *sul ponticello*, glissando, pizzicato, and the use of mutes in certain places. Certain common assumptions underlying the pitch relations in these Berg and Bartók works may also be observed in the concepts of the interval cycle and of inversional symmetry.[2] The latter comparison is not meant to suggest that Bartók was influenced by Berg's use of these concepts but, rather, that these works reveal parallel historical developments; Bartók had already exploited properties of the interval cycles and strict inversional symmetry in the second of his Fourteen Bagatelles Op.6 (1908), and in many following works.[3]

Apparently in connection with his forthcoming American tour during the 1927–8 season, Bartók decided to enter the newly composed Third String Quartet in a competition sponsored by the Musical Fund Society of Philadelphia. Subsequently, Bartók and the Italian composer Alfredo Casella shared the first prize.[4] In interviews during this tour Bartók reasserted his lifelong contention regarding the strong tonal orientation of his music. Notwithstanding Bartók's intensified expressionistic chromaticism in these two quartets, each work remains anchored around a basic tonality – C♯ for the third, and C for the fourth – with subsidiary tonalities for the individual movements. However, the means by which these tonalities are established have nothing to do with traditional tonal or harmonic functions but, rather, point toward a new concept of tonality and progression in twentieth-century music. These new principles of pitch organization are explored within the framework of the otherwise traditional forms of the two quartets.

The intense expressionistic mood of the Third String Quartet is partly due to the condensation of the traditional four-movement sonata plan into a single sonata-*allegro* movement, which is integrated by the cyclic return of themes from the 'Prima parte' and 'Seconda parte' in the abridged 'Ricapitulazione della prima parte' and 'Coda', respectively. This formal approach characterizes many late-nineteenth-century works and stems primarily from the Piano Sonata in B minor and symphonic poems of Franz Liszt. However, traditional tonal functions, which had been so essential in the articulation of the sonata structure, are replaced in this quartet by non-traditional pitch-set interactions. While the sections of the overall sonata plan are articulated by means of thematic–motivic construction and tempo changes, the combined sections form a large arch shape that is integrated by means of special transformational links between Eastern European folk modes and abstract symmetrical or cyclic interval constructions.

The basic principle underlying these transformational processes is described by Bartók as 'extension in range', in which chromatic material is expanded into diatonic themes. (The reverse is called 'chromatic compression'.) Special non-diatonic modes, most notably the octatonic scale – with its regular alternation of whole and half steps – serve as intermediary stages between chromatic and diatonic materials. Through this procedure, Bartók stated, 'we will get variety on the one hand, but the unity will remain undestroyed because of the hidden relation between the two forms.'[5] At the highest architectonic level, this principle is manifested in the relation between the opening held chromatic tetrachord, C♯ D D♯ E (a segment of interval-cycle 1/11),[6] and the closing tetrachordal segment of the cycle of fifths C♯ G♯ D♯ A♯ (cycle 5/7), both built on the C♯ tonic.

Thematic relations within the 'Prima parte' establish the basic premises for this intervallic expansion. The introductory theme, a somewhat amorphous melodic configuration reminiscent of the 'parlando rubato' style of Hungarian folk tunes, is accompanied by a held chord suggesting a typical Eastern European bagpipe (dudelsack) drone. At the same time, both solo and accompaniment are entirely chromatic, complementing each other to produce all twelve notes. However, the registral spacing of the held symmetrical tetrachord C♯ D D♯ E points to the possibility of expansion in two pairs of interval-classes: 1/11 (C♯–D and E–D♯) and 2/10 (D–E and boundary C♯–D♯). Furthermore, the initial thematic segments, A A♯ B♯ and G G♯ A♯ B, which together produce a chromatically filled fourth, G G♯ A A♯ B B♯, imply diatonic and octatonic expansions, respectively. Interactions among chromatic, diatonic and octatonic collections emerge with increasing clarity and are essential in the organic expansion and compression processes.

A phrasal metaphor for these intervallic processes is manifested in a local arch shape (to fig.2) formed by the introduction and first theme. The entry pitches of the opening drone, C♯ D E D♯, which move from low to high, are balanced in the return phase of the arch by the high-to-low entries in the free canon of the first theme. Classically balanced phrases, nevertheless, serve as the framework for this arch. The introductory theme unfolds in antecedent–antecedent–consequent segments, which demarcate the local octatonic and diatonic components. The first theme analogously unfolds two closely related antecedent segments (bars 6–8), followed by a descending consequent.

These phrasal links also support pitch and intervallic connections between these thematic ideas. The initial introductory segment, A♯ B♯ A (in enharmonic spelling, A♯ C A), is expanded to G C A in the basic motif of the first theme, by the replacement of A♯ with G. This new diatonic motif suggests the first significant manifestation of fourths or fifths (cycle 5/7). The addition of note E further expands the motif to a larger 'white-key' cyclic segment: C G [] A E. The three intruding 'black keys' of the first violin (D♯, C♯ and G♯) are expressly reiterated as a 5/7-cyclic adjacency in the second violin (C♯ G♯ D♯). While the consequent phrase of the first violin expands the 'white-key' collection to F C G D A E, the descending fourths of the cello expand the latter 'black-key' collection to B F♯ C♯ G♯ D♯ A♯. Thus, analogously to the introductory chromatic, diatonic and octatonic segments, the complementary relations of the cycle-5/7 segments of the first theme also produce all twelve notes.

Following a return to the chromatically compressed introduction (at fig.2), the first theme reappears intervallically expanded. The viola and first violin are now in canonic imitation at the fourth (C♯–F♯), as both lines together exclusively form the complete 'black-key' cyclic segment F♯ C♯ G♯ D♯ A♯, against the expressed 'white-key' reiterations of the motif G D A.[7] The chords at the final cadence of this theme (*sostenuto*) now sound the expanded open fifths segment C G D A E.

The more compressed intervallic context of the opening is re-established in the second theme (from fig.4), which recalls the 'night music' in other works by Bartók. Transpositions of the original chromatic tetrachord unfold linearly in a more sharply defined dotted Magyar rhythm above the diatonic first-theme stretto, the two ostinato lines providing the clearest polarization thus far of the 'black-key' (F♯ C♯ [] D♯) and 'white-key' cyclic (C G [] A) partitions. An inverted double stretto (at fig.5.4–7) serves as an intermediary stage between the chromatically compressed second theme and the diatonically expanded transformation of the main motif in the closing theme. Inverted dyadic pairings in this stretto form chromatic tetrachords, but each linear pairing produces an expanded octatonic tetrachord: B C D E♭, first violin, F♯ G A B♭, viola, and so on.

The expanded intervals of cycle 5/7 are most systematically established in the development (fig.7). The initial motivic statements unfold successive segments of the 5/7 cycle in three parts: F C G D, D A E and C [] D A [] B, while the alternating *fortissimo* chords combine segments from the 'white-key' and 'black-key' spectra, culminating on a tonic chord of combined fifths a half step apart: C♯–G♯ / D–A (*più lento*). The basic motif then appears in a stretto, the descending perfect-fourth entries outlining the entire 5/7 cycle. Diatonic (cyclic-5/7) expansion is further established in the recapitulation (fig.11.4). The original chromatic tetrachord, C♯ D D♯ E, is replaced by C♯–G♯ in the cello under an extended diatonic statement of the first theme. In its original appearance the motif was embellished by a non-diatonic D♯ (bar 7), which suggested an octatonic colouring (G A C D♯). This note is replaced by D (at fig.11.8) to give us the larger diatonic (cyclic) segment C G D A E.

The octatonic scale represents an intermediary intervallic stage between chromatic and diatonic material. An abridged statement of the introduction moves *attacca* to a D–E♭ trill to begin the 'Seconda parte'. This dyad, which is the axis of symmetry of the original chromatic tetrachord C♯ D D♯ E, serves, as did the latter, to introduce a prominent thematic idea. The diatonic fifths of the original motif of the first theme are now harmonically projected into the parallel triads of this movement's theme 1*a*. While the D pedal supports the D Dorian tonic of theme 1*a*, the E♭ trill supports the E♭ Dorian tonic of theme 1*b* (at fig.1). (The common contour of these subthemes is foreshadowed in the 'Prima parte', in the upper line of the *fortissimo* chords from fig.7 and the *martellato* chords after fig.10.[8]) The E♭ Dorian tetrachord of theme 1*b*, together with the D pedal, forms an octatonic segment, D E♭ F G♭ A♭, so several degrees of intervallic expansion are distinguished in the chromatic trill and octatonic–diatonic thematic segments. Perfect fifths and their diatonic modal forms then prevail harmonically and melodically (fig.3) at a combined statement of a variant of theme 1*b* in E♭ Dorian and a variant of theme 1*a* in D Dorian. These two modes that stem from axis D–E♭ complement each other to produce all twelve notes.

A significant stage in the expansion of intervals is established in the second theme (from fig.9.10). The lower strings unfold the theme in two forms of a special non-diatonic folk mode, first with raised third (C D E F G♭ A♭ B♭), then with normal third (C D E♭ F G♭ A♭ B♭),[9] both thirds of which are articulated in the sforzando chord of the first violin (Ex. 1a). The normal form of this mode implies the presence of three different types of pitch-set segments (Ex. 1b) – diatonic (E♭ F G♭ A♭ B♭ C), octatonic (C D E♭ F G♭ A♭) and whole-tone (G♭ A♭ B♭ C D) – all of which form the basis of scalar interactions in the development section.

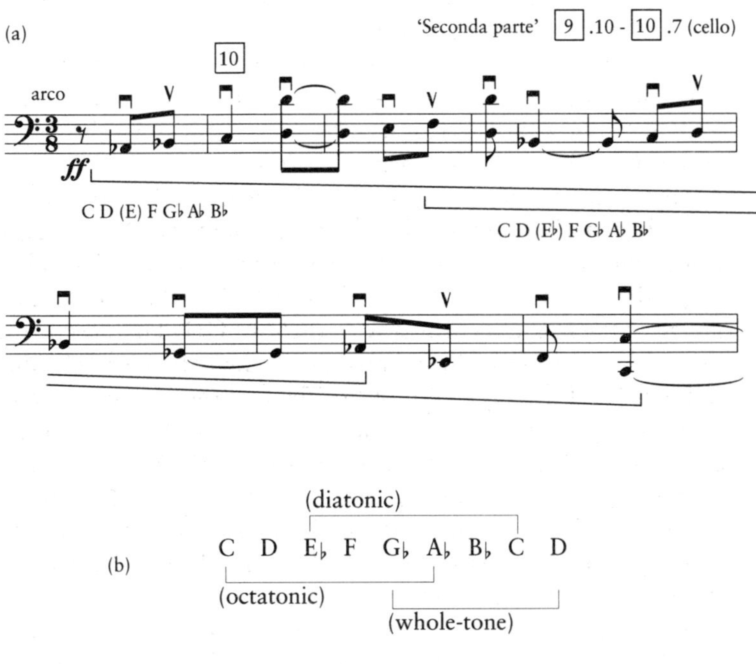

EX. 1

The initial ascent of the theme, with raised third, unfolds five notes of the whole-tone cycle A♭ B♭ C D E. The latter, which appears for the first time in this theme, represents the next stage of expansion in the large-scale progression from chromatic through octatonic and diatonic to the final cycle-5/7 formations. In the following thematic canon (fig.13), based on a permutation of the non-diatonic folk mode E F♯ G♯ A♯ B C♯ D, two of the three modal possibilities are completed. The chromatic D♯ implies the presence of the complete E Lydian mode and the descending phase outlines the complete whole-tone cycle A♯ G♯ F♯ E D C B♭, while the descending lines of the lower strings each outline six-note segments of two different octatonic scales. A stretto (at fig.15) outlines a scale based on two adjacent whole-tone tetrachords, D E F♯ G♯ and A B C♯ D♯, the latter of which is extended to a complete form of the non-diatonic folk mode A B C♯ D♯ E F♯ G.

These pitch-set interactions continue throughout the development section (from fig.23), the last half of which (from fig.31) employs theme 1*b* in the non-diatonic modal form A B C D E♭ F G, as the basis of a fugue with successive entries at the fifth (A, E, A, E). The recapitulation is rounded out by a brief reversal of the process based on the chromatic compression of the second theme (fig.39.10 – fig.41), the coda (from fig.43) further establishing a sense of return to the compressed introductory material of the 'Prima parte'. While the cello glissando outlines the C♯–E boundary of the original chromatic tetrachord, the upper three strings sustain the initial introductory segment B♭ C A. This movement ends with a gapped segment of the original chromatic tetrachord, C♯ D [] E, and G A C of the original diatonic motif. The D♯ missing from the chromatic tetrachord then initiates the 'Ricapitulazione'.

The goals of both cyclic–interval expansion and compression are fulfilled in the 'Coda'. The first return of the second theme in the latter part of this movement (at fig.10.7) serves as a convergent point for these conversely related processes. The second theme (on viola and cello) is initiated precisely by the two 5/7 dyads (C♯–G♯ and D♯–A♯) of the final cycle-5/7 tetrachord. At the same time, the repeated-note figure is based on the original cycle-1/11 tetrachord, C♯ D D♯ E (first violin), and its transposition, F♯ G G♯ A (second violin). While the two polarized cyclic collections (5/7 and 1/11) are separated between theme and accompaniment, the explicit partitioning of the two chromatic tetrachords into their interval-2/10 dyads permits a vertical alignment of the violins at a cycle-5/7 tetrachord, F♯ C♯ G♯ D♯. Interval 5/7 then predominates both in the parallel thematic harmonies of the lower strings and in the root motion to the penultimate G♯ pedal and back to the tonic C♯, preparing us for the final cycle-5/7 tetrachord, C♯ G♯ D♯ A♯. The registral format of these dyads establishes C♯–D♯ as the boundary of the chord as well as its ultimate relationship with the original chromatic tetrachord, bounded by C♯–D♯ by means of octave displacement. Perle states that 'The fact that both sonorities are bounded by the same pitches, C♯ and D♯ . . . is suggestive of the role that the concept of centricity performs in this work, in spite of the quasi "atonal" and even "twelve-tone" character of certain sections.'[10]

Convergence of both the expansion and compression processes is prepared in the most dense and aggressive of contrapuntal textures. Canons, inverted strettos and glissandos, pedal points and repeated-note figures are juxtaposed against the rapid thematic figuration. The E♭ Dorian form of the initial theme 1*b* material is accompanied now by a C pedal, which replaces the 'dissonant' (non-modal) D pedal that produced a prominent octatonic intrusion at the opening of the 'Seconda parte'. Instead, octatonic elements intrude directly into the thematic lines to produce increasingly prominent octatonic overlappings with the E♭ Dorian mode. The first octatonic intrusion is note D (bar 3, cello), the second, note B𝄫 (bar 8). By the end of the crescendo and *sul ponticello* both diatonic and octatonic modes have been mixed thoroughly. Thus, an increasing number of semitones enters into the diatonic lines.

In the next passage (from fig.3) interval expansion occurs against the gradually contracting intervals of the diatonic variant of theme 1*b*. The cello unfolds overlapping octatonic, diatonic and whole-tone segments (Ex. 2), the expanding intervals of which are punctuated by fourths A E B (at fig.4). The latter moves, in turn, to long-note ostinatos that outline two tritones, B–F and E–B♭. Still further expansion occurs in the cello ostinato at the return to theme 1*b* (fig.5). These broken fifths and sixths culminate at the cycle-5/7 segments of the second theme (at fig.11). Conversely, the more rapid lines of theme 1*b* (from fig.3) proceed from diatonic to more compressed diatonic–octatonic overlappings (at figs 7–10). In the climactic passage leading to the second theme (figs 10–11) the ascending scales in

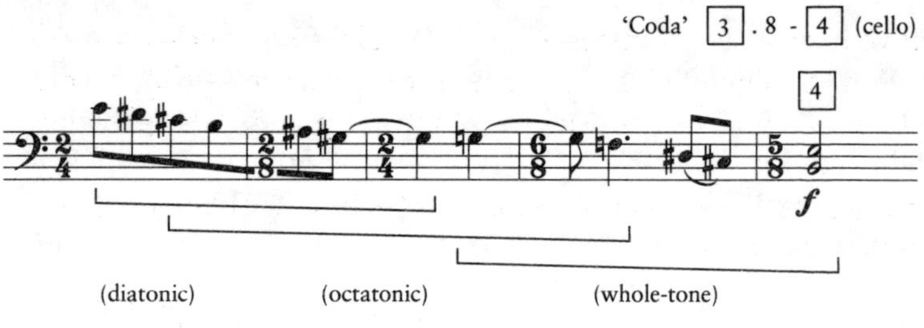

EX. 2

the inverted double canon unfold two complete octatonic scales, while a still more extreme compression is linearly suggested in the descending glissandos. Paradoxically, expansion of range is produced in these inversionally diverging parts as they culminate in the simultaneously compressed (1/11) and expanded (5/7) segments of the second theme.

Bartók's move toward ever greater abstraction and synthesis of divergent art-music and folk-music sources is further epitomized in the rigidly constructed arch form of the Fourth String Quartet. According to Bartók:

> The work is in five movements; their character corresponds to Classical sonata form. The slow movement is the kernel of the work; the other movements are, as it were, arranged in layers around it. Movement IV is a free variation of II, and I and V have the same thematic material; that is, around the kernel (Movement III), metaphorically speaking, I and V are the outer, II and IV the inner layers.[11]

Despite the use of a more abstract musical language, folk characteristics are, nevertheless, still very much in evidence. The *tempo giusto* character of the first movement is balanced by the more complex 'variable' *tempo giusto* of the fifth movement.[12] In the latter a motoric ostinato rhythm in a typical Bulgarian unequal-beat dance pattern of $\frac{3+2+3}{8}$ (from bar 11) accompanies the main theme (bars 15–18), which implies an irregular metre of $\frac{4+3+3}{8}$ as the basis of a folk-like four-line stanzaic structure (unfolding to bar 40). The slow central movement also prominently reveals folk characteristics in its use of a highly embellished *parlando rubato* cello theme, based on an 'old'-style Magyar rhythmic pattern of eight units followed by a cadential figure of a short and two longs (Ex. 3), and a held chord typical of Eastern European bagpipe (dudelsack) drones.

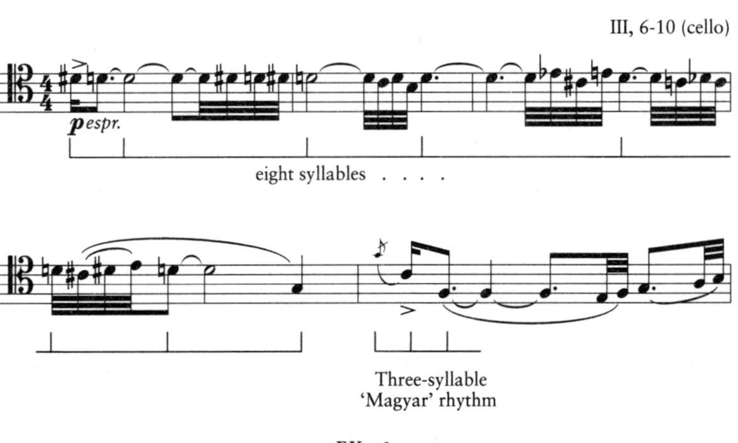

EX. 3

The four-line stanzaic structure of the tune unfolds through the A section of the movement (bars 1–34). The rhapsodic melody itself appears to derive from the *hora lunga* (long song) that Bartók discovered in Romanian folk music.[13]

These folk-music characteristics interact with abstract melodic and harmonic constructions to produce a sense of organic development within the framework of traditional forms. In the central movement the predominating interval is the whole tone. The whole-tone cycles represent, according to the principle of 'diatonic extension' or 'chromatic compression', an intermediary intervallic stage between the predominating cycles (1/11 and 5/7) of the opening and closing movements, respectively. In the first phrase of this movement (bars 1–13), the bagpipe-like drone unfolds two whole-tone trichords, G♯ F♯ E and C♯ B A, which together form a diatonic hexachord. These two trichords are expanded to two whole-tone tetrachords, G♯ F♯ E [D] and [D♯] C♯ B A, by the addition of dyad D♯–D (cello), that is, the 'axis of symmetry' (Ex. 4a).[14] This dyad establishes the 'tonal centre', or axis, of 'sum 5', as demonstrated in Ex. 4b.[15]

Three types of tetrachordal cells, consecutively based on expanding intervals, result from the systematic interlocking of these two whole-tone tetrachords – a semitonal nucleus, C♯ D D♯ E (X-1), the two whole-tone cells, D E F♯ G♯ (Y-2) and A B C♯ D♯ (Y-9), and the combined tritonal boundaries of the latter, A D D♯ G♯ (Z-9/3).[16] These cells, which are themselves segments of the interval cycles, are basic in generating the entire system of interval cycles as well as in establishing axes of symmetry throughout the quartet. In this movement both complete whole-tone cycles are generated from the opening Y–Z construction. As shown in Ex. 4c, the opening Y-2 is transposed by interval 4 to Y-10 (beginning of the middle section, four lowest pedal notes), while the other opening whole-tone tetrachord, Y-9, is analogously transposed by interval 4 to Y-1 (two highest pedal notes and first violin). The transposed Y combination, of B♭ C D E (Y-10) and C♯ E♭ F G (Y-1), significantly maintains the sum-5 axis, D–D♯, of the initial Y-2 / Y-9 combination, both passages commonly intersecting at X-1, C♯ D D♯ E. This background-level transposition from Y-2 to Y-10 adds B♭–C to complete the first whole-tone hexachord, B♭–C / D E F♯ G♯, while the transposition from Y-9 to Y-1 adds dyad F–G to complete the other, A B C♯ D♯ / F–G.

The third phrase (bars 22–9) serves as a link in this background-level unfolding of the whole-tone cycles. The drone contains five notes of one whole-tone cycle, G♯ B♭ C D E, and the solo cello five notes of the other, G A B C♯ D♯, which is completed by the addition of F–G (bars 28–9). While the two odd notes, F and F♯, of the respective cycles are interchanged between the lower viola pedal F and cello F♯ (bar 23), they nevertheless appear in the appropriate registral positions with regard to their respective cycles. At the same time a retention of basic axis-dyad D–D♯ is suggested in the highest and lowest notes of the passage. Thus, both whole-tone cycles are generated from the initial X–Y–Z construction around a single axis of symmetry.

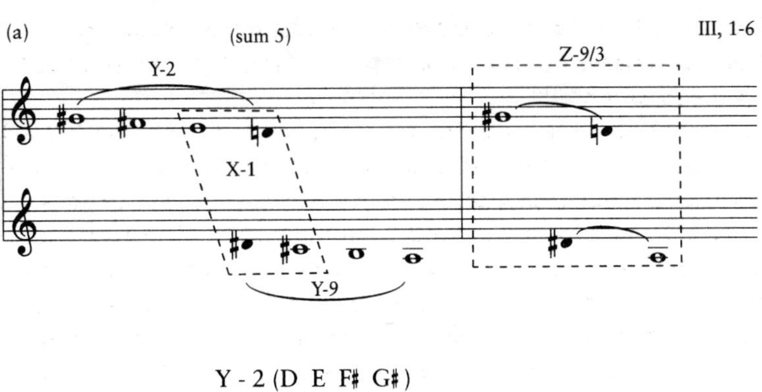

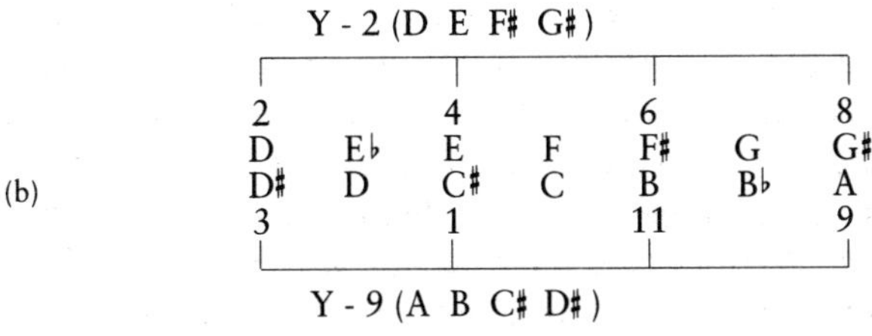

inversionally complementary 1/11 cycles at axis of sum 5 (= 17-12).

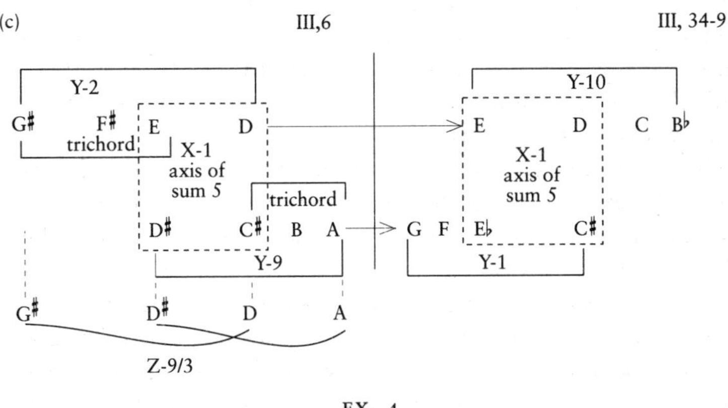

EX. 4

The tendency toward organic expansion within the traditional formal framework of the first movement is established in the opening Classically balanced pairs of phrases and periods.[17] The inward motion at the cadence of the initial antecedent phrase (bar 2, first violin and cello) is balanced by the outward motion at the cadence of the consequent phrase (bar 4).[18] The intervallic properties of cells X, Y and Z are essential in continuing this expansion. The first important harmonic progression (bars 5–6), which initiates the strettos of the next pair of phrases, expands from the semitones of X-0 (C C♯ D D♯) to the whole tones of Y-10 (B♭ C D E: see Ex. 7, below.) The last stretto of the first thematic group (bars 11–13), which is preceded by more rapid cadential X-0 and Y-10 expansions, unfolds linear statements of cell X in the basic rhythmic motif. A viola ostinato begins the transition with the larger whole tones of incomplete Y-10, [] C D E, which then is completed by the addition of B♭ (bar 22, second violin). At this point we get the third, more expanded symmetrical tetrachord, Z-8/2, vertically stated as G♯ C♯ D G (viola and first violin) and linearly as D G A♭ D♭ (first violin). These two tritones of Z, C♯–G and G♯–D, are anticipated in the preceding canon (from bar 15, in the violins), where they form the boundary intervals of the subject and answer, respectively. Thus, the intervallic expansion in the overall X–Y–Z progression of the first thematic group and transition, shown in Ex. 5a, continues the trend initiated by the outward motion of the first consequent phrase.

The construction of the three cells, one from the other according to the equal divisions of the octave, also contributes to the expansion of range. The cadential chord of the first thematic group, B♭ B C C♯ D D♯ E (bar 13), represents a joining of the two X transpositions which are separated by a minor third – X-10, B♭ B C C♯, and X-1, C♯ D D♯ E – to produce the tritonal boundary of basic Y-10, B♭–E. This X-cell combination is explicitly established in the linear motivic statements of the preceding stretto (bar 12), where X-10 (second violin and cello) is motivically inverted by X-1 (first violin and viola). Analogous to the construction of the interval-6 boundary of Y from the two conjunct interval-3 boundaries of X, the tritonal boundaries of Z are formed by joining two specific Y cells near the end of the second theme (bars 40–43, first violin). Here, the boundaries of Y-6 and Y-1 outline Z-1/7 (D♭ G♭ G C).

The structural priority of cells X, Y and Z in the first thematic

X – Y – Z progressions in the first movement
(a) Exposition

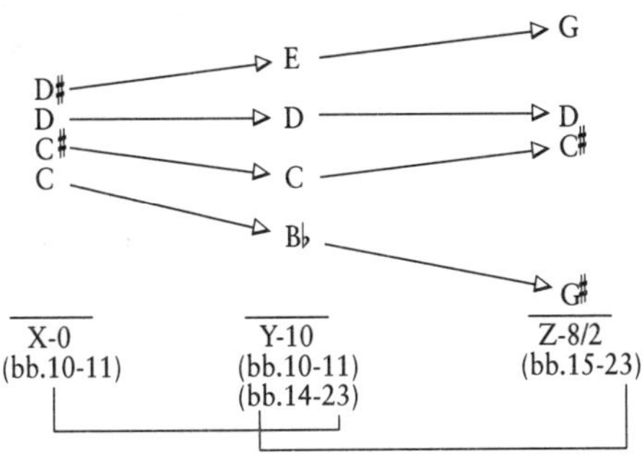

(b) Development

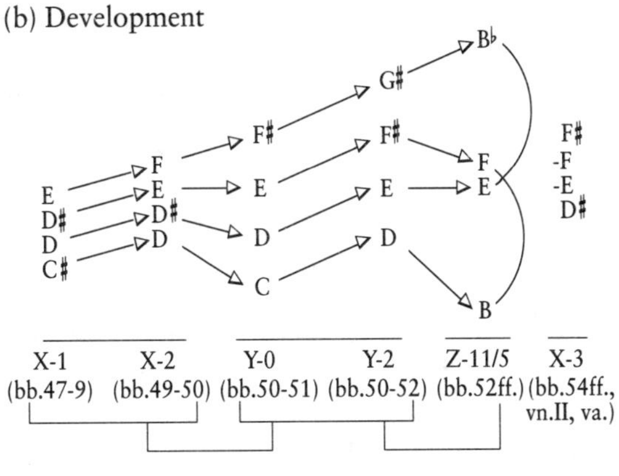

EX. 5

group and transition is supported by the principle of metric departure and return to the regular $\frac{4}{4}$ barring. In the transition (from bar 14) the combined lines produce more complex polymetric patterns, each ostinato implying an unequal-beat metre against the barline. At the first foreground occurrence of Z (bar 22), some metric uniformity appears. The second violin gives us B♭ of cell Y at the barline, the C D E ostinato of cell Y on cello also coinciding with the downbeat and the Z statements on first violin and viola, respectively, subdividing the bar into $\frac{2+3+3}{8}$ and $\frac{3+3+2}{8}$. The viola then establishes regular crotchets (bars 23–4), while the first violin plays a regular syncopation against them. At the opening of the second theme (bar 30) all the instruments are aligned for the first time on the downbeat, on Y-8 (A♭ B♭ C D).

The basic transpositional levels of X and Z share the same axis of symmetry (Ex. 5a), a principle so basic to the new concept of 'tonality' in Bartók's music. The 'key' of the X–Y–Z progression in the first thematic group and transition is sum 3, while the X–Y–Z progression in the development section moves to sum 9, as shown in Ex. 5b. The relationship between these two sets of X–Y–Z progressions is analogous to the tonal relations of the traditional sonata plan. In traditional schemes the common principle of modulation entails tonal motion by the components of the tonic triad. That is, if we move from the tonic area of the first thematic group to the dominant area of the second thematic group and development section, the motion has its reference in the root and fifth degrees of the tonic triad. The same principle is demonstrated in minor keys where the tonality shifts by way of the root to the third degree of the tonic minor triad. Analogously, in the present work, tonal motion from the exposition to the opening of the development occurs by way of the cyclic intervals of the basic cells, as shown in Ex. 5b. Cell X moves up by semitones and Y by whole tones. Cell Y-2 (D E F♯ G♯) then expands to Z-11/5 (B E E♯ A♯), which is the minor-third transposition of original Z-8/2. As shown in Ex. 6, separation by this interval permits both of these Z transpositions to be symmetrically related to each other around either of two different axes of symmetry, C♯–D (or G–G♯) and E–F (or B♭–B) of sums 3 and 9, so that common-chord, Z-cell pivots can be established between these two different 'keys'. The common chord is established at the end of the following canon (bars 53–60), where the inverted stretto between cello and first violin symmetrically contracts from the B–B♭ of Z-11/5, around D–G, to C♯–A♭, producing the sum-9 permutation of original Z-8/2, C♯ D G A♭. At bar 58 a Z-8/2 ostinato is established around the X-3 (sum-9) nucleus which had been unfolding in the two inner

Symmetrical relations between basic X and Z transpositions in the first movement

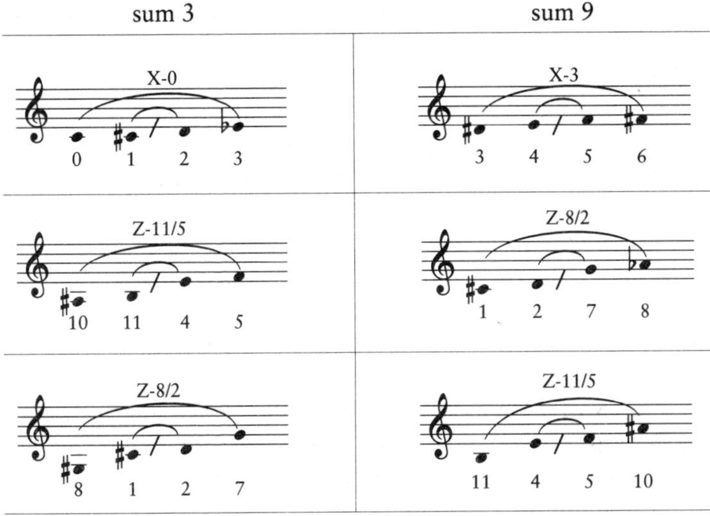

EX. 6

parts. The long-range modulation from axis C♯–D (sum 3) of the exposition to axis E–F (sum 9) of the development is foreshadowed in the opening interaction of X transpositions at these two sums, as shown in Ex. 7.

The key of C represents the basic tonal frame of the quartet, but it also has special connections with the axial concept of tonality. The dual notion of C as the modal tonic of the quasi-Phrygian cadences of the first and fifth movements and as an axis of symmetry is basic to the fusion concept in Bartók's music: C–C (sum-0) is the ultimate axis of the local B♭–B (sum-9) and C♯–D (sum-3) axes. The long-range symmetrical relationship between two basic X-to-Y progressions in the first movement is shown in Ex. 8. Thus, a link between the somewhat traditional tonal frame of C, which is asserted in the first and last bars of the quartet, and the primary odd axes of sums 3 and 9 is suggested in the interrelations of the basic symmetrical cells.

EX. 7

In the fifth movement cell Z is basic in generating two types of intervallic sets – diatonic (cycle-5/7) and octatonic – and, as in the 'Coda' of the Third String Quartet, these two sets represent the final stages of expansion and compression. Cycle 5/7 is generated in two complementary partitions in the ostinato accompaniment from the tritone-separated fourths of initial Z-1/7 (D♭–F♯/G–C), while the octatonic set gradually unfolds in

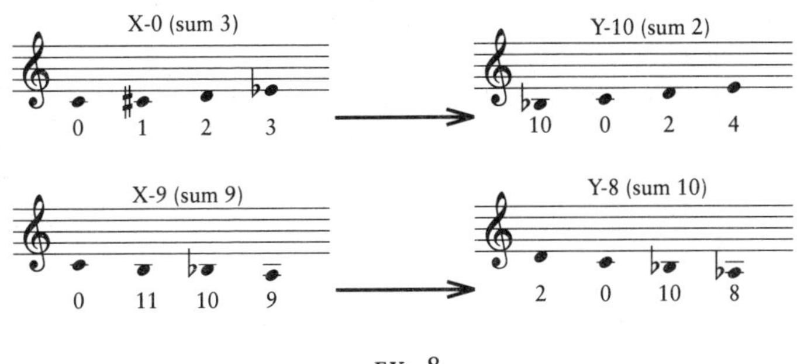

EX. 8

the successive thematic statements. The octatonic theme (C♯ D♯ E F♯ G A B♭ B♯) emerges complete in the violins, then viola (bars 44–75). Basic Z-1/7 (D♭ F♯ G C), which permeates the ostinatos of the opening passages, is joined by its complement, Z-10/4 (B♭ D♯ E A), which first appears in the violins (bar 45) to form the complete octatonic theme. This relationship of two Z cells a minor third apart is the same as that between Z-8/2 and Z-11/5 of the first movement, both of which were subsequently interlocked in the octatonic scale D E F G G♯ A♯ B C♯ near the end of the second movement (bars 243–6, viola).

As part of the final expansion phase in this final movement (bars 357–69) the cycle-5/7 ostinatos culminate in the held notes E A D G C, after which they move to the wider cycle-8/4 pedals G♭ B♭ D (bars 369–74). Conversely, the main octatonic theme, which first appears fragmented and then joined with a diatonic segment (from bar 365), moves toward cell X in the final compression phase (last stretto, from bar 374). The modified linear statements of the X motif first unfold as intervallically wider octatonic tetrachords (G♭ G [] A B♭, etc.), which are then contracted to the original semitonal form of cell X (C♯ D D♯ E and G A♭ A B♭) at the penultimate cadence (bars 384–5).

Such thematic compression is also locally reflected in the middle section (bars 151–236), where the diatonic/whole-tone theme (based on Y-6 and Y-11), accompanied by cycle-5/7 ostinatos, is compressed in the return to linear statements of cell X. The expansion–compression principle is also reflected in the relation between the chromatic arch-shaped theme of the second movement and the fourth movement's expanded hybrid (diatonic–octatonic) arch-shaped theme (A♭ B♭ C D E♭ F G♭ A♭).

Thus, the essence of various Eastern European folk-music styles is absorbed and transformed into a highly integrated system of pitch relations in the middle-period quartets, both based on classically orientated forms that outline an overall arch shape. The latter appears to be a primary manifestation of Bartók's interest in the organic development and transformation of materials, in which he systematically moves between concentrated intervallic constructions and larger ones by means of diatonic (cyclic) expansion or chromatic compression of themes. Cells X, Y and Z, which appear comprehensively in the Fourth String Quartet and to a lesser extent in the Third, are the most systematic manifestations of this procedure.

NOTES

1 The impact of works by Frescobaldi and della Ciaia on Bartók's First Piano Concerto (1926) is demonstrated in Benjamin Suchoff's 'The Impact of Italian Baroque Music on Bartók's Music', in *Bartók and Kodály Revisited*, ed. György Ránki, Budapest (Akadémiai Kiadó), 1987, pp. 189–93.

2 An interval cycle, such as the whole-tone scale, cycle of fifths, etc., is a series based on a single recurrent interval, the sequence of which is completed by the return of the initial pitch class. The components of a symmetrical pitch collection are shown to be derived from the alignment of a given interval cycle and its literal inversion (see Ex. 4b).

3 See my *The Music of Béla Bartók*, Berkeley (University of California Press), 1984, p. 21 and Chapter VI.

4 The first concert performance of the Third Quartet was given in Philadelphia on 30 December 1928 by the Mischakoff/Dubinsky/Lifschey/Van der Berg Quartet. The first concert performance of the Fourth Quartet took place on 20 March 1929 in Budapest, although it was premièred over BBC radio in Britain on 22 February 1929; both these performances were given by the Hungarian (Waldbauer–Kerpely) Quartet. For further historical details see János Kárpáti, *Bartók's String Quartets*, Budapest (Corvina Press), 1975, pp. 197–9 and 209–11.

5 *BBE*, p. 381.

6 Intervals imply their complements or harmonic inversions in the same interval-class and may be more specifically designated by double numbers, calculated in semitones (which will always add to twelve): 0/12, 1/11, 2/10, and so on.

7 These complementary cyclic relations occur still more systematically in the finale of the Fourth Quartet, as first demonstrated in my Ph.D. dissertation, 'Principles of Pitch Organization in Bartók's Fourth String Quartet' (City University of New York, 1975), and further developed in my *The Music of Béla Bartók* in connection with many other works of Bartók. See also Wallace Berry, 'Symmetrical interval sets and derivative pitch materials in Bartók's String Quartet no. 3', *Perspectives of New Music*, vol.18 (1979–80), p. 299.

8 See George Perle, 'The String Quartets of Béla Bartók', in *A Musical Offering: Essays in Honor of Martin Bernstein*, ed. Claire Brook and E. H. Clinkscale, New York (Pendragon Press), 1977, pp. 202–3.

9 See pattern 10 of Table 2 in *RFM*.iv, p. 19.

10 Perle, op. cit., p. 201.

11 *BBE*, p. 412.

12 *Tempo giusto* refers to the strict rhythm of the oldest of the Hungarian dance tunes. 'Variable' or 'adjustable' *tempo giusto* refers to the more complex strict rhythm of the 'new' style of Hungarian folksong, in which 'the crotchet pairs . . . adjust themselves to the quantity, natural or positional, of the syllables of the text.' See *HFS*, pp. xxxvi, 28.

13 See Péter Laki, 'Der lange Gesang als Grundtyp in der internationalen Volksmusik', *SM*, vol.24 (1982), pp. 393–400.

14 We arbitrarily assign 0 (= 12) to the pitch-class C, 1 to C♯, 2 to D, etc. Transposition numbers of pitch collections will also be designated by numbers 0 to 11. We will assume a referential symmetrical order in assigning a transposition number to a collection; the pitch-class number of the 'first' (or lowest) note will designate that collection according to this assumed abstract arrangement. So, X-1 has C♯ as its 'first' note, Y-2 and Y-9, D and A as respective 'first' notes.

15 Any symmetrically placed pairing of pitch-classes within a larger symmetrical collection will have the same sum, that is, axis of symmetry, as any other symmetrically placed pairing in that collection. Ex. 4b shows that a series of sum-5 dyads are generated by aligning two inversionally related semitonal cycles that intersect at D–D♯ (or its dual axis, G♯–A). The sum conveniently represents the axis of symmetry.

16 Cell Z-9 (A D D♯ G♯) is special in that its pitch content remains unchanged at its tritonal transposition, Z-3, D♯ G♯ A D, and so is designated by both transposition numbers, Z-9/3. George Perle was the first to speak of these 'sets X and Y', in 1955; Leo Treitler first referred to 'cell Z' in 1959. All three cells were first discussed in depth and shown to be part of a larger system in my Ph.D. dissertation (see above).

17 For Bartók's brief formal analysis of this quartet see *BBE*, pp. 412–13.

18 See Kárpáti, op. cit., p. 211.

19

Violin Rhapsodies

VERA LAMPERT

The two violin rhapsodies, as with many of Bartók's works written in the 1920s, were conceived with practical ends in mind. During this decade Bartók established himself as a pianist on the European musical scene and, although he loathed concertizing and undertook it mainly for financial reasons, he was aware that his performances gave him the opportunity to propagate his own works and to make himself better known as a composer. In various representatives of the renowned Hungarian school of violin playing he found congenial performing partners, not only in the interpretation of Classical repertory but also in performances of his own compositions. His two violin sonatas of 1921–2, written for his friend from his student years Jelly Arányi, were featured on many programmes in the twenties which he gave with such illustrious Hungarian violinists as Imre Waldbauer, Zoltán Székely, Ede Zathureczky, Joseph Szigeti, Emil Telmányi and Endre Gertler. Soon it must have been obvious that other virtuoso pieces by Bartók, especially shorter and lighter ones, would also be welcome. Firstly, in 1926 Székely transcribed the Romanian Folk Dances for violin and piano, and in 1927 Szigeti arranged some movements from *For Children.* Bartók responded in 1928 with the two violin rhapsodies and, perhaps in recognition of the efforts of Székely and Szigeti or because he felt personally closest to these two, he dedicated the rhapsodies to them.

Bartók wanted to provide versatile pieces which could be adapted to different circumstances, and so both rhapsodies were published in several versions: for violin and piano, violin and orchestra, and the first rhapsody also appeared for cello and piano. There was much guessing in the Bartók literature about the sequence of completion of these different versions. During the past decade, however, many new documents have come to light, particularly items of family correspondence, from which we can today more precisely establish Bartók's intentions and the sequence of events. He wrote to his mother on 26 August 1928:

> I was diligent again during the summer and wrote the following: a piece for violin with piano accompaniment of about twelve minutes. This is an arrangement of folk dances; I will make an orchestral version of it later, that is, I will adapt it for violin with orchestral accompaniment. Then I intend to transcribe the whole thing for violoncello with piano accompaniment.[1]

Instead of working on the planned transcriptions, however, Bartók created another violin rhapsody during the next few weeks. He must have finished it before his trip to Prague on 6 October because his wife gave it to Székely to practise during Bartók's absence. Upon Bartók's return they rehearsed – probably both rhapsodies – and it was then that (according to Székely's recollection) Bartók let him choose which of the rhapsodies would be 'his'. Székely preferred the second one and gave its first performance in Amsterdam on 19 November 1928, with Géza Frid at the piano. Szigeti did not get a chance to play his Rhapsody until a year later, and it was, in fact, Székely who premièred it, on 4 March 1929 in London at an all-Bartók concert, with Bartók at the piano. In the draft of a letter to his publisher, Universal Edition, of 27 December 1928 Bartók mentioned the orchestral transcriptions still as a project for the near future. The cello version was presented to the Budapest public on 20 March 1929 by Jenő Kerpely and Bartók. The orchestral versions were first performed during the autumn of 1929: Szigeti gave the first performance of the First Rhapsody on 1 November in Königsberg (now Kaliningrad), with Hermann Scherchen conducting; Székely played the Second Rhapsody in Budapest on 25 November, with Ernő Dohnányi conducting.

By 1928 Bartók had used more than two hundred folksongs in his compositions, mostly melodies with texts, but also some eighteen instrumental pieces. Yet the violin rhapsodies differ from the earlier folksong arrangements in two significant respects. One is the way of identifying sources. In earlier arrangements Bartók made an effort to give as much information about his sources as possible, either by printing the folksongs used at the beginning of his score (as in the piano Improvisations) or in added notes (as in the Sonatina), or at least in the title or subtitle of the composition (as in the Slovak Folksongs or *Village Scenes*). In these rhapsodies the information is deliberately reduced to 'folk dances', and we can only guess Bartók's reasons for withholding the exact details. In January 1931, when Octavian Beu inquired about the national original of the themes of the rhapsodies, Bartók answered: 'No.1 uses Romanian and Hungarian melodies, No.2 Romanian, Hungarian and Ruthenian.'[2] László Somfai speculates that since some of the dances used in the rhapsodies (which had been performed by Romanian gypsy musicians) preserved an old Hungarian instrumental form, the *verbunkos*, Bartók 'was not quite sure of the nationalities of the themes'.[3] This problem might have strongly contributed to his decision to restrict information about the dances. On the other hand, the Three Rondos on Folk Tunes, finished one year earlier and published a year after the rhapsodies, use exclusively Slovak materials yet show the same reserve in their subtitle: 'on folk melodies'. Obviously, at that time Bartók thought that the results of withholding exact details of his sources would be of greater benefit than those of providing them.

All the sources used in these violin rhapsodies have now been identified in Bartók's various folk-music collections. Most of these tunes – thirteen out of sixteen – appear in the posthumously published first volume of the *Rumanian Folk Music*, which contains more than eight hundred instrumental melodies collected by Bartók mainly between 1910 and 1914 in Transylvania (then part of Hungary). These sources reveal that all the dances used in the violin rhapsodies were collected from peasant violinists. Keeping the instrument of the original source – the violin – in his composition is, again, unique among Bartók's folksong arrangements. It is as if he were aiming for something more than simply using 'folk themes': he wanted to transplant the peasant performance and to preserve for posterity the art of those folk musicians who had amazed him with their skill and repertoire.

Compared with the high standard of classical violin playing, the technique of these peasant players was primitive: they rarely left first position and, aside from a few players, played the frequently used double stops with open strings. Other aspects of the performance, however, rendered this style very exciting and interesting. First of all, its fiery rhythm: 'invigorating accents are frequently put on either odd or even eighths [quavers] of the $\frac{2}{4}$ measure; sometimes the two kinds of accentuation are alternated.'[4] Frequent also were the phenomena of the 'shifted rhythm' (when the same fragment of melody 'is repeated with shifted accents so that accentuated parts lose their accent in the repeat while non-accentuated parts gain one'[5]) and unusual phrasing (the slurring of short, non-accentuated notes to accentuated, long ones). The rich ornamentation of the slow dances, the great variety of motifs and modal scales (Lydian, Mixolydian, etc.), as well as their unusual combinations, and the ambivalent intonation of some scale degrees also enhance the exotic character of the performance. Bartók strove to take over into his rhapsodies as many of these features as he could. He even played the original recordings to his violinist friends to familiarize them with the peculiarities of the original folk performances. Naturally, he exceeded the limitations of the peasant players so as fully to exploit the technical potential of his friends, and used techniques rare or unknown in the peasant players' performances. But often the most virtuoso passages are those which expand the elements of that primitive style.

The violin rhapsodies represent an important milestone in Bartók's *œuvre*. They mark the return to the so-called '"verbunkos" thematic'. At the very beginning of his career Bartók's works – such as the symphonic poem *Kossuth* or the Rhapsody Op.1 – were written in this peculiar Hungarian style, best known from Liszt's compositions of Hungarian character but also prevailing in the popular music of Hungary at that time. After his discovery of genuine folk music, however, Bartók completely lost interest in it and considered it the main obstacle to the wider recognition of his new style. Later, through Kodály's historical research, many documents came to light which preserved the original eighteenth- and early nineteenth-century form of the *verbunkos*, and Bartók himself discovered it among the material he collected from village folk. The inspiration to use *verbunkos*-type melodies might also have come from Kodály, who first used a *verbunkos* melody (taken from a publication of 1802) in his *Háry János* (1924–7), and then again in his Dances of Marosszék (1927).

As Bartók pointed out, there is a close relationship between the Hungarian *verbunkos* and the first few melodies used in his violin rhapsodies. He described these melodies as having 'a rather rugged rhythm as a result of the frequent use of ♪.♬ ♪.♬ patterns, instead of even sixteen-note [semiquaver] values, which give a march-like "heroic" character to these pieces'.[6] In his later compositions (such as *Contrasts*, the Second Violin Concerto and Third Piano Concerto) thematic constructions of this type play an important role.

The '"verbunkos" thematic' and the brilliant presentation must have unequivocally suggested rhapsody form to Bartók. This genre was made famous by Liszt, and if Bartók did not particularly like these works, he none the less knew them well as he had in 1911–17 prepared them for the complete edition of Liszt's works. They consist of two main parts: slow (*lassú*) followed by fast (*friss*). The themes are not developed but are presented one after the other, with occasional recurrences, repetitions or variations. This is exactly the form of Bartók's Rhapsody Op.1 of 1904, but these slow–fast juxtapositions also appear in some other of his early orchestral pieces and in the more recent Second Violin Sonata (1922). Through his folk-music research Bartók discovered that 'the playing of a slower and a faster piece in succession – a composite structure of higher order – is, or was, in frequent use on Hungarian and Rumanian soil',[7] and must have felt that his choice of rhapsody form was even more justified.

Today the First Violin Rhapsody is played more often than its counterpart. It is known and liked better, and considered more

Classical – a natural consequence of its pleasing melodies and concise structure. Its thematic material is more economical than that of the Second Rhapsody: six melodies as against ten. (In fact, there is a seventh melody in the manuscript draft of the First Rhapsody, but Bartók left it out solely for the sake of greater coherence.) The form is symmetrical: the two melodies of the *lassú* result in an *A B A* form, and the *friss*, recalling shortly its third theme after the fourth, concludes the work by bringing back the first theme of the *lassú* movement. The alternative ending, which is obligatory when the *friss* is performed alone, rounds off the form by bringing back the first melody of the *friss*. The melodies themselves are symmetrical and rounded. The five Romanian melodies are chosen from the same, most popular group of dance melodies: those with four equal melodic lines each containing four $\frac{2}{4}$ bars. The second melody, which serves as the 'trio' section of the *lassú*, stands out in several respects: it is the only Hungarian melody of the group; it has a sung variant (a so-called 'wailing song'); structurally it is very similar to the others except that its second and fourth lines have a little extension for the wailing syllables of the text.

It is interesting that Bartók chose the same type of melody to have a similar function in the Second Violin Rhapsody; here the second melody of the work (the first 'trio' of the *lassú*) is a Romanian violin piece which has two textual variants (one Romanian, one Hungarian), both being wailing songs of similar structure. The other two melodies of the first part of the second rhapsody (the *A* and *C* sections of an *A B A C* form) are the same type as the melodies used in the First Rhapsody. The second, *friss* part, however, contains seven melodies, most of which belong to another important group of Romanian dances, those without any determined structure, consisting of 'irregular repetitions, without any plan and co-ordination, of one or more motifs generally composed of two to four bars'.[8] Here the form is left open. Other than creating transitional material between the themes, in the very spirit of the free, improvising character of the sources, there is no attempt to restrict the spontaneous unfolding of ideas. The result is an exuberant dance fantasy, with a seemingly endless heightening of suspense. Bartók was aware of the difficulty of balancing this against the first part of the composition. He made several alterations in the following years and finally, in 1945, a revised, much condensed version was published.

In both violin rhapsodies the piano has a secondary, supportive role and only occasionally is accorded a share in the thematic material. The texture is often chordal, alternating with linear–polyphonic details, and is more daring and varied in the Second Rhapsody, where the piano part is truly brilliant and rich in sonorities, evoking many of the effects of the orchestral version. The orchestral versions are scored to display the different characters of the two rhapsodies: in the first, the only percussion instrument is the cimbalom, which can be substituted by the harp; in the second, a large group of percussion instruments increases the effect of the exotic dances.

NOTES

1 *BBcl*, p. 448.
2 *BBL*, p. 202.
3 'A 2. hegedűrapszódia rutén epizódja', in *Tizennyolc Bartók tanulmány*, Budapest (Zeneműkiadó), 1981, p. 307.
4 *RFM*.i, p. 16.
5 *RFM*.i, p. 45.
6 *RFM*.i, p. 48.
7 *RFM*.i, p. 55.
8 *RFM*.i, p. 13.

20

Violin Duos and Late String Quartets

MALCOLM GILLIES

After the flurry of important compositions in 1926–8, which had culminated in the Fourth String Quartet, Bartók's output dwindled to a trickle. The *Cantata profana* (1930) and Second Piano Concerto (1930–31) were the only major compositions written until he accepted a commission in 1934 to write the Fifth String Quartet. He did, however, in these six years write numerous new folksong settings or arrangements, of which his Forty-four Duos for violins of 1931 are the most significant.

Bartók's Duos were written at the request of the German violin pedagogue Erich Doflein. In December 1930 Doflein had approached Bartók for permission to set various of the composer's *For Children* for two violins and include them in a series of graded repertory for young violinists. Bartók preferred instead to write some new duos himself. Throughout 1931 he was in close contact with Doflein as they worked out the technical needs and ordering of these pieces. In 1932 thirty-two of Bartók's Duos appeared in either the 'first level' volumes of Doflein's *Das Geigen-Schulwerk* or in his edition of easy or intermediate-level violin pieces by contemporary Hungarian composers.[1] The complete collection of forty-four pieces was published the following year through Bartók's usual publisher, Universal Edition. Bartók's purpose in writing these pieces was very similar to that of *For Children*: to present to young players the beautiful simplicity of various folk musics. Here, however, he spread his ethnic net much wider, through including Romanian, Ruthenian, Serbian, Ukrainian and Arabic, as well as Slovak and Hungarian pieces. In all but two of the forty-four pieces Bartók took original folk tunes,[2] and furnished them either with accompaniments of appropriately ethnic origin or extrapolated from their characteristics more or less adventurous accompaniments. Even the two pieces where he did not use original tunes (nos 35, 36) were, nevertheless, imitation melodies in Ruthenian or Hungarian styles. One sample piece, 'Sorrow' (no.28), provides a representative study of Bartók's methods in his Duos. Its original Hungarian *parlando* melody (Ex. 1) had been taken down way back in 1907 during a most fertile period of collecting in Felsőiregh (Tolna county).

EX. 1

Now Bartók presents it in a more drawn-out, halting form (Ex. 2), accentuating the original's sub-phrasing and melodic contours.

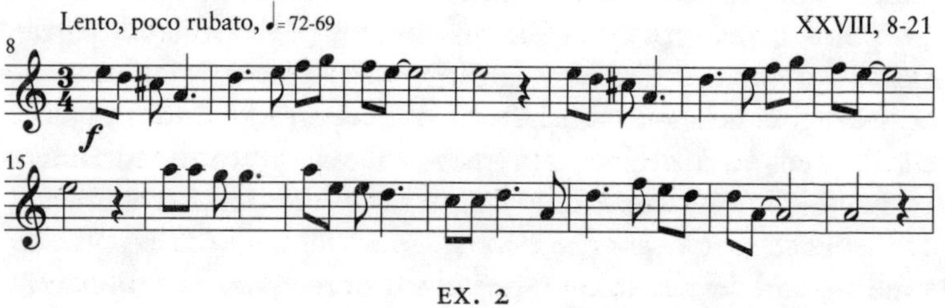

EX. 2

The basis of the tune could be considered Aeolian, but both major and minor thirds, C♯ and C♮, are present. It is played twice, on first violin (bars 8–21) and second violin (bars 25–39). Bartók's setting, however, is chromatically inventive. The first two bars of his quiet introduction establish a collection, <u>A</u> B♭ C D F G G♯, particularly characterized by the tritone D–G♯. From this collection he gradually widens the selection of pitches to include the chromatically remaining notes: C♯ in bar 4, D♯ in bar

6, E in bar 8, B in bar 10, and finally F♯ in bar 13. The accompanying second violin continues to play the smooth, *legato* phrases of the introduction, quite unaffected by the dotted rhythmic patterns of the first violin's melody. At bars 22–4 he inserts a brief, quiet joining passage between the two verses, which, with the semitonal neighbouring notes of G♯ and B♭, points pregnantly across a bar of silence to the second verse, also based on A. Bartók's accompanimental strategy in the second verse is quite different: the parts are more rhythmically bound and create a fuller, more strident harmonic sense through the more frequent use of double stopping. There follows an eight-bar coda, where the material of the opening is varied in such a way as to bring about a slow, contrary-motion resolution: D–B♭, C–B♮, B♭–C, A–C♯. Bartók was clearly pleased with his setting of 'Sorrow'. When in 1936 he turned his mind to a piano arrangement of selected movements from the Duos (which had been selling rather well), he placed this as the first of the pieces in his *Petite Suite*, where he gave it the new title 'Slow Tune'.[3]

Despite their purpose, Bartók's Forty-four Duos cannot be dismissed merely as 'educational music'. They show the continuing development of his compositional thinking, only in a more simple and spare form. As seen in the above survey of 'Sorrow', his variational sense was very much alive and he was happy to explore further manifestations of that technique of chromatic saturation which features in most of his other works of this period. The Duos are historically significant, too, for in 1932, as Bartók came to see his pieces in the published context of Doflein's 'violin school', he warmed to the idea of writing such a graded collection of pieces for piano: the *Mikrokosmos* collection. Even in some aspects of layout and presentation Doflein's 'school' influenced Bartók's. In terms of instrumental technique Bartók had learned many important – and some very basic – lessons about what came truly idiomatically to stringed instruments. The strings become even more securely the backbone of that series of famous compositions initiated by the Fifth String Quartet in 1934 and concluded with the Sixth String Quartet in 1939.

Bartók's Fifth String Quartet was written within just over four weeks during August–September 1934, in response to a commission from one of America's most famous musical patrons, Mrs Elizabeth Sprague-Coolidge. Although the commission had been recommended by the Pro Arte Quartet, to whom Bartók had dedicated his Fourth String Quartet, it was the Kolisch Quartet which gave the work its première, to a reasonable reception, at the Library of Congress in Washington on 8 April 1935. Bartók's quartet shows his superb mastery of string writing, with the widest display yet of technical devices in the service of a startling variety of moods. It is not just a matter of the much-noted 'Bartók pizzicato', where the string slaps back against the fingerboard, but of subtle use of mutes and *col legno* playing, of frequent glissandos, of pizzicatoed arabesques and 'sliding chords', and of glassy *ondeggiando* techniques of accompaniment.[4] The result is a stark characterization of movements according to their distinctive string sound, quite apart from issues of their construction.

The Fifth String Quartet is the ultimate example of Bartók's love of symmetry, tempered by his perpetual inclination towards variation. Both tendencies are evident from the level of momentary embellishing figurations to the arrangements of the work's largest formal blocks. Both constructive ideals have, by this stage, been developing in Bartók's hands through nearly thirty years of composition. In the Fifth String Quartet the static tendency of symmetry is lessened by the flexible, unpredictable variations. Fortunately, it was for this quartet that Bartók left behind the most detailed of his work analyses,[5] which affords great insight into his symmetrical and variational intentions for the work, at least at broader formal levels.

As with the Fourth String Quartet, the Fifth consists of five movements.[6] In the extreme positions are two fast movements, both in a tonality of B♭. The first movement is in Bartók's expected sonata form; the fifth is a type of rondo, known sometimes as a 'bridge' form. These movements are also connected by some common thematic material. Within this external frame, the slow, second and fourth movements share a commonality in form – each is in a ternary (song) form – and motivic or thematic types. They are however in different tonalities: D and G, respectively. Bartók himself described the fourth movement as a 'free variation' of the second. At the kernel of this symmetrical layout of the movements is the Scherzo and Trio, with its expected ternary form. Its tonality is C♯. In tempo, form and some thematic concerns, as well as distinctive string sound, then, these five movements are symmetrically aligned. In tonality, however, they are not, despite the common B♭ tonality of the first and last movements. Such tonal symmetry was an option which Bartók wanted to explore more exhaustively within his individual movements.

The first movement is in broad concept perfectly symmetrical, but on closer inspection always slightly twisted and distorted. Its sonata-form arrangement is modified by an inversion in the order of the themes in the recapitulation, with the second theme preceding the first (Fig. 1).

bar:	1	24	44	59	132	146	159	177
	Exposition			Development	Recapitulation			
	I	Trans.	II		II'	Trans.'	I'	Coda
	B♭	C	D	E	F♯	A♭	B♭	

FIG. 1

At the formal centre of the movement, dominated by the most remote tonality of the tritone relation E, is the development. The three parts of the exposition and recapitulation occur in symmetrical relation to it, at increasing distances according to whole-tone steps. Bartók further reinforces the sense of symmetry in another dimension, too, by reintroducing the themes in the recapitulation in inversion, and what is more, even introduces the first subject in inversion mid-way through the development at the formal pivot point of the movement (bar 126).[7] If any further evidence is needed of Bartók's symmetrical blueprint for the movement it is found in his own analysis, where he noted: 'the beginning, middle part, and end of the movement produce the following tonalities: B♭, E, B♭'. At more local levels of musical construction overt symmetry is a less dominating characteristic. The concluding bars of the movement, however, provide a textbook example of mirrored movements converging on the tonal centre of B♭ (Ex. 3).

EX. 3

The fifth, *allegro vivace* movement is similarly symmetrical in both formal and tonal design (Fig. 2).

bar:	14	202	368	480	546	721
	A	B	C	B'	A'	Coda
	B♭	C♯	E	G	B♭	

FIG. 2

Symmetry is at the core of Bartók's 'bridge' form, which simply builds outwards through three thematic ideas and then retraces its steps. Bartók would use this same form even more cunningly in the third movement of the Music for Strings, Percussion and Celesta, written two years later. Tonally, this Finale's symmetry hinges on the tonality of E, but the surrounding sections' tonalities are distant by steps of a minor third instead of the whole-tone steps of the opening movement. The tonal similarities between the two movements are emphasized by Bartók's comment in his analysis that 'B♭ and E have the same role as in Movement I'. The inner movements exhibit more naturally a sense of tonal symmetry through their common ternary forms: the second movement with D G D tonal sections, the third with C♯ F C♯,[8] and the fourth with G C♯ G.

Bartók undoubtedly planned his quartet very carefully. Once visually pointed out in the score, the symmetries are obvious. But aurally they are less clearly perceived; the formal symmetries are not necessarily reflected temporally within the music. Return sections are, fairly regularly, of lesser duration; the pivot point of the formal symmetry is generally well after the temporal mid-point, reflecting a broad application of natural growth functions in the music.[9] At all levels, too, processes of variation lessen the perception of symmetries, like a vine which disguises the regular features of a brick wall and creates webs of connections between sometimes disparate formal sections.

The highest level of variation within the work, concerning the pairing of movements – first and fifth, second and fourth – has already been described. Within movements, the process of variation is well seen in Bartók's manipulation of his return sections. Exact formal returns are never found. In the recapitulation of the work's strictest movement, the first, for instance, it is not just a matter of thematic inversion and reversal of the order of these entries. Subtle changes are continually being made compared with the exposition, although these changes never threaten the strong sense of identity of each section. The second thematic area (bars 132–46), for instance, compared with its corresponding original passage (bars 44–58), shows these little, but continual changes: a particular, chromatic turn of phrase is sometimes omitted, a stationary part now moves, a bar suddenly acquires another beat, passages previously *arco* are now pizzicato. The sense of section variation is much greater in the *A'* return of the second movement. Here, again, Bartók's strategy was to re-introduce the three original ideas in reverse order, but he was only interested in conjuring up the general sounds of these three ideas. The total length of the passage is cut from the opening section's twenty-five bars to barely eleven (bars 46–56); the sonorous chorale (bars 10–25) and quaver sighs (bars 6–10) are merely represented by a few characteristic gestures, but the opening trill figure (bars 1–3) now assumes grander proportions, being finally exhausted only amid the dying quasi-glissando of the cello. Even more free is the variation of opening material in the *A'* section of the fourth movement (bars 81–101). Bartók has, according to his own analysis, three main ideas to recapitulate, but does not manage this. Instead, this return section becomes a final summary of important materials from both this movement and its spiritual kin, the second. It begins, at bars 81–91, with a combination of figurations taken from its own movement's middle section, set in a chordal milieu reminiscent of the second movement's chorale. Only at bar 92 does he move to recall the opening pizzicato–glissando figure (but now in parallel minor chords on the cello), and then, from bar 95, the *spiccato* chords of his original Part *A*, *più andante* passage. Bartók's *A*' section in this movement is more a free synthesis of relevant ideas than an orderly recapitulation.

This incurable urge to variation is just as evident in his treatment of themes. One of the more important connections between the outermost movements is thematic. The theme of Bartók's central C section in the fifth movement 'bridge' form (Ex. 4) is, as Bartók himself pointed out, derived from the first movement's main theme (Ex. 5).

EX. 4

EX. 5

Although their individual intervals, repetition patterns and rhythms differ, their common identity is beyond dispute. The tritone (E–A♯, B♭–E, respectively) dominates their construction; the concluding, falling intervals of a fourth (A♯–D♯ G♯–C♯, E–A D–G, respectively) add a more specific characterization. Another, more radical example of Bartók's thematic variation is the strange *allegretto, con indifferenza* passage at bars 699–720 of the fifth movement. This is just the endpoint of a series of transformations, from the falling fourth of the movement's opening 'framing' motif, through its following main theme (starting at bar 14) and then that theme's inverted variant (from bar 55). Fig. 3 shows how Bartók has mapped the semi-chromatic scalar basis of that inverted variant on to the fully diatonic (major) basis of the *allegretto* variant to produce the open, gloriously banal sound of this passage.

Bar 55:	G♭	A♭	B♭	C♭	C♮	D♭
Bar 699:	A	B	C♯	D	E	F♯

FIG. 3

Through the use of a *piano*, *meccanico* style of playing and tonic–dominant underlay Bartók reinforces the banal impression, and then sends up his whole technique by allowing the tune's repetition to gravitate to B♭ major while the accompaniment continues resolutely in A major. So different is the following *presto*, with its request for playing *forte*, *con slancio*, that the listener is likely to overlook the exact replaying of the bar-55 variant in the lower instruments.

The most consistent medium for Bartók's variation technique, however, is imitation. This tendency had been growing in his music since the mid-1920s and by the mid-1930s was the most common technique of generating and developing his musical ideas, having grown in tandem with the increasingly linear orientation of his music.[10] It is evident in the presentation of the work's opening, where the theme (Ex. 5) is introduced on the lower instruments but soon overlaps with a further entry of the subject on the violins, and in the hectic play on the fourth interval of the 'framing' motif in the finale's conclusion. In a huge variety of manifestations imitative techniques are present through at least half of the work's duration. Within developmental or central formal sections the imitation tends to be more highly structured and integral to the music's progression, although Bartók is not yet writing the full 'imitation developments' seen later in the decade; in outer formal sections its role is more often one rather of enrichment, ornamentation or transition.

One most intense passage of imitation occurs between bars 103 and 111 in the first movement's development. Bartók's unit of imitation is the second portion of his first theme (Ex. 6). This unit is sometimes presented in full, in ordinary or inverted form; it is sometimes truncated, with Bartók presenting only pattern *a*,

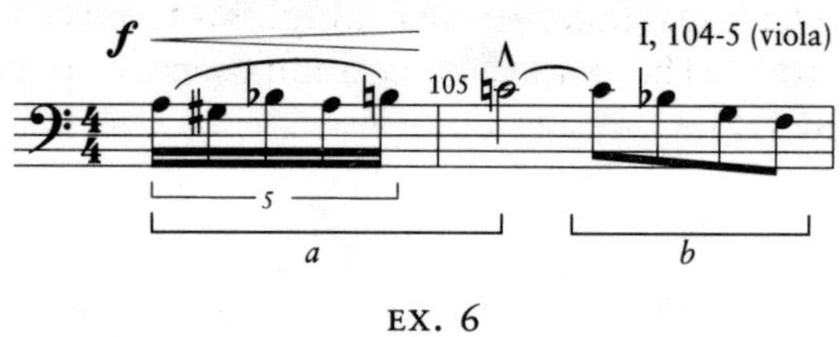

EX. 6

or extended, when he duplicates pattern *b* several times, in an upward direction. But Bartók's purpose is more than light-hearted play upon an important thematic element. The passage is important in the movement's tonal architecture in the battle between tritone and dominant tonal areas, E and F, which creates an important element of tension in this development. The fifth spaces created by the units of imitation are introduced according to the pattern shown in Fig. 4.

<u>F</u>	A	C		
<u>F♯</u>	A♯	C♯		
<u>G</u>	B	D		
<u>A♭</u>	C	E♭		
<u>A</u>	C♯	E		
<u>A</u>	C	E		
<u>G♯</u>	B	D♯		
<u>G</u>	B♭	D	A	E
<u>F♯</u>	A	C♯	G♯	D♯
<u>F</u>	G♯	C	G	D

FIG. 4

Within these spaces the third (the starting note of each unit) is major or minor, according to whether the unit is present in ordinary or inverted orientation. Although disguised by the overlapping and variation of entries this section is a perfect symmetrical structure, in miniature. The pivotal point occurs between the two A-based entries, where the quality of the third changes from major to minor.

A similar, but larger-scale example of variation and imitation in the service of tonal ends is found in the central movement's Trio (a passage which worried Bartók, and which he completely redrafted changing, among other things, his tonal centre from his initial G to F). The element of continuity in this passage is a chromatically infilled space of a fifth (Ex. 7), or its variant, the tritone.

EX. 7

Bartók uses this element to build seemlessly from and back to his tonal base of F, as shown in Fig. 5.

bar:	1	15	24	28	31	33	39	41	44	49	50	51	53
	C	C	D	D	E♭	E♭	E	E	E				
	F	F♯	G	G♯	A♭	A	A	A	A	A			
								D	D	D	D		
									G	G	G	G	
										C	C	C	C
											F	F	F

FIG. 5

As the figure shows, the ascending device is one of semitonal creep, with alternating fifth-range and tritone-range variants. From bar 41 the descent is achieved by a series of simultaneous, entries – both ordinary and inverted – according to a cycle of fifths, which creates an imitational web of twisting chromatic sound. Bartók then gradually sheds the upper entries to consolidate the F–C space with which the Trio began.

Bartók's Sixth String Quartet (1939) is a work of integration rather than innovation. Here is the composer in fullest maturity; that intense concern for intricate motivic or symmetrical structures, seen in his recent quartets, now stands in less stark relief against his other stylistic attributes. During the mid–late 1930s Bartók's writing has attained a new stylistic homogeneity.

On the verge of old age Bartók is, indeed, growing back to a love of extended themes. The tone of the Sixth String Quartet is, in consequence, more relaxed, more nostalgic and less brittle or hectic than that of the Fifth, reflecting Bartók's increasing review of his own output and preparedness to return to ideas first worked out in his earlier compositions.[11] The Sixth's commencement with a slow, chromatic viola theme recalls the opening of the First String Quartet, with its slow, chromatic writing for the two violins; the slow, final movement of the Sixth is paralleled only by the slow finale of the Second; the return of the Sixth's opening theme between each movement clearly invokes the ritornello concept first successfully worked in the Dance Suite of 1923.[12]

The Sixth String Quartet consists of four movements: a sonata form in D; a ternary-form Marcia in B; a ternary-form Burletta in F; a concluding finale in less definite form and key, but suggesting a ternary form ending in D. The tonal plan of the movements is very similar to the symmetrical scheme involving upper and lower minor thirds which Bartók used in the Music for Strings, Percussion and Celesta (A C F♯ A). Here the scheme is less stark, however, because of the quite different, fifth-based tonal scheme followed by the successive ritornello passages: G♯ E♭ B♭ [] C.

In use of the stringed instruments the outer movements (as with the Fifth String Quartet) are more traditional; harmonic and contrapuntal procedures in these movements are also relatively conservative compared with Bartók's immediate past practice. It is in the inner, Marcia and Burletta movements that the technical and stylistic individuality of the work is more expressed. Much of the Marcia is a play of pairs – an idea which Bartók would take up more systematically in the second movement of his Concerto for Orchestra. The result of this pairing is a strange, pseudo-canonic and often tonally confusing texture. At the beginning of the march the leading entry on cello and first violin in B is shadowed by the inner parts in G♯. Later, from bar 35, Bartók's pairs consist of the violins against the viola and cello, but the lower pair now plays the material in inversion, and both pairs are dissonant within themselves: the violin parts are separated by the interval of a ninth (later a second), the viola and cello by a seventh. From bar 44 Bartók initiates a three-against-one texture with the upper three parts forming second-inversion major triads. He pushes his idea one step further in the return section of the Marcia (from bar 122), where through use of double stopping and harmonics he creates an even richer paired texture of fully root-position major triads on cello and second violin against the silvery octave playing of the first violin and viola. The middle section of this Marcia is also notable for an almost Szymanowskian radiance. Against a howling, *forte* tremolo on violins and strummed major chords on viola Bartók introduces an *animato, molto agitato* outcry from the cello. Its line plays on the ambiguity of major and minor thirds before breaking into a passage of sustained glissandos, exploiting the sliding texture which he had already established earlier in the movement. The Burletta is most memorable for its scratching, squawking opening, achieved by much playing near the frog of the bow and repeated down bows. This movement is, from its very name, a satire, and Bartók has other techniques up his sleeve: simultaneous quarter-tone slides (bars 26–9), hysterical *spiccato* passages (bars 119–22, 131–4), and a variety of pizzicato effects of which the boldest is the return of his opening (from bar 97) played in *fortissimo* pizzicatos instead of the original *arco*.

In tempo and mood the quartet involves a curious slowing down and growing resignation of mood. It is as if the *mesto* ritornello gradually infects and, in the end, totally consumes the brighter, faster, sharper sounds of the work. The first movement's predominating *vivace* is replaced by the *risoluto, ben marcato* march – a march of duty rather than of celebratory or funereal significance – and, in turn, the *moderato*, stuttering, Burletta. The ritornello passages, meanwhile, grow inexorably in length: fifty, sixty, eighty seconds, according to Bartók's own timings in the score. He had originally planned for a fast fourth movement, with a bustling main theme similar to that in his *Contrasts* of the previous year and a second theme in a kind of 'Bulgarian' rhythm,[13] but the preceding ritornello passage had taken on such a Beethovenian profundity and grown to such a length – forty-five bars, lasting for some three minutes – that Bartók must have realized that such a finale would have sounded merely frivolous had it followed on as planned. He therefore continued with a *molto tranquillo* middle section, sadly recalling the first movement's two main themes, before reverting to ritornello material (bar 63) and later restoring the original *mesto* tempo, as well (bar 72). The growing power of the ritornello theme through the work is also reflected in Bartók's scoring: solo, on the viola at first occurrence; two-part, led by the cello, at the start of the second movement;[14] three-part, led by the first violin, at the third; four-part, involving independent writing for all four instruments, in the finale.

Other, external factors may have influenced Bartók in his decision to abandon a fast finale. The first three movements were largely sketched in Switzerland during August 1939, before Bartók realized that war was imminent and hurriedly returned home. The fourth movement was drafted and the whole work revised during November, by which time not just had war become a reality but Bartók was suffering the grief of witnessing the slow slide towards death of the one he loved most, his mother. Her death on 19 December 1939, some three weeks after the quartet's completion, would leave him devastated for months.[15] Was the deeply depressed Bartók simply unable to find that joyful expression of optimism which normally characterized his dance-like finales?

Whatever Bartók's reasoning, the result is a work dominated from start to finish by his ritornello theme. Rather than functioning as an occasional interlude it has become the very cement in which the other parts are set. Owing to the good fortune that Bartók jotted down his first ideas for the theme on the concluding page of his Divertimento sketches, it is possible to trace his thinking from germination through the sketches of the quartet into the variety of forms achieved in the score itself.[16] Bartók's original idea (Ex. 8) was for a twelve-note 'new chromatic' theme,[17] strongly anchored in D at both ends. It seems that this theme was initially intended to run straight into the following *vivace* theme, already at this stage in the final form seen at bars 24–5 in the score. Then Bartók began a characteristic process of

EX. 8

expansion and variation with his ritornello theme. While leaving the following *vivace* theme in D, he shifted the opening of the ritornello to D's tritone, G♯, and started to modify and elongate its ending, bringing it to a conclusion on E, and in a later version, on F. He also began to introduce the pattern of descending fourths which, although soon rejected for the theme itself, features dramatically at the first violin's climax point at I, bars 226–9 and in modified form at IV, bars 67–9. Finally, he determined upon the theme's published form (Ex. 9), which ends on E♭, the enharmonic dominant of G♯.

EX. 9

But why has Bartók written such curious pitch notations, in particular the many double sharps, and the shift during the theme's course from sharps to flats? The answer lies in the underlying tonal plan (Fig. 6).

bars 1–4:	G♯	A	A♯	B	[]	C♯	D	[]	E	F	F♯	Fx	G♯
bars 4–9:	D♯	E	E♯	F♯	Fx	G♯	Gx	A♯	B	B♯	C♯	Cx	D♯
bars 9–13:	E♭	F♭	F	G♭	G	A♭	A	[]	[]	C	D♭	[]	E♭

FIG. 6

Instead of remaining in just one tonal system, as with his original D-based version, he has now brought about a crucial modulation, best explained as occurring after the C♯ in bar 4, and a pseudo-modulation between D♯ and E♭-based structures after the E in bar 9. The boundaries of these key areas closely tally with the tripartite partitioning of his theme (see Ex. 9), on the basis of which he conducts much of its development in later ritornello passages.[18]

When the theme returns at the start of the second movement it is based in E♭. Bartók effects changes, both tonal and motivic. The first two sections are maintained virtually intact, but section *c* is extended from five to seven bars, and tonally placed in C, instead of the expected B♭ (or A♭). The ritornello passage at the start of the third movement subjects the theme to more sustained variation. Section *a*, based in B♭, incurs only most minor variations of rhythm and pitch, but section *b*, in the expected dominant tonal area, breaks off in mid-stream (bar 7) to begin a fluid process of development of the theme's opening. Only at bar 14, and in a totally different tonal environment, does Bartók return to the concluding fragment of section *b*, and continue into part of his section *c* material, ending on B♮.[19]

The final movement, of course, draws most of its material from the ritornello theme. In the constantly evolving variational medium the tonal connections between the three sections of the theme are lost but the sense of immensely slow progress through the theme is still maintained. Section *a* is the source of inspiration for bars 1–30: in opening C–F♯ stretto, inverted (bar 13, cello), with expanded intervals (from bar 22). At bar 31 Bartók introduces section *b* in an initially exact reproduction of the pitches and intervals found at the work's opening. This material dominates until the work's most depressing moment is reached, with the *senza colore*, chorale setting of section *a* at bars 40–45. Bartók breaks off, however, to refer to the first movement's two main themes, but returns at bar 63 to introduce a series of variants of the theme's most variable, section *c*. The conclusion of the movement, from bar 72, refers consistently to section *a* and ends with an almost verbatim quotation of the work's viola opening followed by a sardonic turn, imitating that opening, on triple-stopped pizzicato cello.

The Sixth Quartet was originally intended for Zoltán Székely, for whom Bartók had recently written his Second Violin Concerto. Because of some confusion in his relations with Székely in 1939–40, however, Bartók decided upon a dedication to the Kolisch Quartet, which had for many years promoted his string quartets and had premièred his Fifth. That quartet premièred Bartók's Sixth also, in New York on 20 January 1941, in the presence of the composer.

NOTES

1 Published by Schott (Mainz), edition numbers 2201–3 and 2213–14, respectively.

2 For a listing of the original tunes see *DB*.vi, pp. 132–46.

3 The pieces chosen were nos 16, 28, 36, 38 and 43. No.32 was also later included in a revised edition of the suite.

4 Examples of most of these techniques can be found in the fourth movement.

5 *BBE*, pp. 414–15. Bartók was probably prepared to write so starkly about his work because the analysis was intended as a private briefing paper, and not for publication. Of interest, too, among analyses of the work is that by the Hungarian-born composer György Ligeti, found as a foreword to more recent issues of the Universal Edition score, and that by János Kárpáti in his *Bartók's String Quartets*, Budapest (Corvina), 1975, pp. 226–43.

6 The Fifth String Quartet, however, appears to have been conceived as a five-movement symmetrical entity, while the Fourth only became so late in its creation. Bartók, finding it difficult in the Fourth to effect the join between the third movement and his finale, had decided to add in a new, fourth movement with material drawn from the second.

7 Bartók recognized that this entry at bar 126 could be seen as the start of the recapitulation, in which case the formal logic of the movement would require the coda to begin at bar 159.

8 Bartók's own analysis is clearly wrong in claiming that the central Trio is in E. The error and Bartók's highlighting of the significance of this Trio's

tonality in his analysis are instructive, however, as they show his desire to demonstrate (even beyond the realities of the music!) a further tritonal relationship, between the B♭ of the first and last movements and the E of the centre of the central movement.

9 See my chapter 'Masterworks (I): Music for Strings, Percussion and Celesta' in this *Companion* for a brief discussion of Ernő Lendvai's Golden Section theories.

10 For a more detailed discussion of Bartók's techniques of variation at their apogee in the late 1930s, see my chapter 'Final Chamber Works' in this *Companion*.

11 In Bartók's next major work, the Concerto for Orchestra (1943), the review process would continue, with reference to textures and techniques from *Duke Bluebeard's Castle* (1911) and even the orchestral First Suite (1905).

12 Bartók would contemplate such a ritornello again, for his Viola Concerto (left incomplete in 1945), but eventually decided against it.

13 See Benjamin Suchoff, 'Structure and Concept in Bartók's Sixth Quartet', *Tempo*, no.83 (Winter 1967–8), pp. 2–11.

14 The second violin and viola do appear here, but merely shadow at different octave levels the first violin's counter theme.

15 See *BBL*, p. 281.

16 See: John Vinton, 'New Light on Bartók's Sixth Quartet', *Music Review*, vol.25 (1964), pp. 224–38; Benjamin Suchoff, op. cit.; Malcolm Gillies, *Notation and Tonal Structure in Bartók's Later Works*, New York (Garland), 1989, pp. 147–56.

17 See Bartók's discussion of 'new chromaticism' in *BBE*, pp. 376–81.

18 In each case Bartók's tonal closure takes place one note after his phrasing has closed. This overlapping gives rise to a strong feeling of continuity between the different sections.

19 The sketches show Bartók's working of the ritornello theme in inversion, based on a starting pitch of B♭. Perhaps he originally intended this for his third ritornello passage.

1 Bartók aged five, 1886

2 Bartók's mother, Paula, late 1870s

3 Bartók's sister, Elza, aged fourteen, 1899

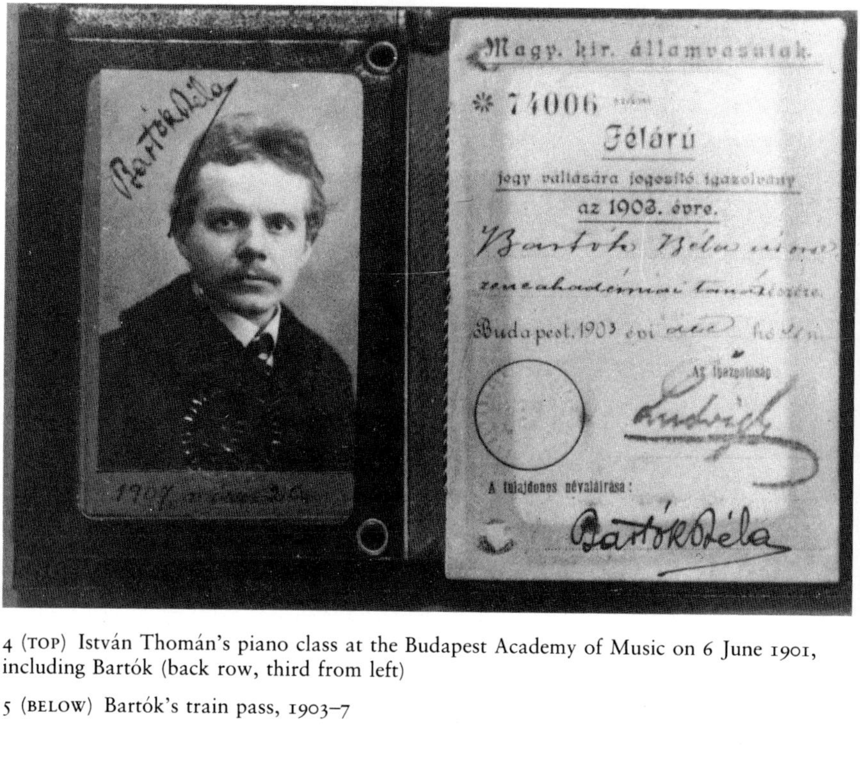

Magy. kir. államvasutak.

74006

Félárú

jegy váltására jogosító igazolvány

az 1903. évre.

Budapest, 1903 évi

Az Igazgatóság

A tulajdonos névaláírása:

4 (TOP) István Thomán's piano class at the Budapest Academy of Music on 6 June 1901, including Bartók (back row, third from left)

5 (BELOW) Bartók's train pass, 1903–7

6 With Kodály (seated, right) and the Waldbauer–Kerpely Quartet, which premièred Bartók's First, Second and Fourth String Quartets, 1910

7 The Waldbauer–Kerpely Quartet (with one change in membership) twenty-five years later

8 Manuscript of the piano piece *Allegro barbaro*, 1911

With his first wife, Márta Ziegler, 912

o Béla Balázs, librettist of Bartók's pera *Duke Bluebeard's Castle* and allet *The Wooden Prince*

11 A family excursion from around 1915, as drawn by Bartók for his son Béla

12 With his son Béla, 1915

3 Two lads from Poniky, Slovakia, uly 1915 (Bartók's photograph)

4 A peasant woman from Poniky, lovakia, July 1915 (Bartók's hotograph)

5 From Bartók's notations of Slovak olk music, 1915

Budapest, I. Gyopár u. 2.; 29. XII., 1921.

Dear Mr. Heseltine,

Your letter and the cheque, included in it, arrived in safety. Many thanks for both! I am a little uneasy with the thought that you were bothered so much with this payment; it was not urgent at all! My Blue Beard and the Wooden Prince will be performed at Frankfort o/M. on the 1. April for the first time. I should be very pleased if you could be present at this performance, and if I could meet you there. Mr. Gray too will be there probably. – It is quite possible that I shall go afterwards or before to England for 10–14 days, and play some works of mine there. A french critic, Mr. Calvocoressi, who lives in London now and Mrs. Fachiri and her sisters try to get some engagements for me. I hope they will succeed. On this occasion I shall bring a new works, composed in the last two months with me: a sonata for piano and violine, and shall try to play it.

In the case you can not go to Franckfort, I hope to see you in London then.

We expect now the visit of Milhaud, Poulenc and Miss Marya Freund, who will give a concert in January at Budapest and perform some works of the „Jeune École Française". I am very curious, for I know only a few and – I hope – not the best of these works.

With the kindest regards yours very sincerely

Béla Bartók.

16 Bartók's letter of 29 December 1921 to the British composer–critic Philip Heseltine (Peter Warlock)

7 With the Hungarian violinist Zoltán zékely, to whom Bartók dedicated his econd Violin Rhapsody and Second Violin Concerto, 1925

18 Frank Whitaker, the English journalist who attempted to write the first book about Bartók in the late 1920s

19 With son Péter, about 1930

20 Ditta Pásztory-Bartók, the composer's second wife

21 The last page of the first movement of the Second Piano Concerto (1930–31) in Bartók's full-score draft, along with preliminary sketches for his second movement

22 Caricature published in *Radio Times*, 18 May 1934

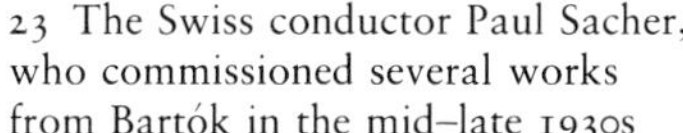

23 The Swiss conductor Paul Sacher, who commissioned several works from Bartók in the mid–late 1930s

24 With his wife, Ditta, and friend Annie Müller-Widmann (centre), Switzerland, 1939

25 Bartók's autograph of an early version of the passage leading to the recapitulation of the first movement of his Sonata for Two Pianos and Percussion (1937)

6 Rehearsing the Sonata for Two Pianos and Percussion, New York, November 1940

27 With Rudolf Kolisch, whose Quartet premièred Bartók's Fifth and Sixth String Quartets; New York, December 1940

28 Bartók's first sketch of the *Allegro vivace* theme for the first movement of his Concerto for Orchestra (1943), with subsequent continuity sketch added in pencil

Yehudi Menuhin, who commissioned
d premièred Bartók's Sonata for solo
olin (1944).

30. During the summer of 1944

31 The cover of the Bartók Records recording of the posthumous Viola Concerto, featuring some of the work's sketches in the background

32 With wife Ditta and son Péter, 1944–45

21

Masterworks (I): Music for Strings, Percussion and Celesta

MALCOLM GILLIES

A peculiar inspiration seized Bartók during the summer of 1936. Between sessions of learning Turkish, in preparation for a folk-music expedition later in the year, he drafted one of his greatest compositions, the Music for Strings, Percussion and Celesta. This work's concept appears to have been complete in his mind almost at the outset, both in its structure and scoring, for he uncharacteristically wrote it down immediately in full score. Since the mid-1920s Bartók's interest in counterpoint had been growing, along with his concern for symmetries in pitch, rhythmic and formal arrangements. In 1936 these tendencies culminated in the Music for Strings, Percussion and Celesta, one of Bartók's few compositions to show great originality at all levels of its construction and to integrate seemlessly the full range of his styles, whether drawn more from folk- or art-music sources. It is also Bartók's most cunning synthesis of opposites, of which the most crucial is chromatic versus diatonic.

The first of the four movements is a tightly constructed fugue with a slow twisting chromatic subject (Ex. 1). In an environment of constantly changing metres Bartók presents four phrases, building from the tonic of A to fill chromatically the fifth space A–E, with a climax in the third of the phrases. The subject is, according to Bartók, an example of his 'new' chromaticism, consisting of 'independent tones having no interrelation between each other'.[1] This is a stage beyond the polymodal chromaticism, so common in Bartók's earlier works, in which the various diatonic modal origins of the notes can still usefully be distinguished. Yet despite this new, modal-free chromatic

EX. 1

independence the sense of resolution to a tonic – in this case, A – is not threatened.

Bartók's subject effectively gives birth to every aspect of this first movement. He introduces his subject entries according to two simultaneous cycles of fifths, both departing from A (Fig. 1).[2]

	Stage 1					Stage 2		Stage 3				Stage 4
bar:	1	4	8	12	16	26	27	33	34	35	35	44
	A	E		B		F♯			C♯		G♯	(D♯)
	A		D		G		C	F		B♭		E♭

FIG. 1

In pursuing both these cycles until they coincide at E♭ (D♯) Bartók includes entries based on all twelve possible chromatic pitches. But such a relentless scheme would become too predictable were it not for Bartók's strategies for varying his subject. The first stage is a formal five-part exposition (bars 1–21), in which the full subject is played with minimal variation. After a brief episode Bartók moves to his second stage, playing the full subject in a close stretto of entries (at the tritone C–F♯). The stretto idea is continued through into the third stage (bars 33–8), in which only phrases from the subject are presented in the individual parts, sometimes with accompanying echo effects. After a further episode (bars 38–44), which develops subject fragments, the final statement on E♭ is reached. This is not a complete statement, but presents only the first phrase literally before becoming part of the intensifying web of chromatic sound which then surges to the E♭ climax at bar 56. But how now to return home from this tonally most distant point? Bartók's solution of retracing his steps with the subject now in inversion (Fig. 2) would, in lesser hands, have been too simple, too tedious.

Stage 4	Stage 3						Stage 2				Stage 1
56	58	58	61	62	64	65	68	69	72	73	77
E♭		A♭		D♭		F♯		B		E	A
	B♭		F		C		G		D		

FIG. 2

This return is abbreviated with such a perfect sense of timing, however, that, without any audible hurrying, home base is achieved within barely twenty bars. Some of the entries within Stage 3 are nominal, with B♭ and F being represented in their turn by the strongly pulsating rhythm just heard at the climax and the D♭ entry only playing part of the subject's fourth phrase (which does not actually include a D♭ at all). The return A-based entry, starting at bar 77, is one of Bartók's most magical moments. Upon an icy, shimmering plateau of sound he plays both ordinary and inverted full subjects on first and fourth violins, but the different forms are separated by a bleak three octaves and are played in rhythmic complementation to prevent the music from momentarily stopping altogether between the phrases. The movement's final passage disintegrates the subject's first phrase in both its ordinary and inverted forms, before Bartók introduces both forms of the second phrase and increasingly augments them rhythmically as they converge from upper and lower E♭ tritones on to the final A tonic.

The listener to this first movement knows little of Bartók's intricate planning, but does experience a remarkable surge and repose over the fugue's six-and-a-half minutes, extending from the *pianissimo*, muted initial playing of the subject on the violas through to the full ensemble's *fff* climax at bar 56 and back to the *ppp* of the final five bars.[3] So naturally does Bartók's movement grow and subside that the question arises: Is there a higher principle governing this movement's construction? In the late 1940s the Hungarian musician Ernő Lendvai first proposed that a number of movements by Bartók, including this one, were structured according to the Golden Section principle.[4] The bar numbers of crucial bars in this movement's development looked uncannily like those of the Fibonacci series, a simple additive series associated with this principle (1, 1, 2, 3, 5, 8, 13, 21, 34, 55, 89 . . .).[5] So was generated probably the most intense debate about Bartók's music, which still lingers and generally centres on two questions: Is such an observation valid or helpful in understanding the music? Did Bartók know about either the Fibonacci series or the Golden Section principle? Unfortunately, a good deal of doubtful arithmetic manipulation, practised above all by Lendvai,[6] deflected attention from the essential truth that this fugue (and some other Bartók movements, too) is an excellent example of natural growth principles in action but that there is no evidence that Bartók was aware of these principles or designed any of his works according to them. The sketches to his later works make it clear that the music just grew this way in his hands. Some innate sense of proportion would alert him to an over-compression or elongation in the phrasing or sectioning of his music and cause him to make appropriate adjustments to fit in with the piece's dynamic.

The second, *allegro* movement is in a C-based sonata form. On the surface it is a model of Classical practice, involving much crisp alternation between the two string groups, situated on opposite sides of the stage. The second subject dutifully appears in the dominant tonality of G (bar 68) and reappears in the recapitulation in the tonic (bar 412); the exposition ends solidly in G major (bars 180–2). The recapitulation of the first subject (from bar 372), too, is almost note-perfect when compared with the exposition, but does show Bartók's constant desire for variation. It is now metrically unsteady, being pushed and pulled into a variety of $\frac{3}{8}$, $\frac{2}{4}$ and $\frac{5}{8}$ barrings before settling into the $\frac{3}{8}$ which dominates most of the recapitulation. As we look more deeply within these neat formal boundaries, however, there is a surprise. Bartók's first subject is none other than a close variant of the fugue subject's second phrase, played in C. This derivation is shown by the circled notes in Ex. 2.[7]

EX. 2

Ex. 2 is, then, itself related by a process of expansion to the movement's introduction (bars 1–4) and, by contraction and compression, to the subject of the fugato (Ex. 3), which Bartók makes a central feature of his development.

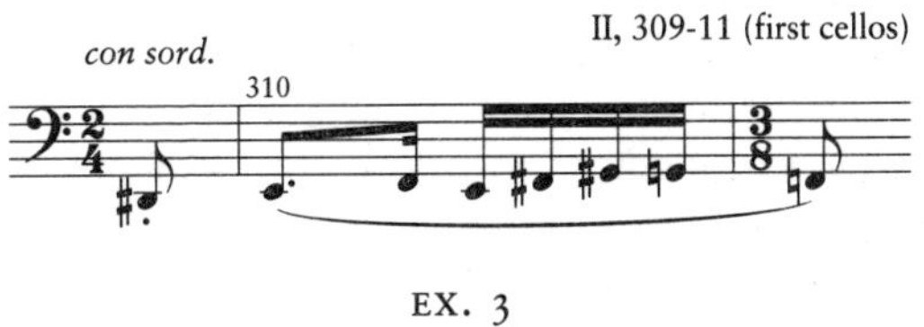

EX. 3

A further connection with the first movement's fugue subject emerges early in the development (bars 199–242), where against a vital five-note ostinato Bartók plays three phrases from that subject, without alteration to their pitches but completely transformed rhythmically into an abrupt, dry passage of 'Bartók' pizzicatos[8] for first-group strings. These three phrases (the first in inversion, the first in ordinary, the second in ordinary) are played in full parallel major chords based on E♭, F♯ and A, respectively, all notes of the dominating A–C–E♭–F♯ axis which tonally controls this work. The following passage in the development, from bar 242, is based on a simple scalar theme, which we later discover to be related to the the main theme of the fourth movement. From this brief thematic survey it is clear that in his second movement Bartók is seeking to effect again that cyclic unity of themes which he had first attempted in his First Suite Op.3 (1905).[9] Now the opening movement's fugue subject is the chief element of that unifying process.

After the mixed chromatic–diatonic writing of the second movement, the slow third movement returns to the world of intense chromaticism. Its tonality is less definite than the other movements, although both its opening and closing feature an emphasis on the tritonal pair of notes F♯ and C. Bartók himself stipulated F♯ in his analyses, which is a conveniently symmetrical counterbalance to the C tonality of the second movement within the framing A tonalities of the outer movements. As in the first movement, the overall structure is quintessentially Bartókian, as shown in Fig. 3.[10]

1	6	20	35	63	76	79
Introduction	*A*	*B*	*C*	*B'*	*A'*	Conclusion

FIG. 3

This is the modified rondo known as 'bridge' form, which can be seen as the model behind the five-movement Fourth and Fifth String Quartets and several multi-partite works as far back as Bartók's ballet, *The Wooden Prince* (1914–16). Its bridging qualities here are reinforced by the dynamics of the movement, which build to a series of fortissimo climaxes in the second C passage, from bars 45 to 54 and then subside to the *pianissimo* of the conclusion.

Bartók's Adagio can broadly be seen as a free study upon the chromatic potentialities of the first movement's subject. Indeed, he uses that subject's four phrases in turn, with only minor modifications of rhythm and ending pitches, as joining material between the movement's five formal sections. They stand there as sacred readings to inspire the 'new chromatic' contemplations of the coming section. Formal section *A* explores the twisting chromatic potential within the medium of brief melodic flurries and arabesques, which he had established in his piano piece 'The Night's Music' of 1926. The Hungarian on-the-beat aspect of these fragments is accentuated by Bartók, which creates a tense and neurotic atmosphere (a feature not missed by several musical directors of Hollywood suspense films).

Bartók is systematic in his chromatic unfolding; during the opening phrase (bars 6–9) he touches on all twelve notes within the E tonal frame of the viola melody. In the return *A'* section (bars 76–80) the chromatic unfolding within the twisting patterns is even more regimented, with each unit of imitation including all seven notes within the tritonal ranges E–B♭ or its complement B♭–E.

The initial *B* formal section (from bar 20) contains three elements: a long twisting chromatic melody which is clearly related to the original fugue subject, even down to its four phrases, although it now uses the full chromatic range; a background of *pianissimo* violin trills which chromatically spans the range B♭ to D♯; a glassy two-bar motif on piano and violin which inverts semitones into major sevenths and is drawn from the conclusion of the fugue subject's first phrase, that provided the join between section *A* and section *B* (see Ex. 4).

III, 18-19 (first violas and cellos)

(a)

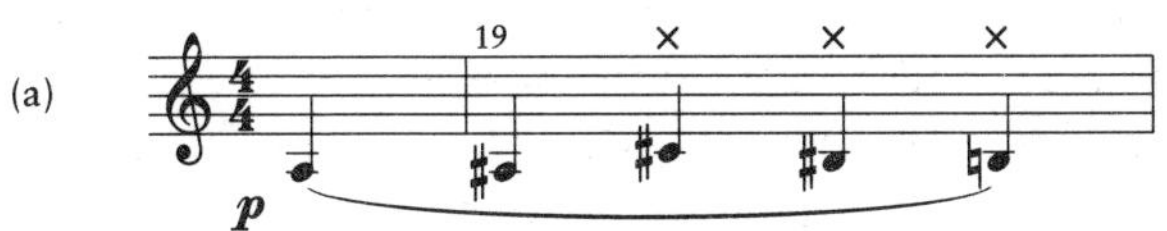

(b) III, 22-3 (second violins and piano)

EX. 4

This section's return *B'*, starting at bar 63, adopts a similar approach. The long chromatic melody is represented, now in a canon at the distance of a tritone (D♭ and G); the violin trills are no longer heard, but are replaced by the buzzing B♭–C♭ on piano, harp and celesta, itself drawn from the end of the preceding joining passage (the fugue subject's third phrase).

The first part of the central C section plays yet another chromatic game. Over an E♭ pedal and a background of complementary pentatonic runs (E G A B D; E♭ G♭ A♭ B♭ D♭) Bartók introduces the short four-note motif (Ex. 5b) which will drive the music through to the section's second part at bar 45. This, again, is just a variant of a portion of the preceding joining passage (see Ex. 5a).

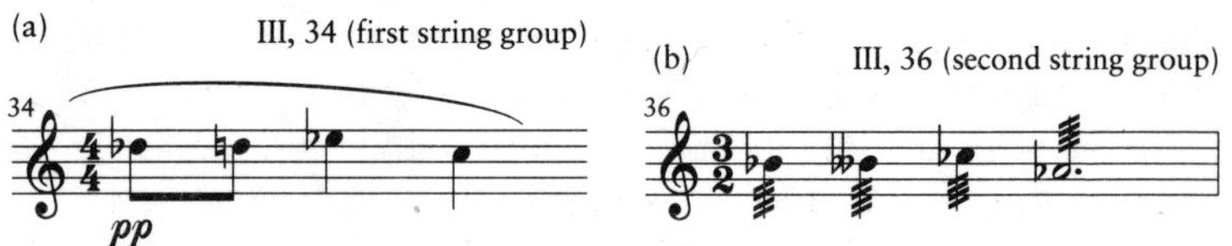

EX. 5

In subsequent bars it is so placed, in ordinary and inverted forms, as to 'saturate' fully the twelve-note chromatic range between A♭ and G. Once that 'saturation' has been achieved Bartók moves to his next chromatic exploration. The second part of section C (Bartók's alternative section *D*) plays a further game that he knew well: creating tension between 'foreground' melodic and 'background' harmonic figures which have no notes in common. These figures are shown in Ex. 6.

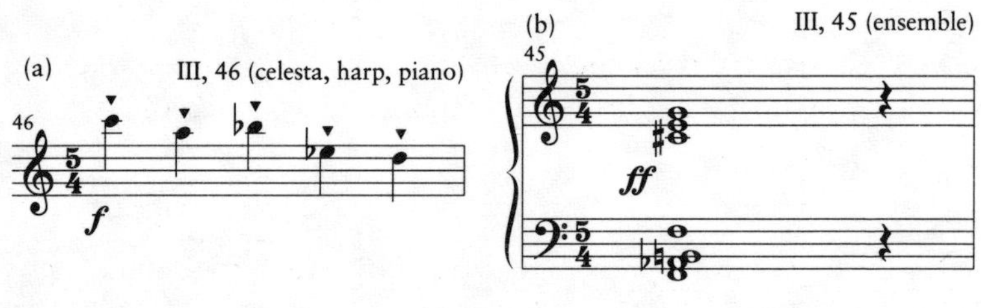

EX. 6

But one note, F♯, remains unplayed; it will appear only at bar 55, in the imitative denouement to the passage.

So has Bartók built his highly chromatic 'bridge'. It is framed by short introductory and concluding passages which feature the xylophone and the timpani. The eerie impression of this movement arises initially through their playing at different ends of the pitch spectrum, with complementary rhythmic and pitch patterns. Much pointed out in the Bartók literature is the perfect example of a Fibonacci series in the xylophone passage in bars 1–4, determined according to the number of notes per crotchet beat: 1, 1, 2, 3, 5, 8, 5, 3, 2, 1, 1. Fragments from this xylophone sequence are later used at section or phrase joins, but it never again returns in such a perfect form.

Diatonic writing is immediately to the fore in Bartók's finale. This is the most open of the movements in pitch, rhythmic and formal considerations. It follows the model of the village dance with its introduction of one dance routine after another and occasional returns to routines already heard. Bartók had evolved this finale model as far back as his *Two Pictures* of 1910 and even his First Suite of 1905. Its particular manifestation in the Music for Strings, Percussion and Celesta is shown in Fig. 4, following Bartók's own analyses.

5	26	44	52	74	83	114	136	203	235
A	*B*	*A'*	*C*	*D*	*E*	*D'*	*F*	*G*	*A''*

FIG. 4

These section distinctions and their broader four-part grouping are reinforced by Bartók's tempo characterizations of the various dances.

The *A* sections are constructed around a bustling, linear tune (Ex. 7) written in the bright, 'super-major' Lydian mode of A.

EX. 7

The tune's hectic impression is created by its irregularly alternating quavers and crotchets, and the complementary 'Bulgarian' rhythm of the strummed accompaniment (using the same 3 + 3 + 2 grouping of quavers found in Bartók's last *Mikrokos-*

mos piece). Not all the movement's passages are as diatonic, however. Sections *B* and *F*, for instance, show signs of the re-emergence of Bartók's chromatic concerns. Section *G* goes one step further, and reintroduces the first movement's fugue subject in its entirety, but now adapted to the finale's more open pitch environment. Since the mid-1920s Bartók had been starting to vary his themes by extending or compressing their intervals, as he described in 1943:

> The working with these chromatic degrees gave me another idea which led to the use of a new device. This consists of the change of the chromatic degrees into diatonic degrees. In other words, the succession of chromatic degrees is extended by levelling them over a diatonic terrain.[11]

Here that extension was to Bartók's 'natural', or 'acoustic', scale, according to the formula shown in Fig. 5.

Chromatic:	A	B♭	B	C	C♯	D	D♯/E♭	E
'Acoustic':	C	D	E	F♯	G	A	B♭	C

FIG. 5

The chromatic range of a fifth has been mapped on to the full octave range of the acoustic scale to produce the gloriously spacious sound of the fugue subject (Ex. 8), now also transformed rhythmically and in phrasing.

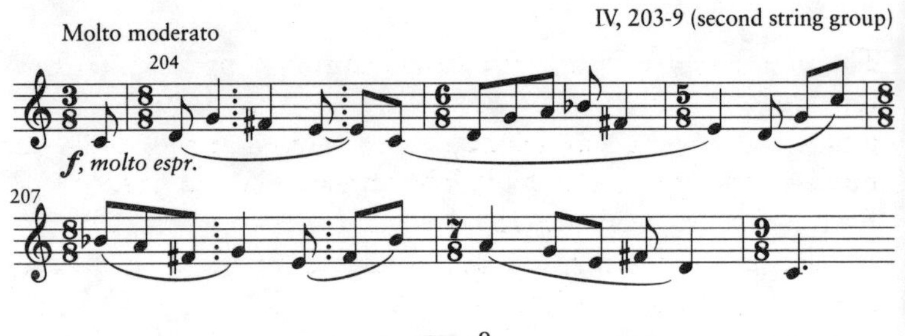

EX. 8

Bartók then moves to a grand replaying of Ex. 8 in parallel chords against its own free inversion, led by the piano. Following subject fragments start to veer towards their original chromatic form and Bartók soon leads the music into the chromatic morass of bars 230–34, against which the solo cello hopelessly struggles. With the work's dominating theme now recapitulated, Bartók moves to recapitulate the movement's main theme: from bar 235 with its characteristic movement but in elongated, ascending lines; from bar 244 complete, but rhythmically levelled to triplet crotchets and played *calmo* on the celesta and harp. In the lively conclusion he finally approaches nearer to the theme's original expression, over strong bass lines moving chromatically, and later, diatonically.

This masterwork of counterpoint, symmetry and scalar flexibility was premièred by the semi-professional Basle Chamber Orchestra in its home town on 21 January 1937. The conductor was Paul Sacher, who had been so impressed by Bartók's Fifth String Quartet (1934) that he had commissioned him to write this new work for the tenth anniversary concert of his orchestra. Bartók went to Basle especially for the final rehearsals and performance. To his wife he reported before the concert:

> Contrary to my expectations, things are going rather nicely, almost perfectly well. We've rehearsed a lot and been very thorough (they've supposedly devoted twenty-five rehearsals to this work, in total); the conductor and orchestra have all worked with me showing the greatest affection and devotion; they claim to be very enthusiastic about the work (I am too!). A couple of spots sound more beautiful and startling than I had imagined. There are some very unusual sounds in it![12]

The première itself met with thunderous applause; Sacher even repeated the final movement. Bartók, too, was pleased and congratulated orchestra and conductor, although he did tell off the pianist, who was 'really bad'. The performance was recorded – Bartók listened with pleasure to its records two weeks later in Amsterdam – but that recording appears never to have been released publicly. Although performed in many European centres before and during the war, Music for Strings, Percussion and Celesta only gained adequate appreciation of its exceptional quality during the Bartók craze which swept America and parts of Western Europe in the later 1940s and 1950s.

NOTES

1 *BBE*, pp. 380–81.
2 Bartók points out this cycle-of-fifths structure in his analyses of the work. See *BBE*, p. 416, and Kroó, p. 184.
3 Bartók creates a subtle aural shift during the movement through his careful placement of the instruments on the stage. The fugal exposition is, in the balance of sound, skewed towards the right-hand side of the stage, while the final bars increasingly emphasize the left.
4 A principle arising from the division of a distance so that the proportion of the larger part to the whole is the same as the proportion of the smaller to the larger part. The proportion comes to the irrational 'golden' number of 0.618 . . . Since Classical times this proportion has been recognized as an ideal proportion in both nature and art. See, further, Roy Howat's following chapter in this *Companion*.
5 The division of successive Fibonacci numbers by the following series number (1/2, 2/3, 3/5, etc.) approaches ever closer to the irrational 'golden' number.
6 See my extended review of Lendvai's *The Workshop of Bartók and Kodály* in *Music Analysis*, vol.5 (1986), pp. 285–95.
7 The original fugal phrase also contains a D♮ before the final D♭.
8 Where the string rebounds upon the fingerboard.
9 See my chapter 'Two Orchestral Suites' in this *Companion*.
10 Bartók's two analyses of this movement diverge significantly here. In one he subdivided the C section into '*C* + *D*', a distinction which is reinforced by the placement of his rehearsal cues and the section timings given at the end of the movement in the score. That extra *D* passage, accordingly, begins at bar 45's *più mosso*.
11 *BBE*, p. 381.
12 *BBcl*, p. 566.

22

Masterworks (II): Sonata for Two Pianos and Percussion

ROY HOWAT

Almost exactly a year after composing the Music for Strings, Percussion and Celesta Bartók wrote the Sonata for Two Pianos and Percussion, in response to another commission from Basle, this time the Basle section of the International Society for Contemporary Music. Although it was this commission that prompted the music's composition in July–August 1937, Bartók admitted that he had already been contemplating such a work for some time.[1] Bartók's interest in this instrumental combination had first shown itself clearly in the slow movement of his First Piano Concerto (1926), which opens with piano and percussion alone before adding wind instruments. A few years later, in the first two movements of his Second Piano Concerto (1931), Bartók focused attention again on piano and percussion, in combination firstly with wind instruments and then with strings. In the Music for Strings, Percussion and Celesta this last combination expanded itself to include a larger range of percussion. From there it was a natural step to the challenge of paring textures back to pure piano and percussion.[2] Having first toyed with the idea of solo piano and percussion, Bartók later decided that two pianos were necessary for balance – allowing the added luxury of antiphonal effects, as with the two orchestras of the Music for Strings, Percussion and Celesta. In coming to this decision Bartók may have been influenced by Igor Markevitch's ballet *L'envol d'Icare*, in its transcription of 1933 for two pianos and percussion.[3] As a further incentive Bartók had in his wife, Ditta Pásztory, an ideal partner for duo performance.

In view of the war clouds threatening Europe by 1937 and already hampering Bartók's professional life, it is a revelation of his inner being that he could produce a work as wide-ranging and exuberant as this Sonata, a veritable celebration in musical dance of the cosmos and nature in all its aspects. A tonal tension between two poles of energy, F♯ and C, animates the work on a large scale, a relationship which reciprocates the similar polarity across A and E♭ in the Music for Strings, Percussion and Celesta.[4] This allows the music two simultaneous planes of tonal tension, for the tritonal relationships run simultaneously with more traditional diatonic relationships.

Bartók was insistent that the percussion and the pianos were of equal importance,[5] an outlook that extends beyond this Sonata to embrace his whole feeling for sound. Accepting the inherently percussive nature of all the instruments in this score, he draws from their percussiveness a wealth of expressive nuances – most explicitly in the melody of quiet percussive colour that opens the slow, second movement (Ex. 1).

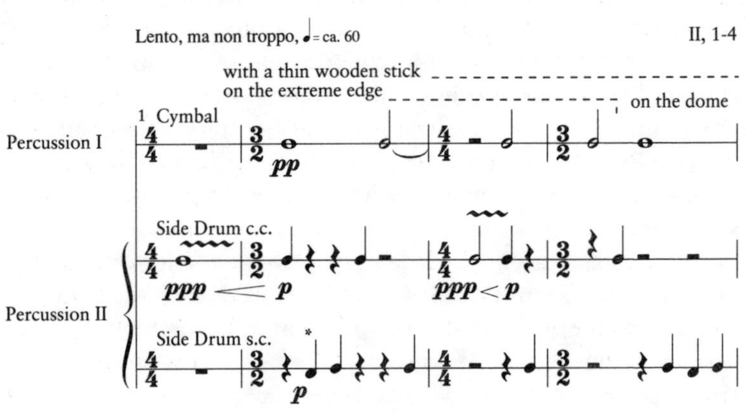

EX. 1

His techniques, as specified in the score, include striking different surface areas of drum skins or cymbals – rim, centre, dome, etc. – as well as using sticks of varying size and hardness, and even, at the very end, a penknife blade (or a fingernail) for special lightness. Bartók had partly explored this area eleven years before, in the First Piano Concerto, whose score requests, altogether, four percussionists. In the Sonata, however, despite its even larger array of percussion, he manages to halve the number of percussionists to two! – the result of much ingenuity, and demanding the utmost from the performers. Bartók also uses the pianos as much for their melodious percussiveness as for their more traditional capabilities. Recordings of his piano playing confirm this trait by revealing Bartók as a pianist of lyrical Romantic tradition – never a hard hitter – with an exceptional ear for fine nuances of timbre, rhythm and melody.

Underneath the Sonata's three-movement layout, the first movement's slow introduction admits another formal element, effectively making the work follow an overall four-part sequence of slow–fast (first movement), slow (second movement), fast (third movement). However, the relationship between slow and fast is different in each case, for whereas the slow tempo of the first movement's introduction gradually accelerates into the ensuing *allegro molto*, the second movement's slow tempo simply becomes the *allegro non troppo* of the finale through an instantaneous equivalence of pulse: ♩ = 66 becomes 𝅗𝅥 = 63–66. If we add to that the frequent fluctuations of tempo throughout the first movement, as against the relatively steady tempo of the finale, we can sense a progressive stabilization of tempo towards the finale, as happens in such works as Schumann's Piano Concerto or Debussy's *La mer*. All this may have its evocative purpose. In his printed remarks about the Sonata Bartók restricted himself to describing formal outlines, and even then often in quite vague terms, characteristically letting the resultant musical intensity speak for itself. However, out of print he appears to have been less inhibited, for several of his students have reported that Bartók described the opening of the Sonata to them in terms of creation archetypes, of a cosmos evolving out of formlessness and timelessness – reflecting Bartók the lover of nature.[6] We can understand why he kept such comments out of print: like most musical analogies, this one becomes slippery if taken beyond a general sense of mood and progression, and, if interpreted *à la* Richard Strauss, could have led to ridicule. It accords well, however, with the spiralling shape of the opening seven-note motif of the first movement (Ex. 2), whose rhythmic 'trip' (the beat shifting by one note on each repetition) intensifies the sense of a nascent form gradually uncoiling.

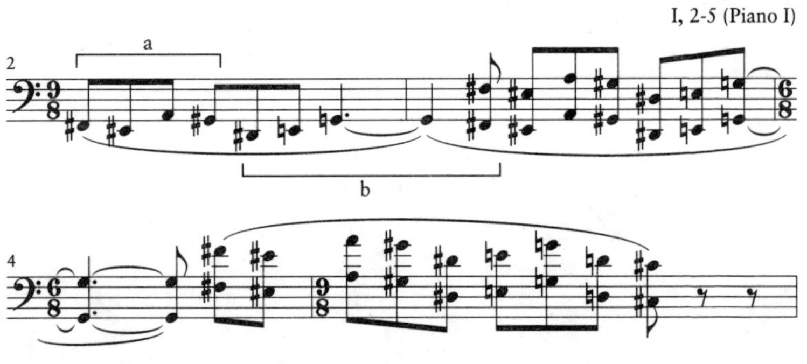

EX. 2

Like the fugue subject of the Music for Strings, Percussion and Celesta this motif uses the modal chromaticism later described by Bartók in his Harvard Lectures, filling in all the semitones of its range.[7] Bartók's love of this device reflects its organic potential, able to open out later into diatonic modes. Its first four notes (bracket *a* in Ex. 2) not only quote the subject of J. S. Bach's C♯ minor Fugue (from Book 1 of the '48'), but also recall a range of Romantic works, from the B–A–C–H motif of Liszt's organ fugue to Chopin's F♯ minor Polonaise (Ex. 3a) and Schubert's 'Der Doppelgänger' from his *Schwanengesang* collection (Ex. 3b).[8] Moreover, the following four notes (bracket *b* in Ex. 2) make the motif itself a 'Doppelgänger' of the fugue subject of the Music for Strings, Percussion and Celesta.[9] Whether or not the affinities with these earlier works were deliberate, they reveal an underlying ancestry of mood, inherent in the circular melodic shape. From this motif Bartók draws some of the most powerful moments of mystery in his music, such as bar 9, where its parallel sixths run in contrary motion (Ex. 4a, in enharmonic reduction). This is one of several passages that suggest Bartók's interest in another work which he later came to

Chopin: F♯ minor Polonaise, Op. 44

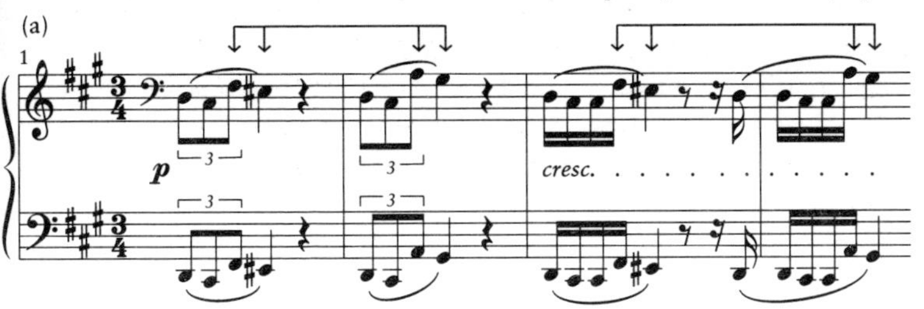

Schubert: 'Der Doppelgänger'
(Schwanengesang)

(b)

pp

EX. 3

perform with his wife, Debussy's two-piano suite *En blanc et noir* (1915), whose third movement similarly exploits parallel and contrary motions (Ex. 4b, also in enharmonic reduction).

The Sonata's slow introduction is worth special scrutiny, for its dramatic power is unusually visible in its architecture. In essence its structure reveals a 1–2–3 progression of the most standard classical type,[10] with a first wave of activity in bars 2–8, a second wave in bars 8–11, and then a third wave from bar 12, which culminates in an *fff* dynamic, its momentum carrying the music through eventually to the *allegro*. Intensity is gradually built up by progressively raising the opening motif by a semitone (F♯ and C in the first wave, G and D♭ in the second, A♭ and D in the third), by introducing parallel sixths and tritones respectively in the second and third waves, and by inverting the motif in the third wave. If we also note the sudden cymbal climaxes in the first two waves, we have a series of events (bars 2–33) that can be shown in diagrammatic form (Fig. 1, measured in units of $\frac{3}{8}$ metre).

I, 9 (pianos in enharmonic reduction)

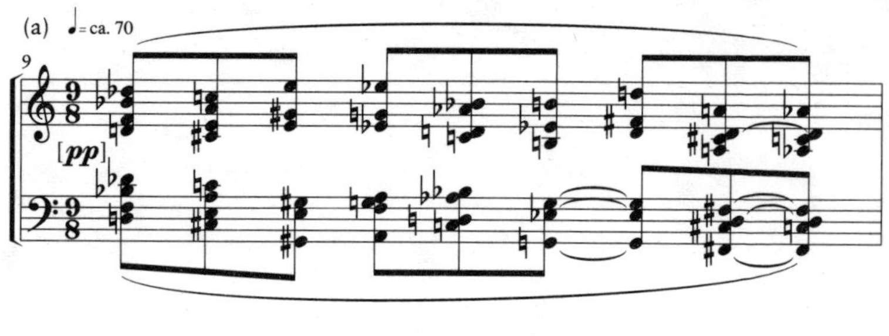

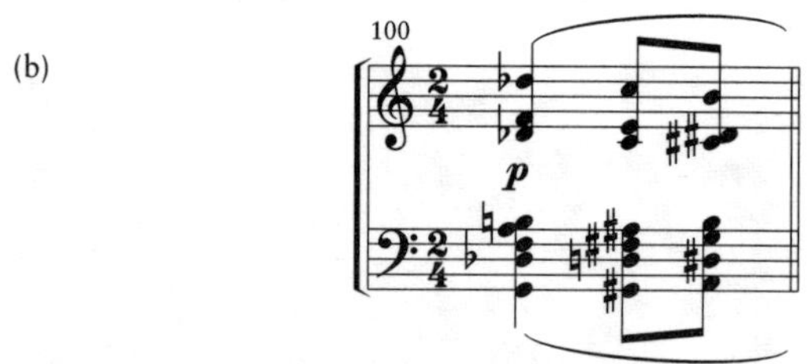

EX. 4

It was Ernő Lendvai who first noted geometric aspects of Bartók's musical architecture which involved the proportion of the golden section.[11] (The golden section divides a length so that the ratio of the smaller part to the larger part is the same as that of the larger part to the whole.) This proportion, whose value approximates to 0.618, occurs widely in organic nature, architecture and the visual arts,[12] and can be represented in whole numbers by the successive terms of summation series such as the 'Fibonacci' sequence (2, 3, 5, 8, 13, 21, 34, etc.) and the 'Lucas'

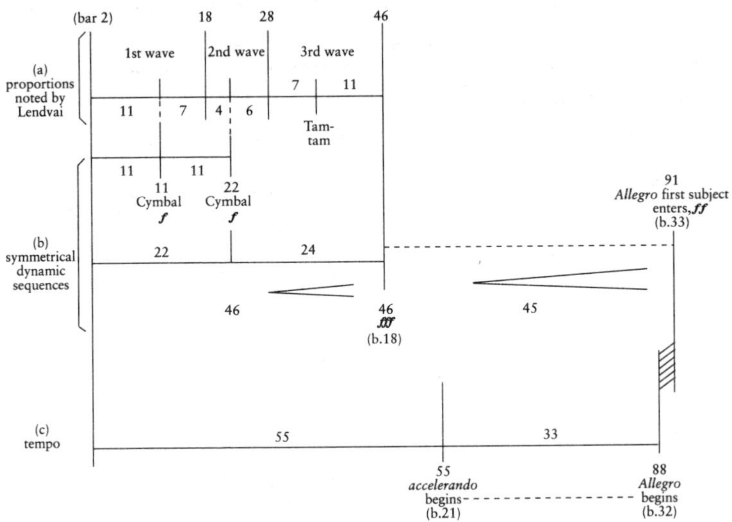

FIG. 1

sequence (3, 4, 7, 11, 18, 29, 47, etc.). Lendvai selects bars 2–18 here as a model example, a network of interlocking golden sections (measured in units of $\frac{3}{8}$) divided principally by the entries of the second and third waves, and then, on a subsidiary scale, by the cymbal climaxes in bars 6 and 10 and the tam-tam entry in bar 14.[13] If we extend our area of measurement to the beginning of the *allegro* at bars 32–3, always measuring in beats of $\frac{3}{8}$ metre, the dramatic purpose of the architecture becomes clearer. This can be seen in Fig. 1. Sequence (a) shows the 'golden' proportions noted by Lendvai, outlining the three opening waves – a close approximation to the Lucas series numbers 4, 7, 11, 18, 29 and 47. From this, the three progressive climaxes can be abstracted down to sequence (b): the first climax occurs exactly halfway to the second (11 : 11 beats); the second occurs within a beat of halfway to the third (22 : 24 beats); and the third occurs again within a beat of halfway (46 : 45 beats) to the introduction's ultimate dynamic goal, the *fortissimo* arrival at C major in bar 33, with the entry of the main *allegro* theme. This is reinforced by the gradation of tempo shown as sequence (c):

the *accelerando* towards the *allegro* begins after 55 beats, and the *allegro* arrives after 88 – within a unit of the Fibonacci golden section numbers 55 and 89. Thus, the golden sections of the more organic sequences work in dialogue with the large symmetrical rhythm of the climaxes, carrying momentum through to the *allegro*. Given the musical intricacy involved, and the metrical framework that accommodates the proportions, their numeric accuracy is remarkable,[14] suggesting the same clarity of organization as has already been noticed in the percussion writing.

Whether the proportions occurred spontaneously or were devised consciously is a question too large to tackle here. Certainly, Bartók never spoke explicitly of them.[15] If they were deliberate, therein may lie another reason for Bartók's interest in Debussy and Ravel: Debussy's *Prélude à l'après-midi d'un faune*, for example, similarly opens out in three waves of increasing intensity, marking out a large-scale rhythm of golden sections and symmetries.[16] Proportions of this type can be found elsewhere in Bartók's Sonata, but not throughout, suggesting not a strict method but rather a dramatic device that can be used (or that occurs) when appropriate.

Bartók's meticulous metronomic indications throughout the following *allegro* are a key to its form, indicating not so much sudden changes as a fluidity of motion, in the performing tradition of that time of bringing sonata architecture into relief through fluctuating tempo. Similar fluctuations can be heard, for example, in Furtwängler's recordings of Beethoven's Third or Schubert's Ninth Symphonies – an apt enough link with Bartók, for it was with Furtwängler that Bartók gave the première of his First Piano Concerto. Bartók's recorded performance, with József Szigeti, of Beethoven's 'Kreutzer' Sonata shows the same flexible moulding of tempo.[17]

Probably most extraordinary of all in the first movement is Bartók's development section, a dramatic *tour-de-force* dominated by an ostinato version of Ex. 2. This long section, like the slow introduction, follows a powerful arch shape, with a climax of enormous intensity in bars 217–30, after which the ostinato figure resumes, but inverted – thus also recalling the arch form of the fugue from the Music for Strings, Percussion and Celesta.[18]

Bartók's working manuscripts show that this whole section found its final form only at a late stage, replacing an earlier version that led into the recapitulation via a straightforward dominant pedal.[19] Since Bartók and his wife used those manuscripts for the first performances (the score was not printed until 1942), it is likely that the final version was not composed until after the première.[20] The final version's superiority is as clear in sound as on paper, most notably at the approach to the recapitulation (bars 264–73). Instead of the dominant pedal the final version tonally surrounds its goal: the timpani begin from E♭ (the mediator between F♯ and C), while imitative entries on the pianos describe a complete tonal cycle of ascending fourths, starting on C in bar 264 and completing itself on C at the recapitulation ten bars later. Anticipating this on a larger scale, the pedal points from the two mirrored ostinato sections, on E and G♯ (from bars 195 and 232 respectively), both surround and approach the C of the recapitulation symmetrically by major thirds. For Bartók the student of natural science, this is perhaps the squaring of the tonal circle, combining the diatonic gamut with two axes of symmetrical relationships. In a similar way, the movement's closing bars sum up with a juxtaposition of F♯–C and G–C tonal tensions, emphasized by the timpani (bars 433–43).

The unusual effect of the second movement has much to do with the way its various sections or sub-sections form a sequence of waves, each rising to a climax before disintegrating into fragments that regroup to begin the next section. This process takes over particularly from the second wave (from bar 28), where the music moves into Bartók's nocturnal world with a counterpoint of two ostinato figures.

EX. 5

The upper one of these (Ex. 5) was for Bartók something of a motto. Having appeared in the main motif of the *Allegro*

molto espr. la melodia
II, 48-51
48
♩= ca. 72
pp
P.I
a tempo ♩= ca. 72
P.II
mf
espr. la melodia
pp
Timp.
Perc.I
p
5
5
50

EX. 6

barbaro of 1911, it also crowns the final bars of *Mikrokosmos* and the Concerto for Orchestra, as well as those of the present movement. By the movement's third episode this figure has shifted to the bass, participating in a counterpoint of octatonic textures again partly borrowed from Debussy (Ex. 6, bars 48–51, xylophone part omitted).[21] After a birdsong-like climax in faster tempo and 'Bulgarian rhythm', again like the final piece of *Mikrokosmos*, the movement folds back on itself with the most magical of transformations, its opening procession-like chant now seemingly entwined in a magic dream.

Ernő Lendvai has drawn attention to the finale's diatonic modes, linear melodic shapes and duple metre, which contrast with the first movement's predominant chromaticism, circular motif and triple metre. This can be seen in its main subject (Ex. 7).[22]

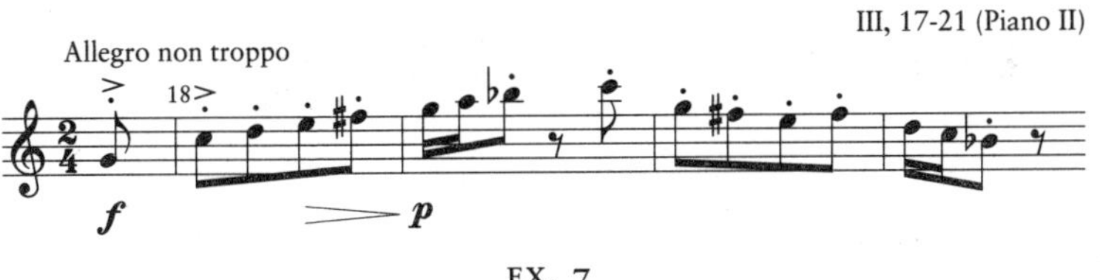

EX. 7

Nevertheless, under the contrasting surface the seemingly new ideas grow naturally out of what has gone before, as can be seen by comparing Ex. 7 with the first movement's second subject (Ex. 8, as it appears in that movement's recapitulation, bars 296–9).

EX. 8

The diatonic mode of Ex. 7, incidentally, is not a standard Western mode but a composite of Lydian and Mixolydian, known in Indian music and also used by Fauré, Debussy and Ravel. As

Lendvai observes, it may have been especially attractive to Bartók as an antithesis to modal chromaticism, because of its close relationship to the open overtone series based on C (Ex. 9).

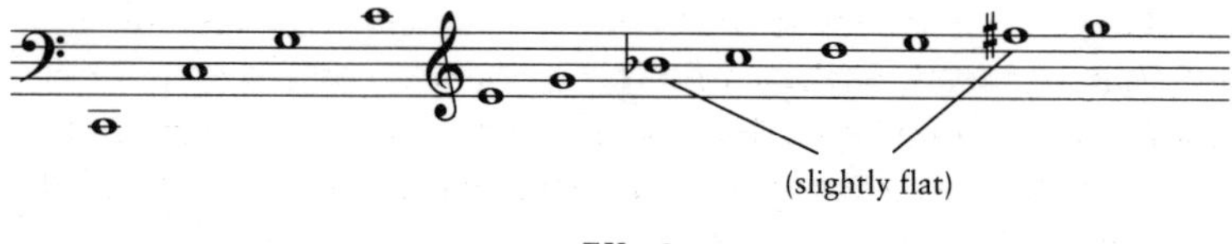

EX. 9

Above all, the Sonata's finale seems dominated by laughter, often in the form of sheer buffoonery akin to that in the finale of *Contrasts*. There can be no mistaking the peasant burlesque that begins to romp from bar 103, completing the exposition in wild merriment by bar 133. (In the one recording Bartók and his wife made of the work,[23] they set this in relief by making a *poco rall.* from bar 100, two bars earlier than printed.) Before long the central episode plunges into a wild dance in the movement's tonal 'counterpole' of F♯ (bars 173–88), accompanied by one of Bartók's most elaborate bagpipe (or barrel organ) effects; derived from an earlier wheezing accompaniment figure (from bar 28), it now rocks antiphonally between the two pianos (bars 173–5, Ex. 10).

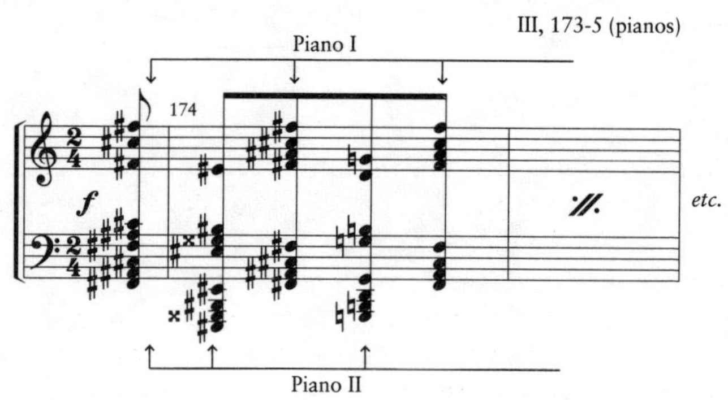

EX. 10

As it dissolves in quasi-glissando raspberries (bars 193–4), its place is taken by the most outright clowning of all, with an episode of rhythmic staggering and cuckoo-like interjections (bars 199–228) that undoubtedly give the impression that the performers – perhaps 'A bit drunk'?[24] – have got lost. The joke can be doubly on the performers, for the rhythmic hiccoughs make this one of the most treacherous passages for ensemble in the Sonata. Indeed, with deadly irony, it is exactly here that the recorded performance by Bartók and his wife, along with two inadequately prepared percussionists, falls apart.[25] Bartók seems deliberately to leave ambiguous the point where the recapitulation proper takes over, as the first subject's treatment at bar 248 is still tonally indefinite and runs on directly from the preceding development. Only by bar 269 is recapitulation clearly under way, and the motif that confirms this (Ex. 11a) is given a new tail that turns it into a diatonic expansion of the Sonata's opening (Ex. 11b).

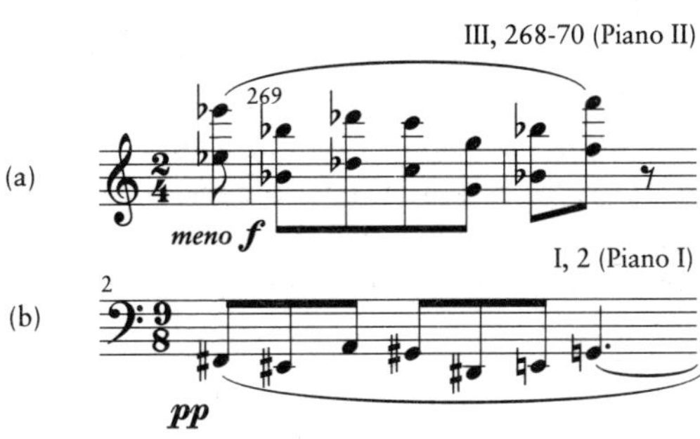

EX. 11

Finally, the main subject returns with a quiet but unmistakable swagger, and, after what seems a single backward glance (bars 409–10), the Sonata dances gently into infinity.

Given the source of the commission, Bartók was assured of good conditions for the Sonata's première on 16 January 1938. In letters to friends he afterwards reported that 'it had a tremendous success', that his wife 'held her own splendidly' and that 'the timpanist was a real virtuoso'.[26] In fact, the Sonata launched a new duo career for the Bartóks, who performed it ten times in several countries over the next year, subsequently adding to their repertoire other two-piano items by Bartók,

Mozart, Liszt, Brahms and Debussy. The one recording they left of the Sonata, despite the ensemble problems already mentioned, reveals beautifully matched piano playing: clear and robust but never hard, flexible but never sentimental. Iambic rhythms in the first movement tend to be strongly accented and slightly compressed (as, for example, from bars 73 or 225), and some melodic lines in asymmetric folk rhythms (notably bars 317–25) are treated in quite a free *parlando rubato*. This just touches on another larger subject, the distinction between the extremely intricate descriptive notation Bartók used for transcribing the rhythms of actual folksong performances, and the simpler 'prescriptive' notation of similar rhythms in his own compositions, whose scores have to be sufficiently 'user friendly' not to inhibit fluency and spontaneity of performance.

Bartók's transcription of this Sonata as the Concerto for Two Pianos and Orchestra was undertaken mainly at the persuasion of his publisher Ralph Hawkes, with a view to securing orchestral performances in the United States, where venues for the Sonata version were sparse. Some of the retouches Bartók made to the piano writing for this version (given in small print in the Sonata's score) are of interest for the light they cast on his intentions in the original version. In particular, Piano I's repetitions of the final chord in the second movement make explicit the acciaccatura effect between the pianos (again evocative of bagpipes).

Just as Brahms's music, regarded a century ago as astringent and even harsh, now conveys to its listeners Romantic warmth and Classical strength, Bartók's music now increasingly comes across to us in its real colours. His Sonata for Two Pianos and Percussion, with all its technical challenge and innovation, and its undoubtedly astringent aspects, is surely just as much one of this century's masterworks for its Classical strength, evocative richness, humour and humanity.

NOTES

1 See Bartók's article about this Sonata in *BBE*, pp. 417–18.
2 See Kroó, p. 192.
3 See Clive Bennett, 'Icare', *Tempo*, no. 133–4 (September 1980), pp. 44–51. This article quotes from a letter, purportedly from Bartók to Markevitch, about *Icare*.
4 See Ernő Lendvai, *The Workshop of Bartók and Kodály*, Budapest (Editio Musica), 1983, pp. 269–317, for discussion of these symmetrical 'axis' relationships. Other symmetries of pitch in Bartók's musical language are investigated in Elliott Antokoletz, *The Music of Béla Bartók*, Berkeley (University of California Press), 1984.
5 *BBE*, p. 417.
6 Sources include Louis Galánffy (reported independently by his friend Ernő Lendvai and his pupil John Aielli, both in conversation with the present writer) and Kroó, p. 193.
7 *BBE*, pp. 376–83.
8 This motif, with its rising minor third sequence, also underpins some prominent moments in the Romantic repertory, including the opening bass line of *Tristan und Isolde*, the beginning of César Franck's Symphony, and the latter's Violin Sonata (at the climaxes of the last two movements). Bartók's affection for Franck's Symphony is documented in an essay of 1920 (*BBE*, p. 465).
9 See Ex. 1 in the preceding chapter, 'Masterworks (I)'.
10 cf. the following standard examples of this progression: the opening phrases of Mozart's Symphony in G minor K550, Debussy's piano Prélude 'Minstrels', and the present movement's fugue subject, starting at bar 332.
11 Ernő Lendvai, op. cit., pp. 33–52 and passim.
12 See, for instance, Samuel Colman, *Nature's Harmonic Unity*, ed. C. A. Coan, New York (Putnam), 1912; Matila Ghyka, *The Geometry of Art and Life*, repr. New York (Dover), 1977; Le Corbusier, *The Modulor*, London (Faber and Faber), 1954; Rudolf Wittkower, 'The changing concept of proportion', *Daedalus*, vol.89 (1960), pp. 199–215.
13 Ernő Lendvai, op. cit., pp. 36–40. Lendvai's omission of bar 1 from the calculation is reasonable, since rhythmic and motivic articulation begin only in bar 2. Perhaps, in terms of Bartók's creation archetype, bar 2 marks the beginning of measured time.
14 None of the slight deviations from theoretical exactitude in Fig. 1 can be 'corrected' without causing either a worse inexactitude elsewhere in the diagram or an intrusive change of metre between bars 18 and 32.
15 See Roy Howat, 'Bartók, Lendvai and the Principles of Proportional Analysis', *Music Analysis*, vol.2 (1983), pp. 69–95.
16 See Roy Howat, *Debussy in Proportion*, Cambridge (Cambridge University Press), 1983, pp. 149–51. Whether or not it implies French musical influence, Bartók did head an early draft of this Sonata 'Sonate pour 2 Pianos et Percussion'.

17 Hungaroton LPX 12331.

18 See also Bartók's comments on the formal outline of this section in *BBE*, p. 417. Again we note how laconically he restricts himself to describing formal outlines, leaving the musical effect to speak for itself.

19 See Illustration no. 25.

20 See pp. 28–9 of László Somfai's commentary in *Bartók's Workshop*, catalogue of the exhibition of the Budapest Bartók Archive (Budapest), 1987. The different bar numbering in Bartók's manuscript arises from his numbering of the bars from the beginning of the *allegro molto*; this early version of the development is also slightly longer.

21 cf. 'Pour un tombeau sans nom', from Debussy's *Six épigraphes antiques* (1914), bars 15–17.

22 The motif's first appearance, on xylophone, has an A in place of the top C. This is perhaps a slip of Bartók's pen, because of the ledger lines involved. Once made, the error would easily have been carried over to later manuscripts because of Bartók's use of lithographic copies.

23 Reissued on Hungaroton LPX 12332. The recording was taken from a CBS live radio broadcast of November 1940.

24 The title of the second of Bartók's *Three Burlesques* Op.8c.

25 The performance would have ground to a halt in this troubled episode had Bartók not played doggedly on by himself – Ditta had lost her place while trying to adjust to one of the percussionists – until the others found their place again at bar 269.

26 *BBL*, pp. 264–6.

23

Final Chamber Works

MALCOLM GILLIES

As with many of Bartók's later works, *Contrasts* (1938), Divertimento (1939) and the Sonata for solo violin (1944) were commissioned, and tailored by Bartók to the specific talents of those who would give these works their premières. His long-time performing partner the Hungarian violinist József Szigeti was the initial inspirer of *Contrasts*, although the formal commissioning of the work was undertaken by the jazz clarinettist Benny Goodman, then renowned as America's 'King of Swing'. For $300 Goodman requested a work of six or seven minutes' duration for clarinet–violin duo, with piano accompaniment, suitable for performance and possibly recording by Szigeti and himself. Bartók promptly obliged during late August and early September 1938 by producing a two-movement work indebted to the traditional bi-partite model of the Hungarian rhapsody, as seen in the movement titles 'verbunkos' (recruiting dance) and 'sebes' (fast dance). But Bartók was worried because each movement took about five minutes to play – too long to fit on to one side of the twelve-inch double-sided 78 rpm records of the day. Writing to Szigeti on 5 September he likened the situation to when clothes are ordered for a three-year-old but arrive fitting an adult. Moreover, by 24 September 1938 he had also composed a slow movement, 'pihenő' (relaxation), for the trio, but kept quiet about this movement until December. The work was, accordingly, premièred in its two-movement form on 9 January 1939 in New York by Goodman, Szigeti and the pianist Endre Petri, but Goodman did later accept the extra movement, which was placed between the two original movements. In that augmented form Bartók's composition was recorded by Goodman, Szigeti and the composer in April 1940,[1] where it lasts for just over seventeen minutes. The work's title had also finally been settled, with Bartók rejecting previous titles of Rhapsody, Two Dances and Three Dances, in favour of *Contrasts*.

The title is certainly appropriate, for several reasons. The tone colours of the three instruments always remain distinct, and only reluctantly convey a sense of ensemble. This strained sense of ensemble may also be attributed to Bartók's inexperience in writing for clarinet – this was his only chamber work to include a wind instrument – and his awkward occasional attempts to imitate something of a jazz idiom.[2] In formal terms the contrast is built into the original slower–faster dance concept of a rhapsody and only heightened by the interpolated slow and flexible 'relaxation'. Bartók's unusual ending of the third movement in B♭, and not the first movement's A, further emphasizes contrast at the expense of structural unity. Within the third movement he seeks contrast in a more subtle way by requiring both violinist and clarinettist to change instruments: at bar 30 from a mistuned violin (G♯ D A E♭) to one normally tuned; at bar 132 from a clarinet in B♭ to one in A, and then back again at bar 169.

Divertimento, for string orchestra, resulted from a commission of Paul Sacher on behalf of the Basle Chamber Orchestra, of which he was conductor. Sacher had commissioned Bartók's Music for Strings, Percussion and Celesta back in 1936, but now wanted something simpler, for an ensemble of about twenty-two players. Bartók's initial response was to write a work of 12–15 minutes' duration, 'something between the Romanian Folk Dances and my two rhapsodies for violin and piano (or orchestra)',[3] but he later moved away from such models to that of a concerto grosso, with alternating tutti and concertino passages. To facilitate Bartók's writing of the work Sacher made available his family's Swiss chalet in Saanen during August 1939. There Bartók rapidly composed his Divertimento, between 2 and 17 August, and immediately played the work, now about twenty-two minutes long, to Sacher to check various of its details with him. He also started to compose his Sixth String Quartet while in Saanen, but broke off on 24 August to return to Budapest as the likelihood of war increased. Given the time at which the Divertimento was composed it is surprisingly radiant in the tone of its outer movements. In the choice of 'Divertimento' as title Bartók perhaps had a Mozartian style in mind; he had certainly been playing more Mozart in his recitals of recent year. The middle movement is, however, a spine-chilling lament for the world crumbling about him. That image was not lost on the hearers of the work's première, in Basle, on 11 June 1940, who already knew of the stunning successes of the German blitzkrieg across northern Europe.

Bartók's final chamber work, the Sonata for solo violin, arose through a friendship established between the American violinist Yehudi Menuhin and Bartók. In November 1943 Bartók had been taken with Menuhin's playing of his First Violin Sonata at a private meeting in New York, and started to consider Menuhin's suggestion of a new work for him to play. Later in that month Bartók heard Menuhin in a New York recital, which included Bartók's First Violin Sonata and Bach's Sonata in C major for solo violin (BWV 1005), and was further impressed. When he could next find peace and quiet, in February–March 1944 while in Asheville, North Carolina, Bartók allowed the experience of Menuhin's Bach performance to mingle with his own compositional ideas in producing the Sonata for solo violin. His score was dated 14 March, although Menuhin and Bartók continued to consult over the work's details for many months, and some aspects of it were not definitively settled even at the time of Bartók's death. But Bartók was proud of this rigorous and intense Sonata, quite out of keeping stylistically with his other, more mellow 'American' works, and wrote shortly after the work's première in Carnegie Hall on 26 November 1944: 'It has four movements, and lasts ca. 20 minutes. I was afraid it is too long; imagine: listen[ing] to a single violin for twenty minutes. But it was quite all right, at least for me.'[4] The work was, in fact, even longer, and takes nearly twenty-six minutes in Menuhin's superb recording of 1947.[5] Of these three late chamber works the Sonata for solo violin is the most significant, revealing the genius of Bartók in a startlingly direct fashion. The work is a *tour de force* of musical concentration and the final fruition of that Bachian style tendency which Bartók had been pursuing over the past two decades.

Despite their obvious differences in instrumentation, purpose and, even, quality, the three works have much in common. All adopt traditional movement patterns, with a moderately-paced first movement, internal slow movement and fast finale. The Sonata contains a fugal, second movement, as well. Bartók's formal scaffolds within the movements are of a predictably narrow range, with first movements in ternary or sonata forms, ternary-form slow movements and loose rondo-influenced finales. Bartók made no attempt to disguise these guiding models, and even listed them bluntly when called upon to say something in explanation of his Divertimento to Paul Sacher.[6]

Once we look within these large-scale structures, however, we find a composer obsessed with exploiting all the potential of variation techniques. In Bartók's hands the music is forever in a state of transformation. As he commented about his string quartets in 1937: 'I do not like to repeat a musical thought unchanged, and I never repeat a detail unchanged.'[7] But he manages to maintain a superb sense of unity to the music through limiting the number of his themes or motifs and ensuring that, whatever processes of transformation they are subjected to, they retain their essential identity. Underlying scalar structures are liable to be expanded or contracted in whimsical ways. The various phrases of his themes rarely involve exact repetition, either rhythmically or in their pitches, but take on a life of their own as soon as they have started. Bartók spins the musical texture within the divisions of his musical forms largely through relentless employment of imitative strategies, with a brief motif frequently generating five or ten bars of music through its varied reiteration in close proximity in any number of parts.

At the level of scalar bases Bartók employs in these works everything from pentatonic through diatonic to chromatic. The twisting, gnarled chromatic theme of the second movement of Divertimento contrasts with his bright Mixolydian opening theme in the third movement and the chromatically tinged Dorian opening theme of the work. Sometimes, as in several earlier works, Bartók is prepared to move a motif or theme from one scalar 'terrain' to another, as in the opening of the first movement's second theme in his Sonata for solo violin, which moves from chromatic (bar 17), to diatonic (bar 21). But he resorts to much more varied structures than these: quarter and third-tone scales, in the variant version to his Sonata's fourth movement;[8] scales which do not duplicate themselves in the octave, such as Ex. 1; those which duplicate an interval pair, as with the minor third – minor second duplication in Ex. 2, or minor third – major second duplication in Ex. 3.

Contrasts, III, 161-2

EX. 1

Divertimento, III, 499-506

EX. 2

Divertimento, I, 167-70

EX. 3

Rhythmically, too, Bartók is fascinated with the duplicative possibilities of simple patterns. Within the 8 + 5-quaver 'Bulgarian rhythm' bars in the last movement of *Contrasts* he maintains an alternating pattern of 3, 2, 3, 2, 3 quavers, but warns the pianist:

> Here it is not possible to count in quavers; instead, he should keep on repeating *m ta ta m ta m ta ta* || *m ta m ta ta*, and practise the rhythm beforehand by tapping etc. anywhere and any time, just wherever possible (it is even possible on the train).[9]

So, too, the disruptive rhythm which obtrudes time and again into the first movement of the Divertimento simply involves the palindromic sequence in $\frac{9}{8}$ time of 1, 2, 3, 2, 1 quaver beats.

With themes Bartók's variational concerns are numerous: to vary subsequent phrases, in contrast with his opening phrase; to vary the theme *in toto* at each return; to exploit its various motivic potentials during transitional or developmental passages. The variation, or development, of his themes therefore generally begins within seconds of the beginning of the theme's first rendition. The opening of the Sonata for solo violin (Ex. 4) shows a four-bar phrase, which is then complemented by a 'dominant' consequent phrase, in true Baroque style.

EX. 4

But Bartók is in his second phrase already starting to turn the original quaver notes of bar 3 into semiquavers, as part of a move towards the freer development of his opening material in the following transition passage (bars 9–16). The development of the movement (from bar 53) starts again with the opening material, but Bartók soon subjects it to much more radical investigation at the basic level of rhythmic and melodic motif. In the recapitulation, however, he presents again the opening theme (Ex. 5).

EX. 5

The sense of recapitulation is undeniable, but Bartók will not allow his theme to return exactly. The supporting harmonies are largely different, and his process of melodic and rhythmic variation begins in the second bar, firstly with rhythmic compression and then a greater pitch rise towards the middle of the phrase, which eventually leads him to lengthen the phrase to five bars if he is to regain his original concluding note of G smoothly. The Sonata's third movement, 'Melodia', follows a similar pattern. Its first phrase (bars 1–6) is increasingly radically varied in the subsequent three phrases. At the formal return (bar 49) Bartók engages in an elaborate embellishment of his original, involving note substitution, rhythmic transformation of quavers into triplets and later semiquavers, interval extrapolations, trills and added unessential notes. But rigorously to apply such embellishment to all four phrases would itself become tedious, so Bartók allows the music to run more freely from within his third phrase (bar 60), thereby liquidating its specific features. The opening of the theme also returns briefly in spare, ethereal form in the work's final bars.

The most striking range of variation techniques is, however, found in Bartók's imitative passages. Here his consummate skill as a contrapuntalist is most evident. His imitative passages range from brief flourishes, for instance where a concluding motif may be echoed at a phrase end by a number of parts, through short imitative patches and whole imitation development sections to the entire movement of fugue in the Sonata for solo violin. Construed broadly, the imitative technique saturates this music. Variational potential is admitted in the opportunity for subsequent entries to differ from the initial subject of imitation in internal rhythm or pitch. Then there is opportunity to vary the pitch relations and distance between the entry points, and to play with their relative dynamics or scoring.

The Divertimento, with its five different instrumental parts, and interplay between tutti and solo passages, afforded the ideal medium for such imitative games, and not surprisingly both its outer movements contain considerable tracts of imitative development. That of the first movement dominates most of the formal development section, from bar 80 to bar 125, and comprises seven different imitative routines, now briefly summarized. Bars 80–87 present a variant of the movement's first theme on the cellos, which is echoed at the fifth on first violins and, in inversion, on violas, each at one beat's distance. The first violins, however, have started chromatically to compress the cello's subject, an idea which the cello then adopts more fully in repetition, with the original B C♯ D E basis being now transformed into D D♯ E F. In the second section, starting at bar 88, a four-part imitation results in a 'seventh chord' of starting pitches F♯ A♯ C♯ E, although not played in that order, followed by a thematic shadowing separated by two octaves and one beat's duration between first violins and cellos. The solo instruments only play the third imitative routine, at bars 95–7, which unfolds through an ascending cycle-of-fifths entry pattern of D♭ A♭ E♭ B♭ F, to be resumed in the next section, at bars 101–4, where the entries follow a descending cycle of fifths, G♯ C♯ F♯ B E. The fifth and sixth, tutti sections (bars 113–14, and from 115) involve a four-part rising pattern of entries separated only by a semitone (A A♯ B C) followed by a similar descending pattern (D♯ D C♯ C), which leads into a tense use of the rhythmic subject in contrary motion. Bartók's most ingenious, final section (bars 122–4) is for solo pairs, where the two violins with simultaneous entry pitches of B♭ and C are followed at one beat's distance by a viola–cello pair with starting pitches at the lower tritone, that is E and F♯. Their subject is a chromaticized version of that used in many of the earlier developmental sections. This passage's eerie effect is then smashed by the rude *fortissimo* tutti passage which breaks in at bar 125, and soon leads the music back to the recapitulation. Imitation is less to the fore within the simpler texture of the third movement, but does feature prominently in the C section of Bartók's rondo (or, alternatively, sonata-rondo) form. There, from bar 184 to bar 235, he includes a fugato full of subtle variation. His strategy is represented schematically in Ex. 6. The first three notes of the eight-bar subject are given in Ex. 6 for each entry, as one of Bartók's subtle changes concerns the 'tonal' answer to his subject (with the original A♭–E♭ interval being answered by E♭–A♭ at bar 192). He also sets out to use a pseudo-'tonal' answer with his third B♭-based entry at bar 200, but in so doing slews the subject back into its original A♭ form. The fourth, E♭ entry then

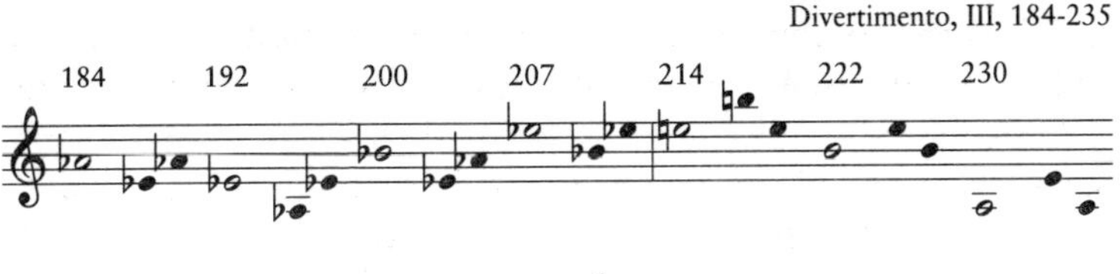

EX. 6

occurs a bar prematurely, and provides a 'tonal' answer to the previous statement. Before its completion, however, Bartók cuts the music off and initiates, at bar 214, an inverted and intervallically expanded subject entry on E, followed by further inversions on B and A. The behaviour of Bartók's countersubject also adds subtle individual colour to his various subject entries.

In the first movement of *Contrasts* Bartók also uses an extended free imitation when bringing back his opening theme (bar 57), to the point where it largely undermines the sense of a formal return. His particular strategies here include interval expansion and interval inversion within the subject's main motif (bars 58, 61–2), use of inversion (bar 65), shortening of the distance between entries (bars 61–2) and a stretto passage with entries based on the whole-tone cycle C♯ B A G F E♭ (bars 65–8).

Two analyses of individual movements, the slow movement of the Divertimento and the Fugue in the Sonata for solo violin, conclude this survey of Bartók's final chamber works. The spiritual kin of the Divertimento's *molto adagio*, second movement is the *adagio (molto)*, third movement of the Music for Strings, Percussion and Celesta. Both share the ghostly texture, in their opening and closing sections, of Bartók's 'night music', and build to strong, granite-like statements of doom in their middle sections. In both Bartók uses sharper keys: the earlier movement is in F♯, while the Divertimento's slow movement is in C♯. Formally, however, the Divertimento movement is less arched, being in ternary form, as against the 'bridge' (*A B C B A*) form of the movement from the Music for Strings, Percussion and Celesta. The opening section of that ternary form begins with one of Bartók's most concise chromatic passages. Within the first ten notes of the second violin's twisting melody the eight notes which comprise the fifth range E♯–B♯ are covered. Meanwhile, the first four pitches of the murmuring accompaniment have provided the remaining four notes, from the tonic of C♯ up to its minor third of E. From bar 6 Bartók begins to introduce imitation as he repeats his melody exactly on the violas but also introduces on the first violins its upper 'shadow', at the distance of two crotchets and the interval of an eleventh. His accompaniment grows more active, chromatically spanning not the tritone (C♯–G) of the opening five bars, but now the full octave C♯–C♯. The following sub-section (bars 11–19) develops two of the movement's key intervals, the fourth and the tritone, within the first violins and cellos, underpinned by a slow bass chromatic descent from D♭ to A. At bars 15–16 Bartók's common technique of interval expansion is well seen, as he expands the original A♭–D♭ fourth to A♭–F♭ and then A♭–G.

The movement's middle section starts at bar 20 and is in three parts – bars 20–32, 33–49, 50–55 – each neatly demarcated by Bartók's sub-section timings. Imitation plays a key role in the first sub-section. Its D-based subject is a halting lament in which the interval of a minor third is crucial. By introducing further upper entries on A (bar 25) and E (bar 27), over a static bass of G, Bartók creates a composite two-octave scalar form, shown in Ex. 7, and generates a wall of tension which only starts to subside at bar 30 where the solo viola is used in an echo effect.

Divertimento, II, 20-29

EX. 7

The second sub-section intensifies the impression of lament and now suggests something more definite: a funeral procession. Over a two-bar ground of groaning open fourth and fifth intervals never departing far from G♯, Bartók introduces a highly embellished melody, which gradually ascends, mostly by chromatic steps, gains in urgency and eventually, from bar 41, is played in parallel perfect fifths, to augment the lumbering, primaeval tone of the accompanying lower instruments. At bar 44 the climax is reached with the ultimate dissonance between the G♯–D♯ of the ground and G–D open fifth of the melody. Over the continuing, but gradually thinning, ground the melody climbs down from its pinnacle, and finally reaches the G♯ of the ground in bar 48. The small, third sub-section of Bartók's middle section of this movement juxtaposes *pianissimo* solo bars, in imitation of the melody which opened the movement, with *fortissimo* tutti bars which recall the peak of the funeral procession. The imitative solo entries, with their encircling motions around transitory 'tonics', define typically Bartókian patterns of diminished sevenths (bars 50, 52) and ditones (D♯ B G; G♯ E C♮, bars 54–5).

The return section of this movement introduces further development of the opening, over a C♯ pedal. The march texture is now more mysterious through the use of tremolos against the double-basses' triplet pattern. Bartók's melody, too, is more ghostly than previously through its playing simultaneously by the two violin parts separated by a distance of two octaves. It has also been transformed into a more systematic chromatic exploration. Its first eleven pitches involve no repetition: only F𝄪 is missing from the full array. The remainder of the movement is strongly based on C♯, reinforced by a conservative functional bass line (bars 62–5) or later, mainly diatonic scalar movement. Bartók winds down the music's tension with an extended play on a small rhythmic embellishing motif (bar 65), which he later augments, turning it from demisemiquavers to semiquavers and, finally, quavers (bar 69). Apart from the *fortissimo* interjection of the middle section's prominent minor third, the movement dies away quietly, concluding simply with a descending C♯ Phrygian scale. The viola's contradictory E♯, however, deliberately held on for a quaver's duration after all the other parts have stopped, is a herald of the tonality of the movement to come, F.

The Fugue from the Sonata for solo violin was Bartók's ultimate offering as a contrapuntalist.[10] Although its exposition is four-part, technical limitations of the instrument meant that such a multi-voiced texture could often only be suggested and frequently – as in the Bach solo violin sonatas – had to be abandoned for simpler single or two-part textures. Bartók's advice to the player is *risoluto, non troppo vivo*, and the resolute impression is reinforced by the *forte* playing of the first four bars of the subject with strong down bows. The fugue subject itself (Ex. 8) is five bars in length and chromatically spans the interval of a fifth, B–F♯, although C is unequivocally the tonic.

EX. 8

Bartók's fugal exposition charges on relentlessly, with following entries, ascending in pitch, on G (bar 5), C (bar 10) and G (bar 15). As to be expected, the variation of the subject is soon forthcoming. The final bar (bar 10) of the second, 'dominant' entry modifies the ending so as to lower it by a tone, thereby gaining the correct tonal relationship with the following 'tonic' entry. But this gives Bartók ideas for further modification of the subject endings at bar 15 and then, with the conclusion of the exposition, at bar 20. Other minor variations of the subject occur in the third and fourth entries, with the introduction of note repetitions, embellishments and rhythmic displacements. Some of these variants, along with those of the countersubject, are suggested by simple playing considerations on the instrument, but most are entirely free-willed. After a long episode of single-line semiquavers alternating with twisting chromatic patterns and more diatonic passages of multiple-stopping, Bartók returns to his subject at bar 37, in the 'polar' tonality of F♯ (a tritone from C), where his subject appears in altered guise. Against a semiquaver accompaniment suggesting an overall three-, then four-part texture, Bartók maintains the pitch integrity of the subject, apart from one octave transfer and one note substitution. But he transforms the rhythm radically. The subject is extended to seven bars, through rhythmic elongation of the concluding bars. Bartók has now reached the tonal 'turning point' of his movement, and at bar 44 introduces the subject again starting on F♯, but now in inversion (Ex. 9) and in the lowest of the parts.

EX. 9

The normalizing of the subject's rhythms started in the ordinary F♯ entry is continued here, with the first six notes being played as even crotchets. In bar 47, and again in bar 48, Bartók transposes his subject lower, resulting in a total range of a minor seventh (A–G), chromatically infilled, as against the infilled perfect fifth of the original subject. After a further episode, Bartók returns at bar 62 with fragments of his subject, and initiates a free development of its opening motifs which involves antiphonal play between ordinary and inverted forms. At bar 76 the opening subject returns in a majestic *fortissimo* three-note chordal rendition, with an ordinary orientation of the C subject at its top and E- and G-based parallel shadows beneath. The technical demands are, however, too great for him to continue the scheme through the entire subject, and he abandons it in mid-course, even eventually cutting off the ending of the C-based subject, which he, after a pentatonic run, introduces as the motif of development in his following coda section. There are no further full statements of the subject, although a brief exchange between ordinary and inverted statements of its opening is found at bars 92–4. And at bars 98–101 Bartók does make one last attempt upon his subject, in the ultimate of forms: four, simultaneous parts. This is, of course, quite impossible to do for the entire subject, yet he takes the third of the subject's motives (C E E♭ D♭) and presents it twice in fifth pairs, C–G with A–E (Ex. 10), before giving up his attempt.

Sonata, II, 99-101

EX. 10

The movement ends with a hugely powerful playing of the opening motif, C–E♭.

Reviewing the movement, the importance of the tritonic frame, C F♯ C, is clear. Within it, however, the most important tonal areas appear to be E♭ (from bar 23) and A (from bar 44, initially overlapping with the F♯), which leads to the suggestion that a 'diminished seventh', C E♭ F♯ A C tonal progression spans the movement, just as happens in the final movement of the Fifth String Quartet. That Bartók did think of the movement in this way is borne out in the movement's sketches.[11] There can be found Bartók's workings on inverted subject entries starting on C, E♭, F♯ and A, although in the end he only fully used a modified inverted entry on F♯. A further point of interest raised by the sketches is his consideration, but then rejection, of an intervallic expansion of the subject, akin to that carried out in the final 'acoustic scale' rendition of the fugue subject in the finale of the Music for Strings, Percussion and Celesta. His thought for this solo-violin theme had been to turn each semitone into a tone, thereby creating an open, whole-tone version of the subject. In that transformation the original opening C–E♭ would have become Bartók's favourite interval, the tritone, C–F♯.

NOTES

1 Columbia Masterworks set X–178, reissued in Hungaroton's *Bartók at the Piano* collection of 1981 (LPX 12329).
2 Szigeti had sent recordings to Bartók of Goodman playing both jazz and Mozart, but these had not arrived by the time Bartók had completed at least his two outer movements.
3 Unpublished letter, to Paul Sacher (NYBA).
4 *BBL*, p. 342.
5 Most recently reissued as EMI References CDH 7 69804 2.
6 Unpublished letter, 15 January 1940 (NYBA).
7 Quoted in Bence Szabolcsi, 'Bartók's Principles of Composition', in *Bartók Studies,* ed. Todd Crow, Detroit (Information Coordinators), 1976, p. 19.
8 This alternative, affecting bars 1–92 and 201–20 (quartertones) and bars 58–63 (third tones), was omitted in the 1947 Boosey & Hawkes edition prepared by Yehudi Menuhin. See Ove Nordwall, 'The Original Version of Bartók's Sonata for Solo Violin', *Tempo*, no.74 (Autumn 1965), pp. 2–4.
9 Unpublished letter, Bartók to Szigeti, 1 December 1938 (NYBA).
10 For a more detailed study of this movement see my *Notation and Tonal Structure in Bartók's Later Works*, New York (Garland), 1989, pp. 157–71.
11 Manuscript 81 FSS1 (NYBA).

MUSIC FOR STAGE

24

Opera: Duke Bluebeard's Castle

GYÖRGY KROÓ

The story of Bluebeard stems from the tale of Charles Perrault, published in 1697 as 'Barbe bleue' in the book *Histoires ou Contes du Temps passé, avec des Moralités*. It led to a veritable avalanche of various literary and musical paraphrases which gave rise in the nineteenth century to monographs discussing the historical antecedents of the tale. It can be traced back, on the one hand, to Gilles de Laval, Baron of Rais, who lived in the fifteenth century, and, on the other, to the figure of the Breton feudal lord Comorre, who lived in the sixth century.[1] Folklorists have also researched the Bluebeard saga and sought to establish its kinship on the basis of its 'forbidden room' and 'test' motifs. Others have looked for companion figures to the 'wife-killer' Bluebeard, and easily found connections in the fairy tales of many different peoples, among them the Hungarian tale of Márton Ajgó, who lured Anna Molnár to beneath the tree on which he had hanged his former lovers. There have also been attempts at tackling the symbolic connotations of the story, which go back as far as the ancient, contrasted notions of Darkness and Light. According to such symbolic interpretation, the figure of Bluebeard stands for the dark and sinful Night, which slays its betrothed. The Light embodies her original curiosity. The 'blue' is the blackish-blue of the Night – the beards of the Egyptian divinity Bes, the Indian Indra and the Greek Zeus were also blue – whereas the embodiments of curiosity in the Bible or mythology were no lesser figures than Eve, Lot's wife and the protagonists of the Pandora story.

There have been many outstanding literary, stage and operatic arrangements of the Bluebeard story, dating back as far as

1789, in which year two three-act operas on the story were written in Paris.[2] Among the nineteenth-century productions was a comic opera by Offenbach dating from 1866. In the first two decades of the twentieth century the following works were written about the legend:

1902 M. Maeterlinck, *Ariane et Barbe-bleue* (play)
1905 H. Eulenberg, *Ritter Blaubart* (3-act drama)
1907 M. Maeterlinck P. Dukas, *Ariane et Barbe-bleue* (3-act opera)
1909 A. France, *Les sept femmes de la Barbe-bleue* (short story)
1910-11 B. Balázs, *A kékszakállú herceg vára* (mystery play)
1911 B. Balázs B. Bartók, *A kékszakállú herceg vára* (1-act opera)
1920 H. Eulenberg E. Rezniček, *Ritter Blaubart* (3-act opera)

The author of Bartók's libretto, Béla Balázs, was a fashionable Symbolist poet in the early years of the century. He was close to the Bartók–Kodály circle, a follower of the Belgian man of letters Maurice Maeterlinck, and friendly with the Hungarian poet Endre Ady. He completed his 'mystery play' *Duke Bluebeard's Castle* in the spring of 1910, and, according to his memoirs, the play was soon performed at a matinée of the most prestigious Hungarian literary magazine of the day, *Nyugat*. The introduction to the play and the Prologue of the Minstrel were published in the 20 April 1910 issue of the Budapest theatrical paper *Színjáték*, with the full text following in an issue of 13 June. The play was dedicated to Bartók and Kodály, although Balázs had originally meant it only for Kodály, before whom he arranged to read it during this year. But Bartók was also present for this reading, and it was he who was more gripped by the subject. Kodály, none the less, did later commend Balázs's work:

> it is remarkable that an opera libretto should stem from a genuine writer, and a dramatist at that. It is therefore Béla Balázs's special merit that he did not hesitate to fashion one of his finest, most poetic ideas into an opera libretto, thus contributing to the birth of a great work of art.[3]

Bartók's draft of the opera includes no indication of when he commenced or completed the work, but the autograph score shows that Bartók started work sometime during February 1911 and completed the opera on 20 September of this same year at his home in Rákoskeresztúr.[4] In the same year he entered the piece (probably in the form of a piano reduction) in an opera competition organized by the Lipótváros Casino. The jury, chaired by the conductor István Kerner, deemed the work unplayable, and rejected it. Bartók was not deterred by the verdict of one of the nation's most prominent musicians and thought of having the work premièred abroad. A German translation of the text was therefore needed, and it was duly prepared by Kodály's wife, Emma, in 1912. That translated text was written into Bartók's autograph draft largely by Zoltán Kodály himself. At the time of this translation work Bartók made a few musical changes in the manuscript (perhaps on the advice of the Kodálys, whose opinion he held in high esteem), and also composed a new ending to the opera. Later, probably during the months prior to the Budapest première of 24 May 1918, Bartók worked out a third, and definitive, ending. He also modified the vocal parts, cutting more than seventy bars from the score and elaborating the dynamic and performance instructions. In the three years between the first performance and the first proofs of the Universal Edition piano reduction Bartók made several changes in the vocal parts, and decided on further last-minute alterations in the last two months of 1921. His final written comments on the work date from 3 December 1921, when he returned the second proofs of the piano reduction to Universal Edition in Vienna. The full score of 1925 was produced on the basis of this piano reduction published in 1921.

The only changes of dramaturgical significance concerned the ending of the opera. Originally it tapered off, leaving a 'pear-like' shape, but then in his first revision, of 1912, Bartók made the ending more weighty, while still preserving its open nature. This second ending took on more of the character of a summary, and he composed thirty-four bars of new material, essentially the apotheosis we now know from fig.135 to the following Andante. This new section sums up the arc of the whole opera, rising *poco a poco crescendo* to the culmination – reminiscent of the C major splendour of the organ at the fifth door (fig.74.19) – and then, after a near-ecstatic, heroic gesture in B♭, falling back in dynamics, texture and tonality to extinguish the light in the 'dark' key of F♯ minor. In 1918 Bartók hit upon the idea of the simultaneity of the vocal parts. This phenomenon occurs for the first time in the opera only after fig.133 in the published score, and creates an extraordinary sense of tension. It serves as a most effective introduction to the apotheosis of the thirty-four bars added in 1912. It was in 1918, also, that Bartók finalized the last phrase sung by Bluebeard, 'henceforth all shall be darkness, darkness, darkness' (from fig.138.4, Ex. 1a), which he had originally introduced in a somewhat different form in 1912 (Ex. 1b).

EX. 1

Balázs's *Bluebeard* begins with a Prologue. A minstrel, in the guise of a latter-day bard, steps in front of the curtain with the purpose of referring the plot to the 'mystery of the soul'. Bartók did not set the minstrel's words to music; instead, he created a ballad-like atmosphere – the mood of a folk tale – with his four-line instrumental pentatonic melody in the nature of a folksong. By repeating this melody at the end of the opera he created a frame for the work. The scene on the stage is a castle clad in the darkness of Night: Bluebeard's home. As the score states,

> It is a vast, circular, Gothic hall. Steep stairs at left lead up to a small iron door. To the right of the stairs seven enormous doors . . . The hall is empty, dark, and forbidding like a cave hewn in the heart of solid rock. . . . Suddenly the small iron door at the head of the stairs is flung wide, and in the dazzling white opening appear the black, silhouetted figures of Bluebeard and Judith.

The duke has brought a new lady to his home. Judith has eloped with him, ignoring the will of her parents and her brother, and only following the call of her heart. She now takes a shy look at the hall: sombre, austere, dank walls all round. The man does not hurry her; he senses that Judith has already heard of his deeds – he has disposed of his previous wives – and waits for the love in Judith's heart to silence the last traces of fear and anxiety. Her confession finally moves the duke: she wishes to share her lover's fate and wants to explore his sad soul. Only at this point does the iron door close: Judith has made up her mind. A tragic struggle is now initiated between them for love complete, without compromise. The secret recesses of the castle, behind the silent, sealed doors are opened now, one after the other, in response to her ardent protestations. Each takes her further and further inside; each explores more of the man's true nature. As each is opened more and more of a burden is placed upon her shoulders, for the castle of Duke Bluebeard is nothing other than man's soul.

The torture chamber behind the first door (fig.30) symbolizes cruelty. The weapons behind the second door are man's requisites amid the vicissitudes of life (fig.42). Both are stained with blood. Blood symbolizes that which separates the two human beings. Its minor-second motif in Bartók's orchestra plays the role of a motto, with its sharp dissonance. Judith clings to her illusion and ignores stark reality: the hard, militant motifs illustrating the first two rooms are repeated now in a soft, transformed guise. The treasures in the third room symbolize spiritual riches (fig.54). Behind the fourth door the noble flowers of masculine tenderness grow in the castle's secret garden (fig.60). The fifth door affords access to everything that gives a man pride – all that he has created (fig.74.19). 'Now behold my spacious kingdom', Bluebeard sings (fig.75), and the orchestra and organ strike up mightily. These three scenes, all in major keys, show the duke stepping once and for all out of his traditional role and being elevated into an ideal. As he reveals more and more of his spiritual treasures to Judith he correspondingly becomes more and more passionate. In this unique moment of his life he yearns to be united with her in an endless embrace.

But Bluebeard knows that love cannot sustain any more light than this. He cautions Judith, forbidding her from finding out the secrets of the remaining two doors. For her, however, their union remains incomplete. She wants to uncover her man's past and to dispel the secrets of the flowers, the blood dripping from the gems or the bloodstained shadow of the clouds. This is the turning point of the opera. These dazzling moments celebrate the greatness of man's ideas and the passion of his love. He has found happiness and a chance of fulfilment. The woman through her faith, trust and devotion has gradually overcome the darkness and sadness of soul, but is now beginning to have doubts. She starts to find the man's secrets a burden, just at the moment when Bluebeard has given her everything that can be shared. From now on her musical portrait expresses more and more her suspicions, curiosity, and the passion of Eve's nature. At her insistence the sixth door opens upon a Lake of Tears – the water of buried grief (fig.91). The light diminishes; doom casts its shadow. Rapture might still save them, but Bluebeard's love-song leaves Judith untouched. She now hurls accusations against him. The theme of Judith's jealousy, which silences the melody of the duke's love, grows out of the motif illustrating the blood stain (fig.112). (Bartók refers here to Ortrud, Wagner's dramatic figure in *Lohengrin*.) The wife-slaying duke of the saga disappears; the only moving force of the tragic denouement will be the woman's blind passion. While woman's mediocrity is being exposed, man's idealism is increasingly glorified. Man's love and heroic character are sublime and pure, and therefore his realization that he can never gain fulfilment in love and is doomed to eternal misery is all the more tragic. The seventh door opens (fig.121) and, instead of bloody corpses, Judith is welcomed by man's one-time loves as they live in his memory – idealized and beautiful. The secret of the last two doors is that tears shed in our solitude and memories enclosed in our souls cannot be shared. The figure of Bluebeard is now cleared of the last shred of suspicion. But now it is too late for Judith to repent. She has lost irredeemably any chance of happiness with Bluebeard. She will become just a dream image of love. The dejected duke leads her to the hall of memories to join the other women. The last door is closed; the castle is once more enveloped in darkness. 'Henceforth all shall be darkness, darkness, darkness.'

This Bartókian interpretation of the libretto highlights the one-act play's strong links with nineteenth-century Romantic opera, in particular Wagner's *œuvre*. Bartók has inherited the motif of 'redeeming love' from Wagner. There is a direct connection to *Lohengrin* not only through the motif of forbidding but also through the basic concept of the work, the love story of the chosen man and the fallible woman. As with Wagner, too, the motif of redemption is not restricted only to love, which is but a symbol of a deeper-seated problem: the isolation of the artist, and his human and social solitude. This pessimistic view of the enveloping of solitude in symbols and representing it as destiny started with Kierkegaard and, through Maeterlinck, became a veritable fashion in literature. Bartók (who had been brought up on the music of Wagner and maintained a great admiration for it) came into contact with this late nineteenth-century train of thought in philosopy, literature and the arts through the mediation of Balázs. This contact occurred around 1906–8, at a most susceptible time in both his personal and his artistic development: in his thinking he was under Nietzsche's influence; his passionate love for Stefi Geyer ended in the tragic break of 1908; his artistic prospects looked bleak because conservative tastes in Hungary rejected the idiom he had developed up to 1906–7 as well as the compositional and folk-music trend which Kodály and he thereafter represented.

Bartók's encounter with the music of Debussy compounded this welter of experiences and sensations. *Pelléas et Mélisande* certainly exerted an influence over both the concept and the music of *Duke Bluebeard's Castle*, yet this opera, above all, stands (perhaps along with *The Wooden Prince* and the Second String Quartet) as the summarizing, representative work of the stylistic period characterized by the discovery of folk music. From the viewpoint of human and artistic conduct, however, that period was still rooted in the nineteenth century, in Romanticism. The works which paved the way to this opera include the last movement (1907) of the Second Suite for orchestra, Op.4, the *Two Pictures* Op.10 (1910), and the *Four Dirges* Op.9a (1909–10). The opera is 'echoed' in the two song cycles of 1916, especially in 'Night of desire' (Op.15 no.3) and 'My bed beckons' (Op.16 no.3).

Bartók's opera is strictly tonal. Its dramatic and musical tension is created between the C major scene placed in the centre (fig.74.19) and the F♯-based passages of pentatonic–minor character at the beginning and ending of the work. The musical structure is articulated by the plot into a three-part Prelude (arrival in the castle, Judith's vow, catching sight of the closed doors) and seven scenes corresponding to the seven doors. Each scene has a key of its own (the third, for instance, is in D major, the fourth in E♭ Lydian, the sixth in A minor, the seventh in C minor), but apart from tonality, they owe their unity also to specific themes, mostly based on instrumental motifs. These themes are partly of an illustrative character (the militant theme of the room of weapons, the basic harmony of the treasure scene) and partly charged with an emotion or atmosphere of their own (the viola theme of the opening, the love theme which precedes the opening of the sixth door). The musical structure is made to conform to the action on the stage. It illustrates the plot and coordinates directly with the lighting effects – indeed, it is reminiscent of a series of tableaux, or a suite. Each tableau is linked symphonically, however; they are not merely placed side by side, but grow one out of the other, following a specific dramatic plan as parts of a symphony-like cycle. What creates the impression of a symphonic construction, in particular, is the presence of the basic minor-second 'blood' motif. This motif, a symbol of the conflict separating man and woman, is superimposed upon the various subjects of the individual tableaux and thereby plays a key dramatic role in the opera. The motif initially appears simply as a musical illustration of images of blood, but in the second half of the scene of the fifth door, when the opera turns towards the tragic and the stage begins to darken, it starts to develop into a self-standing chromatic motif which then dominates the musical material until the opening of the seventh door, in direct correspondence with the development of obsessive jealousy in the woman. Structurally it behaves like the theme of a series of variations in a Romantic symphony or symphonic poem.[5] The dramatic structure of Bartók's next two stage works, *The Wooden Prince* and *The Miraculous Mandarin*, is similarly based on the variation of a basic theme or motif. This procedure can, therefore, be identified as the most essential idea of Bartók's musical dramaturgy.

The vocal parts of the opera have a *parlando* character. Some of them comply with the style of the most ancient layer of Hungarian folksong, being pentatonic and having an overall descending direction. Others develop more immediately out of the chordal progressions but they, too, are mostly descending in nature. Apart from one or two exceptions the phrases are brief and motif-like; they do not add up to strophes. The prosody shows a remarkable mastery even if it is not equal to the perfection of Kodály's choruses, and the music succeeds in offsetting the monotonous pulsation of Balázs's eight-syllable lines. In *Duke Bluebeard's Castle* Bartók puts on the stage protagonists who sing in accordance with the inflections of Hungarian folksong: the first such attempt in the history of opera. The instrumental melodies are of an arioso character and consist of a free concatenation of diatonic motifs, apart from the programmatic chromaticism of the basic 'blood' motif. The vocal and instrumental melodies develop in a complementary fashion, side by side, and the two layers only join in the fourth, garden scene and during the moments which follow the opening of the seventh door.

The harmony in *Bluebeard* is determined by pentatony and the common chords of diatonicism – in keeping with the character of the melodies. The score is replete with well-known Romantic paired chords, related by the interval of a third, as well as solemn second-inversion chords. Chordal passages are frequently articulated by the traditional perfect and plagal resolutions of functional music. The free use of sevenths and ninths recalls the influence of Debussy, while the tritonal key relationships which pervade the structure point to the influential temporal proximity of Richard Strauss's operas, *Salome* (1905) and *Elektra* (1909), as well as the geographical proximity of Romanian and Slovakian folk music. The occurrence of whole-tone pitch patterns is surprisingly insignificant, but fourth chords are much more to the fore (a sign in this particular period more of folk influence than that of the hand of Schoenberg). The most innovative aspects of the harmony, which look forward to the sound world of the more mature Bartók, are the distinctive use of major–minor chords and also the use of chords derived from the harmonic series.

The orchestration is essentially based on the timbres and colour combinations of Wagner and Strauss, but within the framework of a basically homophonic style. Bartók's greatest moments of originality in his scoring are seen in the sheen and radiance of the D major treasure scene (fig.54), the organ glory of the C major scene at the fifth door (fig.74.19), and the A minor harp 'quiver' of the Lake of Tears (fig.91), which was to return over thirty years later in the third movement of the Concerto for Orchestra (1943). The frequency of the middle and lower registers is in keeping with the atmosphere of the opera, as are the solo roles accorded to the clarinet, cor anglais, viola and horn. The many static harmonies, the long sustained notes, and the absence of genuine polyphony all emphasize the static character of the opera and stress both the abstract nature of the stage and the symbolism of the mystery play. The plot is nothing but the spiritual conflict of two characters and the music is a simple abstraction of that conflict. 'Nothing else happens on stage', said the composer of his work in 1917, and in a letter written in 1928 he provided an even more accurate definition of the genre of this work, distinguishing it from traditional opera:

> It would be very welcome if the work were announced in Berlin as a dramatic scene rather than as an opera. . . . Unfortunately, the

> public expects an opera to be something completely different. It is therefore better if the audience is prepared by the title Dramatic Scene for something other than spectacle-opera.[6]

The static effect is offset by the sharp differentiation of the characters, musical images and styles of Bluebeard and Judith. Their realistic dramatic conflict, the dynamic, symphonic development of the opera's basic motif, and the almost Tristanesque intensity of the opera's idiom also work against the impression of stasis. The balance, interconnection and contrast of the two determine the unique effect of Bartók's opera, and make it the only one of its kind in the genre. *Duke Bluebeard's Castle* is, then, a self-standing, complete, closed composition, but it is not isolated within Bartók's *œuvre*. The problems it tackles and its dramatic concept make it the first part of the composer's stage trilogy. The second and third parts of that trilogy, *The Wooden Prince* and *The Miraculous Mandarin*, complement and carry forward the confession of Bartók's opera.

NOTES

1 For a detailed account of these antecedents and of Bartók's opera see my article, 'Duke Bluebeard's Castle', *SM*, vol.1 (1961), pp. 251–340.

2 Ibid., pp. 265–70.

3 'Bartók Béla első operája', *Nyugat*, vol.9 (1918), pp. 937–9.

4 The source material for this work is abundant, and includes the autograph draft (held in the Bartók Archive, Budapest), the autograph score (held by Peter Bartók, Florida), several corrected copies of that autograph score (corrected, at least in part, in the composer's own hand), an autograph fair copy of the piano reduction, proofs of the contemporaneous edition of that reduction (corrected by the composer), and even an autograph listing of Bartók's own suggested alterations to those proofs. In addition, a large quantity of extant correspondence relates to the work. A detailed listing of source material is provided in György Kroó, 'Data on the Genesis of Duke Bluebeard's Castle', *SM*, vol.23 (1981), pp. 79–123.

5 The role of this 'blood' motif and its development into a pervasive melodic motif can be studied by referring to the following passages in the opera: figs 11, 34, 45, 58, 71, 78, 85, 91, 108.

6 Unpublished letter, Bartók to Universal Edition, 1 December 1928 (NYBA).

25

Ballet: The Wooden Prince

GYÖRGY KROÓ

For some years after 1907 Bartók was in the throes of successive personal crises. The unrequited love he felt towards Stefi Geyer provided the emotional background to the First Violin Concerto and the First String Quartet. He overcame that particular emotional upheaval only around 1909–10 with his first marriage, to Márta Ziegler, and the birth of his son Béla. Solitude and a sense of spiritual loneliness, however, continued to haunt him during his work on *Duke Bluebeard's Castle* in 1911. One ingredient of this dejection was his slowly growing disillusionment with the political, social and national ideals which had determined his outlook upon the world some years before, when composing *Kossuth* and his two orchestral suites. He was also bitterly disappointed by the public's rejection of his folk-inspired works after 1908, and, indeed, by Hungarian musical life in general. The New Hungarian Music Society (UMZE), too, which had been organized in 1911 to ensure the propagation and authentic interpretation of new Hungarian music, had soon met with failure. Bartók's response to these failures was to withdraw completely from public musical life, and he thereafter appeared only sporadically in his capacity as a pianist. After nearly a decade on the pianistic stage he had come to realize that his career as a soloist had never really taken off internationally. His creative efforts, too, were bogged down. In 1912–13, then, he became engrossed in the publication of his collection of music from Bihar county, preparations for a tour collecting folk music to north Africa and also plans for a similar expedition to Asia. (In 1913 he did not complete a single composition of his own.) But even his ethnomusicological work led to reverses: he was branded as unpatriotic by some Hungarians because of his collecting of Romanian and Slovak folksongs.

Against this background of growing personal depression, the publication of Béla Balázs's 'The Wooden Prince' in the magazine *Nyugat* must have exerted a considerable influence on Bartók. The writer later commented that he had meant the ballet for Bartók, but, in any case, it appears that the libretto guided Bartók back to creative work and helped to spark off a series of new large-scale compositions, his Opp.14 to 17. Bartók was also motivated by the commission offered by the Royal Opera House in Budapest, and the personal interest of its intendant, the painter Miklós Bánffy, in the stage designs for the ballet. Composition began at Bartók's home in Rákoskeresztúr during April 1914, and then, after a lengthy break (due at least in part to Bartók's worries about orchestration), was resumed in the spring of 1916. Bartók later recalled that the performance in April 1916 of his Op.5 *Two Portraits*, conducted by István Strasser, had inspired him to resume his work on the score of *The Wooden Prince*, and he completed its actual composition shortly afterwards. The orchestration was finished by January 1917, and the work was premièred in the Royal Opera House on 12 May 1917, under the baton of the Italian conductor Egisto Tango. Béla Balázs was the producer.

Before the ballet's première Bartók wrote, 'I am so fond of my opera that when I received the libretto of the pantomime from Béla Balázs, my first idea was that the ballet – with its spectacular, picturesque, richly variegated actions – would make it possible to perform these two works on the same evening.'[1] Bartók may never have stated the matter explicitly, but his friend Kodály recognized that

> the constructive energy of the music [of *Duke Bluebeard's Castle*] becomes even more evident if we hear *The Wooden Prince* immediately afterwards. The playful, mobile Allegro of the ballet serves to balance the desolate Adagio of the opera. The two works fit together like two movements of a huge symphony.[2]

The scores of these two stage works further demonstrate the close links between the works. After the eternal night of *Duke*

Bluebeard's Castle, the music of the Prelude (*A*)[3] of *The Wooden Prince* heralds the dawn and a new awakening. A melody is drawn from the initial C major harmony, based on natural overtones, and this melody comes alive in ever greater spheres of activity. The sound of the violins in the higher register sparkles like the first rays of the rising sun and a marvellously vivid musical picture of nature is unfolded. As the music reaches its climax we hear, once again, the warmest melodic turns of *Duke Bluebeard's Castle* – the music of a man longing for happiness. The dreams and illusions that Bartók buried in the opera's Lake of Tears are wakened once more in the music of the ballet. Balázs's libretto has no trace of this mood of dawn-awakening. It was created by Bartók's poetic genius. On Balázs's stage the action only commences after the stage has been filled with the light of full morning. First, we see the princess, who has just descended from her castle to play in the forest and by the brook (1) (*B*). The gate of the neighbouring castle also opens and the prince sets out on his journey to see the world (2) (C1). The fairy of the forest (representing the fairy-tale world) orders the princess to return to her castle. (Bartók interprets the fairy as the Lady of Nature. The music bears no trace of the libretto's motif of the fairy being in love with the prince or of her ordering the princess to return to her castle so that she, the fairy, can attract the prince's attention.) The prince, however, sees the princess through the window and immediately falls in love with her (C2). The prince tries to follow her, but at the fairy's command the forest bars his way (3) (*D*). He defeats the forest but now the brook overflows its banks (4) (*E*). He therefore carves a wooden puppet, adorns it with his mantle, crown and a lock of his golden hair. It looks exactly like a real prince. He then uses the puppet to lure the princess from her castle, hiding himself behind it (5) (*F*). But the princess is only interested in the gaudy puppet and when, at a sign from the fairy, it becomes animated, she dances away with it towards the forest (6) (*G*). Balázs wrote that the wooden puppet

> symbolizes the creative work of the artist, who puts all of himself into his work until he has made something complete, shining and

> perfect. The artist himself, however, is left robbed and poor. I was thinking of that very common and profound tragedy when the creation becomes the rival of the creator, and of the pain and glory of the situation in which a woman prefers the poem to the poet, the picture to the painter.[4]

Nature embraces the solitary and sorrowful prince – Balázs calls the portrait of the suffering prince 'Intermezzo' – and the fairy covers him with a mantle of flowers, placing a crown of flowers on his head, as if he were the king of the forest (7) (*H*). But the princess returns with the puppet whose 'spring has run down', and who can only stumble about (8) (*G*). It shares the common fate of all discarded playthings. The princess now notices the real prince, and would like to go to him (*F*), but he has been deeply hurt and turns away from her. When the princess wishes to go after him the trees of the forest, again acting according to the wishes of the fairy, bar her way and prevent her from passing through them (9) (*D*). Sadly humiliated, she sinks to the ground, throws away her mantle and crown, and cuts off her lovely hair. Immediately the prince moves to her side, lifts her up and together they depart (10) (*C*). The fairy returns to her customary place in nature, to the realm of flowers, trees and water (*A*).

Bartók himself described the structure of the ballet in this way:

> The music of the pantomime is a kind of elaborate symphonic music, a symphonic poem to be danced to. There are three clearly distinguishable parts, within which are smaller sections, too. The first part lasts till the end of the duet between the wooden puppet and the princess. The second one is far more tranquil, of typical middle-movement character, and it continues to the reappearance of the wooden puppet. The third part is actually the repetition of the first part but in inverse order of subdivisions, a natural requirement because of the libretto.[5]

This analysis of the musical form, provided by the composer, can be made more specific by reference to the sections designated by capital letters in the summary of the plot, above. Bartók's first part encompasses sections *A*–*G*. His second, slower part (*H*) begins at fig.120 and lasts until just before fig.142, where the *accelerando* marks the start of the return to the first part. There is no *B* or *E* section in the reprise (that is, the dance of the princess, and the dance of the brook are omitted), and the return of section *F* is partial, only containing the theme originally presented at fig.74 (the self-humiliation of the princess corresponds, therefore, only dramatically and not musically to that of the prince). Section *C* also omits the music of the prince setting out on his journey. This section, in any case, does not have the character of a reprise since, because of the continuous development of the gestural love theme of the prince, it has the effect of fulfilment. The fact that the musical materials in the reprise appear in different keys from their counterparts in the first part (with the exception of the final *A* section), and develop in a different direction from that originally adopted, encouraged a major Hungarian critic of the day to discern a sonata structure in the piece, and Bartók did not protest at this interpretation.

The function of the love theme (section *C*) appears, however, to be of more importance. The phrase which occurs shortly before fig.21 gradually assumes independence from the 'static' architecture outlined in the composer's self-analysis and develops through various transformations – in a fashion similar to the blood theme in *Bluebeard* – into the basic subject of the composition. This leads to the apparent formal ambiguity of the middle section. That middle section of the 'sonata', built on C♯, is of a typical trio character, in that it does without the themes of the sonata structure although its main material is, none the less, made up of the variations of the 'basic theme'. The order of the themes' returning in the character of a recapitulation bears out the palindromic (bridge) form, referred to by Bartók.

The score of *The Wooden Prince* can, therefore, be interpreted in various ways. It has the character of a symphonic poem and the structure exhibits a complex of transformations of a single basic theme. It can also be considered a sonata or a bridge structure. Yet again, a further approach is suggested by the dramatic construction resulting from the contrast between 'ideal' and 'grotesque' images – a contrast which Bartók had already explicitly exploited in his First Violin Concerto and *Two Portraits* Op.5. Ernő Lendvai has pointed out that the music of the

EX. I

prince (the love theme in my analysis above) and the music of the wooden puppet have the same essential theme, although it varies in character, the prince's expression being more personal and lyrical (Ex. 1a, played by the clarinet) while that of the puppet is more dance-like and grotesque (Ex. 1b, involving full orchestra).

We know that Bartók had been preoccupied with the 'grotesque' character, in particular, at least since 1908, and had perhaps been wrestling with the 'enemy' ever since his parody of the Austrian anthem, 'Gott erhalte', in the symphonic poem *Kossuth*, written in 1903. Even against the background of those antecedents the central dance of the puppet has a few moments that are truly astonishing, where the ironic and grotesque attitude becomes demonic. At such moments we see Bartók embarking on the road that led to *The Miraculous Mandarin*. There, the clarinet melody of the princess is to turn into the street-walker's tune of enticement. Another motif in *The Wooden Prince*, the minor third (or augmented second) which is heard at fig.172 (Ex. 2), when the princess feels most anguished and forlorn, is related to the tense and tragic life-and-death atmosphere of the *Mandarin* pantomime, where, with the same painful downward slide and the same brassy colour, it becomes the symbol of human solitude.

EX. 2

The music of the forest dance is also part of this sombre doom-like dramatic intent. Many similar kinds of music, evoking a nature charged with passion, fear and perils, are encountered in Bartók's later output. At this stage, however, it is just one of a number of possible poetic images of nature. It is contrasted with nature in harmony, the tableau of awakening and slumbering landscape which serves to frame the ballet. Between these two interpretations of nature is a third: the Romantic, dream-like, symbolic, pantheistic 'inner movement' (from fig.120), where the prince, in his Tristanesque agony, is accepted, embraced and consoled by the fairy. In contrast to this Romantic reference, the dance of the brook and the puppet-carving scene are rooted in the style of Hungarian folk music, although the composer does not actually quote a single folk melody. This style is well suited to Balázs's 'naive' story. The near-quotation of 'The Peacock has arisen' at fig.178, however, is anything but naive, as it helps to raise the fulfilment of the lovers' happiness to the level of an apotheosis.

In his letter of 16 December 1924 to Ernst Latzko, then director of the Nationaltheater in Weimar, Bartók requested that in the programme notes for a forthcoming 'double bill' performance of his opera and ballet the following should be noted:

> 1. You should not overemphasize the folkloristic features of my music;
> 2. You should stress that in these stage works, as in my other original compositions, I never employ folk melodies;
> 3. That my music is tonal throughout, and
> 4. That it has nothing in common with 'objective' and 'impersonal' tendencies (therefore, it is not properly 'modern' at all!).[6]

In a letter of 1927 Bartók again emphasized this last-mentioned quality in his music, with particular reference to his pantomime, *The Miraculous Mandarin*: 'In contrast to the current objective, motoric etc. trend, this music actually sets out to express spiritual processes.'[7] As early as 1910, when reviewing Richard Strauss's opera *Elektra*, Bartók had compared that opera with Strauss's earlier *Salome* and ruled in favour of *Salome* because of the strength of its higher, more spiritual inspiration and, also, its greater poetic quality.[8] There is every reason, then, to suppose that in composing his stage works Bartók had sufficient remedy against any kind of simplistic *musique descriptive*, illustrative music or musical naturalism. On the other hand, his autobiography of 1918 makes it clear that, as a musical dramatist, Bartók was educated chiefly in the symphonic poems of Strauss and such operas of Wagner as *Tristan und Isolde*, *Die Meistersinger von Nürnberg* and the tetralogy of *Der Ring des Nibelungen*.[9] From Strauss, above all from his *Ein Heldenleben*,

Bartók inherited that symphonic dramaturgy based on a series of musical characters, in which the characters are not only identifiable but can also be described in words and therefore are almost able to pass for a plot.[10] The composer of *Kossuth* makes consistent use of transformations and combinations of motifs, which he clearly associated in his mind with actual stage scenes.[11] His comments on his own work indicate that he wished not only to express moods and emotions but also to depict human character, actual gestures and plots. It was in this sense that the symphonic poem served as a schooling for Bartók as dramatist.

How did contemporary critics see this relationship between the visual, illustrative nature of the music, the 'spiritual processes' which were so important for Bartók, and the symphonic form which he adopted in *The Wooden Prince*? Erich Katz, in writing a review article of Bartók's three stage works for the December 1927 issue of the Viennese journal *Musikblätter des Anbruch* commented that musical stage works had to give a direct sensory impression to the audience, and had to avoid any difficulties of comprehension of the text. In his opinion the tendency in Bartók's works, as in much contemporary music for the stage, was away from 'music drama' toward a close bond between dramatic material and absolute musical forms, and toward a stylization of the plot. He saw this tendency as favouring ballet over other genres. This perceptive observation of 1927 can be supplemented with two others. The first concerns the enduring propagation of the world of ideas connected with the Romantic music drama. In this sense, Bartók was a Romantic, although he stood at the end of the road outlined above by Katz. Even in the urban hustle and bustle of *The Miraculous Mandarin* he retained the kernel of the 'Liebestod' concept. The second observation concerns the dramaturgy of action and the descriptive character of the Romantic symphonic poem. Bartók was undoubtedly a pupil of that particular school, but his attraction to a concrete musical expression that could be translated directly onto the stage with its gestural nature seems to be rooted in a deeper, highly individual bent and is not inseparable from the genre. This view is supported by the fact that two, and then four decades after his *Kossuth* he wrote symphonic concert works which he accepted as potential ballets: the Dance Suite (1923), and the Concerto for Orchestra (1943).[12]

Bartók himself was concerned at the extent to which the music was tied to the stage, and not only in the case of *The Wooden Prince*. This was the main reason for the dissatisfaction which he expressed with the composition in his correspondence. It also explains why his preparation of a concert version of the ballet took him such a long time, and was undertaken with great thoroughness and tenacity. In a letter to Universal Edition in 1921 he wrote: 'in my opinion such a concert performance of the complete piece would not be advisable, but rather individual sections of the work . . . (forest dance, wave dance, dance of the wooden puppet)'.[13] It is not too extreme to conclude from this statement that Bartók felt the music was too tied to the stage in some places and was afraid that sections highly pantomimic in character, whether linked with gestural series of events or depicting concrete actions, would serve no function in the concert hall. This is what differentiates Bartók's ballet from *Kossuth*: while rooted in the genre of symphonic poem, *Kossuth* is devoid of such ties. This view is confirmed by Bartók's letter from the summer of 1923, which informs his publisher of a ten-minute cut from the score of *The Miraculous Mandarin*. (This is still three years before the controversial première of the pantomime in Cologne, when the work was still in a draft phase.) He wrote to Universal Edition:

> Various experiences have convinced me that the music of this pantomime should be cut considerably (instead of 40 minutes it should last just above 30 minutes) and that I should fashion it so that it can be performed also off-stage, without any changes.[14]

There can be no question here that, in the era of Mahler symphonies, Bartók was afraid of length *per se*. Rather, he wished to rid his score of elements too closely tied to the stage. This sentence about *Mandarin* helps, too, in understanding the nature of the major revision of *The Wooden Prince* which he undertook in 1932.

In this second version of *The Wooden Prince* Bartók certainly made various cuts to bring about a more concentrated musical expression, but, more specifically, he is found consistently omitting three kinds of material found in his first version: (1) internal repetitions serving the form of the plot rather than the musical form (this process also entailed the revision of sections containing only one material and rejection of the laws of stage time in favour of a shaping in accordance with the laws of time in symphonic music – as between fig.121 and fig.126, where Bartók cut the music down to under a third of its original length); (2) lengthy and highly pantomimic sections of quasi-recitative character (more than half of the cuts can be included under this category); (3) sections of closed dance numbers which are not specified in the text but which must originally have been imagined by Bartók as action within the style of the ballet. It is important to emphasize that these numerous cuts were not even related to his forging of a concert version but concerned the revision of the stage version. Bartók clarified this in a letter written to Universal Edition at the time: 'From a musical point of view, but especially with regard to the stageworthiness of the work, these cuts represent an absolute improvement.'[15]

Bartók compiled two concert suites from the music of the ballet. The first, the shorter of the two, consists of three numbers. The dances of the forest and the brook link, through a transition, to a shortened version of the dance between the princess and the wooden puppet, which is followed by a short *pas de deux* composed especially for this suite using material from the dance of the wooden puppet. (Bartók also prepared an even shorter version of this suite, but it has not come to light so far.) The second and longer suite embraces virtually all the important scenes in the ballet. Its construction is as follows: Preludium (Nature awakening), The Princess, The Forest, The Prince's 'work song', The Brook, The Dance of the Wooden Puppet, and the Postludium (using the closing music from the ballet which represents Nature in repose). A newly composed transitional section links the last two of these sections of the suite.

NOTES

1 *BBE*, p. 406.
2 'Bartók Béla első operája', *Nyugat*, vol.11 (1918), p. 939.
3 The bracketed capital letters refer to broad divisions of the musical construction; bracketed arabic numbers refer to the division of Balázs's libretto into dance scenes.
4 'A szövegíró a darabjáról', *Magyar Színpad*, 12 May 1917, p. 2.
5 *BBE*, p. 406.
6 *DB*.ii, p. 128.
7 Unpublished letter, Bartók to Universal Edition, 11 April 1927 (NYBA).
8 *BBE*, p. 446.
9 *BBE*, pp. 408–9.
10 Bartók's programme note on Strauss's *Sinfonia domestica* is found in *BBE*, pp. 437–45.
11 See Bartók's programme note for *Kossuth*, *BBE*, pp. 399–403.
12 The evidence for this view is found in his unpublished letter of 30 October 1927 to Universal Edition (NYBA) and various unpublished letters of 1943–4 to Boosey & Hawkes (NYBA).
13 Unpublished letter, 2 October 1921 (NYBA).
14 Unpublished letter, 31 August 1923 (NYBA).
15 Unpublished letter, 1 July 1932 (NYBA).

26

Pantomime: The Miraculous Mandarin

GYÖRGY KROÓ

In January 1917 Bartók was still orchestrating the last section of his ballet *The Wooden Prince* when the Hungarian literary magazine *Nyugat* published Melchior Lengyel's libretto of 'The Miraculous Mandarin'. This was the same magazine which had first published the text of 'The Wooden Prince' back in 1912. Lengyel had written his libretto having in mind Diaghilev's Russian Ballet, with Ernő Dohnányi as composer. But just as in the case of *Duke Bluebeard's Castle*, where the libretto had gripped Bartók's rather than Kodály's imagination, it was now Bartók and not Dohnányi who was inspired to approach the author and ask his permission to set the libretto to music.

As late as March 1919 Bartók can be found exclaiming 'Listen just how beautiful this story is', in answer to a journalist's question about its plot, and describing the plot in this way:

> Three apaches force a beautiful girl to lure men into their den so that they can rob them. The first is a poor youth; the second is no better off; the third, however, is a wealthy Chinese. He is a good catch, and the girl entertains him by dancing. The mandarin's desire is aroused, he is inflamed with passion, but the girl shrinks from him in horror. The apaches attack him, rob him, smother him in a quilt, stab him with a sword – but their violence is of no avail. They cannot cope with the mandarin, who continues to look at the girl with love and longing in his eyes. Finally, feminine instinct helps, and the girl satisfies the mandarin's desire; only then does he collapse and die.[1]

The chief male figure of the pantomime, the mandarin, is not typical of modern urban society – as are all the other characters – but is a force existing outside society. He is, to some extent, an unreal and symbolic figure. It is this unreality and symbolism which lend him a fearful greatness, enabling him to stand isolated above the world of the vagabonds, and to defy them. But the mandarin's triumph is only symbolic: he raises the girl to his own level of existence by making her aware of herself as a human being and aware of the existence of true love. For this victory, of course, the mandarin has to die, and the girl is left standing beside his body, shocked and lost in wonder, unable now by herself to progress to a better life, unable alone to oppose the evil surrounding her.

The first sketches of *The Miraculous Mandarin* date from August 1917. Bartók described them in a letter addressed to his first wife: 'an awful clamour, clatter, stampeding and blowing of horns: I lead the highly respectable listener from the crowded streets of a metropolis into an apaches' den.'[2] Much of his sketching of *Mandarin* was made in his *Black Pocket-book*, in which he frequently noted down compositional ideas when he was on holidays or otherwise away from home. In total, twenty continuous pages of sketches for the pantomime are found in this pocket-book.[3] The genesis of this work is complicated. A draft was completed by May 1919, but Bartók only addressed himself to writing the actual score more than four years later. He then subjected this score to various cuts and revisions between April and November 1924. By this stage the ending had not been settled, and even the piano reduction published by Universal Edition in 1925 did not contain Bartók's final verdict, which he only arrived at some time between 1926 and 1931.[4] Although early on Bartók did refer to *The Wooden Prince* as a pantomime, he did, both in his style of composition and in later statements, draw a clear distinction between ballet music and music for pantomime. His first comment on this subject dates from 1925 in a letter to his publisher: 'I see that U.E. is advertising Mandarin as a ballet. I have to observe that this work is less a ballet than a pantomime, since only two dances actually occur in it. It would therefore be much more practical to call it a pantomime.'[5] And again, some months later he wrote, 'the piece must not be turned into a ballet-show; it is intended as a pantomime, after all'.[6]

Bartók's awareness of genre distinctions is also documented, indirectly, in the way in which he classified the concert versions of both these works. From *The Wooden Prince* he assembled 'suites', but, in the case of *Mandarin* he took a stand against this term from as early as 1926, and suggested the alternatives of 'Scenes', 'Two Scenes' and simply 'Music from *The Miraculous Mandarin*'. Clearly he attributed to 'pantomime' a more pronounced action and a more dramatic character than that found in a ballet or in an orchestral suite. The very title 'scenes' highlighted the link with the stage. However, in both his pantomime and his ballet, Bartók was aiming at the idea of a stage work (as the title 'Music from the . . .' seems to bear out), although at the same time he wanted the music from these works to be able to be performed in the concert hall, without any reference to the stage. Not only does this music indeed survive by itself, but it has an absolute validity of its own, like a symphonic poem. It was in this spirit that Bartók had cut nearly a quarter of his score of *The Miraculous Mandarin* as early as 1924.[7]

It is particularly instructive to compare the original and definitive versions of the scene of the shy youth – a comparison carried out by John Vinton back in 1964[8] – tracing the transformation of Bartók's pantomimic dramaturgy into a symphonic dramaturgy. In the middle of the *allegretto* dance (starting at fig.27.8, where now one finds the six rustling, quavering bars of *tranquillo*, then *più tranquillo*) there once stood a substantial passage which played the role of a middle section. It contained various elements: a gestural and melodic material of a *molto espressivo* character; the music of the girl stroking the boy. It also reflected the mood of the *tranquillo* as it was carried by sequences to an extended culmination not far from the *a tempo* reprise of the $\frac{5}{4}$ dance (fig.28.3). The formal proportions of the new version are more satisfying than those of this first version. The main dance is given the structural weight compared with the middle section, as is appropriate in a symphonic composition. The 'intonation' of the youth's dance has also changed, as the most sensuous aspects of the harmony and melody, and the *espressivo* character, have all been removed. In this way the portrait of the youth has been rendered more unified: he is nothing more than a shy youth.

The shift from a dramaturgy of pantomime to a symphonic dramaturgy is demonstrated even more clearly by comparing the different versions of the ending. The first ending, from 1919, represents the typical dramaturgy of pantomime. Its character and function are described by the composer as a 'quasi recitative', that is, he relates its nature to vocal genres, and, specifically, to opera. It is, indeed, a dialogue, with the music faithfully depicting the words and gestures written into the score: 'The girl makes an abrupt gesture: I know what we have to do. Cut him down. — The tramps are startled. — The girl: Give me the mandarin. — The tramps retreat in horror. — The girl: Give him to me, give him to me, I want him. . . .' The commanding character of the girl's words is reflected by the *forte risoluto* tone of the music, whereas the instruction 'quasi recitativo' refers to manner of speech. The tramps' state of mind is mirrored by a *piano* dynamic, whereas their reactions (their shuddering, retreating in horror) are consistently reflected by the *tempo giusto* in contrast to the *rubato* of the recitatives. The musical material is gestural, almost illustrative in character. The figure of the girl is allied to whimsical, wilful, recurring leaps of a fourth (the tramps' command of the situation was apparent in this first version in a rising series of fourths before each of the three decoy dances), whereas the tramps are linked to a chromatically shivering chord. The music faithfully follows the direction of stage gestures: the girl's urging fourths and other passages point downwards; we can hear the footsteps of the tramps, then sense as they reach up towards the mandarin (soft, steeply rising staccato chords) and as the mandarin's body falls down (*accelerando*). The experience of the composer at his first creative encounter with the text and the scene shines through this first version of the score. The instructions vary almost from bar to bar, in keeping with the naturalistic dramaturgy of pantomime. This feature, which could be considered a residue of Bartók's own Romantic zeal and exaltation, recurs in the last eighteen bars of the first version of the ending. The text here is a close guide to the score: 'He falls to the ground, pale, his wounds begin to bleed. Agony – he dies.' The music reflects the slackening of the body, the gushing forth of blood, the spasms of the mandarin's limbs. Instructions which determine the character of expression also appear, rather as in pre-Romantic French opera or in Berg's post-Romantic Lyric Suite with its recollection of *Tristan.* (These instructions include *oscuro* written above a bass motif and *dolente* in relation to a motif on the cor anglais.) In the second version of the score, finished in 1924, Bartók sought to free himself from this pantomimic dramaturgy. He cut the entire thirty-eight-bar recitative which had begun the first version of the ending and removed eight of the eighteen bars of the pantomime scene at the end, which illustrate the bleeding, the mandarin's transfiguration and the preparation for this culmination. Along with these changes all instructions affecting the character of expression were removed. In 1931, when Bartók again turned to revise his concluding bars (from fig.111), he merged ideas from both earlier versions in his desire to raise this section to a symbolic, symphonic plane. Against the string and timpani rendition of the death agony's rhythm he has cor anglais, then bass clarinet, play in a descending pattern of fourths the three-note chromatic melody drawn from the 'desire' motif. The naturalistic rhythm of the 'body spasms' is ennobled by the melodic element, which raises it to the realm of love–death, whereas the sequence of fourths and the 'death' rhythm liberate the three-note motif from its original, concrete ('Come closer') meaning at fig.39.

A comparison of Bartók's revisions in preceding sections of the pantomime, likewise, illustrates his desire to distance himself from a pantomimic dramaturgy. Whereas in 1919 the apotheosis (fig.108) was a climax of the preceding action (in particular, the girl's dance, chase, and fulfilment passage), by 1924 it had been refashioned in a major way, and any reference to such action had been replaced by the transfiguration of two musical symbols, of desire and love. In 1931 Bartók again pondered the apotheoses presented in both earlier versions, and made further revisions, removing now every trace of the minor-third 'desire' motif and bringing back a recollection of the girl's dance of the first version, but now diluted and sublimated into something of a presentiment. This *sostenuto* passage, from fig.108, was also transformed, with the *fortissimo* brass fanfare now involving a stylization of the 'chase' motif. Vinton described this solution as 'more transcendental than physical'. We can interpret it as being the final goal of Bartók's dramaturgy, which developed from a concept of stage music based on pantomimic portrayal towards a symphonic treatment based on a symbolic approach.

Bartók's interpretation of the text and the basis of his musical dramaturgy can most easily be grasped through the relationships between certain melodies and motifs. Particularly striking is the way in which Bartók musically identifies the three apaches with the big city. They are its representatives when they seize their 'alien' victims, as can be seen in the use of the work's opening 'city noises' music in a *maestoso* setting at fig.78. The other decisive thematic relationship links elements of the apaches' music to the theme of the decoy dances, for the apaches are the ones who send the girl out on to the street. Later, however, the girl gradually breaks away from her own self as a street-walker and this thematic relationship is loosened. Dramatically and musically she moves closer to the mandarin. The symbolic interval of the mandarin, a descending glissando minor third, unfolds into an ascending minor-third string motif – the two forms are best seen in the voice parts and viola, respectively, from fig.101. This later motivic form is closely related to the girl's character theme, which originates in her dance before the mandarin. They have in common a sad, yearning chromaticism, similar gestures, and paired ascending–descending motions.

Although still operating within the confines of tonal music, by consistently applying the principle of equal usage of all twelve notes and fully exploiting the entire sound spectrum Bartók came closest in this piece to pre-dodecaphonic atonality. In places, the cumulation of the parts adds up to ten or even twelve-note dissonances; subject and accompaniment complement each other in terms of allocation of the twelve available notes; the process of gradual integration of the entire sound material within a formal unit serves as a means of achieving climaxes. Fourth-chords and fourth-based melodies are also signs of that incipient atonality (for instance, at the first culmination of the chase, fig.69, and after the first attempt at murder, fig.81). In an essay which appeared in the April 1920 issue of the Berlin journal *Melos* Bartók discussed this early stage of atonality in detail:

> Previously, fourth chords at the most were fashioned, and those, too, in a certain permissible combination only; nowadays one may even sound all the twelve tones simultaneously in the most varied combinations. We have at our disposal a previously undreamed of wealth of transitory nuances, from the peculiar blankness of a triad such as this [Ex. 1A], or the sonorous daintiness of this chord [Ex. 1B], to the shrill forcefulness of a chord like this [Ex. 1C]. The close position of three or more adjacent tones has the effect of a 'stylized' noise sounding more or less resonant according to pitch position. The slightly narrower position used in lower registers, as in this example [Ex. 1D] is near in sound to a noise-like effect; transposed higher by two octaves, its character alters and becomes more ethereal – its effect approaches that of our second example, above.[9]

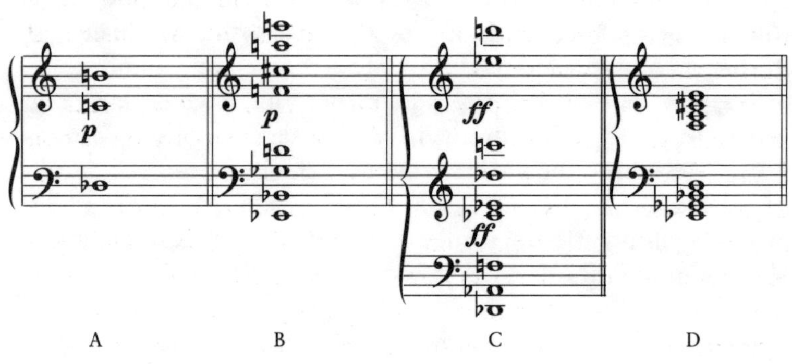

EX. 1

If this fullest possible exploitation of the twelve-note sound spectrum, based on the principle of equality and complementarity, bears witness to a conscious constructional idea, then that idea would be one of selecting atonal harmonies for their particular sonorous qualities. For Bartók the various cited chords evoke moods and expressions with a definite aesthetic value ('blankness', 'daintiness', '"stylized" noise'). The sound of his chord A (in Ex. 1) is highly characteristic of *The Miraculous Mandarin*. Naturally, the major seventh can be broken down into a perfect plus an augmented fourth, and can also be inverted to become a minor second (or ninth). Bartók created a great many, highly diverse examples of such a sonority. The various pedals incorporating tritones in the three decoy scenes and ostinato patterns, such as found in the introduction, also work towards atonality. Nevertheless, in most scenes Bartók provides points of reference, thereby keeping his music within the confines of tonality (in the broadest sense of the term). To create this sense of tonality he uses such techniques as long-term pedal points (the G♯ E♭ A chord which underpins the chase, from figs 61.6 to 69, or the C♭ foundation of the murder scene, from figs 78.3 to 81), reiteration of a note or interval, which assumes the function of a tonal centre or pitch axis within a closed scene (the interval of a perfect fifth which initiates each of the decoy dances; the D axis note at the introduction to the chase), recurrence of certain motifs at absolute pitch (as with the A♭–F + A–C♯–D complex which appears at the mandarin's entry (fig.36), and subsequently in the second half of the chase and during the mandarin's agony).

Tonality cannot be precisely identified in every instance, however. Often a transposition is involved, with a repetition being related to a new axis or centre, so creating a new plane of tonal activity. Examples are found in the migration in the chase of the C-axis note, from an original A, which denotes a new tonal plane and at the same time a formal terrace, and, in the boy's dance, beginning at fig.26.4, where his tonally ambiguous theme is subjected to transposition and then an inversion, indicating a reprise.

The melodic style of the pantomime is characterized by three particular features. Firstly, there are Bartók's model-like themes, which involve series of identical intervals often allied with symmetrical pitch constructions. Ex. 2a shows the alternation of perfect fifth and minor second intervals – expressed here in semitones – which forms the basis of the theme in the decoy dances; Ex. 2b shows the movement of minor and augmented-

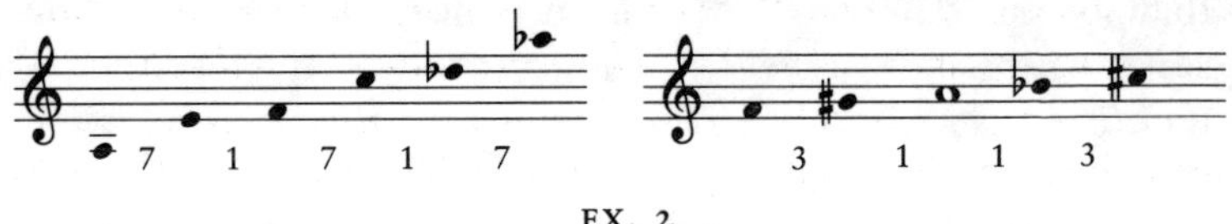

EX. 2

seconds around the pitch centre of A at fig.62, near the start of the chase. The second feature is his expression of 'mistuned' pentatony, linked especially to the figure of the mandarin. Ex. 3, the music accompanying the approach of the mandarin, at fig.34, illustrates this characteristic, with its upper, pentatonic line and 'shadow' a diminished fifth below; the lower lines deform the pentatonic theme, but maintain their own diminished fifth relationship.

EX. 3

Last is his idiosyncratic play with gestures, particularly those representing sighs or shouts.

The minor third has a special function in *The Miraculous Mandarin*. Because of the central role of the 'desire' motif this interval is the *differentia specifica* in the work's score. As Kodály pointed out in 1955, the interval of a third occurs repeatedly in Bartók's music, in both major and minor forms and in both directions.[10] Kodály cited examples from the second movement of the Second String Quartet, various sections of the Dance Suite and the finale of the Second Piano Concerto. We could also add that the glissando character of the minor third (or augmented second), so characteristic of *The Miraculous Mandarin*, is not unique by any means, being found also in the Dance Suite (involving trombones), and in the Third String Quartet, where it is so very striking and can be regarded – as Kodály stated – as a personal stylistic trait.

The music of *The Miraculous Mandarin* is particularly rich rhythmically. In this effervescent, rhythmic–metric atmosphere of the work the 'rigidly' recurring patterns possess a distinctive weight. Examples are the opening $\frac{6}{8}$ rhythm, representing the metropolis and the tramps, and the forceful binary pulsation of the 'chase' theme, which bores itself forward like a bayonet. Apart from the first appearance of the mandarin, perhaps the most highly-charged scene in the work occurs when the suspended mandarin wriggles while the accompanying wordless chorus repeats the 'desire' motif of minor thirds in the background (fig.101, Ex. 4).

EX. 4

At the time this effect was highly unusual, although Bartók had already experimented with it in *Duke Bluebeard's Castle*. He had probably encountered similar effects in the music of some of his contemporaries, such as Delius.

In the stylistic environment of *The Miraculous Mandarin*, Bartók's art of orchestration was fundamentally renewed. As has already been pointed out, the orchestral sound represents the work's last stylistic layer, dating from 1924. Indeed, such a texture would have been unthinkable without the lessons Bartók learnt from orchestrating the Dance Suite in 1923. The orchestral colours and characters are entrusted with organic, dramatic functions. The excitement inherent in the plot requires a sound which lacks definite outlines and seeks to envelop thematic materials in a 'haze'. It is this goal that explains the numerous glissandos, the frequent use of mutes, the pseudo-arpeggios covering the full range of the piano and the celesta, and the sombre, subdued pedal-point colourings. The orchestration also plays an important role in the articulation of form, as seen in the unified clarinet timbre in the three decoy dances and the cymbal clashes which mark the murder attempts. Even more importantly, every character of the drama, every emotion and every action is tied to a specific timbre. It is impossible to forget the *col legno* patter of the feet of the approaching 'old rake' (fig.16), the following cello-viola gestures of his courtship, and the cor anglais timbre of his dance, or the bassoon timbre, accompanied by the harp, at the beginning of the boy's dance (from fig.26). The build-up of excitement in the course of the three decoy dances is also the result of the orchestration. In the first, starting at fig.13, the accompaniment to the A-clarinet melody consists of tremolo and pedal effects on bass clarinet and cello; in the second dance, from fig.22, flute, horn and timpani join the sustained texture supporting the B♭-clarinet melody; the third dance, from fig.30.7, is characterized by an accompanimental texture of string harmonics, *sul ponticello* colours and many piano and harp glissandos, which supports the B♭-clarinet and later the howling E♭-clarinet line. Every detail serves the authenticity of the portrayal. At the mandarin's approach (fig.34) the trombone-tuba theme is surrounded by sonorities which prepare for this extraordinary event: gigantic glissandos on the first violins, timpani tremolos, short flourishes on the piccolo. So, too, when the girl finally starts to dance before the mandarin, the entry of the celesta creates a magical effect (fig.42.9). Similarly characteristic is the cello subject of the mandarin's suffering, which is offset against the brass colour of the murder subject (from fig.78.3). The mandarin's resurrection after the first 'murder' (from fig.84) provides perhaps the richest variety of effects in the service of a highly charged, agitated, almost haunted atmosphere on the stage: quarter-tone slides on the cello and violin; a *sul ponticello* passage on strings; the flourishing motifs on piano and celesta spread over a very wide range; veiled, *sordino* sonorities; hissing (tremolo, glissando), cracking (pizzicato) and other specific timbres on the strings. In total, these techniques complement each other to produce a frightening effect. The second 'murder' is of a similar power and includes graphic illustration of the stabbing through the play with instrumental colours: the *col legno* cymbal effect (fig.91) in association with the overtone glissando on trombone, harmonics on double bass and rough piano chords. After the third 'murder' (fig.97), Bartók arranged for the lowest cello string to be tuned down by a semitone and instructed players of the timpani, piano and trombone to glissando upwards and downwards.

Bartók himself thought very highly of *The Miraculous Mandarin*, writing in 1927: 'in my view this is the best work I have so far written for orchestra'.[11] In many ways it develops practices already established in his earlier works of the 1910s. The chase scene resembles a heightened *Allegro barbaro*, while the clarinet timbre in the decoy dances has its precedent in the princess's ballerina dance in *The Wooden Prince* and the clumsy music of the 'old rake' in that of the wooden puppet. So, too, the painful, glissando minor-third motif of the Mandarin recalls the moment of supreme loneliness felt by the princess when she found she could not pass through the forest. Between 1919 and 1924, while working on this work, Bartók was experiencing a great sense of loneliness. He felt quite isolated in his efforts to warn society of the evils he could see. By setting the 'elemental life force' in opposition to 'degraded emotion', he cried 'No!' to the world of evil, and to the immorality of the dehumanized apaches. And as an example to those who had confidence and hope, he presented the figure of the mandarin who, like Bartók himself, is a constant reminder of courage in opposition, determination in thought and feeling – the very triumph of man.

NOTES

1 *ZT*.vii, p. 113.
2 *BBcl*, p. 242.
3 Facsimile edition, ed. László Somfai, Budapest (Editio Musica), 1987, 15^{r}–24^{v}.
4 The concert version of the pantomime, first published in February 1927, is not affected in this regard as it ends with the chase, that is, in the middle section of the stage version.
5 Unpublished letter, Bartók to Universal Edition, 3 March 1925 (NYBA).
6 Unpublished letter, Bartók to Universal Edition, 22 June 1925 (NYBA).
7 See further comparison between *The Wooden Prince* and *The Miraculous Mandarin* in the final pages of my chapter 'Ballet: *The Wooden Prince*' in this *Companion*.
8 'The Case of *The Miraculous Mandarin*', *Musical Quarterly*, vol.50 (1964), pp. 1–17.
9 'The Problem of the New Music', *BBE*, pp. 456–7.
10 'Szentirmaytól Bartókig', in Zoltán Kodály, *Visszatekintés*, ed. Ferenc Bónis, vol.2, Budapest (Zeneműkiadó), 1982, p. 464.
11 Unpublished letter, Bartók to Universal Edition, 3 February 1927 (NYBA).

VOCAL MUSIC

27

Works for Solo Voice with Piano

VERA LAMPERT

It was for a very short period of time that the mature Bartók felt compelled to choose the most intimate of musical genres, the song, as the vehicle of his thoughts. The ten songs of his two song cycles, Op.15 and Op.16, were written between February and August 1916. Yet, another group of about one and a half dozen songs, which feature in the catalogues of Bartók's works, dates from his youth. Three Songs (1898) and Love Songs (1900) are skilful imitations of German *Lied*, mainly in Schumann's style. Bartók even re-used the texts of two popular Schumann songs, 'Im wunderschönen Monat Mai' and 'Du meine Liebe, du mein Herz', a clear indication of the models for these works. Four Songs (1902) and *Evening* (1903) attempt to give a Hungarian flavour to the genre. A further cycle, *To the Little 'Tót'* (1905), was written for and dedicated to Bartók's newborn nephew. Of these early compositions only the Four Songs (1902) appeared in print during Bartók's lifetime.[1]

Writers about Bartók have suggested that the relatively small number of original songs has a very practical explanation: the difficulties of providing appropriate translations and the rare performing opportunities. The publishing history of the Five 'Ady' Songs Op.16 certainly supports this hypothesis. A further reason for the lack of original songs may have been Bartók's basic predisposition towards instrumental music.

Although Bartók wrote few songs to poetic texts, he did arrange many folksongs for voice and piano. About eighty individual songs are involved, most of them being published shortly after their completion in one of four large sets: Hungarian Folksongs (1906), Eight Hungarian Folksongs (1907–17),

Village Scenes (1924) and Twenty Hungarian Folksongs (1929). Spanning more than twenty years, these four collections reveal how the genre of folksong arrangement evolved from the simplest chordal accompaniments to the highly original and musically complex late settings, which eventually assumed the role of the 'original' song in Bartók's output and are the worthy counterparts of his greatest instrumental compositions.

In the first part of this chapter we shall follow the path of his development through a chronological survey of these four sets of folksong arrangements. Reference will also be made to other partly unpublished or unfinished folksong arrangements. Although the Four Songs (1902) belong to the group of original songs they will be treated here as an introduction to the folksong arrangements since they were an inevitable step towards the discovery of folk music. The two song cycles of 1916 will be discussed separately at the end of the chapter.

Four Songs (1902)

The Four Songs, written to texts by Lajos Pósa, have a special place in Bartók's output for solo voice and piano. Written during Bartók's last year as a student at the Budapest Academy of Music, the set is one of his first experiments in creating a Hungarian national art music. That year coincided with the peak of the nationalist political movement in Hungary. Nationalist politicians were fighting for greater Hungarian independence within the Habsburg dualist monarchy, and in 1903 sparked a parliamentary crisis over the issue of language of command in the common army. Bartók followed the news closely and responded with youthful enthusiasm. He wanted to show his involvement in every way: he wore Hungarian dress and grew intolerant of the use of German within his own family. He also decided to write Hungarian music. His new compositions, in particular the symphonic poem *Kossuth* (1903), attempted to combine the musical vocabulary of Richard Strauss with elements of Hungarian national style.

Models for a Hungarian musical idiom were not plentiful. Liszt's Hungarian Rhapsodies were popular, and Bartók had a faint childhood memory of what he thought to be Hungarian folksongs: the popular art songs of the last years of the nineteenth century. These songs show some of the characteristics of genuine folksong. They have simple four-line structures in which the content of the first line usually returns; they had absorbed some of the rhythmic and cadential elements of the earlier Hungarian instrumental music, the *verbunkos*. Melodically, however, they stand closer to Western music than to genuine Hungarian folk music through the rooting of their harmonic progressions in the major–minor system. Through the frequent and prominent use of certain chords, especially the diminished seventh, they display an affected, mawkish sentimentalism.

Lajos Pósa's texts are typical representatives of simple, folk-like poetry and are of scant artistic merit. Bartók arranged the four texts in two slow–fast pairs, a characteristic structure of *verbunkos* music and also of Liszt's rhapsodies. The texts of the slow movements deal with sorrow: the first song, 'Autumn breeze', is the complaint of an abandoned lover; the third, 'There is no greater sorrow', laments the death of the lover. Love is the subject of the fast songs, 'They are accusing me' and 'Alas, alas', but in a joyful, teasing tone. Each poem has only one four-line strophe. In each of them the first line returns, resulting in the *A A B A* structure of the first two songs and *A A B C* structure of the remaining two. In conformity with the performing customs of popular art song, the second half of each text is repeated in Bartók's setting.

The microstructure of these settings reveals many elements of the popular art-song model: the downward chromatic steps in the cadences, the diminished sevenths, the augmented seconds, the dotted rhythms and the peculiar rhythmic closing figures of the popular fast Hungarian dance, the *csárdás*, which are found even when they do not fit in with the metre of the verse.[2] Yet, on the whole, these are rather attractive compositions within their own terms, and the third song, especially, proves much more than a mere imitation of the Hungarian popular song. The piano's bare fifths frame the melody, which effects bold modulations and implies unconventional harmonies.

The Four Songs were one of Bartók's very first compositions to appear in print, in 1904. A little later, probably in 1905, he made a piano transcription of the first song, which had contained the pianistically most demanding accompaniment.[3]

Hungarian Folksongs (1906)

Two years after completing the Four Songs, towards the end of 1904, Bartók had worked out new plans: 'to collect the finest Hungarian folksongs and to raise them, adding the best possible piano accompaniments, to the level of art song. The purpose of this would be to let foreign countries know Hungarian music.'[4] At that time, however, he did not distinguish between popular art music and genuine folksong: in the same letter as he revealed these new plans he asked his sister to help him out with the text and melody of some fragments, all of them from popular art songs.

This new idea of searching for more songs was triggered by an encounter earlier in 1904 at Gerlicepuszta in northern Hungary. There he had taken down from a Transylvanian servant girl certain songs which were completely unknown to him and totally different from anything he had previously heard. He made an arrangement of one of the songs, 'The red apple has fallen in the mud' ('Piros alma leesett a sárba') – his very first folksong arrangement – and had it published as 'Székely folksong' in the issue of *Magyar lant* of 15 February 1905. About the same time he arranged four popular art songs for voice and piano. These, however, remained unpublished.[5] Bartók put them aside and instead of working on new arrangements sought out ways of finding more 'unknown' Hungarian melodies.

During the spring of 1905 Bartók met Zoltán Kodály, who, besides his studies in composition, was preparing a doctoral dissertation at the university on the strophic structure of Hungarian folksong. His first publication, revealing the results of his earliest folksong collecting trips, appeared during 1905 in the Hungarian journal *Ethnographia*. He called Bartók's attention to existing publications and collections, in particular Béla Vikár's phonograph recordings, then a novelty in the field of ethnography. Bartók applied for a grant to undertake a trip to collect folksongs in Transylvania, and although he postponed this until two years later, he did make some transcriptions during a stay in the country in June 1905, and started his first organized folksong collecting trips using the phonograph during the summer of 1906. He visited villages in the central Hungarian counties of Tolna, Pest, Csongrád and Békés, where he already had connections through relatives or friends.

Bartók and Kodály decided to join forces, and in March 1906 wrote an 'Appeal to the Hungarian public'.[6] They called attention to the hidden treasures of Hungarian folk music, and the urgent need for folk-music collecting in Hungary. As a final goal they anticipated 'a complete collection of folksongs gathered with scholarly exactitude', which would take 'five to ten years to compile'. They turned to the Hungarian public for support of this ambitious plan. As an initial step they offered twenty folksongs,

> partly from the phonograph collection of B. Vikár (in the Hungarian National Museum) and partly choice pieces from our own collection, unknown to the general public so far ... So as to be able to count on the widest possible circle of those interested, simple and very easy piano accompaniments were written to the songs in a way that the tunes were also included in the accompaniment.

This volume of twenty Hungarian folksongs appeared in December 1906, at Bartók's and Kodály's expense. Their expectations were not fulfilled: we know from the postscript to the second edition that it took thirty-two years to sell the 1500 copies. Consequently, all plans to continue the series were abandoned, although Bartók was ready with another set of ten songs as early as December 1906. Except for four of the songs, which were published in *Der junge Bartók* of 1963, these still remain only in manuscript form.

For the first, published set, Bartók chose only one song from Vikár's recorded collection. The rest of the selection reflected the material which he had encountered on his first folksong collecting trips. According to Bartók's later classification of Hungarian folk music there are only two 'old'-style melodies: the first song, 'I left my fair homeland' ('Elindultam szép hazámból'), and the third 'László Fehér stole a horse' ('Fehér László lovat lopott'). The 'mixed' style is represented by one melody, the seventh, 'From the withered branch no rose blooms' ('Száraz ágtól messze virít a rózsa'). Later findings proved that the fifth song of the first edition, 'The street is on fire' ('Ucca, ucca, ég az ucca'), was a popular art song by Elemér Szentirmai. Seven melodies belong to the 'new' style. But even the 'new' songs display traits which differ from Western major–minor tonality. There are several traces of the archaic pentatonic scale (lacking any half steps) as well as Dorian, Mixolydian and Aeolian melodies. Yet the harmonizations mostly follow traditional paths, especially in the fast songs. The harmonizations in the slow songs show more affinity to the peculiar features of the melodies, although they are extremely reserved. Twenty-five years later Bartók thought that they showed an 'unbelievable technical awkwardness', which he explained as being the result of the novelty and difficulty of the task. Although he made only minor alterations in the second printing of the series in 1938, such as adding some original grace notes to the melodies, changing time signatures and replacing a few harmonies, he had substantially reworked the accompaniments in 1928 when recording five of the songs (nos 1, 2, 4, 8, 9) with Vilma Medgyaszay.[7]

Eight Hungarian Folksongs (1907–17)

If the folksong arrangements of 1906 mostly represented the newer kind of Hungarian folk music, in the following cycle, Eight Hungarian Folksongs, the oldest examples predominated. Ever since he had met the Székely servant girl in 1904 Bartók had wanted to go to Transylvania. His historic folksong collecting trip to the Csík district took place during the summer of 1907, with sensational results. He came back with a great number of pentatonic melodies, which immediately made clear the fundamental importance of this previously unnoticed scale.

Beyond its ethnographic significance, the discovery of this layer of folksong had a decisive impact on the development of Bartók's compositional style. Summarizing this influence in an essay of 1928, he wrote:

> in the music of Eastern Europe . . . most of the old modes, such as: Dorian, Phrygian, Mixolydian, Aeolian etc., are robustly alive. Furthermore, we find tonal modes oriental in their colouring (owing to augmented second) and – last but not least – a kind of pentatonic mode. In the majority of these tonal modes the fifth degree in general does not play that dominant part [role] which we can observe in the case of the fifth degree of the major and minor scale. This circumstance has exerted an important influence on our harmonic processes – that reciprocity of effect between tonic and dominant so familiar to us in older art music must here give up much of its sovereignty. In these pentatonic scales the third, fifth and seventh are of equal rank and importance; . . . the modal diminished seventh takes on the character of a consonant interval . . . A visible sign of the consonant character of the seventh is the condition that the regular resolution of the seventh (one degree downward to the sixth degree) does not occur, in reality cannot occur, because the sixth degree is missing . . . When the consonant form of the seventh was established, the ice was broken: from that moment the seventh could be applied as a consonance even without a necessarily logical preparation.[8]

Upon returning from his Transylvanian folksong collecting trip Bartók immediately set several of the most exciting ancient pentatonic melodies. These arrangements show his fascination with the pentatonic scale – a visible, humorous sign of this fascination is a huge handwritten staff representation of the pentatonic notes, written across the back of the first page of his sketch of the work – and the new compositional possibilities it offered. In his detailed analysis of the chord progressions of these songs Elliott Antokoletz demonstrated how in each of them the starting point of the arrangement is the pentatonic core, or the minor-seventh chord derived from it, and how Bartók introduced new notes as the arrangement unfolds, creating different modal segments not necessarily implied by the original tune and sometimes even in direct contrast with it.[9] Two bold solutions well illustrate this point: Ex. 1, from the third song, shows how the pentatonic pattern F♯ C♯ D♯ is contrasted with an E minor triad; Ex. 2, from the fifth song, presents an E Aeolian melody accompanied by five consecutive second-inversion minor triads, descending by whole steps from E, and eventually arriving at F♯ major.

III, 15 (voice, piano)

EX. 1

V, 13-15 (piano)

EX. 2

In addition to the more mature harmonic language, the Eight Hungarian Folksongs manifest the growing importance and independence of the piano in Bartók's technique of folksong arrangement. The accompaniment is still mostly chordal but the texture is richer and more sonorous, or, on the contrary, assumes a transparency, where needed, by contrasting long-held notes with stepwise moving parts or by unfolding chordal progressions through the part-writing. There is usually a short introduction featuring the minor-seventh chord or the pentatonic scale, which sets the mood of the particular song. In the fifth piece, the solo piano interlude and postlude use an instrumental variant of the song, which Bartók had also collected from a peasant flute player (and transcribed for piano as the third piece of the Three Hungarian Folksongs from the Csík District).

The first five of these Eight Hungarian Folksongs, at least, represent the immediate creative reaction to the discovery of the ancient pentatonic melodies. As Bartók later indicated, work on the arrangements was started in 1907 and the first five songs were presented to the Budapest public on 11 November 1911 as Five Old Hungarian Folksongs from the Csík District. Dezső Róna was the singer, with Bartók at the piano. At this early stage they were grouped differently: three slow songs were followed by two fast ones (in order, 1, 4, 2, 3, 5 of the published score). In the slow songs the tempo is 'parlando rubato', the typical style of performance of the 'old' type of folk melodies. Hence, the frequent changes of metre in these songs, which aim to recapture the free, recitative-like character of the original folk performance. In contrast with these, the fast songs have a strict dance-like rhythm (*tempo giusto*). In the texts of the slow songs the main themes are of sadness: the complaint of the betrayed lover (no.1), the lament of the woman forced into an unwanted marriage (no.2), farewell (no.4). The fast songs have humorous overtones. No.3, for instance, is a song which teases spinsters who long to be married, but in vain.

The last three songs of the cycle were written in 1917 for a military concert, which was held in Vienna on 12 January 1918. It is interesting that although Bartók collected folksongs among soldiers in 1916–17, with the permission of the War Ministry, these arrangements use songs collected earlier (in 1907 and 1914). They were also performed in Budapest a few weeks later, at a benefit concert for soldiers. They were then entitled Székely Soldiers' Songs, and each had a distinctive title: 'Recruiting song' (no.6), 'Soldier's farewell' (no.7) and 'Soldier's spring song' (no.8). Ferenc Székelyhidy sang to Bartók's piano accompaniment on both occasions. In 1928 they recorded these three songs; Mária Basilides and Bartók also recorded songs nos 1–3 and 5 of the cycle at this time.[10]

Bartók brought together the two groups of songs in 1918, when he signed an agreement with Universal Edition for publishing his works. It was then that he established the present order of movements: slow–slow–fast; slow–fast; slow–slow–fast. The Eight Hungarian Folksongs were among the first compositions he sent to the publisher, although the score only appeared in 1922 because of difficulties with the translation of the texts. Anticipation of similar difficulties might have prevented Bartók from finishing and publishing two other groups of folksong arrangements for voice and piano. He arranged four Slovak folksongs in 1907 (the second of these is now lost), and another in 1916, all of which were only published posthumously in the volume *Der junge Bartók*. Another set consists of arrangements of nine Romanian folksongs. Composed in 1915, the year of Bartók's three Romanian folksong arrangements for piano – Sonatina, Romanian Folk Dances and Romanian Christmas Carols – they are still in manuscript today. Stylistically both sets are akin to the Eight Hungarian Folksongs. Some of the ideas presented in the Slovak arrangements are particularly resourceful.

Village Scenes (1924)

The *Village Scenes*, finished in December 1924, about halfway between the Dance Suite (1923) and Piano Sonata (1926), can be regarded as an occasional composition, in at least two ways. Between 1922 and 1928 Bartók prepared for publication his Slovak collection of about 2500 melodies. It was only natural that this intensive work quickened his creative imagination and prompted him to share some of his favourite melodies through the artistic medium of arrangement. He especially treasured the ceremonial songs – lullabies, haymaking and wedding songs – which, along with the shepherds' songs, he considered to be the oldest and most original representatives of Slovak folk music.

The year, 1924, may also have been especially appropriate for him to group a few wedding songs and lullabies. In 1923 he had divorced his first wife and remarried. His second son was born in June 1924. He must have had Ditta Pásztory, his new, young wife, in mind when he assembled these songs for the new cycle, for it was dedicated to her.

Of the seven songs, five that feature in the three central movements of the work – 'At the bride's' (no.2), 'Wedding' (no.3) and 'Lullaby' (no.4) – relate to the most important village customs and, at the same time, express the most profound personal experiences in the lives of women: marriage and motherhood. These are framed by two songs which relate to the wider community and symbolize work and entertainment: haymaking (one of the main tasks for village folk keeping animals) in the first song, and 'Lad's dance' (no.5). All the songs were collected by Bartók in the Zólyom county of Old Hungary in 1915–16. Structurally, these Slovak melodies resemble their Hungarian counterparts, with one important exception: the modes used are almost exclusively Mixolydian and Lydian, featuring the interval of the augmented fourth. Bartók attributed great importance to that element of Slovak folk music which encouraged the free use of the augmented fourth, and also to the combination of different fourths more generally in his music. In the piano introduction of the third movement of *Village Scenes* we catch Bartók in the act of extracting the prominent notes from the melody (Ex. 3a) to form a genuine Bartókian harmony (Ex. 3b).

EX. 3

The *Village Scenes* bring several innovations to the genre of vocal folksong arrangement, compared with the earlier Eight Hungarian Folksongs. These innovations, already introduced in

1920 in Bartók's important arrangements for piano, Improvisations Op.20, elucidate the changed role of the original melody in the arrangement. In 1931, in one of his lectures about 'The Influence of Peasant Music on Modern Music', Bartók distinguished two main types of folksong arrangement:

> In one case accompaniment, introductory and concluding phrases are of secondary importance, and they only serve as an ornamental setting for the precious stone: the peasant melody. It is the other way round in the second case: the melody serves as a 'motto' while that which is built round it is of real importance.[11]

Although he goes on to admit that 'all shades of transition are possible between these two extremes and sometimes it is not even possible to decide which of the elements is predominant in any given case', *Village Scenes* clearly represent the second type. Here the original melodies submit themselves to the logic of the composition. They can be transposed (in nos 1, 3, 5), broken up by lines (in the closing sections of nos 1, 4, 5), divided between the piano and voice part (in no.5), and even complemented by original melodic fragments of the composer's invention (at the end of no.2 and within nos 3 and 5).

All the freedom in the treatment of the melody aims at reaching a balance between voice and piano, and at creating an indissoluble unity within the movement. Unity can be established in different ways. In the first two movements the piano has a homogeneous texture with some sort of connection with the melody. The first note of the first song is taken as a pedal point and coupled with other, logically introduced notes found in the song. The stubborn arpeggios seem to evoke the monotony of haymaking: mowing and raking. Thirds and fifths, both deducible from the contour of the melody, alternate in the second song. In the finale the piano's substantial virtuoso introduction alternates with the melody, but during the vocal part's second stanza they take on each other's role: the piano plays the original melody and the voice accompanies it with rhythmic shouting, exactly as happens at the climax of folk-dance gatherings.

In the third and fourth movements Bartók experimented with expanding the formal possibilities in the folksong arrangement, taking two folk melodies as the basis of a single movement and organizing them into simple Classical forms. This practice was introduced in his folksong arrangements for piano from 1915, the most prominent examples being the Sonatina and Three Rondos. In the third movement of *Village Scenes* two contrasting melodies were chosen: a solemn processional melody and a cheerful one. Their alternations result in a kind of rondo form, which is further enlarged by the piano's striking interludes (*x A x B x A x B A B x*), recalling the ostinatos and frequently changing metres of Stravinsky's style of the 1910s. The fourth movement has a ternary form (*A A B B B A*), but here, because the two melodies are very close in character, it is the piano's commentary material which reinforces the three-part form: the first melody is set above long, sustained fifth-chords and rocking chord pairs, while the second melody is embedded in a gently humming background of triplets. Capturing the magical moment at the threshold of sleep, this arresting part of the score is one of the most beautiful representatives of Bartók's 'night music' type of slow movement.

In addition to the effort of creating closed forms *within* movements, a strong connection *between* movements is established through the interrelationship of tempo and mood. This is a real cycle in the Classical sense of the word, and it is to be performed as a whole. The first performance of *Village Scenes* was given by Mária Basilides and Bartók on 8 December 1926. In that same year Bartók transcribed the last three movements for chamber chorus and orchestra. The scores of both versions were published by Universal Edition in 1927.

Twenty Hungarian Folksongs (1929)

It is only a conjecture that the impetus to write this last group of folksong arrangements for voice and piano came from Kodály's *Hungarian Folk Music* (*Magyar népzene*), a large set of fifty-seven ballads and folksongs published in ten volumes between 1924 and 1932. When, in December 1928, His Master's Voice made recordings of Hungarian folksong arrangements for voice and piano, with Bartók's participation, some seven volumes (in total, forty-two folksongs) of Kodály's series were already available. His Master's Voice recorded a selection of twenty. Bartók could participate with only two groups of songs: the ten Hungarian Folksongs from 1906, from which he recorded five (in a newly prepared arrangement, as mentioned above), and the Eight Hungarian Folksongs which, compared with his later folksong arrangements – Improvisations, *Village Scenes* and the violin rhapsodies – did not well represent his new technical conception of folksong arrangement.

During the following year, 1929, Bartók wrote his Twenty Hungarian Folksongs. He chose the melodies from the collection of examples in his book *The Hungarian Folksong* (originally appearing in English as *Hungarian Folk Music*), which had first been published in 1924. Twelve of these songs had been collected by Bartók himself, with the remainder by others. The twenty songs appeared in four books. Except for the fourth, these books were not conceived as inseparable entities but rather as representatives of certain groups of songs displaying common traits. (In fact, Bartók himself generally only played selections from them.)

In the first book, 'Sad songs', four laments are grouped together: the lament of the outlaw (no.1), of the orphan (no.2), the fugitive (no.3) and the shepherd who has lost his sheep (no.4). These songs all belong to the oldest layer of Hungarian folk music, and their performance is 'parlando rubato'. In contrast to this opening selection, the songs of the second book, 'Dancing songs', although still belonging to the old stylistic layer, have a strongly rhythmic character. They most probably originated in instrumental music. 'Slow dance' (no.5) displays the characteristic bagpipe rhythm, with each of its lines consisting of eight accentuated syllables of equal length. The 'Swineherd's dance' (no.7) is representative of a group of Hungarian folk melodies in which Bartók discovered the influence of the Ukrainian *kolomyjka* dance. The 'Six-florin dance' (no.8) has instrumental variants: Bartók collected a version for bagpipe in 1910.

Seven songs are grouped in the third book under the title 'Diverse songs'. 'Diverse' has a double meaning here: firstly, referring to songs dissimilar in subject and character, but also referring to the ethnomusicological term used by Bartók in describing the third stylistic layer of Hungarian folk music. These 'diverse' songs, neither of 'old' or 'new' style, had come into being under foreign influence. Some of them are teasing songs, such as 'The shepherd' (no.9), which is a dialogue with a shepherd whose flock has been attacked by a wolf. In nos 11 and 12, the names are disclosed of a young couple, who are dating. No.15 is a drinking song.

The five melodies of the fourth book, 'New style songs', are grouped somewhat differently from in the earlier volumes. They have no separate titles but are numbered I–V under no.16. Their arrangement is more economical, with each song having only one stanza, except for the last, which has two. They follow each other *attacca*.

With the Twenty Hungarian Folksongs of 1929 the emancipation of the folksong arrangement within the realm of original composition had reached a new stage. The most conspicuous evidence for the new status of these compositions is the extended form – some of the fast songs have four, five or even six stanzas – and the virtuosic texture of the piano part. These songs, as well as the three last movements of *Village Scenes* (1924), transcend the dilettante sphere of music-making and definitively take their place on the concert platform. A closer examination reveals the same stylistic features in the Twenty Hungarian Folksongs as in Bartók piano works of this period: the Sonata, *Out of Doors*, Nine Little Pieces and the First Piano Concerto. To single out the most significant innovations introduced by these compositions for piano one has to refer to the increased role of horizontal elements and percussion-like effects. As John S. Weissmann has pointed out, 'it is counterpoint . . . which is the life-blood of Twenty Hungarian Folksongs: . . . the invigorating dynamism of the music depends a great deal on the impulse behind the horizontal lines.'[12]

Bartók's imagination seems to have been inexhaustible in creating the most varied manifestations of polyphonic organization. The most elemental and most frequent solution is the stepwise melodic or chordal progression, coupled with a pedal point and part-writing in contrary motion. Polyphonic texture is created by entrusting the piano with independent and contrasting material. Many times the motifs receiving polyphonic treatment derive from the folk melody and unfold either between voice and piano (in a canon-like fashion, as in no.6, or with the piano confronting the voice with the inverted melodic progression of the same motif, as in no.16/II), or within the piano part, as in the interlude of no.8.

The polyphony, with its many dissonances created by this 'horizontal logic', is partly responsible for the rich, highly original harmonic language of the Twenty Hungarian Folksongs. Fascinating, bold sonorities are produced by another characteristic feature of Bartók's piano style from 1926: the percussive cluster chord. Presented almost always in the context of an ostinato interspersed with sharp off-beat accents, these chords appear in some of the fast movements, especially in the dance songs (nos 6 and 8). There they impart a tremendous driving force, making these movements some of the most captivating of the series (see Ex. 4).

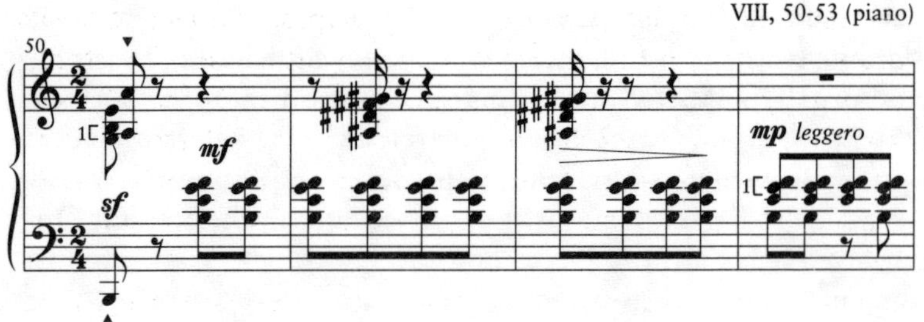

EX. 4

In the Twenty Hungarian Folksongs Bartók did not repeat the solution of *Village Scenes*, of creating more complex formal designs by unifying two melodies within one movement. Here each melody is a self-contained entity, and in making the arrangements Bartók focused on the enhancement of the musical and textual content of the individual melodies. To grasp the essence of the folksong Bartók did not shrink from applying time-honoured 'tonal' effects: tear drops in no.1, the crack of a whip and the ringing of a bell in no.11, laughter in no.12, sighing in no.13. These word paintings are not isolated effects, however; they become an integral part of the movement and serve as unifying elements in the form.

Although the multi-strophic structure of the folksong would suggest a strophic setting, Bartók opted for the method of through composition. This allowed him to follow the text closely, and either to intensify the mood or – as in some of the teasing songs – to illustrate the unexpected turns of the humorous narrative. Two main types can be distinguished among songs displaying an infinitely great variety of designs. The first is a sort of variation in which each stanza of text has its own pattern in the piano (nos 1, 7, 9, 10). The other type is rather monothematic, with only minor alterations, transpositions or enrichments of the texture during successive stanzas (nos 6, 8). Instrumental interludes or framing motifs are almost always present, and contribute significantly to the establishment of the character of the movement and to the overall formal design.

Mária Basilides and Bartók premièred seventeen of the twenty songs on 30 January 1930, in Budapest. Publication was drawn-out, again because of translation difficulties. The songs eventually appeared from Universal Edition in 1932. When in 1933 the Budapest Philharmonic Society asked Bartók to contribute a work for the celebrations of its eightieth anniversary he replied by orchestrating the accompaniments to five of these songs (nos 1, 2, 11, 14, 12).

The Twenty Hungarian Folksongs are the last large set for solo voice and piano in Bartók's output. During the next decade his attention turned toward ensemble singing. In 1930 the *Cantata profana* and Hungarian Folksongs for mixed chorus *a cappella* were written, and between 1932 and 1935 another three significant cycles for *a cappella* choruses were completed: Székely Songs, Twenty-seven Two- and Three-part Choruses and *From Olden Times*.[13] However, Bartók did not abandon the solo song completely. Four pieces of the extensive *Mikrokosmos* collection for piano (1926–39) were written for voice and piano: 'Hungarian song' (no.74), 'Song of the fox' (no.95) and

'New Hungarian folksong' (no.127) are folksong arrangements; 'Dialogue' (no.65) features a symmetrically built four-line melody of Bartók's own invention in which the second and fourth lines are inversions of the first and third lines, respectively, and the accompaniment is built exclusively from fifths. These songs call for a single performer and they were included, as Bartók stated in his Preface, because 'such exercises are very useful as practice in reading three staves instead of two'. But there is an option of playing them without singing: either by one performer (nos 65, 74, 95) or by two performers at two pianos. Bartók himself included a two-piano version of no.127 in his *Seven Pieces from 'Mikrokosmos'* (1940).

Bartók wrote his last folksong arrangements for voice and piano a few months before his death. 'The husband's grief', dedicated to his friend Pál Kecskeméti in February 1945, is a song which mocks the hen-pecked husband, and involves imitations of animal cries. It is based on the same Ruthenian melody which Bartók had arranged for two violins as no.24 of his Forty-four Duos (1931). János Demény published the facsimile of this final work's manuscript in 1951.[14] Another manuscript showing the arrangements of three Ruthenian melodies (probably taken from the collection of eighty-one Ruthenian folksongs which Bartók had recorded in 1912) was found among the papers of his Estate.

Five Songs Op.15 (1916)

From 1912, after his failure to win an opera competition with *Duke Bluebeard's Castle*, Bartók withdrew from public appearances and composed almost nothing for two years. In the spring of 1914 he started to sketch ideas for his ballet, *The Wooden Prince*, but the outbreak of the war again paralysed his creativity and deepened his depression. This crisis ended in 1915, when he arranged more than forty Romanian folksongs (for piano, voice and chorus) and started to work on a new string quartet. February 1916 was the peak time of his renewed activity: he composed the Suite for piano Op.14, and several songs for voice and piano which would feature in the two song cycles he finished later that year. During the summer he also completed the first draft of his ballet.

Bartók's biographers presume that this sudden outburst of energy was fuelled by an episode in the composer's personal life. It was in September 1915 that Bartók met Klára Gombossy, the fifteen-year-old daughter of the chief forester of Kisgaram (one of his hosts during his stay in Zólyom county). She was bright and unconventional, played the piano and had literary ambitions. She accompanied Bartók on the folksong collecting trips which he repeated almost every month during the year of their relationship. After one of their meetings Bartók took home some of her poems and during February 1916 set three of them to music, so forming the basis of his Five Songs Op.15: 'My Love' (no.1), 'Summer' (no.2), and 'In the valley' (no.5). Two more songs were added in August: 'In vivid dreams' (no.4) and 'Night of desire' (no.3), the latter to words probably by Wanda Gleiman, another young friend of the composer.

The precocity of these poems made a sufficiently strong impression on Bartók to turn him to a long-abandoned genre, although the poems themselves are of questionable quality. Bartók's friends soon pointed out to him that they were at best dilettante imitations of poems of the time, disclosing unrestrained feelings of puberty in a crude, almost trivial language. Bartók himself also recognized their shortcomings fairly early. When Universal Edition showed an interest in his unpublished works he mentioned these songs, but finally sent only the first three of them. Later he had doubts even about these: 'it would suit me better if these songs did not appear at all, because the texts are not particularly good'.[15] Nevertheless, he would have consented to their publication – he had even prepared word-for-word German translations of them – but only on condition that the authors of the poems should not be named. The publisher was reluctant to take the responsibility of printing the texts without securing copyright permission. So the songs remained unpublished during Bartók's lifetime, except for a facsimile of the manuscript of the earlier, longer piano postlude of no.1, which appeared on the title page of the 1 February issue of the avant-garde periodical *Ma* (*Today*) in 1917. Nor were the songs performed: there were plans to include the third song in concerts to be given in Berlin and Vienna during the winter season of 1918–19, but these concerts did not take place because of the political situation at the time.

In an essay about the influence of Hungarian folk music on the technique of contemporary composition, written a few years after the Op.15 songs, Bartók complained about the absence of traditions in Hungarian art music on which the composer could rely in developing a specifically Hungarian declamatory style in vocal compositions: 'We Hungarians have nothing but our parlando peasant melodies as the means of enabling us to solve this question.'[16] Indeed, it is not difficult to notice that the vocal part of Op.15 was mostly developed on the model of the *parlando* melodies, even if only no.1 uses the actual tempo designation 'parlando'. The other songs, all within the range of *andante* and *sostenuto*, are equally declamatory in style. They follow the free rhythm of speech which results in frequent changes of metre, note repetitions and irregular divisions of the beat (such as triplets, quintuplets: see Ex.5).

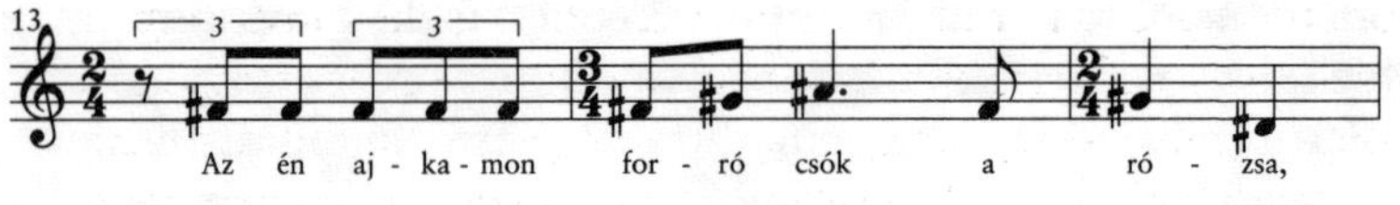

EX.5

In nos 2 and 5, the two earliest songs, the rhythmic profile is smoother and recalls the solution of Kodály's metric songs, which were shaped to highlight the classical metre of the verse, as exemplified in Ex.6.

EX. 6

Both Ex.5 and Ex.6 show other important features of the folk-song model: the pentatonic scale and the descending fourth interval, the latter occurring particularly at the ends of phrases. These are the most important elements in the melodic vocabulary of the Five Songs Op.15.

The rather uniform vocal material is balanced by a bold, impulsive, technically very demanding piano part. This is Bartók's primary vehicle for illustrating the changing mood of the text. Two opposing tendencies can be observed. The first one is the disposition toward improvisatory passages: the most diverse, distinctly pianistic ideas emerge, are repeated or transposed for a while, and then suddenly dropped in favour of other ideas. These mostly arpeggiated passages usually cover the whole range of the keyboard, providing a vibrating, stormy background to the declamatory voice. Its plasticity is in striking contrast to the singularly rhythmic, more economical and lanky style of the piano Suite Op.14, which he was writing at the same time.

On the other hand, it is the piano which brings discipline of form to these songs by repeating similar ideas after each stanza, or by framing the vocal part with a prelude and postlude built from the same material. The only exception is the third song, in which the vocal part also has its own distinctive recurring ideas – such as the descending chain of thirds, recalling Judith's characteristic motif from *Duke Bluebeard's Castle* – to contribute to the overall shaping of the form. Even in the less improvisatory details the texture is homophonic and full of broad gestures and exclamations. Coupled with a bold harmonic language, with harsh clashes of minor seconds and superimposed fourths or fifths, these pages represent a most interesting stage in the development of Bartók's expressionist style.

Five 'Ady' Songs Op.16 (1916)

Although the opus numbers suggest a later date for Op.16, the two song cycles were, in fact, composed almost simultaneously. Two songs of Op.15 were written first – on 5 and 6 February 1916 – but the second song of the Op.16 cycle followed almost immediately in this month. And while the Op.15 cycle was only completed in August, Op.16 was ready as early as April. The appearance of twin compositions, as if the ideas overflowed and could not be contained in a single composition, is a recurring phenomenon in Bartók's career. In the case of these two song cycles, the words of Op.15 prompted the composer to turn his attention to the genre of song, since the immediacy of song promised to be a most appropriate vehicle for conveying his thoughts and feelings of the moment. These thoughts and feelings, however, sought a more profound expression than was possible through the Op.15 texts and called for a deeper poetry.

Endre Ady (1877–1919), the author of the poems Bartók used in this Op.16 cycle, was the leading figure of the avant-garde intellectuals of Bartók's generation. His books of poems, which appeared annually from 1906, introduced a totally new language to Hungarian poetry, which he had developed through his contact with the French Symbolists. In Ady's artistic nonconformism and radical political and social thought, Bartók saw an advocate of his own battles and ideals. He met the poet only in passing, at an art exhibition in the autumn of 1915, but he owned seven of the ten books of Ady's poems and his jottings on the pages of these volumes show the profundity and extent of his interest in the poet's work. When in early 1916 he found himself wanting to express his thoughts through the most personal medium of song, he recalled these poems with which he had felt so much sympathy and which expressed so aptly his current state of mind.

The five poems chosen by Bartók give utterance to the darkest of thoughts: death and the symbols of evanescence. Autumn and night are recurring themes in nos 1, 2 and 5; the love poems (nos 3 and 4) speak of irrevocable separation; nos 1, 3 and 5 conclude with tears, defeat and desperation. Not surprisingly, each of the poems is set to slow music: *andante*, *lento*, *sostenuto* and their combinations are the most frequent tempo designations. Apart from a few notable exceptions there is no steadiness in the tempo. There are constant changes, so as to conjure up the natural declamation of each phrase.

Here we have to mention another possible influence on the melodic style of Bartók's songs, that of the settings of Ady's poetry by Béla Reinitz. Reinitz (1878–1943) was one of those few critics who had immediately recognized Bartók's significance and taken his side in the polemics about his music. He played a key role in the cultural reorganization of Hungary during the short-lived Soviet Republic of 1919, when he had intended to entrust important responsibilities to Bartók. After the fall of the revolution he had to go into exile. He was also well known for the numerous songs in which he sought to imitate Ady's famous poetic recitals. Bartók's warm dedication of his Op.16 'Ady' Songs 'to Béla Reinitz, with true friendship and love, Budapest 1920', was a politically daring gesture at the time, but can also be understood as a recognition of the significance of Reinitz's settings to his own. Apart from the obvious indebtedness of the declamatory passages there is at least one song, 'Alone with the sea' (no.4), in which the subtle sentimentalism of the poem suggested to Bartók a lighter, more melodious setting, reminiscent of Reinitz's style.

If we compare the vocal part with that of the Op.15 songs, the most striking difference is the almost complete absence of pentatonic phrases. The falling fourth also became less frequent although it still plays a prominent role in the last song, 'I cannot come to you'. Another significant difference is that the declamatory writing is occasionally given up in favour of a more melodious vocal line, especially in the first song, 'Autumn tears', but also in the third, 'Lost content', and the fourth. These passages belong to a more traditional style of song writing, where steady rhythm prevails, melodic nuclei reappear and the stretch of the melodic segments is longer than in the declamatory style. An example of this more traditional style is given in Ex. 7.

Each of the above cases occur when the text itself is 'musical' and employs recurring phrases and word repetitions. Equally, inspiration for the concise structure of the first song came from the formal plan of the poem, the three stanzas of which show a *Stollen–Stollen–Abgesang* relationship:

In the autumn noon, in the autumn noon,
Oh, how hard it is
To smile at the girls.

In the autumn night, in the autumn night,
Oh, how hard it is
To look up at the stars.

In the autumn night, in the autumn noon,
Oh, how easy it is,
Weeping, weeping, to fall prostrate.

The music is a true reflection of this formal design. The second stanza is an almost exact repetition of the first, transposed an augmented fifth lower, while the third stanza concludes the piece with transformed but recognizable elements of the first two. Even the slowly dragging waltz rhythm is suggested by the words, although waltz-like segments occur in almost all the Op.16 songs and in other Bartók works of this period, as well. The closest relation of this first song, both chronologically and in mood, is the trio of the fourth movement of the piano Suite Op.14, which was written in the same month. But this characteristic motion also appears in the music of Bartók's pantomime, *The Miraculous Mandarin* Op.19, composed three years later.

The piano part of Bartók's Op.16 is similar to his Op.15, although somewhat less exuberant. It still has its illustrative role, evoking the sound of the swirling fog, the mysterious throbs (no.2) and the roaring waves of the sea (no.4), or generally depicting the changing mood of the text (no.3). Again, the overall formal unity is sometimes secured through the instrumental introductions, which recur at the end, and by the interludes between stanzas (as in no.4). But in the majority of the Op.16 'Ady' Songs the choice of form-building elements is broader, coming from the melody (nos 1, 3, 5), from the rhythm (no.1), or from a harmonic element, as in 'Autumn echoes' (no.2), where the piano part is constructed almost exclusively of superimposed fourths and fourth–second–fourth chains. There is also a more organic link between voice and piano: the refrain of the poem of the fifth song, 'I die', is represented by a falling fourth, and fourths are the most

I, 3-11 (voice)

EX. 7

frequently used intervals in the piano part.

It proved almost impossible to provide adequate translations to Ady's Hungarian poems. Several sets of translations were prepared, but these satisfied neither Bartók nor his publisher, and publication of the cycle was delayed for five years. Meanwhile, three of the songs appeared in different periodicals in facsimile of Bartók's handwriting; one appeared in Vienna and another in Budapest in 1919, in a memorial issue following Ady's death. Universal Edition brought the songs out finally in 1923, but Bartók made several corrections even after the event in his own printed copy.

The first performance of the songs took place in Budapest within Bartók's recital of his own works on 21 April 1919. Ilona Durigó was the singer. An early performance in Vienna, planned by Schoenberg's 'Musikalische Privataufführungen' for January 1920, fell through because of the inadequacies of the German translations. This discouraging experience, along with the miseries associated with the work's protracted publication, might well have provided the strongest incentives for Bartók not to write further original compositions for voice and piano, and to resort to folk music for the rest of his career.

NOTES

1 A selection of the other early works was published in *Der junge Bartók*, ed. Denijs Dille, vol.1, 'Ausgewählte Lieder für Gesang und Klavier', Mainz/Budapest (B. Schott/Editio Musica), 1963.

2 It is interesting to note that the published copy of the second song, held by the Bartók Estate, has several handwritten notes which indicate discrepancies between the lengths of certain syllables and their rhythmic realizations.

3 This appeared as the second movement of *Petits morceaux*, which was published in 1965.

4 *BBcl*, p.125.

5 Only the first song, 'They have mowed the pasture already' ('Lekaszálták már a rétet'), has been published, posthumously, in Denijs Dille, ed., op. cit.

6 Republished in the 'Postscript' to the facsimile edition of Bartók-Kodály, *Hungarian Folksongs*, ed. Denijs Dille, London (Boosey & Hawkes), 1970, p.50.

7 Reissued on Hungaroton LPX 12328.

8 *BBE*, pp. 333–5.

9 *The Music of Béla Bartók*, Berkeley (University of California Press), 1984, pp. 32–50.

10 Reissued on Hungaroton LPX 12328.

11 *BBE*, pp. 341–2.

12 'Notes Concerning Bartók's Solo Vocal Music (I–III)', *Tempo*, nos 36, 38, 40 (1955–6), pp. 16–26, 14–20, 18–23, respectively.

13 For an account of these works see Miklós Szabó's chapter 'Choral Works' in this *Companion*.

14 *BBlev*.ii, plates xiv–xv.

15 Unpublished letter, Bartók to Universal Edition, 14 January 1923 (NYBA).

16 *BBE*, p. 306.

28

Choral Works

MIKLÓS SZABÓ

Béla Bartók was basically an instrumental composer. Apart from his artistic disposition, this was due to his musical education (a typical middle European education of the turn of the century) and to his continuing activities as pianist and pedagogue. As with many of his colleagues he tried his hand with choral music from time to time, but unlike them, he took his major inspiration from folk music. All the works to be discussed here were written to folk texts and, with the exception of the last two compositions, their music was also based on folk melodies, whether Hungarian, Slovak or Romanian.

The choral works listed below follow the order determined by András Szőllősy:

Four Old Hungarian Folksongs, 1910–12, revised in September 1926, for male chorus *a cappella*; premièred in 1911 and 1926 (revised version).

Two Romanian Folksongs, 1915, for female chorus *a cappella*; première unknown.

Slovak Folksongs, 1917, for male chorus *a cappella;* premièred in 1917.

Four Slovak Folksongs, 1916–17, for mixed chorus and piano; premièred in 1917.

Hungarian Folksongs, May 1930, for mixed chorus *a cappella*; partially premièred in 1936.

Székely Songs, November 1932, for male chorus *a cappella*; première unknown.

Two- and Three-part Choruses, 1935, for *a cappella* children's and women's choruses; premièred in 1937.

From Olden Times, 1935, for three-part male chorus *a cappella*; premièred in 1937.

We are not here considering Bartók's juvenile stylistic exercises or the early pieces of instructive purpose. So, too, the *Cantata profana* of 1930 is considered in a separate chapter in this *Companion*, while *Village Scenes* (1924), although mentioned as a 'choral work' in one of Bartók's letters of 1937, was originally written for solo voice and piano, and so has been considered in the preceding chapter.

Little is known of Bartók's motives for composing choral works. As for their place in Bartók's *œuvre*, two thoughts deserve noting. First: that, contrary to common belief, Bartók was a realist, who rarely composed for his own drawer. He usually only turned to choral pieces when there was a hope of their performance. This is proved by the fact that the completion of the works was normally closely followed by their première. There were some exceptions, however. The unpublished Two Romanian Folksongs were probably deliberately withheld from the public by Bartók; the première of the Székely Songs was put off mainly for reasons of copyright. The Hungarian Folksongs (1930), however, did have to wait six years for its première, clearly because of its performing difficulties. Second: an examination of the pieces of similar chronology and style in Bartók's *œuvre* suggests that Bartók wanted to try the same compositional techniques in several genres at the same time. The Four Old Hungarian Folksongs, in both form and harmony, show affinities with Bartók's and Kodály's first collection of Hungarian folksong arrangements of 1906, for voice and piano, and even greater similarities with the first two volumes of his piano series *For Children* (1908–9). The Two Romanian Folksongs are chronologically surrounded by works using Romanian folk melodies or motifs written for either piano or voice and piano: Sonatina (1915), Romanian Folk Dances (1915), Nine Romanian Folksongs (1915). Even the two chorus cycles of Slovak folksongs, from 1917, have their relatives, partly among earlier Slovak folksong arrangements, such as the final volumes of *For Children*, and partly among contemporaneous works, such as the first of the Three Rondos (1916–27). The two chorus cycles of 1930 and 1932 are related to the greatest of the folksong arrangements for voice and piano, the Twenty Hungarian Folksongs (1929) and *Cantata profana* (1930). The last two cycles are full members of the series of masterworks produced by Bartók during the 1930s.

Considering chronology and style further, the eight choral works can be listed in three groups:

Group 1: The four cycles written before or during the First World War. The original version of the folksong is, in most cases, in the top part; introductions, interludes and codas are scarce; the harmonization is simple and mostly chordal.

Group 2: The two cycles of 1930–32. The tremendous stylistic change which had taken place in Bartók's music during the intervening decade is even more vividly demonstrated here than in his instrumental music. Now the folksong material is distributed among all the parts. The formal symmetry is loosened by the motifs of the folk material. The texture ranges from unison to polyphony of six or eight parts, often involving imitations. Harmonizations are complex and, at times, quite dense. The tonal plan involves wider stretches, and is sometimes polytonal but always logical.

Group 3: The two cycles of 1935. In these two works only the texts are of folk origin, and not the music (although Bartók's music does, of course, still contain some folk elements). Some of the Two- and Three-part Choruses start in a closed form, but in the course of the music the structure mostly dissolves. Symmetrical form is entirely avoided in the triptych for male chorus, *From Olden Times*. Apart for a few bars, the number of voices is consistently two or three. The texture is mostly polyphonic, with Bartók writing careful and logical voice-leading. The chords, especially in the Two- and Three-part Choruses, are considerably simpler than those of the choral works of the previous period; at the same time, the crystallization of a specific polymodal sound-structure is found here.

The cycles of the different periods are divergent in the level of performing difficulty, as well. The early works were intended for amateur choirs, so their performance presents no difficulties today. The two series of the middle period, Hungarian Folksongs (1930) in particular, are enormously demanding of vocal technique as well as musicianship, and present frequent melodic, rhythmic and harmonic problems. *From Olden Times*, too, involves a serious trial for singers; in the Two- and Three-part Choruses, on the other hand, the composer evidently avoided technical difficulties, without making any allowances in a musical sense.

Bartók, it seems, differentiated between male and female choral textures. The former are more difficult and their vocal range is much wider than that of the children's and women's choruses written about the same time. The explanation of this lies, at least partially, in the contemporary musical and social conditions of Hungary. During the first decades of the century there were many male choruses, following the German *Liedertafel* tradition. Their members usually could not read music, but through the years they developed a considerable routine in learning by rote; besides, many of them had excellent voices.[1] Children's and women's choruses, on the other hand, were few in Hungary, so it is no coincidence that before 1935 Bartók wrote only one two-movement work for women's chorus, and even that remained unpublished and perhaps also unperformed. As for concert choirs, hardly any were suitable for performing high-level modern compositions.

Turning now to look at the choral works individually, the Four Old Hungarian Folksongs stand as the first fruit for chorus of Bartók's discovery of Hungarian peasant music. A *parlando* folksong opens the cycle (the chordal style is rarely broken by a melisma), then three *giusto* melodies of different character follow, the middle one being in a different key as well (a quasi trio). In the last movement the two outer voices sing the folksong of changing metre in an octave canon, so an interesting metric polyphony results. In the Two Romanian Folksongs a slow, *parlando*, major-key melody with variations and a fast, *giusto*, strophic, minor-key melody confront each other. Such paired movements well represent Bartók's thinking in contrasts, and are also popular in his early orchestral pieces (First Violin

Concerto, Op.posth., *Two Portraits* Op.5, and *Two Pictures* Op.10). The arrangement is very simple and homophonic; the second movement does not even contain an altered note.

The five-movement Slovak Folksongs (1917) uses four melodies only: the slow, lamenting, *parlando* first and fourth movements share the same theme, although in varied versions. But these very movements introduce a novelty compared with the earlier pieces. The Lydian folksong, starting with an augmented fourth interval, obviously excluded any chord-like, Classical harmonization. Bartók himself talked about this arrangement technique in one of his American lectures of 1928:

> many of the melodies may have the most simple 'harmonization': one single chord (that is, one and the same chord) during the whole melody. . . . There are many similar harmonic inspirations we owe to the latent harmonies contained in the peasant songs of ours.[2]

This accompaniment is really a 'vertical projection of the previous horizontal forms', and he adds: 'This result is obtained by a logical process, and not . . . through sheer whimsicality.' The three other folksongs of *giusto* character, which demonstrate the merry side of a soldier's life, follow traditional paths again. (This work was premièred at a military concert in Vienna.)

Four Slovak Folksongs (1917) is the only cycle with piano accompaniment among Bartók's choral works. This circumstance, of course, immediately expands the possibilities. Harmonies are much more colourful; the tonal plan is wider than in the previous compositions. The first three movements follow one another in a gradual increase of tempo, then the cycle closes with a somewhat slower, heavier movement. This sequence of movements is not dissimilar to the cyclic order of the Suite for piano Op.14. The folksong-cum-fugato structure of the third movement and the dance-like, graceful $\frac{5}{8}$ 'Bulgarian' rhythm of the second must have seemed quite novel to singers and audiences of the time. The opening movement is, however, the most significant. The wonderful, rich harmonization of the hauntingly beautiful, sad wedding song and the fine two-part imitation of the second verse distinguish the piece from Bartók's earlier choral essays.

Hungarian Folksongs, composed thirteen years later in 1930, is a large-scale work with professional performers in mind, so the composer felt he could transplant the stylistic characteristics of his instrumental works into the choral language without any compromise. The four movements are built on five folksongs, with the finale's *A B A* form accounting for two of the songs. The cyclic order is arranged around two poles again: two slow, *parlando* pieces (I: 'The prisoner'; II: 'The wanderer'), followed by two fast, *giusto* ones (III: 'Finding a husband'; IV: 'Love song').

The homophonic technique is used as a contrast to free polyphonic writing: in the first two movements, for example, it marks important points of the form; it occurs in the coda of the third and in the trio of the fourth movement. All parts share the folksong material, and there are canons of two or more parts as well. The cantus firmus wanders from key to key, but the tonal plan usually follows strict musical logic, rising by fifths in the first movement and seconds in the second. Primarily in the *parlando* movements, the melody is often accompanied by complex, harshly dissonant chords derived from the motifs of the folksong; but the texture is free, as a result of the dense imitation of the ornamental folksong material. The personal lament of the folksong is surrounded and amplified through the compassionate sighs and comments of the chorus. The interludes, composed of folk motifs, loosen the symmetrical form, and the peasant melody is increasingly integrated into the musical texture. The third movement closes with a graceful coda written in asymmetrical metre; the fourth movement's coda is heavy. In that movement the 'Bulgarian' rhythm of the folksong in the middle section provides a splendid contrast through its *leggero* character.

The treatment of the chorus reveals many similarities with *Cantata profana* (1930); we can almost consider it as a preliminary study to that work. The number of parts is treated in a free manner and Bartók often applies the various contrasts of 'choral orchestration'. In the first and third movements male and female choruses confront each other; in the second the sound gradually expands in both directions from the middle range; in the third the imitations are built upon each other, in a towering fashion. In the same movement the high and low voices represent the snappy dialogue between mother and daughter. In the fourth movement the tutti chorus and the quasi solos bring variety. Thus, in this work, too, we can admire Bartók's 'stereo' dramaturgy.

The same comments are valid, in part, about the Székely Songs, too, although their texture is somewhat simpler. (The Székely people of Transylvania have a particularly old and rich Hungarian folk music.) Bartók arranged five folksongs in the six movements, with each connected by an *attacca*. Nos 1 and 2 are slow, while 3–6 are fast, but before the finale the fifth movement recalls the melody of the third, in a somewhat slower, more restful tempo. The overall form is largely binary here, too.

About the compositional circumstances and motives of the Two- and Three-part Choruses we have more information, through the statements of Zoltán Kodály. In 1946 Kodály said during a lecture: 'from 1925 onwards I often encouraged him to write choral works. For a long time he did not compose any; then (about ten years later) he presented a whole bunch.'[3] It must be noted that in the decade since Kodály's first choruses for children of 1925, an incredibly lively and high-level of musical activity had been developed in the previously stagnant Hungarian schools and choirs. But Kodály, at the same time, referred to the inner motive of the composition as well: 'At that time he [Bartók] began perusing Palestrina's works and was deeply captivated by this art.' Four years later he added that Bartók 'realized that here we can admire what is not to be experienced elsewhere – the highest level of responsibility'.[4]

The series was composed in one creative spell in the summer of 1935, between the masterpieces of the Fifth String Quartet (1935) and the Music for Strings, Percussion and Celesta (1936). That, by itself, was a guarantee of the highest artistic quality in the choruses. Probably only the chorus 'Lánycsúfoló' ('Mocking of girls') was written a little later; its draft is found between the second and third movements of *From Olden Times*, and it was dedicated to Bartók's wife, Ditta, on her birthday: 'To 31 October 1935'. On the evidence of the sketches Bartók worked still further on the series, and then made other slight corrections for its new edition, shortly before he left for the United States.

Kodály greeted the publication of the work in an article of truly poetic beauty:

> The Hungarian child does not know yet that the Christmas of 1936 has brought him a gift that will last him all his life. This is clear to all who seek to take the Hungarian children into a world where the air is clearer, the sky bluer, and the sun shines warmer . . . This is art of full, lasting value, also for the adult world.[5]

Bartók visited the rehearsals before the Budapest première in May 1937, and added to its significance by playing excerpts from the likewise newly composed *Mikrokosmos*. After the première Bartók, who was usually uncommunicative, wrote with great enthusiasm:

> It was a great experience for me when – at the rehearsal – I heard for the first time my little choruses coming from the lips of these children. I shall never forget this impression of the freshness and gaiety of the little ones' voices.[6]

As already mentioned, the musical material of this series was entirely Bartók's compositional invention, but the words derived from Hungarian folklore.[7] According to László Somfai, the majority of the texts came from nineteenth-century collections.[8] His research shows that Bartók used the original, unchanged version of the text only in exceptional cases. Sometimes he substituted just a word, but at other times left out or added whole lines; in some cases, too, he changed the entire structure of the verse. All these changes reflect his refined taste. Through his careful polishing, the beauty, expression and conciseness of the text was increased; its artistic form became more perfect. This 'book of poems', comparable to the work of any great poet, embraces the complete emotional world of childhood and youth. Among them we find playful, dance-like and mocking pieces; energetic, solemn, even dramatic ones; and pieces about farewells, disappointments and loneliness.

Bartók grouped the twenty-seven pieces into eight volumes, each containing three or four pieces. (He proceeded similarly in

For Children, and the Forty-four Duos of 1931, and always grouped smaller pieces into 'suites' in his piano recitals.) The first edition designated the first six volumes as 'for children's chorus', and the final two 'for women's chorus', but a strict line cannot practically be drawn between them. 'Tavasz' ('Spring'), announcing Nature's revival, opens the series vigorously, and 'Isten veled' ('God be with you') closes it with best farewell wishes. In between, the playful, mocking and gentle pieces come first, followed by those of greater dramatic expression, and lamenting or lyrical ones. Although the composer did not plan the series as one continuous cycle, in my experience of many years with these pieces its real significance and unmatched variety is best realized in a complete performance.

Since there is no *cantus prius factus* here, the composer had a greater freedom both formally and tonally. The characteristic variations of his folksong arrangements will not be found, but the thematic materials of different sections of a piece frequently derive from one another through application of a fine variation technique. The range of structures is expanded from one-part, binary and ternary forms to complex, through-composed dramatic forms, although the plan is always logically executed and concentrated. Within these pieces for only two or three parts singing within a relatively narrow range, Bartók developed a polyphony of extraordinary plasticity, taking complete consideration of the vocal possibilities. In this individual sound-world of the mature composer, characteristic stylistic, and sometimes structural, features of the late, great instrumental works appear, but the balance of their occurrence and mode of application is different. In this basic medium of diatony and triadic harmony the effect of alterations and dissonances is multiplied. Perhaps Bartók's studies of Palestrina, mentioned by Kodály, were inspiring him here, too. The harmonic relationship between words and music also deserves special attention. Bartók developed his own *Affekten-* and *Figurenlehre* here, in the spirit of the old masters. It affects the entire series, and enabled him to give musical expression to all textual nuances, mainly through the phenomena of the 'axis system' and 'polytonal alterations'.[9]

It is a pity that this twentieth-century 'madrigal book' has still not received its proper place on the international concert platform. This is probably because of difficulties which choirs outside Hungary experience with the Hungarian texts. The composer Sándor Veress, a Bartók student now living in Switzerland, wrote about the 'Kánon' (Canon) in 1943: 'If nothing else survived from our time but this, musicologists in 700 years' time could still form an idea of today's music, just as *Sumer is icumen in* speaks of its own time to us.'[10]

Bartók wrote a chamber-orchestra accompaniment to seven of the pieces, partly in 1935–6 and partly while in America. This version leaves the original vocal parts practically intact but the instrumental material is independent, too, providing a noble frame for the pieces.

The cycle *From Olden Times – mutatis mutandis* – also displays the stylistic characteristics of the Twenty-seven Two- and Three-part Choruses. But the movements are longer and the overall triptych form was planned by Bartók right from the beginning. The composer indicated in the score that the text consisted of 'transformed words of old folk and art songs'. The outer movements contrast with each other. The two refrains express their basic thought: (I) 'No one is more unhappy than the peasant, for his misery is deeper than the ocean'; (III) 'No one is more happy than the peasant, for his lot is happier than any profession.' The form is reminiscent of Renaissance motets: various imitative sections follow one another; the homophonic or unison blocks emphasize certain parts of the text; the recurring refrains articulate the form, stressing the message of the movements.

The middle movement, in the subdominant C major, is the axis of the work. It starts like an innocent children's ditty but then takes an unexpected turn at the golden-section point of the movement: 'I give the bread to my landlord, / In return he beats me with a stick'. The work is strong criticism of the feudal circumstances of the 'olden times' and, at the same time, is the apotheosis of peasant life idealized by Bartók.

The outer movements create a tonal contrast with each other and a tonal and metric contrast with the middle movement. The first and last movements are written in a broad, often changing metre, at times in *parlando* style, and their metronome numbers (fixing the basic tempo) are close to each other, too. The middle movement is a tight *tempo giusto* in $\frac{2}{4}$ metre. The above-mentioned turning-point of the movement is marked by the stubbornly repeated, tumbling motif of minor thirds. The tonal contrast of the outer movements is symbolic, with the tragically hopeless E minor of the first movement becoming the transfigured, radiant E major of the third. Thus, as with the great instrumental works of the 1930s, this cycle proceeds from the negative to the positive world, from darkness towards light.

The last two works mark the zenith, and also the close, of Bartók's choral art. They warrant inclusion among the classical masterpieces of the composer, then at the peak of his creative career. Bartók's own words in a 1941 American interview might refer to these very works: 'With maturity, it seems to me, comes the wish to economize, to be more simple. . . . Maturity is the period when [the composer] finds the just measure, the middle course which best expresses his own musical personality.'[11]

NOTES

1 Bartók also probably knew through experience that chords must be constructed in wider position for male chorus. If all the notes are presented within a narrow range they tend to grate.

2 *BBE*, pp. 334, 336.

3 *The Selected Writings of Zoltán Kodály*, tr. Lili Halápy and Fred Macnicol, Budapest (Corvina), 1974, p. 100.

4 Ibid., p. 107.

5 'Children's Choruses of Béla Bartók', in booklet to *Béla Bartók Complete Edition*, Hungaroton SLPX 1290, pp. 6–7.

6 *BBL*, p. 257.

7 Ever since the Op.16 'Ady' songs of 1916 Bartók had only used folk texts.

8 'Bartók egynemű kórusainak szövegforrásáról', in *Magyar zenetörténeti tanulmányok*, ed. Ferenc Bónis, Budapest (Zeneműkiadó), 1969, pp. 359–76.

9 See Ernő Lendvai, *The Workshop of Bartók and Kodály*, Budapest (Editio Musica), 1983, and the detailed analyses of this series in my volume, *Bartók Béla kórusművei*, Budapest (Zeneműkiadó), 1985, pp. 37–269.

10 'Bartók Béla huszonhét kórusa', in *Magyar dal* (Budapest), 1 September 1943, p. 3.

11 Friede F. Rothe, 'The Language of the Composer', *Etude*, vol.59 no.2 (February 1941), p. 130.

29

Cantata profana

GYÖRGY KROÓ

As with the best of his contemporaries, the composer of the *Cantata profana* (1930) felt the cold wind of the approaching night of Fascism. In these years at the turn of the decade European musicians seriously set about examining their consciences. In 1930 Stravinsky took up the Bible and composed his *Symphony of Psalms*, a counterpiece to his rebellious masterpiece on pagan human sacrifice, *The Rite of Spring*. Schoenberg, too, began work in this year on his greatest composition, the opera *Moses und Aron*, which centres on the issue of the artist's responsibility and the betrayal of human ideals. In 1931 Honegger produced his 'most tragic composition', the stage oratorio *Cris du monde*, which is a condemnation of the modern society in which art is stifled and destroyed, and man can offer only a cry of despair. Hindemith, in the immediately following years, symbolized the plight of all artists of the twentieth century in his figure of Matthias Grünewald, the genius who is tempted by Satan but resists the forces of night. The *Cantata profana* scored for mixed chorus, tenor, baritone and orchestra, preserves something essential from this momentous period in twentieth-century music, and of all the monumental works written at that time it was one of the few to exhibit a truly inspired quality, a sincerity in its confession, and a perfection as a work of art.

In general, Bartók wrestled a great deal with texts. The creation of a folk-influenced music for Hungarian verse came naturally to Kodály, but for Bartók, a composer of primarily instrumental music, the task usually led to a long-lasting struggle. He fought the first such battle in 1911 over *Duke Bluebeard's Castle*, and his second while composing the Five 'Ady'

Songs Op.16 around 1915–16. For a long time afterwards it was only his work with various Slovak folksongs which indicated any continuing interest in vocal music. Bence Szabolcsi has recalled that after the first performance of the Twenty Hungarian Folksongs, in January 1930, it was as if the composer had burst through that barrier which had prevented him from composing a truly great vocal composition ever since *Duke Bluebeard's Castle*. But it seems that still another vocal test piece was needed: the four Hungarian Folksongs for mixed chorus which were completed in May 1930. József Ujfalussy has described the way in which these beautiful songs and choruses paved the way for Bartók's *Cantata profana*:

> From the Twenty Hungarian Folksongs onwards . . . more and more frequently the vocal works present us with a picture of a suffering and oppressed people. The first volume of the Twenty Hungarian Folksongs consists of sad lyrics gathered together under the title *Szomorú nóták* (Sad Songs): 'A tömlöcben', 'Régi keserves', 'Bújdosó ének', 'Pásztor nóta' ('In prison', 'Old lament', 'The fugitive' and 'Herdsman's song', respectively). The four Hungarian Folksongs for mixed chorus return again to tales of misfortune: 'A rab' ('The prisoner') . . . and 'Bújdosó' ('The rover').[1]

The choice of text also indicates that Bartók had reached the end of one period in the development of his world outlook. His love of the people, his nostalgia for the village and his pantheism became synthesized anew, but more completely than ever before, in an internationalism based both on science and humanism. When this outlook had crystallized in his mind Bartók felt the need to formulate it. Over a quarter of a century after his '*ars poetica* in Hungarian costume', when he had stated his 'one objective: the good of Hungary and the Hungarian people',[2] he now, at the height of his artistic achievement, gave expression to his international objective:

> My creative work, just because it arises from 3 sources (Hungarian, Romanian, Slovakian), might be regarded as the embodiment of the very concept of integration so much emphasized in Hungary today. . . . My own idea, however – of which I have been fully conscious since I found myself as a composer – is the brotherhood of peoples, brotherhood in spite of all wars and conflicts. I try – to

> the best of my ability – to serve this idea in my music; therefore I don't reject any influence, be it Slovakian, Romanian, Arabic or from any other source. The source must only be clean, fresh and healthy![3]

The genesis of the *Cantata profana* actually begins in April 1914, when Bartók recorded on phonograph and notated two versions of the Romanian folk ballad 'The Hunting Boys turned into Stags' in the (Hungarian) county of Maros-Torda. At that time the Transylvanians only sang the ballad as a *colindă*, that is, a song connected with festivities of the winter solstice. They sang it in groups in the houses of hunting families as a monophonic antiphon. The composer himself called attention to the fact that such a *colindă* text rarely had any connection with the Christian Christmas: 'Instead of the Bethlehem legend we hear about a wonderful battle between the victorious hero and the – until then – unvanquished lion (or stag)'.[4] In his long relationship with folklore, Bartók was now for the first time captured more by a folk text than by the music related to it. This is an indication of the degree of Bartók's inspiration by this source as well as of his theoretical and ideological interests at the time. The archaic nature of the text was of at least as much importance to him as its Romanian origin – indeed, he eventually gave up the idea of emphasizing its Romanian character. In 1915 Bartók arranged twenty Romanian *colindă* melodies for piano (later published as Romanian Christmas Carols), and by 1926 had prepared his collection of *colinde* for publication.[5]

Probably in 1929, but certainly by January 1930, he had prepared an initial Romanian-language text for his *Cantata profana*, based on the two versions of the ballad that he had collected himself. Today this original version only exists in a Hungarian translation made by József Erdélyi.[6] Although Bartók was right in rejecting this translation he did, none the less, in preparing his final text for the work, include two passages from it. Having come up with a new 'libretto', in Romanian, he asked his Romanian friend Constantin Brăiloiu to check the text, and probably in July–August 1930 then set it to music. As evidenced in the sketch of the vocal score, it was definitely the Romanian text which Bartók set to music. The Hungarian translation of this text, made by Bartók himself, was first included, alongside the original Romanian, in the sketch of the full score which Bartók completed on 8 September 1930. The Romanian text was only omitted from the final copy of the full score, at which stage the work acquired its published form with Hungarian and German words.[7] This final linguistic form is surprising, given Bartók's plan for the *Cantata profana* to fit into a cycle. He thought of composing a series of three or four cantatas, and even withheld the *Cantata profana* for some years after completing it, in the hope of publishing the whole cycle together. Part of the draft of the text for one of these other cantatas has survived, and from it we can conclude that, in addition to this first 'Romanian' piece, he intended to produce works based on Slovak and Hungarian legends and also, possibly, a fourth cantata summarizing the whole cycle, as an artistic manifestation of his 'brotherhood of peoples' ideal. But Fascism was about to move across Europe, and the plan was, therefore, ill-timed. Bartók was also worried about the actual performance of his work. He was aware of the extraordinarily demanding nature of the composition, and so perhaps never before had he been so concerned about the quality of the performance of one of his works. He only handed over the manuscript to the publisher on condition that any performance would gain his prior approval. Even in 1933 he seems to have harboured hopes of continuing with his cycle of cantatas. He was also now worried about the performance of the work in Hungary because of the Romanian folk source of the text, and late in 1932 had expressed the wish that his cantata not be performed in Hungary then or at any time in the future. The world première finally took place in London on 25 May 1934, using an English translation made by M.-D. Calvocoressi. The first performance in Budapest only occurred two years later, by which time Bartók was already composing his Music for Strings, Percussion and Celesta.

The magical story of the young hunters in the forest is told as a ballad in four verses, most with six-syllable lines. The first verse serves as an introduction; the second is a description of the hunt and the magical transformation; the third is a re-encounter, conflict and solution; the last verse constitutes the end of the story, with a recollection of the introduction providing a structural framework and reinforcement of the moral of the story. This recollection was Bartók's own idea and is not found in the folk sources. His order of musical movements makes the work even more condensed by uniting the first two verses. Thus, the opening movement of the *Cantata profana* consists of two sections (*molto moderato* and, from bar 59, *allegro molto*), which encompass almost half the work and carry the story uninterruptedly to the decisive, dramatic peak of the work, the magical transformation. The other two movements are found beyond this turning point of the work. The second movement is an Andante which functions as a middle section but, in contrast to the narrative outer movements, has the dramatic character of a dialogue. The third movement is a Moderato. Its musical material is a summary of the first movement but, in accordance with the text, it harks back to the second movement as well. This third movement fulfils the function of the reprise in a large ternary form, and also achieves a coda-like effect (from the *poco agitato* at bar 35). This musical structure has the conspicuous feature of not completely tallying with the structure of the text. In particular, the textual reprise does not coincide with the first suggestions of musical reprise, which come in the last section of the second movement.

The opening and concluding key of the work is D, which also functions as a tonal point of reference for the whole composition. The first instrumental melody (I, bar 1) and the last vocal melody (III, bar 72) use mirrored scale forms, based on D (Ex. 1). The latter (an 'acoustic' scale form) is invested by Bartók with an unequivocal meaning through its allied text-content and its integration in the overtone system: it is the symbol of purity, Nature, and the world drawn 'only from a pure source' (alternatively translated, 'from cooling mountain springs') which exists after the transformation (Ex.2, III, bars 72–83).

Other important tonal centres, or complexes of centres, are C♯–E (narrative: the nine youths), B♭–E (C♯) (the hunt and the transformation), G (first tenor aria in the second movement)

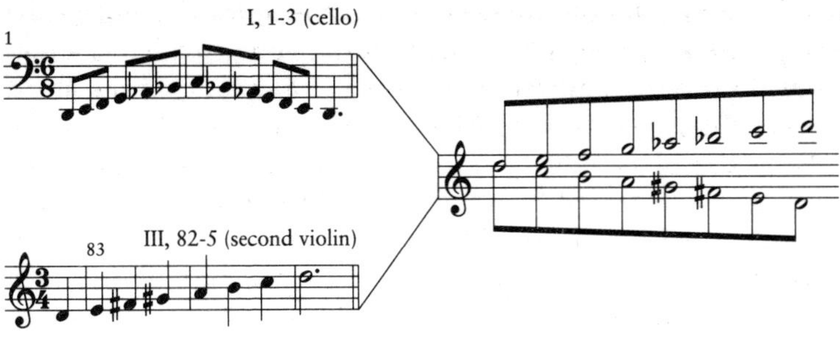

EX. I

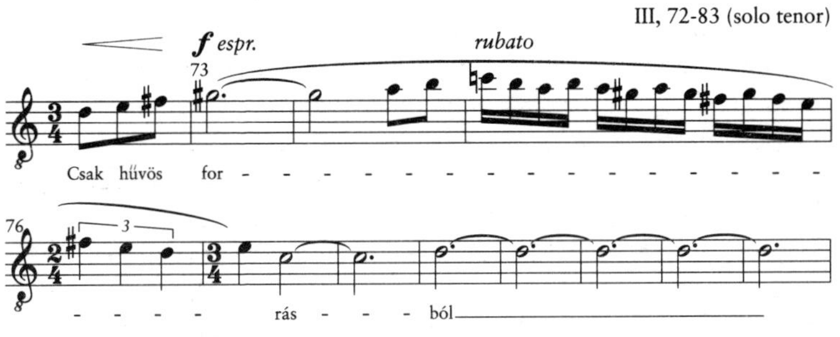

EX. 2

and its pole D♭ (initiating the second movement). A♭ (G♯) and A, function as double dominants, arising from the two forms of the basic D-based scale, as shown in Ex.1. (The D♭–A♭ connection (C♯–G♯ enharmonically) is also important.) In its tonality, motivic material and formal ternary structure the opening *molto moderato* section of the first movement presents all the basic potentialities of the composition. In particular, the motivic relationship between the 'hunt' theme, the music of metamorphosis and the themes of this *molto moderato* gives the unity to the first movement as a whole.

Scholars have interpreted the overall form of the *Cantata profana* in different ways. József Ujfalussy discerned a four-movement structure in this cantata, which is veiled by the inclusion of the extended passage of dialogue in the second movement. László Somfai sees the form as a descendant of the

ABA'B' 'large sonata form' of the Second Violin Sonata and the Third String Quartet. Bence Szabolcsi, on the other hand, discovered the five-act structure of the classical drama behind the façade of the three sections:

> Movement 1. Departure from the ancient world, from the myth, from the vegetational background.
> Movement 2. The hunt. Sin, aggression and murder burst into the peaceful primitive world.
> Movement 3. Transformation. The punitive interference of Nature.
> Movement 4. The father finds his sons but they are no longer his sons. Encounter and clash between old and new, human and metahuman. The summons to return home and the rejection.
> Movement 5. Conclusion and recapitulation.
> Apotheosis: triumph of the new, free world.
> Victorious farewell to the ancient world, that of fathers and mothers. 'The lanterns are lit', in vain; victory belongs to the clear sources.[8]

Szabolcsi, who heard Bartók describe the composition as 'his most profound credo', regarded as most important in the structure the principle of conclusion and recapitulation: that is, the element of Bartók's concept which differed from the folk source. Szabolcsi went so far as to see behind Bartók's inclination for summarizing or reiterative closing movements[9] the inspiration of such great religious pieces of the eighteenth and nineteenth centuries as the 'Gratias agimus' from Bach's Mass in B minor, the Kyrie from Mozart's Mass in C minor, the Kyrie from Mozart's Requiem (all three of which Bartók heard in his youth), or the 'Libera me' from Verdi's Requiem. He held that it was this inspiration that could resolve the *contradictio in adiecto* character of the title '*Cantata profana*'. In Szabolcsi's view this also explained the passion-quotation at the beginning of the work, and took account of the way in which 'in Bartók's hands the great curse-poem of nature turned into a hymn of man'.

The interpretation of Tibor Tallián is based on the ethnological quality and function of the text.[10] He saw the *colindă* used in the *Cantata profana* as a tribal myth of initiation. The mode of initiation is the transformation to an animal state, and the conflict can be grasped as being between those to be initiated and the older generation. The mythical conflict of generations explains a conspicuous feature of the structure of the text, the double hunt. The first hunt was the work of the father, with his bestial, demoniacal, sacral faces. He had cajoled his sons out of his house so that they would become independent men. The second hunt was that of the human-faced father, the father who was ready to shoot at his sons because he did not want to accept the state of old age. With a reference to the figure of Hans Sachs, Tallián also recognizes that in this double hunt, 'the young stags vanishing in the forest and the father who is left behind – they are all Bartók himself. That is why the final conclusion of the work is tragic.'[11]

The central message of initiation is always ritual death and resurrection to a new life. Since as an initiation myth, the winter-solstice *colindă* arranged into music by Bartók is one of those transitional rites which lie at the core of great transcendental religions, it is evident that the symbols of the *colindă*, like those of any typical New Year myth, speak in the idiom of passion symbolism. In other words, there appears in it the sacrifice myth of a religion that has come down to us in fragments, and the story contains the double spiritual moments of punishment and redemption, impurity and purification. Bartók's references to Bach's *St Matthew Passion* in the opening bars of this cantata have truly deep ethnological roots. In Tallián's train of thought the fact that in ancient times initiation into society became abstracted into mythology and the practice of *mystery* religion, has a far-reaching significance which leads directly to Bartók's music. Certain models of the *mystery* have – whether structurally or in a concrete pictorial fashion – been recurring repeatedly in art since the time of mythical cultures. The arch of transitional rites with its five sections (breaking away from customs, initiation into the sacral, transition, breaking away from the sacral, return on a higher plane to customs) is, therefore, something of an archetype of Bartók's most specific form of the palindrome (as seen in his Fourth and Fifth String Quartets, Second Piano Concerto, and Second Violin Concerto), which involved not only the inverted order and mirror inversion of the themes in the recapitulation but also the transubstantiation of the material.

The need for a constructive geometric form, in accordance with the tendency of modern art towards the rationalization of structure, was transmitted to the young Bartók by György Lukács, through his writings on modern drama, and by Béla Balázs, through his mystery dramas. The document of Bartók's first encounter with such formal ideas was *Duke Bluebeard's Castle*, which Tallián interprets as an initiation mystery of an inverted direction (from darkness to light and then back to darkness). It returns in the fairytale-like story of the double initiation, that of man and of woman, in *The Wooden Prince*, where the scene of initiation is – as in the *Cantata profana* – the forest. According to this hermeneutic theory *The Miraculous Mandarin* is also an initiation, having a passion-like ending involving a cruel death and a mourning chorus. As Tallián points out, in this same creative period 'mythological rationality predominates in Bartók's compositional work not only on the plane of the subject but also on that of the organization of material'. He believes that Bartók 'broke down folk music into its basic ingredients: units of intervals, scales and basic rhythms', and built from them a new structure so that 'he projected their fundamental features to an extent which they did not originally possess'.[12] Later, in his great instrumental compositions written from around 1930, he took the geometric, symmetrical forms developed in his youth – which he had in his early stage works used to express a negative attitude to life – and turned them into ideological programmes, as models for constructing, articulating and humanizing of a problematic reality. The open re-emergence of myth in the *Cantata profana* is a declaration of such a programme. Tallián writes: 'It was here that Bartók once again proclaimed in a poetic form his readiness to meet a challenge beyond art (that is, the salvaging of humane values).'[13] And here we have arrived back at our own point of departure: the responsibility of the learned on the eve of Fascism.

Bach's *St Matthew Passion* was mentioned in connection with the beginning of the piece as its background. But in the foreground of Bartók's score a picture of primitive, pagan nature evolves, with the forest being born out of the web of scales. The music creates the inhabitants of the forest through the word of the chorus, which emerges out of the haze of the clusters of scales. Now that the stage has been populated, the first melody can be sounded, one which Bartók had cherished in his memory ever since *Duke Bluebeard's Castle*. The narrative begins: 'Once there was an old man, who treasured nine sons, fair and sturdy . . .' This *più mosso* (from bar 27) is the middle arch of the first formal unit, which unfolds the chorus as an antiphon. The story slowly marches forward in the words of the chorus. The reprise of the surging melody (derived from the forest melody), the pedal point of the timpani and the descending character of the melodic lines all indicate an approach to the boundary of a section, the closing pillar of the first arch in this first formal unit. For the opening minutes the music depicts the figures of the sons, taught naught but 'hill and vale to wander hunting the noble stag' (bars 55–9). At bar 59, immediately following mention of the stag, the scene changes. The forest becomes alive and the hunt begins with a new tempo, new duple metre, new key, and an accompaniment of wild drum beats and horn calls. From bar 74 Bartók introduces a four-part choral fugue – the other Baroque pillar of the composition – involving a wild mood and terrific pace. The forest swallows the swirling group and only their cries and the sound of the hunting horns remain to be heard. Now we can only imagine the chase, but from this moment on we are gradually overcome by a premonition unlike anything else. The sons have reached a bridge and crossed it (bars 164–74). The hunting scene stops suddenly at this culminating point. We have lost our way; the whole world begins to sink around us (represented, from bar 165, by glissando timpani, *portamento* lower strings, horn and harp); the arms of the woodwinds reach out temptingly; the string parts are resolved in rustling; the tam-tam sounds. This is the atmosphere of magic. Here the story of rebirth, or metamorphosis, is depicted: 'All were changed to stags there in the forest shadows' (bars 178–9). The choir hardly dares to utter the words. Everything is lost in a mysterious *piano*; we have arrived at the end of the world. This section closes the first movement. The orchestra recalls ever so softly a descending melodic arch of the forest music heard in the movement's introduction.

The Andante follows the first movement without interruption. These movements are connected not only by the continuous line of one of the parts but also by melodies from the hunt (the fugue subject) and the miracle (the motif associated with the boys going over the bridge). Bartók has good reason for using these former motifs, for it is the boys' father who now takes up his rifle to go hunting, and disappears into the forest. He finds tracks and, not recognizing his sons in the stags, takes aim. The choral section, which persists until the first moments of this encounter, is a film-like recapitulation and montage of the two previous scenes. This new dramatic turn in the action is then emphasized by a change in the tone of the chorus. From bar 38 it starts to recite in the manner of the Evangelist in the *Passion*, and comments like the chorus of an ancient Greek tragedy. The two soloists soon take over the principal roles, and then follow the tenor and baritone arias of the favourite son and the father. This tenor solo (bars 43–95), together with the 'metamorphosis' passages, constitute the *Cantata profana*'s greatest musical contribution. We are suddenly brought face to face with Nature, and hear her voice as the favourite son speaks with the tongues of the trees and the stags. He is given a rubato melody – strange, unique, full of embellishments – and his music seems to depict pointed antler-like branches glowing in a cold light. In the voice of the stag we feel something inexpressible, quite outside human experience, but at the same time profoundly human and reminiscent of the laments.[14] In the father's baritone solo, which is again announced by the chorus-narrator (bars 98–102), we first recognize the figure of the hunter (the melody originates in the first movement's fugue subject), but his words are then strengthened, echoed and softened by the chorus, with its argument for the sons to follow their father home (bars 108–13). The picture of the mother and the home evokes the warmest and most intimate melodic turns of this baritone solo. This kind of lyrical revelation can be compared with that of Bluebeard, in the final section of the opera, when he shows Judith the women of his past made even lovelier by the power of memory. With the words 'the lanterns are lit' (bars 129–31)

Bartók refers to the loves of old by quoting, in reverse direction, the leitmotif of accumulated thirds which he had associated with his own frustrated love for Stefi Geyer back in 1908. Here, too, there is the same resigned, defeated ending. The revelation is interrupted by the sound of trumpets, as if to confirm a decision that was inevitable: behind the monotonously repeated *dolce* baritone motif there is no hope. There is no more need for that wildly emotional tone of rebellion which gave to the first tenor aria such a very human quality (in spite of its abstract 'nature' atmosphere). The boys have come to a decision. They know that there is no way back, and the voice of the second tenor aria comes to the father from beyond the bridge (bars 168–87). The pleading of father and chorus is in vain; and in vain, do they demand an explanation. In the last words of the favourite son the irrevocable determination and judgement sound like a sacred revelation of truth: 'We shall never return, because our antlers cannot pass thy doorway' (bars 193–5). This is something beyond victory and happiness. It is an elevation of spirit which hovers – a union with the stars.

Everything that has happened since the first tenor aria has, in formal terms, comprised the third part of the arch form of this second movement. But with the second tenor solo an anticipation of the overall ternary form of the work is simultaneously enacted. This concealed sense of reprise becomes overt at the start of the third movement when the first line of the cantata's text, 'Once there was an old man', reappears. Yet the starting point of that reprise Bartók had already indicated in an incomplete and condensed fashion both in tonal terms with the passage 'but we cannot go!' (II, bars 186–7) and thematically with 'why not come now?' (II, bars 191–2). This version recalls only the sons' hunt of the first movement, instead of the double hunt. Thereby, in Tallián's interpretation, the moment of actual initiation (of which an important phase is the tempting by the old way of life) becomes the dramatic core of the cantata, separable from the narrative character of the first and third movements with their concentration on the story of metamorphosis. The gesture of softening it all to the level of a fairy tale is undoubtedly there, but this epic character of the final movement is nevertheless not so emphatic as to indicate the meaning of 'return on a higher plane to customs' (as suggested by the arch of transitional rites referred to earlier).

In my opinion, and that of Bartók's contemporaries, the fundamental message of the *Cantata profana* is more than one of pantheistic integration, as it is concerned ultimately with the tragic gesture of breaking away, with representation of a point of no return which has been raised to a transcendental sphere. The great example given by the stag sons to the world becomes part of the chorus's narration of eternal truths in the third movement. Now it is clear that the tale is about ourselves, living in a world in which fathers fail to recognize their sons and take arms against them, living in homes in conditions of servility and compromise, living in freedom only if we abandon both home and family. In return, we cannot hope for human happiness, but can discard this shocking veneer and drink from a pure source, thereby taking on the true garment of the soul. The last line of the tenor's solo, 'from cooling mountain springs' (Ex. 2), which brings the cantata to an end with the notes of the 'acoustic' scale, is part of Nature itself. Within us, however, it becomes the Word. We recognize it as a motto for man as he carries out his life's work, as a command that must be obeyed; for the work itself becomes a magic stag, calling upon us to pursue it until we, too, reach a bridge in the forest of our lives. We have to ask ourselves if we are capable of such a pursuit, and whether it is possible for European art to answer such a call, either then or now.

NOTES

1 *Béla Bartók*, Budapest (Corvina), 1971, p. 273.

2 Letter, Bartók to his mother, 8 September 1903, *BBL*, p. 29.

3 Letter, Bartók to Octavian Beu, 10 January 1931, *BBL*, p. 201.

4 *BBE*, p. 120.

5 *RFM*.iv. The text of the *colindă* in question can be found as 4a, and the melody under 12bb in that study.

6 *Nyugat*, vol.23, no.1 (1930), pp. 60–61.

7 When Universal Edition issued this score in 1934 a poetic German translation of the text, made by Bence Szabolcsi, was provided between the

staves, although Bartók's own literal German translation was also included as a preface.

8 Bence Szabolcsi, 'Bartók Béla: Cantata profana', in *Miért szép századunk zenéje?*, ed. György Kroó, Budapest (Gondolat), 1974, pp. 183–7.

9 As, for instance, in *The Wooden Prince*, Dance Suite, Second Piano Concerto, Third String Quartet, Second Violin Concerto.

10 *Cantata profana – az átmenet mítosza*, Budapest (Magvető), 1983.

11 Ibid., p. 137.

12 Ibid., p. 206.

13 Ibid., p. 210.

14 It was László Somfai who discerned behind the stags' appeal the inspiration of the *hora lunga*, the most amorphous and improvised folk style known to Bartók.

ORCHESTRAL MUSIC

30

Youthful Orchestral Works

GÜNTER WEISS-AIGNER

The Budapest première of Richard Strauss's tone poem *Also sprach Zarathustra* took place on 12 February 1902. According to Bartók's own testimony he was struck 'as by a lightning stroke' by the performance, and was instantly roused from two years of compositional stagnation.[1] He had been disappointed by the strictly traditional teaching of Hans (János) Koessler, his composition professor at the Budapest Academy of Music, and also felt that he had searched in vain for new ideas in the works of Wagner and Liszt. At last he believed he had found a new and extremely promising way in which his own creative output might develop. The twenty-year-old Bartók immediately set to work studying Strauss's scores and, before the year was out, had completed his earliest attempt at writing a piece for orchestra: a symphony in four movements. Three of its movements had been completed in short score by 12 November, and the last was finished on 28 December.[2] This E♭ major Symphony not only reflects the new inspiration of Strauss and the influence of other late-Romantic composers but also contains certain pointers to the national Romantic world of Hungarian music. Most significant of all, however, is the way in which these adopted modes of expression combine to form a network of motivic affinities, which transcends the boundaries of the movements and provides the first large-scale demonstration of Bartók's innate tendency to variation.

Looking at the first movement in thematic terms, it is noteworthy that three of its four themes draw on the same rhythmic impulse. This jagged, rhythmic motif leaps out, as it were in syncopation, from the very first crotchet of the piece. Ex. 1 shows the movement's main theme, in which Bartók, with the stark simplicity of a woodcut, echoes that type of fanfare found in Strauss's *Ein Heldenleben* or *Don Juan*.

EX. 1

The second theme, which develops into a lilting waltz, extends to a typical 'waltz syncopation' at its melodic climax. (Bartók had been familiar with this dance rhythm at least since his Scherzo (Fantasie) of 1897.) The third theme initially soars upwards but then, supported by dramatic trilled chords, ends in a declamatory gesture in the style of Liszt. The fourth theme (from bar 105) remains close to the ascending melodic contour of the minor third (augmented second): its four-bar kernel begins on B♭ and is repeated on C♯ (from bar 109) and E (from bar 113), as shown in Ex.2.

EX. 2

Bartók's creative attentions were directed first and foremost toward the first theme (Ex. 1), especially at the jagged, upward-driving figures (bars 1–2, 5–6) and the 'rolling' movements of semiquavers (bars 4, 6). These latter movements are then passed imitatively to other registers, are augmented rhythmically and are finally combined in a counterpoint of original and augmented forms. The development (with which the sketch of the opening movement ends) is used by Bartók to plunge back immediately to these opening upward figures and rolling movements through a series of fresh attacks on the material. The other themes are not reworked, however.

The following slow movement allows us to see the variational aim behind the work's formal structure even more clearly, but there are also some interesting stylistic excursions. In the first of three clearly demarcated sections, an eight-bar theme is stated, the beginning of which is based on a type of melody then widespread in Europe. Into its melodic return, however, Bartók weaves those ascending upward curves with which he had already become acquainted in Schumann's works and experimented in his own String Quartet in F major of 1898. Repetitions of the theme, motivic transformations and rhythmic diminutions dominate this first section. A dotted figure (from bar 43, Ex. 3), already hinted at earlier, introduces the stylistic shift to the 'Hungarian' central section.

EX. 3

The syncopation, originally found at the end of the second bar of the movement, accordingly acquires a specific stylistic significance. It continues to leave its mark on the music through the expanded dotted figure found at bar 46 (final bar of Ex.3) and following variants, which approach to the basic rhythmic structure of the fragmentary Piano Quintet (1897) and would lead directly to certain of the themes in the symphonic poem *Kossuth* (1903).[3] The 'Hungarian' nature of this passage is also revealed melodically, in the motifs found in bar 43. The recapitulation of the opening material is used by Bartók to write a simultaneous variation of its basic figures; the motivic endings found here reveal rhythmic traits which frequently recur in *Kossuth*.

The theme of the third-movement scherzo was inspired by the 'Tanzlied' from Strauss's *Zarathustra*, although the initial motivic repetitions are also in sympathy with Mendelssohn and Brahms. It is notable, however, that Bartók again introduces the (quasi-Hungarian) closing formula of two quavers followed by a crotchet. He pays lip service to the traditions of the scherzo, with long series of crotchets before the entry of the theme itself, with the culmination in a fugato in the later course of the movement and also – in keeping with his Straussian model – with complex superimpositions of rhythms which even extend into the trio with its simple melody.

The main features of the finale, which runs to no fewer than 638 bars, are its thematic links with the first and second movements, the adoption of the idea of a fugato from the scherzo, and its complex formal design. The initial theme here follows the melodic contours of the slow movement's main theme. Stylistically Bartók is striving to achieve a Hungarian colouring through the sombre minor mood, which is further intensified by the augmented interval in the second melodic arch E♭ D C♭ A♭. The second theme (from bar 18) clearly takes up the fourth theme from the first movement, but by bar 22 is veering surprisingly towards a melodic line from *Zarathustra*. In the third theme (from bar 32) we again find the rolling movement, which is here linked to the rhythmic cadential formula of two quavers plus crotchet. Unlike the first movement, the finale begins with an introductory exposition of all three themes, which are linked together contrapuntally in pairs. (The third theme even assumes the role of main theme of an 'internal' exposition, where both it and the secondary theme are rhythmically diminished and smoother.) This final movement demonstrates all the compositional techniques of Bartók to this time, but now strongly stamped with Strauss's influence. These techniques include the formation of thematic variants, the splitting up of motifs, skilful motivic developments, imitation and the overlapping of thematic entries. In a coda-like recapitulation Bartók attempted to combine structural elements from the introduction and the first subject group. A newly formulated fugato in the development emerges out of rhythmic particles of the 'internal' secondary theme (see above), pointing the way towards the stylistic world of *Kossuth* with its *csárdás*-like rhythm. Broad tonal relations within the movement indicate Bartók's renewed interest in third connections, as, for instance, between the main and second themes: E♭ minor and B major (exposition); E♭ major and G major (recapitulation).

Of course, Bartók himself considered only the scherzo was worth saving, but it was in the other movements that his compositional ideas were more developed and his aspirations to create a new kind of national Hungarian music were more in evidence. The powerful incentive behind his thinking at this time was what Bartók later called 'that well-known chauvinistic political trend',[4] which had been growing in strength in the country since the celebrations of its millennium in 1896. In particular, those celebrations had brought back to public attention the great revolutionary hero of the abortive War of Independence of 1848–9, Lajos Kossuth. The young Bartók took up this nationalistic trend as a personal challenge. Anti-Habsburg slogans appear in his letters, he refused to use the German language and donned Hungarian national dress – all outward signs of an inner search for artistic roots in historic, Hungarian soil. In his symphonic poem *Kossuth* he looked with an idealized gaze upon that heroic Hungarian past, and sought to plot the changing fortunes of the Hungarians in their struggle for national independence. He personally identified with the tragic defeat of the Hungarians in 1849, seeing in the national grief and hopelessness of that time a reflection of his own current inner loneliness and depression.

Bartók's orchestral portrait of the figure of Lajos Kossuth was modelled upon Richard Strauss's hero in *Ein Heldenleben* (1897–8). In orchestration, too, he was largely indebted to Strauss's work, which he knew so well that he could perform it from memory at the piano. These various elements drawn from Strauss encounter a considerable number of Hungarian thematic or motivic forms in *Kossuth*, and also in Bartók's other piano and chamber works from the year 1903.

EX. 4

The main theme (Ex. 4) represents Kossuth's character, as identified by Bartók himself in the programme notes found in the score. This theme is the result of a variational process of growth, the rhythmic basis of which had already been evident in his works for a number of years. The dotting of figures is now found even in the opening A minor triad and at the theme's conclusion, which both help to reinforce the tortured Hungarian style. The rolling semiquaver figure, already seen in the Symphony, is linked in this opening theme with the dotted ending (see bars 5–6) and is developed in the theme's continuation (bars 6–8) until the dotted figure comes to predominate (bars 9–11). The music steers towards the second theme via two modified versions of this first theme, from which the embellishing figure (early in bar 4 of Ex. 4) increasingly stands out. The second theme, 'What sorrow lies so heavily on thy heart, dear husband?' (from bar 29), introduces Kossuth's wife (the equivalent of 'the hero's companion' in Strauss's work). This theme is characterized by syncopations, sharpened *à l'hongroise* at the beginning, and by the long–short / short–long formula typical of the national style at the end (bar 31). (This latter figure, however, assumes an unmistakable overtone of *Zarathustra* when it occurs again, at bar 35). Kossuth's answer, drawing on his opening theme, rises up contrapuntally from the depths. The syncopated texture grows denser and more excited, leading to a *stringendo* and introduction of the third theme (bar 50), 'Danger threatens the fatherland', in which the dialogue is reduced to a development of the initial motifs of both earlier themes. Woven into the dying strains of this dialogue are descending main-theme dotted figures, snatches of which are repeatedly heard. Initially, however, these figures culminate in a nostalgic glance backwards: 'A better fate then was ours' (section IV, from bar 71). Beginning in a wistful minor–major, the new theme presents itself in the guise of the Hungarian long–short / short–long rhythmic pattern (bars 71–2), then of the characteristic syncopated figure (bar 73) and, finally, of the dotted ending, which is now expanded to a perfect fourth (bar 74). At the end of the consequent phrase (bar 78) the opening of the first, 'Kossuth' theme returns and the motif of nostalgia, now melodically transformed, quickly grows also more rhythmically pointed. It ends with descending rolling figures – perhaps referring to the improvisations of gypsy violinists – which are also seen in Bartók's Violin Sonata (1903).

When Kossuth voices his feelings once more and his wife senses his grief (bar 88), the political skies cloud over: 'Yet this brief-lived happiness soon disappeared' (section V, from bar 90). It is in this passage that the 'Kossuth' motif is subjected to its most radical transformations, although without threatening its essential rhythmic and melodic identity. Now, with the rising diminished seventh (B–A♭) in bar 92, the 'adversary' is introduced and heralds disaster with its jagged, sharply articulated figures. It seeks to penetrate the 'Hungarian' motif. This challenger meets his match in the Hungarian general, over a churned-up potential battlefield of motifs. At bar 116 Kossuth briefly recalls the better times of old (themes from sections V and IV are played simultaneously) before summoning his forces 'To the battlefield!' (section VI, from bar 123). In this section the 'Kossuth' motif appears free from dotted rhythm in an *alla breve* metre that brings it close to a *csárdás* dance. The wife's theme is taken up *fff* at bar 146, eventually leading into the seventh section, 'Come, oh come, ye haughty warriors, ye valiant heroes!' (from bar 166). Following an oppressive pause, broken only by isolated drumbeats (cellos and timpani, bars 173–7), these warriors enter the fray with a swift, *allegro* movement, taking up the *csárdás* rhythm once again and introducing what is the last substantial new theme of the work (lower strings, from bar 178). Ex. 5 shows this theme in a slightly varied form, as it appears at bars 195–7.

To the accompaniment of a swelling drumbeat more and more instruments enter this theme's fugato, ready to do battle,

bars 195-7 (strings)

EX. 5

but their movement is gradually reduced to imitations of the concluding fourth interval of Ex. 5, which is finally elongated to become their 'holy oath to fight to the last breath' (bars 264–5). But gradually their confidence in victory begins to die away. After a deathly silence (bars 288–9) the real enemy approaches (section VIII), represented by a minor version of the Austrian national anthem, 'Gott erhalte', a hated piece of music in Hungary at this time. Bartók was, no doubt, encouraged to pen this musical battle of national anthems by Tchaikovsky's *1812 Overture*, with its quotations from the Russian Tsarist anthem and the French *Marseillaise*. After a series of imitative entries the Austrians' motif advances powerfully in the bass, but is immediately attacked by the Hungarians. At bar 319 the 'battle' motif from section VII appears in a new, more hurried form, which leads back to its original form, but now played twice as fast (from bar 322). If the broadening of the theme suggests military ascendancy then the Hungarians clearly win in this battle (see E♭- and F-based bass entries at bars 350 and 362), but they soon find themselves faced by the hero's earlier 'adversary' from happier times (section V). Kossuth still appears confident, as the enemy prepares for the final onslaught. This begins uncannily quietly at bar 393, with the 'adversary' on the Austrians' side, forceful and solid (from bar 398). In spite of the Hungarians' resistance (*più agitato*, from bar 402), the enemy's superior numbers take their toll. The Hungarians' signal for battle becomes increasingly short-breathed until their forces are scattered and put to flight, as depicted by the rolling semiquavers in bars 406–7. The Austrian anthem is triumphantly played (bar 408) but subject to dissonant distortions by Bartók. The 'Kossuth' motif sinks down embittered at the sight of the survivors fleeing 'before the vengeance of the victors' (Ex. 6).

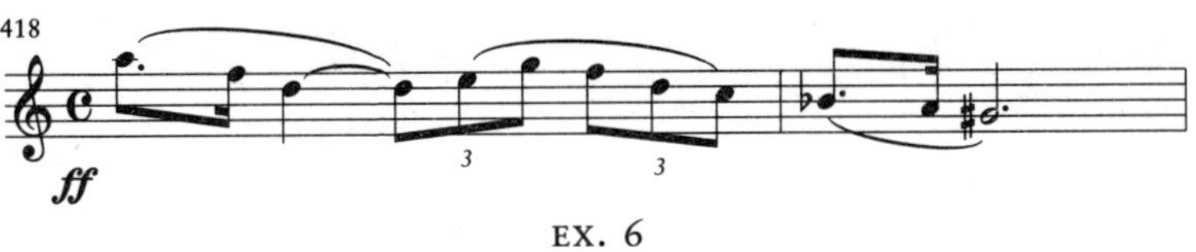

EX. 6

The intervallic inversion is used here (bars 418–19), as also with the 'battle motif' (bar 426). Now that 'All is finished' (section IX), only deep mourning remains. There is a sombre review of the national forces, presented in a slow march: Kossuth himself (bar 438), then his troops (bar 450). The improvisatory figure, once so powerfully articulated, now dies away as a lament (from bar 463). And then, beneath the pressure of a pitiless foe, grief itself ebbs away and 'A hopeless silence reigns' (section X).[5]

Bartók saw this work as a national confession. He felt it was his duty to write something specifically Hungarian in his music,[6] and sought to fulfil this self-appointed task by using the broadest range of compositional techniques at his command and also by drawing freely upon Strauss's music for additional inspiration. To his task he brought, in particular, that ability to vary motifs and themes which was immensely valuable in such highly programmatic music. Also noteworthy in *Kossuth* is the practice of sequencing by successive minor thirds,[7] which is already observable in the Symphony (1902) and in Scherzo, the fourth of the Piano Pieces which he wrote in 1903.

Kossuth was sketched in April and May 1903 and orchestrated between June and August. It was first performed by the Budapest Philharmonic Orchestra, conducted by István Kerner, on 13 January 1904 and, by and large, hailed by the press as a national event. (A handful of Austrophiles did, however, take exception to the distortions of the national anthem.) There was as little agreement on the extent to which the work was influenced by Strauss as there was on the subject of its 'Hungarianness'.[8] Individual exception was taken to certain 'temerities' and 'excesses *à la* Berlioz'.

Liszt's piano works often appeared on Bartók's concert programmes at this time, and it would appear that he felt an affinity with his famous predecessor. With his Rhapsody (1904), Bartók made a clear decision to adopt Liszt's concept of the rhapsody and also various national aspects of his compositional practice. Originally this work was conceived for solo piano, but Bartók then expanded it for piano and orchestra. (Later he entrusted that form to two pianos, and then once again presented it for one piano.)[9] In Bartók's own final scheme of opus numbering it was recognized as 'Op.1'. The orchestral version proved a failure when it was first played at the Rubinstein competition in Paris, in 1905, but Bartók then revised it and it was given the first of a series of successful performances by Bartók himself in Budapest on 15 November 1909. Jenő Hubay conducted the orchestra of the Academy of Music on this occasion.

When Bartók expanded the Rhapsody he took the opportunity to extend the processes of thematic variation. Most noticeably, he extended the range of the opening motif of the work from the piano solo's perfect fifth (Ex. 7a) to a dissonant, major seventh (Ex. 7b).

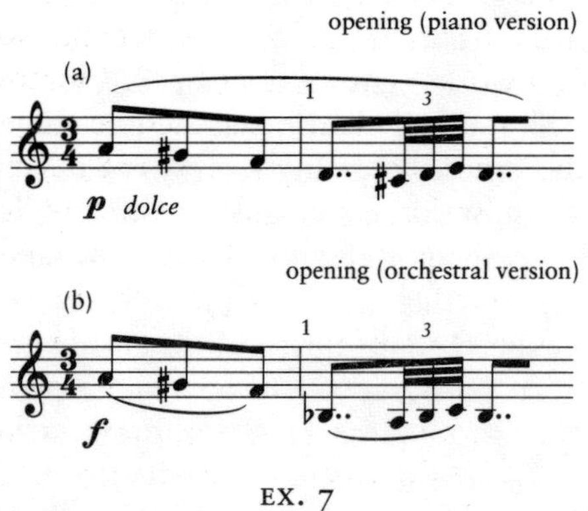

EX. 7

Bartók retained the joined two-movement design of slow–fast found in the piano version, but expanded the opening of the work by admitting an orchestral prelude in which the main theme enters twice, followed on each occasion by a cadenza-like fantasia for solo piano (bar 5 and fig.1.4). There are, otherwise, very few large-scale compositional changes, although various 'corners' of the music are re-worked.

More diverse stylistically was the Scherzo (originally entitled 'Burlesque') for piano and orchestra which Bartók also wrote during 1904, and incorporated into the list of his compositions as Op.2. This work was neither performed nor published during Bartók's lifetime, and only received its première on 28 September 1961 in Budapest, with Erzsébet Tusa as soloist. The Symphony Orchestra of the Hungarian Radio and Television was conducted by György Lehel in that performance.[10] The Scherzo Op.2 is the most idiosyncratic and therefore, perhaps, the most interesting orchestral work from this early period of Bartók's creativity. In it, his struggle to incorporate elements of Hungarian and Western styles finds even more urgent expression than hitherto. The work is characterized by many stark contrasts: bold harmonic advances against the simplest of traditional chordal progressions; subtle motivic formulas against strident tonal gestures that border on the trivial; the grotesque, 'burlesque' impulses drawn from Strauss against a concept of thematic ambivalence, probably drawn from Liszt's 'Faust' Symphony. In this work, too, lie the seeds of the demonizing distortion of 'ideal' shapes which was to become such a potent force in Bartók's works written in 1907–8. Moreover, Bartók's own idea that all musical elements should be subjected to constant change becomes increasingly apparent during the course of his Op.2. Unmistakable, too, is an echo of his rhapsodic plan, where emotionally stated *verbunkos* formulas then return in a form well adapted to the quick, *csárdás* style.

Bartók's Scherzo Op.2 provides further evidence of an imaginative strategy of variation which he had already essayed in the final two movements of his Piano Quintet, written between October 1903 and July 1904.[11] The plan for his Rhapsody Op.1, too, is also related to these two other works of the time. In his Op.2 four thematic ideas are sufficient for Bartók to generate the series of variations necessary to fill out the two basic, scherzo parts of the work. His fundamental idea of contrasting Western and Hungarian styles, and of separating them with the central trio section (bars 498–596), is shown most graphically in the contrast between the $\frac{6}{8}$ metre of the first part (including occasional hemiola implications) and $\frac{2}{4}$ metre of the 'da capo' section. The thematic material is subjected to fantastic variations between the Scherzo and its 'da capo' form. The theme found at the start of the Scherzo proper (Ex. 8a, from bar 104), for instance, reappears later at the start of the 'da capo' in a distorted, whole-tone form (Ex. 8b, from bar 597); the original instrumentation of first violins is now replaced by a combination of the shrill E♭ and A♭ clarinets.[12]

EX. 8

If the *csárdás* pretensions tend to be somewhat pushed aside in the 'da capo' by Bartók's fixation with grotesquerie, he none the less gives them plenty of scope in the first scherzo section, as in the passage from bar 303, where the opening theme of the work is brilliantly worked up in a *rubato, poco a poco accel.* passage.

Bartók concludes his Scherzo Op.2 with an accelerated coda (*allegro vivace*, from bar 847), but this is briefly interrupted by a peaceful dialogue between piano and solo violin (from bar 944), reminiscent of the trio. Most importantly, the first scherzo section is preceded by a slow introduction (bars 1–103) which expounds a *verbunkos* idea in late-Romantic guise. The introduction is also significant in that the 'Hungarian' fourth, which is so prominently expressed in the Scherzo (E♭–B♭ on piano and timpani, from bar 476), had already been integrated into the B♭–E♭ upbeat formula found at bars 74–5 (first trombone) of the introduction.

Given the wealth of ideas in this Scherzo, we must return to investigate why it was never performed by Bartók. The première performance was certainly planned for 15 March 1905, during a concert at which István Kerner was conducting the Budapest Philharmonic Orchestra. (Kerner had already conducted the premières of *Kossuth* and the 1902 Scherzo.) But at the first rehearsal Bartók found the orchestra unprepared and contemptuous of his new work. It is reported that he left the rehearsal hall, slamming the door behind him, and refused to allow the work to be performed. Neither Bartók nor any other pianist found any need to return to this stylistically transitional work, and it would probably have become just a footnote of history had it not been rediscovered by Denijs Dille among Bartók's papers during the late 1950s.

NOTES

1 *BBE*, p. 409.

2 Only the third movement, a Scherzo, was orchestrated. This was done as an exercise in orchestration for the Academy examinations of mid-1903. It was performed in Budapest on 29 February 1904, but met with little response. It was not until 1959 that the Symphony was discovered by Denijs Dille among Bartók's papers. Dille orchestrated the other movements – Bartók himself had started to orchestrate the first movement – but this score remains unpublished. A complete performance of the work, in Dille's orchestration, took place in Budapest on 30 October 1968 under György Lehel's direction. A recording of the Scherzo movement may be found on Hungaroton LPX 11517.

3 See, *Kossuth*, bars 3, 418 and 450, for instance.

4 *DB*.ii, p. 114.

5 From sections IX and X Bartók extracted a *Marcia funèbre* for piano solo, DD75b, which he had privately published in 1905.

6 See, for instance, *BBL*, pp. 28–31.

7 See, for instance, the succession of entries at bars 50–59 (A C E♭ F♯), bars 343–6 (B D F A♭), bars 450–55 (C E♭ F♯ A).

8 See the collected reviews in *DB*.i, pp. 30-63.

9 For a more detailed account of the Rhapsody Op.1, and specifically of its solo piano version, see my chapter 'Youthful Piano Works' in this *Companion*.

10 A recording of the Scherzo Op.2, with Tusa, Lehel and the Budapest Symphony Orchestra is found on Hungaroton LPX 11517.

11 For an account of this work see my chapter 'Youthful Chamber Works' in this *Companion*.

12 A further variant of this theme in the coda (from bar 847) combines these high clarinets with the original first violins.

31
Two Orchestral Suites

MALCOLM GILLIES

Bartók's first five opuses fall awkwardly between his apparent coming of age as a composer in 1904 and his successful adoption of folk music as a root inspiration for his composition around 1908. These five works, all written for orchestra, were later a frequent source of embarrassment to him, either because of their compositional shortcomings or because of their very popularity compared with his more recent, more radical compositions. His Scherzo Op.2 (1904), for piano and orchestra, and original Op.5, a Violin Concerto (1907–8), were withdrawn even before they reached a first performance. The Rhapsody for piano and orchestra Op.1 (1904–5) and First Suite Op.3 (1905) did gain reasonably frequent performances from 1909 onwards, but regularly caused confusion for listeners and critics between their Hungarian Romantic style and the Hungarian folk-based style, which predominated in Bartók's works starting with his Fourteen Bagatelles Op.6 (1908). In 1918 Bartók would state that he considered these two works of no real musical significance, but by 1935 had come to recognize the Op.3 Suite, at least, as 'an outstanding achievement for a young man of 24'.[1] Bartók's insecurity about his Second Suite Op.4 was more deep-seated, taking hold even before he had completed it. After drafting three movements in late 1905 he put the work aside and only returned to write its fourth, final movement in mid-1907. By that time his folk-music experiences were already undermining his former Romantic style so fundamentally that no stylistic return was possible. Like Schoenberg in the final movements of his Second String Quartet Op.10 (1907–8), Bartók had at this same time also sensed the attraction of another sound world. Bartók's Second Suite was poorly received and little played, but ever remained in his affections because of its historical significance.

Both Bartók's suites, then, share the common heritage of that diversity of stylistic characteristics which the composer had been accumulating since 1902. To an originally Brahmsian base he had grafted important aspects of Strauss's symphonic poems and Liszt's large-scale works, and further added recognize Hungarian national features, drawn from patriotic compositions of Liszt, Mihály Mosonyi and Ferenc Erkel, and from stylized *verbunkos* and *csárdás* dances, popular songs and gypsy embellishment figures.[2] Although Bartók would later reject so much of this Romantic Hungarian legacy, many of the compositional strategies worked out in his two suites would be invoked repeatedly in his compositions over the following forty years.

Bartók's two suites show different approaches to non-soloistic writing for orchestra. His thinking for the five-movement First Suite was along symphonic lines, while he thought of the four-movement Second Suite as more of a serenade (by which title he called this work while composing it). The First lasts for almost forty minutes and is for large orchestra; the Second, lasting about twenty-five minutes, is for a smaller, late-Classical period orchestra. In the domain of pitch constructions, his concern was primarily with thematic connections in the First, and upon motivic connections in the Second. His formal concept for the First was a multi-movement one, with strong thematic links between the various movements resulting in an overall impression of an extended sonata form, of the sort pioneered by Liszt; with the Second Suite he paid more attention to the balance within individual movement forms, whether sonata or ternary.

Within the ambit of these generalized polarities, many shifts, developments and continuities of compositional technique are evident. In both works the dominating influence in orchestration is Richard Strauss, as seen in the use of finely divided string sections, E♭ and D clarinets and closing solo violin passages in several movements. Strauss's previously strong influence over Bartók's forms and themes is waning, however, in comparison with Liszt's. Brahms's influence, too, is increasingly moving to the background, and is probably now much mediated by the Brahmsian style of Bartók's colleague Ernő Dohnányi.

Bartók's own originality is most evident in that movement type with which he had the most experience by this time: the scherzo. His humorous, whimsical treatment of this movement type, with frequent distortion of theme and motif, is seen in both the third movement of the First Suite and the second movement of the Second. In treatment of rhythm and tempo Bartók's originality is also noteworthy, as he instinctively develops the potentialities of those free (*rubato*) and strict (*giusto*) rhythms which would so characterize his later folk-influenced works. Those potentialities are best seen in the final two movements of the Second Suite. The later suite also shows Bartók's increasingly radical approach to interval usage. Whereas the First Suite places much emphasis on the 'dissonant' interval of the major seventh, in the Second Bartók becomes obsessed with the minor seventh and an attempt to make it consonant. His third, *andante* movement is so saturated with the descending motif, E C♯ A F♯ (Ex. 1), that Bartók ends up presenting the seventh note, E, as a consonance in the final F♯-minor chord.[3]

EX. 1

Bartók himself saw this as an historic move. In 1928 he commented: 'the ice was broken: from that moment the seventh could be applied as a consonance even without a necessarily logical preparation'. In use of interval cycles Bartók's range is extended between the two suites. The First presents occasional whole-tone scales and diminished seventh constructions, while the Second introduces substantial segments of both fourth (Ex. 2a) and third cycles (Ex. 2b).

One common deficiency in both suites was long-windedness, a surprising characteristic in a composer later known for over-

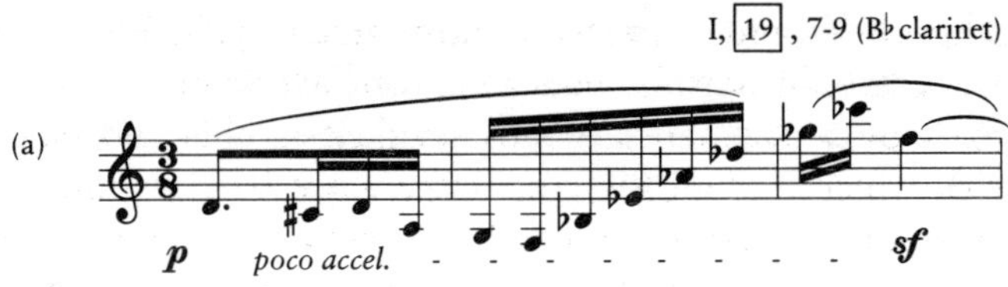

EX. 2

compression and terseness of musical utterance. Bartók certainly worried about the flabby underbelly of these compositions. He came to find these works tedious and, through frequent recourse to Lisztian sequential passages, overly repetitive of unremarkable thematic or motivic material. In 1920, therefore, he effected extensive cuts to the second and third movements of the First Suite, removing several minutes of music; so, too, in 1920 and 1941–3 he revised the Second Suite most substantially and introduced major changes into the second and fourth movements. But despite Bartók's surgery the works remain flawed. Their insurmountable problem is that their forms do not arise naturally from their contents but present themselves as pre-arranged shells awaiting their sometimes grandiose fillings. It would take twenty years – until the Fourth String Quartet (1928) – for Bartók to evolve an ultimate, truly original synthesis of form and content.

For both suites he wrote reasonably detailed programme notes.[4] Although the analytical value of such notes is limited by the conventions of the time, which looked upon music essentially through formal–thematic binoculars, Bartók's comments provide a useful starting point for any investigation of the broad properties of these works.

The five movements of Bartók's First Suite present the tonal scheme E major, E major, C major, A minor, E major, in association with a fast–slow–fast–moderate–fast pattern of tempos. The thematic connections in the work are underpinned by a basic motif (Ex. 3), which introduces all three notes of the tonic triad.

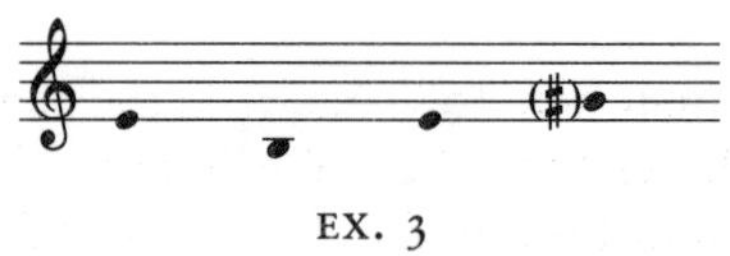

EX. 3

From such a common, tonally strong motif Bartók constructs a web of specific themes that touches every movement and is augmented by subsidiary themes of less clear parentage. The American musicologist Halsey Stevens described Bartók's thematic technique as 'a primitive sort of thematic interreference, not in the Franckian manner but somewhat less obviously and, it must be admitted, less efficiently'.[5] As further reinforcement of his thematic web Bartók ensured that, as in a symphony, the first and last movements played the most important roles in expounding and recapitulating the work's variety of themes. His programme notes even used the titles 'Introduction' and 'Finale' to stress these buttressing roles. Bartók strongly viewed his suite as a unity and was, therefore, incensed at the early practice of orchestras to play only a selection of its movements. In 1915 he explained to the directors of the Philharmonic Society in Budapest that 'certain bars of some of the movements cannot be understood unless one has already heard the preceding movements' and condemned their 'zoo' performances of 'anthology' items.[6]

The First Suite's opening movement is bold and luxuriantly scored in the heroic key of E major. It is a stylistic mix very similar to Stravinsky's opening to his Symphony in E♭ major Op.1, also started in 1905. Both have the smell of dutiful lessons in orchestration (with Strauss and Rimsky-Korsakov, respectively), applied to self-conscious, four-square 'international' thematic material, to which national figurations are later occasionally added. Bartók's formal sections are as aurally obvious, following this design:

	(Exposition				Development		Recapitulation)	
Fig.:		5	10	18	24	29	32	36.5
Theme:	I	II	I	III	I	I	II	I
Key:	E	G	G	c/C	C	C/E	E	E

FIG. I

The tonal movement here to C major in the centre of the movement loosely follows that of the entire Suite. The most significant supporting motif is found at fig.5, where Bartók introduces the ascending major seventh, in dotted rhythm, which will recur most prominently in the second movement. Of the various ethnic features the most intriguing is the slipping between minor and major third, which occurs first at fig.18, in the accompaniment to Bartók's third theme, and more persistently at fig.20, where it momentarily destabilizes the sense of tonal security.

The suite's second, *poco adagio* movement is more overtly programmatic in intention and more freely constructed than the first. In the composer's own analysis it consists of four 'musical pictures', or only three if Bartók's recommended cuts are adopted. These scenes are joined together by the movement's main theme, itself a version of the second theme of the opening movement. The two themes of the first picture are highly expressive, *rubato* melodies – Bartók's original tempo designation for the movement appears to have been *andante rubato* – played haltingly upon the cor anglais and clarinets, respectively. A Hungarian flavour is injected into their accompaniment by the harps, which imitate the Hungarian form of dulcimer known as the cimbalom. Bartók's second musical picture commences mysteriously at fig.9 with the murmur of muted, *pianissimo*, tremolo strings divided into eighteen distinct parts *à la* Strauss. Against this backdrop Bartók paints a woodwind tune of lamentation, loosely constructed around the work's basic motivic shape (Ex. 3). A further Straussian resonance emerges at its repetition, where the shrill clarinet in D is added to the chorus of lament. Before progressing to his third picture Bartók recalls both his first picture's themes and his main, binding theme. The third picture, which Bartók later omitted, begins shortly after fig.18 and evokes a patriotic, nostalgic mood related to that of the section 'A better fate then was ours' in Bartók's symphonic poem *Kossuth* of 1903. After a further playing of his main theme Bartók presents at fig.27 his fourth picture, a recollection of the first. Here, to end the movement, the solo violin is introduced and plays an eerily distorted version of the main contours of the movement's opening theme. Such soulful, solo violin coda passages are common in Bartók's writing at this time.[7] His own analysis poetically sums up the movement's final image, with the solo violin 'magically illuminated by the tremolos of the upper strings, as if by the blood-red embers of the sinking sun. A final flash of the main theme – the sun sank!'

The third and fourth movements are less adventurous in formal, tonal and thematic terms. The third is, according to Bartók, a 'jumping dance', a 'wild boisterous Scherzo' solidly in C major, with its main theme following the shape of the work's basic motif. Its originally clear-cut ternary form, with coda, is deformed by Bartók's cuts of 1920, leading to a hurried sense of exit from the first section and a confused join between the return passage and the coda. (This latter cut Bartók only suggested, while all others in the work he requested.) The fourth movement, a *moderato* Intermezzo, begins with a wistful clarinet melody, which again conforms to the work's basic motif. The form is that of theme and four variations, with the theme's unusual construction from four three-bar phrases being the most immediate source of variation, by phrase elongation. To lessen the predictability of the movement's course Bartók introduces sharper-toned interludes after fig.4 and fig.11, and concludes with a humorous dialogue between the phrases of the theme, played lugubriously on the solo horn, and interspersed with *vivo* echoes on woodwind instruments. By this time the original three-bar phrases have been extended to six bars, except for the final phrase, which Bartók runs to fourteen bars.

With the *molto vivace*, fifth movement in E major, Bartók initiates his work's reprise. This takes the loose form of a series of dance-like passages, not dissimilar to the final movement of his Music for Strings, Percussion and Celesta. Little by little material from all preceding movements is recalled, although the fourth movement is less well represented than the other movements. The opening melody, as Bartók himself proudly pointed out in his analysis, is drawn from a moment towards the end of the first movement (fig.32.8–10), which is now developed into a bustling theme for full orchestra. He conscientiously manipulates his themes to transform or distort earlier materials. Ex. 4 shows how he has transformed the opening phrase of the second movement's initial *rubato* melody into the *molto vivace*, second theme of this Finale.

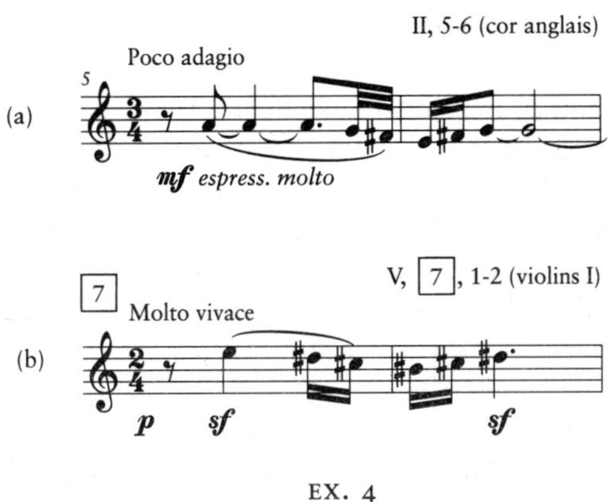

EX. 4

At fig.21.7 there is a similar thematic transformation, of the second theme of the third movement. This melange of themes continues into the work's coda, where (from fig.28) he presents the ultimate synthesis by playing the opening themes of his outermost movements simultaneously. After a short, quiet interlude featuring the solo violin the suite closes with an exact quotation of the final fifteen bars of the first movement.

Bartók's First Suite was premièred in a concert of orchestral 'novelties' in Vienna on 29 November 1905. Probably for reasons of time, in both the concert and rehearsing, the most difficult, second movement was not played on this occasion. Bartók was evidently depressed at hearing his work, but in writing a biographical note soon afterwards allowed no expression of his private misgivings: 'A week ago my orchestral suite, in all its Hungarianness, caused a sensation *in Vienna*.'[8] Despite its late adolescent status the Suite proved an important work for promoting Bartók's compositions abroad. Sir Henry Wood gave an early performance of it on 1 September 1914 in London, which he repeated six years later when the wartime embargo on 'enemy' works was lifted. The work also provided an initial foray into integrated five-movement composition which Bartók would follow up in his Fourth and Fifth String Quartets and in his Concerto for Orchestra.

The Second Suite is conceived on an altogether more modest scale than its predecessor. Bartók's intention of writing a serenade probably owed most to Brahms's two early serenades for small orchestra, Opp.11 and 16, although Dohnányi's string Serenade Op.10 (1902) might have been another influence. He only definitely rejected the title of 'serenade' early in 1908, perhaps following the great success of the Serenade for small orchestra, Op.3, by his younger Hungarian contemporary Leó Weiner at its première in 1907. Bartók's suite reveals a composer increasingly dissatisfied with his existing style and trying to work his new fascination with folk music into his composition. The work's first three movements, written at the end of 1905, still cling, albeit sometimes tenuously, to national Romantic tenets. But between them and the fourth movement, written during the summer of 1907, Bartók did gain the confidence, musically and ideologically, to express something of that rustic simplicity in his own work. As with Stravinsky, returning to complete his opera *The Nightingale* after writing his three famous Parisian ballets, so too did Bartók in 1907 find it impossible to resuscitate in his finale the full stylistic range of his earlier movements. Not only was his love of the peasantry in full bloom during 1906–7 but his dislike of popular urban culture – the breeding ground of his own national Romantic style – had become equally intense. In late 1906 he wrote:

> When I come to Pest next time I'm going to compare the peasantry and the average of the Hungarian intelligentsia! I'm starting to develop a well-nigh pathological hatred toward the latter. Least of all can I understand the thinking of the provincials on the question of the peasants. How can people know so very little about something they constantly see, as a provincial gentleman does about a peasant?[9]

Although the permeation of folk elements is only relatively superficial in the Suite's fourth movement – the pentatonic opening tune and harmonically more spare and static accompaniment – it gave Bartók the impetus to essay bolder experiments in the following year.

In contrast to the variety of forms presented in the First Suite, Bartók's Second Suite invokes only two formal models: ternary form (first and third movements) and sonata form (second and fourth movements). Bartók was little interested in inter-movement connections, although he does create a sense of affinity in texture and tempo between the outer movements through the simple chordal accompaniments featuring the harp. The greater constructive role of motifs is also neatly played out within rather than across the movements. Tonal relations between movements are less clearly established than in the First Suite, with the distantly related tonalities of G major and F♯ minor being found within the outer movements' B♭ majors.

The first movement is constructed around a collection of four motifs, all of which are unveiled within the first sixteen bars of the music. The rich patriotic tone of earlier compositions is played down by Bartók as he develops his various motifs amid a more sparse texture. The quiet opening, featuring solo cello with harp accompaniment, provides a foretaste of the textural understatement which characterizes all but the second movement of the Suite. Of most interest in the movement is the slight middle section of the ternary form, from fig.8, which is largely an outgrowth of the fourth of Bartók's motifs, and the extensive coda, from fig.15, which presents four little studies on various motivic combinations.

Liszt hangs as a continuing influence over the second, *allegro scherzando* movement, and nowhere more than in the wild fugato found at the start of the development. In an autobiographical essay of 1921 Bartók claimed that around 1904–5 the magic of Strauss was evaporating for him, and Liszt's works, such as the 'Faust' Symphony, *Totentanz* and *Années de pèlerinage* were revealing to him 'the true essence of composing'.[10] His model for this fugato appears to have come from the third movement of the 'Faust' Symphony, but was perhaps also conditioned by the fugato of Liszt's Piano Sonata in B minor, which Bartók was playing in concerts during this year. In his analysis Bartók described his fugato passage, the theme of which is shown in Ex. 5, as a 'great raging', and a whirlwind in which 'peculiar chords are wildly thrown about'.

EX. 5

He uses irregular barring initially to reinforce the lurching quality of his theme, but at subsequent entries makes rhythmic modifications to accommodate the theme to a more regular triple metre. The passage reaches its most concerted phase at fig.15, where the lower instruments play the theme in unison, against shrill off-beat punctuations from their upper-range colleagues. Bartók finally jettisons his theme at figs 19–20, by which time it has been thoroughly distorted in both rhythmic and pitch qualities and is being rendered in $\frac{5}{8}$ metre. At this point the original version of the suite contained at least another fifty bars, but in Bartók's revision – now the only version available – he soon moves to his recapitulation, although inverts the order of entry, presenting his secondary theme before his primary. The coda is characterized by a richly Hungarian *ritenuto molto* section, a solo violin rendition of the fugato theme, which gradually disintegrates, and final, *fortissimo* Lisztian chords.

Wagner on the Hungarian Plain is the immediate image presented by Bartók's third, *andante* movement. Its first thirty-four bars for solo bass clarinet are in obvious imitation of the extended cor anglais solo at the opening of *Tristan und Isolde*'s third act. But Bartók appears to be trying to imitate the sound of the Hungarian *tárogató*,[11] and, more specifically, to transform the style of the late nineteenth-century writer of popular song Elemér Szentirmai. Midway through the bass clarinet solo he introduces the motif of falling thirds (Ex. 1), which so dominates the rest of the movement. This is the precursor of the 'love' motif, specifically associated with the violinist Stefi Geyer, which occurs time and again in Bartók's compositions of 1907–10. Even the middle section of his ternary form, from fig.2, is but a display of its potency, as are the final dozen *quieto* bars of coda, which conclude in its simultaneous expression in the famous 'consonant' seventh chord, discussed above.

The discovery of the summer of 1907 by Bartók was the fundamental importance of pentatony in the oldest stratum of Hungarian folk music. The employment of a short, pentatonic melody in the opening bars of the fourth movement (Ex. 6) is a celebration of that realization, rather than anything relating to Debussy, whose music Bartók only appears to have come to know through Kodály later that year.

EX. 6

Bartók's approach to this melody is not a purist one, however. The continuation of the melody on two B♭ clarinets, while retaining the pentatonic outline, does admit non-pentatonic passing notes, and from fig.2 his opening melody is subjected to increasing chromatic distortions. In his development section (from fig.8), the theme is further modified, with the opening falling fourth, for instance, becoming a diminished fifth. In further altered guise it introduces the recapitulation at fig.11.7, amid a 'celestial' Lisztian setting built upon a static second inversion B♭ tonic chord, and does also feature prominently in the coda. Bartók's second subject in this sonata form is not much exposed. Indeed, his later cuts to the work have left hardly more than a vestige of it in the exposition – just four bars from fig.6 to fig.7 – although it does occur more fully in the recapitulation at fig.15 and gains its own 'celestial' setting in the following *molto quieto* passage. The texture of this movement is starkly spare, even compared with Bartók's less than full textures in his earlier movements. There is a good deal of unison or open octave playing, especially on the strings; the rate of harmonic change is frequently very slow. The new Bartók is more concerned to expose solos and to subdue his accompaniments.

Bartók's Second Suite gained him few friends, particularly because of its 'new world' finale and its twisted second movement. That second movement was first performed on its own in Berlin on 2 January 1909. On this occasion Bartók took the podium (for the only time in his life) before the Berlin Philharmonic Orchestra. The audience was deeply split in its verdict. 'Two camps', reported Bartók the following day, 'hisses on the one side, a storm of enthusiastic applause on the other, and I had five curtain calls'.[12] When performed in its entirety in Budapest on 22 November 1909 the suite's reception was chilly and sceptical. The critic of *Pester Lloyd* concluded in the following morning's issue: 'This music is a malevolent, ingenious monstrosity.' Hoping for a more sympathetic appreciation Bartók sent the score to his newly-found friend Frederick Delius during the summer of 1910. Delius ranked the quality of the movements in the order III, I, II, IV. He found the third movement 'tremendously atmospheric', but from his other comments clearly heard too much of Berlioz and Strauss in Bartók's score, composers whom Delius considered 'purely intellectual' and lacking knowledge of 'the soul of music'.[13] Bartók, nevertheless, continued to cherish the work, and, when encouraged in 1941 by Boosey & Hawkes, arranged and revised it to produce the Suite for Two Pianos Op.4b, from which he later drew his final revision of the orchestral version. That two-piano version met with only modest success the few times it was played in early 1942 by Bartók and his second wife, Ditta Pásztory. Its movement titles, however, help to sharpen understanding of Bartók's intentions in his Suite: I. Serenata, II. Allegro diabolico, III. Scena della Puszta,[14] IV. Per finire.

NOTES

1 *BBL*, p. 245.
2 For further description of Bartók's Romantic national style see Vera Lampert's chapter 'Works for Solo Voice with Piano' and the chapters by Günter Weiss-Aigner in this *Companion*.
3 *BBE*, p. 335.
4 *BBí*.i, pp. 51–60, 205–9. These notes are not yet available in English translation.
5 Stevens, p. 260.
6 *BBL*, p. 132.
7 See, for instance, the conclusions of Op.2, the fifth movement of Op.3, and the second movement of Op.4.
8 *BBL*, p. 54.
9 *BBlev*.v, p. 115.
10 *BBE*, p. 409.
11 An instrument originally double-reeded, but from 1900 also manufactured with a single reed.
12 *BBL*, pp. 93–4.
13 *DB*.iii, p. 57.
14 'Scene of the (Hungarian) Plain'.

32

The 'Lost' Violin Concerto

GÜNTER WEISS-AIGNER

A great deal had changed in Bartók's career between the writing of his symphonic poem *Kossuth* in 1903 and the commencement of work on a violin concerto during the summer of 1907. The thunderous applause that had greeted the young composer's demonstration of musical nationalism in *Kossuth* had now died away. That work had successfully caught the mood of large sections of Budapest's population, but now there was scarcely anyone seriously willing to lend an ear to Bartók's artistic aspirations – aspirations which had quickly outgrown the medium of symphonic poem. Bartók perceived an intellectual stagnation hanging over Budapest's cultural life, to which was added his personal disappointment at his lack of success as pianist or composer in the 1905 Rubinstein competition in Paris. A crisis loomed as he sought a release from this depression. Rational and irrational ideas alike combined to produce a tormented state of mind. The feeling of growing isolation made Bartók receptive to the philosophy of Friedrich Nietzsche, which encouraged him 'to rise above everything' and not to allow himself to be affected by anything. His flight from 'bourgeois' desolation led him in other directions: he had just encountered the first traces of autochthonous peasant music, and he now discovered in his rural seclusion that 'lowest' stratum of society which seemed to Bartók to be an integral part of all-embracing Nature. This idealizing attitude towards 'the folk' prompted a growing rejection within him of urban society. The erstwhile herald of a resounding national Romanticism now became the socio-Romantic rebel striking out against injustice, insincerity and ignorance. He was overcome with despair at the prevailing 'system' of human relationships, a despair which was balanced by his yearning for a 'pure and noble society'.[1]

It was at this stage that he came to know the young violinist Stefi Geyer. He felt passionately drawn to her and involved her, no less passionately, in philosophical debate, vainly hoping all the while that love would bridge the evident differences between them. The girl's parting letter of 13 February 1908 marked the inevitable end of a hopeless love, but its artistic fruit had been a highly unconventional work for solo violin and orchestra.

Bartók had jotted down the first 11½ bars of his new work on 1 July 1907, while spending a number of days in the Hungarian provinces in the company of Stefi Geyer and her brother. By January 1908 he had drawn up the plan for a violin concerto of three movements. Its first two movements were already finished and only needed to be orchestrated. Bartók characterized these movements as musical portraits: the 'idealized Stefi Geyer, celestial and inward', and the lively, society artist who conformed to the picture of a 'cheerful, witty, amusing' person. Geyer later recognized in the first movement 'the young girl whom he had loved', and in the second movement 'the violinist whom he had admired'. She saw the work, however, not as a 'proper' concerto, but rather as a fantasy for violin and orchestra. Bartók sought to explain its two movements to her from the viewpoint of pictorial contrast, having by now decided to reject his original idea of depicting the 'indifferent, cool and silent Stefi Geyer' in a third movement (the music of which would have been 'hateful').[2]

Bartók himself called the first movement (an idealizing piece in the spirit of *Tristan und Isolde*) his 'most direct' music to date, which had been 'written exclusively from the heart'. Its forms are melodic, developing variationally and moving in waves. In this way he continued to nurture a method of composition which increasingly clearly reflected in sound his inner vision of the plasticity of all 'natural' growth. The expositional nucleus is formed by the seven bars of the main theme (Ex. 1), which are performed alone by the solo violin. The various parts of this nucleus illustrate musical concerns of Bartók at this time: the diatonic, chordal cumulation of thirds (bars 1–3); scalar

EX. 1

movement, involving some chromatics (bar 4); a two-level pentatonic movement emphasizing the fourth intervals D–G and E–A (bars 5–6); a Hungarian-style syncopation (bar 7). The opening D F♯ A C♯ motif is of central significance to the work, although it appears in several variants. Already in bars 3–4, for instance, its direction and intervallic structure are changed (B♭ G E♭ B♮). He had described its minor form, C♯ E G♯ B♯, as 'your leitmotif' to Stefi Geyer in a letter of September 1907,[3] and its variants recur not only in following letters but also in several piano works written around the painful time of the conclusion of their relationship.[4] Even more far-reaching are certain procedures in these opening bars, which fundamentally affect the melodic *Gestalt* of this 'first portrait'. The D- and B♮-based major-seventh chords unfolded in bars 1–4 are linked together by a short arch figure (bars 2–3), from which the subsidiary theme of bars 7–9 (first violins) is developed. In contrast with the uni-directional leitmotif, this short joining figure, with its twisting motion and intervallic compression (B–F♯, bar 2; G♯–F♮, bar 3), provides the basis for much of the movement's development, and the specific means in the following passage, bars 7–16, for passing the leitmotif between upper and lower lines (C A F♯/ D, bars 9–10, etc.). While all the melodically important elements are clearly distinguishable in the movement's opening passages, the chromatically tight counterpoint which develops from bar 13 introduces a new emphasis on the dotted rhythm (originally found in bars 5–6). These dotted figures relate to scherzo-like ideas which Bartók had been harbouring for some years. They return many times in this movement, as, for instance, at fig.2 and fig.4.

In the formal planning of his works during this period Bartók included not only strict, fugue-like structural models, with themes of varying length, but also free variations involving important tonal and thematic transformations. In this movement of the concerto the first section, played solely by the violins, presents a modified thematic exposition. The second and third entries of the theme are delayed (fig.1 and fig.1.8), so that the solo violin reaches its first melodic climax during the course of the third entry (fig.1.10). The leitmotivic outline is transformed at this point by the B♭ and F♯ octave leaps and their immediately following dotted rhythm. The second section of the movement, from fig.2, involves a slow increase in volume from its opening *pianissimo*, and extends the timbral palette by introducing firstly the woodwind instruments and then the lower strings, which in their turn intone the principal theme in unison. The dynamic is developed, above all, by the solo violin, which descants high above the orchestra until it finally reverts to something of the intervallic outline of the leitmotif in the bar before fig.3. Here the fugal exposition comes to an end. The thematic entries over its course had started on either the tonic (D) or the upper or lower dominants (A or G).

The third section, starting at fig.3, is conceived solely as a number of variations. It involves a vast dynamic arch and draws on all the sound resources of the orchestra. It is the solo violin which takes the lead in expounding the various transformations of the theme. The original form of the leitmotif appears at fig.4 (A C♯ E G♯), although it is preceded by a gapped descending variant at fig.3 (F D [] G). Even more than in the preceding section the solo instrument here expresses itself in complex dotted rhythms, which are further complicated by a series of metrical changes. In tonal terms the opening D centre has been forsaken for F (at fig.3), which then modulates to B (minor) (see fig.4.11). In other words, during this third section the music moves tonally to the opposite (tritonal) pole on the circle of fifths. During the movement's second part A♭ is also established as a tonal centre (at fig.6.1), suggesting a new tonal principle of tritone associations (D–A♭ and F–B) across the movement, in stark opposition to the traditional progressions of perfect fifths (D–A, D–G) established in the fugal exposition.

The middle of the movement suggests both a new beginning and a turning point. At fig.5 the subsidiary theme (which had been held in reserve until now) is reintroduced, combining linearly, however, with elements of the leitmotif and the arch figure. The interweaving of themes and motives here is typical of Bartók's procedure in many of his early works. After entries of the subsidiary theme on the cor anglais and then oboe that theme becomes the basis for a brief imitative section (from fig.5.8) on the strings, with the twisting opening motive being introduced in close succession from lower to higher instruments.

At fig.6 the main theme returns, but soon moves via a series of upward sequences of the leitmotif (descending form) to a powerful climax for soloist and then full orchestra. The last section of the movement begins at fig.7.6 with a variant of the arch figure in the solo violin over a lower-string accompaniment of the main theme. Finally, at fig.8, the solo violin restates the D-based main theme over an accompaniment characterized by the sound of the harps. The closing bars exhibit a sustained *pianissimo* texture, providing only the lightest of chordal support for the solo violin, which eventually dies away as the leitmotif, D F♯ A C♯, achieves final resolution on high D.

The second movement did not become a 'hateful' music, although into the 'cheerful' portrait of the virtuoso postulated by the composer are injected 'witty and amusing' features. It is imbued with impulses already evident in Bartók's earlier output. Released from the world of the scherzo, these impulses point with increasing forcefulness to that sense of burlesque, and the grotesque, which have so often become the goal of deliberately contrasting transformations of material. Bartók's ideas drew particularly on the music of Liszt and Richard Strauss, to which he was clearly receptive during this period of personal turmoil. It was almost to be expected that he would, in this second movement, seek to extend the technique of variation which he had used in the first movement, but to employ it here in an obviously contrasting way.

Bartók's second movement is almost three times the length of the first, in number of bars, and gives him the scope to carry to extremes various processes of thematic transformation, interpenetration and contrapuntal juxtaposition. It is in this movement that the full potential of the thematic exposition in the first movement is realized. Comparison of the openings of the two movements reveals that bar 2 of the second movement (Ex. 2) is directly derived from bar 4 of the first (see Ex. 1), and that bars 3–4 (Ex. 2) are somewhat more freely drawn from bars 5–7 of the first movement (see Ex. 1). Of central importance, too, is a process whereby bars 1–3 and 12–14 of the first movement have prepared for the transformed bar 1 of the second movement (Ex. 2).

EX. 2

Even during the years before this concerto was written this type of jagged opening figure was frequently found in Bartók's output.[5] We now find him seeking more strenuously to come to terms with such figures, both compositionally and psychologically. He had already worked the shape into his First String Quartet Op.7, the opening two-voice motif of which he described as his 'funeral dirge'. In a letter to Stefi Geyer he expressly emphasized its thematic identity with the opening theme of the concerto's second movement.[6]

During this second movement Bartók works to exhaust all possibilities of the jagged figure. The reformulations of its distinctive contour begin as early as the fifth bar, where its first and third crotchets are rhythmically filled out with semiquavers (see

Ex. 2). This transformation leads to further rhythmic 'mirror-image' changes at fig.10.2–3, where the rhythmic infilling now takes place during the weaker beats.[7] The dotted rhythm found in bar 3 of Ex.2 tends toward the popular Hungarian *verbunkos* style, thereby providing further specific characterization of this jagged figure, as at fig.23.5–7. But the number of possible transformations is almost infinite: the extension of the opening parallel sixth movement, at bars 14–15; the complex variation of bars 1–2 at fig.17.19–fig.18.1, where the descending figure of B C♯ D retains the same rhythm and turns into the ascending counter-figure E♯ F♯ D, meanwhile allowing the opening thematic motif to ascend in a simple jagged pattern of quavers C G E B. The arch figure, which had similarly been developed in the course of the first movement is further developed in the second to become a broad subsidiary theme (Ex. 3).

EX. 3

Now Bartók tries various procedures in his attempt to produce a rapprochement between the melodic *Gestalt* of the subsidiary theme and that of the two, alternative main themes of the concerto. The jagged figure, for example, is expressed in triplets at fig.13.5–9 and is 'stretched out' to form a variant of the initial leitmotif; at fig.15.4–5 the arch figure hints at a similar thematic destination. Only toward the end of the movement does the primal relationship between this subsidiary theme and the leitmotif become clear, in the contrapuntal mirror imaging which occurs at fig.34 (Ex. 4). A third, Straussian theme, drawing its inspiration from bar 2 of the opening theme, is also introduced, at fig.15.9 of this movement. It plays only a secondary role in the compositional development, however.

Ever since Bartók's first symphonic attempt in 1902 a

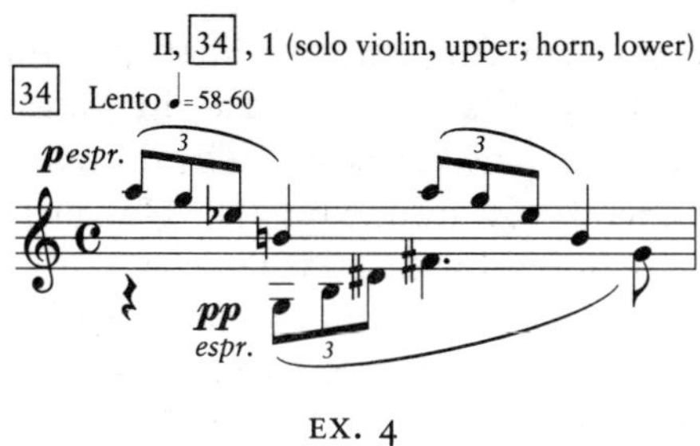

EX. 4

tendency is discernible in his compositions of overlaying traditional sonata form with several transitional thematic sections. That tendency assumed a more definite form in this second movement. Of course, the two passages of development of the subsidiary theme (from fig.12.11 and fig.28) and of the third theme (from fig.15.9 and fig.30) can be interpreted entirely within the return relationship expected between exposition and recapitulation, just as the entry of the main theme at fig.25 (linked contrapuntally with the third theme) can be taken as the beginning of the recapitulation. But the many 'development sections' which begin afresh from the initial motif of the movement can only be accommodated within this sonata-form framework with considerable difficulty. The brief fugato in the middle of the movement (from fig.20) well exemplifies Bartók's free developmental practices; so, too, does the insertion of a brief quotation from the song 'Der Esel ist ein dummes Tier' ('The donkey is a foolish beast') at fig.30.6–8, which simply reflects the composer's memory of happy hours spent singing in the company of the violinist and her brother.[8]

The tonal relationships differ from those of the first movement. Fifth relations are identifiable at certain points of formal juncture, but the centre of G, which is the unequivocal final tonal centre of the movement, is quite frequently veiled through chord alterations and substitutions. Bartók's tendency to tritonal relations, already seen in the first movement, is also observed here: the main theme moves between C and F♯ before modulating to E, from where the subsidiary theme in B♭ is then reached.

Although Bartók retained the same instrumentation as in the first movement he made considerably greater technical demands upon his soloist. The various passages referring to the main and the subsidiary themes repeatedly use double stoppings, from thirds to tenths. At the opening of the movement, too, he calls for a series of brilliant, rapidly ascending diminished sevenths, which lead to a passage where the intended soloist could display that rapid staccato playing which Bartók so admired.

But Stefi Geyer, to whom Bartók gave the manuscript in February 1908, never played the work. Equally unsuccessful were the composer's attempts to have it performed by other violinists. Apparently no longer wholly convinced of the musical quality of the second movement, he decided to combine the expressive first movement with his grotesque first Romanian Dance Op.8a, but later replaced this coupling with another: the first movement (now renamed 'Ideal') was contrasted with an orchestrated version of the last of the Fourteen Bagatelles Op.6 (renamed 'Grotesque'), to produce the *Two Portraits* Op.5.[9] Only after Stefi Geyer's death did the violin concerto receive its première, in the original two-movement version. On the dedicatee's recommendation the soloist was Hans-Heinz Schneeberger, and the conductor Paul Sacher. That performance took place in Basle on 30 May 1958. The work was published the following year by Boosey & Hawkes under the title 'Violin Concerto no.1'.

NOTES

1 For a selection of letters from the 1903-7 period see *BBL*, pp. 20–88.

2 See *DB*.ii, pp. 91–103.

3 *BBL*, p. 87.

4 See Benjamin Suchoff's chapter 'Fusion of National Styles: Piano Literature, 1908–11' in this *Companion*.

5 See, for instance, the opening of his Symphony (1902), bars 92–3 (flute, piccolo), of *Kossuth* (1903), and several instances in the Op.3 and Op.4 suites for orchestra.

6 *DB*.ii, p. 92.

7 These rolling semiquaver figures, seen at fig.10.2–3, would remain a characteristic feature of Bartók's style at least until the time of his Second Violin Concerto (1937–8).

8 The score dutifully places this two-bar quotation in inverted commas and adds the note 'Jászberény, 28 June 1907'.

9 See the following chapter, 'Portraits, Pictures and Pieces', in this *Companion*.

33

Portraits, Pictures and Pieces

MALCOLM GILLIES

Bartók's pre-war orchestral works, the *Two Pictures* Op.10 (1910) and Four Orchestral Pieces Op.12 (1912), are 'melting pot' rather than fully mature works. By the time of their composition Bartók had a good experience of Hungarian, Slovak and Romanian folk music, which he had used effectively to compositional ends in his many piano pieces of 1908–10. He had also, since late 1907, been a devotee of Debussy's music. In these two orchestral works – along with his intervening opera, *Duke Bluebeard's Castle* Op.11 (1911) – Bartók tried hard to bring together these two lines of his recent musical experience. He was encouraged to effect their mutual accommodation because of the similarity he observed between many of Debussy's melodic lines and those found in much East European folk music. But, while *Bluebeard* is a triumph of adaptation to Hungarian medium of that principle of musical recitation which Debussy had forged in *Pelléas et Mélisande*, the *Two Pictures* and Four Pieces are less aesthetically successful. Their different lines of influence have not well combined together. The American composer Halsey Stevens early identified their 'undigested Debussyisms', and even went so far as to point out the 'disaster which might have overtaken their composer' had he continued in the direction indicated by the Four Pieces.[1] Before examining these works, however, some mention is needed of another pre-war orchestral work, the *Two Portraits* Op.5, which Bartók had early in 1911 crafted from two already existing sources.

The *Two Portraits* arose through Bartók's attempt to salvage the best material from his original Op.5, the First Violin Concerto. By late 1910 he appears to have realized the inadvisability of releasing this concerto, which he had written in 1907–8 while besotted with the violinist Stefi Geyer. So he extracted the concerto's first movement, titled it 'Une idéale' and coupled it with an orchestration of the last of his Fourteen Bagatelles Op.6 (1908), a wild Valse which used the same 'love' motifs to represent his lover dancing. This he retitled 'Une grotesque'. The paired caricature, graced with the Op.5 designation, was published in 1911 but appears to have been first performed only on 20 April 1916, by the Opera Orchestra in Budapest under the direction of István Strasser. The violin soloist in the first movement was Emil Baré on that occasion. That first movement, had, however, been independently performed under the title 'Portrait' on 12 February 1911 in Budapest, with Bartók's friend Imre Waldbauer as soloist.

Bartók appears to have remained diffident about his *Portraits* and their very personal inspiration. When asked in 1914 by the American violinist Arthur Hartmann about his works for solo violin he wrote back mentioning his 'most "ineffective" kind of "Romance"'.[2] Thirteen years later, when the English journalist Frank Whitaker asked him about their inspiration, his response was testy; he advised Whitaker that such inspiration was of no importance and that the piece should only be viewed from a strictly musical perspective.[3] Whitaker still concluded, unsurprisingly, that the work represented two different aspects of a woman's character, but did not consider that it might equally represent a woman seen by an artist when in two different frames of mind. Bartók appears not to have actively promoted the work's performance in later years, preferring for orchestras to play his *Two Pictures* Op.10. By the 1930s certainly he was back in friendly relations with Stefi Geyer and would not have wanted unnecessarily to open up old wounds.

The constructions of the *Portraits'* two movements are discussed under the chapters devoted to the First Violin Concerto and the Fourteen Bagatelles, respectively. Here there is need merely to consider the ways in which the *Two Portraits* differ from their original forms. This is primarily a matter of instrumentation and orchestration. The first *Portrait*'s changes are most minor: a shortening of the length of the soloist's final note;

an occasional slight thinning of the orchestral texture, as in the violas and cellos at fig.8.5–6 (bars 95–6); slight differences in placement of performing instructions, or their omission, as with the '*sempre sostenuto*' instruction at fig.8.8 (bar 98). The second *Portrait* is a faithful realization for full orchestra of the original piece for solo piano, with only slight changes to the actual notes of the work, such as the simplification of an original triplet minor-seventh figure to semiquavers at fig.9 (from bar 151, bassoon) and occasional changes in pitch spellings. Bartók's instrumentation is, however, quite distinct from that of the first *Portrait*. To achieve his sense of the grotesque, he withdraws the cor anglais, A clarinet, A bass clarinet and placid solo violin found in the first movement and adds in the sharper sounds of piccolo, E♭ clarinet, B♭ bass clarinet and several percussion instruments. The harps, trumpets and trombones, sparingly used in the first movement, are here also given freer rein. The result is a shrill, hysterical tone, resembling that of Strauss's *Till Eulenspiegel* and even the 'Witches' Sabbath' from Berlioz's *Symphonie fantastique*. This dance could, indeed, be seen as Bartók's answer to the 'Dance of the Seven Veils' in Strauss's opera *Salome*, a work which Bartók admired at this time.[4] The orchestral medium allows him to add fantastic colours to the originally rather gaunt piano version. At fig.11.2 (bar 172), for instance, the original's simple three G♯ quavers are now set in a swirling atmosphere created by the glissandos of the harps, trills, tremolos and harmonics of the lower strings, ringing of the triangle, snarl of the horns and rapid open-fifth oscillations of the bassoons. The movement shows just how much Bartók had learnt from the study of the scores of Debussy, and others, in the three years since orchestrating the first *Portrait*.

That influence of Debussy is more obvious in the *Two Pictures*, which were composed during the summer of 1910. Even the title (originally *Deux images*, in French) seems to have been inspired by Debussy's sets of piano *Images* (1905–7),[5] although, as György Kroó points out, it is the first *Nocturne* for orchestra, 'Nuages' (1899), for which the closest parallels can be drawn with Bartók's first *Picture*, 'In full flower': 'The similarity between these two works is not confined to the pastel colours, the orchestration and tonal system. There is also a similarity in the melody.'[6] Both works begin in $\frac{6}{4}$ metre, with a very quiet, oscillating accompaniment against which descending fragments of melody are introduced. Bartók's initial fragments are less conjunct than Debussy's in their descent, and establish the two scalar elements which are most characteristic of the piece, the pentatonic and the whole-tone. Both works soon then progress to movement in parallel chords. Rhythmically, Bartók's writing is more ambiguous than Debussy's, as a result of his changes of time-signature in each of the first eleven bars. At the other end of this first *Picture*, from fig.12.5, Debussy's influence is also clearly seen in the soloistic play of woodwind instruments against a shimmering accompaniment on strings and harp, with nearly all parts sharing the notes of the whole-tone scale on D.

'In full flower' is formally unadventurous. It has an undisguised ternary form, with an abbreviated return (starting at fig.11) but substantial coda. With the benefit of hindsight the piece can be seen as a testing ground for ideas and atmospheres which would later appear, more successfully, in both *Bluebeard* and Bartók's ballet, *The Wooden Prince* (1914–16). The biting G–A♭ figure on the horns at fig.5 points to the recurring semitone figure of the 'blood' motif in *Bluebeard*; the interlocking fourths, C♯ G♯ A E, at fig.6.3, suggests the C G A E pattern of Judith in the 'Lake of Tears' episode of the opera. The horn melody, which commences the middle section of the ternary form, in rhythm and mood, is a precursor of the same instrument's representation of downcast moods of the prince in *The Wooden Prince.*

The second *Picture*, 'Village dance', is designed as a stark contrast. The Debussyan effects are less important here, as Bartók develops his pseudo-folk materials with their clear-cut articulations and off-beat accents. The form is rondo (*ABACA*), although between these formal sections Bartók provides generous joining passages, either functioning as mini-codas or motivically looking ahead to the incoming section. Tonally, the *A* sections progress from an F–D complex to endings in G, while both *B* and *C* sections are established in A♭. Ex. 1 shows the movement's first two phrases, which are notable for their whole-tone content.

EX. 1

In the first phrase only the final note, D, does not fit the underlying scalar pattern of F G A B C♯ E♭, and even this Bartók subverts by the introduction of D♯ in the first bar of the second phrase. It is probably by design that this whole-tone pattern complements that D-based pattern which brought the first *Picture* to a close. The opening of the second phrase, A B C♯ D♯, soon becomes one of the movement's most popular motifs, and at the first return of the *A* section (fig.13) is played along with its inversion for thirty bars as a shrill whole-tone woodwind accompaniment to the strings' renewed playing of the main theme. The *B* section (starting at fig.6) is itself in a well-demarcated ternary form in which the return (at fig.9) introduces the section's theme in free inversion. The only substantial link back to the first *Picture* occurs in section C (starting at fig.16.14), through its static bass, slower tempo, prominent use of the harp, and intervallically compressed versions of the earlier movement's opening melodic fragments. With the final *A* section the real jollity of the 'Village dance' emerges, particularly at fig.28 where Bartók pulls all stops out and invites the entire large orchestra, including its membership of triple woodwind and dozen brass players, to play *fff* in the final statement of the main theme.

Although now seen as a transitional work in Bartók's long quest for truly mature expression in the genre of orchestral music, *Two Pictures* was important for furthering Bartók's career. The work was published in both orchestral and piano solo versions by Rózsavölgyi in 1912 and first performed on 26 February 1913 by the orchestra of the Philharmonic Society in Budapest, conducted by István Kerner. Its fame must have spread, for it was scheduled for performance in London on 16 September 1914 at Sir Henry Wood's Promenade concerts, and only cancelled because of the introduction of a wartime embargo on 'enemy' works. (Joseph Holbrooke's jingoistic *Imperial March* replaced it on that programme.) It was also performed in Zürich during 1916 and was probably the first orchestral work by Bartók to be performed in America when Edgard Varèse conducted it in New York on 11 April 1919. In Budapest *Two Pictures* was Bartók's most performed orchestral work during his lifetime, gaining thirteen performances with the Philharmonic Society's orchestra alone between 1913 and 1940.

Four Orchestral Pieces, Bartók's next orchestral work, was composed as a two-piano score in 1912 but not orchestrated until the late summer of 1921. It was a victim of the long years of isolation and depression, to which Bartók started to succumb in 1911–12 and which were then prolonged by the war and its chaotic aftermath in Hungary. Only with the prospect of performance did he undertake the scoring, for a large orchestra including mainly quadruple woodwind and brass. That first performance was mounted by the Budapest Philharmonic Society's orchestra on 9 January 1922. The Four Orchestral Pieces need, therefore, to be viewed with an eye to their different chronological frames. In pitch, rhythmic and formal characteristics they are definitely pre-war – somewhat curious, in some regards even regressive, successors to Bartók's opera and *Allegro barbaro* of the previous year. In use of instruments and colour effects the pieces are definitely post-war, betraying in subtle ways his new knowledge of such works as Stravinsky's *The Rite of Spring*, Schoenberg's *Pierrot lunaire* and some later works of Debussy. Between the two stages of the work's creation Bartók himself had also gained much extra experience as a composer and arranger, most significantly with his ballet *The Wooden Prince* Op.13 (1914–16), the Second String Quartet

Op.17 (1915–17), and the short score of his pantomime *The Miraculous Mandarin* Op.19 (1918–19).

Bartók's four pieces do not comprise a tightly unified opus. He appears originally to have thought of a slower–faster succession of two movements, similar to his Op.5 and Op.10, and so written his Preludio and Scherzo. But he then added in two short concluding pieces, the *moderato* Intermezzo and *maestoso* Marcia funèbre. The resultant tonal scheme of the movements Bartók himself identified as E major, B♭ major, G minor, C♯ minor, that is, two tritone pairs (E–B♭, G–C♯) with the four tonal centres according to a 'diminished seventh' pattern. Thematically, there are few inter-movement connections of importance, although a weaving secondary theme in the first piece, at fig.8, is closely related to the theme at fig.5 in the final piece. In mood the *moderato* pieces, Preludio and Intermezzo, are heavily indebted to Debussy, albeit sometimes through the intermediary of *Duke Bluebeard's Castle*.[7] Their soft, autumnal characters are announced in their first bars as much by the instruments employed as pitch or rhythmic features. Harp and horn feature prominently, in a shimmering, harmonically static texture. The Scherzo and Marcia funèbre are quite different in mood; they are rhythmically sharper and more genuinely Bartókian, exemplifying movement types established by the composer as far back as his student years. The Scherzo is a fierce, rambling piece, less overtly intellectual than the second-movement Scherzo of the Second Suite with its fugal development, but equally as diabolical. Its brass chorus work and sections of rapid, *fortissimo* jostling between lower and higher instrumental groups (as, for instance, from fig.25.6), however, suggest Stravinsky's *Rite*, which Bartók had come to know in about 1917. The *maestoso* funeral march has a predecessor in the conclusion of Bartók's early symphonic poem *Kossuth* (1903) but is more closely related in its rhythmic patterns to the grim, stuttering, final bars which Bartók would write for *The Miraculous Mandarin*. This finale's slow tempo,[8] 'postlude' status and lack of tonal connection with any of the other pieces all suggest why Bartók did not represent his opus as a 'symphony', 'suite' or even 'serenade', but simply as 'four pieces'. Other composers, such as Schoenberg, Webern and Stravinsky, were also moving towards less strongly structured works with similarly neutral titles in their pre-war output.

In tempo and metre Bartók's pieces lack the flexibility found in at least the opening movement of his *Two Pictures*. His Four Pieces are starkly characterized in these musical parameters. Changes in time-signature are rare; the outer movements maintain a consistent duple pulse against the triple of the inner movements – frantic in the Scherzo, waltz-like in the Intermezzo except for its brief, *agitato* interlude. The sense of a dominating tempo is likewise well established and maintained in each piece. Bartók does, however, frequently pull back or hasten his tempos to underscore the music's flow into or out of formal sections or to assist in the delineation of particular themes or motifs. Even the Marcia funèbre, despite the march-like rhythmic strictness demanded of its various figures of anacrusis, does sometimes unbend. Bartók introduces a dozen subtle changes in pace during its seventy bars.

Harmonically and melodically, the writing in these pieces is diverse. The first and third pieces, apart from the latter's *agitato* passage, are underpinned by slow-moving bass lines supporting both traditional and non-traditional harmonies. Traditional chords of accumulated thirds, such as sevenths and ninths, are common, as in the dominating sonority of the Intermezzo's first eleven bars: G B♭ D♭ F A♭. The melodies constructed over such traditional harmonies tend to be little more than linear expressions of these harmonies, giving the music an uninnovative, even pianistic feel. The effect of Bartók's 'love' motif, originally associated with Stefi Geyer, is still strong in this third piece, as is seen in the bass line's descending D B♭ G D♯, at fig.6, and C♯ A F♯ D♯, at fig.11. The first movement's opening and closing sonority, similarly, is a tonic seventh in E major but with added sixth, E G♯ B C♯ D♯, against which the implicitly pentatonic (E G A B D E) melody line clashes. At fig.13, the point of recapitulation in the movement's ternary form, Bartók reconciles his opening melody and harmony to a G-based pentatonic structure, G B♭ C D F. The whole-tone interest, seen in the first *Picture*, is also present in this movement, as, for instance, at fig.3.5, where the gapped whole-tone melody starting with G♯ F♯ [] D C is simultaneously harmonically projected into the strings. A further technique considerably exploited by Bartók in the first piece to create a hazy, impressionistic glow about his harmonies is that of semitonal 'shadows'. This is usually associated with quiet, *sul ponticello* tremolo playing on the strings or flutter-tongue playing on the flutes (as from fig.4.2 and fig.16.3). The first violins and flutes at fig.5, for instance, proceed in vertical semitonal clusters – D E♭ E, E♯ F♯ G, F♯ G A♭ – thereby muddying the underlying G major triad maintained in the other parts. Bartók's Scherzo is harmonically more spare and generally employs ostinato figures in support of his melodies. On several occasions the constant repetition of ostinato patterns is used to move the music forward to a climax, the most impressive of which occurs between fig.11 and fig.17, where the dynamic builds inexorably from *ppp* to *fff*. The Marcia funèbre has a more established sense of triadic harmonic progression, quite frequently involving seventh or ninth chords. Its climax, initiated at fig.5, is, however, driven by ostinato movement.

Given that Bartók was thirty-one when he composed the Four Orchestral Pieces and forty when he orchestrated them, the result is surprisingly immature. Charges can be sustained against his Op.12 both that it is frequently little more than orchestrated piano music and that it fails to submerge the various stylistic influences being brought to bear upon it within Bartók's own creativity. The composer was clearly finding the genre of abstract orchestral music more difficult than other genres – solo piano music, chamber music, stage music, for instance – where he had already achieved works of compelling maturity and originality. It was only with the Dance Suite of 1923 that his mastery of this orchestral medium would be placed beyond question.

NOTES

1 Stevens, pp. 41, 267.
2 Unpublished letter, 22 May 1914 (Free Library of Philadelphia).
3 See British Library, Add. MS. 51023.
4 See *BBE*, p. 446.
5 Debussy's orchestral *Images* were only completed after Bartók's, in 1912.
6 Kroó, p. 57.
7 Compare, in particular, fig.4.2 with fig.91 in the opera.
8 See slow final movements, similarly, in the piano Suite Op.14 and Second String Quartet Op.17.

34

Dance Suite

MALCOLM GILLIES

On 17 November 1873 the three sister cities of Buda, Óbuda and Pest effected a long overdue union officially to create the metropolis of Budapest. The following fifty years witnessed an explosion in its population from around one quarter of a million to nearly 1,200,000 inhabitants. Budapest joined with Vienna as a twin capital of the Austro-Hungarian Empire and assumed an increasingly dominant role in the economic development of the empire's multi-ethnic eastern division. By 1923 that empire, economic prosperity and multi-ethnicity had been shattered, swept away in the aftermath of the First World War. Budapest stood as the capital of a country barely one-third of its original size and stripped of most of its ethnic minorities as well as over nearly one-third of its own ethnic kin. As in most of the defeated nations, inflation was rampant and the population's standard of living was plummeting. The press and the right-wing government, which had emerged after a brief flirtation with Communism in 1919, were now beating the drum of Hungarian nationalism. Bartók had already himself been the butt of this chauvinism in 1920 when he was accused of lack of patriotism because of his work with Romanian and Slovak folk music.[1]

It was surprising then that in April 1923 the conservative municipal authorities drawing up plans for the celebration of the city's fiftieth anniversary should have commissioned three composers associated with the former Communist government to compose works for the occasion. Ernő Dohnányi responded with his Festival Overture Op.31; Zoltán Kodály composed one of his most famous and popular works, the *Psalmus hungaricus* Op.13; Bartók decided on a suite of dances for orchestra. All three works were premièred at a celebratory concert on 19 November 1923, under Dohnányi's direction.

At the time of composition Bartók was tight-lipped about the inspiration for his Dance Suite. His few sentences for the concert programme merely described the work's architecture and pointed to its 'original, folk-like, but not folk' themes.[2] By 1931, however, in a passage later deleted from an essay draft, he explained: 'The aim of the whole work was to put together a kind of idealized peasant music – you could say an invented peasant music – in such a way that the individual movements of the work would introduce particular types of music.'[3] Those 'particular types' were ethnic types, and Bartók went on to enumerate the instances in the work where Hungarian, Romanian and Arabic folk music had served him as models. By 1931 the climate in Hungary was somewhat more tolerant than in 1923; Bartók himself had even been appointed to a committee of the League of Nations. He was prepared to write unguardedly to a Romanian acquaintance of his belief in a 'brotherhood of peoples', of his own artistic debt to Hungarian, Romanian, Slovak and Arabic folk music, and of his aim of drawing inspiration from any source as long as it was 'clean, fresh and healthy'.[4] The Dance Suite can, then, be interpreted as an early musical expression of Bartók's evolving cultural pluralism, which he had, however, refrained from explaining to his less broad-minded public at its time of civic pride. While Kodály remained happily rooted in Hungarian folk traditions Bartók had through a decade of personal disillusionment and war lost much of his national faith and was by the early 1920s looking idealistically towards a music of all humanity.[5] That ideal he would develop further in planning a cycle of three or four 'Danube Basin' cantatas, of which only the *Cantata profana* (1930) was ever written, and in his Forty-four Duos for violins of 1931.

The Dance Suite consists of six movements which run from one into the other, often through the mediation of a ritornello passage (R). The overall plan of the movements is shown in Fig. 1. The slow, tranquil Ritornello theme (Ex. 1), a G-based imitation of an eight-bar Hungarian folksong in Aeolian mode, is an important unifying device, not just through its recurrence but also through its tonal role in bringing about a smooth link between one dance and the next.

Movement design:	I R	II R	III	IV R	V	VI
Tonal plan:	G	B♭	B	G/A♭	E	. . . G

FIG. 1

I, 132-9 (first violins)

Tranquillo

p

poco rit.

EX. 1

It provides, additionally, an element of contrast and relaxation between the generally fast-paced movements. Only the fourth movement is of a similarly slow tempo. Characteristically, Bartók varies his ritornello at each appearance – indeed, only the rhythm of the theme's first bar remains intact throughout – but not to such an extent at any one time that its essential identity is threatened. He also introduces it mid-way through the finale (at bar 112) as part of his culminating roll-call of the work's themes. Bartók was pleased with his counterfeit tune and commented in his 1931 essay draft: 'The ritornello theme is such a faithful imitation of a certain kind of Hungarian folk melody that its derivation might puzzle even the most knowledgeable of musical folklorists.' In fact, the melody and its setting nostalgically recall the tone of the nineteenth-century stylized *verbunkos* dance, and present a first sign that Bartók was prepared again to invoke those Romantic Hungarian styles which he had forsaken around 1907 when he had committed his musical future to peasant music.

An important element in the success of this suite is the stark characterization of the individual dance numbers. This is achieved by various correlations of tempo, dynamics and scoring, but principally by the distinctive use of intervals. The first movement's opening, bassoon theme is a chromatic melody, based on Arabic precedent. For most of its course it moves symmetrically inwards and outwards using the four-note semitonal set A♭ A B♭ C♭, although Bartók does finally expand this range outwards to include D♭ and the note of tonal resolution, G. The interest in symmetrical semitonal movements is immediately projected into the accompaniment, as in the concertina-like alternation between the opening G–D fifth and F♯–E♭, and later movement around axes of A–D (from bar 9) and F C G (from bar 15). Bartók maintains this symmetrical chromatic concern throughout the movement's succession of themes and accompaniment patterns, even at the movement's climax (bars 88–102), where the main melody becomes diatonic but the accompaniment patterns remain chromatic or play with major sevenths (inverted semitones).[6]

The second movement is a loud, harsh Allegro molto of Hungarian inspiration. Its characterizing interval is the minor third, which establishes an immediate kinship of mood with the pantomime *The Miraculous Mandarin* Op.19, which Bartók was also orchestrating during the summer of 1923. Symmetrical concerns continue through this movement although in a different guise and less relentlessly than in the first movement. The main theme (Ex. 2) is tonally in B♭ and features upper and lower minor thirds, D♭ and G. Within this frame he introduces B♭'s upper and lower major seconds, C and A♭. Bartók reinforced the final B♭–G–B♭ cadential movement with glissandos (or *portamenti*) on the violins and trombone. This technique, also used in *Mandarin*, raised some eyebrows. Of a Birmingham performance of the work on 25 February 1926, *The Times*'s critic commented: 'We shall slip away before it, next time it occurs. It is time that some protest was registered against glissandos on the trombones, even if every other atrocity is admitted to the concert room.'

Given Bartók's acknowledged debt to Slovakian folk music and this work's composition while he was staying at Radvány in

EX. 2

southern Slovakia, the lack of a movement in Slovakian style is surprising. Bartók had intended that such a movement come after this second movement of the suite, and appears even to have drafted it, but then, for whatever reason, decided to omit it. The following movement in the finished work is an Allegro vivace, which begins with an imitation of Hungarian bagpipe music. The *giocoso* tune, initially played by the bassoon, is in a pentatonic mode, B C♯ E F♯ A B, with emphasis on the intervals of a fourth, B–E, E–A and F♯–B (Ex. 3, as marked).

EX. 3

It is accompanied by a tonic–dominant drone on horns and piano, which is spiked by off-beat string pizzicatos. In contrast to the earlier two movements, with their single returns of opening themes, the bagpipe melody returns twice, creating a bi-ethnic rondo form (*A B A C A*). The melody of the *B* section, which starts abruptly at bar 46, is in a Romanian folk-violin style and irregular metre. It is built over a D–G drone. It and another Romanian violin-drone theme, which initiates the formal *C* section at bar 94, are both diatonic in construction but feature sharpened seventh or fourth degrees prominently. Bartók then follows with a *scherzando*, E♭ Dorian variant of his main theme (from bar 125), where he ingeniously uses these same seven diatonic notes in a cycle-of-fourths accompaniment based on C: C F B♭ E♭ A♭ D♭ G♭. This C-based pattern of fourths – an outgrowth of the emphasis on fourths in the movement's main theme (Ex. 3) – will return more dramatically later in the work. The movement ends with a *vivacissimo*, *fortissimo* playing of the main theme.

Of the six movements the fourth is the most significant from the viewpoint of development of Bartók's mature style types. Here he unveils a static, symmetrical 'frozen architecture', an initiative which he follows up in many works over the coming decade to culminate in the miraculous first and third movements of his Music for Strings, Percussion and Celesta (1936). The music of this dance moves stealthily from quietness to a *fortissimo* climax (at bar 16) but then retreats along the same path. It leaves the uncanny impression of a music that just *is* rather than one that *progresses*. It exists in time rather than moves through time. The woodwind's seven melodic passages, scattered between muted chordal passages, graphically illustrate the game of 'slow change' in which Bartók is engaging with his pitches (Fig. 2).

(1) bars 3–4:	F	A♭	B♭	C♭											
(2) bars 7-8:	F	A♭	B♭	C♭	D♭										
(3) bars 11–12:		G♯	A♯		C♯		D♯	E		F♯					
(4) bars 15–19:					C♯	D	D♯		E♯	F♯	G	G♯	A	B	C
(5) bar 21:		A♭	B♭		D♭		E♭	F♭		G♭					
(6) bar 23:	F	A♭	B♭	C♭	D♭										
(7) bars 25–30:	F	A♭	B♭	C♭											

FIG. 2

The pitch symmetry here is total as far as scalar bases to the melodic passages are concerned, hence the perfectly balanced 'rocket' shape in Fig. 2. Bartók builds steadily to his climactic passage (4) by removing some of the lower and adding some higher pitches; he then leads away from it by invoking the process in reverse. The tonal centres of his melodies (underlined in Fig. 2), in each case the last note of the passage, form an underlying ascending pattern of perfect fourths, A♭ C♯ F♯, with following identical descent, F♯ D♭ A♭. The movement to and from the central focus is further reinforced by the growth and then decay in scoring and dynamics: passage (1) *mf espr.*, 2 instruments; (2) *mf espr.*, 3 instruments; (3) *f*, 4 instruments; (4) *f*, 5 instruments, then *ff*, 6 instruments, then *dim.*, 5 instruments; (5) *mf espr.*, 4 instruments; (6) *p*, 3 instruments; (7) *p–pp*, 3, then 2, then 1 instrument. But within this inexorable pitch structure there is variation, in the contours, lengths and ornamentation of individual melodic passages, and in the subtle differences in the way in which the most important melodic intervals, in particular the minor third, are represented. The point of Bartók's climax, too, is not centrally placed in the movement but comes a little later, in accordance with the general psychological rule that the way out should take longer than the way back.[7] Against this foreground activity there remain the intervening background chordal passages, which operate according to their own rules (Fig. 3).

(I)	bars 1–2:	<u>G</u>	A	C	D						
(II)	bars 5–6:	<u>G</u>	A	C	D						
(III)	bars 9–10:				<u>D</u>	E		G	A		
(IV)	bars 13–14:				<u>D</u>	E		G	A		
(V)	bar 20:						<u>F</u>	G		B♭	C
(VI)	bar 22:			<u>C</u>	D		F	G			
(VII)	bar 24:	<u>G</u>	A	C	D						
(VIII)	bars 26–8:	<u>G</u>	A	C	D						

FIG. 3

The movement of these clusters through the piece is only imperfectly symmetrical and their dynamic rarely departs from a level of *pianissimo* or less. Nevertheless, Bartók does allow the number of instruments to grow, peaking in passages (IV)–(VI), and requires the strings' mutes to be removed for passages (V) and (VI). For variety he introduces chromatic neighbouring clusters in contrary motion and in passage (IV) even writes in a small excursion for these clusters. Bartók's model for this movement was one of 'quite complex Arabic music, perhaps of urban origin'. Such tunes were not of the narrow-intervalled type that he had himself noted down during his 1913 visit to French north Africa, and used as a model for his first movement, but rather ones he remembered from a brief visit to Tangier in May 1906 and had otherwise read about in volumes of tunes taken down in the cities of Algiers and Tunis.

The fifth movement is barely more than an extended formal up-beat to the finale. The characteristic interval of its theme is the semitone (Ex. 4), and the ordering principle for thematic entries is one of ascending fourths (E A D G C), although there is always a melodic return by steps of a fourth to the fundamental E at the end of each entry.

EX. 4

In Bartók's analysis the movement lacks any particular ethnic model: 'the theme of no.5 is so primitive that one can only speak of a primitive peasant character here'.[8]

With the *allegro*, sixth movement Bartók brings to final success a medley technique which he had attempted as early as 1905 with his First Suite Op.3. In theory this movement should be of a pan-ethnic flavour, reflecting the variety of sources which had inspired the earlier five movements, but Bartók gives a strong preference to his imitation Hungarian and 'primitive' themes. Only the Arabic theme of the first movement features prominently here; the two Romanian violin tunes from the third movement and the 'urban Arabic' melody of the fourth movement are not reheard. This finale begins with a continuation of the 'primitive' theme of the fifth movement, now rhythmically regularized and presented in nine successive entries separated according to an ascending cycle of fourths: C F B♭ D♯ G♯ C♯ F♯ B E. Bartók then runs seamlessly into a brass call upon the first movement's chromatic theme (bar 9) and on to sections which recall themes and motifs from all but the fourth movement in varying degrees of transformation, development and disintegration. The tempos are carefully calculated by Bartók to lead up to the *presto* playing of the second movement's main theme (from bar 94), where the trumpets and trombones triumphantly play *pavillon en l'air* for more dramatic effect. The tension then dissolves, allowing the Ritornello theme to enter *molto tranquillo* on the first violins. Such a lull becomes common in Bartók's finales of later years, but it is only ever momentary. He soon starts again to gear up his tempos, firstly in developing material from the second Ritornello passage (II, bars 106–10) and then in reintroducing the main themes of first and third movement before the impetuous *allegro molto* peroration. Bartók's ending is abrupt, slewing the music back into the tonality of G only at the last moment. Given the mass of excitement that he has generated in this movement, its ending sounds too abrupt and suggests that same weakness in resolution of momentum which caused him twenty years later to revise the ending of this composition's spiritual successor, the Concerto for Orchestra.

There is a radiance and mildness in the Dance Suite which does not emerge altogether naturally from his preceding compositions, the First and Second Violin Sonatas (1921–2). Their stiffness, entrenched dissonance and segregation of performing roles slipped into the background as Bartók turned away from his goal, stated in 1920, of 'equal treatment of the twelve semitones'.[9] The Dance Suite marks his decisive move towards the recognition, baldly stated in 1928, that:

> Our peasant music, naturally, is invariably tonal, if not always in the sense that the inflexible major and minor system is tonal. (An 'atonal' folk music, in my opinion, is unthinkable.) Since we depend upon a tonal basis of this kind in our creative work, it is quite self-evident that our works are quite pronouncedly tonal in type.[10]

The Dance Suite allowed him to idealize certain of the tonal qualities in his favourite folk musics. In those of his following works which are not direct settings of folksongs that idealizing tendency would be continued, laying the foundations for his secure, but varied tonal practice of the 1930s and 1940s. But there is also another, more personal reason for Bartók's new radiance: he was in love. His marriage with Márta Ziegler had been strained for the best part of a decade and ended abruptly with their separation and divorce in the summer of 1923. This freed Bartók to marry his new love, the nineteen-year-old piano student Ditta Pásztory. The Dance Suite was largely composed in the weeks between the separation from Márta Ziegler and formal union with Ditta Pásztory.[11]

Despite the new mildness of this work it gained a lukewarm response at its première. Bartók put this down primarily to the inadequacies of the orchestra and shortness of rehearsal time,[12] but the work also appears to have been overshadowed by Kodály's hugely well received *Psalmus hungaricus*, which immediately preceded it on the programme. The Dance Suite might not have caught the public imagination were it not for Václav Talich's excellent rendition on 19 May 1925 in Prague, where the Czech Philharmonic Orchestra was participating in a festival of the International Society for Contemporary Music. The suite's strong but accessible nature was perceived and news of it quickly spread. Before the end of the year it had been performed at numerous venues in Europe and America, and Bartók's Viennese publisher, Universal Edition, was heading its advertisements with the claim that it was to be heard in sixty cities during the coming season. A piano solo version of the suite was also produced in 1925, although Bartók never played it in public. It appears to have been premièred only on 20 February 1945 in New York by the Hungarian pianist György Sándor.

NOTES

1 See *BBE*, pp. 201–3.
2 *BBí*.i, p. 66.

3 See Tibor Tallián, *Béla Bartók: the Man and his Work*, Budapest (Corvina), 1988, p. 133.
4 *BBL*, p. 201.
5 See, further, the questions raised about Bartók's attitudes to ethnic and national questions in this *Companion*'s opening chapter.
6 See the piano and first violin figures of G–F♯, E♯–F♯, G–F♯ at bars 88–91.
7 The point of climax, at the end of bar 16, is however still several per cent short of the Golden Section point of the movement, whether measured in beats or bars.
8 *BBL*, p. 202.
9 *BBE*, p. 459.
10 *BBE*, p. 338.
11 It was, however, his first wife Márta who dutifully copied out the full score of the suite for her, by then, ex-husband.
12 Unpublished letter to Universal Edition, 13 January 1924 (NYBA).

35

The First Two Piano Concertos

JÁNOS KÁRPÁTI

Ever since the early writings of the Hungarian critic Aladár Tóth, in the 1920s, it has been stated repeatedly in the Bartók literature that the composer's piano music has played a pioneering role in the development of his art. An especially good example of that pioneering role is seen in the period from 1926 which, following two years' silence, was opened by such significant piano pieces as the Sonata, *Out of Doors*, Nine Little Piano Pieces and the First Piano Concerto. It is also well known that the demand for Bartók as a performing artist contributed to the creation of these works. In the 1920s Bartók was very active as a pianist, playing frequently in the cities of Western Europe, and making concert tours to the Soviet Union and the United States as well. It was natural, then, for the pianist–composer to extend his repertory with his own new works; this desire was particularly strong in terms of orchestral works, since when asked to perform with orchestra Bartók could only present his Rhapsody Op.1, of 1904. That is why we can consider Bartók's First Piano Concerto – his first real attempt in the concerto genre – the most significant result of 1926. The assumption that he composed it for the concert stage is supported by the fact that shortly after the world première of the work in Frankfurt am Main on 1 July 1927 it was performed in London, Prague, Warsaw and Vienna, and in 1928 was presented in New York, Boston, Cincinnati, Budapest, Cologne, Berlin, Amsterdam, The Hague and Erfurt. Each time, Bartók himself was the soloist and his partners included such conductors as Furtwängler (for the première), Clark, Strasser, Fitelberg, Reiner, Koussevitzky, Dohnányi, Abendroth, Kleiber and Monteux. Despite these many distinguished names the performances were less than outstanding. The orchestras found the parts difficult and the conductors themselves were not always comfortable with the language of this new music. Bartók himself was only satisfied with the conducting of Reiner, Monteux and the young German conductor, Franz Jung.

Bartók's performing experiences with the First Piano Concerto probably persuaded him to begin composing another piano concerto fairly soon afterwards, as he himself explained in an article of 1939:

> I wrote my First Concerto for Piano and Orchestra in 1926. I consider it a successful work although its writing is a bit difficult – one might even say very difficult! – as much for orchestra as for audience. That is why some years later (1930–31), while writing my Second Concerto, I wanted to produce a piece which would contrast with the first: a work which would be less bristling with difficulties for the orchestra and whose thematic material would be more pleasing. This intention explains the rather light and popular character of most of the themes of my latest concerto: a lightness that sometimes almost reminds me of one of my youthful works, the First Suite for Orchestra Op.3 (1905).[1]

This second concerto also gained an international reputation fairly soon, even though the composer's performing activities had been somewhat curtailed in the 1930s. The world première was again given in Frankfurt am Main, on 23 January 1933, with Hans Rosbaud conducting. It, too, was soon associated with many famous conductors: Klemperer in Vienna, Vilmos Palotai in Strasbourg, Boult in London, Scherchen in Winterthur, and Talich in Stockholm and Prague. Unfortunately Bartók's own opinions of these performances are not known. It is also regrettable that no recording survives of these many, significant performances of the concertos, apart from a fragmentary amateur attempt with parts of the second, so we have no authentic aural image of these two works which were, in many ways, nearest to the personality of the composer.

The most important message in Bartók's quotation above is that he intended to make his Second Piano Concerto the counterpart of his first. This attitude is characteristic of Bartók throughout his career. Such complementary works include the First and Second Violin Sonatas of 1921–2, the Third and Fourth String Quartets of 1927–8, and the two Violin Rhapsodies of 1928. Although the dates of composition of the two piano concertos are not as close as in the case of these other paired works, analysis of the two concertos and Bartók's own statement bear out a similarly close connection. Bartók said that he wanted to write a lighter, more pleasing companion piece to the First Piano Concerto, but he had basically to cope with the same compositional problems and remained in the same stylistic sphere as he had with the first concerto. So it would be wrong to think that by 'more pleasing' he was indicating any compromise with the taste of the general musical public. The Second Piano Concerto is more 'pleasing' in one sense only: in contrast to the passionately impulsive presentation of musical ideas in the First Concerto, he took to shaping these thoughts in a more mature, more assertive, perhaps more Classical, way in the Second Concerto. This new technique of artistic expression he had mastered through such intervening works as the Third and Fourth String Quartets and *Cantata profana*.

Bartók himself recognized the significance of the stylistic turn that he had taken in 1926, writing in a letter of two years later:

> In my youth my ideal of beauty was not so much the art of Bach or of Mozart as that of Beethoven. Recently it has changed somewhat: in recent years I have considerably occupied myself with music before Bach, and I believe that traces of this are to be noticed in the Piano Concerto and in the Nine Little Piano Pieces.[2]

Consequently, Bartók intentionally turned to examples of Baroque music and adopted their concision of theme, contrapuntal technique and motoric, toccata-like movement into his own style. This was, of course, a general feature of the 1920s; many composers were trying to shed the lengthy, digressive style of late Romanticism or art nouveau that had been so dominant at the turn of the century.

This change in Bartók's musical ideals coincided with the development of a greater sensitivity towards contemporary artists. The first signs of this were Bartók's theoretical articles in leading musical journals of the time, such as that on Schoenberg's reception in Hungary, for the Viennese *Musikblätter des Anbruch,* and one in Berlin's *Melos,* about the problems of new music and the relationship between folk and composed musics.[3] At the same time, a new period was beginning in Bartók's life, during which he made a great number of concert tours and eagerly participated in the activities of the International Society for Contemporary Music. Because of this exposure, by the mid-1920s he well knew his contemporaries' artistic goals and could make very well based judgements about them. He considered Stravinsky to be the closest of all the composers to his own beliefs, and almost no publication or statement of the 1920s passed without some reference to the Russian composer. This is fully understandable since in Stravinsky's works Bartók could find support and justification for his own aspirations both in terms of a folk-music basis to composition and concerning attempts to revive Classical and Baroque forms. What Stravinsky accomplished in two different decades of his own artistic development, however, Bartók set to achieve simultaneously in the 1920s.

In 1931 Bartók observed:

> The right type of peasant music is most varied and perfect in its forms. Its expressive power is amazing, and at the same time devoid of all sentimentality and superfluous ornaments. It is simple, sometimes primitive, but never silly. It is the ideal starting point for a musical renaissance.[4]

During the period between the two piano concertos Bartók did not compose any folksong arrangements, apart from the two violin rhapsodies. None the less, as the quotation shows, folk music was a dominating source for him since in it he found those massive yet simple principles of structure which were also to feature in his music of this period, even though folksongs were not actually present by direct quotation or even imitation in these compositions. The following analysis does not deal with the two piano concertos separately, but presents a comparative approach, concentrating on the connections between them. Its purpose is to elucidate how Bartók managed to accomplish his main goal at this time: a musical renaissance based on a synthesis of the structure of folk music and the technique of Baroque music.

As is well known, to Bartók folk music did not mean just the songs of the peoples of the Carpathian Basin, but also included a number of ancient traditions which he came to know either through personal experience (as with north Africa) or through the publications of the emerging new musical discipline of the period, ethnomusicology. The rich culture of percussion that he encountered through the music of various primitive tribes led him to an unadorned rhythmic music lacking any melodic dimension whatsoever. However, in contrast to many of his contemporaries or followers, he did not want merely to imitate, for instance, African drum music, but sought to bring about a fundamental integration of its ideas into a basically European musical system, using European instruments. Thus, he created a musical conception in which the backbone of the composition is represented by a clearly rhythmic form – a kind of proto-rhythm – from which the whole work, or at least a considerable part of it, unfolds.

This process of creating a composition from a single rhythm is clearly recognizable in the First Piano Concerto. The entirely rhythmical proto-idea, or proto-motif, starts in the deepest register of the piano and the brass instruments, to the accompaniment of the monotonous pulse of the timpani. This serves as a basis from which a number of themes of the composition set forth. The adjectival prefix 'proto' is important here, because not only is it the utmost reduction – the most essential idea – of the work but also originally one of the most ancient forms of music.

The first subject of the First Concerto's first and third movement is the logical consequence of this introductory 'proto-rhythm'. In each case, one note is repeated throughout several bars, showing that the rhythm is dominant. This 'hammering' thematic concept, it seems, is an important invention of 1926, as it plays a significant role in the Sonata for piano, as well. It must have been this concept that Bartók was describing when he answered a questionnaire of the *Musikblätter des Anbruch* in 1927: 'The neutral character of the piano tone has been long recognized. Yet it seems to me that its inherent nature becomes really expressive only by means of the present tendency to use the piano as a percussion instrument.'[5]

In his First Piano Concerto Bartók also uses actual percussion instruments frequently, and not in the background as part of the general orchestration as much as in prominent positions, often as if in a chamber-music setting with the piano. The first part of the second movement, for instance, is nothing but a dialogue between piano and percussion. This shows that the idea of this particular combination came to Bartók over ten years before composing the Sonata for Two Pianos and Percussion (1937). Another usage of the piano as a percussion instrument is seen when Bartók mixes dissonant notes, such as 'grating' seconds, into the firm chords of the piano, thereby stressing the rhythmic, percussive functions of the music over its melodic functions. By this method an exceptionally expressive part is constructed in the middle of the second movement; the piano plays an ostinato motif in $\frac{3}{8}$ metre for no less than 58 bars, with an ever-growing sonority and dynamic, all serving as a background to a gradually extending, orientalized multi-part melodic texture played entirely by the wind instruments.

The 'hammering' rhythm and the use of the piano as a percussion instrument are probably the most characteristic features of the First Piano Concerto. They recur again in the Second Piano Concerto, but in a more refined, less impulsive and dynamic way. The element in the Second Concerto that refers back to the First most conspicuously is the 'framework' theme of the third movement, a 'barbaric' Allegro introduced by the timpani and continued by the piano, but the second subject of the first movement also provides another example of this type of music. There, with repeated full chords, the piano 'beats out' a characteristic rhythmic pattern (Ex. 1). This rhythmic pattern bridges the gap between 'barbaric' and 'Baroque' rhythm. The peculiar rhythmic atmosphere of the first movement which, similar to a Baroque concerto, pulses from first note to last, is created by the alternation of anapaestic and dactylic rhythmic patterns. A miniature sample, bars 60–63 of this first movement of the Second Concerto, affords some idea of the wider process (Ex. 2).

EX. 1

EX. 2

Looking now at both of the concertos, the same important, not to say dominant, role is ascribed to the firm, sharp and 'hammering' rhythm. In the First Concerto this rhythm is combined with a passionate, 'barbaric' feature, whereas in the Second it has been tamed to some extent and is expressed in Baroque-like variants. It is surely not accidental in the First Concerto that beside the 'proto-rhythm' there appears a 'proto-tune', a seemingly primitive, elemental, shapeless, fragmentary tune that moves in a narrow range and constantly returns to itself. Perhaps the most characteristic example of such a 'proto-type' is found in the framework theme of the first movement. It is played firstly *fortissimo* by the horns, at fig.1, and then by the bassoons at fig.2, in a version which shows that a low register is part of its essential character (Ex. 3). This type of tune has already been met in the opening bars of the Dance Suite (1923), where the bassoon intones a similar, almost shapeless theme in a deep register. A more rhythmic example of this type of elemental tune is found at the start of the third movement of the Second Concerto, where the pulsing 'proto-rhythm' is combined with a 'proto-tune' dominated by the E♭–G♭ interval of a minor third, as shown in Ex. 4.[6]

EX. 3

EX. 4

In these extremely simple, ultra-reduced musical cells we experience the most characteristic feature of Bartók's musical mind. And it is always the *process* which is so important. In some works, such as the Third String Quartet (1927), the transformation starts with a more complicated form and moves towards the simpler, more essential and abstract forms. For instance, it is through the deconstruction of a folk tune, or a scale-like passage, that the music can arrive at the most conventional and simplest of straight lines: the glissando. In the piano concertos, however, the process is reversed: the starting point is a simple 'proto-music', and through the succeeding stages of the compositions its variations add more and more to the original material, leading to an increasing complexity and refinement. In this way the 'simple and pleasing' Second Piano Concerto becomes an excellent example of Bartók's mastery of monothematic compositional technique, through its demonstration of the infinite number of rhythmic and melodic variations possible with a single theme. At the beginning of that work, when the short two-bar melody is played by the trumpet, we can hardly guess that here is such a tight nucleus of rhythm and melody that it will serve as the basis of the entire composition. The affinity of Bartók's theme (Ex. 5a) with that of the finale to Stravinsky's 1910 ballet *The Firebird* (Ex. 5b) is easy to recognize, although it is not clear whether the allusion is intentional or coincidental.

EX. 5

The only difference between these two themes is that Stravinsky's is *lento maestoso*, creating a Russian national or folk atmosphere – one is reminded of Musorgsky's 'Great Gate of Kiev' or Rimsky-Korsakov's Overture on Three Russian Themes – while Bartók forces these same notes into a firm, hard, Baroque rhythm. This character is maintained in the piano's continuation of the theme (as if in explanation), and with a contrary-motion scale passage in full chords it carries on that most essential quality of the music: the rhythm. As it turns out, the future of the whole movement is decided in this opening section, since every subsequent detail of the music is based upon the rhythmic patterns exposed there: ♫♩ ♩ (anapaest), ♩♫♩ (dactyl), ♪♪ (spondee), ♩♫♫♩ (combination of the above three). It is immediately apparent that these rhythmic variations, with their constant pulsation and in-filling of each other's gaps, evoke the atmosphere of the Baroque concerto. Baroque technique, furthermore, suggested to Bartók a number of possibilities besides rhythmic variations: mirror inversion, in which the direction of every step or leap in the melody is changed; retrograde inversion, in which the melody starts with the last note and moves backwards; and the combination of the two.

Within the twentieth century the main group of composers adopting Baroque contrapuntal techniques was the dodecaphonists, but while these composers provided variations of the abstract series through various inversion processes, Bartók created real, tangible and recognizable variations. It is typical of Bartók's way of thinking that he even used these variations to build new forms. They appear, for instance, in the recapitulation of a sonata, and, later on, are used to create the formal homogeneity of a whole work by combining inversion technique and rhythmic variations. In this way, the anapaestic–dactylic themes of the Second Concerto's first movement return in a triplet form in its third movement.

Besides inversions and rhythmic transformations of the melody Bartók practised another variation process, especially in the Second Concerto: compression and extension of the melody. This practice goes back to the 'maggiore–minore' variations of previous eras, when the composer presented the same melody in the major then the minor key. Technically speaking, it was not the whole melody but only the important interval of the third that was being compressed or extended. A similarly transitional technique, practised by Bartók is that of 'mistuning', where a selection of the extremity notes of the melody are extended or compressed. As a result, a diatonic structure becomes partially chromatic. Such a variation technique is carried to its logical conclusion with the compression of a diatonic scale into a chromatic one, or the extension of a chromatic into a diatonic or even whole-tone scale. Bartók applied this method systematically in the second and fourth movements of his Fourth String Quartet (1928); these two movements are, in fact, variations of each other in that the melody of the second movement consists entirely of semitones, which are regularly extended into whole tones in the fourth movement.

Looking back over his *œuvre* in his Harvard Lectures of 1943 Bartók commented on this compositional technique:

> You know very well the extension of themes in their value called augmentation, and their compression in value called diminution. These devices are very well known, especially from the art music of the seventeenth and eighteenth centuries. Now, this new device could be called 'extension in range' of a theme . . . As you will see, such an extension will considerably change the character of the melody, sometimes to such a degree that its relation to the original, non-extended form will be scarcely recognizable . . . And this circumstance is very good indeed, because we will get variety on the one hand, but the unity will remain undestroyed because of the hidden relation between the two forms.[7]

Bartók was speaking here mainly about extension, since his starting point with this process had been a 'chromatic' melody, the bassoon theme at the start of the Dance Suite which was inspired by Arabic examples. Later on in his lecture he spoke about the reverse process, the compression of diatonic melodies into chromatic ones. As far as the Second Piano Concerto is concerned, we are dealing with this latter process of compression. To trace that process through the work is not easy, however, because simultaneous changes in texture and orchestration are also involved.

At the end of bar 81 of the Second Concerto's first movement (Ex. 6a), a second or episodic theme appears, in *tranquillo* tempo. It is found at the upper extremity of the arpeggiated chords of the piano. This is the most spacious, diatonic version of this theme. Later, at bar 99 (Ex. 6b), this same theme appears, this time played by horns, but its melodic character has changed. The diatonic structure of the theme has been compressed ('mistuned'), and its continuation has become entirely chromatic.

EX. 6

Finally, near the end of the movement, after the cadenza (from bar 254, Ex. 6c), the theme appears again, played by clarinets and bassoons, but this time the head of the theme is fully chromatic as well. Bartók's ability for variation is shown by the fact that this is still not the last phase of the process. In the third movement – itself a thematic variant of the first – a further form of this theme appears (from bar 278, Ex. 6d). It uses both compression and extension, with two minor seconds surrounding the perfect fourth, F–B♭, in the head of the theme, whereas its continuation is again consistently chromatic.

Having now surveyed the microstructures of these works, we turn to look at larger units of their construction. Bartók himself provides an initial orientation. Writing in the brochure for his performance of 22 February 1939 with the Orchestre de la Suisse Romande, he observed:

> As regards form, the Second Concerto on the whole is written in Classical sonata form. Movement I: exposition, development, recapitulation. Movement III: rondo; it should be noted that only the exposition of this movement has the character of a rondo. A few observations on the form should be made: (1) . . . [movement] III is really the free variation of I, with the exception of one new theme, which serves as a 'frame' . . .; (2) In the recapitulation of the first and third movements the themes appear in inversion.[8]

Although this rather concise analysis is actually of the Second Concerto, it is generally valid for the first, as well. As emerges from Bartók's own analyses and writings, in his works of Classical genres (such as concertos and quartets) he observes the structural principles of the Classical sonata to a remarkable extent. Yet we still find important references to original solutions, as seen in his mention of the 'framework' theme, which provides the Bartókian sonata form with a quite specific character. The 'framework' theme has an important role in the construction of Bartók's music, and more broadly than in just the piano concertos. The idea may go back to the extension of the introductory section. There, a musical material of secondary importance compared with the first subject, but yet preparing for and highlighting it, is integrated into the composition. That is why we can regard the 'hammering' first subject of the First Concerto both as an introduction and as a 'framework'; the 'proto-rhythm' and the 'proto-tune' jointly prepare the real musical plot. There is another detail here, the significance of which is shown by a similar detail in a much later work: the last eight bars of the introductory part of the First Concerto (from fig.3) lead to the *allegro* first subject with the same turbulent excitement and acceleration as at the corresponding structural point in the Sonata for Two Pianos and Percussion, composed a decade later.[9] It is also relevant that this remarkably rhythmic introductory music returns at several other points in the movement. That is what turns an apparently traditional and ordinary introduction into a Bartókian 'framework' theme: it is a structural element which provides the articulation of the thematic sections. In traditional structures the transition between the thematic sections takes place through gradual development; the audience arrives at a new section without actually noticing it. Bartók prefers to give a more conspicuous outline to his formal units, and places emphasis on these connecting points through his repeated use of recurring motifs or interpolated themes. Many such examples can be found in the Second, Fourth and Fifth String Quartets, and also especially in the third movement of the Second Piano Concerto, where the opening 'barbaric' minor-third motif (Ex. 4), with its duple metre, contrasts with the themes in triple metre. Throughout the movement it remains distinctly identifiable, appearing at the major articulation points in the form.

The other important aspect of Bartók's short analysis is that concerning the rondo hidden within a sonata form. It is noteworthy here that he does not mean the traditional sonata-rondo, the typical form for the final movement of a Classical concerto, but a rondo-like structure which relates to the structural model of Baroque concertos and in which the contrast of the 'rondo' theme and the episode is marked by a difference in the scoring; the rondo theme is played tutti, while the episode is played by a concertino group of instruments. It is again evident that Bartók's formal concerns, also, serve his firm intention of getting closer to the model of the Baroque concerto.

Orchestration plays an important role in creating the distinctive character of both these concertos. In the first work the second movement is noteworthy, with the piano being combined initially with a small group of percussion instruments, which only the wind instruments later join. In the outer movements of this concerto the composer uses a traditional, full orchestra, but still exercises a preference for percussion and wind sounds. In the second concerto his determination to create an unusual mix of sound is even more evident. To quote Bartók's own analysis:

> The orchestra for the first movement is comprised of wind and percussion instruments; that for the Adagio, the strings (muted) and the timpani; strings and a group of wind and percussion instruments for the scherzo; only the third movement employs the full orchestra.[10]

Given Bartók's special interests in Stravinsky's works, it is highly probable that the Russian maestro's Piano Concerto, premièred in 1924, influenced Bartók considerably in scoring the first movement of the Second Concerto. Nevertheless, the orchestral dramaturgy in this concerto is fully Bartókian, especially in the middle movement, where the instrumental alternation creates a unique structure. Bartók wrote: 'Movement II is a scherzo within the frame of an Adagio or, if you prefer, an Adagio containing a scherzo as its nucleus.'[11] An important innovation here was the idea of dividing this middle movement into three movements, which bears in itself the conception of the wholly symmetrical five-movement 'bridge' form, since the first and last movement also have a balancing role. Bartók was fully aware of this potential, since in his analysis of this Second Concerto in 1939 he referred to his two similarly structured works, the Fourth and Fifth String Quartets (1928, 1934). In these works, then, the symmetry is not of a simple *A B A* type, but exhibits a complex palindromic *A B C B A* scheme, with processes taking an opposite direction from the middle axis onwards.

Besides this most important and individual structural model, the Second Piano Concerto also illustrates the emergence or maturing of other important structural types. The *adagio* second movement, for instance, is opened by the chorale-like sequence of muted, *pianissimo* chords of the strings. This chorale is a rather strange, even cold and mysterious, piece of music because its chords are but empty fifths stacked one on top of the other, and they are played *non vibrato*. The reply to this massive block is the piano solo which starts at bar 23: a series of descending, exquisitely decorated melodies played *dolce* and in a rather speech-like style. These two passages – the chorale and the declamation – together create something of a dialogue, just as in the second movement of Beethoven's Fourth Piano Concerto. At this point an unusual system of correspondences occurs. This Bartókian dialogue anticipates the dialogue of the Adagio religioso of the Third Piano Concerto (1945), where we hear the conversation of strings and the solo piano. (And the structure of the dialogue in that later work definitely alludes to the 'Heiliger Dankgesang' movement of Beethoven's String Quartet in A minor Op.132.)

The *presto* section in the centre of Bartók's slow movement in the Second Concerto cannot be considered a trio, or the middle part of a ternary form. Bartók himself maintained that this was, in fact, an independent scherzo movement. But this scherzo is far from the joking, original type of the Classical Viennese composers. Already by Beethoven's time the character of the scherzo was starting to change to something sarcastic and demonic. Bartók, so to speak, continued that process here in translating horrifying nightmares, wild chases and portraits of a savage Nature into music. A quite detailed genealogy can be drawn up for this fearful Bartókian scherzo, from his early burlesque pieces, through the grotesque dance of the wooden puppet of *The Wooden Prince,* to the chase passages of *The Miraculous Mandarin* and, looking forward, to the Third Piano Concerto with its more peaceful representation of the night and its 'bird music'.

The Second Piano Concerto is a particularly complex and ambiguous work. Its first movement is a clear example of the Bartókian version of a Baroque concerto, while the remaining movements leave behind the strict, austere, 'hammering' style of the 1920s and anticipate the more flexible and melodic style of Bartók's development in the mid-1930s. By the time of composition of this concerto Bartók had already completed the *Cantata profana,* and its flowing vocal melodies were increasingly competing with his earlier percussive pianistic intentions. In the pastel tone clusters of the second movement as well as the powerful and barbaric *allegro* of the third can also be recognized the roots of some of the essential ideas of his Music for Strings, Percussion and Celesta (1936). From the peak of the

Second Piano Concerto it was only one further step to those compositions of the mid–late 1930s which stand as the masterworks of Bartók's *œuvre*, and of twentieth-century music.

NOTES

1 *BBE*, p. 419.
2 Quoted in Stevens, pp. 231–2.
3 See *BBE*, pp. 467–8 and pp. 316–19, respectively.
4 *BBE*, p. 341.
5 *BBE*, p. 288.
6 The immediate 'ancestor' to the tune shown in Ex. 4 is the dance melody which opens the second movement of the Dance Suite. See Ex. 2 in the chapter 'Dance Suite' in this *Companion*.
7 *BBE*, p. 381.
8 *BBE*, pp. 419–20.
9 This structural similarity provides further reason for believing that the basic ideas for that later Sonata were born with the First Piano Concerto.
10 *BBE*, p. 423.
11 *BBE*, p. 422.

36

Second Violin Concerto

VERA LAMPERT

Although Bartók marked the period for composing his Second Violin Concerto as 'Aug. 1937 – 31 Dec. 1938' at the end of the work's score, the history of the work goes back at least one year further. It was, in fact, on 10 August 1936 that the idea of composing a violin concerto was proposed to Bartók by one of the most eminent Hungarian violinists, Zoltán Székely. Székely had, since the early 1920s, been a frequent chamber music partner of Bartók. Their professional relationship soon developed into friendship, as evidenced by their many exchanges of correspondence, Bartók's dedication of the Second Violin Rhapsody (1928) to Székely, and the unusually warm wording of the dedication of this Second Violin Concerto: 'To my dear friend, Zoltán Székely'.

At the time of Székely's proposition Bartók was working on his Music for Strings, Percussion and Celesta. But on 1 September 1936, some days before that work was completed, he decided to pursue the idea of the violin concerto and asked his publisher, Universal Edition, to send him the most recent relevant literature in their catalogue. They mailed him the violin concertos of Berg, Weill and Szymanowski.

Other than in the months of summer, Bartók usually had insufficient free time to write major compositions. The impending season of 1936–7 was no exception. He had concert engagements, private piano students, and his work at the Academy of Sciences (his regular job since 1934), where he was preparing several thousand Hungarian folk melodies for publication. In addition, for November 1936 he organized a trip to Turkey to collect folk music among the nomadic Anatolian tribes. Consequently, when he met up with Zoltán Székely in January 1937 for a concert tour to Paris, Brussels, London and Hilversum, it was only the overall plan of the work that they could discuss.

Székely recalls that Bartók's first plan was to write a one-movement piece in variation form. Since the second movement of the concerto is a theme with variations one can speculate that this represents the oldest layer of the work. Recent investigations also suggest that it may be built on a never-realized composition: an orchestral work consisting of 'a series of short pieces' which Bartók reported to his publisher on 1 September 1936 as being partially ready in draft. Székely wanted to have a 'real', three-movement concerto, however, and Bartók consented. But first, in May 1937, he accepted another commission, for the Sonata for Two Pianos and Percussion, written during July–August of that year. While working on the Sonata the principal themes of the Violin Concerto came to his mind. The first sketches of the two themes of the first movement were written on the back of a sheet of music used for the Sonata. This is the time – August 1937 – that Bartók recorded as the starting point of his composing of this concerto. He must have been working on it seriously during the last stages of composing the Sonata, or, at least, immediately after finishing it. He presented a good part of the first movement to Székely on 20 September, as Székely has recalled: 'Already during my first visit Bartók pulled out the beautifully copied first two pages of the concerto and we played it through. Of course, only the violin part was copied. He accompanied from a sketch.'[1] Nevertheless, it took Bartók about a year just to complete the first draft of the whole work. During the last month or so of its composition, Bartók's attention was again divided, as he fulfilled a new commission from Benny Goodman and Joseph Szigeti for a trio. That work, *Contrasts*, was composed in a matter of weeks, and finished on 24 September 1938.

Bartók worked on the orchestration of the concerto during the autumn of 1938. He finished it on 31 December and started to send lithographs of the fair manuscript copy to Székely on 9 January 1939. During the first days of March 1939 they had 'very good and long rehearsals together' in Paris, and effected some important changes. It was then that Bartók added the two semiquaver upbeat notes to the main theme and probably provided the alternative ending involving the solo violin, again at Székely's suggestion. (The original ending of the finale – the second version in the published score – had no role for the solo violin, and Székely wished the work to end 'like a concerto, not a symphony'.)

The prolonged, frequently interrupted creation of the Violin Concerto had no effect upon its spontaneity and freshness. From the start it has been one of the most popular of Bartók's compositions. In the Bartók literature it is considered as one of the first representatives of Bartók's later style, which Tibor Tallián describes as 'transfigured, ambiguous and sublime concert music, with bright and transparent harmonic language and texture, with polished characters, their elegance, abstraction and restraint reminiscent more of Mozart than Beethoven'.[2] In the concerto this new intonation is immediately apparent as the six introductory bars present the airy, serene B major background to the main theme, a broad, self-assured and spirited song which – together with the theme of the second movement – belongs among Bartók's most inspired and memorable melodies.

A closer look reveals that the specific flavour of these melodies comes from the deep roots that they have in the traditions of folk music. The opening theme is modelled on certain folk dances that Bartók collected from Transylvanian peasant violinists. This particular type of melody, a slow dance with 'heroic, march-like character' (Bartók's description in his book *Rumanian Folk Music*) preserved the tradition of *verbunkos*, the Hungarian national dance that flourished at the turn of the nineteenth century and had since then dominated every aspect of the musical scene in Hungary. The young Bartók originally adopted this style as the ground upon which to build his nationalistic style. Later, when he discovered the musical tradition of the primitive village people, he turned his back on the popular, Romantic *verbunkos*. But when he encountered the peasant version of this music he used it as his source of inspiration once again, first in arranging this music for the concert podium in his violin rhapsodies, and then in absorbing its features into his own themes. During one phase of the composition of the Violin Concerto (in September 1937, when he copied out the first two pages of the solo violin part for Székely) he even wrote 'Tempo di verbunkos', but did not retain this, probably because he named the first movement of his *Contrasts* 'Verbunkos'. But the syncopated, dotted rhythm and characteristic, rich ornamentation leave no doubt about the theme's *verbunkos* origin. Further features recalling folk music are the melody's four-line structure, with a fifth relationship between the first two lines,[3] a frequent structural characteristic of the 'new'-style Hungarian folk melodies. The peculiar scale, with its Dorian colour (involving a raised sixth degree) and stress upon the pentatonic main degrees and alternating major–minor thirds, could also be found in a typical folk-dance melody in Bartók's collection.

This extraordinary opening theme stands at the head of a concentrated sonata form of Classical simplicity, where the subsequent elements are clearly defined and easily recognizable. The main theme is followed by an energetic transitional section (*risoluto*, from bar 56), which leads to the secondary theme, a lonely, hesitating melody (Ex. 1) set within a soft, mysteriously distant orchestral texture.

EX. I

This theme attracts special attention because of its connection to the dodecaphonic technique of composition. It is built on a 'row' containing twelve different notes, and on the various inversions and transpositions of this 'row'. Bartók used the twelve-note technique rather freely, however. The sequence of the notes is not stable; they are interchanged from section to section for the sake of melodic contour. Also, the sections are clearly separated, not only in texture, by the alternations of solo violin and orchestra, but also because each 'row' contains a thirteenth note, which brings a return of the initial note and so provides a tonal frame. Significantly, the fifth and sixth sections make use only of ten notes, exactly as shown in Bartók's very first sketches. (His original idea was for a ten-note theme, but at a later stage in his preparation he added in the missing two notes.) Zoltán Székely remembers that Bartók asked him jokingly if he had noticed the twelve-note structure of the second theme but 'he did not seem to give great importance to the matter. He was rather pleased to show that one can compose tonally even using twelve tones.'[4]

The second unit of the form, the development, starts at bar 115 with a reference back to the movement's introductory bars. Now the solo violin picks up this pentatonic fragment of melody, extemporizes upon it with triplets and stretches fourth intervals over a bucolic background.

Not long before he started work on this concerto Bartók called attention to an important feature of his style in an interview:

> It has probably been observed that I place much of the emphasis on the work of technical elaboration, that I do not like to repeat a musical thought unchanged, and I never repeat a detail unchanged. This practice of mine arises from my inclination for variation and for transforming themes.[5]

Nowhere does this principle hold better than in the recapitulations of Bartók's sonata forms, where he strove to find unique ways of bringing back the themes of his expositions. In earlier compositions he reversed their order, used their inversions and changed their rhythmic or metric profile. In the Violin Concerto several of these methods are combined in another unique solution: the themes first return in inversion (see Ex. 2, for instance) but after that the original form is also repeated. In addition, the segments of the transitional, *risoluto* theme and the twelve-note theme return woven one with the other.

A substantial coda (from bar 363) balances the structure, corresponding to the development section. It starts with a brilliant cadenza emanating from quarter tones – a novelty in Bartók's

EX. 2

output which occurs again in his Sonata for solo violin – and leading to the movement's culminating point, the apotheosis of the main theme, which is characteristically of a strong Hungarian flavour.

Other than in a few short piano pieces, Bartók rarely used variation form. The concerto's second movement is his only large-scale exercise in this form, a surprising fact in light of his stated inclination towards variation procedures. In his exhaustive analysis of this movement László Somfai argues that Bartók's choice of variations has to be seen as a manifestation of his attempt to break away from the strict, palindromic form which had been the structural 'solution' in his most important works of the preceding decade.[6]

The theme is a warm, tender melody of arresting beauty. As the first sketches testify, it was born in a single wave of inspiration: Bartók did not even have music paper to hand when it came to his mind.[7] Folksong reminiscences play an important role again in this seemingly simple, but infinitely complex theme. Six variations follow. In each of them the solo violin is kept in the foreground and the proportions and contours of the theme are throughout preserved. In spite of the differing characters of the variations there are many extremely delicate cross-references, which result in a highly complex structure. Somfai's unorthodox analysis, which goes beyond the traditional description of the character of each variation to consider tonal structure, phrase structure, instrumental groupings and registral formations as aspects of the variation procedure, concluded that in this movement, 'Bartók forged far ahead, and reached certain abstractions in the problem of filling in musical space'.[8] He also stated:

> As regards its instrumentation, the second movement constitutes one of Bartók's best works and not only because of its faultless perfection but mainly because the principles it embodies are already virtually unBartók-like in foreshadowing the purposefulness, the permutations and the graphic ideas of the serial composers.[9]

In the first variation the theme's song-like character is changed to a more agitated recitative monologue. Then, in the second variation, the smoother, singing tone is recalled but the intervals are broader and the orchestral texture is different, bringing in the woodwind instruments which were previously absent. Abrupt contrast appears with the third variation's *forte* double stoppings. Its drone-like repetitions of notes come from the style of peasant violinists, a technique that has its counterpart in the outer movements of the concerto. The fourth variation goes even further. The theme's simplified chorale-like version appears in the low strings of the orchestra; above it the solo violin's part is reduced to organ-points with trills and embellishments reminiscent of filigree work. In the second part of this variation the solo violin joins the strings in the imitative elaboration of the chorale theme, leaving the trills to the woodwinds. An anapaestic rhythmic figure dominates the fifth variation, the scherzo part of the movement. The last variation recalls the fourth by its imitative presentation of the theme – this time on plucked strings – and with the soloist's light and graceful ornamentation. Then it leads back to the main theme, which reappears an octave higher, soaring to and then dissolving in unworldly heights.

When Bartók broke the news to Székely that he was just finishing the sketch of the third movement, he referred to the formal relationship of the first and third movements: 'strictly speaking, it is a free variation of the first movement (so I managed to outwit you. I wrote variations after all.)'[10] The existence of thematic relationships between outer movements is not a novelty in Bartók's *œuvre*: the finales of his most concentrated cyclic works in palindromic form written over the preceding decade (the Fourth and Fifth String Quartets and Second Piano Concerto, for instance) all cited material from their first movements. In this Violin Concerto (and in the following composition, the Divertimento), however, there is more than occasional reference to the themes of the first movement. Here, the finale is constructed exclusively from transformed first-movement thematic material: all the themes return; they have the same place and function in the structure of the movement as originally, and even the transitional and developmental sections show similar traits.

On the basis of the sketches it is most probable that Bartók did not have a preconceived idea of the close relationship of variation between the outer movements when he started to work on the concerto. At least, at the time of sketching the first two main themes of the first movement he was not yet concerned about his finale. The first theme of the third movement – and thereby the idea of a free variation of first-movement material – occurred to him during the later stages of composing the first movement. He wrote the main theme of the finale hastily into the first continuous sketch of the first movement, in the empty staff under the first section of the first theme, as shown in Ex .3.[11] (The 'corrections' in the third bar are Bartók's.)

EX. 3

It did not come to him as easily as the original theme: the first and last thematic sections do not show much hesitation, but the second section has several 'corrections' and the third is missing altogether at this point. Nevertheless, the theme's character is already there and, with it, the character of the whole finale: a boisterous, stamping dance. The relationship to the original theme is clearly recognizable: the first seven notes are identical but the rest is extremely compressed. It is like a miniature folk-song, consisting of four isometric, seven-syllable lines. The $\frac{4}{4}$ metre is changed to $\frac{3}{4}$, which recalls the proportional relationship of Renaissance dances.

The orchestra's refrain brings a new transformation of the main theme, with a waltz-like rhythm (Ex. 4a). The same rhythm is then attached to the second, twelve-note theme (Ex. 4b).

EX. 4

The first movement's transitional thematic material is brought to the common denominator of triplets – a very efficient unifying rhythmic element. Besides being in sharp contrast with the main and secondary themes, it also has a tremendous driving force, with its note repetitions and long linear scalar sections. The fourths which added a characteristic touch to the profile of the work's main theme and gained significance in the development section of the first movement, receive an increasingly important role in the finale. They reach a particularly memorable conclusion during its coda, with a diminutive, rocking melody built exclusively of perfect fourths (Ex. 5).

EX. 5

Once again the structure is a blueprint of a folk melody. It has four lines of only four syllables, with an *A A B A* content – the quintessence of a folksong.

The first performance of the Second Violin Concerto took place in Amsterdam on 23 March 1939, with Zoltán Székely as soloist and Willem Mengelberg conducting the Concertgebouw Orchestra. Bartók could not be present; he had another concert engagement in Budapest the following day. The only time he heard his Violin Concerto was in New York during 1943, with Tossy Spivakovsky as soloist. Bartók was rather pleased with the work, and wrote to Joseph Szigeti on 30 January 1944: 'My greatest joy was that there was no trouble with regard to the instrumentation. Nothing had to be changed. For an orchestral "accompaniment" to the violin is a very delicate matter.'[12]

As it happened, Székely's world première of the work was recorded by the Hilversum studios and, to the good fortune of succeeding generations, the original shellac recording survived in Székely's keeping. This recording is of priceless documentary value, not only because of Székely's excellent performance and the active role he played in bringing the work to life and shaping its final form, but also because it bears witness to the composer's personal intentions concerning tempo, character and other details. It was reconstructed and distributed by Hungaroton in 1971 as a supplementary volume to the complete recorded edition of Bartók's works.[13]

NOTES

1 Quoted in László Somfai, *Tizennyolc Bartók tanulmány*, Budapest (Zeneműkiadó), 1981, p. 107.
2 *Bartók Béla szemtől szemben*, Budapest (Gondolat), 1981, p. 249.
3 That is, the second line is the virtual repetition of the first but is placed a fifth higher.
4 Quoted in Somfai, op. cit., p. 110.
5 As quoted in Bence Szabolcsi, 'Bartók's Principles of Composition', in *Bartók Studies*, ed. Todd Crow, Detroit (Information Coordinators), 1976, p. 19.
6 'Strategics of Variation in the Second Movement of Bartók's Violin Concerto 1937–1938', *SM*, vol.19 (1977), pp. 161–202.
7 See the facsimile of this sketch in Somfai, *Tizennyolc Bartók tanulmány*, p. 106.
8 László Somfai, 'Strategics of Variation', p. 196.
9 Ibid., p. 190.
10 Quoted in László Somfai, *Tizennyolc Bartók tanulmány*, p. 105.
11 This sketch is now in the possession of Péter Bartók (Homosassa, Florida).
12 *BBL*, p. 329.
13 LPX 11573.

37
Concerto for Orchestra

ELLIOTT ANTOKOLETZ

The Concerto for Orchestra, one of Bartók's most popular works, was composed between 15 August and 8 October 1943 at Saranac Lake, New York, during the composer's self-imposed exile from Nazified Hungary. The circumstances surrounding its composition were among the unhappiest in Bartók's life. His health began to decline in 1942, and he soon gave his last concert, during January 1943, in which his wife and he played the concerto arrangement of his Sonata for Two Pianos and Percussion. The general lack of acceptance of his performances of his own music during this final period in the United States, together with his illness and isolation from his native national folk-music sources, were the main causes of his anguish during such uncertain times for Europe and the rest of the world. His only contact with Eastern European folk-music materials was permitted by a grant from Columbia University, which made it possible for him to work on the Milman Parry collection of Yugoslav folk-music recordings (held at Harvard University) from March 1941 until the end of 1942, while he was also editing his own Romanian and Turkish materials.

This research was one of several significant events that led to the composition of the Concerto for Orchestra.[1] While transcribing the Yugoslav materials from the recordings he made his first discovery of Dalmatian two-part chromatic folk melodies. This provided him with a broader spectrum of divergent Eastern European sources, which he was now able to synthesize in the Concerto with some of the most abstract contemporary art-music techniques, as well as traditional Classical forms and procedures.[2] The idea for the work was directly sparked in 1942 when his London publisher Ralph Hawkes asked him for 'a series of concertos for solo instrument or instruments and string orchestra ... or combinations of solo instruments and string orchestra', although the actual commission came in 1943 from Koussevitzky, who sought an orchestral work to be performed by the Boston Symphony Orchestra.

Within the traditional forms and procedures the varying themes, each of which is derived from a specific national folk-music style that characterizes a given section or movement, generate the larger harmonic fabric based on both traditional (diatonic) and non-traditional (cyclic-interval) pitch formations.[3] Special interactions and transformations occur among these pitch collections to produce a highly integrated yet organically evolving form. The significance of these developments is that diatonic as well as octatonic and whole-tone collections,[4] whether employed as the basis of traditional folk-like themes or as abstract scale patterns, primarily function as pitch sets. That is, they are independent of traditional major–minor harmonic roles.

In the first movement the two introductory themes (from bars 1 and 30) each unfold in the four-line stanzaic structure of Hungarian folksong, the opening one of which is in the pentatonic mode and *parlando rubato* rhythm of the 'old'-style Hungarian folksong.[5] A connection between the folk-like pentatonic structure of this theme (F♯ A B C♯ E) and the more abstract cycle of fourths is expressed in the ordering of the pentatonic theme as a series of perfect-fourth segments. These together imply the presence of the five-note cyclic collection C♯ F♯ B E A. A further cyclic-interval transformation of the pentatonic theme occurs in the consequent tremolo phrase (bars 6–10). The upper strings unfold a symmetrical pattern around an axis of symmetry, C–C, the entire semitonal content of which is encompassed by A♭ and E. While the perfect-fourth cyclic segments in the antecedent phrase (C♯–F♯–B / A–E / F♯–C♯) are interconnected by two whole-tone dyads (B–A and E–F♯), the semitonal cyclic-interval content (A♭ A B♭ B C D♭ D E♭ E) of the expanding and contracting phases of the consequent phrase is partitioned into mutually exclusive segments of the two whole-tone cycles (A♭ B♭ C D E and A B D♭ E♭). The whole tone (interval 2/10),[6] a common property of the opening pentatonic theme and the chromatic symmetry of the contrasting tremolo phrase, therefore serves as a link between the interval-5/7 (perfect fourth/perfect fifth) and 1/11 (minor second/major seventh) cycles.

These cyclic interactions are further developed throughout the introduction (to bar 75). For instance: the arpeggiations at bars 35–6, shown in Ex. 1, which are rhythmic diminutions of the opening perfect-fourth (pentatonic) theme, as well as a foreshadowing of motif *b* in the main theme of the exposition (see Ex. 2), are also based on intercalations of interval-5/7 and 2/10 cyclic segments. The first arpeggiation unfolds two ascending perfect-fourth segments (E A D and C F B♭) that intersect at a whole tone (D–C); the following inverted arpeggiation (C G D and E B F♯) transposes the initial one up by a whole tone.

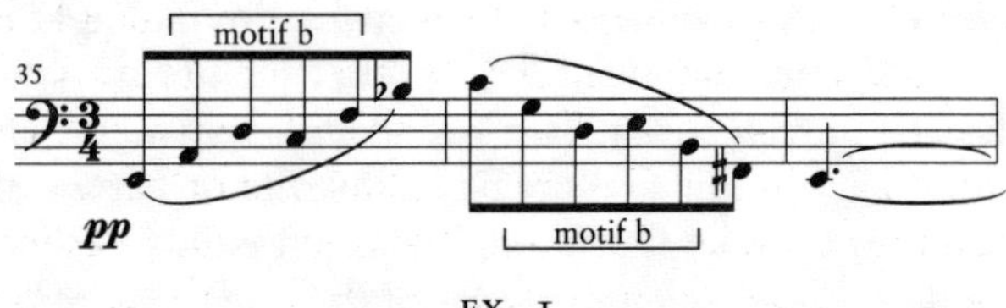

EX. 1

In the main theme of the exposition, beginning at bar 76, these cyclic-interval interactions are again fused with folk-music elements, in this case with the *tempo giusto* rhythm and tritone so characteristic of Slovak folk tunes. As shown in Ex. 2, the first of the theme's two contrasting motifs (*a*), is based on a tritone-bounded segment of an octatonic scale, F G A♭ B♭ B, which intercalates whole tones and semitones (interval ratio 2:1); motif *b* is based on an ambiguous segment of either an octatonic or diatonic scale, C F E♭ A♭, which contains two perfect fourths intersecting at a whole tone (interval ratio 2:5). Thus, these interval ratios in the main themes are a more systematic manifestation of the cyclic-interval relations of the introduction, in which cyclic-interval 2 commonly interacts with cyclic-intervals 1 and 5.

I, 76-8 (violins)

Allegro vivace ♩. = 83

motif a — 2 1 2 1

motif b — 5 2 5

EX. 2

In the organic unfolding of the theme both motifs are expanded into larger diatonic and octatonic collections, respectively, each of which is also transformed into the other of these two collections by means of special pitch-set interactions. Both motifs are most prominently and completely expanded into the larger sets in the development section (from bar 231). A stretto based on motif *a*, at bars 246–8 (strings), results in expanded octatonic scales. The final ascent of the violins in this stretto (at bars 247–8) expands motif *a* into a larger octatonic segment, C♯ D♯ E F♯ G A [] [], while the violas and cellos expand the motif into a complete statement of another octatonic collection: B C♯ D E E♯ F𝄪 G♯ A♯ (B). The last five notes of the latter, in enharmonic spelling F G A♭ B♭ B, outline the original transposition of motif *a*. Whereas motif *b* was expanded earlier into a larger F Phrygian collection – F G♭ A♭ B♭ C D♭ E♭, at bars 86–91, near the ending of the first theme – and subsequently into an ambiguous C♯ Aeolian or Dorian segment – C♯ D♯ E F♯ G♯ [] B, at bars 134–44 (transitional trombone theme) – the next stretto in the development (from bar 248) now draws motif *b* into the octatonic sphere by means of sequential extension. Here, the first six bars expand motif *b* to a larger segment of the remaining octatonic collection, A D C F E♭ A♭, and, at the end of this stretto (from bar 258) to a complete octatonic collection: G C B♭ E♭ D♭ G♭ E A (in scalar ordering, G A B♭ C D♭ E♭ E G♭). Thus, this octatonic reinterpretation of the ambiguous diatonic/octatonic motif *b* permits it to have a closer association with octatonic motif *a*.

The relationship between the interval ratios of the two motifs (2:1 and 2:5) is one of cyclic-interval expansion, a trend already explicitly established at the opening of the development (from bar 231). Successive statements of motif *a*, each bounded by a tritone cycle, are transposed up by semitones, D♭–G and D–G♯ in the ascending forms being followed by E♭–A in the descending ones. From bar 242 the ascending statements of motif *a* on the strings in the inverted stretto then proceed by whole steps through one of the complete whole-tone cycles (E♭–A, F–B, G–C♯, A–D♯, B–E♯, C♯–G), against the modified descending whole-tone transpositions. The development section ends (bars 316–85) with a fugato based on the earlier transitional trombone theme. The succession of interval-5/7 entries is altered at two points by interval 2/10 (F B♭ F B♭ / C G C G / F), suggesting a projection of the 2:5 interval ratio of motif *b*. Thus, the overall development reflects the local motion from the cyclic-interval properties of motif *a* to those of motif *b*.

Diverse folk-music sources, which also characterize the successive themes of the second movement, are further absorbed into abstract pitch formations and procedures. Theme *a* (bassoons in parallel sixths, from bar 8) is in the style of the Yugoslav *kolo*, or round dance. Ambiguous octatonic and diatonic segments that simultaneously unfold in each of the opening bassoon lines are more completely realized in the closing phrase of this thematic group, at bar 18 (Ex. 3), where basic motif *a* from the first movement returns as an octatonic segment in the first bassoon (C♯ D♯ E F♯ G) and as a diatonic segment in the second bassoon (E F♯ G♯ A♯ B).

The octatonic form of the motif is melodically enframed by two interval-3 cycles – B♯ D♯ F♯ A and A♯ C♯ E G – which together produce a complete octatonic collection to fulfil the octatonic implications of the motif: C♯ D♯ E F♯ G A A♯ B♯. The diatonic form of the motif is similarly enframed by two dominant seventh chords, D♯ F𝄪 A♯ C♯ and C♯ E♯ G♯ B. The contrapuntal alignment of the latter two diatonic constructions with the interval-3 cycles of the first bassoon draws these dominant sevenths into two distinct seven-note octatonic segments: C♯ D♯ [] F♯ F𝄪 A A♯ B♯ and C♯ [] E E♯ G G♯ A♯ B.

Theme *c* (bar 52, clarinets in parallel minor sevenths) is in the style of the *sopel* (folk oboe) of Dalmatian folksong, while theme *d* (bar 60, flute duet in parallel fifths, major mode, and

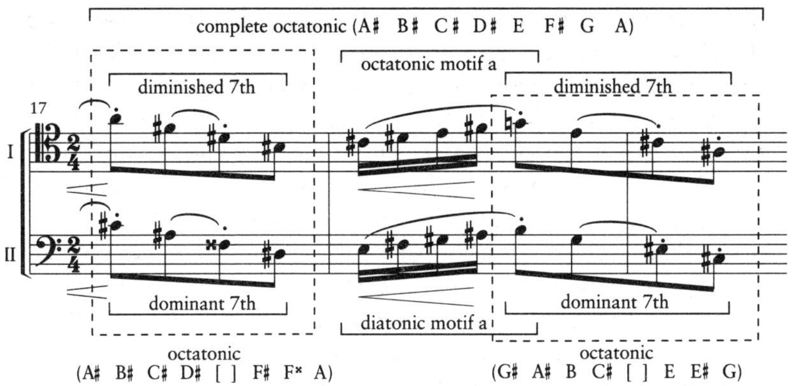

EX. 3

dotted rhythm) reveals influences from Western Europe. Segments from all three octatonic collections are separately outlined in the two flute lines (bars 60–61) and accompanying harmony (bars 60–62): A♯ B♯ C♯ [] E (first flute), D♯ E♯ F♯ [] A (second flute) and G♯ A♯ B C♯ D (strings), the flutes then unfolding two complete, ascending octatonic scales. The cadence of theme-group *d* (bars 82–3) is a special adumbration of the more intense melodic fusions of diatonic and octatonic sets that will permeate the last two movements of the Concerto. The parallel ascending flute lines each overlap complete major and Mixolydian scales with octatonic statements of motif *a* (Ex. 4).

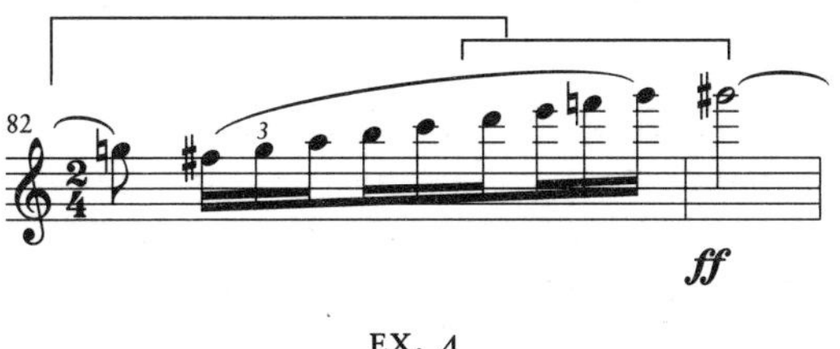

EX. 4

At the opening of the trio (bar 123) a chorale-like brass theme now unfolds pentatonic lines in the tuba and second trombone, harmonized by triads. This is cadenced by the progression F♯ A C♯ E, A C♯ E G♯, B D♯ F♯ (bars 125–6), the first two chords of which produce a kind of semi-cadence close of the melody (the so-called Yugoslav cadence that had infiltrated Romanian Transylvania).[7]

The third movement, which is the nucleus of the five-movement arch form, provides the most abstract manifestations of the cyclic-interval relations discussed thus far and, at the same time, expresses a 'lugubrious death song' that includes a chromatic viola theme in the style of a folk lament (bars 62–3). Following the opening inverted statement of motif *b* from the first movement a string stretto unfolds four complete linear transpositions of cell Z, as shown in Ex. 5.[8]

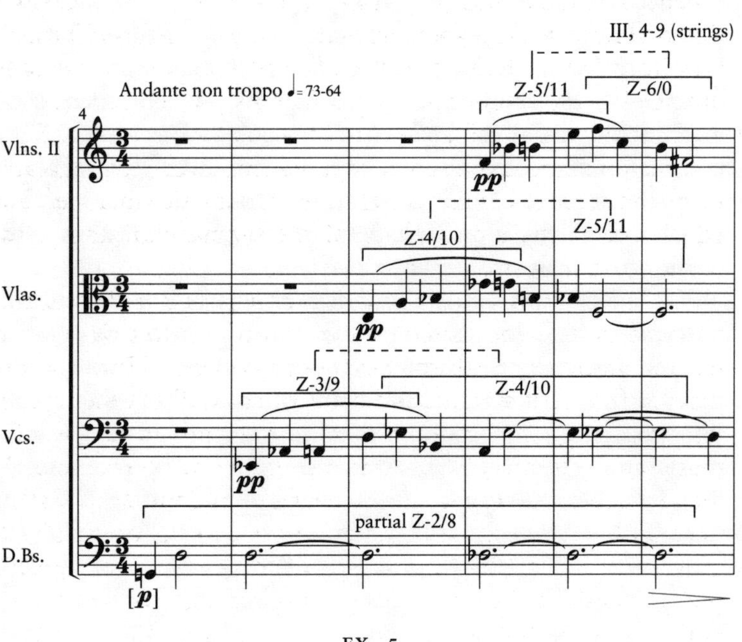

EX. 5

The interval ratio of this double-tritone cyclic tetrachord is 5:1, that is, both orderings of cell Z – a semitonal gap between two perfect fourths, or a perfect-fourth gap between two semitones – are manifested in each line. The adjacency of ascending and descending forms of cell Z produces a secondary symmetrical cell, based on a contraction of the Z interval ratio to 4:1 (such as A B♭ D E♭, on cellos). While the 5:1 ratio interlocks two interval-6 (tritone) cycles, the 4:1 ratio suggests an interlocking of two interval-5 (perfect-fourth) cyclic segments. A further intervallic contraction occurs in a new, rhythmically diminished figure, C E♭ E G A♭ B (from bar 10), based on interval ratio 3:1 interlocking two interval-4 (major-third) cycles. The lyrical oboe theme that unfolds against this figure (bars 12–18) is based on a final contraction to interval ratio 1:1 (X-8: G♯ A B♭ B). This semitonal theme is locally partitioned into its two interval-2 (whole-tone) dyads, B♭–G♯ and A–B, thereby suggesting a transitional stage between ratios 3:1 and 1:1. The theme is cadenced in the winds (bars 19–22, first quaver) by C D♭ E♭ E (interval ratio 2:1), before returning to the 3:1 figure. Thus, all the interval ratios between cell Z and cell X have systematically unfolded to the end of this section (bar 33), which cadences on a return to partial cell Z, D♭ G♭ G (piccolo) of ratio 5:1. Such contractions and expansions continue more or less regularly throughout the remaining sections, the chromatic viola theme of which begins the return phase of the symmetrical arch form of the movement (from bar 62).

The last two movements tend toward a more popular character in their thematic materials and return to a less rigidly systematic unfolding of abstract cyclic-interval sets. However, the greatest fusion of diatonic and octatonic as well as other cyclic-interval collections occurs in these movements, in which folk-music and other popular features continue to be prominently manifested. In addition to the emphasis on the tritone as well as unequal-beat patterns in the opening oboe theme of the fourth movement, which suggests a Slovak folk style, a composed, pseudo-folksong melody of Zsigmond Vincze, 'You are lovely, you are beautiful, Hungary', appears as the main viola theme of the middle section (bars 42–50). Furthermore, Bartók's use of quotation of another type of music is also employed in this fourth, 'Intermezzo Interrotto' movement. In a 1942 broadcast of Shostakovich's ('Leningrad') Seventh Symphony Bartók was very surprised to hear repetitions of a theme that 'sounded like a Viennese cabaret song', and was to satirize the work by using a variant of this theme as an interruption (from bar 76).

The opening diatonic oboe theme, ambiguously in B major/minor, is gradually joined with and transformed into the octatonic sphere. The minor mode is more explicitly established by the contrapuntal alignment of an unambiguous B minor flute segment against the third statement of the theme (from bar 32). However, longer segments of these two lines (bars 33–8, third quaver) before the chromatic shift in the flute, together reveal a permutation of a special non-diatonic folk mode, E F♯ G♯ A♯ B C♯ D E, the first six notes of which outline an E Lydian segment, the last six an octatonic segment.[9] Such diatonic–octatonic overlappings are implied in the popular viola theme of the serenade-like trio (Ex. 6), which is otherwise traditionally harmonized by dominant–tonic progressions.

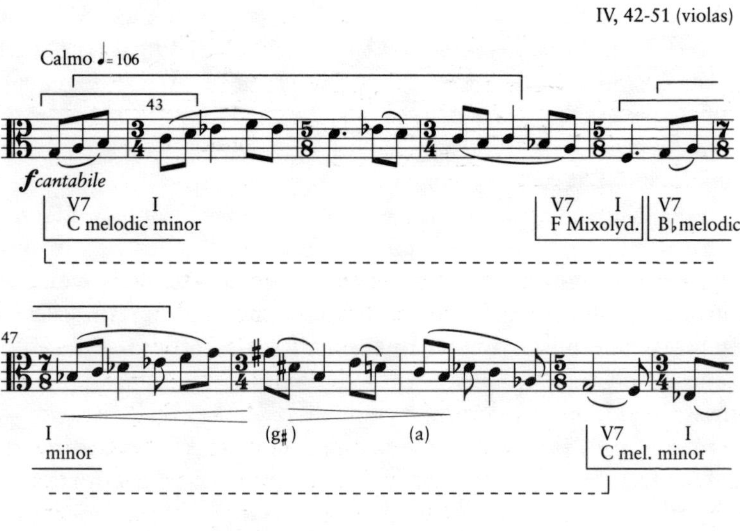

EX. 6

The C melodic minor scale of the first phrase of this theme, G A B C D E♭ F (bars 42–5),[10] implies the presence of overlapping diatonic and octatonic segments G A B C D and A B C D E♭ F. The tune shifts to B♭ melodic minor at the beginning of the next phrase, F G A B♭ C D♭ E♭, similarly implying the diatonic and octatonic segments F G A B♭ C and G A B♭ C D♭ E♭.

Complete octatonic collections are unfolded in subsequent passages of this movement, but literal extensions of the hybrid diatonic–octatonic theme to the complete forms of the two overlapping sets are most explicitly and thoroughly manifested in the fifth movement. These are part of a larger context pervaded by transformed bagpipe motifs that Bartók had collected from Romanian Transylvania,[11] the development section (from bar 96) further suggesting the Balinese gamelan (tuned percussion) orchestra. The final flourish of ascending scales just prior to the coda (Ex. 7) is initiated by a reappearance of the permuted C melodic minor mode of the popular viola theme from the fourth movement (G A B C D E♭ F).

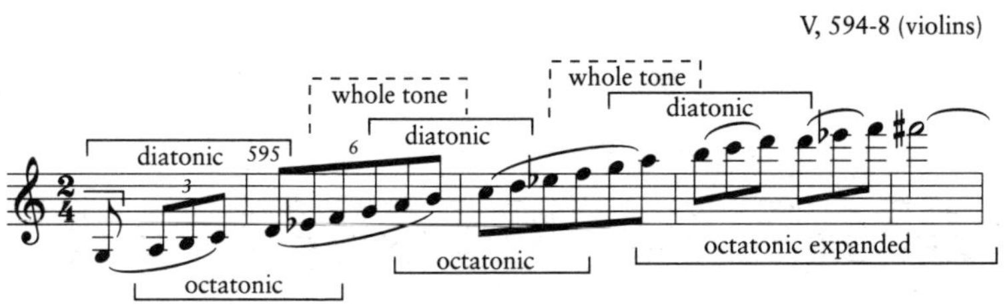

EX. 7

The six-note octatonic segment of the mode is extended at this cadence to seven notes by the addition of the final F♯ (A B C D E♭ F F♯ []). The projection of this modal scale through several octaves also brings into adjacency the five notes of the whole-tone segment contained within the scale (E♭ F G A B []).

The complete forms of all three pitch-sets implied in the non-diatonic folk mode – diatonic, octatonic and whole-tone – are generated in the extensive scale passages accompanying the central fanfare theme (bars 482–555).[12] Each of the entry statements of the fanfare's accompanying scalar stretto is based on a permutation of the non-diatonic folk mode A♭ B♭ C D E♭ F G♭, against which the violas add the tritonal transposition, D E F♯ G♯ A B C (bars 484–5). While the initiating A♭ Lydian (A♭ B♭ C D E♭ F) and D Lydian (D E F♯ G♯ A B) segments of the two larger modal transpositions are linearly overlapped by the octatonic segments C D E♭ F G♭ and F♯ G♯ A B C, respectively, the contrapuntal alignment of these octatonic segments jointly produces the first complete form of the octatonic set in this passage: C D E♭ F G♭ / F♯ G♯ A B C. Furthermore, the alignment of the two Lydian tetrachords analogously produces the complete whole-tone cycle A♭ B♭ C D / D E F♯ G♯. The basic mode is then linearly extended to the complete octatonic scale, as A♭ B♭ C D E♭ F G♭ A♭ A B (from bar 486). Significantly, the descending scales in first violins and cellos (bars 491–2) bring back the two transpositions of the non-diatonic folk mode of the popular viola theme (as shown in Ex. 6, above), but now extending their octatonic segments through the entire octatonic scale. At this point the inner voices simultaneously provide the respective tritonal transpositions of the outer voices, so that a succession of whole-tone (French-sixth) tetrachords is harmonically generated.

More abstract cyclic-interval transformations of the mode are introduced at the cadence of the bass clarinet fanfare statement (bar 498), where the octatonic interval ratio 2:1 of the mode is expanded in the inversionally related scales to interval ratio 3:1. This expanded interval ratio, which is reminiscent of the more systematic contracting and expanding procedures in the central movement, implies the presence of interlocking interval-4 cycles (for instance, that A♭ F E C♯ C A G♯ is a joining of A♭ E C G♯ and F C♯ A). The latter, which represent segments of the two whole-tone scales, respectively, foreshadow the next significant transformation into both complete whole-tone cycles (from bar 533), in the ascending and descending scalar phases. At the final return of the fanfare section the theme itself expands the ratio to 4:1 (from bar 573, upper strings, flutes and piccolo) and to 5:1, or overlapping Z-cell transpositions, F B♭ B E and E A B♭ E♭ (bar 583, second beat, to bar 585, same instruments). In the remainder of the work the diatonic implications of the mode are increasingly realized as complete diatonic scales in alternation with the non-diatonic pitch-set components. Thus, the Concerto for Orchestra represents one of Bartók's most extensive fusions of diverse Eastern European folk-music sources and contemporary art-music principles.

NOTES

1 See Benjamin Suchoff, 'Program Notes for the *Concerto for Orchestra*', in *Béla Bartók: A Celebration*, New York (Book-of-the-Month Records), 1981, pp. 6ff.

2 Bartók stated: 'The title of this symphony-like orchestral work is explained by its tendency to treat the single instruments or instrumental groups in a *concertant* or soloistic manner.' *BBE*, p. 431. Bartók also provided a brief formal analysis of the composition.

3 An interval cycle is a series based on a single interval, the sequence of which is completed by the return of the initial pitch-class. Whole-tone scales or cycles of fourths are examples.

4 The octatonic collection – an eight-note scale alternating whole and half steps, or alternatively, half and whole steps – can be formed by interlocking either two minor-third or four tritone cycles.

5 These, and subsequent references to the various folk-music sources for the Concerto's themes are outlined in Suchoff, op. cit.

6 Intervals and their harmonic inversions in the octave are here calculated in semitones.

7 See *RFM*.iv, p. 20.

8 See my chapter 'Middle-period String Quartets' in this *Companion* for a description of the properties and numerical nomenclatures of cells X, Y and Z.

9 See *BBE*, p. 363.

10 If we rotate this scale to F G A B C D E♭ we see that it is a permuted transposition of the non-diatonic folk mode E F♯ G♯ A♯ B C♯ D referred to above.

11 Suchoff (op. cit.) refers to Bartók's transcription of an 'Ardelenescu' ('Transylvanian', or round dance) for comparison.

12 This theme, which introduces the movement, intermittently recurs between or within the sections of the sonata plan.

38
Final Concertos

SÁNDOR KOVÁCS

After the première of the Concerto for Orchestra and the Sonata for solo violin at the turn of 1944–5, it seemed that a calmer and more carefree period had started in Bartók's life. He found his financial situation more settled than a few years earlier; his illness seemed to have abated; his working mood remained tireless and he now had the opportunity to choose from commissions as he wished. His publisher, Ralph Hawkes, hoped for a new string quartet and offered him a considerable advance payment. The viola player William Primrose asked him for a viola concerto, and others encouraged him to write concertos, either for one or two pianos. These favourable developments he acknowledged with satisfaction in his correspondence, but added: 'the only obstacle is that I don't know where and when I could write this huge mass of scores!'[1] After a brief consideration he rejected the plan for a two-piano concerto. He accepted the advance payment sent for the string quartet (and noted down some ideas for the piece), and, likewise, sent a favourable answer to Primrose. But, first of all, he set to composing a new piano concerto. This concerto was not even intended for a client, but rather, as a surprise for his wife: 'If she could play it in three or four places then it would bring in about as much money as the one commission I refused', he wrote in February 1945 to his son Péter, then in armed service.[2] Even if he did not speak about it, he probably thought a good deal about the future: what would happen to his wife is she were left on her own and had to live by giving concerts (performing primarily his works, of course)? In the past year he had become convinced that Ditta had real difficulties with the piano part of the Second Piano Concerto. She was diligently rehearsing the work, but her strength was not sufficient for the dense octave and chordal passages. Perhaps this was the catalyst for his decision to write another concerto, still of virtuoso character but, nevertheless, technically easier than the Second.

It is not known when he noted down the first musical ideas for this work, but he certainly carried out the bulk of its composition during his summer vacation at Asheville, in North Carolina, and even worked intensively upon it during September, as far as his deteriorating health allowed. As was his custom, he first wrote a continuity draft in *particella* form, then added his notes about orchestration, and finally set about preparing the full score. All this he managed to do apart from the last two pages of the full score of the final movement. He had his son Péter draw the bar-lines on these final pages, and himself started to fill in bars 752–5 with their tremolo timpani figure, although in a rushed and scrawly hand. The orchestration of the remaining seventeen bars was completed by Tibor Serly, who happened to be with Bartók on the last afternoon he spent at home, and felt that it was partly owing to his visit that the composer had been prevented from completing the score.

As with the last works of other great composers, the Third Piano Concerto has frequently provided grounds for speculation during the decades since its première. In the 1950s a genuine cult emerged around it in Hungary, and abroad, unfortunately mainly at the expense of the previous two piano concertos. Many people were inclined to see the crown of the entire *œuvre* in this composition and, at the same time, the beginnings of a new style-period which would have surpassed everything before, had it not been interrupted so tragically. In order to justify their opinions, the supporters of this concept frequently quoted the words which were allegedly uttered by Bartók on the day of his death: 'the trouble is that I have to leave with my suitcase full'.[3] Others, including analysts of the Schoenberg school, generally evaluated Bartók's works written in the United States in a much more sceptical manner, referring in particular to the Third Piano Concerto. They believed that in the interests of success and popularity Bartók had been excessive in his attempt to adapt himself to the tastes of the average American public. Undoubtedly there lies some truth at the bottom of both arguments. Like many other European composers searching for shelter in the New World at this time, Bartók had attempted to adjust himself to the expectations of his new environment. But it is also a fact that, quite independently from his American experiences, he had already in the late 1930s been assaying a path towards a simpler and more Classical (perhaps, even Romantic) style. The Second Violin Concerto (1937–8) is the first work along this path towards the 'genial simplicity' that he acknowledged as his aim in a Belgian newspaper article of 1938. Nevertheless, the extreme evaluations of the Third Piano Concerto usually originated in a basic misunderstanding. This piece is essentially a 'feminine concerto',[4] and if this fact is overlooked then its key features, in particular its one-sidedness of tone, will not adequately be understood. Put another way: the fact that the dark colours, the customary 'barbaro' rhythms and the 'nocturnal' sounds are conspicuously absent from this Concerto is by no means proof that at the end of his life Bartók was giving up the rougher dissonances, or spectacularly withdrawing from his avant-garde past. It is improbable that he would have denied anything. Quite simply, on this occasion he did not strive for the 'completeness' which characterized his other large-scale and representative works, such as the earlier concertos. One could say that this composition consciously illustrates only the brighter, sunnier and more relaxed half of Bartók's artistic world.

The fundamental key of the concerto, E major, is not new among Bartók's works. But in contrast to his earlier E-based works – the First Piano Concerto, the Sonata for piano – this work has strong affinities with nineteenth-century music in that key, such as Mendelssohn's *A Midsummer Night's Dream* and the Wagnerian *Waldesrauschen*. (The string introduction to the first movement particularly recalls the latter.) The piano's main first movement theme, which enters at the end of the second bar with its stately dotted (sometimes double dotted) rhythms, revives the nineteenth-century Hungarian *verbunkos* dance. The *verbunkos* had come a long way in Bartók's *œuvre*: as a youth he enthused about it, but around 1904 or 1905 he turned away from it, or at least from its contemporary urban music-hall renditions. In the mid-1910s he recalled the dance in *The Wooden Prince*, but cast it in a negative role, using it to characterize the cold and rigid princess. From the late 1920s, from the time of the violin rhapsodies, he again began to change his opinion. That change is reflected in the noble and elegant main theme of the Second Violin Concerto,[5] the opening movement of *Contrasts* (1938), and, finally, in the Third Piano Concerto, in which the theme of *verbunkos* rhythm appears as a heavenly phenomenon over the rustling string background (Ex. 1).

With its whimsical lurches and sudden stops, this melody gives the impression of an improvisation, although after thorough study of the score it is not difficult to discover that its fluttering changeability masks a specific system and regularity: each of the bars of the opening builds a different scale or portion of a scale over the keynote of E, although the major character of these modes remains clearly observable throughout. Four different pitches can be heard in the string introduction: E, F♯, A, B. In the second bar the piano adds C♯, momentarily creating a pentatonic structure, until the G♯ is added in bar 3. Only the seventh degree, D♯, is missing for the complete major scale. Instead, however, bar 4 supplies a D♮, which, added to the existing pitches, completes a Mixolydian scale. G, instead of G♯, in bar 5 suggests a Dorian mode, while the G♯ and A♯ of bar 6 introduce a Lydian characteristic. All this play with the modes deserves attention because it is a particularly clear example of the 'polymodal chromaticism' about which Bartók spoke in his Harvard Lectures of 1943.[6]

In bar 18 the orchestra also begins to play this opening theme, thereby introducing the transition section of the sonata form. In fact, the theme appears in a variegated form in the orchestra, but in a version which none the less suggests in advance the aim of the transition: the key of the second theme, G major, or, at least, its opening interval. Bartók's first and second themes are thereby linked: the movement's opening B A C♯ B motif (Ex. 1, bars 2–3) is changed into B A D B at the start of the transition (Ex. 2a, bars 18–19). At the introduction of the second theme

EX. I

this final D–B is recalled and expanded into a playful chain of thirds (Ex. 2b, bars 54–5). At the same time this tiny transformation in the first four notes of the first theme also launches another process.

At the end of the exposition we hear this motif on the horn, with intervals further expanded (Ex. 2c, bars 73–4). Directly afterwards, at the beginning of the development, another variation of the main theme can be heard, at the beginning of which we can recognize the inversion of the basic motif (Ex. 2d, bars 76–8). This inverted variation will be unified with its original at the point of recapitulation (Ex. 2e, bars 118–20). Thus, every important theme of the movement can ultimately be interpreted as the variation of a single melodic cell.

In the literature it is customary to compare this concerto with Mozart's concertos. This comparison is justified from many viewpoints. Bartók's handling of the piano, the transparent and thrifty orchestral writing, the relatively short but condensed nature of the movements, and the formal proportions are all reminiscent of Mozart's compositions. However, the manner in which Bartók creates a motivic link between the different themes, and the way in which he unfolds one motif from another, cannot be described as Mozartian. His principle is essentially one of 'developing variation', as developed by Beethoven and frequently mentioned in twentieth-century theoretical texts.[7]

The second movement also associates itself with Beethoven's art, in fact with an unusual openness. Here, the Beethovenian features can be found not only in the motivic texture but also in the direct reference of the imitative introduction of the strings and following chorale on the piano to the famous third movement of the String Quartet in A minor Op.132. That movement had been explained by Beethoven as a 'hymn of thanksgiving to the divinity, from a convalescent, in the Lydian mode'. The opening performing instructions for Bartók's slow movement, *adagio religioso*, were rather laconic, but compared to his legendary taciturnity, surprisingly confessional. The biographical references are so evident that it is almost superfluous to speak of them: in the summer of 1945 Bartók may genuinely have believed for a time that he had hopes of full recovery. At the same time, he could see the future of the world in a more optimistic manner than earlier, for that acute danger which had caused him to flee Europe had come to an end. The thought of returning to Hungary may have emerged – of course, for the

I, 18-20 (violins I)
(a)
19
f
(b)
I, 54-5 (piano)
scherzando
54
tr
tr
p
I, 73-4 (horn I)
(c)
74
p
I, 76-8 (orch.)
(d)
77
f cantabile
etc.
I, 118-20 (piano)
(e)
119
mf
etc.

EX. 2

time being, only as a distant possibility. Perhaps those analysts are correct who hear a nostalgia for the abandoned homeland in this music which, although starting with a disciplined, dispassionate C major, gradually assumes a pathos and emotion rarely found in Bartók's composition. The intensification of tension can be clearly followed through the changes of the lengths, rhythms and harmonies of the different chorale lines. The settings for piano of the first three chorale lines have the same rhythm, but the fourth line (from bar 38), although starting in a similar manner, is expanded to nine bars and introduces new types of rhythm, such as triplet crotchets, in some of the parts. The fifth, final chorale line (bars 48–56) is different from the rest, both in regard to its rhythm and its harmony. The four relaxed minims which began the earlier statements are left aside; the first chord involves not a unison or triad, as before, but a characteristically sad and yearning harmony of Romanticism related to the 'Tristan chord'.[8] We hear this chord, in various transpositions, on no less than four occasions before the final calm resolution to C major (bars 53–4), or, more accurately, to a C-based pentatonic mode. For no matter how strong the major feeling, the motif with which this movement starts and to which it now returns is clearly pentatonic. It can be interpreted as a musical symbol of the 'Hungarian homeland', for Bartók always considered pentatony as a chief characteristic of ancient Hungarian folksong.

In the middle section, a 'scherzo', the sounds of nature emerge, in similar fashion to the second movement of the Second Piano Concerto. In contrast to that earlier music, however, this 'nature music' is far from fearsome. It is not the 'night's music', but that of broad daylight. These noises are not mysterious – rustlings, chirpings of the crickets, croakings of the frogs, as in the *Out of Doors* cycle – but rather songs of the birds. According to Péter Bartók, while in Asheville his father noted down bird music in a pocket notebook, employing the same precision as was the case with his folksong notations. This notebook has not yet been found, but recently a slip of paper was discovered with several short melodies upon it, undoubtedly Bartók's notations of bird songs. They include the main theme of this 'scherzo' entitled '6. Parting in peace', regrettably without naming the 'singer'. This melody (bars 60–63) could with some plausibility be considered the musical basis of the entire second movement, for the opening two chorale lines (starting at bars 16 and 24) are obviously derived from it (Ex. 3).

EX. 3

The *attacca* finale propagates that *joie de vivre* and sense of optimism frequently found in his Bartók's last movements.[9] In contrast to many other finales by him only its rondo-like returning main theme is of folk-music inspiration. This theme is a stylized folk-dance tune of Hungarian flavour, its rhythm being one of the 'softer' variations of the Hungarian dotted rhythm identified by Bartók (Ex. 4, bars 141–4). The episodes, instead of folk music, remind the listener of 'early music', primarily of the Baroque. The first episode, starting at bar 228, is a playful fugato launched by the piano, whose theme later also appears as an inversion. At bar 392 the second episode starts. As Tallián aptly states, it is a 'menuet antique' with Bach-like imitation in the

EX. 4

accompaniment and a strange $\frac{2}{4}$ 'trio' section, whose main motif (Ex. 5, bars 427–30) seems a kin of the brass fanfare in the last movement of the Concerto for Orchestra.[10]

EX. 5

Bartók did not write any tempo indications for this movement, and other performing instructions were clearly missing from the score. These deficiencies, along with minor omissions in the first two movements and the lack of metronome numbers, were remedied variously by Tibor Serly, the pianist Louis Kentner, the Boosey & Hawkes editor Erwin Stein, and the Hungarian-born conductor Eugene Ormandy. Ormandy conducted the première in Philadelphia on 8 February 1946, with György Sándor as soloist. Ditta Pásztory, for whom it had been intended, withdrew from public life for many years after her husband's death, and did not publicly perform the work until the 1960s.

The word *vége*, the Hungarian equivalent of 'the end', can be read in both the draft and the full score copies of the Third Piano Concerto on their last pages, next to the closing double bar-line. As no similar practice is found in any other Bartók manuscript there is a strong temptation to attribute a symbolic significance to this word which, it must be remembered, follows bars left empty in the score. We are tempted to presume that in this way Bartók put a symbolic full-stop after his entire *œuvre*. This, of course, would also mean that the Viola Concerto, the other piece on which he was working during 1945, could only be considered a type of 'after the last' composition, to some extent locked out from the legitimate *œuvre*. Grave reservations can certainly be admitted concerning this composition, which was reconstructed by Tibor Serly and premièred four years after Bartók's death, although it is clear that, whatever its status, this work has irrevocably become part of the concert repertoire over the last four decades.

Its origin can be traced to the beginning of 1945. The first documentary evidence of the work is found in a letter dated 22 January of that year, in which William Primrose expressed his gratitude and pleasure that Bartók had accepted the commission. That Bartók was soon occupied with the work is indicated by the request to his publishers for study scores of Berlioz's *Harold in Italy* – a composition with viola solo – on 27 January.[11] It seems that after this, however, work was halted for some months. Major progress was first reported in a letter of 5 August. In that letter Bartók admitted to Primrose that around mid-July he had almost given up composing the work, when he suddenly had some new ideas:

> However embryonic the state of the work still is, the general plan and ideas are already fixed. So I can tell you that it will be in 4 movements: a serious Allegro, a Scherzo, a (rather short) slow movement, and a finale beginning Allegretto and developing the tempo to an Allegro molto. Each movement, or at least 3 of them, will be preceded by a (short) recurring introduction (mostly solo of the viola), a kind of ritornello.[12]

One month later, on 8 September, Bartók reported that the Viola Concerto was 'ready in draft, so that only the score has to be written, which means a purely mechanical work, so to speak'.[13] Not one bar of a fair copy of the score was completed during the remaining couple of weeks of Bartók's life, however. When visiting Bartók on 21 September Serly saw the pages of the Viola Concerto's draft on a table beside Bartók's bed, and asked whether the Concerto was ready. Bartók's answer was laconic, yet puzzling: 'Yes and no'.

How far it was 'yes' and how far 'no' remained a puzzle for a long time for musicologists. The manuscript was not accessible for research, and the only information about the reconstruction came from what Tibor Serly wrote in the score's Foreword and in various interviews and articles. A contradictory picture emerged of the work: on the one hand the composition seemed 'strange' and, in many respects, unBartókian; on the other hand, in the absence of decisive counter-evidence, Serly's declaration that the work was essentially an opus of Bartók had, at least provisionally, to be accepted. Many people tried to resolve the dilemma by suggesting that Bartók's creative powers had perhaps started to decline towards the end, and that he had used up all his remaining energy on the Piano Concerto, which was nearer to his heart. During a short visit to Hungary in 1963, Serly presented a photocopy of the thirteen-page draft manuscript to the Budapest Bartók Archive and, finally, more scientific analysis of the work became possible. Recently, László Somfai's thorough analysis of the original manuscript safeguarded in the United States has opened a further level of research.

The manuscript consists of sixteen pages from four bifolios, that is, from four double-sided folded sheets of manuscript paper. Of these, Bartók left two blank, and one contained the first version of the beginning of the first movement. Thus, for the work of reconstruction only thirteen pages could play any role. On the pages of the first and second bifolios, Serly's numbered pages 1–7, the draft of the first movement can be found. At the bottom of page 7 a strongly soloistic material starts, which seems in its character to tally with the description of a 'kind of ritornello' mentioned in Bartók's letter of 5 August 1945. After a lengthy passage it ends on the lowest note, C, of the viola. Directly before this note, however, the draft specifies a change of metre, from $\frac{4}{4}$ to $\frac{2}{4}$. Here the draft ends and the fourth page of this second bifolio is left empty. Serly's page 8 belongs to the third bifolio, which involves a different brand of manuscript paper. Bartók drew up his slow movement on this page. At the bottom of that page, linked to the slow movement, is new material, which continues on to page 9, but is then broken off. At the bottom of this page, however, various thematic drafts can be read, but they are written 'upside down'.[14] Page 10 is filled with the draft of the last movement and the fourth page of this third bifolio Serly ignored (as he found there essentially the same material as Bartók had copied on to his page 1). Finally, the closing movement continues on the pages of the fourth bifolio (marked pages 11–13). The last page of this last bifolio is blank.

From this account it is clear that there are certain obscure sections in the manuscript. Bartók, according to György Kroó, was motivated by 'a desire to reassure' his client when, in his letter of 8 September 1945, he wrote optimistically saying that the draft was ready.[15] In fact, only the draft of the first movement can be considered as more or less complete. The draft of the slow movement, only two-thirds of a page, is a mere sketch, and that of the closing movement is in most places only an outline of the viola part. The most acute problem, however, is caused by the 'incomplete' parts written at the bottom of pages 7, 8 and 9. In view of Bartók's August letter, then, the question can justifiably be asked: was not the 'kind of ritornello' found on page 7 originally planned for the introduction of Bartók's intended second movement, the Scherzo, which is missing from the manuscript? Perhaps it was lost, but it is more probable that Bartók had meanwhile amended his compositional concept and given up the plan for a four-movement work. This view is supported by a calculation found on page 5 of the manuscript. There, Bartók worked out a duration of 10 minutes 20 seconds for his first movement, 5 minutes 10 seconds for a second movement, and 4 minutes 45 seconds for a third.[16]

A bolder, yet supportable hypothesis is suggested by the particular connection between two of the more perplexing parts of the manuscript. The section after the slow movement (starting with *allegretto* at II, bar 58 in the published score) is of C tonality and in $\frac{2}{4}$ metre. The material which immediately precedes the slow movement (the score's *lento parlando* passage) prepares exactly for such a section, as shown in Ex. 6. At the same time, it is undoubted that that same C-based $\frac{2}{4}$ material (at the bottom of manuscript page 8) is also the organic continuation of the slow movement. It fits well in both places. Is it, perhaps the 'recurring' material, which Bartók, for want of time, only wrote down at the point of its recurrence? In this case it is possible to imagine a combined

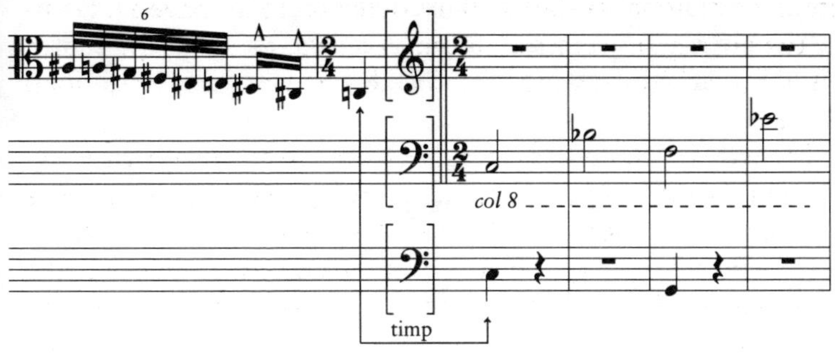

EX. 6

form between the large-scale opening movement and the finale along the following lines:

a soloistic introduction (the published score's *lento parlando* section)
a section of 2/4 Scherzo character in C (similar to the score's *allegretto* passage, from II, bar 58)
a slow middle section (the score's *adagio religioso* passage, from II, bar 1)
a section of return of Scherzo material.[17]

Whichever way the arguments are taken – and there are other possible hypotheses, as well – one thing is certain: the solution chosen by Serly was not planned by Bartók. In an understandable manner, especially in light of the prevailing circumstances, Serly sought to 'save' the largest number of bars written down by Bartók, and to 'interfere' as little as possible. Thus, he did not reject any of the 'problematic' material, but also did not undertake larger-scale supplementation of it. As he probably did not know of Bartók's letter of 5 August 1945 (and hence, of the four-movement concept) at this time, he hardly had any choice but to link the soloistic 'introductory' material on page 7 directly with the beginning of the slow movement. He undoubtedly acted with discretion when he used a melody of the first movement as a linking chain, although this does not excuse the clumsiness of the modulation. It is very strange that the viola solo aims at and powerfully prepares for a C tonality, but on reaching this goal the bassoon melody immediately leads from it to the distant E tonality of the slow movement (Ex. 7).

EX. 7

The incorporation of the other 'mysterious' material is similarly unfortunate. Serly developed this material (introduced at II, bar 58 of the published score) into a type of 'transition' from the slow movement to the finale, although the material is far from being of transitional character, and, from the viewpoint of key, does not lead anywhere. Its beginning is linked with a dominant upbeat chord on G (bar 57) and it, likewise, runs out with a G upbeat (bar 85). In effect, it does not modulate, thereby failing to fulfil the main function of a transition in tonal music.

With regard to orchestration and sound quality some of Serly's solutions are definitely fortunate (for example, the enrichment of the central part of the slow movement with excited wind flourishes), but others were regrettable, unjustified or, simply, incomprehensible. In the Romanian-type dance finale, for instance, he changed the key of a longish section (bar 114 and following) from A♭ to A; he designated the slow movement 'Adagio religioso', although Bartók would certainly not have used this designation again so soon after the Third Piano Concerto. And although in the first movement he generally adhered to Bartók's manuscript, where he did consciously make amendments they were mostly unnecessary. On occasion he ignored Bartók's sporadic instructions regarding orchestration, as at the work's opening where Bartók clearly specified that the viola should be accompanied, first of all, by timpani alone. Serly sacrificed this potentially unique opening, preferring to create a much less original one involving pizzicatos on the lower string instruments.

In summary, the Viola Concerto played in concerts today is not an authentic composition of Bartók. In fact, Serly undertook an impossible task. Given such a contradictory and incomplete manuscript he could not, despite the best of intentions, produce a work comparable to the great compositions of Bartók. None the less, he could have produced a more appealing, better-proportioned and more skilful version. Perhaps in the not so distant future the possibility for such a version will present itself. As the hopes for publication of Bartók's manuscript in facsimile form brighten it is not unimaginable that a fertile discussion will be provoked amongst musicologists, similar to that of past years in connection with Mozart's Requiem. Just as there continue to be new versions of Mozart's final work, so too can a new, more convincing version of Bartók's Viola Concerto be produced.

NOTES

1 Kroó, p. 242.
2 Kroó, p. 242.
3 See Tibor Tallián, *Béla Bartók: the Man and his Work*, Budapest (Corvina), 1988, p. 238.
4 See Kroó, p. 243.
5 According to manuscript sources, the tempo instruction for the first movement was originally 'Tempo di Verbunkos'.
6 *BBE*, pp. 361–83.
7 In particular, Arnold Schoenberg's posthumous *Fundamentals of Musical Composition*.
8 Bartók's chord has the same interval construction as the 'Tristan chord', although it fulfils a different tonal function.
9 Bartók's bar numbering continues through the second into the third movement.
10 Tallián, op. cit., p. 237.

11 See Kroó, pp. 246–7, for an account of these initial exchanges of correspondence. It is noteworthy that Bartók studied the violin concertos of Berg, Weill and Szymanowski (his First) in a similar fashion before composing his Second Violin Concerto.
12 From draft of letter (MTA BA-B).
13 Quoted in Tibor Serly's Foreword to the pocket score.
14 These drafts include a few bars from the beginning of the first movement and a theme probably intended – but then rejected – for the finale.
15 Kroó, p. 247.
16 A further calculation on the bottom of page 8 perhaps illustrates his hesitation between a three and a four-movement concept. There, the sum of the three movements' durations is given as 18 minutes 30 seconds, but on the side, bracketed and with a question mark, the number 25 can also be read.
17 Such a form would have been the 'negative' of that found in the Second and the Third Piano Concertos, for in both of these works two slow parts frame the central 'scherzo'.

Chronology: Bartók's Life and Works

1881 Born Béla Viktor János Bartók on 25 March in Naygszentmiklós, Hungary (now Sînnicolau Mare, Romania), son of Béla Bartók (1855–88) and Paula Bartók (née Voit, 1857–1939), both teachers and amateur musicians.

1884 Receives his first musical instrument, a drum.

1886 Begins piano lessons with his mother.

1888 His father dies of Addison's disease in Nagyszentmiklós; the family moves frequently in the following six years as Bartók's mother seeks work in various provincial Hungarian towns.

1890 Starts first opus numbering of compositions, with Waltz Op.1.

1892 First public performance as a pianist, in Nagyszöllős, including his own piece *The Course of the Danube.*

1894 The Bartók family settles in Pozsony (Bratislava), allowing for his more orderly musical and general education; he starts second opus numbering of compositions, with the Piano Sonata in G minor Op.1.

1895 Succeeds Ernő Dohnányi as his school's organist.

1898 Performs his own Piano Sonata (DD51) and parts of his Piano Quartet (DD52) in Pozsony; visits Vienna, where he is offered a scholarship at the Conservatory.

1899 Completes secondary education in Pozsony; commences studies in piano and composition at the Academy of Music in Budapest; serious lung problems develop.

1901 Gains first major success as a pianist in Budapest with a playing of Liszt's Piano Sonata; his interest in the works of Liszt and Wagner grows.

1902 Hears Strauss's *Also sprach Zarathustra* and resumes serious composition under its influence.

1903 Performs Strauss's *Ein Heldenleben* in his own transcription for solo piano in Budapest and Vienna; presents first public solo recital, in Nagyszentmiklós; completes his Academy studies; visits and performs in Berlin.

1904 His symphonic poem *Kossuth* (1903) is performed in Budapest and Manchester; his interest in genuine folk music is aroused; last opus numbering of compositions begins, with the piano Rhapsody Op.1, and Scherzo Op.2.

1905 Competes unsuccessfully in the Rubinstein Competition in Paris, both as pianist and composer; starts folk-music collaboration with Zoltán Kodály, composes his orchestral First Suite Op.3, and first three movements of the Second Suite Op.4.

1906 Tours Spain and Portugal as accompanist to the Hungarian violinist Ferenc Vecsey; with Kodály, publishes first Hungarian folksong settings; starts annual expeditions collecting folk music using an Edison phonograph.

1907 Accepts appointment to the piano staff of the Academy of Music in Budapest; realizes the pentatonic basis to much Hungarian folk music; his interest is aroused in the works of Debussy and Reger; he completes his Second Suite as well as sets of Hungarian and Slovak folksong arrangements.

1908 His first article about folk music and also his first of many instructive editions of piano classics are published in Budapest; he starts to investigate Romanian folk music; completes his First Violin Concerto (Op.posth.) and composes many piano pieces, including his Fourteen Bagatelles Op.6.

1909 Marries Márta Ziegler (1893–1967); completes his First String Quartet Op.7, and a variety of short piano pieces; first complete performances of his two orchestral suites.

1910 His works feature in a 'Festival Hongrois' in Paris; he composes *Two Pictures* Op.10.

1911 With Kodály and friends, founds the New Hungarian Musical Society, which soon fails; commences editorial work for the Liszt critical edition (to 1917); completes orchestration of his *Two Portraits* Op.5, and composes the opera *Duke Bluebeard's Castle* Op.11, and *Allegro barbaro*.

1912 Starts his withdrawal from public musical life, although continues to teach at the Academy; composes his Four Orchestral Pieces Op.12 (orchestrated in 1921).

1913 Collects folk music in French north Africa (now Algeria); his first ethnomusicological book, about Romanian folk music from Bihar county, appears through the Romanian Academy in Bucharest.

1914 Rejected for military service; he starts to compose his ballet *The Wooden Prince* Op.13.

1915 Collects folk music during several visits to Slovak regions; composes many piano works including Sonatina, Romanian Folk Dances, Romanian Christmas Carols (*colinde*).

1916 Composes Suite Op.14 for piano, and Five 'Ady' Songs Op.16; completes *The Wooden Prince* (except for some orchestration), Five Songs Op.15, and several Slovak folksong settings.

1917 Well-received première of *The Wooden Prince* in Budapest; he completes the Second String Quartet Op.17.

1918 Première of *Duke Bluebeard's Castle* (1911) in Budapest; he undertakes final folk-music collecting expedition in Hungary; contracts Spanish influenza; concludes negotiations with Universal Edition, Vienna, to publish his compositions; completes Fifteen Hungarian Peasant Songs and Three Studies Op.18, both for solo piano.

1919 Re-emerges into Budapest's concert life; accepts a position on the Music Directorate of the short-lived Communist Republic of Councils; completes initial composition of his pantomime *The Miraculous Mandarin* Op.19 (orchestrated in 1923–4, with revisions to 1931).

1920 Starts to re-establish connections with Western Europe cut off by the war; thinks of emigrating; writes of approaching a 'twelve-note' goal in his recent compositional work; composes his piano Improvisations Op.20.

1921 Plans international concert tours and writes many articles for foreign journals; completes his study, with Kodály, of 150 Hungarian folksongs from Transylvania (soon published in Budapest); contracts for publication of his Slovak collection (eventually not realized); composes his First Violin Sonata, dispensing with opus numberings from here on.

1922 Undertakes highly successful concert tours of Transylvania, Britain, France and Germany; participates in the founding of the International Society for Contemporary Music (ISCM) in Salzburg; composes his Second Violin Sonata.

1923 Divorces, and marries Ditta Pásztory (1903–82); tours further as composer–pianist in Western Europe; his volume of Romanian folk music from Máramaros county appears in Munich; he composes orchestral Dance Suite, in a more accessible and tonal style.

1924 His most widely known folk-music study, *The Hungarian Folksong*, appears in Budapest (also in Berlin, 1925, and London, 1931); he composes his *Village Scenes*.

1925 Continues with European concert tours; his Dance Suite gains much popularity internationally.

1926 Completes his important study of Romanian Christmas songs; makes his first radio appearances as a pianist; attends the controversial première of his *The Miraculous Mandarin* (1918–19) in Cologne; composes many works for piano, including the Sonata, *Out of Doors*, Nine Little Piano Pieces and First Piano Concerto, which reflect his growing interest in Baroque stylistic models.

1927 Premières his First Piano Concerto in Frankfurt am Main; undertakes tour of the United States, to mixed reception; completes his Three Rondos for piano, and Third String Quartet.

1928 Makes first commercial gramophone recordings of his own works; composes First and Second Violin Rhapsodies and Fourth String Quartet.

1929 Tours the Soviet Union and widely in Western Europe; composes Twenty Hungarian Folksongs.

1930 Decides not to perform his own works any more in Budapest (this ban lasts for six years); the first full-length study of his works, by Edwin von der Nüll, appears in Halle; he composes *Cantata profana*, for chorus, male soloists and orchestra.

1931 Joins the Permament Committee for Literature and the Arts of the League of Nations' Commission for Intellectual Co-operation; teaches at an Austro-American summer music school; completes his Second Piano Concerto and Forty-four Duos for violins.

1932 Attends a conference on Arabic music in Cairo; moves to his final home in the Buda foothills; composes Székely Folksongs for male chorus.

1933 Premières his Second Piano Concerto in Frankfurt am Main (his last appearance in Germany).

1934 Attends première of his *Cantata profana* in London; negotiates his release from teaching duties at the Budapest Academy of Music and attachment to the folk-music section of the Hungarian Academy of Sciences, where he works until 1940; composes his Fifth String Quartet.

1935 Refuses award of the Greguss Prize for his First Suite Op.3; publishes in Vienna, at his own expense, his study of Romanian Christmas songs; composes Twenty-seven Two- and Three-part Choruses, and *From Olden Times*, for male chorus.

1936 Presents his inaugural address, about Liszt's music, before the Hungarian Academy of Sciences; visits Turkey to perform, collect folk music and advise on music education; composes the Music for Strings, Percussion and Celesta and arranges his *Petite Suite* for piano.

1937 Première in Basle of the Music for Strings, Percussion and Celesta; he forbids relay broadcasts of his concerts over German or Italian radio stations; composes Sonata for Two Pianos and Percussion.

1938 Première in Basle of Sonata for Two Pianos and Percussion, with Bartók and his wife as pianists; he starts negotiations with Boosey & Hawkes of London to take over publication of his works from Universal Edition, because of its Nazification; starts to send valuable manuscripts out of Hungary; performs for the last time in Britain; completes the Second Violin Concerto and composes *Contrasts*.

1939 Makes final concert tours of France, Switzerland and Italy; formally contracts with Boosey & Hawkes; his mother dies, freeing him to accelerate plans to leave Hungary; he completes his six-volume *Mikrokosmos* collection of graded piano pieces; composes the Divertimento and Sixth String Quartet.

1940 Undertakes his second concert tour of the United States and later in the year emigrates there with his wife, settling in New York; receives an honorary doctorate from Columbia University; arranges his Sonata for Two Pianos and Percussion as a concerto.

1941 Takes up post as a research fellow working on Serbo-Croatian folk music at Columbia University and gives occasional concerts, many with his wife; arranges his Second Suite Op.4 for two pianos.

1942 Experiences depression at dwindling concert, lecturing and publishing opportunities, and onset of illness.

1943 Gives his final concert appearance, with his wife, at the American première of the Concerto for Two Pianos, Percussion and Orchestra in New York; takes up a visiting professorship at Harvard University but soon has to relinquish his responsibilities because of ill health; completes his study of Turkish folk music (published in 1976); experiences strain in relations with his wife, leading to their occasional separations; composes Concerto for Orchestra.

1944 Completes his study of Serbo-Croatian folksongs (published in 1951); moves into his final New York apartment, after many months of recuperation at health resorts; première in Boston of Concerto for Orchestra; he composes and hears Menuhin première his Sonata for solo violin in New York.

1945 Completes his monumental study of Romanian folk music (published in 1967–75); composes his Third Piano Concerto; drafts his Viola Concerto and starts to sketch his Seventh String Quartet; dies of leukaemia in New York on 26 September.

Select Bibliography

I: BARTÓK'S WRITINGS

LETTERS

Béla Bartók Letters, ed. János Demény, London (Faber and Faber), 1971

Bartók Letters: The Musical Mind, ed. Malcolm Gillies and Adrienne Gombocz, Oxford (Clarendon Press), forthcoming

Bartók Béla levelei [Béla Bartók Letters], 5th edn, ed. János Demény, Budapest (Zeneműkiadó), 1976

Bartók Béla családi levelei [Béla Bartók Family Letters], ed. Béla Bartók Jun., Budapest (Zeneműkiadó), 1981

Béla Bartók: Ausgewählte Briefe, ed. János Demény, Budapest (Corvina), 1960

Béla Bartók: Briefe, ed. János Demeny, Budapest (Corvina), 1973 (2 vols)

'Korrespondenz zwischen Bartók und der holländischen Konzertdirektion "Kossar"', ed. János Demény, in *Documenta Bartókiana*, vol.6 (1981), pp. 153–229

'Bartóks Briefe an Calvocoressi (1914–1930)', ed. Adrienne Gombocz and László Somfai, in *Studia Musicologica*, vol.24 (1982), pp. 199–231

ESSAYS

Béla Bartók Essays, ed. Benjamin Suchoff, London (Faber and Faber), 1976

Bartók Béla összegyűjtött írásai I [Béla Bartók's Collected Writings I], ed. András Szőllősy, Budapest (Zeneműkiadó), 1967

Bartók Béla írásai I [Béla Bartók's Writings I], ed. Tibor Tallián, Budapest (Zeneműkiadó), 1989

Béla Bartók: Musiksprachen, Aufsätze und Vorträge, ed. Bence Szabolcsi, Leipzig (Philipp Reclam, Jun.), 1972

'Vierzehn Bartók-Schriften aus den Jahren 1920/21', ed. László Somfai, in *Documenta Bartókiana*, vol.5 (1977), pp. 15–141

FOLK-MUSIC STUDIES

Rumanian Folk Music, ed. Benjamin Suchoff, The Hague (Martinus Nijhoff), 1967–75 (5 vols)

Turkish Folk Music from Asia Minor, ed. Benjamin Suchoff, Princeton (Princeton University Press), 1976

Yugoslav Folk Music, ed. Benjamin Suchoff, Albany (State University of New York Press), 1978 (4 vols)

The Hungarian Folk Song, ed. Benjamin Suchoff, Albany (State University of New York Press), 1981 (originally published in English as *Hungarian Folk Music,* London (Oxford University Press), 1931)

Erdélyi magyar népdalok [Transylvanian Hungarian Folksongs], ed. Béla Bartók and Zoltán Kodály, Budapest (A Népies Irodalmi Társaság), 1923 (repr. Budapest: Állami Könyvterjesztő Vállalat, 1987)

Magyar népdalok: Egyetemes gyűjtemény I [Hungarian Folksongs: Universal Collection I], ed. Sándor Kovács and Ferenc Sebő, Budapest (Akadémiai Kiadó), 1991

Béla Bartók: Ethnomusikologische Schriften Faksimile-Nachdrucke, ed. D. Dille, Mainz (B. Schott's Söhne), 1965–8 (4 vols)

Slovenské l'udové piesne / Slowakische Volkslieder, ed. Alica Elscheková, Oskár Elschek, Jozef Kresánek, Bratislava (Academia Scientiarum Slovaca), 1959, 1970 (2 vols)

'Musique paysanne serbe et bulgare du Banat (Budapest, 1935)', *Documenta Bartókiana,* vol.4 (1970), 221–44

SELECTED WRITINGS

Bartók breviárium, 2nd edn, ed. József Ujfalussy, Budapest (Zeneműkiadó), 1974

Béla Bartók: Weg und Werk, rev. edn, ed. Bence Szabolcsi, Kassel (Bärenreiter Verlag), 1972, pp. 153–306

Musique de la vie: Béla Bartók, ed. Philippe A, Autexier, Paris (Stock), 1981

2: WRITINGS OF OTHERS

Antokoletz, Elliott: *The Music of Béla Bartók,* Berkeley (University of California Press), 1984

——: *Béla Bartók: A Guide to Research,* New York (Garland), 1988

——: *Twentieth-Century Music,* Englewood Cliffs, NJ (Prentice-Hall), 1992, pp. 106–140

Bárdos, Lajos: *Selected Writings on Music,* Budapest (Editio Musica), 1984, pp. 373–479

Bartók, Béla, Jun.: *Apám életének krónikája* [Chronicle of My Father's

Life], Budapest (Zeneműkiadó), 1981
——: *Bartók Béla műhelyében* [In Béla Bartók's Workshop], Budapest (Szépirodalmi Könyvkiadó), 1982
Bator, Victor: *The Béla Bartók Archives: History and Catalogue,* New York (Bartók Archives), 1963
Béla Bartók: A Memorial Review, New York (Boosey & Hawkes), 1950
Bónis, Ferenc: *Béla Bartók: His Life in Pictures and Documents,* 2nd edn, Budapest (Corvina), 1981
—— ed.: *Így láttuk Bartókot* [So saw we Bartók], Budapest (Zeneműkiadó), 1981
Breuer, János: *Bartók és Kodály* [Bartók and Kodály], Budapest (Magvető), 1978
Brown, Christine: *Bartók's Mikrokosmos: A Guide for Piano Teachers,* London (Boosey & Hawkes), 1988
Citron, Pierre: *Bartók,* Paris (Editions du Seuil), 1963
Crow, Todd, ed.: *Bartók Studies,* Detroit (Information Coordinators), 1976
Csende, Béla, ed.: *A népdalkutató Bartók Béla* [Béla Bartók, the Folksong Researcher], Békéscsaba (Kner), 1981
Demény, János: 'Bartók Béla tanulóévei és romantikus korszaka' [Béla Bartók's Student Years and Romantic Period], in *Zenetudományi tanulmányok*, vol.2 (1954), pp. 323–487
——: 'Bartók Béla művészi kibontakozásának évei (I)' [The Years of Béla Bartók's Artistic Development (I)], in *Zenetudományi tanulmányok,* vol.3 (1955), pp. 286–459
——: 'Bartók Béla művészi kibontakozásának évei (II)' [The Years of Béla Bartók's Artistic Development (II)], in *Zenetudományi tanulmányok*, vol.7 (1959), pp. 5–425
——: 'Bartók Béla pályája delelőjén' [Béla Bartók at the Height of his Career], in *Zenetudományi tanulmányok*, vol.10 (1962), pp. 198–727
——: *Bartók Béla, a zongoraművész* [Béla Bartók, the Pianist]; Budapest (Zeneműkiadó), 1973
——: 'Zeitgenössische Musik in Bartóks Konzertrepertoire', in *Documenta Bartókiana*, vol.5 (1977), pp. 169–76
Dille, Denis: *Thematisches Verzeichnis der Jugendwerke Béla Bartóks, 1890–1904*, Budapest (Akadémiai Kiadó), 1974
——: *Généalogie sommaire de la famille Bartók,* Antwerp (Metropolis), 1977
——: *Het werk van Béla Bartók*, Antwerp (Metropolis), 1979
——: *Béla Bartók: Regard sur le passé,* Louvain-la-Neuve (Institut Supérieur d'Archéologie et d'Histoire de l'Art, Collège Erasme), 1990

Engelmann, Hans: *Béla Bartóks Mikrokosmos*, Würzburg (Konrad Triltsch), 1953

Fassett, Agatha: *Béla Bartók's Last Years: The Naked Face of Genius*, London (Victor Gollancz), 1958

Fuchss, Werner: *Béla Bartók und die Schweiz*, Bern (Hallway), 1973

Gergely, Jean: *Béla Bartók: compositeur hongrois, La revue musicale*, nos 328–35 (1980)

—— ed.: *Béla Bartók vivant*, Paris (Publications orientalistes de France), 1984

—— and Jean Vigue: *Conscience musicale ou conscience humaine? Vie, œuvre et héritage spirituel de Béla Bartók*, Budapest (Akadémiai Kiadó), 1990

Gillies, Malcolm: *Bartók in Britain: A Guided Tour*, Oxford (Clarendon Press), 1989

——: *Notation and Tonal Structure in Bartók's Later Works*, New York (Garland), 1989

——: *Bartók Remembered*, London (Faber and Faber), 1990

Griffiths, Paul: *Bartók*, London (J.M. Dent), 1984

Haraszti, Emil: *Béla Bartók: His Life and Works*, Paris (Lyrebird), 1938

Helm, Everett: *Bartók*, New York (Crowell), 1972

Howat, Roy: 'Bartók, Lendvai and the Principles of Proportional Analysis', *Music Analysis*, vol.2 (1983), pp. 69–95

Hundt, Theodor: *Bartóks Satztechnik in den Klavierwerken*, Regensburg (Gustav Bosse), 1971

Hunkemöller, Jürgen: *Béla Bartók: Musik für Saiteninstrumente*, Munich (Wilhelm Fink), 1982

Juhász, Vilmos, ed.: *Bartók's Years in America*, Washington DC (Occidental), 1981

Kapst, Erich: 'Stilkriterien der polymodal-chromatischen Gestaltungsweise im Werk Béla Bartóks', *Beiträge zur Musikwissenschaft*, vol.12 (1970), pp. 1–28

Kárpáti, János: *Bartók's String Quartets*, Budapest (Corvina), 1975

——: *Bartók kamarazenéje* [Bartók's Chamber Music], Budapest (Zeneműkiadó), 1976

Kodály, Zoltán: *Visszatekintés* [A Retrospective], ed. Ferenc Bónis, Budapest (Zeneműkiadó), 1982–9 (3 vols)

Kristóf, Károly: *Beszélgetések Bartók Bélával* [Conversations with Béla Bartók], Budapest (Zeneműkiadó), 1957

Kroó, György: *Bartók Béla színpadi művei* [Béla Bartók's Stage Works], Budapest (Zeneműkiadó), 1962

——: *A Guide to Bartók*, Budapest (Corvina), 1974

Lampert, Vera: 'Zeitgenössische Musik in Bartóks Notensammlung',

Documenta Bartókiana, vol.5 (1977), pp. 142–68
——: 'Quellenkatalog der Volksliedbearbeitungen von Bartók', *Documenta Bartókiana*, vol.6 (1981), pp. 15–149
—— and László Somfai: 'Béla Bartók', in *The New Grove: Modern Masters*, London (Macmillan), 1984, pp. 1–101
László, Ferenc: *Bartók Béla: tanulmányok és tanúságok* [Béla Bartók: Essays and Testimonies], Bucharest (Kriterion), 1980
—— ed.: *Bartók-dolgozatok* [Bartók Studies], Bucharest (Kriterion), 1974
—— ed.: *Bartók-dolgozatok 1981* [Bartók Studies 1981], Bucharest (Kriterion), 1982
Lendvai, Ernő: *Béla Bartók: An Analysis of his Music*, London (Kahn & Averill), 1971
——: *The Workshop of Bartók and Kodály*, Budapest (Editio Musica), 1983
Lenoir, Yves: *Folklore et transcendance dans l'œuvre américaine de Béla Bartók (1940–1945)*, Louvain-la-Neuve (Institut Supérieur d'Archéologie et d'Histoire de l'Art, Collège Erasme), 1986
Lesznai, Lajos: *Béla Bartók*, London (J.M. Dent), 1973
Lindlar, Heinrich: *Lübbes Bartók Lexikon*, Bergisch Gladbach (Gustav Lübbe), 1984
Masotti, Franco, ed.: *Bartók e la didattica musicale*, Milan (Edizioni Unicopli), 1984
McCabe, John: *Bartók's Orchestral Music*, London (BBC), 1974
Michael, Frank: *Béla Bartóks Variationstechnik*, Regensburg (Gustav Bosse), 1976
Milne, Hamish: *Bartók: His Life and Times*, Tunbridge Wells (Midas), 1982
Moreux, Serge: *Béla Bartók*, London (Harvill), 1953
Nüll, Edwin von der: *Béla Bartók: ein Beitrag zur Morphologie der neuen Musik*, Halle (Mitteldeutsche), 1930
Oramo, Ilkka: *Modaalinen Symmetria: Tutkimus Bartókin kromatiikasta*, Helsinki (Suomen Musiikkitieteellinen Seura), 1977
——: 'Modale Symmetrie bei Bartók', *Musikforschung*, vol.33 (1980), pp. 450–63
Perle, George: 'The String Quartets of Béla Bartók', in *A Musical Offering: Essays in Honor of Martin Bernstein*, ed. Claire Brook and E. H. Clinkscale, New York (Pendragon), 1977
Petersen, Peter: *Die Tonalität im Instrumentalschaffen von Béla Bartók*, Hamburg (Karl Dieter Wagner), 1971
Pethő, Bertalan: *Bartók rejtekútja* [Bartók's Secret Path], Budapest (Gondolat), 1984
Queffelec, Yann: *Béla Bartók*, Paris (Mazarine), 1981

Ránki, György, ed.: *Bartók and Kodály Revisited,* Budapest (Akadémiai Kiadó), 1987

Saygun, A. Adnan: *Béla Bartók's Folk Music Research in Turkey* Budapest (Akadémiai Kiadó), 1976

Seiber, Mátyás: *The String Quartets of Béla Bartók,* London (Boosey & Hawkes), 1945

Serly, Tibor: 'A Belated Account of the Reconstruction of a 20th-century Masterpiece', *College Music Symposium,* vol.15 (1975), pp. 7–25

Somfai, László: *Tizennyolc Bartók tanulmány* [Eighteen Bartók Essays], Budapest (Zeneműkiadó), 1981

——: 'Manuscript versus Urtext: The Primary Sources of Bartók's Works', *Studia Musicologica,* vol.23 (1981), pp. 17–66

——: *Bartók's Workshop,* exhibition booklet, Budapest (MTA Institute of Musicology), 1987

Spangemacher, Friedrich, ed.: *Béla Bartók: zu Leben und Werk,* Bonn (Boosey & Hawkes), 1982

Stevens, Halsey: *The Life and Music of Béla Bartók,* 3rd edn, ed. Malcolm Gillies, Oxford (Clarendon Press), 1993

Suchoff, Benjamin: *Guide to Bartók's 'Mikrokosmos',* 2nd edn reprint, New York (Da Capo), 1983

Szabó, Miklós: *Bartók Béla kórusművei* [Béla Bartók's Choral Works], Budapest (Zeneműkiadó), 1985

Szabolcsi, Bence: *Béla Bartók,* Leipzig (Philipp Reclam, Jun.), 1961

——: *Kodályról és Bartókról* [About Kodály and Bartók], ed. Ferenc Bónis, Budapest (Zeneműkiadó), 1987

Székely, Júlia: *Bartók tanár úr* [Professor Bartók], rev. edn, Budapest (Kozmosz), 1978

Takács, Jenő: *Erinnerungen an Béla Bartók,* Vienna (Ludwig Doblinger), 1982

Tallián, Tibor: *Cantata profana – az átmenet mítosza* [*Cantata profana* – the Myth of Metamorphosis], Budapest (Magvető), 1983

——: *Béla Bartók: the Man and his Work,* Budapest (Corvina), 1988

——: *Bartók fogadtatása Amerikában, 1940–1945,* [Bartók's Reception in America, 1940–45], Budapest (Zeneműkiadó), 1988

Traimer, Roswitha: *Béla Bartóks Kompositionstechnik,* Regensburg (Gustav Bosse), 1956

Travis, Roy: 'Tonal Coherence in the First Movement of Bartók's Fourth String Quartet', *Music Forum,* vol.2 (1970), pp. 298–371

Uhde, Jürgen: *Béla Bartók,* Berlin (Colloquium), 1959

Ujfalussy, József: *Béla Bartók,* Budapest (Corvina), 1971

—— and János Breuer, ed.: *International Musicological Conference in Commemoration of Béla Bartók 1971,* Budapest (Editio Musica), 1972

Vinton, John: 'Bartók on his own Music', *Journal of the American Musicological Society*, vol.19 (1966), pp. 232–43

Waldbauer, Iván F.: 'Bartók's First Piano Concerto: A Publication History', *Musical Quarterly*, vol.51 (1965), pp. 336–44

Walsh, Stephen: *Bartók Chamber Music*, London (BBC), 1982

Wangenheim, Annette von: *Béla Bartók: 'Der wunderbare Mandarin'*, Overath bei Köln (Ulrich Steiner), 1985

Wilson, Paul: *The Music of Béla Bartók*, New Haven (Yale University Press), 1992

Yeomans, David: *Bartók for Piano*, Bloomington (Indiana University Press), 1988

Zieliński, Tadeusz A.: *Bartók: Leben, Werk, Klangwelt*, Zürich (Atlantis), 1973

Contributors

ELLIOTT ANTOKOLETZ studied violin at the Juilliard School of Music and musicology at the City University of New York. In 1976 he was appointed to the University of Texas at Austin, where he is now professor of musicology. His research includes many analytical articles about Bartók's music and two books, *The Music of Béla Bartók* (1984) and *Béla Bartók: A Guide to Research* (1988). His monumental study of *Twentieth-Century Music* appeared in 1992.

BÉLA BARTÓK JUN. is the composer's elder son, by his first wife, Márta Ziegler. An engineer by profession, he attained a senior rank in the Hungarian State Railways and taught at the Technical University in Budapest. Since retiring he has worked for the Unitarian Church in Hungary, compiled two chronicles of his father's life, edited a volume of Bartók family correspondence and, in 1992, published a book about his own numerous travels.

JÁNOS DEMÉNY was a pioneer of Bartók research in the immediate post-war years. He wrote some of the earliest accounts of Bartók's life and works and has edited his correspondence through five Hungarian editions. His detailed study of Bartók's career, published between 1954 and 1962 in the series *Zenetudományi tanulmányok*, has provided a basis for all subsequent studies of the composer. Demény's English-language edition of Bartók's letters appeared in 1971 with Faber and Faber.

MALCOLM GILLIES is professor and dean of the Faculty of Music, University of Queensland. His books include *Bartók in Britain: A Guided Tour, Notation and Tonal Structure in Bartók's Later Works* and *Bartók Remembered*, as well as collections of writings concerning the Australian musician Percy Grainger.

ADRIENNE GOMBOCZ is an assistant keeper at the Budapest Bartók Archive, where she has worked since 1962. As translator, editor or transcriber, she has contributed to most of the Hungarian volumes of

Bartók documentation. Adrienne Gombocz is co-editor with Malcolm Gillies of a forthcoming volume of Bartók's correspondence, to be issued by Oxford University Press.

ROY HOWAT is a concert pianist and writer living in London. He took a doctorate at Cambridge University with a study of Debussy which formed the basis of his book *Debussy in Proportion*, published by Cambridge University Press in 1983. Between 1979 and 1987 he held various university positions at Cambridge and in Australia. He has performed Bartók's Sonata for Two Pianos and Percussion in several countries, notably with Erzsébet Tusa, the former duo partner of Ditta Pásztory-Bartók.

JÁNOS KÁRPÁTI studied musicology at the Liszt Academy of Music in Budapest, where he now teaches and holds the position of director of the Academy's library. His main musicological interests are twentieth-century music and Asian musical cultures. In Bartók studies he is probably best known for his analyses of the chamber music; his English-language volume *Bartók's String Quartets* was published by Corvina Press in 1975.

SÁNDOR KOVÁCS teaches at the Liszt Academy and also works as a researcher at the Bartók Archive in Budapest. In recent years he has been preparing a comprehensive edition of Bartók's collection of Hungarian folk music, ordered according to Bartók's own system. Its first volume appeared in 1991.

GYÖRGY KROÓ, a professor of the Liszt Academy in Budapest since 1961 and leading official of Hungarian Radio, has published widely on nineteenth and twentieth-century music. As a writer about Bartók he is best known for his early studies of the stage works. In 1974 his *Guide to Bartók* was issued in English.

VERA LAMPERT studied at the Liszt Academy in Budapest; she then worked at the Bartók Archive there between 1969 and 1978. Since 1983 she has been a librarian at Brandeis University in Massachusetts. In her research she has focused on Bartók's writings and ethnomusicological activity, and has documented all the folk melodies used in Bartók's compositions.

LÁSZLÓ SOMFAI is professor of musicology at the Liszt Academy and since 1972 director of the Bartók Archive in Budapest. His prolific output includes several books about Haydn and articles about almost all aspects of Bartók's activity. His latest collection of essays about Bartók is forthcoming from the University of California Press. Professor Somfai is chief editor of the Béla Bartók Complete Critical Edition.

BENJAMIN SUCHOFF was curator of the New York Bartók Archives from 1953 to 1967 and then successor-trustee of the Bartók Estate until 1984. He simultaneously held a position as adjunct professor of arts and letters at the State University of New York at Stony Brook. Among his many contributions to Bartók studies are editions of the Romanian, Turkish, Yugoslav and Hungarian folk-music collections, a *Guide to Bartók*'s '*Mikrokosmos*' and an edition of Bartók's essays, published by Faber and Faber in 1976.

MIKLÓS SZABÓ was educated at the Liszt Academy in Budapest. Since 1953 he has taught in Győr and Budapest, and also appeared internationally as lecturer and performer. In 1982 he was appointed a professor at the Liszt Academy. As a conductor he has appeared on many discs, including recordings of nearly all of Bartók's choral works. In 1985 his definitive study of Bartók's Two- and Three-part Choruses was published in Hungarian.

GÜNTER WEISS-AIGNER, the German musicologist from Ingolstadt, has been one of the few scholars to look in detail at Bartók's early works. His doctoral dissertation from the University of Erlangen-Nürnberg in 1971 considered Bartók's early creative development in light of Western and Eastern musical traditions.

PAUL WILSON is associate professor of music theory at the University of Miami's School of Music in Coral Gables, Florida. He received his doctoral degree in music theory from Yale University. He has published several essays and reviews on Bartók's work. In 1992 Yale University Press published his book *The Music of Béla Bartók*.

Index of Bartók's Works

Note: Works are entered under their full English-language names, e.g. First String Quartet *under* F. *Page references in* **bold** *indicate detailed discussion of the work.*

General Index